LOOK FOR THE WOMAN

A Narrative Encyclopedia of Female Poisoners,
Kidnappers, Thieves, Extortionists, Terrorists,
Swindlers and Spies from Elizabethan Times to the Present

JAY ROBERT NASH

M. EVANS AND COMPANY, INC.
New York

Library of Congress Cataloging in Publication Data

Nash, Jay Robert.
  Look for the woman.

  Bibliography: p. 397
  Includes index.
  1. Female offenders—Biography—Dictionaries.
I. Title 2. Crime and Criminals
HV6245.N38 R 364.3'74'0922 [B] 81-2868

ISBN 0-87131-336-7   AACR2

M. Evans and Company, Inc.
216 East 49 Street
New York, New York 10017

Design by RFS Graphic Design, Inc.

Manufactured in the United States of America

9 8 7 6 5 4 3 2 1

LOOK FOR THE WOMAN

BOOKS BY JAY ROBERT NASH

Fiction

On All Fronts
A Crime Story

Nonfiction

Dillinger: Dead or Alive?
Citizen Hoover, A Critical Study of the Life and Times
    of J. Edgar Hoover and His F.B.I.
Bloodletters and Badmen, A Narrative Encyclopedia of American
    Criminals from the Pilgrims to the Present
Hustlers and Con Men, An Anecdotal History of the
    Confidence Man and His Games
Darkest Hours, A Narrative Encyclopedia of Worldwide Disasters
    from Ancient Times to the Present
Among the Missing, An Anecdotal History of Missing Persons
    from 1800 to the Present
Murder, America, Homicide in the United States from the
    Revolution to the Present.
Almanac of World Crime

Poetry

Lost Natives & Expatriates

Theater

The Way Back
Outside the Gates
1947 (Last Rites for the Boys)

This book is for Judy

ACKNOWLEDGMENTS

My deep gratitude goes to my deadline-racing typist, Sandy Horeis, and to Judy Anetsberger, who had the devastating job of proofreading the manuscript. Challenging graphic work was completed by Tom Buckley and Bernard Van Marm, the best in the business. Also of great help with photographs were Bill Kelly of Wide World, Ed Kita, and P. Noel Hepp.

I am also indebted to scores of people who provided printed source material, correspondence, and memorabilia—Neil H. Nash, Jack Jules Klein, Jr., Leonard Des Jardins, Phil Krap, Edgar Krebs, Bob Howe, Jerry Goldberg, Sydney Harris, P. Michael O'Sullivan, Hank Oettinger, Curt Johnson, Dan McConnell, Jim and Edie McCormick, Neal and Joan Amidei, Marc Davis, Bob Abel, Jack Conroy, Ray Peekner, Raymond Friday Locke, Jay Odell, Bob Connelly, Arnold L. Kaye. Also Lynette Francis, librarian for the San Francisco Chronicle; Susanna Shuster, editorial research librarian for the Los Angeles Times; Dorothy Frazier of the Denver Post library; Paul Cook of Parade magazine; Jennie DeLanctd of the Miami Herald; Gloria Osborne of Sentinel Star in Orlando, Florida; Dennis Laurie, newspaper curator for The American Antiquarian Society in Worcester, Massachusetts; George O'Neal of the Pinkerton Detective Agency; and Scott Baker, chief of the reference department of the Troy (New York) Public Library.

Other librarians, from all over the country, were exceedingly helpful. These include John Edwards and Tom Hanley, School of Law, University of Missouri at Columbia; Pat Wilcoxson, Regenstein Library, University of Chicago; Peter Weil, microfilm, and the staff of the Newberry Library of Chicago. Invaluable assistance was also given by the staff at the School of Law, University of Chicago; the staff of the New York Public Library; the staff of the John Crerar Library at Chicago's Illinois Institute of Technology; the Chicago Historical Society; the New York Historical Society; and the San Francisco Historical Society.

I would especially like to thank correspondents living abroad—Paul Allen (Paris), Roger Madden (London), David Halliday (Berlin), and G. Caetani (Rome).

PREFACE

My reasons for writing this book are quite simple. Out of pure interest, I had been gathering information, both hard facts and anecdotal material, on women criminals for more than a decade. With such a monumental amount of information at hand, and in view of the increasing number of crimes committed by women today, as well as the increasingly sensational nature of those crimes, to write a book, an encyclopedia, in fact, on the subject seemed clearly in order.

To say that the number of crimes committed by women today is increasing is not to say that the percentage of all crimes that are committed by women has increased. It is still the men who commit from eighty to ninety percent of all serious crimes. (I quote the statistics, and yet statistics in the crime field can seldom be taken seriously, arrived at, as they are, for often specious reasons. Prepared and offered on federal, state, and local levels, they are typically manipulated either for political reasons, as is the case with the FBI's forever seeking to increase its annual budget by juggling "fright statistics," or by state and local agencies tenaciously competing for funds and jobs.)

Interestingly, it is the off-beat and the inexplicable that dominate among the crimes of female offenders. In all recorded history, the female criminal has many times over excelled her male counterpart in daring robberies, labyrinthine confidence schemes, and heinous murders. In fact, the female murderer has proved herself easily as deadly as any male and certainly more insidious. Her motives, as a general rule, lack the clearheaded and darkly reasoned purposes of the male. Whim and fancy often rule here. Long-smoldering emotions often burn themselves out only after the victim of the female killer—whether male or female—has been subjected to excruciating agony. Seldom is there the quick, clean stroke of death as with the male. It is almost the exclusive province of the woman who commits homicide, as was the case with

Martha Grinder, Jane Toppan, Helene Jagado, and dozens more, to display an obsession to witness the slow death of the victim, most often by poison, although some atypical cases have involved use of the more manly axe, knife, or gun.

Historically, even the world of crime has proved male dominated, and the female criminal has been kept in her place, with little opportunity to follow certain criminal pursuits exclusively practiced and guarded by males. Notorious exceptions include pirate Anne Bonny, counterfeiter Ann Carson, stagecoach robber Pearl Hart, and pickpocket/fence Moll Cutpurse.

Through the centuries women were kept uneducated and close to the hearth. They saw little of the "wicked" outside world, and therefore their most serious crimes were domestic. Sensational early-day women criminals were the killers of husbands and lovers—Alice Arden, Mary Blandy, Ann Bilansky, Edith Carew, Augusta Fullam. Their punishments, moreover, were much more severe than those meted out to males committing similar offenses. Husband-killer Catherine Hayes, for instance, instead of merely being hanged, was strangled and burned to death before a great throng as a public warning, a governmental caution to any woman who might momentarily run a finger down the sharp edge of a kitchen knife while eyeing the throat of an oppressive spouse. In the twentieth century, details of such sordid murder cases as those of Ruth Snyder, Grace Lusk, and Wanda Stopa, who ostensibly killed for love, glutted the newspapers.

From the beginning, to be sure, there were phalanxes of female monsters who slew without any love or compassion, committing mass murder for obscure reasons, usually for the vague and perverted sense of power they held over their many victims. Of these, there were the poisoners La Voisin, La Spara, and La Toffania; the berserk aristocrat, Elizabeth Bathory; and the Nazi concentration camp ogres, Irma Grese and Ilse Koch. These women, however, retained vestiges of sanity. Others were totally unbalanced—Margaret Allen, who bludgeoned an old woman to death because she was "feeling kind of funny" one morning and had an urge to kill; Gertrude Baniszewski, who tortured a teenage girl to death to "teach her a lesson"; Lydia Sherman, "America's Lucrezia Borgia," who poisoned her husbands, children, anyone in sight who displeased her, as did mass killer Marie de Brinvilliers of France; Winnie Ruth Judd, who chopped up her two best friends and shipped them piecemeal in a trunk by rail to a distant city; and Jeanne Weiss, perhaps the most frightening female murderer on record, a demented, if shrewd, French housewife who became a *cause célèbre* even as she continued to slaughter children.

When women have murdered for gain, they have generally been more successful than the male in that their careers in crime have often lasted longer. Among this breed have been excellent actresses whose astoundingly brazen ways have carried them past suspicion and accusation, enabling them to kill for profit over many years. Examples of this type include British-born Mary Ann Cotton, Mrs. Archer-Gilligan of Connecticut, Mrs. Belle Gunness of Indiana, and Miss Kate Bender of Kansas. Others of a long-term career in crime merely blundered down the decades unnoticed by an indifferent society. The most notorious of these was Chicago's Tillie Klimek, who disposed of husbands with her poisoned stew, ordering coffins even before her doltish spouses succumbed to her terrible meals, and collecting insurance money with which to snare yet another unsuspecting mate.

With the coming of women's suffrage in the United States, female malefactors became even bolder, taking gun in hand and rivaling men in their success at armed robbery. Margie Dean was not only a member but a planner and leader of the crimes of the ruthless Sherrill Gang. Cecelia Cooney, Brooklyn's electrifying "Bobbed-Haired Bandit," joined her husband in a crime spree that became the subject of national headlines in the early 1920s. Then the female superstars of the crime-ridden 1930s emerged with a vengeance—Ma Barker, Kathryn Kelly, Bonnie Parker, and "Duchess" Spinelli.

By the late 1940s and early 1950s, women were killing, kidnapping and robbing with the same alacrity and audacity as males. Martha Beck and Bonnie Heady inspired their weak-willed lovers to assist them in committing crimes that earned them worldwide notoriety and hurried them to death chambers. A decade later female terrorists were capable of any crime that, in their minds, was justified by their political ends. The Manson women, devoted to a warped love cult, murdered as willfully as Mississippi bargemen had murdered their way through the whorehouses of New Orleans a century earlier. And, in 1980, Priscilla Bradford, a Florida housewife, conspired with two other women to batter her husband to death so that her spouse's business could become an "all-female" enterprise.

In all ages, however, there have been women criminals of great intelligence who operated alone, for the most part clever, steel-nerved women who managed to retain great feminine charm and grace. In one form or another of white-collar crime, usually sophisticated confidence schemes, they have tended to surpass the male in ability to plan and carry out successful crimes. Such women include the beauteous Mary Moders, the bizarre Edith Salomen, the energetic Ellen Peck, the calculating Mildred Hill, and the inventive and unforgettable Sophie Lyons, who gathered a fortune through swindling until she abruptly decided to reform and then made another fortune in the legitimate world before her death.

The murderers, the bandits, the confidence artists, the spies, and the monsters are presented in this book as a cross section of female criminals from all lands and ages. (Over the years, they have not changed much in personality, only technique.) Naturally, it would have been impossible to include in one volume every female criminal of note who ever lived. Beginning with more than ten thousand entries from which to choose, I selected those hundreds that were the most notorious of their day, those who established landmark cases, such as Marie Lafarge, at whose murder trial the science of toxicology made its debut in criminal law, those who set a precedent in criminal history and law, and those whose case best represented some particular field of crime.

It is interesting to note that in the course of my research in this broad field, certain historical patterns emerged:

■ The most popular names of women criminals are, in order of frequency, Catherine, Elizabeth, Mary, and Ann.

■ Women criminals are in some ways no different from their law-abiding sisters; they consistently lie about their age, which explains many of the large number of question-marks where the subject's birth date should appear.

■ Although there are notable exceptions, a predominant number of the more outrageous female criminals were middle-aged during their period of greatest activity. (Some, such as Ma Barker, Ma Beland, and Nannie Doss, were even old enough to be grandmothers, and indeed were.) This trend seems to be lessening a bit, with younger women increasing among the numbers of those who commit serious crimes today.

■ Compared with males, female murderers confronted with absolute proof of guilt are less likely to confess. Throughout history, the convicted female killer has seldom repented, even while standing on the gallows; unlike most males, she has consistently denied her guilt, angrily going to her death as one persecuted, lashing out with threats and physical abuse against the executioner.

■ In the past, women consistently used their sex as a way to save themselves from capital punishment, pleading pregnancy in order to stall execution when no such physical condition existed. (A tragic exception was Bathsheba Spooner, who was convicted in Massachusetts of the murder of her husband; she claimed pregnancy but was nevertheless hanged. When her corpse was examined she was discovered to have been telling the truth.)

■ Most female criminals are unattractive, many of them even physically repulsive. Some, from Moll Cutpurse to Margaret Allen, shunned female garb, wearing men's clothes and abandoning their sex altogether. Belle Starr, portrayed by the ravishing actress Gene Tierney in a motion picture loosely based on her life, was, as her photo herein will testify, a hatchet-faced harridan with a maniacal stare. Ruth Snyder had a jaw of granite. Bonnie Parker, also used as a role model in many movies and played by a bevy of beautiful Hollywood stars, chiefly Faye Dunaway, was, in reality, a lean-faced, squinty-eyed killer with the body of a young boy, her facial features further mottled when she was burned in a car explosion while escaping a police trap with her equally repugnant-looking boyfriend, Clyde Barrow. There have, of course, been rare exceptions. Mary Moders, the confidence artist of early-day England, was reported to have been a great beauty who even appeared on stage in a play based upon her criminal career. Kidnapper Kathryn Kelly was sleek, sophisticated, and physically alluring. Killer Barbara Graham, and, especially, mob girl Virginia Hill, were extremely attractive women criminals.

■ Most women criminals retain their motherly instincts, showing loyalty and love to their children irrespective of the terrible crimes they commit. "Iron Irene" Schroeder, shooting her way through police blockades across the country during the late 1920s, was typical. She refused to abandon her little boy, who sat in the back seat of her bullet-riddled car witnessing one battle after another, thinking it all great fun.

■ In instances where female criminals have operated in tandem with male counterparts, the female has most often remained loyal to her partner. She often willingly attempts to take all the blame committed by the pair to try to save the male. This kind of fidelity on the part of the hardened, professional criminal was exemplified by "Chicago May" Churchill, normally a bank burglar and confidence artist, who returned to a French jail to visit her fellow thief and paramour, Eddie Guerin, even though she knew it would mean her own imprisonment.

These are but a few of the most intriguing points in a work I believe to be the most definitive to date. There have been other books in the field, most of which are sociological diatribes or one-sided polemics, short on information and research, long on personal theories, and so fragmentary in true study as to provide only a narrow glimpse of certain types of female criminals. It is hoped that the reader will find this book a far broader view of women in crime, and will discover the lives portrayed herein to be as revealing of human nature and as fascinating as I did.

Jay Robert Nash
Chicago, 1981

LOOK FOR THE WOMAN

ADAMS, MARY

Thief ■ (? –1702)

Born in Berkshire, England, Mary Adams at an early age went to work for a grocer in Reading and was soon seduced by the man's son, giving birth to an illegitimate child, which was a great shame in those days and which caused her to leave for London in social disgrace. In London she worked briefly for a shopkeeper, who also seduced her, then kept her in separate apartments. Mary's second child was born dead, and the shopkeeper thought to abandon her after giving her some money.

Mary by then had grown street-wise, and began to blackmail the shopkeeper, threatening to inform his wife of his indiscretion. The man paid her off again but thwarted any further blackmail by informing his wife himself of his sexual liaison with Mary Adams.

Mary next moved into an inn and became the proprietor's mistress, then the consort of one of his customers. Abandoned once again, and penniless, she went to work for an ancient crone in Drury Lane, working as a sort of call girl, servicing high-born gentlemen. She picked the pocket of one of these men, obtaining several checks. The man notified authorities, and when Mary went to the victim's bank to cash the checks she was arrested.

Quickly tried and condemned, Mary Adams was taken to Tyburn on June 16, 1702. She was at the time in her late twenties and the thought of her death seemed not to bother her; she was more concerned about smoothing out the wrinkles of her new mourning dress, purchased for her by an admirer, than about the hooded hangman who solemnly came forward to place the noose about her lovely neck.

ADAMS, MILLICENT

Murderer ■ (1942–   )

Raised in an upper-class world of Eastern Establishment values, Millicent Adams, blonde, post-debutante Bryn Mawr student, first met Axel Schmidt, a promising postgraduate student of engineering, at a charity function in Philadelphia, and the two soon fell in love. The girl from snobbish Chestnut Hill later discovered that Schmidt intended marrying someone else, someone whose background was more socially prominent, who had more money, who offered him a better career. He jilted Millicent, not knowing she was pregnant. (Judging from his avaricious, ruthlessly ambitious attitude, such knowledge would probably not have made a difference to the callous Schmidt anyway.)

Millicent sought the age-old revenge of the woman scorned. She purchased a .22-caliber Smith & Wesson, thinking at first to commit suicide, it was later alleged. To make sure the weapon would do the job, Ms. Adams bought a St. Bernard and, taking the animal to an unused servant's room in her house, shot and killed it. In October 1962 she took the same weapon to bed when she and Schmidt partook of their farewell sexual encounter in Millicent's Philadelphia townhouse. Instead of killing herself, Ms. Adams sent one bullet into Schmidt, killing him.

Through her attorneys, Millicent Adams pleaded temporary insanity and entered a plea of guilty to manslaughter, requesting a ten-year probation during which she would voluntarily commit herself to a mental-health center. And that was her fate. After spending three years in the center—she was allowed to go home on weekends to visit her child, Lisa, the daughter of the man she had killed—Millicent Adams was released as "rehabilitated." She moved to the West Coast and took up residence with a rich relative, a destiny that would surely not have befallen a girl lacking her social prestige and money.

ADLER, LYDIA

Murderer ■ (1704– ?)

Lydia was a London housewife whose temper was forever getting her into trouble, especially with her husband, John Adler, who had been married three times before taking Lydia as his wife. They fought constantly, with Lydia, a large woman, usually getting the upper hand. On June 11, 1744, Lydia was seen to attack her husband, "throwing him on the ground, kicking and stamping him in the groin."

Hours later Adler staggered to the house of a friend, Benjamin Barton, holding a handkerchief to a bloody head and shouting, "This eternal fiend [meaning Lydia] will be the death of me!" He was taken to a hospital where he lingered near death, calling friends and constables to arrest his wife, begging a warrant be issued. Lydia visited him and laughed at the stricken Adler. "I am a dead man," Adler said to a nurse, "and this woman has killed me."

Only minutes before he died on June 23, 1744, Adler cried out, "Do you have the warrant yet?" Upon his death Lydia was arrested and tried at the Old Bailey for murder, her daughter Hannah stating that her mother had willfully attacked her father. The woman was saved from the gallows by a Dr. Godman, who testified that Adler was suffering from a rupture (hernia) and that the kicking blow administered to his groin by Lydia would not have killed a healthy man.

Lydia Adler was convicted of manslaughter and was ordered to be burned on the hand, then set free. As the wardens were bringing the branding iron to white heat, Lydia Adler grew impatient and snapped, "Hurry it up—I have my linen to do!"

ADLER, POLLY

Madam ■ (1900–1962)

Perhaps the most notorious madam in the history of American prostitution, New York's Polly Adler (born April 16, 1900, in Russia as Pearl Adler) opened her first brothel in 1920 with three girls servicing the rich first-nighters Polly snared from Broadway. She had fitted out a lavishly decorated apartment on Manhattan's Riverside Drive as her first bordello. She was later to write, "I didn't invent sex, nobody had to come to my apartment who didn't want to, I was really doing them a favor . . . but I had a bad conscience when I thought of my parents, and I used to have terrible nightmares in which my father would chase me down the streets yelling, *'Kirva! Bliad!'* ('Whore! Bum!') . . . But no matter how I viewed my conduct, I was the proprietress of a whorehouse."

Polly's brothel moved from apartment to apartment, a sort of floating bordello, for more than twenty years (1920 to 1944), after which she officially retired. In the interim she accumulated a small fortune and a blazing reputation. Her first serious arrest came in 1928, but she was released "for lack of evidence." In reality she was freed without trial thanks to her powerful underworld protectors to whom she kicked back fifty percent of her income, her chief sponsor being Charles "Lucky" Luciano, king of prostitution not only in New York but throughout the country by the mid-1930s.

During the Seabury Investigations of 1931, which subsequently brought about the ruination of the administration of the dapper and much loved Mayor James J. Walker, Polly Adler became a criminal celebrity overnight, first going into hiding when summoned to testify, then dramatically surrendering. As with all her subsequent statements about Luciano and other kingpins of New York crime, she shielded her protectors to her dying breath.

A typical example of her testimony during the Seabury Investigations:

Madam Polly Adler in 1931, during one of her many court appearances.

Q: Do you know Mr. Director? [Undoubtedly Luciano]
A: No. Who is he?
Q: He spoke to you a few weeks ago on the street.

A: I meet a lot of people and don't remember their names.

Q: Mr. Director was here and told us that you once called police headquarters to remove cops from the premises.

A: I don't recall that.

Q: Do you know the number Spring 3100?

A: Yes, police headquarters.

Q: How did you know that?

A: Saw it in the book.

Q: Did you look for it?

A: Any child knows Spring 3100.

Q: Didn't you call a Mr. Johnny to remove cops [from her brothel during a raid]?

A: No.

Q: Who do you know at headquarters?

A: Nobody.

Polly's last important arrest was on March 5, 1935, a Tuesday, the madam's jinx day. It was an arrest that heralded the vice investigations that would subsequently bring Luciano and others long prison terms. Polly got thirty days and the inexplicable support of the *New York Daily News*, which, on March 12, 1935, ran an editorial under the headline *Polly Adler's "Little Black Book,"* reading, in part, "Here is a woman who keeps an expensive house of ill fame, conducting it on the quiet, without complaints from the neighbors, and with every regard for outward decency. . . . The police tap this woman's wire, set spies on her, and in other ways keep her under surveillance as if they suspected her of being the Lindbergh kidnapper. They seize, without a vestige of right to do so, her 'little black book' containing the names and addresses of various well-to-do patrons of her establishment. Thus they obtain opportunities for blackmail for anybody who can get a peek at this book. Already whispers are going the rounds that the book contains the names of a motion picture star and a Broadway stage favorite.

"It is this crusading against personal and private habits and instincts—the sex instinct . . . which is futile and sickening, just as the prohibition of drinking of liquor was."

The notorious Polly Adler could not have said it better in her own defense. Further, she took perverse pride in her bordello, as illustrated when a customer once exclaimed, "Say, Polly, this is one swell joint."

"Joint!" she roared back. "You've got a nerve calling this a joint. This is an A-number-1 house of assignation!"

In 1950, six years after Polly's reported retirement from prostitution, she wrote a best-seller, *A House Is Not a Home*, the profits from which kept her in comfort, if not the grand style of her salad days, until her death on June 10, 1962. For years afterward gentlemen in esteemed clubs would proudly withdraw her card—showing a parrot on a perch—and exhibit this cherished memento which simply declared, "LExington 2-1099, New York City."

ALLEN, MARGARET

Murderer ■ (1906–1949)

Of all the female murderers of twentieth century England, none remains more enigmatic than Margaret Allen, who apparently never really knew whether she was male or female. All her life she manifested a personality that was decidedly male, yet her lone, horrifying murder of a sixty-eight-year-old woman had all the earmarks of a female killing, a fatuous, inexplicable murder, a purposeless, mad act, the motive for which is agonized over to this day.

Margaret Allen was born into a huge family, the twentieth of twenty-two children, and even as a child she preferred the dress and company of men. Shunning female chores, Margaret enjoyed any work that required muscle and stamina, from hauling coal to repairing the house. As a young woman, she worked in a Lancashire mill close to her home in the borough of Rawtenstall. She later took on the job of bus conductor but was dismissed when passengers reported her for pushing them about and cuffing them on the back of the head when they moved too slowly for her.

By the late 1920s Margaret made no pretense of her love for all things masculine. She

British slayer Margaret Allen in her customary man's suit.

1935, and a claim thought to be absurd in that no such operation had as yet proved successful (not until decades later in the day of Christine Jorgensen would such medical miracles be heralded). The sex change may only have been in Margaret's mind, but the very idea seemed to enable her to move more easily through a man's world, convincing her that her body was in unison with her mental attitude.

Margaret remained an oddity in Rawtenstall, taking up residence in an old building once used as police headquarters, fronting on Bacup Road, the borough's main street. The men she befriended shunned her company, except in the pubs—she usually bought the drinks—and women found her strange, repulsive, and argumentative. Only one female, her only real friend, Mrs. Annie Cook, spent time with her. Even this relationship was almost severed when Margaret proposed a lesbian love affair with Mrs. Cook while the pair were on vacation at Blackpool, Margaret having registered at the resort hotel as "Mr. Allen."

Later, at Margaret's trial, Mrs. Cook was asked, "Did she suggest that something should happen while you were there?"

Replied Mrs. Cook, "She did, but I refused at once."

Refusal and rejection were everyday occurrences in Margaret Allen's peculiar life, a life she turned into a nightmare on August 28, 1948. On the morning of that day Mrs. Nancy Ellen Chadwick, an eccentric, cantankerous old woman, who was thought to be a rich miser, was seen walking toward Margaret Allen's house on Bacup Road, a knitted shopping bag on her arm. It was the last time anyone saw the old woman alive. Early the next morning, a bus driver named Herbert Beaumont noticed what appeared to be a sack lying on Bacup Road. Inside the sack was the body of the reclusive Mrs. Chadwick. Police found that the old woman had been battered to death, ten vicious head wounds made by what a pathologist later determined to be the pointed end of a coal hammer. Her face was coated with ashes. From the beginning, the police suspected Margaret Allen; bloodstains and other marks trailed from Margaret's house to the curb of the roadway where the body had been discovered.

wore men's clothing and had her dark, wavy hair cut short. She drank in pubs with workingmen, who referred to her as "Bill Allen," and played darts with them, cursing and swaggering her short, squat frame about like a sailor on leave.

At twenty-nine Margaret entered a hospital under mysterious circumstances. She later confided to a friend that a delicate operation had been performed on her which had changed her from a woman to a man, a shocking statement in

Further, Margaret proved more talkative than usual when reporters and customers in the pub where she drank brought up the murder. At one point she laughingly ventured, "She was an old fool to sit on a roadside bench counting her money." Everywhere investigators from Scotland Yard went in Rawtenstall, they found the mannish Margaret Allen at their side, hands deep in her pockets, her wide, unblinking eyes staring at their every move. When constables dragged the river Irwell behind Margaret's house, she was the first to point out a bag floating in the water, tugging at an officer's sleeve and shouting, "Look, there's something there!" It was Mrs. Chadwick's knitted shopping bag, empty of the money she was known to have carried.

At almost every turn the woman was on hand to help the police track down the murderer, suggesting to constables to take plaster casts of footprints in the vicinity, trailing officers into nearby woods where they searched fruitlessly for the weapon. Her actions were almost identical to that of Richard Loeb, of Chicago's infamous child-killing team of Loeb and Leopold in 1924, when Loeb dogged the steps of investigating officers, so ingratiatingly helpful in providing clues to the kidnap murder that he implicated himself. But, unlike the quick-acting Chicago police, Scotland Yard detectives took their time, apparently preferring the cat-and-mouse game.

Thinking the police had given up the hunt, Margaret sauntered into her favorite pub, and, after gulping down several pints of ale, belched out the fact to one and all that she was "the last person to see the old woman." Further, she revealed that Mrs. Chadwick was wearing an underskirt when she was murdered, one in which the old lady had sewn a secret pocket. Her remarks, of course, were an open challenge to police, who visited her on September 1, 1948; a search was supervised by Chief Detective Inspector Stevens of Scotland Yard. A bag with ashes and rags was brought to him. He held up the bag to Margaret's bland face. "Where did these come from?"

"From the fireplace upstairs." As Stevens examined the rags, Margaret smiled and added, "I use them for floor swabs." The detective stared at her wordlessly. Suddenly, Margaret grabbed her man's overcoat, threw it over her shoulders, and said in her best lumberjack's voice, "Come on, let's get out of here. I'll tell you all about it." She passed the cellar door and nonchalantly pointed to it, saying, "That's where I put her."

Without her confession, detectives would nevertheless have presented an airtight case against Margaret in court. The bloodstains found on her "swabbing" rags matched the blood type of Mrs. Chadwick. The ashes in Margaret's cellar matched those ground into the victim's face. Hairs from Mrs. Chadwick's head and fibers from her coat were found on Margaret's pants, blazer, coat, and shoes.

After being formally charged with murder, Margaret nodded and said stoically, "I did." The slight smile on her face never drooped. Later she recalled how she had found Mrs. Chadwick sitting on a bench outside her house. "I was in a funny mood. . . . She seemed to insist on coming in. I just happened to look around and saw a hammer in the kitchen. . . . On the spur of the moment I hit her. . . . She gave a shout and that seemed to start me off more and I hit a few times, I don't know how many."

Her trial was brief, only five hours. Not even her attorney could offer a suitable defense, remarking, "I do not seek to deny that the hand of Margaret Allen caused the death of Mrs. Chadwick." He did make an attempt to prove his client insane, but experts testified to the contrary. She was condemned to death.

Great speculation was made about Margaret's motive for murder, since she never volunteered the slightest hint of what compelled her to bash in the head of old Mrs. Chadwick. She was heavily in debt, some said, and she murdered for the money, but it was later proved that the victim was carrying only a few coins when she was killed.

The residents of Rawtenstall had little sympathy for Margaret in her fate. When the ever loyal Mrs. Cook attempted to get up a petition to save her friend from the gallows, only 162 persons out of a community of 28,000 would sign.

Margaret's volatile temperament did not desert her in her last moments. She was cranky and mean to her keepers at Strangeways Prison.

On the morning of January 12, 1949, the dawn of her execution, a female guard brought Margaret her last breakfast. She stared at the food she had requested and then, with a sudden movement, kicked the tray high into the air, splattering the wall with scrambled eggs. "At least no one else will enjoy that meal," sneered Margaret Allen.

ANDERSON, BELLA

Kidnapper ■ (1864– ?)

One of the early-day kidnappings in America took place in New York City in mid-May, 1899, when twenty-month-old Marion Clarke was taken from her modest home by a trained nurse, Bella Anderson. Newspapers ran the child's photo and offered substantial rewards for information leading to her kidnapper's arrest.

Public reaction to the crime was enormous, and whipped to a frenzy by the press. In late May, local residents of Garnerville, New York, identified the Clarke child when a woman carried her into a grocery store. Police followed the woman to a farmhouse where they arrested nurse Anderson and George and Addie Barrow. Barrow was the son of a socially esteemed family in Little Rock, Arkansas, who had left that city after running afoul of the law. His wife worked for a New York printing firm.

Cheering crowds greeted the baby, who was returned to New York on a special train. More than five thousand people milled about the Clarke home to wish the family well. The passion of the day was captured by *The New York Times*, which reported on June 2, 1899, "During the second act of *The Man in the Moon* at the New York Theatre last night, comedian Sam Bernard stepped down to the footlights and told the audience that Marion Clarke had been found. The audience broke into a demonstration such as has not been witnessed since the days of the war."

Nurse Anderson confessed to a bizarre plot; she and the Barrows thought to kidnap children throughout the country, holding these victims for small ransoms, but intending to reap great amounts through mass kidnappings. It was Bella Anderson's job as a nurse to take positions with those families to be victimized and make off with the children to hideouts where the Barrows would be waiting. The Clarke family, one of only average means, was the first trial run in the scheme. The kidnappers had asked for only a $300 ransom.

Quick trials found all three kidnappers guilty. The Barrows were given long prison terms. Bella Anderson, who cooperated with prosecutors, received four years.

ANSELL, MARY

Murderer ■ (1877–1899)

In 1899 a London domestic servant, Mary Ansell, put in motion a bumbling plan to murder her half-witted sister, Caroline, so that she could obtain twenty-two pounds from a small insurance policy. Mary sent her sister a cake on March 9, 1899, mailing it to the Leavesden Asylum in Watford where Caroline was confined. The weak-minded Caroline, who was wholly devoted to her older sister, squealed with delight upon receiving the gift and joyfully shared the cake with other inmates. A few hours later, several inmates grew ill, and Caroline, who had eaten most of the cake, endured paroxysms of pain before dying in agony. Asylum doctors declared that they intended to perform an autopsy on Caroline. Hearing of this, the illiterate Mary wrote the head of the asylum pretending to be her mother:

Dear Sir,—For why do you want a post-mortem examination on the body after she had been under your care for years? We decline to give you the authority to hold one. I remain, yours,

Mrs. Ansell

Using her own name, she next wrote a letter to the insurance agent with whom she had taken out the policy on Caroline's life, demanding payment.

Meanwhile, Dr. Blair of the asylum analyzed some of the remains of Caroline Ansell and found that she had died from phosphorus poisoning. This led to the prompt arrest of Mary Ansell, who denied any guilt in her sister's death, angrily asking police, "Why was we not sent for to see my sister before she was dead, so we could have had a word with her about who sent the cake?" After being formally charged with murder, Mary replied, "I am as innocent a girl as ever was born."

The jury, at her trial in June 1899, thought differently. Though Mary shouted in court, "I bought it for my own protection against them [rats], as I was frightened of them!" her denial was to no avail. It was quickly concluded that Mary had purchased the phosphorus for the explicit reason of killing her sister. The evidence against her was overwhelming and she was convicted.

The judge in this case, Justice Mathew, took his time in reading the girl's death sentence: "Prisoner at the bar, it was impossible for a jury of reasonable and conscientious men to return any other verdict than this. It has been shown to their satisfaction that you deliberately took the life of your sister, an afflicted woman, who had never been a burden to you, and who had a peculiar claim on your affection. You were moved to this terrible crime for the sake of a small sum of money which you would receive on the policy of insurance. Never in my experience has so terrible a crime been committed for a motive so utterly inadequate. It is no part of my duty to add to the misery of your position. Your time on earth is short. Let that time be employed in seeking mercy where alone mercy can be found. I have only to pass upon you the sentence of the law—that you be taken hence to the place whence you came and thence to a place of public execution where you shall be hanged by the neck until you are dead, and your body buried within the precincts of the prison. And may the Lord have mercy on your soul!"

No sooner was this sentence uttered than shrieks and wails from Mary's mother were heard from where she stood in a nearby corridor. Mary Ansell cried out in response from the dock, "Mother! Mother! Mother!" The hysterical twenty-two-year-old had to be dragged from the court. Her attitude was unchanged when she went to her death on July 19, 1899, in St. Albans Prison. An enormous crowd swarmed around the gallows to see the young woman half carried to the hangman. As the rope went around her neck, Mary Ansell cried out, "Oh, my God in Heaven!" and "Lord have mercy on my soul!" With that she collapsed in a faint, the rope supporting her in a sagging position until the trap shot open to the hoots and howls of the callous crowd.

ANTONINI, THERESA

Murderer ■ (1785–1809)

A dedicated and professional criminal all her life, Theresa Marschall was born and bred in Berlin, and at an early age married a Sicilian bandit and pirate named Antonini. Both Antoninis robbed and burglarized throughout Germany and had twice been imprisoned together. In November 1809 the venomous pair found themselves in a coach heading from Danzig to Vienna, Theresa's fifteen-year-old brother Carl accompanying them. The fourth passenger in the coach was a beautiful young woman named Dorothea Blankenfeld, whose rich clothes and jewelry attracted the thieves, who quickly resolved to kill her and make off with her valuables at the first opportunity. The murderous traveling companions doubled their efforts after learning she had money, more than 2,000 talers, sewn into the stays of her corset.

When they stopped in Hof, the trio thought first to set a small fire in the victim's room, allow her to suffocate to death in the smoke, then filch her belongings, but the plan proved awkward. At Nuremberg Carl proposed putting ground glass into Dorothea's soup, but Antonini shrugged off the suggestion, saying, "I've swallowed broken glass for sport without ill effects."

At each stop the plotters devised new ways to kill their victim but found none suitable. Finally, at the last station, Maitingen, near Augsburg in Bavaria, they resolved to enter the woman's room that night and simply batter her to death. According to one chronicler, "The boy Carl was to be the principal agent in the crime; it was thought that his youth would save him from capital punishment, an inevitable sentence for the others if convicted." On the pretense of bathing her feet, Theresa Antonini ordered hot water sent to her room; this was really meant to wash away the bloodstains the trio would incur when murdering Dorothea. Theresa also dosed the victim's brandy and water with laudanum so that she was in a drugged state; she was half carried to her room.

The trio entered Miss Blankenfeld's room and sat about her bed, in which she lay in a stupor, thinking of how to kill her. "Let us pour molten lead into her ears and eyes," volunteered the inventive Theresa. Her brother attempted to melt pieces of a spoon over a large candle but a drop falling on a sheet only scorched the material, proving that the metal cooled too soon to kill a person.

They waited until 4:00 A.M. pondering their next move. Antonini finally threw up his hands in frustration and said, "Carl—bash in her head!" Wielding a mattock with three iron prongs, the boy struck Dorothea on the head, but she bolted upright and begged for her life. Theresa ran to the bed and began striking the woman with a poker. When the victim proved too strong, Antonini walked to the bed, took the poker from his wife's hands, and caved in the hapless girl's skull. They then wrapped the body in a blue cloak. The next morning they carried the corpse like a piece of baggage, along with Dorothea's goods, to the coach.

The innkeeper was suspicious immediately, noting that two women had arrived the night before and only one was leaving. He and his servants rushed to the rooms occupied by the travelers, finding Dorothea's room—the walls, floor, and bed—drenched with blood. The alarm was sent out, and the dragoons were soon galloping after the coach, catching up with it before the Antoninis had time to toss the body along-

side the road, which was part of their imperfect plan.

Taken to Nuremburg, the trio stubbornly insisted they were innocent. The woman had been murdered in the inn, they said, and, fearing they would be suspected, they had no choice but to remove the body and dispose of it somewhere. After hours of interrogation, the boy Carl broke down and confessed. Theresa also confessed, but her husband refused to admit his guilt. Carl Marschall was given ten years in prison and the Antoninis were condemned. Antonini cheated the executioner by dying in his cell, having starved himself to death.

Theresa Antonini was not as fortunate. She was tied by the hands and led by a rope up a high scaffold. A towering executioner, his head covered with a black mask, threw her to the blocks, and, his foot on her neck, held her head down. He then raised his wide, gleaming sword. "Mercy!" screamed Theresa Antonini. "None," murmured the executioner, and with one terrible downward movement she was beheaded.

ARCHER-GILLIGAN, "SISTER" AMY

Murderer ■ (1869–1928)

Decidedly a nymphomaniac, Amy Archer-Gilligan, known to her unsuspecting nursing home charges as "Sister Amy," opened a rest home for the elderly in Windsor, Connecticut, in 1901, and commenced marrying old men entrusted to her case, insuring them heavily, and then poisoning them, five marriages in all.

Women in her care also became her victims, poisoned after she had become the beneficiary in new wills she instructed them to make. This was done with the approval of relatives whom Sister Amy convinced that this was the only just way in which she could be compensated for caring for elderly persons not able to pay the proper costs of upkeep. But no sooner was a new will drawn than the person mysteriously died.

A relative of one of the home's residents finally alerted authorities to the suspiciously high death rate at Sister Amy's establishment, compared with that of other institutions for the aged. Placing an undercover policewoman in the home, Sister Amy's poisoning techniques were soon revealed. She was tried in 1914, found guilty, and sent to Weathersfield Prison for life. Sister Amy was later removed to an insane asylum where she died in 1928.

ARDEN, ALICE

Murderer ■ (1516–1551)

A handsome, high-born woman, Alice Arden was the stepdaughter of Sir Edward North, whose father was the translator of Plutarch. Having married Thomas Arden, Alice moved to Faversham, England, in 1544, where she continued her affair with Richard Mosby, a tailor. Mosby (or Mosbie) had been a servant in the North family and Alice had begun her long-standing affair with him when she was a teenager.

Not long after moving to Faversham, Alice decided that her husband must die so that she could be with the love of her life, and she conspired to have Thomas Arden murdered. To that end, Alice tried for years to kill her husband, a man twice her age and who suspected nothing of her marathon affair with Mosby. At first Alice went to a painter named Clark who dabbled in poison. According to one report, "The painter suggested that he should paint a portrait of Alice and temper the oil with poison, so that her husband might perish by the fumes when he gazed upon the picture." This bizarre plan was dismissed as being haphazard.

Knowing of a man named Green who hated her husband over a land dispute, Alice went to Green, giving him ten pounds to hire assassins to murder her husband. Two desperate characters aptly named Black Will and Shakebag were employed, and these men trailed Arden for days, following him to London and back to Faversham. Mosby, hearing of the plot, at first declined to participate, then succumbed to Alice's entreaties, as well as her considerable sexual persuasions.

Black Will and Shakebag hid in the Arden mansion, Alice "visiting them with food and drink." On Sunday evening, February 15, 1551, Mosby conspired to invite Arden to a game of backgammon with Arden's back to a closet in which Black Will was hiding.

Suddenly Mosby exclaimed, "Now I may take you, sir, if I will!" (This was the prearranged signal to Black Will to kill Arden.)

"Take me which way?" replied the perplexed Arden, uttering his last words.

Black Will jumped from the closet and strangled Arden with a towel. Mosby helped out by striking the victim with a fourteen-pound pressing iron. The killers, aided by a servant named Michael, dragged the body into Arden's countinghouse. When Arden was heard to moan, Black Will slashed his skull, killing him. Alice rushed in and, to make sure the deed was done, stabbed her husband seven or eight times.

Dragging the victim by his heels, the killers took the body to the garden outside the house, leaving it to be found by neighbors, as was Alice's plan. Waiting only a few hours, Alice Arden sent messengers to look for her "lost" husband. Family servants told the local mayor that Arden had not returned to dinner that night and his wife was worried that he might have been waylaid by highwaymen. The villagers of Faversham then commenced a night search by torchlight. Arden's mutilated body was found shortly by a local grocer named Prune.

Everything about the killing appeared suspicious; the mayor noticed bloody strands of carpet on Arden's shoes that had come from his own house. There was a trail of blood from the house to the garden which the mayor and other officials followed. Along the same route, a tub near the well yielded the bloody towel and knife used by Black Will and Alice to murder Arden.

The murder of Thomas Arden, February 15, 1551.

The impetuous killers, for all their plotting, had committed a blunder-filled murder.

Confronted by the mayor, Alice at first appeared insulted that she should have anything to do with such a heinous crime: "I would you should know that I am no such woman!" The bloody knife and towel were shown to her, along with the bloody carpet strands.

Alice Arden shuddered, then confessed, pressing the bloody towel to her beautiful face and moaning, "Oh, the blood of God help, for this blood have I shed." She and her servants were arrested. Mosby was found in bed by arresting officials, his hose and purse coated with Arden's blood. He, too, confessed.

The killer-for-hire, Black Will, along with the man who had purchased his services, Green, had fled on horseback. The trials and executions of the others were swift and horrible. The servant Michael was hanged in chains in Faversham. One of Alice's maidservants who had had nothing to do with the killing was also executed, burned at the stake while she screamed curses at her mistress for not saving her. Mosby and his sister Susan, who had helped plot Arden's death,

were taken to Smithfield and hanged. Alice rode to Canterbury in an open cart and with great pomp on March 14, 1551, was burned at the stake while hundreds cheered her miserable fate.

Besides executing the maidservant, another great injustice involved in this crime was the condemning of one George Bradshaw, who had innocently carried messages between Alice and Mosby, not knowing the contents to be murder plans. He was hanged. Such was the rage of local authorities—it was unthinkable to murder a high-born man in those days—that even the keeper of the local inn, the Fleur de Lys, one Adam Fowl, "was taken to London with his legs bound under the horse's belly," where he was tossed into the Marshalsea Prison. His only crime was having served a tankard of ale to Mosby and Alice at one of their clandestine meetings. He was later released.

Green, who was not the brightest of men, appeared in Faversham some years later, and was instantly seized and hanged. Black Will, who had looted Arden's countinghouse before fleeting Faversham, attempted to escape England but was found near Flushing. He was hanged and his body burned. Shakebag, who apparently had not taken any actual part in the killing, was nevertheless tracked down in Southwark where local authorities didn't bother with a trial; they simply ran the ruffian through with swords and left his carcass to rot alongside the road. Only Clark, the painter of the poison fumes, escaped the wrath of the authorities.

Alice Arden's unspeakable crime was portrayed in a play, published in 1592, whose author is anonymous, though it is said to have been edited by Shakespeare, and which was immensely popular for several decades. Part of the play's lengthy title describes "the great malice and dissimulation of a wicked woman, the insatiable desire of filthy lust and the shameful end of all murderers."

BANISZEWSKI, GERTRUDE WRIGHT

Murderer ■ (1929–)

An aging, embittered, divorced housewife, Gertrude Baniszewski, to supplement a meager income, took two teenage girls, the sisters Sylvia and Jenny Likens, ages sixteen and fifteen, into her Indianapolis, Indiana, home in 1965, their traveling parents paying $20 a week board. When Mrs. Baniszewski failed to receive the upkeep for the children, she mercilessly beat them. Later she hit the children with boards, and, manifesting her considerable sadism, burned Sylvia's fingers with matches for the warped amusement of cretinous neighborhood boys.

Mrs. Baniszewki encouraged the local roughnecks to use Sylvia as a punching bag and a helpless opponent in bone-breaking judo exercises. All the woman's bestial inclinations surfaced at once on October 26, 1965, when she encouraged and aided several teenage boys in torturing Sylvia, after branding her stomach with the words, "I am a prostitute and proud of it." The beating administered by Mrs. Baniszewski was so severe that Sylvia died.

Panicking, the hollow-eyed, sunken-lipped housewife called police, reporting that her boarder had been the victim of a gang of youths. Sylvia's sister, Jenny, a cripple, who had witnessed the awful torture-murder, narrated the entire sordid story.

Mrs. Baniszewski offered no defense at her trial and was sent to prison for life.

BARBERI, MARIA

Murderer ■ (1855– ?)

Jilted by her lover, Domenico Cataldo, thirty-year-old Maria Barberi went into a bar in New York's Little Italy. Walking over to Cataldo, who had his back to her, she slit his throat with a razor. It was early April 1885.

It was a clear case of murder and Maria was quickly convicted. Sentenced to death, she was to be the first woman scheduled to die in the new electric chair. Female reporters, however, rose to defend the so-called "Tombs Angel," and, rattling off a series of maudlin stories in her defense, the "sob sisters" managed a new trial for Maria. Through the fanatical pressure of the sob sisters of the press, Maria was acquitted. The murderer later appeared on stage to tell the tale of how a scoundrel had wronged her name and wounded her heart. The show closed in less than a week.

BARKER, ARIZONA DONNIE CLARK ("MA")

Gangleader, Murderer ■ (1872–1935)

A vicious harridan, born in Missouri in 1872 and claiming kinship with the James and Younger brothers, Ma Barker raised a murderous brood of sons—Arthur ("Dock"), Fred, Lloyd, and Herman—who began, at her encouragement, with petty thievery and graduated to bank robbery, kidnapping, and murder, especially during the early 1930s, when her sons became known, with the help of Alvin "Old Creepy" Karpis, as the terrible Barker Gang.

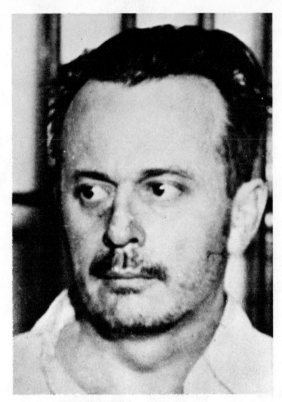

Arthur "Dock" Barker, the only one of Ma's sons who was heterosexual.

If not the direct planner of the notorious Hamm and Bremer kidnappings of 1933 and 1934, which brought the gang more than $300,000, Ma Barker was certainly the inspiration and architect of those crimes, along with the numerous bank robberies committed by the Barker Gang.

Ma proved her ability to use weapons when she and her youngest and dearest hellion, Fred, were trapped at a Lake Weir, Florida, resort on January 16, 1935, by a small army of FBI agents and local police. Their cottage was surrounded and an agent called upon the pair to surrender. Agents distinctly heard Ma shout to her killer son, "All right, go ahead!" With that, Ma and Freddie opened up on the agents with a Thompson submachine gun and a .300 gas-operated rifle, battling to the death for forty-five minutes in a nonstop shoot-out. Both Ma and

Two snapshots of the infamous Ma Barker, shown with her lover, Arthur V. Dunlop, whom she had killed after tiring of him; "Ma" preferred women.

Freddie were put on display at the local mortuary, their bodies riddled with bullets. The other Barker sons were soon killed or captured, Dock Barker shot to death in 1939 when he tried to escape Alcatraz.

Unlike the other notorious bandit gangs of the era, those of Dillinger, Floyd, and Underhill, the Barker Gang was made up almost exclusively of homosexuals. Fred Barker and Alvin Karpis were lovers, although they occasionally maintained girl friends, chiefly for the purpose of providing bail or smuggling weapons to them while they were in jail. (Dock Barker was decidedly heterosexual, staying away from his awful mother and brothers until summoned to participate in a robbery or kidnapping.)

Although Ma Barker dragged about an elderly man named Arthur V. Dunlop during the many years she and her boys ran wild—she tired of Dunlop and had Fred and Karpis murder him—Ma preferred the company of young women. "The whole mob was a bunch of fags and Ma was the biggest fag of them all—a bulldog dyke who liked to work over unsuspecting girls." These were the words of James Henry "Blackie" Audett, told to the author in 1979. Audett had robbed several banks with the Barkers in 1932 and 1933 and was later an inmate of Alcatraz when Dock Barker and Karpis were also confined on The Rock. "Karpis was a sneaky little fag," Audett declared, "and it was his job to go out through the Minnesota countryside—the Barkers always hid out in country places up there—and find these poor, dumb farm girls, and bring 'em back to ugly old Ma, and, God, she would abuse these poor girls terribly—it was disgusting, sickening what she did to 'em—and then Freddie and Karpis and that fag Volney

Alvin "Old Creepy" Karpis, staunch member of the Barker gang, Fred Barker's lover, and procurer of young girls for "Ma."

Davis [another member of the gang] would kill the girls at Ma's orders when old lady Barker was done playing with them, and get rid of the bodies. Why, there must be thirty or forty bodies of young girls, or their bones, still at the bottom of a half dozen Minnesota lakes to this day!"

BARRY, MARY ANN

Murderer ■ (1855– 1874)

Mary Ann Barry and her common-law husband, Edwin Bailey, both alcoholics and petty thieves, murdered their one-year-old child in London—they considered the child a nuisance—and were quickly arrested, tried, and condemned. They were hanged

alongside one Edwin Butt, who had strangled his sweetheart, a rare triple execution.

BATEMAN, MARY

Murderer ■ (1768– 1809)

She was known as the Yorkshire Witch, and in England she earned an eerie reputation, especially among the uneducated and the naive, as a worker of evil magic. Yet there was no magic about this woman, only a greedy hand and a malignant heart, which, from childhood to the hangman's noose, worked against the gullible to fill her own pockets.

Mary Bateman was born in 1768, at Aisenby in Yorkshire. Her father, James Harker, was a small well-to-do farmer, and both her parents were highly respected. At age five, Mary gave strong evidence of the pathological criminal she was to become. She stole a pair of expensive morocco shoes, hiding them in her father's barn, waiting for weeks before producing them and telling her parents without the blink of an eyelash that she had found them. For this deceit, according to one chronicle, "she forfeited the confidence of all her friends."

Such thieving went on throughout Mary's childhood until her parents, incapable of curing her sneak thievery, sent her off at a young age to work as a domestic. But Mary's stealing did not stop, and, having bungled so many petty thefts and being fired from so many jobs, there was no one who would hire her.

Moving in 1778 to Leeds, Mary took up dressmaking and was somewhat successful at the trade. She supplemented her income by advertising to her customers that she possessed supernatural powers and made money on the side as a soothsayer, telling her simpleminded customers whatever spiritual drivel charmed them.

A relative of one of her customers, an unsophisticated wheelright named John Bateman, fell under Mary's spell. Her gentle demeanor so disarmed him that after a three-week courtship he married the twenty-four-year-old schemer. For John Bateman, the time-ragged proverb, "Marry in haste, repent at leisure," could have served as his spiritual epitaph.

No sooner were they wed than all manner of complaints were registered against Mary by other lodgers living in the inn where the Batemans dwelled. She had stolen small objects, from tools to cheap jewelry, the residents accused. Nothing could be proved, but John Bateman thought it best they move. No doubt his neighbors were jealous of his gifted wife, he concluded, and he soon found a small house where they settled down.

Weeks later Mary burst into the small plant where Bateman worked, weeping and carrying a letter she said had been sent by his relatives and begging John to rush home to his father in Thirsk; the old man was at death's door. Borrowing money from his employer, Bateman traveled to Thirsk only to find his father, the town crier, at his job, crying out a brisk auction. The elderly Bateman was surprised to see his son and when asked about his ailment shrugged and told the son that he had never felt better. No, no one in the family had sent his wife a letter asking him to come. Bateman, thoroughly perplexed, returned to Leeds.

When he arrived home days later, he entered a house that was barren except for the presence of his wife, Mary, who sat in the middle of the living room on a single pillow. All their furniture, curtains, lamps, even Bateman's entire wardrobe down to the last button, was gone, sold by Mary. The wife smooth-talked her husband out of his wrath simply by telling him that she had gotten into some trouble and had had to "buy herself off." Bateman accepted the explanation without threats. His wife, he knew from her own mouth and the wagging tongues of his neighbors, was a practicing witch. "Possibly he was too afraid of her to protest over-much," reported Richard Hyson in *Sixty Famous Trials.* "Be that as it may, he continued to live with her, and remained with her to the end."

When a large factory in Leeds burned down, killing several workers and leaving many families without support, Mary developed a

Mary Bateman, circa 1805, shown dispensing some of her magical charms.

sinister plan to pay her debts and fill her coffers. She went from door to door, asking for linen, foodstuffs, and money, saying she was a nurse at the hospital, and the injured from the fire, along with their suffering families, desperately needed aid. Her baskets were filled to brimming through her heart-rending speeches. Mary Bateman promptly sold these goods and pocketed the money, never telling her husband of the vile scheme. Oddly enough, even though a known thief, the woman went on living in Leeds unmolested by police. It was later concluded that the simple working people of the district feared her witchcraft and for that reason refused to inform on her.

Mary's so-called powers were taxed increasingly as she sold her supernatural gifts to servant girls and other young women eager to know of impending marriage proposals, selling these easily duped females all manner of charms and love potions. She became so successful that she turned her full-time attention to fortune-telling and witchcraft. But, carefully eliminating herself from direct responsibility for her predictions and soothsayings, she put the burden of her statements upon a Mrs. Moore, a reclusive old lady who saw no one and who acted as Mary's contact with the spiritual world. Mrs. Moore, of course, was a convenient figment of Mary's inventive imagination, and, if necessary, a scapegoat who could never be apprehended.

By 1799 Mary Bateman's so-called magic involved extortion, abortion, and outright theft. One of her clients, Mrs. Greenwood, was told that her husband, who was away on a business trip, was being held for ransom by four men and that Mrs. Moore insisted four gold coins be produced or Mr. Greenwood would be killed. The gold, the client was informed, would be melted down by Mary, and used as a sacrificial offering to mystical powers to effect the husband's release. When the terrified Mrs. Greenwood told Mary she had no money, she was given the typical response, "Then you must steal it." The woman did, giving Mary the money. Mr. Greenwood returned home safe and sound some days later. The fact that he had never been in jeopardy by any kidnappers was no business of her own, Mary Bateman told the irate Mrs. Greenwood. Her information had come from Mrs. Moore, her oracle, and the poor old dear could sometimes be wrong. The matter was dropped.

Mary's invention of events proved so effective that she began to make up stories frequently. A Mr. Stead was about to run off with another woman, she told Mrs. Stead. For three half crowns, Mrs. Moore would send up a protective magic umbrella which would cause the lust-driven Mr. Stead to give up the girl. Upon receipt of the money, Mary informed the naive Mrs. Stead that her husband had not only lost interest in the bawdy wench but that he no longer had any memory of her. This of course, was true, in that Mr. Stead, who was serving in the army at the time, was carrying on no love affair.

The heartlessness of the would-be witch was exemplified in her treatment of a young girl who came to her for help with her lover. Mary first sold the girl charms, and then extorted money from her by threatening to expose her affair if she did not comply.

Mrs. Bateman went further with this client, performing an abortion on the girl that eventually cost the girl her life. Her lover, in guilty conscience, did marry the girl, but by then she was dying, cursing the Yorkshire witch and saying, "Had I never known Mary Bateman my child would now have been in my arms and I should have been a healthy woman."

In December 1806, William and Rebecca Perigo came to seek Mary's help. Rebecca complained of a "flacking" in her breast and was convinced that some vicious neighbor had put the evil eye on her. By then Mary had a new oracle, a Mrs. Blythe, who was as mythical as Mrs. Moore had been.

"Bring me one of your petticoats," Mary told Rebecca Perigo, "and I will send it to Mrs. Blythe for study."

As one might expect, Mrs. Blythe responded with a letter full of bad news. Powerful magic had to be worked fast to rid the Perigos of an evil curse. It would take money to propitiate the forces of evil. Mary instructed the Perigos to give her four guinea notes to be sewn into the couple's pillowcases. Mrs. Bateman was also proficient at sleight-of-hand, it seems, because she pocketed the notes, substituting crumpled newspaper for them, even as the Perigos watched. Sleeping on the money would somehow ward off Mrs. Perigo's pains, Mary told the dupes.

So artless were the Perigos that they came to believe anything Mary told them. The greedy witch immediately saw an opportunity to bilk the couple over a long period of time. In the months to come, as she prescribed all manner of ridiculous charms—from bent horseshoes to be placed over the front door of the Perigo home, to chicken necks kept in closets to turn back evil spirits—Mary Bateman robbed the couple of all their savings, clothing, even food. When she had drained them dry Mary decided to poison them. Mrs. Blythe was her prophet of doom.

Mary went to the couple in mid-April 1807, showing them a letter she claimed Mrs. Blythe had sent them. It read—

My dear friend:
    I am sorry to tell you you will take an illness in the month of May next, either one or both of

An artist's conception of Mary Bateman and her sister witches reveling in the rites of black magic, 1809.

you, but I think both, but the work of God must have its course. You will escape the chambers of the grave and though you seem to be dead, yet you will live. Your wife must take half a pound of honey to Mary Bateman, and it must remain there until you go down yourself, and she will put in such-like stuff as I have sent from Scarborough to her. You must eat pudding for six days, and you must put in it such stuff as I have sent to Mary Bateman, and she will give your wife it, but you must not begin to eat of this pudding until I let you know. . . .

This pudding, of course, was liberally peppered with poison, mercuric chloride, by Mary Bateman. On May 11, 1808, the gullible Perigos began eating it. When both became sick, Mary administered an antidote, which was arsenic. William Perigo ate little of the pudding or antidote, yet his lips turned black and he was deathly ill for days. Rebecca Perigo, who was totally in Mary's sway, forced herself to eat everything. She died in agony on May 24, 1808.

William Perigo, who had been cautioned by Mary never to consult a physician if he grew ill, disregarded her advice and on October 19, 1808, went to Dr. Thomas Chorley, who promptly told the man he was being poisoned. Perigo rushed home, tore open the charmed pillowcases on his bed and found useless paper in place of the guinea notes. He confronted the Yorkshire Witch, telling her how he had torn open the pillowcases to discover his money gone.

Cried Mary Bateman, "You've opened them too soon!"

"I think it is too late!" Perigo shouted back, finally coming to his senses. On October 21, 1808, Perigo asked Mary to meet him on the Leeds and Liverpool canal bank. Perigo asked Constable Driffield to wait in hiding nearby as he approached the woman, hoping to engage her in conversation that would fix her guilt.

But Mary Bateman was shrewd; she suspected a trap. Perigo found her sitting on a rock at the appointed place, but no sooner did he approach her than she began to vomit, shouting at him, "That bottle which you gave me has almost poisoned me! ... I would scorn to give a dog such a bottle!" Her plan then was to put all the responsibility for the poisonings on her own victim.

Constable Driffield nevertheless stepped from his hiding place and arrested Mary on a charge of murder. While she was imprisoned in York Castle, authorities searched Mary's house and found Perigo's possessions, along with all types of poisons.

The trial of the Yorkshire Witch caused a great sensation. People gathered outside the courtroom in great numbers, many believing Mary had, indeed, dark powers. Mary insisted that she was innocent of any wrongdoing, that if evil had been done, it was all the doing of that old crone, Mrs. Blythe. It was easily determined that there never had been a Mrs. Blythe, except in Mary's stormy imagination.

Witnesses by the score testified as to Mary's abortions, frauds, and extortions. Servant girls who had worked for Mary testified that she kept and administered poisons to her clients. Following a quick deliberation, the jury returned a verdict of guilty on the charge of murdering Mrs. Perigo. When the judge asked the Yorkshire Witch if she had anything to say before he sentenced her to death, Mary burst forth with a river of tears, crying out that she was pregnant.

The judge then asked that several women in the courtroom examine Mary to verify her claim. So frightened of her were the women that they jumped from their seats and bolted for the doors. The judge leaped up and ordered the courtroom doors locked and the women returned to their seats. He selected several of them to inspect the Yorkshire Witch, which they did in a small antechamber and with much hesitation, fearing she would bring her powers of black magic down on them. A little later these women informed the court that Mary had lied. Mrs. Bateman was sentenced to die on the gallows.

While she waited for the rope, Mary was not idle. She ruthlessly swindled several of her fellow prisoners out of their last pennies with lying promises about reprieves and releases. She was allowed to keep her twenty-two-month-old child with her until the morning of her execution.

At 5:00 A.M. on March 20, 1809, Mary Bateman kissed her baby before placing the child in the arms of a matron, then stoically stepped from her cell and was taken to the scaffold.

The enormous crowd that attended Mary's hanging was hushed, having a strange awe of her. Like her victims over the years, the spectators were simple folk who thought the woman to be a mystic, even a martyr, especially when she shrieked her innocence to the last.

Ironically, the end of the Yorkshire Witch served an honest and useful purpose. Her body was displayed to the public to obtain money for charities. Thousands of superstitious people filed past her bloated corpse, and hundreds more later paid handsomely for strips of skin cut from her body, these grisly remains sold as charms to fend off evil.

BATHORY, ELIZABETH

Murderer ■ (1560–1614)

A mentally unbalanced Hungarian countess, Elizabeth Bathory believed that her complexion would remain smooth and her body young if she bathed in human blood. For that purpose she dispatched several of her servants over a period of years to waylay and return to her hundreds of servant girls, whom she butchered like cattle in her remote castle, 610 being the final count of her victims.

Countess Bathory was brought to trial in 1611 and found guilty, along with three of her servants. Her servants were executed. Through her high political connections, she was spared, but was walled up in her rooms where she died raving three years later.

BECK, MARTHA

Murderer ■ (1921–1951)

O bese, emotionally unstable Martha Beck, a registered nurse living in Pensacola, Florida, where she supervised a home for crippled children, answered an ad for the lovelorn. Her reward was the appearance of the man who had paid for it, confidence swindler Raymond Fernandez, a sleazy, run-down romancer who patterned himself after the faded jazz-age sheiks of the 1920s, a man with a cheap wig who promised marriage to any woman over the age of fifty. Of course, the woman's money must be turned over to him before the parson was called.

Oddly enough, Fernandez fell in love with dumpy Martha, and she was overjoyed when he

Martha Beck and Raymond Fernandez, the doomed "Lonely Hearts Killers," shown flanking their lawyer, Herbert Rosenberg, while awaiting a verdict in their 1949 murder case.

asked her to join him in his lovelorn scams. The couple embarked on a shabby career of swindling elderly women, then began murdering these hapless females for whatever stored treasures they might have, brutal murders that later earned the unseemly duo the nickname "The Lonely Hearts Killers."

During the late forties, the couple conned and killed Mrs. Myrtle Young of Chicago; Mrs. Janet Fay, a sixty-nine-year-old widow from New York; Mrs. Jane Thompson; and perhaps two dozen more. In January 1949, Beck and Fernandez killed Mrs. Delphine Dowling and her two-year-old daughter, Rainelle, in Grand Rapids, Michigan. (Mrs. Beck drowned the child in a washtub, then looked up, her hands still holding the dead girl underwater, to mutter to her lover, "Oh, come and look what I've done, sweetheart.")

Apprehended for this double murder, the Becks pleaded guilty, but Michigan authorities allowed the couple's extradition to New York, where they would stand trial for the killing of Mrs. Fay. Michigan has no capital punishment, which Beck and Fernandez knew full well. They fought the extradition and failed.

Tried in New York, Beck and her boyfriend were found guilty of the Fay killing and sentenced to death. They were both sent to Sing Sing, where they passed long love-hate notes to each other, wiggled their bodies at each other when passing open doors between the men's and women's quarters, and made an ongoing spectacle of their absurd relationship.

On March 8, 1951, Fernandez was taken to the electric chair; he had to be supported, his legs bending like rubber bands. Martha followed him after wolfing down two complete chicken dinners.

Her final message to the world was contained in a posthumous note to the press, handed to reporters minutes after the current had been sent through her enormous body. It read—

My story is a love story. But only those tortured by love can know what I mean. I am not unfeeling, stupid or moronic. I am a woman who had a great love and always will have it. Imprisonment in the "Death House" has only strengthened my feeling for Raymond.

BECK, SOPHIE

Swindler ■ (1858– ?)

A minor confidence artist most of her life, Sophie moved to Philadelphia from New York at the turn of the century, using her savings to establish an impressive but hollow firm she called the Story Cotton Company, advertising for investors and promising a fifty-percent return on all money within weeks. Suckers by the droves showered her with cash—she insisted on cash-only investments—and, in return, received useless stock certificates. Pocketing more than $2 million in early 1903, Sophie sailed for Europe and sumptuous retirement.

BECKER, MARIE ALEXANDER

Murderer ■ (1877– ?)

An aging, graying housewife in Liège, Belgium, Marie Becker, at fifty-three had never done a wrong thing in her life. But life itself had conspired against her, she began to think in 1932, and love and youth had passed her, leaving her with a plodding, unromantic husband, a stoic cabinetmaker. Marie was the perfect love victim for Lambert Beyer, a middle-aged rake who propositioned her while she was selecting cabbages from a street stall one day. The lovesick Marie responded immediately, hurling herself into a tempestuous affair that left the scheming Beyer gasping for relief.

Marie Becker's first affair awoke in her a wild desire to capture anything that smacked of youth that she could attach to herself, make part of herself as it were. She not only poisoned her husband with digitalis, but quickly tired of Beyer and dispatched him in a similar manner. Neighbors were shocked to see this once matronly woman performing wild dances with men half her age in the local nightclubs. To dissuade her young male partners from leaving her at the edge of the dance floor, Marie paid these indifferent gigolos to accompany her home to her bedroom. Her new sexual habits cost Marie money she did not possess.

She solved her problem by poisoning the elderly women who patronized the new dressmaking shop she opened, stealing from these women what she could. From the ten known victims who swallowed her digitalis, Marie Becker enjoyed only small amounts of money.

A friend of Marie's then complained of her husband, adding, "I wish he were dead."

So easily had Marie committed murder that she responded with a statement that indicated her feelings of immunity from any kind of punishment, telling her lady friend, "If you really mean that, I can supply you with a powder that will leave no trace."

Some days later the friend informed police of her suspicions. Marie was arrested, while the bodies of her husband, Beyer, and some of her shop matrons were exhumed and examined, poison found in all.

Marie's trial was theatrical and bizarre. Corrupted with murder as her mind was, Mrs. Becker hid nothing, gloating over the deaths of her victims. She laughed when she described how one of the ladies who took her digitalis "looked like an angel choked with sauerkraut." Another victim she described as "dying beautifully, lying flat on her back."

Witnesses then told of seeing Mrs. Becker attend the funerals of each and every victim, dressed in black, kneeling at the gravesides, weeping great tears, then leaving the ceremonies to scurry off with the victim's money, spending that money on young men before the next dawn.

Belgium's mass poisoner Marie Becker at the time of her trial.

Marie Becker was found guilty and sent to prison for life, the most severe penalty possible in Belgium, which had long ago abandoned capital punishment. She died in prison some years later, the exact date lost in the chaos of World War II.

BEDDINGFIELD, ANN

Murderer ■ (1742–1763)

John Beddingfield was a well-to-do farmer of twenty-four when he married pretty young Ann and moved to a large farm in Suffolk, England, an estate purchased for him as a wedding gift by his wealthy parents. Several servants were employed at the couple's large manor house, one being a handsome nineteen-year-old named Richard Ringe.

Ann Beddingfield soon tired of her husband and seduced the naive Ringe, imploring the teenager to murder her husband so that they could be together, promising Ringe half her husband's estate once Beddingfield was safely out of the way. For three months the mistress and servant carried on a less than discreet affair, Ringe sneaking into Ann's bedroom each night. They were both also indiscreet in their murder plans, in fact, downright blatant.

One morning, while dressing, Ann called a servant to her, saying, "Help me put on my earrings, but I shall not wear them much longer, for I shall have new black ones. It will not be long before somebody in the house dies, and I believe it will be your master."

Ringe was even more obvious, purchasing some poison and imprudently begging a kitchen maid if she would stir it in with the rum and milk drink she customarily served Beddingfield. "I will be your constant friend," implored Ringe of the girl, "if you will but do this for me." The girl refused but did not inform authorities until after murder charges were brought against Ringe and Ann Beddingfield.

The plotters abandoned all subtlety and, in March 1763, resolved that Ringe would simply strangle the master while he slept in his own room. The youth did exactly that, then burst into Ann's room to exclaim, "I have done for him."

"Then I am easy," replied Ann, bundled beneath some quilts. Oddly enough, Ann did not mention the fact to Ringe as he stood sweating in the dark room that a servant girl was in bed with her (as a bedwarmer, which was then the custom). Ann thought the girl was asleep, but, after Ringe left the room to go to his own chamber, the servant, who had heard the strange conversation, jumped from the bed and ran to Beddingfield's room to find him lying dead beside his bed, black welts about his throat.

A coroner's jury some days later determined, oddly, that Beddingfield had "died a natural death," surmising that the wealthy farmer had somehow strangled himself in his own bedsheets after having a nightmare. None of the Beddingfield servants testified as to their suspicions.

A few weeks went by, and during this time Ann and Ringe fell out, the mistress telling the youth that he was a bumpkin and had almost gotten them hanged. She hated him, she said. Well, he hated her, too, he replied.

The servant girl who had slept with Ann on the night of the murder apparently hated both of them. She waited until she was paid her monthly wages, then raced off to the authorities to tell what she knew. Ringe and Ann Beddingfield were arrested and placed on trial in early April 1763. After several of Beddingfield's servants testified against them, Ringe confessed to his part in the murder; Ann, however, insisted that she had nothing to do with killing her husband. Both were convicted and sentenced to death, taken by sledge on April 8, 1763, to Rushmore, near Ipswich, where Ringe not only confessed again but gave a lecture to the large crowd assembled, warning young men to avoid the snares and pitfalls of wicked women and to "consider chastity as a virtue." He was then hanged.

Ann Beddingfield's fate was grimmer than that of her unseasoned lover; she was to be burned alive at the stake, a form of capital punishment reserved for unfaithful and murderous wives. As she was tied to the stake she suddenly repented and confessed her crime, telling all assembled there that she "deserved to die for being privy to the murder of her husband and for having had criminal intercourse with Ringe."

BELAND, MRS. LUCY ("MA")

Narcotics Peddler ■ (1871–1941)

Known as "Ma," Mrs. Lucy Beland was as terrible an influence upon her six children as Ma Barker had been on hers. The only difference in the criminal bent of Ma Beland was that she preferred the sale of illegal narcotics to the more hazardous occupations of kidnapping and bank robbery. Texas-born and -bred, Ma Beland and her family resided in Grandview, Texas; her husband, J. H. Beland, was an engineer for a cotton-oil mill. Nothing in the family's makeup suggested criminal tendencies until Ma grew restless in 1908 and insisted on moving to Fort Worth.

Within a year, J. H. Beland, his energies and bank account bled white, complained to a friend about his wife's excessive demands. "She's got me about crazy. . . . She gets greedier every day. . . . She says that if I can't give her the things she wants, she'll use the girls. She says that she's going to have a fine home and everything like that, and if she has to she'll send our daughters, Cora and Willie, on the streets to get them."

To Beland it was a losing battle. He left the family in 1912 and died a few years later. Ma did exactly as threatened, sending her girls onto the streets to shoplift and walk the streets as prostitutes while still in their early teens. Moving into a house in Fort Worth's red-light district, Ma began to deal in dope, especially heroin and morphine, instructing her sons to peddle the drugs throughout Texas. Her prostitute daughters became addicts, a condition that was to kill Cora, who was arrested for soliciting and overdosed in her cell after her mother smuggled morphine to her.

Willie Beland was also addicted to morphine, as were her brothers Charlie and Joe. Ma felt that her children would be more agreeable to her instructions if they were chained to her through drugs. Her sons became the most notorious drug pushers in the Southwest, particularly after the passage of the Harrison Narcotics Act of 1914 when drugs became scarce.

Of this period, Willie was later to state, "When dope became hard to get, Ma said that here was a real way to make money. When we girls would go out to work the streets at night, she'd parcel out some cubes of morphine for us to sell. Of course, now, we only do a wholesale business because Ma kept her word to us. Just as soon as we had made a lot of customers she moved out of the district and we Beland girls got off the streets."

As the major wholesaler of illegal drugs in the Southwest, the Beland family grew rich and powerful, Ma bribing highly placed Texas officials to overlook her blatant operations. However, agents of the Federal Bureau of Narcotics worked doggedly against the Beland clan and with occasional success. In 1931 Willie Beland and her husband, Lester James, both addicts, were caught selling heroin and sent to jail. Ma's son Charlie was sent to prison in 1935 for the same offense. FBI agents were tightening the ring around the Beland clan. But not until 1937 was the notorious Ma trapped by her own greed. An agent, working under cover, simply walked into the dry goods store she ran as a front in Fort Worth and boldly asked to buy seven ounces of heroin, showing a roll of hundred-dollar bills. Ma could not resist making such a profitable sale directly to a customer. She and several of her accomplices were arrested. She was given a two-year sentence because of her advanced years and died in 1941, two years after her release.

BENDER, KATE

Murderer ■ (1849– ?)

Little is known of Kate Bender before she and her father, mother, and brother moved into rural Kansas in 1872, setting up a two-room inn outside Cherryvale. Over the period of a year, the Benders killed more than a dozen travelers who had the bad luck to stay at their inn.

While curvacious, buxom Kate distracted the traveler, seating him against a canvas wall and serving him a hot meal, her father and brother would strike the victim's head, which rested against the canvas wall, with sledgehammers, then steal the victim's goods and bury the body on the plain near the small log cabin.

Kate appeared in many small towns at the time, giving séance and healing lectures, billing herself as "Professor Kate Webster." Many young men attracted to the voluptuous spiritualist were subsequently enticed to her murder inn. One of the Bender victims, Dr. Wil-

Kate Bender, leader of the "Bloody Benders" of Kansas.

liam York, proved the undoing of the murderous clan; he had informed his brother, Colonel York, that he would be staying with the Benders in early spring 1873. When the doctor failed to return home from his travels, the brother visited the Benders, making inquiries. Kate and her family knew nothing, but did offer to drag a stream nearby, Kate suggesting that "he might have fallen off his horse and into the water."

The suspicious Colonel York departed but promised to return shortly. It was enough to cause the Benders to panic. They packed up their supplies and stolen goods and fled on May 5, 1873. York returned with a posse to find the inn abandoned. Strange mounds of earth dotting the surrounding countryside were obviously graves and the posse members soon uncovered eleven bodies. (Perhaps two dozen more deaths were later attributed to the "Bloody Benders.")

None of the Benders was ever seen again, although reports from all over the country were

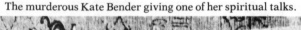

The murderous Kate Bender giving one of her spiritual talks.

made for decades, placing Kate in Detroit, St. Paul, and even San Francisco. In the late 1880s, one rumor had it that a posse did, indeed, catch up with the Benders and hanged them, except for the beauteous Kate; she was the last to be executed, burned at the stake for her crimes. This story was never substantiated, but given the fact that the possemen would themselves be held for murder if the story proved true, it was understandable that the tale remained apocryphal.

BEVAN, CATHERINE

Murderer ■ (1680–1731)

A woman over fifty, living in Delaware, Catherine Bevan carried on an affair with husband Henry's servant, Peter Murphy, then decided to murder the husband, first by poison, which Murphy purchased and Catherine gave to her husband with his morning coffee. When this failed, Murphy pounced on the sixty-year-old man, beating him unconscious while Mrs. Bevan strangled her husband to death with a handkerchief.

Catherine then sent her young lover to town to inform officials that her husband had died of a fit. A quick funeral was held, but a local judge thought it suspicious that the coffin was nailed shut; it was then the custom to view the deceased before burial. The judge ordered the coffin opened, and Henry Bevan's battered corpse testified to the real cause of his death.

Both the wife and lover were arrested, Murphy confessing almost immediately. The couple faced execution on June 10, 1731. Catherine's fate was especially gruesome. She, like Catherine Hayes in England five years earlier, was to be strangled to death at the stake and then her body burned. As with Catherine Hayes, the rope extending from Catherine Bevan's neck was burned away by the fire, which had been prematurely set, and the murderer was burned alive in horrible agony, the only woman in America to meet such an execution.

BILANSKY, ANN

Murderer ■ (1820–1860)

A nother love triangle found Mrs. Bilansky (née Mary Ann Evards Wright), of St. Paul, Minnesota, tiring of her saloon-keeper husband, Stanislaus Bilansky, and desiring the affections of her handsome nephew, John Walker, a carpenter by trade. After complaining to her friend, Mrs. Lucinda Kilpatrick, that the elderly Bilansky was nothing but a nuisance to her, Mrs. Bilansky dosed the old man's soup with arsenic; he was dead in a matter of days.

Mrs. Kilpatrick, after a few bad dreams, told her husband that her friend Ann had probably murdered her husband. Mr. Kilpatrick went to the police, who dug up the deceased, finding the arsenic.

Walker, who was arrested with his forty-year-old paramour, was released for lack of evidence. Ann was found guilty and sentenced to be hanged. She mounted the scaffold on March 23, 1860, and made her confession to a large throng. As the only woman ever hanged in Minnesota history, the thought of her execution was repugnant to the gray-eyed blonde. She snapped at the executioner, "How can you stain your hands by putting that rope around my neck?"

The hangman told her it was his job, no more.

"Be sure my face is well covered," she told him in a quieter voice.

A black cap went over the woman's face. Minutes later she was dead.

BJORKLAND, PENNY

Murderer ■ (1941–   )

Rosemarie Diane "Penny" Bjorkland, a resident of Daly City, California, was obviously in a demented state on the morning of February 1, 1959. When she awoke that day she told herself, "This is the day I will kill someone; if I meet anyone, that will be it." She left her parents' house with a .38-caliber pistol, and walked through the hills of San Francisco.

She found an unlucky gardener, August Norry, the father of two children, dumping refuse from his car on a remote road. He offered her a lift, thinking she was stranded. "Thank you," replied Penny who jerked forth her pistol and emptied it into the startled gardener. She pulled his body from his car, reloaded her weapon twice, and fired another twelve bullets into the dead man. Then she took Norry's car for a thrill ride through the hills.

Police traced the slugs taken from Norry's body—they were unusual "wadcutters," used for target practice—to a gun shop, and the proprietor, Lawrence Schultz, reported that Penny Bjorkland had purchased the special bullets.

The girl confessed the senseless murder following her arrest. She was tried and convicted, given a life sentence.

"This is not what I expected," mumbled the eighteen-year-old blonde.

BLANDY, MARY

Murderer ■ (1719–1752)

As the only daughter of the esteemed lawyer Francis Blandy of Henley on Thames, Mary Blandy received the best in home life and education, schooled as a reader of the classics. Her father touted her dowry of 10,000 pounds, although he found no suitor worthy of his daughter's affections. Mary was rather plain but had a winning personality; by the time she was twenty-six she was growing desperate, thinking her father intended to discourage any future husbands. At this time the Blandys met one Captain William Henry Cranstoun, the son of a Scottish peer who was recruiting in the area. He soon ingratiated himself to Blandy and his wife, who snobbishly thought him a worthwhile candidate for their daughter's hand by virtue of his noble ancestors. Mary thought so, too, despite the fact that Cranstoun was almost twice her age.

Cranstoun thought only of the huge dowry he would pocket after marrying Miss Blandy, a temptation great enough for him to forsake his wife and two children living in Scotland. He wrote his wife, begging her to sign documents, which he provided, wherein she would disown him. She did. Next Cranstoun wrote imploring the woman to have their marriage annulled. Mrs. Cranstoun balked at this and brought legal action against her straying husband.

Blandy heard of these odd arrangements and raged against Cranstoun, who had been his house guest for more than a year. By this time it was clear that he was a cad and a rake and Blandy would never allow such a man to marry his daughter. Cranstoun departed to live with a mistress nearby, then returned to Scotland.

From Scotland, Cranstoun sent Mary some powders she later claimed were ancient "love" potions designed to soften her father's heart toward the errant lover. Mary slipped the powders into her father's tea and gruel, and after taking them he grew ill, as did some of the servants who finished Blandy's poisoned meal.

Physicians were called, one telling Mary that if her father died, she would stand accused of murdering the old man. Miss Blandy quickly burned her letters from Cranstoun and threw the rest of the "love" powders into a fire, her actions witnessed by servants, who had also seen her dose her father's food.

When Francis Blandy was dying he called his daughter to him. She feigned ignorance of the cause of his impending death but, oddly enough, begged his forgiveness. Blandy did forgive her and gave her his blessing before dying

Mary Blandy begging her father's forgiveness for poisoning him.

He became ill and died on November 30, 1752, never having enjoyed a pound of Mary's dowry. Had he managed to murder and marry, however, he would have been cheated, for there was no 10,000-pound dowry. Blandy's entire estate when he died was less than 4,000 pounds.

on August 14, 1751. Mary, as everyone predicted, was arrested and tried, but not until March 3, 1752. The Blandy household servants testified against her. (Her mother had died from natural causes by this time.)

Mary Blandy defended herself with intelligence and zeal, but the testimony against her was too strong. She was convicted and condemned to death. Taken to an open field near Oxford, where she had been tried, Mary was ordered to mount a crude scaffold. As she awkwardly climbed a tall ladder, ruffians in the crowd attempting to peek beneath her skirts, Miss Blandy said to the executioners, "Gentlemen, don't hang me high, for the sake of decency." As the rope was placed about her neck, Mary covered her face with a handkerchief. Her body was allowed to hang for a long period of time to edify the enormous and unruly crowd. When finally taken down, she was buried next to her parents.

Cranstoun, the co-murderer, upon hearing of his sweetheart's arrest, fled to France and went into hiding behind the walls of a monastery, where he converted to the Catholic faith.

Shown with leg irons, Mary insisted on modesty at her hanging in 1752.

BLUFFSTEIN, SOPHIE ("GOLDEN HAND")

Swindler ■ (1854–1891)

One of Russia's most notorious female swindlers was Sophie Bluffstein, referred to as "the Golden Hand" by her underworld peers. A stunning, dark-haired beauty, Sophie married a small-time banker, but when her husband's future looked dim, she deserted him, traveling to the capitals of Europe, living on the income of her witty frauds. Through accomplices, she managed to present the appearance of a lady of quality, arriving at jewelry salons where she would order exquisite gems. These rare jewels were delivered to her suite, always in the best hotel, but when the jewelers arrived some days later to collect payment—a discreet period of time between possession and payment was then the custom when dealing with royalty and wealth—they found that Sophie had fled. She soon became wanted by the police of every capital in Europe—London, St. Petersburg, Paris, Vienna.

In Smolensk, Russia, Sophie was apprehended while trying to swindle another jeweler and was thrown into the local prison. Her beauty saved her as she seduced the governor of the area, persuading him not only to set her free but to desert his wife and children and accompany her. When she was finally trapped, it was through an accident of the police, who were looking for political terrorists at a party she happened to be attending. This time Sophie was sent to Siberia and locked up in the Alexandrovsk Prison. Authorities there thought so much of her guile and ability to escape that Sophie was kept constantly handcuffed for more than two years.

When freed, Sophie Bluffstein traveled to Vladivostok where she opened a successful inn, regaling guests with tales of her confidence games until her untimely death in 1891 at age thirty-seven.

BOGLE, HELEN McDERMOTT

Kidnapper ■ (1871– ?)

Mystery surrounded the life of Helen McDermott Bogle (the press sometimes referred to her married name as Boyle), and the lack of knowledge about her background vexed the press of 1909 as reporters attempted to explain her motives for becoming the infamous kidnapper of eight-year-old Willie Whitla in March of that year. Willie was the son of well-to-do James P. Whitla, a lawyer in Sharon, Pennsylvania, who was related to steel tycoon Frank Buhl.

The boy was picked up at his school by a man saying that he had come to take the boy to his father's office. Willie's teacher bundled up her student and took him to a buggy where the short, dark man waited. As he drove off with Willie, the teacher cryptically remarked to the school janitor, "I hope that man doesn't kidnap Willie."

That afternoon Mrs. Whitla received in the mail the following note:

> We have your boy, and no harm will come to him if you comply with our instructions. If you give this letter to the newspapers or divulge any of its contents, you will never see your boy again. We demand ten thousand dollars in twenty dollar bills. If you attempt to mark the money, or place counterfeit money, you will be sorry. Dead men tell no tales. Neither do dead boys. You may answer at the following address: Cleveland Press, Youngstown Vindicator, Indianapolis News, and Pittsburgh Dispatch in the personal columns. Answer "A.A. will do as you requested, J.P.W."

The family, remembering how Charley Ross had been kidnapped and had vanished forever in 1874, made preparations to pay the ransom, though Buhl gave out statements that no ransom would be paid. To assure the terrified parents that the Whitla boy was still alive during the negotiations through the personal columns, the kidnappers sent along the following note, signed by Willie:

> Two bad men have me. They will kill me if you don't send $10,000.

After police botched several of his attempts to pay the money, Whitla finally delivered the ransom to a candy store in Cleveland, and went to the Hollenden Hotel to await his son's delivery, as instructed by the kidnappers. Three hours later, a small boy got off a streetcar and walked slowly into the lobby of the hotel wearing a cap and goggles. By then the entire country had been alerted to the kidnapping, and the clerk at the hotel desk recognized the child instantly, taking off the boy's goggles and asking, "Aren't you Willie Whitla?"

"Where's my daddy?" said Willie through a wide smile.

Only hours later a man and woman entered a Cleveland saloon in a drunken state, flashing crisp new five-dollar bills and loudly ordering drinks for the house. The bartender set up the drinks and then checked the bills the couple threw on the bar, noting that they had consecutive serial numbers. He supplied the couple with free drinks, and when they finally staggered out after closing time, the bartender called police.

Taken to the station, the couple identified themselves as James H. Bogle and his wife, Helen. Police matrons found $9,790 sewn into Helen Bogle's clothes, every bit of the ransom money except what the two had spent in the bar. When reporters swarmed into the station to interview the wobbly-legged pair, Helen Bogle pushed aside her weak-willed husband to brag, "I planned the whole thing!"

She gave varying stories about her background. She had respectable parents. She had also spent fifteen years in a convent, receiving a classical education. None of this showed in the speech or mannerisms of Helen Bogle, who conducted herself more like the "loose woman" she was known to have been by police throughout the Midwest. Bogle was a simple-minded man, whose father had been a plumber in Shar-

on. He had been easily led by his wife into the kidnapping.

Both were quickly tried and sentenced to life in prison.

BOLTON, MILDRED MARY

Murderer ■ (1886–1943)

Chicago businessman Charles Bolton married an attractive but flighty girl from Kalamazoo, Michigan, in 1922. Before long he discovered her to be insanely jealous of his every move. The bespectacled Bolton, an innocuous-looking stay-at-home, never really gave his wife, Mildred, cause for her maniacal jealousy, but she nevertheless accused him of having affairs with every woman he encountered, from saleswomen to his secretaries.

The couple moved to Chicago in the early 1930s, living in Hyde Park, a quiet residential area. Police were summoned to the Bolton house on more than one occasion to find the much harassed husband bruised and bleeding, having been attacked by his raging wife as she screamed her fantasies of his infidelities. One time Bolton fled the house, his arm slashed so badly that he had to be hospitalized. An investigating officer found Mildred calmly smoking a cigar in her living room, explaining that her husband "cut himself while shaving." She did not bother to tell the officer why Bolton would be shaving at three in the morning.

On June 15, 1936, Mildred visited her husband's office at 166 West Jackson in the Loop. She walked softly into an inner office, where her husband sat looking at her from behind his desk, and emptied a revolver into him. Bolton managed to crawl into the outer hallway, where he begged startled elevator operators to "keep that woman away from me."

Mildred Bolton thought it funny that she be tried for the murder of her husband in 1936.

Mildred followed the man into the hallway, saying to the office employees, "Don't you mind! He's putting on an act!"

It was the final act; Bolton died some hours later and Mildred was quickly tried and condemned. Governor Henry Horner converted her sentence to 199 years, specifying that she was never to be paroled. Mildred was sent to the women's penitentiary at Dwight, Illinois, where on August 29, 1943, she ended her own nightmare-ridden life by slashing her wrists with a pair of scissors she had filched from the fabric shop.

BOMPARD, GABRIELLE

Murderer ■ (1869– ?)

A down-and-out trollop, Gabrielle Bompard became the mistress of ne'er-do-well and bully Michel Eyraud, a married man who was more than twice her age and had failed at numerous businesses. Both prepared to murder the first wealthy man who made Gabrielle's sexual acquaintance. On July 26, 1889, the luckless victim was Toussaint-Augustin Gouffe, a forty-nine-year-old bailiff, who was known to sip too much wine and wave about the funds he had collected during his day's work. Encountering Gouffe on the street, Gabrielle, who had wined and dined with the bailiff on numerous occasions, told him how Eyraud was mistreating her and that she would much prefer Gouffe's company. She invited him to her small apartment to share a bottle of champagne that night.

At eight o'clock Gouffe entered Gabrielle's tiny one-room flat on the rue Tronson-Du-Coudray. She manipulated him to a chaise longue behind which was a curtain, and behind the curtain hid the brutish Eyraud. As if toying with Gouffe, Gabrielle undid the silk belt from her kimono, opening the gown wide to reveal her naked body. She then encircled the drooling bailiff's neck with the belt, handing the end of the belt behind the curtain to Eyraud, who attached it to an elaborate pulley and rope system (which had taken the pair days to construct in the room). Eyraud then yanked downward with all his might. The bailiff was abruptly pulled upward by the neck and hanged.

The pair then took Gouffe down, placing his body in a canvas sack, which Gabrielle had spent hours sewing. The sack was lowered into a trunk at the foot of the strumpet's bed. Having gone through Gouffe's clothes and not finding the 14,000 francs he had foolishly shown to Gabrielle earlier that day, Eyraud raced off to the bailiff's locked offices. He broke inside and rifled the drawers of Gouffe's desk but found no money. Interrupted by a watchman, Eyraud dashed from the building. He returned to Gabrielle's room in a frenzied state, so excited that he insisted his accomplice have sex on the floor with him immediately; she reluctantly agreed, later claiming that Eyraud forced her.

The next day, having gotten only a small amount of money from Gouffe, the couple took the trunk by carriage to Millery, near Lyons, and dumped it on the bank of the Rhone River. They then fled, first to Marseilles, then to London, and finally to New York and Canada, traveling with funds borrowed from relatives. Meanwhile, the trunk and its grisly contents were discovered and authorities went to work identifying the corpse.

Gabrielle and Eyraud traveled to western Canada, visiting Vancouver, then to San Francisco, where the twenty-year-old vixen seduced a naive young American businessman. She confided to her new lover that Eyraud intended to kill her. They traveled east, Gabrielle insisting that they return to Paris. Once back in her homeland, Gabrielle informed her lover that she was wanted for murder, and promptly went to the police, confessing the killing of Gouffe, but putting the blame on Eyraud, and stating that she had been an unwilling dupe in the crime.

Eyraud, who had been following his faithless mistress across America, read of Gabrielle's testimony in the Paris newspapers, then wrote a twenty-page letter to the Paris police, insisting that the woman was framing him. He was arrested in Havana, Cuba, and returned to Paris where he and his elusive girl friend were put on trial.

At the end of five days, a jury returned a verdict of guilty for both. Eyraud was sentenced to death by guillotine; Gabrielle was given twenty years' hard labor. She smiled and thanked the jury. Eyraud sneered and mumbled as he was being led away, "It was *her* idea, not mine. Why should I forfeit my life alone? Why not the woman, too?" The answer was in Eyraud's question, because Gabrielle Bompard, no matter how heinous her crime, *was* a woman, and that stood for as much with French juries then, as it does now.

BONMARTINI, COUNTESS LINDA

Murderer ■ (1873– ?)

The partly decomposed corpse of Count Bonmartini was found in his house on the Via Mazzini, Bologna, Italy, on September 2, 1902, by neighbors investigating an overpowering smell. Police were astounded to discover that the dead man had fifteen wounds, undoubtedly dagger thrusts, that had entered his breast, arms, face, even the back of his neck. At first, investigators thought the deed had been committed by thieves; the room was in disorder and jewel cases and the count's pocketbook had been emptied.

The only real clue was the bloody imprint of a woman's hand on one wall of the murder room. This was photographed and studied without results. Two towels soaked with blood were also found. Police, knowing the count had the habit of patronizing whores, speculated that he had been killed by a streetwalker. Efforts to discover the guilty strumpet proved fruitless.

On September 11, 1902, a bewhiskered gentleman, Professor Murri, walked into the office of the magistrate in charge of the case, and stated with great formality, "Seek no further for the assassin of Count Bonmartini. I have come to tell you his name. It is my son Tullio."

Through the old professor the police heard the vicious murder tale. His daughter, Linda, had married Bonmartini but found him not only her intellectual inferior but a skirt chaser, and she had taken up with her old lover, Dr. Carlo Secchi. Moreover, the moments she did spend with her husband were filled with political tirades. Countess Linda was a liberal, the count an arch-conservative. Linda complained bitterly to her family about her marriage, once crying out to her brother Tullio and his mistress, Rosina Bonetti, "My God! Would that someone rid me of that soft-brained bigot!" Brother Tullio, who also hated the count over money matters, readily agreed to kill the husband, and thus the murder plot was born. Dr. Secchi and Tullio first thought to poison the count but abandoned that method as being too slow. Next, they asked a Dr. Naldi to stab their intended victim to death, telling Naldi that his pay would be "anything you can find in the place." The physician declined.

Frustrated, Tullio decided to kill the count himself. He used his mistress, the attractive Rosina Bonetti as bait. The woman enticed the count into a bedroom where Tullio, Linda, and Secchi were waiting. When the count was undressed, the gang attacked him with daggers, stabbing him to death.

Professor Murri uncovered the plot when, over several bottles of wine, his son Tullio weepily informed the old man of the killing. Tullio, his mistress Rosina, Countess Linda, and her lover Dr. Secchi, were placed on trial, found guilty, and given long prison terms.

BONNER, ANTOINETTE

Jewel Thief ■ (1892–1920)

Antoinette Bonner's entire world revolved around diamonds. An immigrant from Rumania, the girl learned early how to determine the value of fine diamonds, her father, an expert in the field for years, teaching her how to determine the proper color and purity of the gems. In an era when lapidaries were rare, Miss Bonner became a great asset to the top jewelers of New York City. She established an office, and through her contacts with wealthy women in search of perfect diamonds, she conducted sales ranging into the millions. At the time Antoinette was in her early twenties.

For four years, 1910 to 1914, Antoinette was known as "the Queen of Diamonds." Jewelers trusted her implicitly, turning over their diamonds to her without being paid and awaiting her spectacular sales. She would invariably re-turn within a few weeks with their cash, hundreds of thousands of dollars; her commissions averaged $100,000 a year. There were those in the gem business, however, who warned that at some point the temptation of the diamonds would prove too great for Antoinette. Such temptation seemed apparent in early 1914 when she disappeared with diamonds estimated to be worth more than a million dollars. Detectives were put on her trail, which ended in Paris in May 1914. The gems were recovered—they were still in Antoinette's possession—and she was arrested, protesting mightily that she had merely gone to Paris to negotiate a difficult sale, as was her usual custom. She was released, but it was several years before Antoinette regained the confidence of New York jewelers.

By 1920, her re-established reputation was such that a group of jewelers trusted her with seventy-five rare uncut diamonds, the value of which exceeded $500,000. These stones were sold to customers other than those specified by Antoinette, the jewelers learned. They were further alarmed when detectives in their employ reported that Miss Bonner had booked passage for Europe under an assumed name and had closed out her bank accounts. Police were alerted and soon burst into Antoinette's posh New York offices.

They found her seated at her desk, jamming important papers into a briefcase and preparing to flee. When she was informed of her arrest for jewel theft, Antoinette Bonner opened a desk drawer, took out a small bottle, uncorked it, and saluted the officers, saying, "Go to hell!" With that she swallowed the contents of the bottle, strychnine, stood up, walked toward the dumbfounded officers, and then fell dead at their feet. The beautiful Queen of Diamonds was only twenty-eight when she finished her career with the kind of heady drama that typified her life.

BONNY, ANNE

Pirate ■ (? −1720)

Contrary to all the bestial rules scratched down upon the scrolls of piracy, at least two women were allowed to join the motley ranks of seagoing cutthroats during the golden age of buccaneers. For Anne Bonny and Mary Read, leading the lives of female pirates was an enviable though hazardous ambition, and these two hellions proved to be more terrible than any of their cutlass-wielding messmates sailing the Caribbean.

Of the pair, Anne Bonny's early life gave no hint to the wild future she would embrace. Her father, William Cormac, was a successful lawyer in Cork, Ireland, but a roving eye and a reckless sexual appetite ruined that career when he and his attractive housemaid, Peg Brennan, produced a child out of wedlock, Anne. Cormac, to stifle gossip, first dressed the child as a boy, pretending that Anne was the small son of friends who had been left in his care. Growing disgusted with this farce, Cormac moved away from his wife, taking his child and his mistress with him, openly living with her in a small cottage. His heavily Catholic patronage disappeared and Cormac, to survive, sailed with Peg and Anne for Charleston, South Carolina, seeking a fortune in the New World.

The disgraced lawyer became a successful merchant in Charleston, and, after amassing a great fortune, purchased a huge plantation. When Anne's mother died, the young girl was thrust into the position of her father's housekeeper, prematurely assuming arduous adult duties. As such, Anne toughened in her early teens. At age fourteen, she was described as having a robust body, one larger and stronger than expected for her years. The great chronicler, Daniel Defoe, who was to lionize Anne Bonny and Mary Read in his romantic *General History of Pirates*, portrayed Anne in these formative years as having "a fierce and courageous temper."

Anne Bonny, the Irish-American female pirate, terror of the Caribbean.

More than once Anne lived up to that description. It was alleged that, in a raging fit, Anne scooped up a carving knife and slashed a serving girl to death, but this whispered gossip was never proved. It was known, however, that when a strapping Charleston youth waylaid Anne on a back road of her father's plantation one night, the girl lashed out at her attacker with such fury and force that she broke the young man's jaw and gave him so many other wounds that he was hospitalized for three months. The manner in which Anne used her fists would have been the envy of any latter-day John L. Sullivan.

Only a few years later an impoverished sailor, James Bonny, won the girl's heart, and the two were married without Cormac's approval. But Bonny was "not worth a Groat," according to one historian, his real aim being to obtain Anne's considerable inheritance. Her angry father reacted to the marriage by disowning Anne and forcing her and her avaricious husband from his plantation.

Bonny, ever the fortune-hunter, heard that Governor Woodes Rogers of New Providence in the Bahamas was determined to wipe out the pirates infesting the West Indies. The enterprising young man sailed for New Providence with Anne, applying to Rogers upon arrival for a position as informer. He was paid handsomely to loiter about the many brothels and taverns, turning in any cross-eyed sailor he suspected of piracy. All this disgusted his teenage bride, and more than once, she publicly upbraided her sleazy husband for his back-alley occupation.

When Governor Rogers declared an amnesty, pirates by the droves sailed into New Providence to claim royal pardons. One of these was the colorful brigand, John "Calico Rackham, so nicknamed because of his addiction to striped trousers, later to become part of the attire symbolic of pirates.

Rackham spotted the amply endowed Anne Bonny in New Providence and pursued her as would a cultured cavalier, plying her with expensive gifts and jewels he had filched throughout the Bahamas. Rackham had been the quartermaster for the much feared pirate Charles Vane. When Vane was captured and executed, Rackham took command of his sloop and crew, proving himself twice as dangerous as his one-time commander.

Anne quickly succumbed to the romantic overtures of the pirate, moving into a small house with him on New Providence. When her husband came to retrieve her, Rackham offered to buy Anne, exercising a then common though illegal practice of divorce by sale. Bonny not only refused to sell his wife but raced off to Governor Rogers to report his wife's infidelity. Rogers had the young woman brought before him, thundering that she would be flogged unless she returned to her husband. Instead, Anne went back to Rackham, and both decided to go to sea, taking up the ways of the pirate.

Anne, Rackham, and some of Rackham's old crew crawled undetected aboard the fastest sloop in New Providence one night, overpowering the guards and setting sail. Wearing

The "Jolly Roger" flag flown by Calico Jack Rackham, Anne Bonny's pirate lover.

the clothes of a seaman, and developing great skill with cutlass and pistol, Anne not only aided Rackham and his pirates in looting scores of merchant and fishing ships but more than once showed that she could be as terrible as her foul-smelling shipmates.

Anne, as would be Mary Read after joining the crew, was a fierce and uncompromising warrior who on boarding a ship wouldn't hesitate to kill anyone in her path. Wrote Hugh R. Rankin in *The Golden Age of Piracy:* "One witness at their trial stated that the two [Anne Bonny and Mary Read] cursed and swore with the best of males, and never cringed from murder." Though she sometimes wore female garb, Anne preferred men's clothing, especially when in battle, wearing a man's jacket, long trousers, and a handkerchief about her head. At such times she bristled with pistols, cutlasses, and knives.

One prize taken by Rackham was a Dutch ship. As was the pirate custom, the crew of the captured vessel was pressed into service aboard Rackham's ship. Anne Bonny spotted a fair-complexioned youth among the new seamen, one so attractive that she inveigled the youth into her cabin. As she began to slip off the sailor's jacket, Anne, "who was not altogether so reserved in point of chastity," jumped back at the sight of female breasts.

The first two female pirates, Anne Bonny and Mary Read.

Mary Read (left), fighting a duel to the death to protect the good name of her male lover.

Anne Bonny visiting her condemned lover Calico Jack and wearing female clothing, a rare occurrence.

The sailor revealed herself to be Mary Read, who, like Anne Bonny, had been given to wearing men's clothing most of her life, having served aboard a British man-of-war, and later as a cadet in an infantry regiment, and still later in the cavalry. Mary had fallen in love with one of her messmates and they had been married, settling briefly in Holland where they opened an inn, the Three Horseshoes, near Breda. When her husband died of illness, Mary, after several adventures, again donned the clothing of a sailor, and shipped aboard a Dutch vessel, the very one Rackham and Anne Bonny attacked and sank.

Anne took an immediate liking to Mary, promising to keep her secret from the lusty crew members. She did not count on Rackham, who, noticing the small kindnesses his mistress bestowed upon the young seaman, threatened to kill Mary. When Anne told the pirate his new conscript was female, Rackham swore the trio to secrecy.

The secret was short-lived. Mary Read fell in love with another seaman, one who had been pressed into service by Rackham, after accidentally revealing her womanhood to him—"she suffered the discovery of her sex to be made by carelessly showing her breasts, which were very white." The two became lovers, but the young sailor had no stomach for combat, and, when he was challenged by another pirate, the fearsome Mary Read took up the duel and, wielding a sword with the skill of a master, ran her lover's opponent through, killing him instantly.

Rackham and his cutthroats drove Governor Rogers on New Providence to raging tirades over their attacks upon peaceful merchant ships. Rogers vowed to rid the Caribbean of these pirates and, in late October 1720, ordered a Captain Burnet to arm his sloop and capture the brigands.

On the day Burnet chose for his attack, Rackham's ship lay off Jamaica, the crew half drunk, celebrating the capture of a merchantman that very day. They were also occupied in debating the fate of a Mrs. Dorothy Thomas, who had been taken capture in the raid. Most of the pirates, undoubtedly because of her sex, wanted to spare her, but two of the crew members viciously insisted the woman be made to walk the plank. Mrs. Thomas was later to state in court as she testified against Anne Bonny and Mary Read that she noticed their sex almost immediately: "By the largeness of their breasts I believed them to be women."

As the crew debated Mrs. Thomas's fate in a lower hold, Burnet and his men crept aboard Rackham's ship, surprising the guards on deck. Mary, Anne, and one other sailor rushed to the deck, slashing out at the attackers with swords, battling wildly. Mary Read turned to glance down into the hold where the rest of the pirate crew were cowering. "Come up, you bastards, and fight like men!" she shrieked at them. When they refused, Mary withdrew two pistols and fired down at them, killing one pirate and wounding another.

The three were finally overpowered, and all the crew put in chains. Captain Jack Rackham, who had locked himself in his cabin, surrendered meekly to Burnet, his mistress Anne so disgusted that she spat in his face.

Frontispiece of the 1725 edition of Defoe's *General History*, showing Anne Bonny and Mary Read.

The entire lot was taken to St. Jago de la Vega where they were put on trial and quickly convicted. All were to be hanged, including the murderous amazons. When the judge asked if there was any reason why they should not be executed, Anne and Mary replied in unison, "We plead our bellies," insisting to the court that they were both pregnant. Under British law, no woman with child could be executed until delivering the infant. The flabbergasted judge stayed the execution of the two women.

On the morning of his execution, Anne Bonny was allowed to visit her pirate lover in prison. Rackham sat blubbering on his prison cot while his one-time paramour eyed him with contempt. Her only comment to him before wheeling about and leaving was, "Had you fought like a man, you need not have been hanged like a dog!" She was returned to her cell and Calico Jack was marched to the gallows.

Mary Read's lover, being an impressed seaman, was set free, but Mary was held for execution pending the birth of her child. She never saw the hangman's rope, dying of fever before her child was born. The fate of her female co-pirate, Anne Bonny, was enigmatic. After several stays of execution following the birth of her child, Anne suddenly disappeared from the New Providence jail. It was generally believed that her father, repentant at having sent his daughter away and into a life of crime, bribed the local officials and spirited Anne and her child back to South Carolina, where, under an assumed name, she lived deep into the eighteenth century, dying a grand dame of a vast southern plantation with nothing but female finery in her stunning wardrobe.

Both hellions were specially marked for historical note, being among the rare pirates to be given a ballad to themselves:

> *With pitch and tar their hands were hard*
> *Tho' once like velvet soft,*
> *They weigh'd the anchor, heav'd the lead,*
> *And boldly went aloft.*

BORELLI, LaVERNE

Murderer ■ (1909– ?)

Discovering that her husband, Gene, had been making love to another woman, LaVerne Borelli, after fortifying herself with whiskey, returned to her San Francisco apartment on the night of May 9, 1946, removed her husband's automatic from a bureau drawer, and shot him to death while he slept. Gene Borelli was younger than LaVerne, and her jealousy stemmed from that fact.

LaVerne was defended by the notable criminal lawyer Jake Erlich but proved reluctant to help in her own case. She had, in fact, attempted suicide after murdering her husband by swallowing strychnine and firing two shots into her own breast but to no avail. She sneered and jeered at her own counsel throughout the trial, and it was a wonder that Erlich managed to reduce the charge against her to manslaughter, for which the woman received a light sentence in California's prison for women at Tehachapi. She was paroled on March 10, 1953.

BOTKIN, CORDELIA

Murderer ■ (1854–1910)

Mistress of John Presley Dunning, AP Bureau Chief in San Francisco, Cordelia Botkin was a self-styled Bohemian, who had left her husband in Stockton, California, for the revelries of the Barbary Coast. Dunning's long-suffering wife, Elizabeth, left her straying husband in 1896 to return to Dover, Delaware, the home of her father, who was a U.S. congressman.

Throughout the following year, Mrs. Dunning received anonymous letters from San Francisco, taunting the woman with Dunnings' extramarital relationships. The same letter writer later sent a box of candy to Mrs. Dunning, which arrived in Dover on September 9, 1898. Mrs. Dunning and some friends ate the candy, thinking it from a family friend. Elizabeth, along with Mrs. Joshua Deane, died in agony, three days later. Attending doctors determined that the women had been poisoned.

The candy was traced to George Haas' candy store in San Francisco and subsequently to the overweight Cordelia Botkin, who not only had mailed the box of poisoned bonbons to Mrs. Dunning but proved to have been the anonymous letter writer who had so harassed the abandoned wife. Cordelia was tried and given a life sentence, dying in San Quentin in 1910.

BOUVIER, LEONE

Murderer ■ (1929–   )

The tragedy of Leone Bouvier's crime was that the absence of love on every level of her life was what drove her to her crime. Born of alcoholic parents in the French village of Saint-Macaire-en-Mauges, Leone's childhood was lonely and loveless; her parents ignored the girl, and she and her older sister, Georgette, had to fend more or less for themselves. Georgette escaped the poverty and misery of her home by entering a convent and becoming a nun. Leone took work in a factory.

Ugly and ignored, the girl attended a local dance one night in 1951 and met Emile Clenet, a twenty-two-year-old garage mechanic who appeared attracted to her and proposed that they meet on Sundays at a local hotel. Leone felt Emile loved her, but after three or four meetings, he brutally told the twenty-three-year-old girl that he found her looks repulsive.

On one occasion a street photographer snapped the couple together. When they went to the photographer's office to see the prints, Emile threw the photo into a garbage can. "I don't want it," he said.

"Why not?" Leone asked.

"Just look at that face and you'll understand," the callous mechanic said, pointing to Leone in the photo.

A few weeks later Leone discovered that she was pregnant. Emile told her to have an abortion, in fact, arranged for a crude operation that left the girl desperately ill. Recovering in her squalid home, she sought comfort from her drunken mother. (The Bouviers drank nothing but a vile homemade cider known in the region as *gniole*, which was known to have driven some people mad and killed others.)

Mrs. Bouvier was less than sympathetic with her depressed daughter. Finding the girl weeping in bed, the mother inquired, "What the devil's wrong with you, girl?"

"Leave me alone," replied Leone, "I want to die."

Mrs. Bouvier nodded. "Go ahead and die then and stop disturbing everyone."

The abandoned Leone was crushed when she learned that she had been fired from her job for taking time out for her abortion. In desperation she bicycled to Nantes to visit Emile at the garage where he worked.

The reluctant boyfriend blew up. "Now get this into your head. There's plenty of time on Sundays for making love. The week, that's for work. Understand that once and for all if you still want to go on seeing me!"

The next day when Leone again came to visit him at the garage, Emile sent a friend out to see the girl waiting at the gate with word that she should never bother him again, they were finished.

For almost a month the girl lived as a lowly prostitute and from her earnings she purchased a .22-caliber automatic pistol. She had the weapon in her purse when next she saw the mechanic, on February 17, 1952, meeting Emile at a mid-Lent dance in the small town of Cholet. The mechanic took the girl for a spin on his motorcycle. As she held on to him, the cycle roaring over hills, Emile shouted to her that he was about to leave for the United States to earn more money.

"But what about me?" Leone asked.

"What about you?"

"But what will I become without you?"

"Anything you like."

"But we were going to get married."

"So what?"

"You don't want to marry me anymore then?"

"One day you want to, the next you don't. That's life. And the more I see of you, the less I want to marry you!"

The mechanic brought the motorcycle to a stop on the remote road. Leone shook her head sorrowfully, then pulled the pistol from her purse. She kissed Emile from behind on the cheek, raised the weapon to his neck and fired a shot into his head. He toppled dead from the cycle. Leone ran back down the road to her bicycle and pedaled madly to her sister's convent, begging for help. Police picked her up a few hours later.

Beginning on December 10, 1953, Leone's murder trial was devastating; the presiding magistrate, Judge Diousidon, mercilessly attacked the girl from the bench. When Leone's mother appeared in court she offhandedly condemned her ugly-duckling daughter by saying, "But my other daughter is a nun. . . ."

"You see!" cried Judge Diousidon, wagging an accusing finger at the girl cowering in the dock. "There is no need for you to go wrong! . . . Your behavior was not that of a proper young girl! Your gesture, and I am duty bound to put it thus, was atrocious. You kissed him, you kissed Emile Clenet and at the same time, with your right hand, you drew your pistol from under your coat. You placed it behind the head of this unfortunate man, you rested it on his coat collar. Then you pressed the trigger! Atrocious, I repeat, atrocious! . . . Why did you kill him?"

"I loved him," whispered Leone Bouvier.

"You loved him, you loved him," raged the judge. "So that's why you killed him!" Diousidon sneered. "The classic reply, I loved him!"

Despite a heroic attempt to defend her, Leone's lawyer, Claude Fournier, saw her case as hopeless. So did the jury. She was convicted of murder and sent to prison for life.

BRADFORD, PRISCILLA

Murderer ■ (1944– ?)

John Young Bradford trembled as he spoke, his hands shook and his face twitched. "They're after me," the fifty-three-year-old optometrist said in a quavering voice. "I think they plan to kill me."

The employees of the Budget Rent-a-Car agency in Orlando, Florida, were nonplussed. It was 4:00 A.M. February 23, 1980. Bradford, whose practice was based in Melbourne, Florida, insisted that he was marked for murder and needed a car, any car, right away, so that he would not be recognized. The badly frightened man was asked if he had a credit card. Bradford replied that he didn't use credit cards.

"No credit card, no car, it's our rule," he was told.

"But I have money." Bradford opened a wallet that bulged with crisp fifty-dollar bills. "I'll leave the wallet, all the money, just give me a car. The people who want to kill me will surely recognize mine." Then Bradford asked for some paper and a pen. He sat writing for some minutes, filling up two pages with a hurried scrawl. Finished, he looked up at the bewildered car-rental employees. "This is my will. Would you gentlemen be good enough to sign it?" The two men signed the document.

Instead of renting a car to Bradford, the rental agents drove the nerve-wracked doctor to his hotel, stopping first at a mailbox where Bradford sent his new will to his lawyer in Palm Bay, Florida. The agents watched the doctor walk unsteadily into his hotel but knew he was not crazy or drunk. Said one agent to the other, "Wouldn't it be just too weird if we read in the paper that this guy's been killed?"

On March 30, 1980, the car agents picked up a paper to read that Dr. John Young Bradford, Jr., fifty-three, had been found beaten to death in his Melbourne, Florida, home on the evening of March 28, 1980. Police had been summoned to the Bradford home that Friday evening to find the man a bloody pulp on the kitchen floor of his swanky suburban home. At first, police thought the optometrist had died as the result of a domestic quarrel with his wife, Priscilla, the dumpy, myopic woman who had summoned them. Only the day before, the thirty-six-year-old Priscilla had filed a formal complaint against her husband, saying that he had beaten her unmercifully. Neighbors could tell little to investigating officers, saying merely that Bradford was a quiet, peaceful man, never known to show violence. Priscilla Bradford, on the other hand, portrayed her husband as an inhuman monster who had pummeled, slapped, and slugged her about as if she were a punching bag. She admitted that she had struck the blows that had killed her husband in a terrific domestic battle. "But I was fighting for my life," she insisted.

Police at first nodded sympathetically. Acting Police Chief C. W. "Jake" Miller told the press that Bradford's tragic death developed from "a domestic situation that has progressively gotten worse."

But from the moment investigators entered the Bradford home at 208 Dubber Road, Melbourne, they suspected Mrs. Bradford's conduct was something other than a woman merely trying to defend herself against a brutal husband gone berserk. The woman seemed to be sorrowful, but she sobbed without tears. Her two friends, Joyce Lisa Cummings, 18, and Janice Irene Gould, 34, also contorted their faces in remorse, but their gestures appeared synthetic, practiced. Police found these women wearing bathing suits and dripping wet when they arrived. They had just come in from the pool in back of the house, they said, in response to the fight the Bradfords were having. Mrs. Bradford's fourteen-year-old daughter from a previous marriage, Eden Elaine, stood near the body of the dead man without a trace of emotion. She stared at the body without a whimper.

Mrs. Bradford adjusted her glasses in front of narrow staring eyes. Her granite-like oval face showed no strain, and from turned-down lips she repeated her statement blurted over the phone to police at 6:15 P.M. that Friday night: "My husband attacked me. I was fighting for my life. I had to do it." Bradford, she said, arrived home that night and, grabbing a bottle capper, shouted, "I'm going to kill you!" The struggle commenced. Cummings and Gould, hearing the commotion, ran from the swimming pool and into the house. They told detectives they had heard Mrs. Bradford scream, "No! Don't, John!" Both women claimed that they had no choice but to help Mrs. Bradford defend her life. "We all fought furiously in self-defense," one of the women volunteered. And they had won.

Both women worked with Mrs. Bradford in her husband's lucrative optical lab. Janice Gould, known as "Gouldie" to her friends, had moved from Everett, Massachusetts, and had been hired by Mrs. Bradford six months earlier. The 180 pounds on her five-foot-two-inch frame gave her the appearance of a fireplug with legs. Joyce Cummings was a high school dropout from upstate New York who had had a drug problem and a juvenile police record. She lived in a nearby mobile-home camp. As she stood in her bathing suit, dripping onto the handset dining room floor, one of the detectives noticed she had a rose tattoo on her right shoulder.

Bradford's body was removed that night, and police informed the women that they would be wanted later for further questioning. None of the events surrounding the gruesome death of Dr. Bradford seemed to fit the right patterns, according to investigating officers, Detective Earl Petty and Lt. Darrell Parsons. Both men became suspicious when Mrs. Bradford ordered a quick-as-lightning funeral, and then had her husband's remains cremated, despite the fact that the optometrist owned an expensive crypt at Fountainhead Memorial Park. The officers began to dig deeper into the background and character of Dr. John and Mrs. Priscilla Bradford.

The doctor had been extremely well-to-do. Besides having an estate worth more than $300,000, his home was definitely country club, situated on a golf course and boasting a large swimming pool. Bradford's lab, according to John Lockhart, the manager, showed profits of more than $12,000 a month. He owned and operated a 36-foot boat and belonged to several exclusive clubs. Born in Crowell, Texas, Bradford had been educated in Tennessee. None of his patients, business associates, or fellow club members found him to be anything but a mild-mannered, almost meek man, including his former wife, Deenie, who shook her head in wonder when hearing how Bradford had inexplicably changed into a frothing-at-the-mouth brute. "He never once struck me in twenty-eight years of marriage," she said.

But apparently all that had changed when Bradford married Priscilla Ann Hadley Smith, on November 5, 1976, about five months after Bradford's divorce from his first wife. Priscilla had always been unattractive but had been compensated in life by growing up rich in Trenton, New Jersey, living in a large white house next to a duck pond, wearing the latest fashions, and excelling in high school, acting in the class play, writing the yearbook, and singing in the glee club. She was a brainy person, a clever person, a calculating woman by the time she met John Young Bradford. By then, she, too, had been divorced, having married a soldier and moved to Florida, her first union producing one child, her daughter, Eden Elaine.

The relationship between John and Priscilla Bradford—the names put one in mind of the Pilgrim founders—was at first peaceful. But in the last six months of the Bradfords' life, the marriage had become a nightmare. More and more Priscilla spent most of her time with female friends, Gould, Cummings, and others, using them as a wall between herself and Bradford, her women's liberation sentiments mounting to shrieking crescendos. Priscilla's female friends were in the Bradford home at all hours of the day, and more than once Priscilla announced that her loyalty and love belonged to them, not to her husband. In frustration one day, the normally placid Bradford slaughtered a pig in the backyard for a roast given in honor of *his* friends. The sight of the bleeding pig enraged Priscilla, who rushed into the bedroom, dumped Bradford's belongings on the floor, and coated them with shaving cream, delighting her man-hating friends who squealed with laughter. Then came the attacks.

About a month before his death Bradford went to his lab late one night to retrieve some notes. He walked through the reception area, then into the large laboratory but neglected to turn on the lights. In the dark someone struck him a blow so hard that he crashed to the floor in a semi-conscious state. He heard the sound of what he thought to be the clatter of a woman's high heels running on the hard floor. On March 27, 1980, Bradford dressed in a hurry to get to his office; he was late and had no time for breakfast, just some orange juice. He gulped down a glass from a fresh batch made by Priscilla, and rushed to his lab. By the time he arrived, he was ashen-faced and so weak and ill that he collapsed on the floor of his office, lying there for two hours before he managed to take something to wash out his stomach. Next he called his lawyer.

"I think my wife is trying to poison me," Bradford told Nicholas Tsamoutales. He related the story of the spiked orange juice.

"Quick. Go home and get that glass so the contents can be analyzed."

Bradford drove home but the glass had disappeared. So had the orange juice. The optometrist filed for divorce the next day, the last day of his life, a day that for him was crowded with too many women.

Some days after Bradford's speedy cremation, police began to interrogate Bradford's employees and friends. Tracy Smith, one of the lab employees, pointed the finger at Priscilla Bradford and talked of premeditated murder. The murder plot was enlarged by John Lockhart, Bradford's lab manager, who had overheard Priscilla talking to Gould and Cummings in the lab, saying, "These two know that if I fry, they fry, too." Reported Lockhart, "She said she would do anything for the lab—to keep Dr. Bradford from getting it."

Then came the star witness, Priscilla's teenage daughter, Eden, who had been present at the time of Bradford's death. Police interviewed the girl who first told of her mother's heroic stand in defending herself from her terrible stepfather.

"That's not the way it really happened, is it, Eden?" an officer said slowly.

The girl broke into tears. No. Her mother meant to murder her stepfather. It was all planned, an ambush in which Gould and Cummings were integral parts. The teenager was obviously disturbed, her background as unstable as her mother's thinking. Eden admitted that she was "a weird person, you know. I acted much different than the other kids, and much older. I just, I don't know, I had a lot of problems." Her problems included smoking marijuana by the time she was thirteen, shoplifting, taking pornographic pictures of herself, and writing "dirty" letters to a Melbourne disc jockey she admired. She stated that she had been sexually attacked by a classmate at school and had since carried a Girl Scout knife for protection. And she had helped murder John Young Bradford.

The girl helped only in the last attack, ordered to do so by her mother, Eden said. They had tried everything else so the plotters concluded that the only sure way to kill the optometrist was to beat Bradford to death and make it appear self-defense, a common occurrence these days, when the trend, as Priscilla pointed out, was to free the battered wife. Months earlier, Priscilla, Gould, and Cummings had planned an elaborate death for the doctor.

Priscilla purchased a rifle in Miami, using a false name so it "couldn't be traced." Mrs. Bradford then gave the rifle to Joyce Cummings who practiced with it until she became an expert shot. Next Priscilla and Gould took Mrs. Bradford's car out into the country, faked a breakdown, then called the doctor to come to their assistance on the special two-way radios the Bradfords had installed in their cars. Cummings, hiding in the bushes nearby, was to shoot Bradford when he arrived to help. "But he would never come alone," Gould was later to admit, so the conspirators resorted to other measures. They long debated cutting the brake line of Bradford's car so that he would have an accident and hopefully be killed. "He might only be crippled," one of the women volunteered.

It was then decided to dose Bradford's morning orange juice with speed; he would surely black out at the wheel, and the resulting crash would most probably kill him. Joyce Cummings obtained a hundred amphetamine tablets, paying a friend $90 for the "black beauties." These were mixed into the orange juice, but to the women's astonishment, Bradford survived the massive poisoning. Bradford, on the other hand, acted like a man in a piece of bad fiction. Though he had made out a new will deleting Priscilla as a beneficiary, and though he had clear evidence that she was trying to murder him, he continued to live with her. Even after the poisoned orange juice incident, Priscilla convinced him that it was all a mistake. They would have a wonderful dinner the next night, just the two of them, and forget about all this attempted murder nonsense. Incredibly, the victim-to-be agreed.

On the morning of March 28, Priscilla met with Cummings and Gould at a Burger King, telling the conspirators, "It is going down tonight. Are you ready now? You realize it's going down tonight? I'm going to kill Bradford." The three women next went to a grocery store, purchasing filet mignon steaks and asparagus. One of the conspirators began to pick up a pack of paper plates, favored by Priscilla who hated washing dishes or doing housework of any kind. "No, put those back," Mrs. Bradford ordered. "I'm going to use the best silver tonight. It's going to be like the Last Supper." Gould and Cummings laughed long and hard at that one.

That night, according to Eden, all was in readiness. Only minutes before Bradford was due home, Eden was told to take her dog, Eeyore, into the bathroom, turn on the shower, and stay there. She, Gould, and Cummings had just finished slapping and punching Mrs. Bradford in the face, Priscilla insisting that they bruise and welt her body to prove to the police that Bradford had mercilessly attacked her. Earlier, Priscilla had furiously rubbed washcloths and fingernail files on her face and arms "to cause abrasions and make it look like she had been hit."

Eden was to stay in the shower, keeping the water running. Priscilla had ordained this so that her daughter would not hear Dr. Bradford's screams, nor would the dog get upset by the noise. The running shower would also serve another purpose. Immediately after Bradford had been killed, Gould and Cummings, wearing their bathing suits, could quickly wash away any blood from the wounds they were to inflict on Bradford, and make it appear to police that they had just run in from the swimming pool.

With Eden in the bathroom, the women waited in the kitchen, each selecting a large blunt instrument. Priscilla Bradford chose a huge cast-iron frying pan—the killing would later be dubbed by the press as "The Frying Pan Murder"—while the other two women armed themselves with two apothecary jars and an antique cast-iron bottle capper. The last item was normally used to cap bottles for homemade juices and other foods. Now it would be used to batter a man to death. The plan called for Mrs. Bradford to greet her husband pleasantly as he came into the house, then lead him into the kitchen where "a punch to his privates" would be delivered and render Bradford helpless. The three women would then kill the man, "bash him to pieces."

Everything went according to plan. Bradford came into the house. Priscilla smiled and kissed him, gently taking his hand and leading him toward the kitchen to see "some beautiful steaks." Eden, her dog tied to a towel rack in the bathroom, turned on the shower full blast, but the water did not drown out the awful screams and moans that continued for more than fifteen minutes. Inside the kitchen the women had gone wild and in a frenzy were striking Bradford, who was writhing on the floor in agony; they struck out with anything handy, the apothecary jars, the frying pan—which was finally splintered into seven pieces, broken on the doctor's caved-in skull—a wooden stool, golf clubs, and the metal bottle capper.

Bradford was tough, clutching on to life. Joyce Cummings, sweat pouring from her face, an abandoned look in her eyes, screamed to Janice Gould, "Hit him again, Gouldie! Hit him again!" Gould struck down at the twitching Bradford, fresh blood squirting onto her thick bare legs. Worn out, Gould staggered to the bathroom, threw open the door, and said to Priscilla's daughter, "Eden, the son-of-a-bitch won't die!"

Eden walked into the kitchen. "I saw him lying there. He was trying to breathe. It was a mess . . . it sounded like he was trying to say something. He was probably just gurgling. He was drowning in his blood and he started to move his hand and, well, my mother had the frying pan, which had the bottom of it broken out . . . she was hitting him with that."

Mrs. Priscilla Bradford then assumed her motherly duties by handing her teenage daughter the heavy bottle capper and snapping an order, "Keep hitting him—anywhere!"

Eden later remembered in a 6-hour testimony that would fill a 324-page deposition, that "I, really, you know, thought, okay, it wouldn't faze me or anything, so I took the bottle capper and hit him a couple times, just to keep him down."

The man was obviously dying but continued to fight against it. Disgusted, Priscilla ran to the phone and called her sixty-nine-year-old mother, Mildred Hadley, shouting over the phone, "We've been beating and beating him but he won't die!"

According to a later report, Mrs. Hadley replied, "Just beat him some more until you're sure he's dead. Then call the police."

While this call was going on, Eden stared down at her stepfather, compassion rising. "I really was looking at him, you know. His eyes were open and he was looking at me and I remember I started to cry, but then I stopped. I don't know. I just stopped probably because if I started to cry or something or I started to maybe help him, maybe they would have turned against me.

"And I wanted, I think I really wanted to help him. There was nothing I could have done. Even if he had survived, he would have just been a total mess, you know. No way really to put him back together, I don't think."

Bradford, with superhuman strength, tried to rise from the floor. "He didn't even look like a person in his condition," Eden recalled. "He didn't look like a person at all. And I didn't know what to do, you know? So I took the bottle capper and hit him a few times on the neck." A second before Eden struck her stepfather, Bradford stared into her eyes, a look that seemed for her to "last an hour. It really seemed like a long time I was looking at him. . . . He had a look in his eyes, you know, why did you all do this to me? What did I do?"

The nightmare gripped the child as it had the adults who created it, and later Eden was to think back about her mother's conduct, how for months she had nagged the teenager into hating her stepfather, preparing her. "Before the killing, when she had been saying all these things to me, I turned against him, because I believed her. But when I think of it now, I think that eighty to ninety percent of it was really just outrageous, I mean. I don't believe it. I don't see how he could have been that awful. I don't think I really hated him." But Priscilla Bradford, and Cummings and Gould, as later testimony pointed out, did hate Bradford, who represented all men to them, these women liberationists gone wrong, turned to blood-dripping murderous banshees, taking a human life to control an optical laboratory.

Before investigating officers answered Priscilla's call, Mrs. Bradford said to her daughter, "I want you to start crying when the cops get here. I want real tears!" But the act was a disaster. "I couldn't cry," Eden later told police. "I couldn't even fake it. Janice and Joyce did a lousy job. They couldn't even tear."

Police removed the body to the morgue, where pathologist Dr. James B. Adamson listed Bradford's death as due to asphyxiation; he had swallowed his own tongue. He had been struck fifteen times. His head had been caved in, his jaw broken twice.

On April 10, 1980, Priscilla Bradford, Joyce Cummings, and Janice Gould were charged with murder and jailed. Eden was given immunity as a witness for the state. Her grandmother, Mrs. Hadley, who had reportedly encouraged her daughter to finish off Bradford over the phone, an unsubstantiated report, was released.

It appeared that Priscilla Bradford and her female friends were finished, but the harrowing housewife was far from giving up. Priscilla reasoned that her daughter would recant her massive admissions in court. That left only Lockhart and Tracy Smith as witnesses against the murderous trio. They could be eliminated. Miss Smith was the most dangerous, Priscilla thought, and so she asked a cellmate, Ursula Mattox, a prostitute, if she "knew anybody who could kill somebody."

"Are you kidding?"

"No, I'm serious. You've got to know somebody. You've been on the street." Priscilla insisted that Ursula contact a "professional killer" who would murder Tracy Smith, someone who could make her death appear accidental, hide her body somewhere for a few months. Perhaps the killer could burn down the trailer Tracy lived in, even though Tracy's husband, Joe, might be inside the trailer. "He's nothing but scum anyway," Priscilla added, dismissing the husband's possible death as anything to be considered. "The way Tracy likes men," Mattox later quoted Priscilla, "it would be very easy for a man to pick her up, rape and kill her."

Mrs. Bradford confided to Mattox, "I'm rich. Do this for us and I'll give you some priceless jewelry and a share—make it a quarter interest—in my optical business."

Gould encouraged Mattox to do Mrs. Bradford's bidding: "We don't have anything to lose anyway. We're already going to the electric chair."

Mattox nodded agreement but it was a ruse. She informed jail authorities of the plot and they allowed the farce to continue. Grandmother Hadley, they later reported, visited the Titusville Jail where the women were being held, and was told by Priscilla to obtain $2,000 in hundred-dollar bills, and to place this money in a plain envelope and drop it in a phone booth near a Dino's pizza parlor. Grandmother Hadley nodded, apparently not knowing what it all meant. Janice Gould's mother, Virginia, would accompany Mrs. Hadley.

Next Priscilla wrote a note to the would-be killer-for-hire, giving this to Mattox who, in turn, said she would pass it along to her contact. The note read, "Tomorrow, 2 p.m., Dino's, 2 old ladies, white haired one drop bottom phone booth white envelope, do not do until $ in your hands, accident, at your convenience."

Mattox slipped the note to jail guards when Priscilla wasn't looking. Mrs. Bradford and her friends chuckled at the idea of using two elderly women in the plot. "Between the two of them," laughed Priscilla, "they should have a brain working."

The elderly women did as they were told, dropping the package of money in the phone booth where it was retrieved by police officer Robert Carrasquilloa, dressed in shabby clothes and pretending to be the professional killer. Mrs. Hadley walked back to the phone booth after Carrasquilloa departed to make sure the package had been picked up. Other officers, hiding nearby, took dozens of photos of the drop-off. No charges were made against the old ladies since authorities considered them dupes, but the note and delivery of the mony were used in evidence against Mrs. Bradford and friends on charges of conspiracy to commit murder, making for six trials.

There were only three, and all were brief. Before the trials commenced, the conspirators decided to put on brave faces for the cameras that would be trained on them by Central Florida Television. "We're gonna smile and not worry about what anybody thinks," Priscilla told her co-defendants in jail. She snorted a laugh. "Maybe we ought to wave and say 'Hello, Mother!' "

"Maybe I ought to shoot a bird," laughed Cummings.

But there was no smiling when Mrs. Bradford came to trial, not a snicker. In August 1980, Mrs. Priscilla Bradford, saying that she did not wish to hear her teenager daughter condemn her in court, pleaded guilty to the murder charges. Cummings and Gould were also convicted. All three were sent to prison for life.

Joyce Cummings summed up the motive for the three man-killers at the conclusion of her trial: "All we wanted was an all-female lab."

BRANCH, ELIZABETH AND MARY

Murderers ■ (Elizabeth, 1673–1740; Mary, 1716–1740)

Born in Phillips-Norton, Somersetshire, England, Elizabeth Branch had always manifested a cruel streak in her unpredictable nature. It was a wonder to most that a wealthy farmer married the sadistic young woman, and, indeed, he soon had cause to regret his action. His wife not only beat their servants but made them sleep outside when they displeased her. Her daughter, Mary, grew to be her exact likeness in temperament, as mean and vicious as her mother.

When Branch died, leaving his wife and daughter a sizable estate, the women began to persecute their servants, beating and torturing them in every conceivable way. One teenage girl, Jane Buttersworth, who had been placed as an orphan in the Branch home, was the particular object of the women's wrath. The girl was too slow in performing her chores and was beaten senseless at every turn.

When Jane spent too much time buying yeast one day, Elizabeth and Mary attacked her with fists and broomsticks. They stripped her and continued to beat her, pouring salt on her open wounds as they attacked the poor girl in a frenzy.

A milkmaid, Ann Somers, entered the Branch house to find Elizabeth quietly seated before a fire, the battered body of the girl lying on the floor in a pool of blood. (Oddly, Somers

Elizabeth and Mary Branch shown beating the hapless Jane Buttersworth, 1740.

later declared, the Branch women had put a clean cap on the girl's head and "blood had run through it.") Mrs. Branch pointed to the girl, cursing her and saying that she thought she had died. That night the Branch women ordered Ann Somers to sleep with the dead girl. In the middle of the night the women apparently came to their senses and dragged the body to a pasture where they buried it in the moonlight.

Thinking she would be the next victim of these maniacs, Ann Somers raced to the police at the first opportunity and told her story. Elizabeth and Mary Branch were arrested and taken to Taunton for trial in March 1740. After Ann Somers and others testified against them, both women were condemned to death. Mrs.

Branch appeared unconcerned while awaiting execution, but her terrified daughter begged all who spoke to her in prison to pray for her.

The Branch women were taken to Ovelchester to be hanged, authorities having warned that the residents of Sumersetshire intended to "tear them apart while alive" before their execution there. Mrs. Branch confessed to her crime on the gallows in a long speech, admitting that she had considered her servants "as slaves, vagabonds, and thieves; it was these that made me despise them, and led me on from one degree of cruelty to another." As her daughter, twenty-four years old, wept loudly at her side, Mrs. Branch asked that the executioner perform his duty quickly.

Both women were allowed to hang for more

than an hour while several clergymen harangued the huge crowd, stating that servants should not be beaten. From most reports, the spectators were only concerned with the grim deaths of these horrible women.

BRECOURT, JEANNE

Blackmailer ■ (1837– ?)

Like Marie Lafarge before her, Jeanne Amenaide Brécourt had grand illusions about herself, but, unlike Madame Lafarge, who *was* related to French royalty and murdered out of fear that her delicate dream world would collapse, Jeanne Brécourt only pretended an aristocratic background, and destroyed her lovers out of sheer hatred of men and love of self. She was a lethal vixen, who became France's most infamous courtesan of the nineteenth century.

Jeanne was born in Paris in 1837. Her father was a printer, and her mother sold vegetables from a pushcart. Both parents worked so many hours a day that each night they dropped from exhaustion. There was no time for the little girl; there was only survival to think about. A titled lady chanced to meet little Jeanne when she was five years old and adopted the neglected child. Within three years the girl had changed from a meek-mannered street waif to a haughty, spoiled child who refused to play with other children because she deemed them socially inferior. To another eight-year-old Jeanne was heard to pronounce imperiously, "The daughter of a baroness cannot play with the daughter of a wine merchant."

Jeanne's original parents fell on even harder times in 1848 and insisted that their daughter be returned to them to help support the family. At age eleven the confused child was torn away from a life of ease and culture and returned to poverty, compelled to sell gingerbread in the streets of Paris. The girl slaved at this miserable trade for seven years, learning the mean ways of the gutter. At eighteen, Jeanne implored the baroness to take her back, telling the kindly old aristocrat that if she had to spend another day trying to survive in poverty row of Paris she would end her life. The baroness took the girl under her wing once again, finding her a job in a silk plant.

Pretty, imaginative, and full of the craft and wiles of the street, Jeanne continued to live with the baroness but began to scheme of a way to better her station. Her early years of drastic changes, black and white existences, had formed in her an abiding fear of losing the comforts that money and status could ensure. At eighteen, Jeanne attended the wedding of a friend and returned after the nuptials to tell her benefactress that she was desperate to marry.

The baroness had heard Jeanne's whims expressed countless times and always treated these impulsive comments lightly. When a grocer arrived delivering goods, the baroness pointed to him and remarked flippantly, "You want a husband? There's one." To her amazement, Jeanne married the grocer, a man named Gras, within weeks. The marriage was doomed from the outset.

Though the baroness supplied money for the couple to open a grocery store, the differences between them were insurmountable. Gras was a crude, ugly peasant whose only real interest in his young bride centered about his insatiable sexual appetite. He would drag the girl into the small bedroom behind their grocery store at all hours of the day and night, treating her more as a common street slut than his wife. Often as not, Gras would rush into the grocery after having made a delivery, shout for the customers to get out, and rudely lift Jeanne's skirts, taking her behind the counter or even on it.

In contrast to her doltish husband, Jeanne had had the benefit of enough schooling—the baroness had provided her with a private tutor, who had instructed her in the ways of etiquette, and had given her an appreciation of the fine arts—so that she towered intellectually above her spouse and resented his common ways. In no time, the couple fell to bitter arguments. Jeanne found Gras' constant drinking offensive and told him so. Gras sneered at his wife's high airs and branded her a schemer to her face.

"You will die in a hospital," Jeanne told Gras. "A drunk."

"You will land your carcass in prison," he spat back. "A criminal."

Within the coming decades, both would discover just how accurate these impulsive prophecies actually were.

When Jeanne began to refuse his sex-at-all-hours, Gras packed a bag and vanished. The young woman went back to live with the baroness and some months later sold the grocery. With the proceeds from this sale, Jeanne left the baroness, never to return.

Not for some years did Jeanne again surface in Paris. When she did, it was as an entirely new person, a beautiful, irresistible courtesan with a new name, Jeanne de la Cour. Before this, Jeanne had tried all manner of professions. She had acted with several troupes, using a different name. She had attempted to write novels, also under another name. She had tried her hand at journalism, using still another name. Jeanne had failed miserably at everything.

Once back in Paris, ensconced in a luxurious suite, she reverted to becoming the alluring sex symbol that had driven Gras mad. By then Jeanne was a heartless creature, without passion, without sympathy for her fellow human beings. She had given herself wholly to eroticism, enjoying it for its own sake, perhaps developing a latent nymphomania, some reports have it. She became wealthy from the favors of men, and she grew to despise all men. She pretended love for men but developed a deep desire to see them suffer.

To a young sister she wrote, "All is dust and lies. So much the worse for the men who get in my way. Men are mere stepping-stones to me. As soon as they begin to fail or are played out, I put them scornfully aside. Society is a vast chessboard, men the pawns, some white, some black; I move them as I please, and break them when they bore me."

The siren viciously carried out her philosophy through the heyday of her high-priced prostitution. One of her lovers, a German merchant, gave Jeanne all his riches and, after she had milked him, she refused to see him

again. He committed suicide. Her only comment was, "One less German in Paris!"

A young scion of an aristocratic French family showered gifts on Jeanne, even stealing the family jewels to place about her lovely neck. When he had no more to offer, Jeanne told him he was sexually inadequate and dismissed him. The injured youth died the next day of an overdose of cantharides. Informed of his death, Jeanne laughed, remarking that "it was bound to happen—he had no moderation."

Another lover, his fortune also depleted by the gold-digging harlot, drank himself into a hospital where he perished blessing Jeanne's name. Said Jeanne, "He was a fool who, in spite of all, died respecting me."

But Jeanne had little respect for her own body. She used it as a weapon against men to obtain her riches and, after ten years of neglect, she entered a private asylum posing as a lady of quality. Not only did she suffer from rampant venereal disease but her nervous system seemed to be affected by all her years of debauchery. Attendants patiently helped her through convulsions, hysterical fits, and deep depression during which she completely lost her speech. A doctor's report of that period describes Jeanne as "dark in complexion, with dark expressive eyes, very pale, and of a nervous temperament, agreeable and pretty."

Late in 1865 Jeanne was released, told that she was cured, and advised to rest. Using the fake title of baroness, Jeanne traveled to Vittel, a resort town, and took rooms in the largest hotel-spa. There she played the grande dame, but her funds became low and so she returned to Paris. To support herself in luxury, Jeanne went back to her old ways, but her looks were fading. She resorted to blackmailing her clients and in this way built up a new fortune. One of her victims, an aging count, paid her an enormous amount of money to buy off her claim that she was having his child. Of course, the pregnancy was faked, but it worked to Jeanne's end nevertheless.

Fielding about for more victims, in 1873 Jeanne attended a ball, where she was introduced to a young well-to-do gentleman named Georges de Saint Pierre. Though Jeanne was sixteen years older than he, Georges fell madly in love with this worldly woman. He became her only lover and supported her richly.

Georges idolized the woman, who was both mother and lover to him, his own mother having died when he was five years old. His letters to her were slavish in expressing his total devotion. One read—

It is enough for me that you love me, because I don't weary you, and I, I love you with all my heart. I cannot bear to leave you. We will live happily together. You will always love me truly, and as for me, my loving care will ever protect you. I don't know what would become of me if I did not feel that your love watched over me. . . . Your form is ever before my eyes; I wish I could enshrine your pure heart in gold and crystal.

Georges went to Egypt in 1876 for a six-month visit, but he did not forget his precious Jeanne, begging her to use his Paris apartments whenever she pleased. He also continued to make sure she received her handsome monthly allowance from him. Jeanne, however, became uncomfortable with the affair. Though Georges had never once indicated a loss of interest in her, the woman worried. Their affair was approaching its fourth year and there was no assurance that it would continue indefinitely. The thoughts of her security with Georges, or lack of it, became an obsession. She knew full well that his family disapproved of her and that his relatives would object violently to any marriage plans the lovers entertained. Jeanne herself entertained them hourly; she did not know what was in Georges' mind.

Just after Georges returned from Egypt in late 1876, Jeanne went with friends to an afternoon party in the home of a famous ballet dancer. While there, she watched, fascinated, as a friend of hers entered the salon leading a young man who was totally blind. Jeanne's friend made the young man comfortable on a sofa, then tended to his every need. The young man expressed profound gratitude for every small kindness, kissing the hand of his female companion, murmuring his devotion to her.

Jeanne called her friend to her. She, like Jeanne, had once been a ravishingly beautiful courtesan, and, also like Jeanne, her beauty was fleeing. Yet she seemed perfectly happy in the company of the young blind man. She quickly explained to Jeanne: "I love this victim of nature and look after him with every care. He is young, rich, without family, and is going to marry me. Like you, Jeanne, I am just on forty. My hair is turning gray, my youth vanishing. I shall soon be cast adrift on the sea, a wreck. This boy is the providential spar to which I am going to cling that I may reach land in safety."

Jeanne Brécourt found the story more than charming. "You mean then that you will soon be beyond the reach of want?"

"Yes," sighed the friend, "I needn't worry anymore about the future."

"My congratulations," said Jeanne, and then the thought came to her, an incredible thought. "And what is all the more wonderful—your lover will never see you grow old!"

The scene of the friend and her blind lover never left Jeanne's thoughts. To have such a devoted and *helpless* lover was the perfect answer to her horrible doubts about the future. Such total dependence of such a stricken man would guarantee security for life. That was the answer, Jeanne concluded, she was sure that was the answer. Slowly, a plan, sinister and hideous, took shape in Jeanne Brécourt's mind.

To help that plan to completion Jeanne sought out an old friend, Nathalis Gaudry, who had been her childhood playmate in the streets of Paris. But to Jeanne, Gaudry would not act as a friend—he would serve as her weapon. She had seen Gaudry on the street in 1875. The uncultured, rough and burly man had almost swooned when he beheld Jeanne as a beauteous lady of the world. He had mumbled something about his wife dying earlier that year and how he worked in an oil refinery at Saint-Denis. Jeanne sent for him, and soon the ugly, good-natured man stood before her, his eyes filled with affection.

"It is so good to see you again, Nathalis," cooed Jeanne as she motioned him to a chair, her skimpy chemise arranged in such a manner that Gaudry had a long look at Jeanne's ample breasts and curvacious legs. She was thinking that she might need some help with her apartments, Jeanne told Gaudry, and had remembered him. Would he like to make some extra money helping her with odds and ends?

Anything, the workingman nodded. Gaudry filled all his spare hours after that by dutifully laboring for Jeanne. He scrubbed her floors, carried coal, and even bottled her wine. No job was too menial for him. Weeks went by before Gaudry worked up enough nerve to ask the woman of his dreams if she would marry him. No, Jeanne said gently, she was not the woman for him. Kissing him sweetly on the cheek, Jeanne told Gaudry they must remain friends, but that she had many beautiful acquaintances and that she would arrange some meetings.

On the pretext of introducing Gaudry to prospective wives, Jeanne invited friends for lunch while Gaudry was in her apartments. He met an actress, a seamstress, and several rich prostitutes, whom Jeanne introduced to him as merchants. These women generally found Gaudry ugly, even repulsive, but their visits served Jeanne's insidious purposes. Gaudry became convinced that his darling Jeanne was attempting to find him a good wife, which increased his blind devotion to her.

On November 17, 1876, Jeanne sent an urgent message to Gaudry at the oil refinery where he worked. "Come at once," the note read. "I want you on a matter of serious business. Tell your employer it is a family affair; I will make up your wages."

Gaudry arrived in Jeanne's apartments in a breathless state. He had run all the way. Jeanne came to the point immediately. She had been terribly wronged and could think of nothing but revenge. She had entrusted money to a man, Jeanne confided to Gaudry, and he had cruelly defrauded her, refusing to return the loan. "I will strike back at his dearest possession," Jeanne said. "And that is his son. You, my dear Nathalis, will be the instrument of my revenge."

With that Jeanne led the dumbfounded brute to her waiting carriage and drove to an exclusive men's club. Hiding behind the shades of the carriage, which was parked across the street from the club, Jeanne and Gaudry waited for some hours until a handsome young man appeared. "That is the man's son," Jeanne said to Gaudry. "Burn his image into your brain." She

had pointed out her devoted lover, Georges de Saint Pierre.

It was some months, however, before Jeanne put her complete plan into operation. Georges complicated matters by leaving for his country estate to visit with his family over Christmas.

In early January, Georges wrote lovingly to his mistress from his country estate. But the letters contained certain things that alarmed Jeanne and made her all the more resolved to go through with her brutal plan.

Georges had written:

I cannot bear leaving you, and I don't mean to. We will live together. . . . I have difficulties with my family which have made me depressed. The difficulties do not concern money or business but are of a kind that I can only communicate to you in person.

Jeanne knew what that meant. His family was opposed to any kind of liaison between them and would certainly tolerate no marriage. Perhaps they have discovered my real past, Jeanne's thoughts nagged. She had to act soon.

Jeanne wrote back, imploring Georges to return to Paris on the night of January 12, 1877. She told him that she was desperate to attend the masked ball at the opera house on January 13, since friends she hadn't seen in years would be on hand. Naturally she could not go alone, but must be escorted, as befitted a lady of quality.

Georges wrote back, his missive displaying reluctance:

I don't understand why you are so anxious to go to the opera. I can't see any real reason for your wanting to tire yourself out at such a disreputable gathering. However, if you are happy and well, and promise to be careful, I will take you. I would be the last person, my dear little wife, to deny you anything that would give you pleasure. . . . I am depressed this evening. For a very little I could break down altogether and give way to tears. You can't imagine what horrid thoughts possess me. If I felt your love close to me, I should be less sad.

As soon as Jeanne received this letter, she got in touch with the giant Gaudry and instructed him to appear promptly at 2:00 P.M. at her apartments on January 11. As usual, the devoted laborer arrived on time. Jeanne took him into the parlor and carefully picked up a small bottle.

"Do you know what this is, my dear Nathalis?"

Gaudry shook his head.

Jeanne removed the cork from the bottle. "I am suffering because of the injustice done to me. It has made me physically ill. I *must* have revenge upon the son of the man who has cheated me! Make him suffer, if you love me, Nathalis." She held up the bottle and dropped a splash of acid onto the edge of a carpet. It ate through the thick fibers in seconds.

"Here is the means. Use it and I swear I will be yours. I will become your lover." She handed the bottle to Gaudry.

Gaudry, an honest soul, stood in horror. He then blurted out, "I would do anything for you—but this. I am a soldier. I was given a medal for valor in the Italian war of 1859, which you know, madam. Using acid is not the work of a soldier." He thought for a moment. "I will provoke the young man to a duel. I will kill him that way."

"No, no!" Jeanne's careful plan was suddenly crumbling under the weight of Gaudry's own awkward honor. She never meant for Georges to be murdered. That wouldn't do at all. "He is not of your class. He would refuse to fight with you." She approached the man, taking up his giant paw of a hand, placing it against her breast. "I ask that you play the cowardly ruffian for me. I know you are a gallant soldier, but you must play the role I assign you—and then you can have me."

Gaudry was lost. He agreed to throw the acid into the eyes of the young man Jeanne had pointed out in the street. They went into rehearsal, Jeanne acting as director, Gaudry the grim cast of one. Jeanne Brécourt's experience as an actress stood her in good stead as they made their preparations; her attention to the details of her plan put Gaudry in awe.

She had arranged for her deadly enemy's son to take her to the opera ball, Jeanne explained to Gaudry. They would arrive home late in the evening of January 13. Gaudry would hear Jeanne ring the bell for the porter to open the outer gate to the courtyard leading to her apartments. The porter would then go back into the building, leaving this gate open until Jeanne rang for him to close it. He was then to rush from hiding in the courtyard and throw the acid in the young man's face, taking care to aim the vitriol into his eyes.

"But some of it might strike you," Gaudry worried.

"I will be behind him, closing the small inner gate. I shall not really close this gate, but keep it open so that you can make your escape."

Georges called for Jeanne early Saturday evening, January 13. Before leaving for the ball, they dined in Jeanne's apartments on the rue de Boulogne. Gaudry was already present, hiding in a closet. Through the keyhole the obedient loveslave had a perfect view of Georges, the man he was to disfigure for life. At the last minute, Jeanne had thought it a good idea to have Gaudry wait concealed in her apartments. The dull-witted fellow would make no mistake about Georges' identity that way. When Georges left to get madame's carriage, Jeanne let Gaudry out of the closet. She adjusted her gown in such a way as to whet her obedient thug's appetite for her. Then she clung to Gaudry for a moment, kissing him long and passionately on the mouth. "It will soon be over—and then you will be my lover for life, darling Nathalis."

Gaudry stayed in the apartment, sitting by a window and waiting for the ball to be over and the couple to return. He nodded off to sleep while reading the essays of Montaigne, a book Jeanne had given him to while away the hours, one Gaudry could hardly have been expected to understand.

Sometime around 2:30 A.M. the next morning, Gaudry was awakened at his window perch by the sounds of horses and a carriage stopping in the rue de Boulogne. Hurriedly, he took up the bottle of acid and rushed downstairs, waiting in the shadows of the courtyard. Georges de Saint Pierre entered the dark courtyard alone; Jeanne Brécourt stalled, pretending to close the gate. In a moment, Gaudry dashed forward, uncorking the bottle as he ran, and sloshing the searing liquid into the face of Jeanne's lover, before rushing past Jeanne, through the gate and down the rue de Boulone.

Jeanne went to the side of the screaming Georges. Police and doctors were called. No, the couple knew nothing. It was all a terrible mistake. They had gotten the wrong man, whoever the attackers were, Jeanne said. Georges had no enemies. He was much loved.

By the following day, Georges talked through incredible pain to his devoted Jeanne from a hospital bed. He had been totally blinded in one eye; the other eye was so badly burned that what Georges saw out of it for the remainder of his life would be nothing more than a blur. His once handsome face was scarred, horribly disfigured for life. In this helpless state, Georges was indeed totally dependent upon Jeanne Brécourt, which, of course, was exactly what she had planned.

Her lover's relatives attempted many times to see Georges, but Jeanne managed to keep them away, and with Georges' consent. The only nurse he required, the melancholy young man insisted, the only person he wished to have in his presence, was the kind and beautiful woman who had been his lover and friend for the past four years.

Word reached one of Georges' relatives that Jeanne intended to take her blind lover away, perhaps to Italy. This so bothered the relative that he went to the police, telling officials that there were "suspicious circumstances" surrounding the entire acid-throwing event.

The police assigned a magistrate to investigate. This official turned the case over to a young detective, Gustave Macé, who would later become France's most able sleuth and the pride of the Sûreté. By then Jeanne had removed Georges to her suite of rooms on the rue de Boulogne. Macé went to the suite to find Jeanne spraying the air with some antiseptic liquid. As the detective began to question her, Jeanne all but ignored him, continuing to spray the room.

Macé was a straight-to-the-point man and angrily ordered Jeanne to "leave that spray alone—it might shoot over us, and then, perhaps we should be sprinkled as De Saint Pierre was."

The semi-accusation stunned Jeanne. She dutifully put down the spray bottle and, at Macé's orders, led the detective into a bedroom where he could talk with Georges.

De Saint Pierre told Macé in a weak voice that he had no enemies and was positive that the attack was a matter of mistaken identity. He did not want the affair made into a police case, preferring his bad luck to remain private. "All I require, inspector, is to be left alone with my brave and devoted nurse, Jeanne."

"What about your family?"

"I do not wish to see them. I wish to avoid the nervous excitement such a meeting would bring. I intend to leave Paris shortly."

Jeanne suddenly cut in, telling Macé, "You can see he is tired. It is inhuman to make him suffer through these stupid questions."

"Where do you intend to take this patient?" Macé asked Jeanne.

"To Italy."

"That's out of the question. You must remain within the Department of the Seine until my investigation is over." Macé went on to add that he intended to keep Jeanne under surveillance and would enter and leave her apartments as he saw fit as he put together evidence in his case.

Two detectives were assigned to follow Jeanne wherever she went. On February 11, 1877, one of these officers watched her drive alone in a rented carriage to the Charonne Cemetery where she met a hulking man dressed in the soiled clothes of a laborer. She was seen to give him money before he raced off.

Some days later Jeanne left Paris with Georges, going to the suburb of Courbevoie. Macé and his men continued to dig for facts. Interviewing the porter at Jeanne's Paris building, Macé learned that Georges had gone ahead of her into the courtyard on the night of the attack, something no gentleman would normally do, and that Jeanne had lingered at the heavy inner gate which she had apparently held open and through which the attacker had made his escape. Such information further cemented the strong suspicions Macé had about Jeanne Brécourt, who struck him as desperate to cling to Georges de Saint Pierre as her permanent provider. Also, the porter informed Macé, Madame's "brother" had visited Jeanne on January 13. The detective concluded this mysterious man to be the woman's accomplice.

Macé requested a magistrate to order Jeanne back to Paris. She arrived, much agitated, presumably at having to leaves Georges, on March 6, and was taken to police headquarters to face Gustave Macé.

"You must consider yourself under provisional arrest," he told her.

"But who will take care of Georges?" She was almost hysterical.

"His family," Macé curtly told her.

Pacing the detective's office, Jeanne threatened him with retribution from high government places. He would not remain a detective for long, that was certain. He would be back in the uniform of the gendarme shortly.

Macé ignored her. "Why did you insist on going to that ball in January, Madame Brécourt?"

"I did nothing of the kind," Jeanne snapped back.

"Can you explain how the attacker made such a quick getaway? It was convenient, your holding open the gate for him that way, was it not?"

"I don't know what you're talking about."

"I would like to know the name and address of the man who calls himself your brother."

Jeanne gave Macé a murderous look. "I will not deliver the honest father of a good family into the clutches of the police, I assure you."

"Why did you go to the Charonne Cemetery on February 11?"

"What?" The question shook Jeanne for a moment.

"You met a man in that cemetery."

"I—I go to the cemetery to pray, not to meet men, not to keep assignations! And if you want to know, I have had typhoid fever, which makes me often forget things. So I shall say nothing more—nothing—nothing!"

Macé took Jeanne before an examining magistrate. Her defiance blistered the ears of the police judge. "Your cleverest policemen," she yelled at him, "will never find *any* evidence against me! Think well before you send me to prison. I am not the woman to live long among thieves and prostitutes!" Apparently the judge took Jeanne's remarks somewhat seriously, because he instructed Macé to search Jeanne's apartments for more evidence before taking her to prison.

A short time later, Jeanne, accompanied by Macé and other detectives, entered her suite. To her maid, Jeanne shouted, "Open all the windows—let in the air—the police are coming in. They make a nasty smell!"

Carefully the detectives sifted through Jeanne's papers as she sat in a chair glaring at them. Inside the covers of her Bible, Macé found letters from her lovers of old, including an affectionate missive from the elderly count she had blackmailed with the false tale of being pregnant. There was a card from another lover, a young gentleman who had sent a bullet into his brain for the love of her. The card read, "Jeanne, in the flush of my youth I die because of you, but I forgive you.—M." Also pressed into the Bible were letters to Jeanne that were nothing more than obscene poems written to her by her less cultured patrons describing every gyration of the sex act imaginable.

Macé placed these items, one by one, in front of Jeanne, saying nothing, looking for a response. Other detectives placed on the same table her account books, paints, pomades, and a great number of drugs in little jars. They included belladonna, cantharides, and hashish.

Jeanne merely glanced at the items in front of her and then asked calmly, "Are the current prices of the stock exchange up or down?"

Macé went back to work, searching with his men every cranny of the suite. In a linen closet, beneath some blankets, the detective found a small leather case. Inside was a sheaf of papers burned at the edges.

"You are not to look at that!" protested Jeanne. "That is the property of Georges de Saint Pierre."

The detective shrugged and began to examine the letters in the case, all of them, it appeared at a glance, being of an intimate nature.

"I found them on the floor near the stove in the dining room," Jeanne hastily explained, "and I kept them. I admit it was a wrong thing to do, but Georges will forgive me when he knows why I did it."

"A wrong thing to do," repeated Macé, looking at his deadly suspect. "Is it possible?"

An hour later, Jeanne was placed in detention, and Gustave Macé was traveling to Courbevoie, the burned letters in his hand. The detective sat at Georges' bedside, slowly getting to his point. "I have come to tell you the truth about Madame Brécourt."

"I will hear no word said against that woman," insisted the loyal Georges. "She is my Antigone. Jeanne has lavished on me all her care, her tenderness, her love, and she believes in God."

"Yes, lad, the god of money, the god of power—and of vengeance." Piece by piece, Macé brought forth the damning billets-doux he had found in Jeanne's Bible, telling the blind man, in great and painful detail, about Jeanne's scarlet past.

Nothing could shake Georges' love for the woman. "I forgive her past," he said. "I accept her present, and please understand me, no one has the power to separate me from her."

Then Macé pulled forth the letters burned at the edges and began slowly to read them. Georges bolted upright in bed, hands trembling as he groped for the letters. "She promised me—she told me she had destroyed those letters!" He collapsed.

Later, in an agonized voice, Georges related to Macé that after his being blinded and moving to Jeanne's suite, he had asked her to go to his apartment and retrieve some letters he had written ten years before meeting Jeanne, letters that would damn the reputation of another woman, an aristocrat, should they be made public. At the time, Georges told Macé, he had thought he was going to die from the acid attack and he wanted the letters destroyed. With his eyes bandaged he had instructed Jeanne to take the letters to the dining room stove and burn them. He had heard the fire crackling and then he had heard Jeanne take up some tongs. "Why have you picked up the tongs?" he remembered asking her. "The papers are fluttering inside the stove—I must use the tongs to keep them inside," she had replied.

"Now I understand," Georges told Macé. "She used those tongs to take the papers *out* of the fire, to keep for her own use. . . . Later, if things went bad between us, she would use those letters . . . to . . . blackmail me!" Georges paused for a long time, thinking. Then he exclaimed, "To blind me! To torture me! And then profit by my condition to lie to me, to betray me. It's infamous! Infamous!"

Only hours later, Jeanne Amenaide Brécourt was taken to St. Lazare Prison. Instead of the arrogance initially displayed to the police, Jeanne kept silent, for she knew that only in silence could she sidestep a conviction and a future in prison. They would have to find Gaudry, and they had no way of knowing where the man might be unless she told them. And she intended to say nothing—nothing—nothing.

But as the weeks went by, prison life began to jangle Jeanne's nerves. Her smallest doubts grew into overwhelming obsessions. The silence of the guards, the silence of her fellow prisoners, her own silence worked against her will to remain silent. That she remained uninformed of any developments in her case drove her even closer to madness. She wrote constantly to Georges but received no reply. This, too, caused her sleepless nights. Finally, Jeanne believed that only one person in the whole world would help her—Nathalis Gaudry.

Knowing that another female prisoner, an Italian dancer who had been convicted of stealing, was about to be released, Jeanne asked the woman to smuggle out a letter for her, to take it to Gaudry at Saint-Denis. She would be well paid for taking such a chance, Jeanne promised. Gaudry would pay her, and when Jeanne was freed, she would give her a priceless bracelet. The dancer agreed.

Jeanne poured her heart out to the man she had duped and used, telling Gaudry that she was starving to death in prison, that when she had refused to eat the matrons had force-fed her, that she had dashed her head in frustration against the stone walls of her cell, and God forbid, if she were driven to such madness again, she would no longer be beautiful for her dear Nathalis when she was released. Only he could save her, she wrote. He must come forward and admit to the police that he was the man they were seeking, the man that she, Jeanne Brécourt, had sheltered and for so doing had been thrown into prison, and humiliated, and humbled, and tortured. If luck went against him, Jeanne promised that she would adopt his young son and leave her fortune to the boy.

A few days later the dancer was released and took Jeanne's letter with her. But she never delivered it, reading it instead to her husband who told her she was crazy for getting involved with such a terrible person as Jeanne Brécourt. The husband grabbed the letter and burned it. The dancer, a born gossip, told her friends about the letter, and the story finally found its way to the ears of the police. When Macé interviewed the dancer, the woman could recall little of the letter's contents, but she did remember the unusual first name of the man to whom she was to take the letter—Nathalis. She also remembered that he worked in an oil refinery.

Armed only with this information, Macé tracked down Gaudry at the Saint-Denis plant in a few days. Once letters from Jeanne were found in his home, he was easily trapped—letters that cautioned him to stay sway from her apartments after "the incident" of his blinding Georges. There was also a letter instructing him to meet her in Charonne Cemetery where she would give him some money.

The broad-shouldered Gaudry quickly confessed to Macé. "I have such a passion for that woman," he whined. "She promised to marry me—one night with her would have been enough to live off the rest of my life. It was the passion that drove me to do such a monstrous deed. You're a man, inspector, you can understand how reason leaves the mind when passion takes over."

Macé understood too well the workings of Jeanne Brécourt upon the passions of men. He ordered Gaudry taken to Mazas Prison. Macé went to St. Lazare Prison and confronted Jeanne with the facts he had learned. She refused to say a word. Hours later she attempted to kill herself by swallowing powdered glass but was revived. Two days later she attempted suicide with verdigris, but that too failed.

On May 12, 1877, Jeanne was brought before a magistrate. Gaudry was brought into the court to face her. Without looking at the woman he desired more than anything on earth, Gaudry spilled out the entire wretched plot.

In mock surprise, Jeanne drew back, saying, "It is inconceivable how a dear friend of my childhood could malign me so cruelly." She placed a hand gently on his shoulder. "Please, Nathalis, none of this is true, you must tell them. I am not involved in your madness—you must tell them that."

Gaudry's massive head rested on his chest as he continued to stare at his own enormous feet, his toes almost breaking through the rotting leather of his shoes. "It is too late," he mumbled. He was crying.

Both were brought to trial before the Paris Assize Court on July 23, 1877. For three days, Jeanne Brécourt heard herself damned, even though she was defended by the most able lawyer in France, Charles Lachaud, who had defended and loved the infamous Marie Lafarge. Monsieur Demange defended Gaudry. He would later become famous for his defense of Alfred Dreyfus.

In the spectator's gallery sat half of all the intelligentsia of Paris. Conquelin and Mounet-Sully from the Comédie Franscaise were there. So was the playwright Halévy. Jeanne's manner and looks inspired many a journalist of the day to write long profiles of her. Fernand Rodays of *Le Figaro* described her like this: "She looks more than her age, of moderate height, well made, neither blatant nor ill at ease, with nothing of the air of a woman of the town. Her hands are small. Her bust is flat, and her back round, her hair quite white [it had turned completely white during Jeanne's stay in prison]. Beneath her brows glitter two jet-black eyes—the eyes of a tigress that seem to breathe hatred and revenge."

Gaudry's testimony overwhelmed the court; the man's naiveté, his innocence of love was pathetic.

"What is the motive for this crime you have committed?" asked the judge.

"I was mad for Jeanne Brécourt. I would have done anything she told me. I had known her as a child. I had been brought up with her.

Then I saw her again. I loved her. I was mad for her. I couldn't resist it. Her wish was law to me."

"Does this man speak the truth?" the judge asked Jeanne.

She gave Gaudry a sneer. "He has lied."

"What is his motive for lying?"

Jeanne did not answer.

Charles Lachaud, her lawyer, stood up, pleading, "Please answer the president of the court."

"I cannot," said Jeanne Brécourt.

"Was Gaudry at your house while you were at the ball?" the judge went on.

"No, no! He cannot look me in the face and say so."

"But he is looking at you now," the judge pointed out.

Jeanne fixed her eyes on Gaudry with such a smoldering stare that he lowered his head. "He dares not look at me!"

The judge, though, could not be cowed by Jeanne's piercing look. "I, whose duty it is to interrogate you, look you in the face and repeat my question: Was Gaudry at your house that night?"

"No!"

"You hear her, Gaudry?" asked the judge.

"Yes, monsieur," replied the accomplice in a low voice. "But I *was* there."

"It's absolutely impossible!" raged Jeanne from the dock. She looked imploringly about the courtroom. "Can anyone believe me guilty of such a thing?"

Said the judge, "You prefer to feign indignation and deny everything. You have the right. I will read your examination before the examining magistrate. I see Monsieur Lachaud makes a gesture, but I must beg the counsel for the defense not to impart unnecessary passion into these proceedings."

Lachaud, who had thrown up his arms in frustration, replied to the court, "My gesture was merely meant to express that the woman is on trial, and that under the circumstances her indignation is natural."

"Very good," hrummphed the judge.

Then Georges de Saint Pierre was called. A gasp came from the courtroom as the tragic young man was led to the witness box. Hesi-

tantly, Georges told his story, leaving nothing out. At the end, Jeanne became hysterical.

"Georges! Georges!" she yelled to him. "Defend me! Defend me!"

He moved his head in the direction of her voice and faced her with sightless eyes. He said to her in a voice without passion, "I state the facts."

Then both defendants, through their lawyers, attempted to place the greater burden of the crime on the other. But it was clear that Jeanne Brécourt had masterminded the heinous offense. The jury found both guilty. Jeanne was given fifteen years in prison, Gaudry five.

Little is known of Jeanne Brécourt after she entered prison. The records are sketchy, but one report has it that she was released only after serving every day of her sentence. Reduced to an old hag with stringy white hair and a bent frame, she now crept along the cobblestone streets of her childhood peddling fruit, later dying in abject poverty, a destiny she had fought against all her life.

In the last years of her life, Jeanne certainly passed a small playhouse that was still standing in her old neighborhood. It is not known whether or not she remembered having acted out roles in that theater during her brief career as a struggling actress, or if she recalled one of the dramas in which she acted, a play ruefully ironic in its title: *Who Puts Out the Eyes Must Pay for Them*.

BRINVILLIERS, MARIE DE

Murderer ■ (1630–1676)

Rich, spoiled, born of a noble French family, the attractive vixen Marie de Brinvilliers took on a lover soon after marrying the Marquis Antoine de Brinvilliers. The lover, Gaudin de Saint-Croix, aided Marie in obtaining poisons with which to murder her father, the wealthy Dreux d'Aubray, in order to inherit her estates. (She had depleted her husband's funds in short order.)

Marie first experimented with various poisons, searching for the most undetectable one by pretending to nurse patients at the Hotel Dieu, the public hospital in Paris. During her time there she poisoned scores of patients; at least fifty deaths were directly attributed to her. She finally murdered her father in 1666. Having spent the fortune inherited from her father, Marie next poisoned her two brothers, also to get hold of their estates.

Socially prominent at the French court, Marie could tolerate not the slightest insult or rebuff; she took to poisoning anyone who displeased her, usually dosing the coffee she served to those who had offended her. The lover Saint-Croix was kept so busy in a laboratory perfecting poisons for the murderous Marie that he accidentally inhaled some deadly fumes and died. Officials discovering the body uncovered Marie's sinister activities; a servant confessed under torture, describing in detail the many murders committed by Marie.

Marie was tried and condemned in 1676, and forced to make a public confession in front of Notre Dame Cathedral, her beautiful body almost naked. She was then beheaded and her body burned before a great throng.

BROADINGHAM, ELIZABETH

Murderer ■ (? –1776)

Tiring of her husband, John Broadingham, a British smuggler, Elizabeth Broadingham took up with a younger man, Thomas Aikney. While living with Aikney, the attractive Elizabeth begged the lover to murder her husband so they could be wed. Aikney, horror stricken, at first refused. But the woman pressured him daily. He finally agreed. Elizabeth returned to her husband's home in York, England.

On February 13, 1776, she slapped her husband awake, telling him that someone was knocking at their door. Broadingham, sleepy-eyed, stumbled downstairs and threw open the door. Aikney rushed inside, slashing out with a large knife, cutting Broadingham in the leg, then gashing his belly, leaving the knife plunged into the fatally stricken man before dashing down the street.

Broadingham staggered down the street after his assailant, shouting, "Murder! Murder!" According to an old account, "some neighbors came to his assistance who found in one hand the bloody instrument which he had just drawn out of his body, and the other supporting his bowels, which were dropping to the ground." Broadingham died the following day.

The knife was traced to Aikney, who confessed when arrested. He was hanged on March 20, 1776. Elizabeth Broadingham, who had confessed to planning the murder of her husband, was first strangled to death and then her body was burned to ashes. The good citizens of York who witnessed the execution scooped up the woman's ashes as souvenirs. Aikney's body served a more practical use; it was taken to the Leeds infirmary and dissected by medical students.

BROWNRIGG, ELIZABETH

Murderer ■ (1720–1767)

Inhuman monsters who inflict terrible punishment upon the flesh of other people are generally rooted out of the ranks of male miscreants. Seldom do women, no matter their prey or their dark ambitions, physically abuse another for any prolonged period except with poison. There have been exceptions, of course, and, of these, Elizabeth Brownrigg is the most notorious.

Elizabeth Brownrigg, shown as she exercised her murderous sadism on one of her apprentices.

As is the case with so many arch-criminals, no real motivation for Elizabeth's crimes can be found in her personal history. Born in 1720 to a family named either Harkly or Hartley, Elizabeth spent a normal childhood among working-class people. Her conduct in youth was reported as nothing out of the ordinary. She was married young, to James Brownrigg, an apprentice plumber, and the pair produced a staggering number of offspring, sixteen in all, thirteen of them dying while still youngsters. (In light of

Elizabeth's subsequent sadistic bent, we can speculate that these deaths may have been caused by the baby-plagued woman herself.)

In the mid-1760s, the Brownriggs moved from their original homesite in Greenwich to a handsome home in Fleur de Lys Court, Fetter Lane, in London. James Brownrigg had prospered so that he not only bought considerable real estate in London, but maintained a country retreat in Islington.

Elizabeth kept busy in the role of midwife, proving to have exceptional skills in handling pregnant women. She was held in such high esteem that the overseers of St. Dunstan's-in-the-West parish appointed her an official midwife to look after destitute women in labor. All reports of Elizabeth's attitude in this period reflect great kindness and consideration on her part.

Elizabeth's midwifery practice became so successful that, by 1765, she was forced to seek assistance, going to the workhouse, where unwanted children were kept. These young people, for five pounds paid to their impoverished mothers, would be bound over as apprentices to any upstanding citizen who took them in to a trade. It was the custom then that the youngster was assigned to a tradesman or tradeswoman for a month "upon liking." This meant that at the end of a month's residence with the supporting family and providing that "both maid and mistress were satisfied the indentures were signed and the apprenticeship began."

The first apprentice taken in by Elizabeth Brownrigg was fourteen-year-old Mary Mitchell. Some have suggested that the spark of sadism was ignited in Elizabeth with the discovery that she had absolute control, complete authority, over this totally dependent waif, a latent compulsion she had not exercised with her own children.

At the end of a month, the child, having been treated kindly and fed well, happily agreed to be bound over as an apprentice to the Brownriggs. Only days following the agreement, however, treatment of her worsened by the hour. Elizabeth made of Mary Mitchell a drudge, scoffing at her inability to lift heavy objects, jeering at her complaints of hunger, for by then she was no longer permitted to sit at the table when the rest of the family dined, but was thrown scraps of food from their plates as one would toss leftovers to a dog.

Entering the kitchen, Elizabeth shouted at the girl to take off her clothes, replacing them with foul-smelling rags recently discovered in the basement. Elizabeth then took to berating the frantic girl in front of her husband and son, who grinned through the ordeal, watching and delighting in the new family diversion. Mrs. Brownrigg would slap, punch, and kick the girl about the kitchen, screaming, "You're nothing but a dirty slut!" The only rest afforded Mary Mitchell was when she sank down to a dirty mat in the kitchen late at night. Elizabeth worked her eighteen hours a day.

Horror-filled months followed. Elizabeth used whips and broomsticks with which to flog the girl until her back was raw and bleeding. Her sense of power over the girl, her taste for tyranny, was so acutely whetted that Elizabeth resolved to obtain another servant victim and arranged to take in one Mary Jones from the foundling hospital.

Mary Jones became Mary Mitchell's companion in misery and suffered even more. But Mary Jones sought to escape the clutches of the monster, which when she found out infuriated Elizabeth all the more, and she devised a special torture for her. The girl was stripped naked, placed between two chairs, and whipped mercilessly until Mrs. Brownrigg dropped from exhaustion. When she learned that Mary Jones had a great fear of drowning, Elizabeth repeatedly shoved the girl's head into a large vat of water, holding her until Mary was at the edge of death, at which time she would finally lift up the gasping child.

On other occasions, the poor slave girl would be scrubbing floors when Mrs. Brownrigg, and sometimes her husband and son, would suddenly snatch her up by the ankles and drive her head into the water bucket so that she came near drowning. This lethal game was played countless times each day.

But unlike the submissive Mary Mitchell, Mary Jones still vowed to escape her evil torturer. The girl was forced to sleep beneath a dresser in the Brownriggs' bedroom. She had tried all the doors each day to find them locked; the windows were barred. One morning, however, the girl awoke early and went downstairs, again tiredly pulling at the front door. To her amazement, it was unlocked. James Brownrigg, off on a crack-of-dawn business appointment, had left the door ajar. Mary Jones sprang into the street, running for her life.

The emaciated waif wandered about for hours until a kindly peddler took her back to the foundling hospital. In shock, doctors inspected her horrible wounds. Half starved, the girl was covered with cuts and bruises. She was blind in one eye and deep wounds from the water tub she had been shoved into had become infected. Mary told her tale of the bestial Mrs. Brownrigg, begging authorities to free her friend Mary Mitchell.

Hospital authorities wrote to James Brownrigg, demanding he pay damages for mistreating the girl, but the rich plumber never bothered to respond. Incredibly, the matter was dropped, the hospital authorities merely notifying the Brownriggs that Mary Jones's apprenticeship with them was terminated.

Mrs. Brownrigg by then had obtained another apprentice, fourteen-year-old Mary Clifford. Because rumors were spreading about her harsh treatment of her apprentices, she had been careful to go to a different workhouse for this girl, one in Whitefriars parish.

Mary Clifford, too, was given lice-infested rags to wear, and was whipped several times a day, tied to a hook in the ceiling. Mrs. Brownrigg truly hated this girl for her stupidity and reserved her most inhuman punishments for her, whipping her until she bled, all in sight of James and John Brownrigg, who thought these beatings a form of amusement. Such was Elizabeth's black humor that while she administered these savage attacks, she joked and laughed like a lunatic. At times she beat the naked girl, strung up like a side of beef, her feet swinging in midair, with an iron pipe, until Mary Clifford collapsed into unconsciousness.

A French woman came to stay at the Brownrigg home to deliver a child. While there she encountered the battered Mary Clifford. The child begged her help in escaping her fiendish captor. The woman upbraided Elizabeth for her treatment of the girl. Mrs. Brownrigg's response was to snatch up a large pair of scissors and rush to the kitchen where she grabbed Mary Clifford, screaming, "I will cure you of your tattling!" She cut the girl's tongue in two places and then yelled, "Next time I will cut that wagging tongue out completely!"

On July 12, the unexpected happened. Mary Clifford's stepmother called at the Brownrigg house, asking to see the apprentice.

"We have no apprentices," lied Mrs. Brownrigg.

"But I know the girl is here," responded the stepmother. "The workhouse authorities directed me to your house."

"If you don't leave us in peace," threatened Elizabeth, "I'll call the police." With that Mrs. Brownrigg slammed the door in a rage.

Before the stepmother departed the area, a neighbor, a Mrs. Deacon, stopped her, telling her that, indeed, the Brownriggs did have girl apprentices. She had heard the girls groan and moan in the Brownrigg basement. (The two Marys were kept in the basement without light, food, or water during the weekends when the family went off to their Islington retreat.) It could mean only that they were being horribly mistreated, concluded the neighbor, Mrs. Deacon and the stepmother agreed to go to the authorities.

Meanwhile, a servant girl was told to watch through a skylight of the Brownrigg house for any signs of the girls. She "presently saw . . . a shapeless mass, which turned out to be the bare, raw, half-mortified body of Mary Clifford. It seemed impossible to attract her attention, and when endeavors to do so were made by some men, who descended onto the leads for the purpose, no response other than inarticulate sounds were given."

Mrs. Clifford, with the neighbor, Mrs. Deacon, at her side, went to parish officials, and all together they descended upon the Brownrigg home. James Brownrigg opened the door a crack.

"We demand to see the apprentice girls in your charge, Brownrigg. We have reports that they are terribly mistreated and we intend to inspect them."

"We have no apprentices."

"Show us Mary Clifford!" shouted the stepmother.

Brownrigg, his hands shaking in a nervous twitch, opened the door but barred the way with his body. "We have a Mary Mitchell as an apprentice, but no Mary Clifford."

Elizabeth Brownrigg and her son John, hearing the commotion while secreted in another room, hurriedly snatched up some belongings and a tin box containing gold and raced from the house through the back door.

"All right, Brownrigg," said a man named Grundy, one of the overseers of the parish, "produce Mary Mitchell."

Brownrigg had no choice but to call the wretched girl to the door. She was immediately taken away by coach to a hospital, where doctors slowly peeled her rags from her body; dried blood from her wounds had caked her clothes to her skin. Grundy and others raced back to the Brownrigg house, knocking down the door. They found a terrified James Brownrigg at a table, gulping ale. "Get out of my house!" he roared. "My lawyers will be summoned. I'll drag you all into court to pay for this invasion. Call the police!"

"The police are already with us," said Grundy.

A constable stepped forward. "We're going to search your house, Brownrigg." With that a dozen people carefully went through each room. Mary Clifford was found crammed into a small cupboard. Her rescuers soon realized that the poor girl was more dead than alive. Her body was covered with ulcers. There were dozens of gashes on her head and her mouth had been cut so that she could not speak.

As the girl was taken outside and put into a coach to speed her to St. Bartholomew's Hospital, one of the men in the crowd stepped again inside the house, grabbed Brownrigg by the throat, and hurled him against a wall. The constable stopped the man, who shouted, "I'd like to give the bastard what he gave that girl."

"Not me," gasped Brownrigg. "It was the wife who done it all."

The wife, Elizabeth Brownrigg, was in hiding. She and her son, disguised in clothes hurriedly bought at a nearby rag fair, had made their way to Wandsworth, registering under assumed names at an inn run by a man named Chandler.

On August 9, 1767, despite the heroic efforts of many doctors to save her, the hapless Mary Clifford died of her horrible wounds. James Brownrigg was already in custody. The public outcry against Elizabeth Brownrigg, once her tortures became publicized, was so great that a nationwide search for her ensued.

Newspapers blared descriptions of the culprits, especially Elizabeth. One read that she was "a middle-sized woman of a swarthy complexion near 50 years of age, remarkably smooth of speech," and that she was wearing upon her escape, "a black silk crepe or bombazine gown, a black silk whalebone bonnet, and a purple petticoat flounced."

Innkeeper Chandler read this description and turned in his two guests, telling arresting constables that the woman and boy had stayed in their room for five days, having their meals served to them, showing great fear when approached. Mrs. Brownrigg was taken to Newgate where, for a month, she awaited trial. The crowds that assembled around the prison each day became so incensed at her crimes and made so many threats of storming the prison to hang the murderer that authorities were unsure of their ability to guard the woman.

Tried at the Old Bailey, Elizabeth Brownrigg stood in the dock without uttering a word as the barely surviving Mary Mitchell testified against her, detailing the sickening cruelty she had inflicted on the girls, particularly Mary Clifford. Mrs. Brownrigg offered no defense. Also in the dock with her were her husband and son. At the end of the eleventh-hour trial, Elizabeth was found guilty of murder and condemned. The male Brownriggs, both blaming Elizabeth for all the crimes inflicted against the girls, were fined one shilling each and given six months in prison.

On September 14, 1767, Elizabeth Brownrigg was taken from her prison cell and put into an open cart. In her last day of imprisonment, she had frantically turned to God, begging forgiveness from the Newgate chaplain, the Reverend Joseph Moore, who accompanied Mrs. Brownrigg to the site of her execution at Tyburn. The crowd assembled to see this most detestable of women die was enormous, reportedly the largest throng ever assembled for a public execution in England. And the spectators were

Mrs. Brownrigg in her prison cell, sketched on the morning of her execution.

beside themselves with outrage over Elizabeth's savage cruelty, fighting the companies of mounted troops protecting the cart to get at the woman.

"Close ranks!" shouted one captain. "They will tear her limb from limb if we do not get her to the hangman soon!"

The soldiers had to fight their way through the swelling, roaring crowd, infantry clearing the way at bayonet point.

The Reverend Moore was appalled at the cries of vengeance of those close to the rumbling cart. "Pray for that bitch's damnation," screamed one man at the chaplain, "not her salvation!"

"She's going to hell!" yelled a woman.

"The devil will fetch her this day!" cried another.

Moore later wrote: "This unchristian behavior greatly shocked me, and I could not help exclaiming, Are these the people called Christians?"

Once on the scaffold, Mrs. Elizabeth Brownrigg, to appease the surging crowd, shouted, "I freely admit my guilt!"

The executioner, fearing for his own safety, quickly hanged the awful creature while the mob tore at the troopers in its attempt to dismantle the scaffold and shred the corpse. Elizabeth's body was quickly taken down and removed to the Surgeons' Hall where it was dissected. Her skeleton was hanged in a niche facing the front door of the anatomy theater where it remained for decades to haunt all would-be child-beaters.

The likes of this degenerate beast would not be seen again for centuries, until, at the end of World War II, the soldiers of the Allied armies fell back in shock from the gates of Nazi concentration camps and took into custody the savage Nazi matrons who had returned sadism to the incredibly evil art practiced by Elizabeth Brownrigg.

BRUHNE, VERA

Murderer ■ (1910– ?)

Mistress to a wealthy physician, Dr. Otto Praun of Munich, Germany, Vera Brühne was still a radiant, cool blonde of exceptional beauty at age fifty. Praun lavished furs and jewels on Vera and kept her in luxury in his rich estate outside Munich and the sprawling villa he also kept on Spain's Costa Brava. Tiring of Vera in 1960, the suave, well-dressed sixty-five-year-old doctor calmly told his mistress that

it would be better if she got out of his life. He also informed her that his $250,000 estate in Spain, which he had given her as a present, was no longer hers. Praun had habitually bestowed this estate on his mistresses over the years, all of them tall, cool blondes like Vera, and then taken the property back when he had grown bored with them.

Vera seemed to accept the dismissal with grace, so much grace that she offered to provide Praun with a buyer for his Spanish estate since he was thinking of selling the property. She sent her contact, one Dr. Schmitz, to see Praun to arrange the purchase. The following day the police found the physician dead, along with his housekeeper, who was also a sometime mistress. Praun was lying dead in his lavishly appointed bedroom, the housekeeper in the basement of the Munich mansion. Police quickly concluded that Praun had suffered a nervous breakdown, killed the housekeeper, then committed suicide. They closed the case.

Disturbing reports then began to trickle into the Munich police, dozens of residents implicating the attractive Vera. Authorities dug up Praun's body, and a closer inspection revealed that the doctor had been shot twice in the head, ruling out suicide. Vera was picked up for questioning, but she gave the police nothing. Her fourteen-year-old daughter, Sylvia, however, had much to say. Her mother was a perverted creature, said Sylvia. Vera had hidden in a large Renaissance chest in her apartment many times as Sylvia seduced teenage boys, the sons of Vera's high society friends. The daughter had performed at her mother's instructions, because "she liked to watch," the girl said. Further, Vera had many lovers besides the picky Dr. Praun who kept her in style and money. She also maintained her own lover on the side, an unschooled giant named Johann Ferbach. This man had deserted the German army in 1944 and was taken in by Vera who not only hid him until the close of the war but kept him as her lover and stooge through two marriages and countless affairs, including that of Dr. Praun.

Vera Brühne had planned Praun's death, her publicity-seeking daughter insisted, sending Ferbach to see Praun while posing as the purchaser of his Spanish estate. Vera had written a letter to Praun which introduced Ferbach as Dr. Schmitz. Once inside Praun's mansion, Ferbach simply murdered the housekeeper, dragged her body to the basement, and waited for the doctor to return home. When Praun entered his home, Ferbach killed him, too, making it appear as if Praun had gone berserk, killed his housekeeper, and then shot himself. Besides shooting him twice, he made the further mistake of leaving his letter of introduction behind. The handwriting in the letter was compared with Vera's and proved identical.

The defense counsel stated that Praun was undoubtedly killed by German gangsters since it was through rum-running, abortions, smuggling, and dope peddling that he had amassed his fortune. The jury paid no attention to this smoke screen and quickly convicted both Vera and her non compos mentis lover Ferbach. Both were given life sentences. While fistfights broke out in court between her supporters and antagonists once the sentence was given, Vera screamed through tears, "Please, I am not guilty!" She was led from court, listening to the chant of "Killer, killer, killer!"

BRYANT, CHARLOTTE

Murderer ■ (1904–1936)

Illiterate and promiscuous all her adult life, Charlotte Bryant married a mercenary, Frederick Bryant, who at the time was serving in the British forces occupying Ireland during the early 1920s. After moving to England, Charlotte produced a total of five children. When not having babies, the woman sought in Dorset's public houses any sexual liaison available, becoming the most notorious woman in the village of Coombe.

Frederick Bryant passively ignored his wife's nymphomania and did not object even when she brought other men home to share her bed. One of these was a crude, unschooled gypsy named Leonard Parsons who took up residence in the Bryant home sometime in 1933. Charlotte's affair with the gypsy lasted for two years. So much was the woman attracted to this unwashed, uncaring man that she resolved to murder her husband and run off with Parsons. It apparently never occurred to the scatterbrained Charlotte that her much cuckolded husband would have readily agreed to a divorce. She poisoned her husband with arsenic and, after a long period of illness, Bryant died on December 22, 1935.

An inquest raised suspicions about Mrs. Bryant and the body was examined. Not only was the arsenic found in the corpse of the dead husband, but traces of the poison turned up in the Bryant cottage. Charlotte was placed on trial the following year. She showed remarkable un-

Charlotte Bryant with her third child.

The Bryant cottage outside the village of Coombe.

Charlotte Bryant's sloppy kitchen, where she brewed tea mixed with arsenic for her cuckolded husband.

concern during the proceedings, chewing candy and gossiping in court.

The lover, Parsons, was totally disinterested in the fate of the slovenly Charlotte. He registered no emotion whatever when informed that she had been condemned to death; the gypsy paused only to swallow the beer he was drinking in a pub on July 15, 1936, when he was told that Mrs. Bryant had been hanged that morning.

During the six weeks between her conviction and execution, Charlotte Bryant's raven black hair turned completely white.

BURDOCK, MARY ANN

Murderer ■ (1805–1835)

An attractive, thirty-year-old landlady living in Bristol, England, fell in love with Charles Wade, a young sailor who had come to live in her house. Wade told the woman that he wanted to open a lock shop but lacked funds, which was also the reason why he could not marry the pretty housekeeper.

Mary, driven to desperation, poisoned one of her roomers, the elderly Mrs. Clara Smith, taking several thousand pounds from her room. (Mrs. Smith, like many in those days, did not trust banks and kept her savings in a cash box beneath her bed.) After giving the money to Wade, Mary planned her wedding. A man named Read, however, upset the scheme. A relative of Mrs. Smith's, Read grew suspicious when he heard from Mary that the deceased "died very poor." Read knew Mrs. Smith had considerable funds, and took this information to the police.

The victim's body was exhumed and arsenic was found. Mary Ann Burdock was arrested, tried, and condemned to death, hanged in April 1835, the place of her execution only a block from the rooming house she had operated. Her betrothed, Charles Wade, did not attend her execution.

BUTCHILL, ELIZABETH

Murderer ■ (1758–1780)

A young unwed servant working at Trinity College in England, Elizabeth Butchill became pregnant, and, only hours after delivering a baby girl, bashed in the child's head and threw the tiny corpse into the nearby river. The body was found and doctors easily determined that the child had been murdered.

Ester Hall, the wife of a local brewer and employer of the twenty-two-year-old Elizabeth, came forward to tell authorities that the dead baby had been born to Elizabeth. (Mrs. Hall was also Elizabeth's aunt.) The girl confessed and was tried and convicted. She begged for mercy, telling the court that she did not want her child to grow up fatherless. The presiding judge shook his head and said that since she had "been deaf to the cries of the innocent" he could show her no mercy. She was sentenced to be hanged on March 17, 1780, at Cambridge.

One chronicler stated, "Desiring her example might be a warning to all thoughtless young women, and calling on Jesus Christ for mercy, she was launched into eternity amidst thousands of commiserating spectators, who, though they abhorred the crime, shed tears of pity for the unhappy criminal."

CAILLAUX, HENRIETTE

Murderer ■ (? –1943)

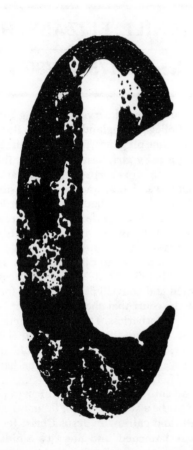

Joseph Caillaux, France's Minister of Finance, finished reading another splenetic editorial aimed at him, then slammed the newspaper down on the dining room table, cursing under his breath. Gaston Calmette, the brilliant editor of *Le Figaro* and Caillaux's archenemy, had gone too far this time, slandering in his invective-filled editorial the personal character of Caillaux and his second wife, the volatile and attractive Henriette.

The thirty-six-year-old Henriette attempted to soothe her husband's wrath, but the minister was beyond reason; Calmette's ceaseless attacks had made his life miserable. "If there's no solution, at least I won't let him attack you with impunity," Caillaux told his wife. "I'll wring his neck!"

For two months, Calmette had derided Minister Caillaux incessantly, publishing 138 articles and sneering cartoons depicting the minister as a bandit, and more than suggesting that Caillaux was a traitor in that he was dealing with enemy agents of Germany—France at the time was on the brink of war with Kaiser Wilhelm. The *Le Figaro* editor then resorted to publishing letters Caillaux had written years earlier to his first wife and to Henriette Rainouard when she was his mistress, indiscreet letters written on the official stationery of the Chambre des Députés, in which he injudiciously discussed his private love life and affairs of state.

In one letter written by Caillaux, which he signed with the lovename "Ton Joe," Caillaux gushed, "...a thousand million kisses on every part of your adorable little body," and had then confided, "I have crushed the Income Tax Bill while appearing to defend it, thereby pleasing the Centre and the Right, without too much upsetting the Left." When this letter appeared in *Le Figaro*, a public storm burst over Caillaux's head, citizens everywhere branding him a hypocrite and the most ruthless politician in French history.

Henriette Caillaux at the time of her notorious murder of Gaston Calmette in 1914.

found the weapon difficult to handle, the clerk substituted a Browning revolver. "Much nicer," she said after firing two rounds. "Less noise." Henriette bought the revolver and returned home.

As she bathed and changed into a new gown, Madame Caillaux could not make up her mind whether to go to the tea party being given that evening, or to go to the offices of *Le Figaro* and deal with the upstart editor Calmette.

When her husband threatened to "wring" Calmette's neck, Henriette thought to save him from his own anger, or so she later said. Henriette visited with a judge named Monier, a family friend, asking if the Caillaux family could not sue *Le Figaro* for libel. Monier waved his hands to signify his helplessness, telling her that public figures could not sue for libel. Henriette in the afternoon March 16, 1914, then went to the shop of Gastinne-Renette, a gunsmith, and asked for a weapon. An accommodating clerk first offered her a Smith & Wesson revolver. Henriette was cordially invited to try it out in the small shooting gallery in the shop's basement. When she

Gaston Calmette, the esteemed editor of *Le Figaro*, whose editorials were silenced by a woman's wrath.

By the time she went downstairs to her husband's study, attired as she was in an exquisite evening dress, Madame Caillaux had made up her mind. Going to his desk, she wrote him the following note:

My beloved husband—

When I told you this morning of my interview with Judge Monier, from whom I learnt that in France there is no law to protect us against the libels of the press, you told me that one of these days you would break the vile Calmette's neck. I know your decision to be irrevocable. From that instant on, my mind was made up. I will see that justice is done. France and the Republic have need of you. I will carry out the task! If you should receive this letter, it will mean that I have obtained or tried to obtain justice. Forgive me, but my patience is at an end. I love and embrace you with all my heart.

Your Henriette

Madame Caillaux then ordered her car to take her to the offices of Le Figaro at 26 rue Drouot.

Once in the offices Henriette asked to see the editor and chief columnist, Calmette. She was told to take a seat outside the editor's office and while waiting, overheard some of the newspaper employees gleefully discussing the "big story on Caillaux" Le Figaro would be publishing the next morning.

Calmette's voice was heard to say, "Show in Madame Caillaux." Office boy Adrien Sirac showed the distinguished visitor into Calmette's office.

Henriette stood before Calmette, calmly saying, "No doubt, you are surprised by my visit?"

Calmette, every inch the gallant, motioned her toward a chair. "Not at all. Please be seated."

As Calmette began to walk behind his desk, Henriette eased the Browning revolver from her handbag, pushed over the safety catch, and fired a shot. Sirac dove to the floor. So did Calmette, trying to hide behind his desk, but Henriette pursued him, firing four more shots into the editor. The office boy finally summoned up enough nerve to jump the woman, grabbing her

arm and wrenching the weapon from her hand.

Henriette gave the youth a withering stare and said with great indignation, "I am Madame Caillaux. Don't be afraid."

Newsmen and secretaries rushed into the editor's room and lifted the bleeding Calmette to a chair. "Forgive my causing you so much trouble, my friends," the editor told his employees with the grace of an Arthurian knight.

Henriette watched it all silently and then announced to the shocked reporters, "It was the only way to put an end to it all. There was no justice—so I gave it."

A burly newsman grabbed her, saying he was going to drag her to the police.

"Let me go!" cried Henriette. "I am a lady! I am Madame Caillaux. I have my car waiting downstairs to drive me to the police station." She spotted an office boy examining her revolver and told him with a great deal of authority, "Be careful with that—it might still have a bullet in it."

Gendarmes swarmed into the office moments later. Henriette turned to an officer and exclaimed, "There is no justice in—"

"Shut up, will you?" said a reporter. "After what you've done, the least you can do now is to remain silent."

"I was not addressing you, monsieur," huffed Henriette.

Calmette was taken to the hospital at Neuilly with four bullet wounds; one in the abdomen proved fatal and he was dead a little after midnight. Madame Caillaux was by then under arrest and in a comfortable jail cell. Her meals were later catered to her by Paris's finest restaurants. News of the murder stunned the entire continent and remained the story until Henriette came to trial on July 20, 1914. Madame Caillaux appealed to the jury in highly emotional terms, eloquently defending herself in testimony, describing what, for her and her husband, had been excruciating persecution at the hands of that viper, Calmette.

The killing had not been premeditated, Henriette insisted. "I lost my head when I found myself in the presence of the man who had done us much harm, who had ruined our lives for thirteen months. The gun went off accidentally. The bullets seemed to follow each other automati-

Calmette's funeral in Paris was attended by the country's most important dignitaries, except for Minister Caillaux.

Henriette Caillaux shortly before her death.

cally. ...'' She did not take pains to point out that she had carefully and with premeditation bought the revolver for only one purpose—to kill Calmette.

A jury spellbound by the sweet words of Henriette Caillaux quickly agreed with her that she had done the only expedient thing in ridding herself of a wretched tormentor. To a member, the jury felt that Henriette was innocent of committing murder and shooting the editor with premeditation, a decision that shocked the nation and the press. The killer went free, returning to her luxurious home without making any further comment on the act that made her name notorious until her death in 1943.

Caillaux was as aloof from the crime as was his wife. He remained a public official in France, though he was later charged with treason, and died in 1944. The minister's only remark about an affair he considered beneath discussion was made shortly after his wife's release. Said Caillaux, "If Calmette had walked right up to her to disarm her as any man of courage would have done, instead of running away, or even if he had just not crouched down, he would have only been wounded in the legs, if indeed, touched at all."

To Minister Caillaux, the killing of one of France's most respected journalists was nothing more than the high-strung act of a beautiful, frivolous woman.

CALVERT, MRS. LOUIE

Murderer ■ (? −1926)

Following the death of her husband, Mrs. Lily Waterhouse of Leeds, England, spent most of her evenings holding séances and entertaining men into the wee hours. Her days, however, were empty and boring, and, to fill the emptiness, Mrs. Waterhouse arranged through friends to have a Mrs. Louie Calvert stay with her. Mrs. Calvert, who arrived on March 8, 1926, was an odd, middle-aged woman. It was later learned that she had told her friends that she had recently married and intended to have her forthcoming baby at Mrs. Waterhouse's home.

The women proved unsuitable companions, arguing and bickering constantly. The arrangement called for Mrs. Calvert to act as a sort of maid, but instead she behaved as her hostess's equal, refusing to do any work. Worse, she began to filch Mrs. Waterhouse's bedding and silverware, which she pawned.

Discovering the thefts, Mrs. Waterhouse went to the Leeds police to complain. To constables interviewing her, she was a woman of minor notoriety, according to one chronicler, who reported that "it was known to the police that she was suffering from a social disease." Mrs. Waterhouse was told to return the next day and sign a complaint against Louie Calvert.

The following day neighbors heard banging sounds from the Waterhouse premises. Minutes later, Louie Calvert was seen leaving the home carrying a baby. A Mrs. Clayton asked Louie what the noise was all about. Replied Mrs. Calvert, "I put up the baby's bed, and it fell when I was folding it."

Mrs. Clayton said she thought she heard Mrs. Waterhouse make some strange sounds.

"Yes," answered Louie with a sad shake of her head. "I have left her in bed crying because I am leaving her."

A few hours later a constable appeared at Mrs. Waterhouse's home to find out why she had not appeared to sign a complaint against her pilfering lodger. Upon hearing the complaints of noise from neighbors, the officer obtained a key and entered the home. He found Mrs. Waterhouse shoeless, lying on a bed. Her head had been battered, and she had been strangled to death.

Police instantly sought out Louie Calvert, finding her in her own home at Railway Place, Leeds. The stories Louie gave to arresting officers were confusing and bizarre, all of them lies. Investigators soon learned that she had borrowed a baby from a woman in a neighboring town and for some reason passed the child off as the one she had given birth to in Mrs. Waterhouse's home. Confronted with items belonging to Mrs. Waterhouse, found in Louie's own low lodgings, the woman shrugged, stating that Mrs. Waterhouse was most certainly muddled, that she had asked Louie to peddle the items and had no doubt forgotten about it.

By this time police had looked into the strange past of Mrs. Louie Calvert, learning that she had been involved in the 1922 death of a man named John Frobisher. At the time the suspect was known as Mrs. Louie Jackson and was Frobisher's housekeeper in Leeds. Frobisher's body had been found floating in a canal, and, though Louie had first appeared to be involved in the death, Frobisher's demise had been ruled a simple drowning.

As officers quizzed Mrs. Calvert about the Waterhouse murder, one remembered the odd fact that Frobisher had been found barefoot.

"Take off your boots," ordered the constable. He inspected the boots and soon learned that they had belonged to Mrs. Waterhouse. The boots had been stripped from the victim's feet, it

The home of Mrs. Lily Waterhouse in Leeds. Louis Calvert boldly stood outside these double doors and told a neighbor that the woman she had just murdered was inside weeping over her departure.

was concluded, after Louie Calvert murdered her, the killer slipping them onto her own feet. Louie was wearing Mrs. Waterhouse's boots when arrested.

Mrs. Calvert was quickly tried and condemned. Upon hearing the sentence, Louie cried out from the dock that she was pregnant and could not, under the law, be executed until her child was born. Matrons examining the woman testified that Louie *might be* in the early stages of pregnancy but that her condition was not such where her execution would take more than one life. Despite public criticism, the execution was ordered to take place. Hundreds of petitions demanding a reprieve flooded the office of the Home Secretary; all were denied and Mrs. Louie Calvert, a murderer with a boot fe-

tish, was executed at Strangeways Jail in Manchester, the first woman to be hanged in that prison since 1886.

CAREW, MRS. EDITH MARY

Murderer ■ (1868– ?)

The luxuries and conveniences of upper-class British society life of 1889 belonged to Edith Mary Porch, the attractive twenty-one-year-old daughter of John Albert Porch, mayor of the town of Glastonbury. She had been provided with the finest education, the best wardrobe, the warmest attention from her doting parents. When she attended a ball at Bridport, a dozen young swains from socially prominent families flocked to her side. Her most ardent admirer was W. R. H. Carew, son of an esteemed military officer. The couple fell in love and were married in May 1889, leaving for Japan, where Carew intended to seek his fortune, his pockets already lined with considerable family money.

The Carews moved into the elegant European quarters of Yokohama in Japan, living in great style. Their parties in the district were the events of the season, and the beautiful Edith Carew was a radiant and envied hostess. Five years flitted by in relative peace for the Carews as the husband prospered and Edith enjoyed the many comforts his business afforded them. In 1894, Mrs. Carew returned briefly to Glastonbury, England. From all appearances it seemed to be a state visit. The town was decked out in Japanese and British flags, and, in honor of the married young daughter of the mayor, the residents walked about wearing kimonos and Japanese headgear.

After Edith returned to her husband in Japan, the citizens of Glastonbury followed her glamorous social life closely, hanging on to every word sent back from the Orient. Many of Edith's flowery letters were read publicly to scintillate the enraptured townsfolk. In late 1896, however, a cable from Yokohama stunned the citizens of Glastonbury, informing them that their darling Edith was a murderer, that she had poisoned to death a kindly, devoted husband.

The shock among the great numbers of Europeans in Yokohama was even more devastating. An upper-class white woman had defamed the good name of Europeans before polite Japanese society. The details came slowly to light, indicating that the beautiful Edith Carew was a cunning, crafty, unpredictable killer.

Carew had grown ill in mid-October 1896. His physician, a Dr. Wheeler, first diagnosed the problem as a diseased liver, but Carew did not improve when given the medicine appropriate to that illness. About that time Edith sent the Carew governess, Miss Jacobs, to a local druggist to purchase a large supply of arsenic. When

filling the order the druggist remarked that Mrs. Carew needed a great amount of the poison in that this was her third order in recent days. (There were few or no restrictions on the sale of such poisons in Japan at the time.) Miss Jacobs turned over the arsenic to Edith and a few hours later, through a nurse, informed Dr. Wheeler of the purchases of poison ordered by Mrs. Carew.

Wheeler, suspecting Mrs. Carew of poisoning her husband, ordered his patient removed to the naval hospital. His action came too late; Carew died on October 22, 1896. On the night of Carew's death, Edith went to Dr. Wheeler and said, "There is one thing I would like to tell you which I suppose I ought to have told you before. Mr. Carew asked me if I would get him a small bottle of arsenic. He also wanted some sugar of lead." In this way, it was later reasoned, Edith Carew had thought to offset charges of murder against her by implying that Carew alone was responsible for the poison that might later be found in his body.

A coroner's jury at first thought Carew had engaged in arsenic eating, a peculiarly popular habit among Victorian men suffering from stomach ailments, the theory being that small doses of the poison would allay pain. This belief of the jury's was based upon Edith Carew's testimony alone, with no other evidence to indicate its truth.

It was, however, linked with a much debated murder case of 1889, the year the Carews were married. That case, which also involved arsenic eating, dealt with Florence Maybrick and the death of Mrs. Maybrick's husband by poisoning, a case with which Mrs. Carew was well acquainted. In that instance Mrs. Maybrick was convicted of poisoning her husband and, though most probably innocent, was sent to prison for life. The coroner's jury hearing the Carew case declared that Carew had died from poisoning but failed to indict anyone, leaving the verdict open.

Police began to investigate and some weeks later arrested Edith Carew, charging her with murder. Her trial began on January 5, 1897. Mrs. Carew shocked the court by declaring that the governess, Miss Jacobs, was really one "Annie Luke" who had not only been carrying on an affair with her husband but had been the real culprit in his death. Mrs. Carew's lawyer then produced a letter, which Mrs. Carew had somehow unearthed, that clearly implicated Miss Jacobs. Its penny-dreadful prose read:

Dead men tell no tales—no, nor dead women either, for I am going to join him. Do you know what waiting means for eight long, weary years? I have watched and waited—watched till I knew he would grow tired of her, that silly little fool, and then I came to him. What is the result? We, between us, electrify Japan. By the time you get this I shall be well on my way to join him, my twin soul. I have bamboozled (1) the chemist, (2) the doctor, and last, but not least, that fool his wife, and I am now going to join him, my twin soul. A.L. [The signature meant "Annie Luke."]

With that Miss Jacobs was arrested. The terrified woman denied any guilt in the death of Carew, but before she could be charged, the prosecution produced further evidence against Mrs. Carew in the form of letters between her and her secret lover, a man named Dickinson.

The lover was brought to court and testified that he and Edith had been carrying on an affair for several years. He further admitted that he had encouraged her to divorce her husband, but only while under the false impression that Carew was a petty tyrant who treated his wife cruelly, a portrait painted completely from Edith's own imagination. When he had discovered Carew to be a loving and kind husband, he had broken off with Mrs. Carew. Just weeks later the husband had died of arsenic poisoning.

Further, the prosecuting attorneys provided handwriting experts who asserted unequivocally that the "A.L." letter was written by none other than Edith Carew in a desperate attempt to shift the blame for her husband's death from herself to the hapless Miss Jacobs. Mrs. Carew's lawyer, upon hearing this evidence, withdrew from the case.

Edith Carew was convicted and sentenced to be executed, but the British ambassador later commuted her sentence to penal servitude for life. Returned to England by ship, she was confined in Aylesbury Prison, where, ironically, she became friendly with the very Florence Maybrick whose tragic story she had attempted to

use toward her own ends. Edith Carew served thirteen years in prison before being released.

CARSON, ANN

Counterfeiter ■ (? –1838)

John Carson, an adventurer who had been married to Ann Baker for nine years, suddenly departed in 1810. Not hearing from her husband for several years and presuming him dead, Ann wed Lieutenant Richard Smith in Philadelphia. Four years later, on January 20, 1816, Carson appeared at the Smith home, insisting that Smith clear out and leave Ann to him.

Contrary to the portrait drawn in a recent book of social apologia for female criminals, Ann Carson's attitude by this time was decidedly criminal. She not only encouraged her second and illegal husband, Smith, to kill Carson, but gave him the weapon with which he shot dead the long missing Carson. Smith was quickly tried and condemned.

In an attempt to save her second husband, Ann Carson, with the help of some Philadelphia ruffians she had hired, tried to kidnap Simon Snyder, the governor of Philadelphia, planning to hold Snyder captive until Smith was released and returned to her. The plot was detected at the last moment and several of the would-be kidnappers were shot and jailed, Ann Carson fleeing. Smith was hanged a short time later.

As the daughter of a navy officer, Ann knew well how to organize, and used these particular talents to put together a band of white-collar thieves who specialized in counterfeiting. Ann headed the ring for a number of years, successfully directing the group's activities from hiding (she was still wanted on attempted kidnapping charges). The gang included Sarah Maland, Sarah Willis (alias Kelly), William Butler, and a Dr. Loring.

Ann planned to pass a series of large counterfeit notes on Philadelphia's giant bank, Girard's, but these notes were detected and the entire gang rounded up and tried on July 2, 1823. Ann Carson was sent to the Philadelphia jail where she died after writing her memoirs, a lurid and untrustworthy document in which she blamed the state for her turning to a life of crime after the execution of Smith.

CHADWICK, CASSIE L.

Swindler ■ (1859–1907)

Born in Strathroy, Ontario, in 1859 as Elizabeth Bigley, this remarkable con artist traveled the United States for decades, using assumed names for the many swindles she perpetrated. She was known as Lydia de Vere in San Francisco, where she bilked suckers through mystical schemes, passing herself off as an all-powerful clairvoyant and hypnotist who could cure any disease, make any fortune. She would best be known some time later in Ohio as Cassie Chadwick, after marrying the gullible Dr. Leroy Chadwick in Cleveland.

In 1894 she traveled to New York and connived to have an Ohio bank president with her when she visited the luxurious mansion of Andrew Carnegie. The bank official waited in a carriage while Cassie, under some pretext or other, was admitted into the mansion. Half an hour later, she came out again, waving farewell to a man who appeared to be Carnegie but who was really the Carnegie butler. She not only convinced the Ohio banker that she was the illegitimate daughter of Andrew Carnegie but that she had promissory notes from her so-called father that amounted to millions. (Carnegie was a confirmed bachelor, and when Cassie's bubble burst, he indignantly told the press that he never sired a single child.)

Cassie, using her banker dupe, was able to take out enormous loans, millions of dollars, which she used to establish herself as the

Con woman Cassie Chadwick, whose spectacular fraud brought banks in Ohio to ruin. (UPI)

"Queen of Ohio," spending as much as $100,000 for a single party, and buying grand pianos, which she never played, by the half dozen, and diamond necklaces, which she wore to bed. Whenever her bankers got edgy, she flashed her fake promissory notes from Carnegie, one alone in the amount of $2 million, before returning the notes to her safe-deposit box. The bankers themselves were a greedy lot; they were more than willing to advance Cassie whatever she desired, thinking to reap enormous amounts of interest. Even a private millionaire, Herbert Newton, loaned Cassie more than $500,000 on her phony notes. When this hard-edged Massachusetts businessman demanded his interest, Cassie exploded, waving away his demand, saying that all her securities, which amounted to $10 million, were in the Wade Park National Bank in

Cleveland. Upon inspection of Cassie's safe-deposit box in that bank, it was soon learned that her Carnegie notes were inept forgeries.

On December 7, 1904, police burst into Cassie's lavish suite in Cleveland's Hotel Breslin. There they found Cassie in bed wearing a money belt that contained $100,000. She was tried, convicted of fraud, and given a ten-year prison sentence. She died in prison three years later.

CHESIMARD, JOANNE

Terrorist ■ (1948–   )

A member of the so-called Black Liberation Army, a minor terrorist group active in New York and New Jersey in the early 1970s, Joanne Chesimard proved to be the only member of this fanatical organization recruited from the ranks of non-felons. She had been a student at City College of New York.

On May 2, 1973, Chesimard, in company with James Costan (alias Zayd Malik Shakur) and Clark E. Squire, both members of the radical group, was stopped by state police on the New Jersey Turnpike for a traffic violation. State trooper James Harper approached the car and got into a scuffle with Squire. He later testified that Joanne Chesimard and Costan reached under their seats and drew weapons. They exchanged shots with Harper, who was wounded and escaped the scene on foot. Another state trooper, Werner Foerster, who had been summoned by Harper, arrived to exchange shots with the terrorists. Foerster and Costan were killed. The twenty-nine-year-old Chesimard and Squire were wounded and were found later, trying to escape.

Though defended by William M. Kunstler, the self-appointed defender of the violent radical left in the 1970s, Joanne Chesimard was given a life sentence in 1977. She escaped from Clinton Correctional Institution for Women on November 2, 1979, and at this writing is still at large.

CHIVERS, ELIZABETH

Murderer ■ (1682–1712)

Terrorist Joanne Chesimard in 1973. (Wide World)

E lizabeth Chivers was born into poverty in Spitafields, England, and went to work at age fourteen as a domestic servant. At age thirty, having never had any relationship with a man, Elizabeth was seduced by an attorney named Ward in late 1711. She delivered his child, Elizabeth, the following year. At first, Ward cared for both mother and child but three months later his wife discovered the liaison, and the lawyer broke off his support. Mrs. Ward further made life miserable for Elizabeth by spreading the word of her affair and illegitimate child. Shamed and afraid to show her face, Elizabeth took her infant to a nearby pond and drowned the girl, thinking in that way to somehow end her disgrace.

Some witnesses, seeing Elizabeth drown her baby girl, made a citizen's arrest and took her immediately to a magistrate. She was tried and condemned to hang. Before her execution on August 1, 1712, Elizabeth confessed to her attending parson. The clergyman later released her last words: "Oh, sir! I am lost! I cannot pray, I cannot repent; my sin is too great to be pardoned! I did commit it with deliberation and choice, and in cold blood. I was not driven to it by necessity. The father had all the while provided for me and for the child, and would have done so still, had not I destroyed the child, and thereby sought my own destruction."

CHOATE, MRS. PEARL

Killer ■ (1907– ?)

A giantess, Pearl Choate stood well over six feet and weighed more than 250 pounds during her heyday. The Texas-born Pearl was married to six men, all of them rich and in their nineties, and all of them dying shortly after wedding the behemoth private nurse. (Pearl's penchant was applying as a private nurse to ancient Texas millionaires, marrying them, and, if it could be arranged, inheriting their fortunes. One of Pearl's husbands appeared reluctant to depart this best of possible worlds, but finally died when, in the heat of an argument with the towering Pearl, the woman sent four bullets into him. Though Pearl claimed self-defense, she was convicted and served twelve years for the man's death.

When released, Pearl took up various forms of grand larceny in Houston, Texas, and served more time in jail. She was released and promptly married her star patient, ninety-five-year-old A. O. Birch, a retired millionaire living in Grand Prairie, Texas. A few months later, in March 1966, Birch too died. Though she was suspected of having brought about Birch's demise, nothing in this instance could be proved against her. To one reporter at the time she sneered, "They keep bringing up my six other husbands. What's that got to do with today's love? . . . They were all about Mr. Birch's age when I married them. So what? I done the decent thing. You never heard of Pearl Choate not marrying a man. Pearl Choate don't shack up!"

CHRISTOFI, MRS. STYLLOU

Murderer ■ (1900–1954)

A Cypriot Greek, Mrs. Christofi had not seen her son Stavros for twelve years. He had moved from Cyprus to England and married a beautiful German girl, Hella Bleicher. By the time Mrs. Christofi could afford passage to England in July 1953 to visit her son, he had three children.

The mother and daughter-in-law did not get along. Mrs. Christofi tried to bully and manage Hella at every turn in the small Hampstead flat occupied by the Christofi family. Stavros was working as a waiter and insurance salesman most of the time, and was not present to keep peace between the two women. Hella finally put her foot down and told her husband that she was taking the children to see her parents in Germany and when she returned she expected to see the stern-faced Mrs. Christofi gone, sent back to Cyprus. Stavros nodded agreement.

Homicide altered the plan on the night of July 29, 1953. Her husband at work and the children asleep, Hella Christofi informed her mother-in-law that she was going to take a bath. The tall, attractive brunette stripped to her panties and entered the bathroom, thinking Mrs. Christofi was going upstairs to sleep. In moments, the unwanted mother-in-law rushed into the bathroom and slammed an ash plate from the kitchen stove down onto Hella's head, knocking the woman unconscious. She next dragged her hated daughter-in-law into the kitchen, strangling her to death with one of Hella's own scarves. To hide the crime, Mrs. Christofi poured paraffin over Hella's half-naked corpse and lit it. The flames shot up, threatening to ignite the entire kitchen.

Fearing for her grandchildren asleep upstairs, Mrs. Christofi lost her head and ran into the street, hailing a man named Burstoff who was sitting in a car parked nearby. In her poor English, Mrs. Christofi shouted to him, "Please come! Fire burning, children sleeping!"

Burstoff ran after Mrs. Christofi who led him into the flat. The man took one look at the body smoldering before him and gave the lean-faced Mrs. Christofi a suspicious glance. Hella's body lay in a pool of blood on the kitchen floor near some French windows. Her body was charred in spots, but the red welt around her neck was clearly visible. A constable entered the flat and Mrs. Christofi blurted out, "Me smell burning, me come down, me pour water, but she be died. My son married Germany girl he like, plenty clothes, plenty shoes, babies going to Germany." The motive for the murder was instantly apparent to the police. Mrs. Christofi had convicted herself out of her own mouth.

Further ensuring the woman's murder conviction, was the testimony of a neighbor, John Young, who stated that on the night of the killing he had seen Mrs. Christofi through the French windows as she stirred the fire about the body of her daughter-in-law. Oddly, he had thought the burning form on the kitchen floor was a tailor's dummy.

The defense tried to assert that Mrs. Christofi was insane, but she herself refused to allow experts to so testify, telling her attorney, "I am a poor woman, of no education, but I am not a mad woman. Never, never, never!" But Mrs. Christofi had been touched with some sort of maniacal urge most of her adult life, the prosecution insisted, pointing out that the killer had, in 1925, been acquitted of murdering *her* mother-in-law on Cyprus by ramming a burning torch down the woman's throat.

Mrs. Christofi was condemned. As she awaited her execution, she wrote bitterly to her

Cypriot-born Mrs. Styllou Christofi under arrest in London for murder, 1953.

son, her hatred still seething for being replaced by another woman in Stavros' heart, wrath that would be stilled only by the rope. Stavros Christofi received the following written words from his mother in her final hours:

It doesn't matter what is going to happen to me. You have tried too hard to hang me, in order to put around my neck the noose, so that you may rest.

I am not obliging you to come see me, my son.

The son did not attend the hanging.

CHURCHILL, DEBORAH

Pickpocket ■ (1677–1708)

Though born into a good family and given a superior education, Deborah Churchill, in the words of one chronicler, "abandoned herself to all manner of filthiness and uncleanness which afterward proved her shame and ruin." After marrying John Churchill, an ensign in the army, Deborah soon departed for the streets of London where she became a common whore, picking the pockets of her customers as well. She practiced the badger game with her pimp and lover Richard Hunt, blackmailing rich merchants for a number of years.

Arrested many times, Deborah Churchill always managed to escape any severe punishment, usually through the efforts of Hunt who bribed officials to release her. In early 1708, Deborah was strolling through Drury Lane looking for another pickpocket victim, three male friends—Richard Hunt, William Lewis, and a youth called John Boy—trailing behind her. She bumped into a merchant, Martin Were, and propositioned him. The merchant said he wanted no part of "a diseased whore." When he found Deborah's hand in his pocket, he knocked her to the ground. Her three thug friends came up on the run. Deborah cursed Were and demanded that her friends kill him. They ran him through with swords.

Officials ran forward but only caught the slow-moving Deborah Churchill. She was tried for the murder of Were and condemned on February 26, 1708, but was reprieved when she convinced prison authorities that she was pregnant. After seven months, officials realized they had been duped, that Deborah was not with child. She was taken in a coach to Tyburn on Friday, December 17, 1708, and promptly hanged.

CHURCHILL, MAY ("CHICAGO MAY")

Swindler, Bank Burglar ■ (1876–1929)

The woman in the dock, facing charges of attempted murder, on June 25, 1907, was considered by the British court and the press of three continents to be one of the worst female criminals the world had ever seen, a red-headed, beautiful woman of thirty-one who had trimmed thousands of unsuspecting lusting men in one of the oldest rackets on record. She had many names, but lawmen everywhere knew her by the cognomen of Chicago May, and to the professional criminals of Europe, and North and South America, she was "Queen of the Badgers."

No great childhood tragedy contributed to the construction of May's criminal character; she had wanted it that way from the start, when, as a teenager, she stole her mother's meager savings and sailed to America from Sligo, Ireland, where she had been born May Lambert in 1876. At the end of her evil career, and close to death, May Vivienne Churchill—the name she chose to go to the grave with—hurriedly penned her somewhat unreliable memoirs, expressing not a single thought of remorse for her horrendous deeds. "I have never suffered from the qualms of conscience," May wrote. "I have had no regrets—except when I was caught. I am not really sorry I was a criminal."

Arriving in New York at fifteen in 1891, May changed her name to Latimer and applied for a job as a chorus girl, taking advantage of the dancing lessons her mother had scrimped to pay for years earlier in Ireland. Lying about her age, the statuesque girl with flaming red hair and a pure white complexion landed a spot in the chorus of a new musical, *The Belle of New York*. No one seeing this energetic Irish colleen with spry, long legs at the premiere of this musical ever thought she would someday become the notorious Chicago May.

One man who did see the girl, going to the

show night after night, was a handsome young army officer named Sharp, who came from a wealthy New York family. Sharp proposed to May one night in her dressing room, oblivious to the squeals from the other chorus girls present who overheard his sincere words of love. May was never one to miss an opportunity. After learning the young man was rich, she accepted. The marriage lasted only a few months. May had bled the young man of nearly $10,000 before she told Sharp that she was bored with living in a fine home and having servants. "I'm for myself," she said. "I want to risk myself in the world. The thought of having security annoys me." She left Sharp and took up lodgings in the old Tenderloin district of New York, an area of jewel-bedecked courtesans and luxurious, wide-open gambling dens and brothels, all patronized by the most famous high rollers in America, from Richard Canfield to Diamond Jim Brady, and, for payment of enormous sums, protected by a thoroughly corrupt New York police department. (The name for the district came from a police captain who, having been transferred to the area from a remote New York post, was heard to quip, "I've been eating pork chops for years. Now I'm going to have nothing but tenderloin.")

Using Sharp's money, May moved through the Tenderloin as would a visiting princess, dressed in the finest gowns as she made her grand appearances in the most fashionable clubs on the arms of hired escorts. Her beauty was such that she completely stupefied the elegantly attired males in her presence. Some fifteen years later *The New York Times* was to describe her at this time as having "eyes that were large and brilliant and teeth wonderfully white. Her features were baby-like in their soft roundness, and she made a picture of sweet innocence."

May was far from innocent by that time. She had several lovers, all wealthy, who showered jewels upon her, and offered her their family fortunes if she would wed them. She simply dangled them, enjoying watching their agonies. In fact, May's pronounced dislike of men in general undoubtedly brought her to the criminal profession in which she became the reigning queen.

One night in her travels through the casinos and clubs, May met Max Shinborn, a confidence

Queen of the badget game, May Churchill, standing next to her last lover and co-author of her *Memoirs*, Netley Lucas.

artist, bank burglar, and gambler who himself was considered "the King of the Badgers." Shinborn had no real interest in May as a woman—his singular interest in life was money, and he would retire to the Riviera shortly after purchasing the title of "Baron Shindell"—but he found May's driving desire to swindle rich men amusing and taught her every trick of the badger game. It was the simple, ageless method of blackmail with many variations, all of which were practiced and many invented by Chicago May.

She would begin by inviting a wealthy admirer to a smartly decorated apartment used only for business purposes. May would make passionate love to the gentleman, emotions she later claimed she never felt, while plying her lover with drugged champagne. When the caller passed out, May would take his valuables and wallet, throw his clothes out the window, and depart. When the swain awoke, his head throbbing, he would find a strange man sitting next to the bed, staring dully at him. The stranger, a Chicago May confederate, would then inform the sucker that he was in serious trouble—May's "husband" had unexpectedly returned from a business trip and had found them in bed, dragging off his wife and leaving the unconscious man alone. "May's husband intends to inform your wife and sue your entire family penniless," the confederate would explain to the pop-eyed gull, "but I think I can fix things."

The confederate would then explain that for a certain price he could convince the husband to keep quiet about the entire affair. The sucker invariably paid the required amount, making many blackmail payments over a period of months. This then was the old badger game that May played, and she played it with a vengeance, blackmailing dozens of New York's most esteemed citizens, for tens of thousands of dollars.

In one instance, May compromised a New York millionaire and blackmailed the young gentleman for $5,000. When the victim's check bounced, May, unperturbed, went to her victim's father, showing the elderly man his son's check and threatening a suit for fraud, in addition to revealing his scandalous affairs. The man's father gave May a check for $10,000.

There were, however, those rare times when a sucker did stand up to May's badger-game blackmail, one being the brother of a New York judge, who brought her into court. When asked by a magistrate how he could have been so easily hoodwinked, the victim replied in a sincere voice, "I tell you, when I looked into her eyes, I was transfixed." He pointed a finger at May who was dressed in conservative black, a veil hiding her pretty face. "That woman is a vixen of the worst kind. Why, she hypnotized me, your honor, mesmerized me right out of my mind, and she got me to give her five thousand dollars besides!"

As in almost all her court appearances during her badger-game heyday, May again escaped with only a light reprimand. Of the twenty cases of grand larceny brought against her in New York and later in Detroit and Chicago, she was given negligible sentences for theft, or for dealing in firearms, or for prostitution, or, the most common charge, for working the badger game. Sometimes she spent only a week or so in confinement. She worked six cities in South America in the mid-1890s before going to Chicago from New York, without one charge being brought against her. And not one dime of the fortunes she bilked was ever returned.

Her undoing in New York, however, came about through May's double-dealing the very people who had provided her protection—the police. May was approached by some reformers working for the Reverend Parkhurst, a zealot, who had vowed to close up the Tenderloin. She was asked to compromise some powerful police detectives in the district and, for some very mysterious reason, May agreed. It was later reported that May had been shaken down by Lieutenant Charles Becker of the New York Police Department, and had developed a seething hatred for all police officers. (Becker, known as "the crookedest cop in New York," would later die in the electric chair in 1912 after ordering the murder of Herman Rosenthal, a gambler who had refused to pay him off.)

May arranged for a powerful police captain and his top aides to visit her to discuss the amounts she should pay for protection. Handsome kickbacks were expected from May, as the reigning queen of the badgers, for the enormous profits the police allowed her to glean from suckers. While the captain and his men conversed with May about these financial arrangements, Dr. Parkhurst and several witnesses hid behind a curtain in May's apartment, finally stepping forth to catch the shocked policemen red-handed. The captain and his men were fired from the force, but Chicago May had little joy in helping the reformers. The police made life so miserable for her that she was prevented from working her unsavory trade. Her accomplices were warned by detectives that they would be arrested on sight if seen in May's company. The rich courtesan was finished in the Tenderloin.

Packing her bags, May departed for Chicago, and, once there, became the darling of the bunco artists, who infested the town like fleas; hundreds of confidence swindlers worked in the open and under the powerful protection of Big Mike McDonald, America's first crime czar, who controlled every action of the city's mayor, police and legislators. Here May improved upon her badger game, swindling Chicago's pillars of society and business, aided in her efforts by a congenial con man named "Kid John" McManus. It was while working with McManus that May developed the idea of using cameras in her game.

Cameras in the late 1890s were cumbersome affairs but May, always inventive, had special walls erected in her apartment, behind which the cameras were set up, focusing from three sides of the room on a bed into which May would bring her rich victims and where she would shamelessly perform acrobatic sex acts for her shuttering accomplices, the photos taken through peepholes. Enormous sums were paid to May when these photographic plates were shown to the duped lovers. "They can go into your wastecan or to the newspapers," May would inform her blackmail victims, "I don't care which."

When McManus and "Dutch Gus" Miller, another of May's confederates, were hounded out of Chicago by the Pinkertons, May decided to join them in the greener fields of England, traveling to London in 1900. By then the twenty-five-year-old stunner had an endless trail of broken bank accounts and countless tales of incredible badger-game feats to leave behind in the windy city. She was forever after known as Chicago May.

Once in London, May set up shop with several harpies acting as decoys, hiring male accomplices to handle the heavy traffic May provided. This group was soon known to Scotland Yard as "the Northumberland Gang," but gang efforts to evade detection were so adroit that May and her minions operated without police interference. Typical of Chicago May's lightning speed in rolling British suckers was this first-hand report: "I got a bottle of brandy and then steered the john into a room in a side street. He was lit up by the time he got there, but I shot a few more Mickey Finns into him. I slipped some little drops [chloral] into the last drink. In a few minutes he was gone, dreaming no doubt of conquests. All I had to do was to pull the rings off his fingers. He had a lovely horseshoe pin, a diamond-studded watch, and about a thousand pounds in notes which I also took."

But despite the enormous riches she was accumulating, May was unhappy. Her life seemed without purpose. She sought solace in opium, smoking as many as thirty or forty pipes a day, a drug debauch that "made London's pipe fiends open their eyes," according to *The New York Times*. She soon quit the drug and went back to work.

The rich and the powerful fell victim to the tireless May. She blackmailed the son of an earl for a fortune. A noted British lawyer paid her another fortune not to turn over photos of him and May frolicking in her bedroom. Peers of the realm and titled gentlemen, scores of them, fell for May's badger game. For these whirlwind scores, Detective Inspector Stockley of Scotland Yard would label her "the worst woman in London."

May then moved about on the continent, working her smooth game in Vienna and Paris before returning to London. It was at this time in London that she chanced to meet her old friend "Kid John" McManus. May entered a gambling den near Charing Cross and was greeted with a crushing hug from McManus. He then turned to introduce a tall man with a sincere face. "Meet a doctor friend of mine," McManus said. The tall man held out his hand.

"Doctor, hell," said May. She stared the man square in the eyes. "I know who you are—you're Eddie Guerin."

"And you're Chicago May." Guerin, an international jewel thief who had served a long prison term for robbing a bank in Lyons, France, in 1888, was as infamous as May. From that moment the two entered into a love-hate relationship that brought both of them to destruction.

McManus saw the sparks igniting between the two and leaned next to his friend's ear, whispering, "Leave this dame alone—she'll take you for all you've got."

"I've got nothing," Guerin whispered back, "so what?"

Guerin could only gaze in rapture at May as the vixen sat down at his table to sip champagne. In the words of Guerin, she was "radiant, elegantly attired, lovely, blazing with valuable jewelry." The man who was regarded as a master thief on two continents would never forget that moment, whatever the pain Chicago May brought him later. He would always remember her as "tall and beautifully proportioned, with an abundance of golden-red hair—the real thing, not the peroxide variety—and a complexion of delicate pink and cream, large blue eyes shaded with long dark lashes, and her mouth, the upper lip of which formed a perfect Cupid's bow, while the lower was straight and full and ripe. Such was the vision of loveliness I beheld, and, beholding, instantly coveted."

Then, for a few sober moments, Guerin thought about the wild reputation this woman had, scandalous even for the underworlds of New York, London, and Paris. "My ardor cooled a bit at that," Guerin bitterly remembered years later. "As it chanced I had never met her before, but I knew her by reputation and I knew also she had not then had it smirched by the five years' captivity she was afterwards to undergo in a French prison. But of her moral character the less said the better. And not only was she a wanton, but she was treacherous into the bargain. Many a man, as I was well aware, was even then serving out the last years of his life through her in jails of Europe and America. This I knew full well. Yet knowing it, I could not leave her alone. Her beauty held me spellbound—as it had held many another in years gone by."

It was not known to Guerin at the time that five men had already taken their lives over the woman's vicious blackmailing, one, an elderly Manchester merchant whom May had bankrupted, having blown out his brains only two days before Guerin met her.

May's version of the meeting was altogether different. She later claimed that she had met Guerin in Dublin after visiting with her mother, a bold lie; May never returned to Ireland to see her family, but she did send money to her mother, undoubtedly as retribution for her initial theft. "Guerin brought me back to London and then to Paris," May insisted in her highly suspect autobiography. "He never gave me the slightest idea of what he was doing. He used me as his dupe!"

Whatever the truth as to the circumstances of their meeting, the two fell madly in love with each other and instantly established a professional as well as a romantic union. They agreed to pull a big job together. Only days after Guerin and May moved into the same hotel room, "Dutch Gus" Miller arrived from Paris to tell them about the "most beautiful safe in the world, an enormous old-fashioned safe that is in the offices of the American Express Company in Paris on the rue Scribe."

Miller, who had been trained as an engineer in Pittsburgh, had cracked safes in New York and Chicago before meeting up with May and McManus to work the badger game. He knew Eddie Guerin was a master safecracker and the American Express job was too big for anyone except Guerin. After Miller finished describing every detail of the safe over which he had drooled for several weeks while visiting the Paris office, Guerin agreed to the robbery. Eddie would use McManus also, he said, because he had steel nerves and was a good "crackman." And May would be part of the job, insisted the lovestick Guerin. She would act as a lookout, Eddie told Miller. As it turned out, Chicago May served far beyond that capacity during the spectacular robbery.

The foursome traveled to Paris. Guerin studied the safe himself for weeks. He would mail letters to himself in care of the American Express office, then pick these missives up, which gave him ample time to case the office and study the safe. He learned that a Negro watchman was the only person on duty at night, although gendarmes regularly patrolled the area, paying particular attention to the American Express office on the corner of rue Scribe and rue Auber. The Negro watchman, a seventeen-year-old named Merl Segar, who slept in one of the rooms on the first floor, would have to be gotten out of the way, Eddie figured. And one of the gang members would have to get inside the bank before it closed for the day, hide somewhere, then open the door for Guerin and the others when it was safe. According to her version, Chicago May was the inside person. The gang struck on the night of April 26, 1901.

"At the appointed time," May later related, "having previously studied the layout [of the express office], I went to the company office. It was near closing time and I asked the clerks a lot of inane questions. They shunted me from one to the other, each one wanting to be rid of me and clear up his work for the day. As everyone was more or less distracted, and going out of his way to avoid me, I found it very easy to hide myself. I squeezed under a counter in an out-of-the-way corner, used only for storing extra packages during the rush hours."

"The place was closed for the night, leaving only the Negro watchman, and me, inside. I had to wait, crouching, a couple of hours before the Negro went upstairs to attend to his watching business. When he did, I shifted a large inkstand near one of the windows [which was the agreed-upon signal to Guerin, Miller, and McManus that all was going as planned inside the office]. Then I drew back the bolts of the designated door. In came my confederates. They, too, had to wait for the Negro. He took a long time to come downstairs. Finally, he came like a good fellow, and was trussed up proper. It took a couple of hours to drill and charge the two safes. In the meanwhile I went to the lookout beat, outside."

Segar had been tied hand and foot and dragged by Miller to his room where he was placed on a cot. Miller sat next to the terrified guard, gun in hand, saying nothing as Guerin and McManus worked on the ancient safe in the outer office. The safe was situated so that passersby could not see it from the street.

May stood across the street, pretending to be a common prostitute waiting for a trick to appear, a role she undoubtedly played to perfection. A muffled explosion went off at about 2:00 A.M., and soon May saw a gendarme running down the street toward the American Express office.

"Where was that explosion, miss?" the gendarme politely asked May in French.

"It was over there," May replied, also in French, pointing to a direction away from the

May Churchill at the time of the infamous robbery of the American Express in Paris.

express office. The gendarme moved off, in the direction she had indicated.

May continued to keep her vigil, growing nervous. "It seemed like an age before I heard the next shot fired. [It was almost three hours later, close to 5:00 A.M.] Shortly thereafter, the inkwell was moved back into place. My work was finished then, so I went home to bed."

Guerin arrived some hours later. He stood at the foot of May's bed and laughed wildly, throwing money over her, a shower of francs, pound notes, and dollars. Eddie beamed, reporting to a sleepy Chicago May that they had made the strike of their lives. He laughed as he described how he and McManus had shoveled francs and pounds and dollars into suitcases they had brought along for that purpose, a haul of about $600,000 in traveler's checks and $40,00 in cold cash. May sewed a great deal of cash into the lining of her favorite coat, while Guerin packed his share of the traveler's checks in a trunk. McManus had already left for Italy, and Miller had fled also, Guerin told May. They must hurry out of France and return to the safety of London. He had purchased train tickets days earlier and the boat train for Calais and England would leave in only a few hours.

By that time detectives from the Sûreté were swarming all over the American Express office. Segar, the watchman, was found shivering on his cot. He stated that the man who guarded him cut the ropes on his hands and feet about 5:00 A.M. that morning, telling him, "I'm going to stand across the street for an hour. If you run out and give the alarm I will put a bullet in your head." The youthful watchman stayed on his cot and was discovered by an office boy named Charpentier an hour later.

The thieves had left no clues, but Segar was able to give complete descriptions of the three male intruders. He thought he had seen a woman when he had been overpowered, but was uncertain as to her appearance. The police accurately figured the thieves would depart Paris immediately, and scores of detectives were sent to the train stations.

By then Guerin and May, pretending to be British tourists, were aboard a speeding train headed toward Calais, a train that two French detectives, Debishop and Thevenot, had caught on the spur of the moment. The detectives had no idea Guerin and Chicago May were actually on the train but had simply played a hunch. As they were making their way down a corridor, they paused for a moment, meeting a well-dressed couple going in the opposite direction. According to May, "everything might have gone well, if it had not been for Eddie's infernal conceit. He was very proud of his ability at slinging French. The two French dicks happened to ask him, in broken English, where they could find the dining car. We had been posing as English travelers, but what does the chump do but answer the detectives in French that would do credit to an educated native. At that, the *sans culottes* did not know who they had in their clutches. They thought he was a French criminal they were on the lookout for."

May was allowed to go on alone. Taken off the train at Amiens, Guerin merely nodded in May's direction. She was safe for the moment and took the boat to England, arriving with the major portion of the loot, which she im-

mediately hid. Guerin was returned to Paris. There he was confronted with a whimpering Dutch Gus Miller, who had been arrested on the very day of the robbery at the Gard du Nord railway station as he prepared to leave Paris, identified by detectives through the watchman's description. He was not hard to pick out in a crowd; Gus had an eight-inch scar, livid red, across his forehead. Miller instantly informed on McManus and Guerin, but had gallantly forgotten Chicago May's name.

McManus successfully fled Italy to London and went into hiding. May spent nervous weeks worrying if Guerin, confined in La Santé Prison and awaiting trial, would implicate her. She finally decided to make sure she was not wanted and that her lover had not "squealed" on her. May foolishly took the boat back to France and the train to Paris. She argued her way into visiting Guerin by telling the warden that she was his sister.

"Are you crazy coming here?" Guerin said to her through the bars of his cell. "Beat it!"

"I want you to know I'm loyal to you, Eddie. I won't desert you."

"You damned idiot! They saw you on the train with me, and now here. That'll add up to you being involved in the robbery."

Impetuously, May reached into her handbag, withdrew $500 in cash, and thrust the money through the bars and into Guerin's hands. "You'll need this cash for a lawyer. I'll get you all you need. The money is safe in England."

A moment later the warden and two detectives surrounded Chicago May, lightly holding on to her arms. "You spoke of some money, mademoiselle?" inquired the warden politely.

"Now you've done it, May," Guerin said through gritting teeth, tossing the money onto the floor of his cell.

May faced trial with Miller and Guerin. Both men insisted that May had had nothing to do with the robbery, but she was clearly implicated by her own actions. On June 29, 1902, she was sentenced to five years in prison. McManus and Guerin were sent to the penal colony in French Guiana for life at hard labor. This was the most dreaded penal colony in the world, of Devil's Island fame. No one expected to see

Eddie Guerin again, least of all Chicago May Churchill.

May worked her feminine charms on the doctor in Montpellier Prison where she had been held captive for almost three years. The doctor, after trysting with May in her cell, an act witnessed by another female prisoner at May's insistence, was promptly blackmailed into signing a phony medical certificate for Chicago May's release in 1904. The badger game had worked for May even behind bars. The French authorities warned her that if she ever set foot on French soil again, she would be locked up for life. She returned to London.

A year later the impossible happened; Eddie Guerin escaped from the penal colony in Cayenne, French Guiana. He simply bribed a guard to look the other way and walked off into the surrounding jungle. Two other prisoners saw Guerin leaving and insisted they escape with him or else give the alarm. He agreed, and the three men, after miraculously crossing hundreds of miles of dense jungle in Surinam (Dutch Guiana), came to a river where they found a dugout which Guerin bought from a native standing nearby. The source of Guerin's money was never revealed, but May later claimed that she had raised $50,000 from her underworld contacts, which was smuggled to him, money that effected his escape, but Guerin later heard and instantly branded the story a lie. Guerin's companions never survived the ordeal. One man fell out of the dugout during a storm and drowned. The other committed suicide by diving out of a high tree when cornered by a jaguar, the jewel thief later told a British court. May, who was no friend of Guerin's at the time he related the fanciful fates of his companions, placed the deaths of Guerin's fellow escapees in his hands. Said May, "It would not surprise me to learn that Guerin killed the two men, either in a fight, or when they were off guard. I wouldn't blame him for it. They forced their company on him, and they were a menace to his safety."

Going to the American consulate in British Guiana, Guerin convinced authorities that he was an American citizen who had been stranded in the jungle, a member of a lost archeological party. His transportation was arranged to America. Guerin traveled to Chicago to work a

few safes but quickly left for London when he heard that French authorities had tracked him down and were preparing extradition orders for him. In London, Eddie Guerin met the faded love of his life, Chicago May.

Looking thin and pale, Guerin walked into the Horse and Groom Pub on Portland Street and ordered a beer. The milky arms of a woman soon hugged him wildly as Chicago May kissed him, chirping, "My God, Eddie, is it you? I'm glad to see you!" Guerin wasn't sure he was happy to see May, but in a short while they were a couple again. Fearlessly, they returned to France, pulling off minor confidence games to

Eddie Guerin, "Chicago May's" lover and master bank burglar.

keep themselves going, but the great days for Eddie Guerin were obviously over.

Since her own release, May told Eddie, she had pulled off some big scores in South America, taking one millionaire in Rio de Janeiro for $100,000. This was gone, of course, as was the loot from the Paris robbery. "They were mostly useless traveler's checks," May reported. "I threw those checks out the train window after you and the detectives got off."

In Aix-la-Chapelle, the two argued. Guerin wanted to continue his career alone. "If you leave me," May vowed, "I'll inform the authorities—I'll send you back to Devil's Island. You'll die like a dog!"

Guerin left Chicago May, returning to London. She followed and, when arriving, promptly informed authorities that Eddie Guerin was a fugitive from French justice. Guerin was jailed pending a hearing. Though the French fought hard to have Guerin returned to them, the British courts refused to grant extradition. Guerin proved he was a British subject and not liable to extradition. He was set free.

A few days later, on the night of June 16, 1907, the forty-seven-year-old jewel thief was walking through Russell Square. A cab suddenly came abreast of him and a woman's voice shouted, "There his is! Shoot him!" It was the voice of Chicago May; the woman was leaning from the window of the halting cab, a man named Cubine Jackson, alias Charlie Smith, leaping from the cab with a revolver in his hand. Smith had at one time been a cellmate of Guerin's and was now May's lover.

Guerin began to run, looking for cover, but Smith was close after him, firing all the shots in his revolver as May shouted over and over again, "Shoot him! Shoot him!"

One of the bullets found its mark, striking Guerin in the foot. By then May had taken refuge in a doorway and was screaming, "Kill him, Charlie!" But Charlie Smith couldn't kill anyone. He had been thrown to the ground by a constable answering the alarm, then dozens of passersby jumped on the burly would-be assassin. "For God's sake," Charlie called to the constable, "take these people off me—they're choking me!"

Guerin, in agonizing pain, hobbled to the doorway where his former lover stood glaring hate at him. "When you couldn't send me back to Devil's Island," he spat in her direction, "you stoop to murder, you whore!"

"I'm only sorry Charlie didn't finish you," May said through gritted teeth.

Another constable arrived just as Guerin collapsed. He pointed to May Churchill, telling the officer she was behind the shooting.

"I had nothing to do with it," May said. "I was alone in the cab when a man shot this gentleman."

Charlie Smith was brought forward under arrest. He leaped to May's defense. "She has done nothing," he shouted. "I fired the shots. She has done nothing. I don't see how you can charge her."

Both May and Smith were arrested. They were tried nine days later, Guerin testifying against them. May remained calm during the proceedings, showing no emotion as the tempestuous former lovers glared at each other in court. Guerin had his revenge. May Churchill was given fifteen years in prison and Smith was sent away for life for attempted murder. Smith hurled curses at the judge before being led away.

The Queen of the Badgers served twelve terrible years in Alesbury Jail, being released in 1918; Smith was released in 1923, a broken man. When May arrived in New York she gave an interview to newsmen curious about this once ravishing courtesan of the underworld, now faded and a bit dumpy. May still lashed out at Guerin, who was dead, saying that her ex-lover had writtern her parents in Ireland, telling the Lamberts the entire story of May's sordid past and including press clippings in his missive. "My mother died from the shock," May lamented.

May tried her hand at small confidence games over the next decade, but her luck was miserable and she was invariably caught. Sick, and broke, Chicago May sat down in 1928 and wrote her memoirs, most of her remembrances being nothing more than romantic fiction. The book was not a success. The following year, Chicago May Churchill was found dead in a run-down Philadelphia boardinghouse. Inside her drab room there was nothing to suggest the memories of a woman who had bilked countless lovers out of a million dollars. There was, though, a faded photograph on her bedside table, a picture showing May standing next to a dapper-looking fellow sitting in a chair. The man was, of course, Eddie Guerin.

CLARK, LORRAINE

Murderer ■ (1926–   )

Bored with her ten-year marriage to Melvin Clark, an electronics worker who spent most of his spare time running a boat rental service on Lake Attitash, Massachusetts, Lorraine Clark began having extramarital affairs in 1954. It so happened that the town of Amesbury, where they lived, was awash just then with the new cult of spouse swapping. Lorraine attended countless parties where the husbands would throw their house keys into a hat and the wives would pluck out a key and meet the man later. Her husband wasn't aware of his wife's indiscretions until the night of April 10, when he walked into his home and found her with another man.

Just minutes after the offending man sheepishly left the Clark house next to Lake Attitash, Lorraine exploded, attacking her husband with razor-sharp darning needles, which she twice plunged into his chest. She then grabbed a .32-caliber pistol and shot Melvin Clark dead with two bullets. For hours that night Lorraine labored to dispose of the body, trussing the corpse in chicken wire, then rolling it to her car and packing it into the trunk. Next she drove the six miles to the Merrimack River, where she tied three fifteen-pound weights to the body, and then dumped it from a bridge, thinking it would be carried out to sea.

Some days later Lorraine began complaining about her "cruel" husband, and that they had argued. She filed for divorce on April 17, 1954, saying that Melvin Clark had abused her. The "abusive" Melvin Clark washed ashore in some marshlands on June 2, 1954, his unrecog-

nizable body found by birdwatchers. He was identified through fingerprints.

Confronted with the bullet-torn body, Mrs. Clark hastily wrote out a confession, including a sordid account of the sleazy sex practices of her Amesbury neighbors. She was sentenced to life imprisonment in the Women's Reformatory at Framingham, Massachusetts.

CLARKE, MRS. MARY ANNE

Swindler ■ (1776–1852)

A British courtesan of exceptional beauty, Mary Anne Clarke, born Thompson in London, received a modest education at Ham, her schooling allegedly paid for by a man named Day who thought to marry her someday. Instead, Mary Anne, at sixteen, wed a youth named Clarke. In five years the young man had turned into a drunken sot and was bankrupt. Mrs. Clarke began her rise through the backstairs of the British aristocracy, becoming the mistress of Sir Charles Milner, then Sir James Brudenell, both of whom she bilked out of large sums before discarding them as lovers. She next seduced and milked the son of a wealthy wine merchant.

For a brief period Mary Anne took roles on the Haymarket stage, an endeavor that enabled her to select her noble victims from an admiring male audience. Among such victims were Lord Barrymore and the Duke of York, the latter becoming her most lasting lover.

The Duke of York, as commander-in-chief of the British army, wielded enormous power, a fact known well to the conniving Mary Anne Clarke. She began to sell favors to anyone rich enough to buy them, favors she whispered were endorsed by the Duke of York. She sold commissions in the army as one would apples on the street corner, competing successfully with the standard purchases of such commissions available through the government. A man could buy a

The beautiful con artist, Mary Anne Clarke, circa 1814.

association with the Duke of York. Although the duke was subjected to a hearing, he was exonerated.

Owing to her powerful connections, Mary Anne Clarke was not prosecuted but, having lost those connections, she was shunted to the backwaters of British society to dabble in petty intriques and larceny. In 1814, Mrs. Clarke received a nine-month prison sentence for libeling the Irish Chancellor of the Exchequer. Following this humiliating imprisonment Mary Anne left for Europe, in disgrace but extremely rich. She set up a sumptuous salon in Paris where she reigned in comfortable exile for several decades, one of the most sought-after mistresses of the day. She died at her estate in Boulogne on June 21, 1852.

COLUMBO, PATRICIA

Murderer ■ (1957–   )

The brutality of the slayings was nothing less than awesome, and even the hard-boiled cops found themselves recoiling from the terrible sight. Three bodies lay sprawled before them inside the posh suburban home at 55 Brantwood in Elk Grove Village, a bedroom community west of Chicago. The police arrived on the night of May 7, 1976, called by suspicious neighbors. Slowly, officers began to check each body. They determined the victims had been dead since May 4.

Frank Columbo, 43, was hardly recognizable. He had been shot four times, bullets sent through both cheeks, the mouth, and behind the left ear. Burning cigarettes had been extinguished on his chest, and his head had been crushed as if someone had struck him repeatedly with a baseball bat. Columbo's wife, Mary, 41, had been shot once between the eyes. She lay with her nightgown and robe torn open, her panties yanked to her ankles, but she had not been raped. The Columbos' son, thirteen-year-old

majority for 900 pounds through Mary Anne whereas the government would charge 2,600 pounds. Pocketing the money, Mrs. Clarke promised that the commission would be arranged through her lover, the all-powerful Duke of York. More often than not, the commission would be awarded, although the duke's complicity was never proved.

Over the years, Mary Anne grew enormously rich and maintained one of the finest mansions in London, as well as a stunning country estate. Not until January 27, 1809, when Colonel Gwyllym Lloyd Wardle made a shocking speech in the House of Commons, was Mary Anne's mighty graft exposed. Wardle outlined the many years of Mrs. Clarke's selling of positions through her

Patricia Columbo, the attractive Illinois killer who traded sexual favors for having her parents and brother murdered.

Michael, had received the full vent of the killer's wrath—he had been stabbed eighty-four times, eight wounds puncturing his lungs, seventy-six other stab wounds slashing his entire body.

At first police thought they had another berserk Manson-like family of cult killers on their hands, especially since the Columbo home had not been ransacked; more than $4,000 in a small safe and expensive jewelry had not been touched. The killings appeared to be the work of psychopaths bent only on thrill murders. This was also the expressed belief of nineteen-year-old Patricia Columbo, the only family member to survive. Patty, who lived apart with her thirty-nine-year-old boyfriend, Frank DeLuca, sobbingly told police that she guessed it was "kids in the area" who had committed these horrible slayings. A few days after the murders Patty called a police reporter, offering whatever help she could in solving the case. Stifling tears, Patty told the reporter that the killers must have been "the young punks" in the suburb, and that they were "probably high on drugs" when they killed her family. "They're very sick people."

The statuesque, voluptuous brunette murmured similar accusations as she wept bitter tears while watching three coffins lowered into graves hours later. She begged authorities to track down the lunatics who had wiped out her family. "Find them," she implored, "please find them!"

Police did find Frank Columbo's car, which had been missing since the night of the murders. On the steering wheel of the car lawmen discovered a bloody smear left by someone who had only three fingers on one hand. They began a systematic check for anyone known to the Columbos who was missing an index finger. By the time investigators knocked on the door of Patty Columbo's apartment at 2015 South Finley Road in Lombard, Illinois, they had not only learned the identity of the three-fingered man, but had listened to shocking testimony by one of Patty's girl friends. Even after the detectives identified themselves, Patty Columbo took several minutes before opening the door to the police. Investigators later claimed that she was busy destroying evidence during those precious minutes.

Patty was arrested for the murder of her parents and brother. Frank DeLuca was picked up a short time later and charged with the same heinous crime. Both denied the charges with angry, startled shouts, both insisting that they had been with each other on the night of the murder. Officers only nodded, then one grabbed DeLuca's hand. He had only three fingers, having lost one in a skydiving accident years earlier.

Even more damning were the statements of Patty Columbo's friend. The friend had gone to the Elk Grove police department after reading about the Columbo slaughter and reported that Miss Columbo had hated her family, chiefly her father, ever since she had taken up with DeLuca, and that she had been planning the murder of her family for months, even hiring two hit men to perform the slayings. All this Patty had confided to her friend, who remembered the name Lanyon Mitchell.

Checking through their files, police discovered that Lanyon Mitchell had been hired under a federal government work program and had worked in the Cook County sheriff's office. Mitchell was brought in for questioning. Meanwhile, other investigators interrogated Patty Columbo. After some hours, according to an Elk Grove police official, the raven-haired beauty admitted that, yes, she had planned to have her father killed, but had abandoned the idea. "I wanted to beat my father to the punch," she blurted out, adding that Frank Columbo had hated her boyfriend, DeLuca, and had ordered a syndicate "hit" on the thirty-nine-year-old pharmacist. "Father had a contract on Frank." Moreover, Columbo had attacked DeLuca in the parking lot in front of the Elk Grove Village drugstore when the pharmacist had left work, slamming the butt of a rifle into DeLuca's mouth and knocking out two teeth. Then there was the $250,000 life insurance policy held by Columbo, his savings, his stocks, a considerable estate Patty feared she might not be left because of her common-law marriage to DeLuca. Hatred, revenge, money, these were the motives that spurred Patty Columbo to have her family murdered, police concluded.

But she denied going through with her plans. She had changed her mind and had cancelled the "hit" on her father. "Dad's attitude had changed. I was going to call it off." She insisted that her boyfriend did not know of her lethal plans. "I never told him about the contract." To police, Patty's statements were almost cryptic. On May 17, 1976, while being kept without bond in the women's center of Cook County Jail, she told Detective Gene Gargano that she had a "vision" of the slayings. "I felt that I was there. I'm confused. I see someone there with me. I believe I was there and did it." All this Gargano was later to insist Patty had said, along with showing him many color snapshots of herself, Frank DeLuca, and Patty's dog, Duke. The photos showed Patty and Frank in the nude, the dog paying tribute to the naked Patty. Some of these photos were reportedly sent to a wife-swapping magazine. Police also obtained many pornographic films featuring DeLuca. "I guess our senses of morality are different," Patty said through a smile to Gargano.

Her sense of morality, or rather her sensibility to human life, proved indeed to be quite different from society's, as her sensational trial revealed. Both Patty and DeLuca were staunchly denying any guilt when their six-week trial commenced in 1977 before Judge R. Eugene Picham. But by then a waterfall of testimony had cascaded against them. Lanyon Mitchell, one of the two would-be hit men hired by Patty, was the first to condemn her. During her lengthy trial, the long-legged Patty made a habit of wearing tight skirts, boots, and clinging blouses to court. Most reporters in the court spent more time ogling the twenty-year-old sexpot and marveling at her "almond face," and "Farrah-like curls," than listening to the testimony, describing Patty as "a Barbie-doll-faced brunette," and "a suburban sylph."

The twenty-five-year-old Mitchell took the stand to declare that Patty had asked him to kill her parents a week after he had met her in October 1975. As Patty stared icily at Mitchell in the courtroom, he stated calmly, "Her parents were bugging her and giving her and Frank a hard time, and she wished that they could be killed, dead and gone." Mitchell told the jury that, in return for sexual favors, he and thirty-five-year-old Roman Sobcynski, a recruiter for the county personnel department, and a former Cook County deputy sheriff, promised to kill her parents. Michell hastily added that he and Sob-

cynski only pretended to be hit men with syndicate ties to "impress" Patty.

Mitchell spared the jury nothing in his raw statements. He described how Patty met Sobcynski at a party he gave. "I told her I was with Roman and he was heavy [with mob connections]. I told her that if she took care of Roman, there would be favors for her [such as the killing of her parents]." He described how Patty got excited and agreed enthusiastically, quoting Patty as saying she would "fuck his eyes out." All of it was pretense on their part, the witness insisted, a device by which they induced Patty to participate in sex orgies with them. The three of them met countless times. and after each acrobatic bout with the leggy brunette, Patty pressed the men to move in on her family. In November 1975, Patty met with Mitchell, giving him a floor plan of her family's home in Elk Grove Village, along with details of her family's schedules and habits. Some weeks later, according to Mitchell, Patty gave him color photographs of her father, mother, and brother, so he and Sobcynski could identify their victims when they entered the house. "She told us we had to do it before Christmas and it would be a Christmas present for her." Patty had thought to spare her thirteen-year-old brother, but later changed her mind, according to Mitchell. When Michael Columbo grew up, "he might put two and two together and figure out Frank and Pat did it."

Yet the men delayed, which had been their intention all along. They told Patty that a payment of $10,000 a head on each family member she wanted killed would have to be paid, knowing she could not pay such sums. She paid sexually at first and, according to Mitchell, agreed that "there would be money after they're dead," a sum of $50,000, which she would give the killers from her inheritance.

As the early months of 1976 went by, Patty Columbo showed her irritation with Mitchell and Sobcynski. She sneered at Mitchell, he said, calling him "chicken," and carping, "I've been putting out sexwise for you two and you haven't done anything for me yet!" Some days later when meeting Mitchell, Patty suddenly pulled out a derringer and aimed it at him, saying, "See how easy it is to kill someone? All you have to do is pull the trigger!"

Mitchell had had enough of the charade. He remembered going to Sobcynski and telling him, "She's crazy. I want out." (Sobcynski would later testify and support Mitchell's statements.)

Although claims were made that Frank DeLuca knew nothing of Patty's sex parties with Mitchell and Sobcynski and her "arrangement" with them to kill her family, Detective Gargano took the stand to report how he had interviewed DeLuca on many occasions while the defendant was in jail. DeLuca had told him how Columbo had ordered a hit on him, cancelled it, then ordered another hit. The swarthy pharmacist knew all about the for-hire killers, saying they had deserted him and Patty and that he knew that "these guys are just jagging us around . . . we'll just have to do the job ourse—"

"Do you mean 'ourselves'?" Gargano asked him at the time.

"You said that, I didn't," DeLuca had hastily answered.

A moment later DeLuca had quizzed the policeman: "Hypothetically speaking, if this guy and this girl did commit these murders, what would be the penalty?"

Judging from his past actions, Frank DeLuca's question was in keeping with an unpredictable personality. Married and with five children, the pharmacist had hired Patty when she was eighteen. While working in his drugstore, she moved into his home, where he carried on an affair with her, finally leaving with her, deserting his family and moving into an apartment with Patty in Lombard. He had been with her ever since, and, as all the evidence later pointed out, he gave up on the phony hit men and invaded the Columbo home, killing the entire family, as Patty stood by encouraging him.

Although on the witness stand he steadfastly denied being at the murder site, more witnesses were ready to place him in the home where he made of himself "a bloody mess." While he was awaiting trial in Cook County Jail, DeLuca promised his cellmate, Clifford X. Childs, $10,000 to murder two other witnesses against him. This claim seemed to be supported when DeLuca's former wife, Marilyn, posted a $4,250 bond for Childs' release. Childs insisted that he had no intention of murdering anyone, that he promised to murder the witnesses only "as a

way out of the Cook County Jail." Childs added that DeLuca considered himself a master criminal and had boasted in his cell that he had committed "the perfect murder. Frank told me he shot the whole family."

Two people on DeLuca's hit list provided the prosecution with the final damning testimony in the Columbo case. Mrs. Joy Heysek and Bert Green, both employees in DeLuca's drugstore, informed the jury that the pharmacist had not only told them that he had killed the Columbo family a day after the murders but described how he had done it, all the while threatening both with extermination if they ever talked.

"I took them all down last night," Mrs. Heysek quoted DeLuca as telling her only twelve hours after the murders. "He said old man Columbo had really given him a rough time." DeLuca had also told her that the two hit men had deserted him and Patty, so he decided to perform the deed himself. He took special revenge on Frank Columbo, sending a bullet through the back of his head so that Columbo's teeth would be knocked out, just as Columbo had knocked out DeLuca's. "And he said that his [Columbo's] teeth are the same as his own." After telling Mrs. Heysek these horrors, DeLuca threatened her, saying that if she went to the police "he would have my son run over on his bike, my daughter raped, and have me beat up so badly that no one would ever recognize me."

Bert Green, the assistant manager of the drugstore, was next. He remembered going into the basement of the store on the morning of May 5, and finding DeLuca burning his clothes in the incinerator. Green asked what DeLuca was doing and his boss calmly replied that he was burning the clothes that he had worn the night before. "He said that the Columbo house was a mess. He said he was a mess and said that he was covered from head to toe with blood." DeLuca described to Green in graphic detail how he had blown out Columbo's teeth. "He said he then went up and shot the old lady. He said Michael was easy. He said, 'All I had to do was stand him up and shoot him.' "

On July 1, 1977, the jury retired for only two hours, returning a verdict of guilty on three counts of murder for both Patty Columbo and her lover Frank DeLuca. Hearing the verdict, Patty merely dropped her head and said nothing. Both Patty and DeLuca were sentenced to two hundred to three hundred years in prison. Neither admitted their guilt at the time, and both claim innocence to this day.

Patty Columbo made headlines again in September 1979 when she was accused of organizing sex parties in the women's prison at Dwight, Illinois, procuring attractive inmates for two prison officials. As inmate No. C77200, Patty Columbo denied further accusations that, in return for sexual favors, she had been allowed such privileges as dining with prison officials. Two of these officials were later suspended. Patty's prison life goes on.

In September 1980, the tall brunette, her hair grown to waist length, told a reporter that she had no idea who killed her family and her conviction was all a mistake. She did admit to one indiscretion. "I did something once that I'd change if I could. I left home when I found out my mother had cancer." Then, remembering her father with warmth, she smiled. "I had a great life. I had never been to a wake or a funeral. I never had anything happen to me. My father protected me from any hurt. . . . My life was a bed of roses, but Daddy didn't tell me about the thorns."

But Patty Columbo does not dwell on the past. She's looking to the future, working on a two-year associate of arts degree. "I want to be a journalist," she said sweetly to an interviewer. "I want to show all of you how to do it right."

COO, EVA

Madam, Murderer ■ (? −1935)

Canadian born, Eva Coo moved to the United States some time in the early 1920s, an attractive and calculating woman whose eyes were riveted on money. After spending several years as a prostitute in cities along the East Coast, Eva opened a roadhouse and bordello outside Cooperstown, New York, which she ran successfully through the Prohibition years, becoming the most notorious madam in the district.

When repeal of Prohibition went into effect, Eva Coo's business dropped off. Within a year she was in desperate need of funds and thought to enrich herself by collecting the life insurance of an alcoholic handyman, Harry Wright, who sometimes worked for her. Getting Wright drunk on the night of June 15, 1934, Eva led him outside her remote roadhouse where she hit him over the head with a heavy mallet. As the man

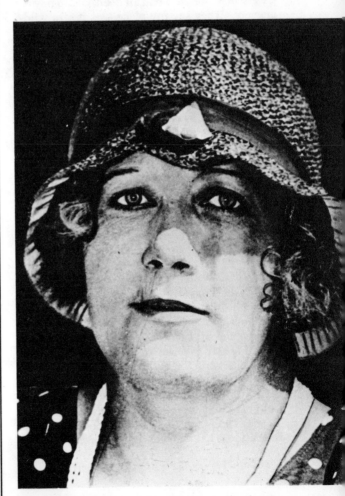

Murder for profit sent madam Eva Coo to the electric chair in 1935.

lay unconscious in the road, Eva ordered her best friend, Martha Clift, to run over Wright in her car. The body was later found by state police only 100 yards from Eva's establishment.

She was arrested, along with Martha Clift, after Eva put in a claim for Wright's insurance. Martha Clift immediately implicated Eva and later, as a state's witness and to save her own life, testified against her friend.

Eva Coo was found guilty and condemned. Martha Clift received a light prison sentence. Eva awaited execution in Sing Sing, hoping for a reprieve and giving countless interviews to news-hungry reporters: She complained that her jewels, furs, and cars had all been sold to pay her lawyers. "They say my place was pretty wild," Eva smirked. "I didn't do anything to make it that way. It was the men of the country who did it. I took care of Harry Wright for four years after his mother died. They say I killed him. It's a damn vicious lie. I wish to God the men I know would help me now."

But there was no help. Eva—though she weighed 170 pounds, she was referred to by the press as "Little Eva," after the hapless heroine of *Uncle Tom's Cabin*—went to her death in Sing Sing's electric chair on June 28, 1935, waving to prison matrons and giving them a cheery "Goodbye, darlings!"

Warden Lewis E. Lawes of Sing Sing held a press conference after the execution, telling reporters, "I don't know if she was innocent or guilty. But I do know that she got a rotten deal all around. Rotten. She told me that after her arrest she signed a power of attorney for a lawyer so that he could collect three thousand dollars a man owed her. She gave them everything to defend her. I suppose I ought not to say anything. My job was to kill that woman, not defend her. And I'm not defending her—she may be guilty as well, but she got a raw deal. Her trial attorneys—do you know what they did to help her lately? Know what? One of them wrote to me, saying he'd like four invitations to her execution. That's the kind of defense she had."

COONEY, CECELIA

Bandit ■ (1904– ?)

She burst upon the New York crime scene like a time bomb going off. From January 5 to April 1, 1924, the "Bobbed-Haired Bandit" struck terror through Brooklyn. Hundreds of befuddled policemen searched in vain for her. At first glance, the exploits of this lady bandit had all the elements of the movie or short-story plot, especially for the hectic Jazz Age: a flapper and her bandit lover, money, excitement, and the mystery of the crimes they committed in whirlwind moves. But at the end of the mean street chase was actually an ignorant girl whose entire life was a tragedy. Cecelia Cooney, commonly called Celia, was the epitome of the female criminal carved from her environment, one who struck back in one fierce sweep of petty vengeance at the society that had forsaken her.

Celia Roth, born in a Manhattan basement in 1904, was one of eight children. Her parents, Michael and Annie Roth, were miserable creatures and wayward parents who let their children fend for themselves when still far too young. Celia, along with the other children, spent most of her time in and out of orphanages and foster homes, taken back periodically into the hovel of a home her parents barely maintained. At these times Celia slept in a coal bin. Her breakfast consisted of scraps from garbage cans which she and her sisters and brothers scouted down nearby alleys.

At age twelve, Celia was taken in by an aunt who put the undernourished child on a proper diet and sent her to school. The aunt bought Celia a white lawn dress and new stockings and shoes and had the girl photographed, a lean, dark-eyed little girl with a large white ribbon in her hair. When her parents spotted the photograph they demanded Celia be returned to them. They were the natural parents. Celia was their child. A day after the girl returned to the basement apartment, her mother sold the lawn dress, stockings, and shoes, replacing them with rags. After another two years of misery, Celia went to live with an older sister in Brooklyn, leaving school and working in a brush factory. Her income was less than three dollars a week. At fifteen, the girl was bringing home sailors at night, and her sister asked her to leave. Again living with her mother in a furnished room in Manhattan, she went to work in the laundry of the New York Hospital in 1919 and remained a laundry worker, slaving over steaming tubs of dirty linen for twelve hours a day.

In early 1923, Celia moved into a furnished room on Franklin Avenue in Brooklyn, living as the common-law wife of a man named Cherison. Some months later she met and married an unemployed garage mechanic, Edward Cooney. She was twenty, he twenty-five. They took a furnished room for eight dollars a week. Though Celia was pregnant, she continued to work in the Foster Laundry, her meager salary the only means of support for the pair; Ed Cooney spent most of his days looking for a job. Their situation worsened by the week, a hopeless future, they felt, for their unborn child.

At the beginning of January, Celia and Ed Cooney thought of committing suicide together but dismissed the idea as unfair to the child Celia was carrying. One or both of them suddenly got the idea to use the suicide gun Ed had purchased to "rob stores, take from the people who have taken from us." They launched their career as bandits on January 5, 1924, running into the Roulston Store on Seventh Avenue in Brooklyn. Celia stood by the door wearing a pink turban and a sealskin coat, holding the pistol on several customers and the proprietor. "Stay where you are," Celia told those standing before her, "and you won't get hurt." Ed ran behind the counter and scooped up $688. They fled, running out of the store and down the block. They could not afford a getaway car for their initial robbery.

The Cooneys returned to their cheap room to count their take, amazed at their good fortune. Ed bought a new pair of shoes and another pistol. Celia purchased a new dress and, in the tradition of the flapper, had her dark hair bobbed. The couple, frugal in their new career, put away half their stolen money as a nest egg for their unborn child. Seven days later at 9:40 A.M. they went through the same routine, Ed taking $113 from the cash register of a Brooklyn

A&P store run by Richard Ohlandt, while Celia calmly held two pistols on those in the store. They then strolled outside and casually walked a few blocks to the Bohack Store on Brooklyn Avenue, arriving there twenty minutes later and robbing the till of $250. On January 15, the Cooneys looted the till of a drugstore, holding up clerk Louis Hecht for $60. Five days later they struck another drugstore on New York Avenue, taking $160 from Benjamin Josprey.

By now the Cooney crime wave had police scurrying throughout Brooklyn. Celia was described as the "Bobbed-Haired Bandit," by a press that romanticized her hit-and-run tactics. Husband Ed was merely described as "her tall, dark companion." The newspaper stories got more colorful as the robbery spree continued, reporters profiling the unknown female bandit as a professional criminal.

Celia Cooney read these stories as she and Ed feloniously built up her child's savings account; she began to act the part on January 22 when she entered alone the grocery store on Albany Avenue run by Abraham Fishbein. Wearing a sealskin coat and a black fur hat, the slim, dark Celia walked to the counter and asked for a bar of soap. Fishbein got it for her.

"What's in there?" she said, pointing to a barrel.

"Herring."

"Open it up, let me see if they look good."

Fishbein stooped to remove the barrel lid. When he stood up he was greeted by an automatic pointed at his nose. The girl holding it smiled sweetly. "Stick up your hands and keep quiet," Celia told Fishbein, then added in true crime-detective dialogue, "or I'll fill you full of lead." The grocer's quavering hands shot above his head. "That's a nice little boy," said Celia. "Now get into the back room." After marching Fishbein into a storage room, Celia went through his pockets, taking $600 in checks and $35 in cash. Through the open door the grocer saw Ed Cooney come into the store, walk behind the counter, and rifle the cash register, snatching $85. Suddenly, Anne Phillips, a customer, entered the store. Cooney whirled about, pointing a revolver at her. "Shut up and get in the back room or I'll kill you," he ordered. Mrs. Phillips did as she was told.

"You'll be all right," Celia told the grocer and his terrified customer. "Just stay back and keep quiet." She waved her automatic at them. "And don't cry for the coppers too soon." She closed the door to the storage room and fled with her husband.

Again the female bandit was described as the Bobbed-Haired Bandit, and again police doubled their efforts to track down the girl, but she was only another girl in thousands. Since she and her accomplice never seemed to use a car, escaping on foot into the backstreets of Brooklyn, tracing an auto was out of the question.

Again the couple struck, on February 2, robbing a Bohack chain store of $150. The take was diminishing as their reputation spread. The chain stores began to employ armed guards, so the couple preyed upon Mom-and-Pop stores, small establishments owned by people like themselves. They took $60 from a grocer on Third Avenue on February 22 and on March 25 held up druggist Samuel Weiss for $35.

The Bobbed-Haired Bandit became an obsession for Captain Daniel Carey of the Brooklyn Police who was assigned to head up the "bobbed" squad. Carey thought the woman was a skirted Dr. Jekyll and Mr. Hyde. "She consorts with bandits at night," Carey told reporters, "and probably lives respectably during the daytime." The frustrated captain went on to add that police had been arresting bobbed-haired girls for weeks, but none of them were recognized by the victims. The victims themselves were confused about the girl, some claiming she was tall, others that she was short. The only thing all the victims agreed upon was that "she has a wicked way of saying, 'Hands up!'"

More than five hundred Brooklyn detectives and police officers were assigned to hunt down the Bobbed-Haired Bandit. Carey ordered them to shoot to kill. But the grim reality was that several bobbed-haired bandits had now taken to robbing stores, particularly the lucrative chain stores. They would all be Celia Cooney in the end, even though the obviously professional doubles stole thousands of dollars in robberies involving whole gangs of men, robberies for which Celia and Ed were blamed.

Not only the professionals, but an army of local youths also cashed in on the Bobbed-Haired Bandit's fame, using her as a guise to mask their own robberies. Two Brooklyn teenagers, Clarence Wilson and Fred Martini, dressed up in knee-length skirts and wigs of bobbed hair and attempted to rob a store, but detectives caught them in a street chase; the boys had found it impossible to escape wearing high heels.

"Who is the Bobbed-Haired Bandit?" asked *The New York Times* in late February 1924. "Who are her people? Nobody knows who she is. She may be a he. She may be two or three or any number of hardy young adventuresses. But one thing is certain: After only a few weeks of rapid and efficient pillaging she is already a tradition, the symbol of a reckless age." The *Times* went on to liken Celia to Moll Cutpurse and Jenny Diver, but admitted that she had developed a style of her own, concluding that "her effrontery is amazing."

Celia was herself offended when reading about one innocent girl who was arrested merely for having bobbed hair. She wrote to the police, "You dirty fish-peddling bums! Leave this innocent girl alone and get the right one which is nobody else but us! . . . We defy you to catch us!"

Everywhere Celia Cooney went now she feared police. Though she and Ed were still unknown, their descriptions were printed almost daily in the New York papers. And the very people they had been robbing, the little business people, had begun to arm themselves, preparing to fight back. Later Celia was to remember how, "along toward the first of April, Brooklyn began to get too hot to hold us. Nobody was talking about anything but the Bobbed-Haired Bandit. I went into our own butcher shop one night to get Ed a steak, and there, lying beside the cash register, was a blue-steel forty-five, big enough to have blown the head off a horse." Then some victim noticed that Celia was pregnant, and the newspapers printed that report. The "gun-girl" was almost afraid to go out into the street. "Every cop had orders to shoot us on sight. They weren't looking for us to arrest us. They were looking for us to kill us, like they do out West."

Ed Cooney was just as worried and nervous

as his pregnant wife. One night he told Celia, "We're in dutch, so dutch that we can't stay here even if we quit. It's too late to quit. And we've played a piker's game. What have we got? Pretty good that first night, but since—a hundred dollars, fifty dollars, sometimes not as much as twenty-five. And some people got thousands. We got to beat it and we got to have money. I been thinking hard. We got to pull one more big one, careful and different, and then blow."

The big job was the robbery of the National Biscuit Company at 1000 Pacific Street, Brooklyn. The office of this firm, Ed Cooney had heard, always contained large amounts of money from daily receipts. Using some of their hoarded loot, the couple arrived at the Times Square Hotel in Manhattan, registering as Mr. and Mrs. Parker from Boston. That afternoon they hired a limousine from the F. J. Wilmarth Motor Renting Service and had driver Arthur West take them on a sightseeing tour. The limousine, thought the Cooneys, would not be traceable by the police. After the robbery, they would go to Jacksonville, Florida; Ed had worked there as a mechanic just after getting out of the navy; it was a good, quiet town where they could have their baby in peace and enjoy the sunshine.

That day, during their seemingly aimless sightseeing tour through Brooklyn, was the best day Celia Cooney ever remembered living. "It was fine going through Brooklyn that way—me now riding in a limousine where I used to work in a laundry. And I felt safe. No cop was going to look for me sitting back in the cushions of a big Packard with a chauffeur, and besides I had the veil on my face."

The next day, April 1, 1924, the hired car arrived at the Times Square Hotel early in the morning to pick up Mr. and Mrs. Parker. Ed told West to drive into Brooklyn. While going through a park, Celia told West to pull over. Ed got out, as if to stretch his legs. He went swiftly to the driver's side of the limousine and thrust a pistol in West's face, ordering him into the spacious backseat and to lie down on the floor. Celia tied West's hands with picture wire and stuffed a handkerchief into his mouth. Ed then drove to the offices of the National Biscuit Company.

Celia stared down at the helpless West curled up at her feet and took an odd delight in the chauffeur's hapless plight. "I had to move my feet so he could turn, and I got to looking down at my own feet. I had on new high-heeled pumps and pretty stockings, and they looked so little with him all hunched there, that I thought how funny it would be if I put one of them on his neck, like Cleopatra I once saw in the movies. And the more I thought of it, the more I couldn't help doing it, so I put one foot easy and rested it right on his neck, and then I pressed the heel down a little, but not enough to hurt him.

"And that's the way I rode through the park, piled back in a limousine, with my foot on a man's neck. We passed two or three cars, and I thought wouldn't it be a joke if they knew."

Cooney pulled the big Packard in front of the biscuit company offices at exactly 9:50 A.M. Celia and Ed got out of the limousine, Ed telling West, "If you move or make a noise I'll come back and kill you."

A minute later Celia was inside the offices. William Christie, an order clerk, approached her. Said Celia, "I'd like to see the manager."

Seconds later, before the manager, Joseph A. Enslow, could respond from a nearby desk, Cooney burst into the office, a gun in each hand.

"You came too soon," Celia scolded in a hushed voice.

Ed ignored her remark and shouted to several persons in the office, "Hands up, everybody, and make it snappy."

Celia drew an automatic pistol from her coat pocket, and held it on the office workers. "Now line up, all you people." She spotted two elderly females shaking with terror and whispered to Ed, "Be gentle with the ladies."

The employees lined up in front of the cashier's cage, hands stretched in the air. "Not there," Ed said, waving his pistols, "get back in the corner."

Ed handed one of his guns to Celia and the girl trained two guns on the office workers cowering in ths corner. Ed went into the cashier's cage and began to ransack the place, wildly throwing about business papers, documents, reports. "There isn't a dime!" he said through teeth gritted in frustration. The open safe yielded nothing, not a single bill. Had Cooney looked a bit closer he would have spotted a bag just beneath the safe which contained $5,900, receipts that had just minutes before been prepared for a bank delivery.

Celia began to get nervous. "We better go, honey," she called out to him.

"I don't understand it!" Ed shouted, still ripping apart drawers.

Just at that moment, Nathan Mazo, the twenty-two-year-old assistant cashier, realized that Celia's attention was distracted. "I saw a chance and tried to grab her wrist," Mazo later said. He struggled with Celia, pushing her backward and sailing forward on top of her as she fell over a chair and onto the floor. But she held on to the gun, wrenching her hand from Mazo's grasp and firing at the scurrying cashier as she stood up. Her shot went wild. Losing her temper, Celia lashed out at Mazo and Enslow, pistol-whipping both men into a back room where the rest of the employees were already huddled. She closed the door and locked it.

By then Cooney had rushed from the cashier's cage and had learned of Mazo's attempt to disarm his wife. "Why that bastard!" Cooney uncontrollably sent two bullets through the door. Mazo, directly on the other side, was wounded in the left hip and the stomach. (He would survive.)

"It's a mess," Celia said and with that she and Ed dashed for the entrance, fleeing to the limousine. While West still lay helpless on the floor of the backseat, Ed drove slowly to Atlantic Avenue where the couple abandoned the car. The badly frightened chauffeur was found a few hours later. Once rescued, the man spat out his gag and shouted to a startled policeman, "Why would anyone want to kidnap me? I got nothing!"

The Cooneys could only run. They took several taxis to Pier 36 and the Clyde Line Boat, boarding a small vessel that was sailing for Florida. Both wept in their cabin, jumping at the slightest noise on deck.

"Maybe we killed that fellow," Celia volunteered.

"If we did, it's the electric chair for both of us."

"Murder." The Bobbed-Haired Bandit drew

the word out with a frightened voice.

When they arrived in Jacksonville, the couple, with only $50 between them, took a cheap room, "one that was worse than any I'd lived in when I used to work in the laundry," Celia later remembered, "The baby was coming soon, Celia reminded Ed, and they had to eat. He'd find work in a garage, he was sure of it. The following day Ed Cooney started looking for work. "But he never went to any garage," Celia was to remember with a shudder. "He didn't dare."

Cooney bought a New York newspaper. Pictures of him and Celia were on the front page, complete descriptions, backgrounds, everything. He raced back to his wife. How had it happened? How were they identified? As they began to think Celia suddenly remembered a little black address book she had had in her coat pocket during the robbery. She checked the coat and found it missing. "It must have dropped on the floor of the biscuit company when that fellow knocked me backward."

On April 10, Celia gave birth to a baby girl in a small clinic. She took the child back to the furnished room. "It was dirty and I had no proper things for the baby, not even a can of talcum powder. And you could see it was sick all the time and I didn't know what to do for it. I wanted my baby to have a chance and look at the chance it had." Five days later Catherine Cooney was dead. Ed and Celia took the little corpse to a Jacksonville undertaker, begging him for a coffin and telling him that they were expecting money from home and would pay him in a few days. "There was nobody at the funeral but Ed and me." A few hours later the undertaker called police in New York, reporting that he knew where the Bobbed-Haired Bandit and her friend could be found.

On April 21, New York detectives Frank Grey and William Casey burst into the room occupied by the Cooneys. Celia held up a pistol, Ed pointed two weapons in the direction of the officers who faced them with drawn guns. There was no gunfire. The detectives stared in disbelief. The Cooneys were emaciated, their hands trembling with weakness; they were starving.

"It ain't worth it," Casey told them.

"Sure, you're right," said Celia in a thin

voice. The twenty-year-old woman threw her pistol on the bed. Ed tossed his guns next to hers.

On the train back to New York Celia read detective magazines. The couple ate ravenously in the dining car. Detective Grey tried to puzzle out their crime spree and finally asked Celia, "Why did you do it? One day you're working in a laundry, the next day you become a lawless thing. Bobbed-Haired Bandit, hell! You ain't nothing more than a girl. Why did you do it?"

Celia put down her magazine and said solemnly, "We didn't want our baby born in a furnished room."

During the brief time of their trial the Cooneys received enormous publicity, newsmen paying special attention to Celia. The gun-girl grew annoyed at the newshounds, especially photographers standing outside her jail cell, asking her to pose. "Is this what you crumbs want?" she said and did a bit of the Charleston, but before photographs could be taken, Celia insisted that she be paid for posing. "What's in it for me?"

A photographer offered her $25.

"Piker—that's only cigarette money."

The *New York American* finally paid Celia $1,000 for her life story. The noted attorney Samuel Liebowitz defended her and Ed but could do little for them. Both confessed to taking $1,601 in ten armed robberies. Judge George W. Martin, before whom they pleaded guilty, gave them the maximum sentence, ten to twenty years. Celia was to be sent to Auburn Prison, Ed to Sing Sing.

Both thanked the judge, telling the magistrate that he was right in sending them to prison for their crimes. Celia then handed Judge Martin a scrap of paper. "I'd appreciate your honor giving this to the newspapers," she said. On it, in a childish scrawl, the Bobbed-Haired Bandit had written, "To those girls who think they would like to see their names in the paper as mine has been, or think they would like to do what I have done, let me say: Don't try to do it; you don't know what you suffer. While I smile, my heart is breaking in me. Cecelia Cooney."

She and Ed were allowed a brief visit with each other before being sent off to their separate prisons. Through sobs, Conney told his wife, "It'll be a long, long time, a long time before I see you, but we gotta make the best of it."

"Yes, we got to," choked Celia Cooney. "But the time ain't gonna be so long, Ed. We'll soon be together."

The time amounted to six years. The Cooneys were released and reunited in 1931. Ed was no longer a complete man. The mechanic had lost an arm in Sing Sing's machine shop. He was given $12,000 in compensation from the Empire State, and with this money the Cooneys purchased a small farm in upstate New York. Celia had another child, one who was not born in a furnished room and who lived.

The story of the Bobbed-Haired Bandit was typical of the Roaring Twenties, of the sudden eruption of violence in the form of an obscure laundry girl gun-clutching her way toward what she thought to be a better life. Before Celia's criminal saga faded, then disappeared from the headlines that fed off her tarnished exploits, an editorial appeared in the pages of the *New York World*, written by the great journalist Walter Lippmann. Here was a girl, said Lippmann, who "at twenty was married, had borne a child, had committed a series of robberies, and is condemned to spend the rest of her youth in prison. . . . This is what twentieth century civilization in New York achieved in the case of Cecelia Cooney. . . . Fully warned when she was still an infant, society allowed her to drift out of its hands into a life of dirt, neglect, dark basements, begging, stealing, ignorance, poor little tawdry excitements and twisted romance. . . .

"The absent-minded routine of all that is well-meaning and respectable did not deflect by an inch her inexorable progress from the basement where she was born to the jail where she will expiate her crimes and ours.

"For her crimes are on our heads too. No record could be clearer or more eloquent. None could leave less room for doubt that Cecelia Cooney is a product of this city, of its neglect and its carelessness, of its indifferences and its undercurrents of misery. We recommend her story to the pulpits of New York, to the school men of New York, to the lawmakers of New York, to the social workers of New York, to those who are tempted to boast of its wealth, its magnificence and its power."

CORDAY, CHARLOTTE

Assassin ■ (1768–1793)

Charlotte Corday as a young girl in Caen, France.

Much has been written of Charlotte Corday (Marie-Anne Charlotte Corday D'Armans) in which she is likened to Joan of Arc, making of her another great savior of France. In truth, she was a naive young woman of noble birth who committed a stupid, albeit sensational, murder when, on the evening of July 13, 1793, she plunged a carving knife into the chest of Jean-Paul Marat, one of the most powerful leaders of the French Revolution.

The fact that she was exceptionally beautiful cannot be denied. The residents of her home town, Caen, considered her the most attractive female in the province of Calvados along the Normandy coast. Her passport describes her as standing only five feet one inch, but she was undoubtedly taller since the inch measurement in use at the time was much longer than the modern inch. She may have been as tall as five feet six or seven inches. Her hair was a radiant chestnut, her Latin nose was long, her forehead high, her deep-set eyes a piercing gray, and her average mouth pursed above a rounded, cleft chin, on an oval face that would be immortalized by scores of French painters. Charlotte's body was lithe and somewhat voluptuous by virtue of her large breasts, a body likened to great Roman statuary.

Convent educated, Charlotte Corday possessed a fine mind. She was an intellectual, partial to the scribes of Rome, especially Plutarch. Though her noble family was impoverished, she was nevertheless raised in relative comfort. She nourished a deep sense of patriotism and, while still a teenager, thought of herself as another Joan of Arc. At the onset of the French Revolution, Charlotte's family and friends, along with almost everyone else in her native province, joined the Girondist party, a revolutionary middle-class faction which was anti-democratic and desired the wrecking of the central government in Paris. By 1792 the Girondists were considered anti-revolutionary, and its members were hounded and persecuted by the Parisian leaders of the Revolution, chiefly Robespierre, Danton, and the scientific genius turned witch-hunter, Jean-Paul Marat.

Charlotte's hatred for Marat as a bloody oppressor of France, one who fed the guillotine with the lives of innocent people, prompted her actions in early July 1793. With only one change of clothes and without announcing her intentions to her parents, Charlotte left home and walked the two hundred miles to Paris in three days. She had been recently inspired to make this journey by reading the words of a young Girondist named Barboux: "Without another Jeanne d'Arc, without some deliverer sent from heaven, without some unexpected miracle, what is to become of France?"

Arriving in Paris, she took a room at the Hôtel de la Providence on the rue des Vieux-Augustins. She next checked on Marat's movements and learned he was ailing and confined to his house. Early on the morning of July 13, 1793, Charlotte went to a cutler's shop in the Palais Egalité (now the Palais Royal) and purchased a carving knife with a six-inch blade, an ebony handle, and a shagreen sheath. She ordered it honed on a grinding stone to razor sharpness before paying for it.

At about 9:00 A.M. she arrived in a fiacre in front of Marat's home at No. 20 rue des Cordelières and asked to see the powerful revolutionary leader. Inside the bodice of her dress was the knife she had just bought. Catherine Evrard, sister of Simone Evrard, Marat's devoted mistress, answered Charlotte's knock but turned the woman away, telling her that Marat was too sick to see anyone.

Undaunted, Charlotte immediately returned to her hotel room where she wrote Marat the following note:

> I come from Caen. Your love of your country must make you wish to know the plots that are hatching there. I await your reply.
>
> Charlotte de Corday, Hôtel de la Providence

She posted this letter minutes later. Given the chaos then rampant in Paris, it was a wonder that the mails functioned so well; the letter was delivered, as Charlotte was promised, only a few hours later. Again Charlotte returned to her room, this time dressing in her best clothes—a gray underskirt over which she wore a spotted Indian muslin gown. Around her shoulders she placed a delicate rose-colored scarf called a fichu. She combed her long, beautiful hair and then placed a tall hat with a black cockade and green ribbons on her head. Snatching up her best gloves and a fan, she departed again for the home of the hated Marat; she had dressed to kill, donning her finest clothes to murder a man she had never met.

Charlotte arrived at Marat's home at 7:00 P.M. The cook answered the bell and told her to go away. She stood her ground, insisting that she see Marat. Simmone Evrard came to the door and said that her lover was too ill to meet with her. Perhaps she could return in a few days? Charlotte refused to budge. Marat, who was taking his bath, heard the disturbance and called out to his mistress, who informed him that the caller was the woman from Caen who had sent the letter he had received only hours earlier. The revolutionary leader felt that such an ardent supporter of his bloody regime deserved an audience and asked Charlotte inside.

Stepping inside a small bathroom, Charlotte found Marat seated in a slipper bath of copper, a board laid across the tub and on this a stack of papers, pen, and ink. He was busy signing the orders of execution for more traitors to the Revolution and was eager to have any names Charlotte could add to his list. He was an odd sight, this ugly little man, his head wrapped in a bandanna soaked with vinegar to relieve his terrible headaches; but to Charlotte Corday he was undoubtedly the epitome of a cancerous political evil.

Marat motioned her to sit on a nearby stool. He asked her for the names of traitors in Caen, and Charlotte, as she edged the stool closer to the tub, rattled off the names of persons who did not exist. Marat scribbled the names violently, saying, "Excellent. In a few days' time I shall have them all guillotined in Paris!"

With that Charlotte Corday reached into her bodice, withdrew the carving knife and removed the scabbard. Reaching over Marat's bare shoulder, she plunged the knife to the hilt into the startled man's chest, an incredibly lucky thrust in that it pierced the heart squarely. Withdrawing the bloody knife, Charlotte let it drop to Marat's writing board. The victim's last seconds were condensed into a scream for his mistress, Simmone, "Help, dear friend, help!"

Simmone Evrard raced into the bathroom to see the wall splattered with her lover's blood and Chalotte Corday standing stoically near the tub. With a scream Simmone knelt, placing her hands against the gushing wound to staunch the flow of blood, but it was useless. By the time Marat was taken from the tub to his bedroom he was dead.

Charlotte walked into another room and was struck over the head by Laurent Bas, a cretinous servant, who held on to her breasts until

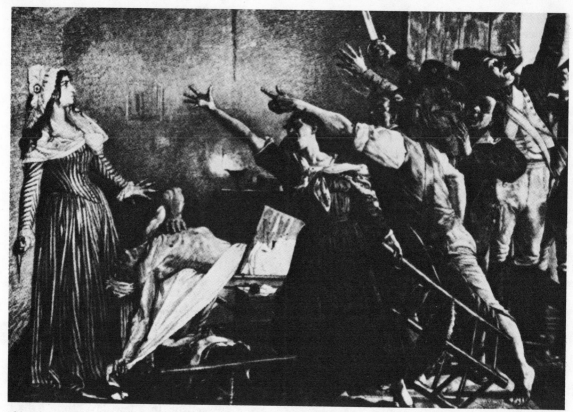

Charlotte Corday, the dying Marat before her, as she is besieged by revolutionaries crying for her blood.

other revolutionaries stormed in from the street to tie the woman to a chair.

The local chief of police, Guellard, arrived with some soldiers. He inspected the blood-splattered bathroom and Marat's corpse, which was being embalmed on the spot in a bedroom. He quizzed the bound Charlotte, who said she had come to Paris only to kill Marat, and that she had no accomplices, a claim no one believed. Men with pikes stood around the woman and lasciviously peered down the torn front of her dress. A defrocked priest, one François Chabot, asked her, "How was it that you were able to strike him to the heart at one blow?"

Charlotte replied with the kind of cool reasoning that was to be the hallmark of her conduct to her last moments, "The anger in my own heart showed me the way to his."

Reporters had filled the room, amazed at this beautiful, intelligent woman and the calm manner she exuded, as a great mob outside the house howled to have her thrown to them. Wrote one journalist, "She has the gentleness of a cat which offers a velvet paw in order to scratch better. She appears no more troubled than if she had just performed some good deed. She went to prison as though she were going to a ball."

Jean-Baptiste Drouet, who had arrested King Louis XVI at Varennes, arrived and led Charlotte into the bedroom to view Marat's corpse and Simmone Evrard still clinging to it, weeping uncontrollably.

"Yes, yes, I killed him," Charlotte said in a small voice. She was led outside to a coach and only with great difficulty did Drouet manage to get the woman unharmed to Abbaye Prison.

Four days later Charlotte Corday was placed on trial before Judge Montane and a jury of fourteen, blood-lusting revolutionaries. She was amazingly clear-headed and resigned to her fate. She spoke defiantly to her tribunal and with a logic that astounded the kangaroo court.

"What did you hope to gain by killing him?" Montane asked Charlotte.

"Peace for my country."

"But do you believe that in killing him you have killed all the Marats?"

"This one dead—the others perhaps will be afraid."

"How could you regard Marat as a monster when he generously gave you an interview after you wrote him that you were persecuted?"

Charlotte stared back at Montane for a moment and then said, "What could his humanity to me matter if he had been a monster for so many other people? . . . It is only in Paris that people have been hypnotized by the man. In the provinces he has always been regarded as a monster. . . . I knew that he was perverting France. I killed one man in order to save a hundred thousand. I was a Republican long before the Revolution, and I have never lacked energy."

"What do you mean by 'energy'?"

"That resolution which is given to people who put their private interests aside and who know how to sacrifice themselves bravely for their country."

Her prosecutor, Antoine-Quentin Fourquier-Tinville, held up the knife with which Charlotte had killed Marat. She admitted that it was the murder weapon. The prosecutor shook his head and remarked how skillfully Charlotte had used the knife, killing her victim in one blow. "You seem to be very well practiced in this sort of crime."

Charlotte expressed shock. "Good heavens! He takes me for an assassin!"

Her lawyer, Claude-François Chauveau-Lagarde, was powerless in defending the woman, although he did plead her insane in a subtle summation that portrayed her as one whose reason was clouded by political fanaticism. (The court had instructed him to plead insanity in order to reduce Charlotte's fast-developing stature as a martyr.)

As expected, she was condemned to die on the guillotine, her execution to take place that evening. In her prison cell, Charlotte cut her

long hair and gave the locks as presents to her keepers. She put on the red chemise that all condemned murderers were compelled to wear and, at a little after 6:00 P.M., was taken to a cart that carried her to the place de la Révolution (now the place de la Concorde). Her executioner, Samson, rode with her in the cart. He later expressed great respect for her courageous attitude. With the cart rattling through the jeering crowds, Samson said to Charlotte, "It seems like a long trip, doesn't it?"

"We're certain to get there eventually," she said through a thin smile.

The cart rumbled into the rue Royale, and the compassionate Samson stood in the cart in such a way as to block the vision of the towering guillotine that awaited her. The young woman brushed his shoulder, asking him politely to move aside. She wanted to see it. "I've never seen one of them before," she said, as if she were coming upon the reconstructed bones of a museum dinosaur. "In my situation I'm naturally curious."

It began to rain. Charlotte stood defiant in the cart, soaked, her hands tied to her back. In the words of one chronicler, "The thin red smock clung wetly to her body, outlining every contour of it like the draperies of a statue."

The crowd was immense but strangely quiet, almost respectful toward the brave young woman mounting the scaffold. They began to cheer her, some even throwing roses on the wooden planks at her feet. In a nearby building the leaders of the Revolution—Robespierre, Danton, and Desmoulins—watched nervously from a window, feeling that this woman was a greater threat to their Revolution than the monarchists had ever been; they were anxious to see her executed and had personally decreed that she be guillotined without delay following her trial that morning.

Charlotte wordlessly assumed the position on the plank, embracing the wood "almost with joy," according to Samson. With one swoop of the descending blade, Samson decapitated her. A half-wit named Legros, who had been hired as an assistant only for the day, thought to please the crowd by seizing Charlotte's head and holding it up. He gave it a savage punch, and the enormous crowd later swore that the face blushed at such an outrage. The crowd hissed and booed Legros with such anger that the assistant hastily replaced the head in the basket. His act had gone unseen by Samson, who cuffed Legros from the scaffold; he was later rebuked by revolutionary leaders and sent to prison for a short while.

Charlotte's body was removed to a hospital where the fanatical, brutal Jacques-Louis David, later famous for his majestic canvases extolling the glory of Napoleon, performed an autopsy on the corpse. David grudgingly reported that Charlotte Corday had been a virgin at the time of her death. Her remains were buried in the Madeleine Cemetery, near those of Louis XVI, removed in 1815 to a new site in the Plaine Monçeau. The arch-assassin remained an enigma to the end and even now many in France consider her a patriot instead of a cold-blooded murderer.

Her final words in prison after she refused to see a priest and make a last confession testified to Charlotte Corday's resolve, "I have hated only one person in my life and I have proved the strength of my hatred."

CORNELYS, MADAME

Madam ■ (? –1779)

One of the most notorious procurers in England, Madame Cornelys ran a salon that attracted the wealthy and the noble. Her Carlisle House in Soho, London, opened with great pomp in 1763, offered gentlemen great balls and masquerades at which Madame Cornelys provided scores of beautiful whores at great prices. An Italian girl from Tyrol, she herself had been the mistress of the great Casanova, giving him a son years earlier.

Madame Cornelys' place was the most talked-about salon in Europe. Horace Walpole wrote that she catered to "both righteous and ungodly" customers. Royalty and members of parliament attended her masquerade balls religiously.

Indignant churchmen, however, pressed the novelist and magistrate Sir John Fielding to close down this glorified house of prostitution. Fielding charged Madame Cornelys with presenting dramatic performances without a license, this, of course, being a pretext to open an investigation into her real activities as a brothel owner. A grand jury indictment later charged that "she does keep and maintain a common disorderly house, and does permit and suffer divers, loose and idle persons, as well as men and women, to be and remain during the whole night, rioting and otherwise misbehaving themselves."

Though she was not imprisoned, Madame Cornelys was ruined. She soon sold off the lavish furnishings of Carlisle House to support herself. She moved to Knightsbridge and opened another bordello but the operation failed, mostly because her notoriety prevented the wealthy from openly patronizing her. Madame Cornelys fell so low that she was sent to debtor's prison in 1772 and died there seven years later.

COTTON, MARY ANN

Murderer ■ (1833–1873)

She was by all standards an inhuman beast without conscience or a sense of morality, and Mary Ann Cotton is today still considered England's worst mass murderer. Born Mary Ann Robson in the mining town of East Rainton in 1833, her father and mother being working-class people, Mary Ann attended chapel each Sunday and grew to love the church so much that by the time her father was killed in a pit accident, she was working regularly in the chapel. She was then fourteen and considered to be the prettiest and gentlest child in the area.

At sixteen Mary became a domestic servant in South Hetton. Here, at twenty, she met and married a young miner named William Mowbray. In five years Mary produced four children but all of them died at an early age. Her husband, desperate to quit coal mining, became a sailor, but he too, died soon after returning from a voyage. His death and those of Mary Ann's children were all diagnosed by doctors as the result of gastric fever.

Using the insurance money from the deaths of members of her family, Mary Ann moved to Seaview Harbor, where she met Joseph Nattrass. She fell in love with Nattrass but, fortunately for him, he was married. Mary Ann moved on, taking a job as a nurse in a Sunderland infirmary. George Wade, one of her patients, fell in love with her and upon his recovery the two were married. Wade fell ill of gastric fever shortly after making out his will in which he left everything to his beautiful twenty-five-year-old wife.

Next on Mary Ann's lengthening list of victims was James Robinson, a foreman in a shipbuilding yard, widower, and father of four. The Robinson children, two boys, two girls, and a child Mary Ann bore her third husband, all died of gastric fever. Robinson himself escaped only because he learned that Mary Ann had been stealing his money and kicked her out of his house.

She held odd jobs after that. Ironically this Lucretia Borgia of North England was briefly a matron in the Sunderland penitentiary, but left this post after meeting a ship's captain for whom she worked as a housekeeper. When the captain left on a voyage, Mary Ann sold off all his household goods and departed. She worked as an office employee for a Dr. Hefferman in Spennymoor for some weeks but was caught taking money from his cash box and fired. On to the mining town of Walbottle in Northumberland went the tireless Mary Ann.

Here she met and married another young widower, Frederick Cotton, who had two young sons. It didn't seem to bother Mary Ann that she was still married to Robinson, but what was bigamy compared with mass murder? The couple moved to Newcastle when Mary Ann gave birth to a boy, her sixth child. The family moved again to Bishop Auckland, where Mary thought it a good idea to take out insurance on the entire family, except herself.

Weeks later Frederick Cotton was whistling his way to work in a mine when suddenly he keeled over, doubled up, and screamed in agony. He was carried home, his body wracked with sharp spasms of pain and incessant diarrhea. Gastric fever claimed his life within hours. Mary Ann collected his insurance. Some time later Joseph Nattrass appeared, explaining that his wife had died. He moved into Mary Ann's large house at her warm invitation. The deaths of the oldest Cotton child and her own baby followed in days. Nattrass, once insured by Mary Ann, also succumbed to the ever present gastric fever; she collected 30 pounds on his life.

Mary Ann had saved the youngest of the Cotton boys for a greater profit than any insurance policy would then bring. She dragged the boy to the workhouse, offering him as a servant, whatever wages he earned to be returned to her. The supervisor of the workhouse, Thomas Riley, informed Mary Ann that he could not take the boy in unless Mary Ann herself accompanied him.

With a sneer, Mary Ann said, "I could have married again but for the child. But there, he won't live long and will go the way of all the Cotton family."

Some days later, on July 12, 1872, Charles Edward Cotton died, the result of that indefatigable gastric fever. Upon hearing of the child's death, Riley went to the police, repeating Mary Ann's prophetic remarks. The police began an investigation. The body of the Cotton boy was exhumed, and arsenic was found riddling his body by a Dr. Kilburn. Mary Ann's other victims, twenty in all, were likewise examined and found to have been poisoned with arsenic.

At her trial for the murder of the last Cotton boy, which began in Durham in March 1873, Mary Ann's lawyer, Campbell Foster, presented an ingenious if not convincing argument for the defense. Foster stated that the Cotton family had all died in the same room which had green floral wallpaper which contained arsenic. When, as was customary, this paper was washed with a soap, also containing arsenic, a poisonous dust was created in the room, and this was inhaled by the victims, causing their deaths.

Sir Charles Russell snorted at that one, the prosecutor pointing out that more than a dozen other victims of Mary Annn Cotton had never been in the "arsenic room." A jury quickly found Mary Ann guilty and she was sentenced to death.

Upon hearing her fate, the forty-year-old woman, who had shown no emotion throughout the trial, cried out, "Oh, no! Oh, no!" She then fainted and had to be carried from the dock by guards to her cell.

She delivered her seventh child, the bastard of an excise officer named Quick-Manning, while awaiting execution in Durham Prison. The baby was taken from Mary Ann five days before she was scheduled to hang. On the morning of March 24, 1873, prison guards entered her cell to fetch her to the gallows. Mary Ann Cotton turned her back to them for some minutes as she carefully brushed her long, lustrous black hair. She admired herself in a small window mirror for a moment, then whirled about, saying, "Now I am ready!"

CRIMMINS, ALICE

Murderer ■ (1941–)

One of the most sensational murder cases in New York City during the 1960s involved the attractive Mrs. Alice Crimmins who stood accused of murdering her two small children on July 14, 1965. A resident of Queens, the twenty-six-year-old Alice had been separated from her husband, Edmund, at the time her son Eddie, age five, and four-and-a-half-year-old Alice were found dead.

Mrs. Crimmins' reputation was described by her own lawyer as "amoral," and she was known to have had numerous affairs, all the while treating her children with indifference if not outright neglect. She was thought to have killed her children in order to be free of the responsibility of caring for them. Edmund Crimmins first reported the children missing to police on the morning of July 14, 1965. Alice, called Missy, was found a short time later in a vacant lot. She had been strangled to death with her pajamas. Eddie was located a week later about a mile from the Crimmins' home; the

Convicted child-killer Alice Crimmins of New York.

cause of death was never determined owing to the advanced stage of decomposition of the boy's corpse.

Alice Crimmins convicted herself of her daughter's murder out of her own mouth. She insisted that she had fed both children manicotti and string beans at 7:30 P.M. the night before, had looked in on the children in their room around midnight, did not fall asleep until about 4:00 A.M., and that the children were taken from their bedroom after that time.

These time periods fixed so firmly by Mrs. Crimmins were absolutely refuted by Milton Helpern, one of the most esteemed pathologists in America, and considered by most authorities, including the author, to be the foremost medical detective in the United States. Helpern performed the autopsy upon Missy Crimmins and found that a meal of manicotti and string beans had indeed been consumed by the child, but that the meal had certainly *not* been served to her at the time specified by Alice Crimmins. The food was barely digested, according to Dr. Helpern's meticulous autopsy, proving that the food was consumed only a short time before the little girl's murder (the body was still warm when found). Dr. Helpern called Mrs. Crimmins' statements "impossible—just impossible. If she said she saw them alive before midnight, how could the stomach of Missy show that she must have died within two hours of taking a meal at 7:30 o'clock. It is patently absurd to think that death might have occurred in the pre-dawn hours after her mother had gone to bed."

Further, when police took Mrs. Crimmins to the site where her small daughter lay dead, the woman seemed to go into a faint, but showed no real emotion and shed not a single tear. Much was later claimed by radical feminist writers that Mrs. Crimmins was railroaded during her two trials, but a careful study of the evidence in this case clearly points to her unquestioned guilt.

Alice Crimmins was eventually convicted of manslaughter and sent to prison on May 16, 1975. She was paroled on September 7, 1977.

CUTPURSE, MOLL

Pickpocket ■ (1589–1662)

The first great professional female criminal, and, in many ways, the most spectacular on record, was the legendary Mary Frith, popularly known to the underworld and the police of her day and to modern historians as Moll Cutpurse. Any psychiatrist worth his analysis would be hard pressed to explain Moll's emergence as a super-crook, for there was nothing in her background to suggest the astounding criminal career her seventy-three years would produce.

Born in London's Aldersgate Street about 1589, Mary Frith was an extremely homely child, whose looks did not improve with age. Her parents, however, who were hard-working, God-serving subjects of the British Crown, the father a shoemaker, the mother a gentlewoman, lavished attention on their only child. The girl was given more than generous affection; Mary's parents scrimped to adorn her in garments far superior to the typical ones of her caste. Special tutors were hired to provide her the best education. Yet, from the time Mary could talk, she inexplicably defied her parents and teachers, heaping abuse upon them. "She was above all breeding and instruction," wrote Edwin Valentine Mitchell. "She was a very tomrig, rump-scuttle, or hoyden."

Refusing to play with girls her own age, Mary the tomboy found pleasure only in the rough games of boys. When her mother insisted

Seehere the Prefideſſe o'th pilfring Trade
Mercuryes ſecond; Venus's onely Mayd
Doublet and breeches in a Uniform dreſſe
The Female Humurriſt a Kickſhaw meſſe
Heres no attraction that your fancy greets
But if her FEATURES pleaſe not read her FEATS..

The infamous Moll Cutpurse, dressed in men's clothing, as usual.

that she devote time to sewing and stitching, Mary angrily wielded her bodkin and needle as one would slash with a sword and dagger. Discipline was unknown to her. From age three on, Mary would randomly bite, scratch, kick, spit, and, an invention of her own, distort her homely features into an appalling face that horrified all who looked upon her, causing family friends to whisper to her parents that their daughter was possessed of the devil. By the time she was twelve, one of her favorite pastimes was to stand at the entrances of pubs, making this monster's face at the men entering and leaving. Her extreme ugliness undoubtedly led the girl to believe no man would ever find interest in her, let alone take her for a bride. Her reaction to this idea was to compete with all the lusty youths in her neighborhood, using her fists and well-built teenage body to best them. "She would fight with boys and courageously beat them," reported Captain Alexander Smith in his *History of the Highwaymen*, "run, jump, leap, or hop with any of the contrary sex, or recreate herself with any other play whatsoever."

Mary's parents died of illness when she was in her early teens, and family members, especially an elderly uncle who was a parson, undertook her upbringing. For a while Mary held her minister uncle in some awe but soon returned to her hellion ways, abandoning the dress of her sex, and purchasing from a second-hand dealer a suit of men's clothing—she was to wear breeches and a man's doublet until her dying day.

Realizing he could not control the wild girl, the uncle decided that Mary would be better off in the new settlements of America, strongly suggesting she emigrate to New England. Hard work in the colonies would cure her of her reckless ways. Mary agreed at first, boarding a merchant ship at Gravesend, its first destination being Virginia. But just as the vessel set sail, she changed her mind, diving overboard and swimming to shore. She later wryly commented: "I escaped the voyage, alike hating Virginia and my virginity."

The girl returned home, and friends found a job for her as a domestic servant, but Mary was discharged within weeks for cursing her employer. Again outfitted in men's apparel, Mary became a fortune-teller. This career was

also brief. So amused was she with her own outrageous lies to customers devoted to the cult, she drove off patrons with her uproarious laughter. Mary began drinking in the pubs and, needing money for her unquenchable thirst, she decided on a career of pickpocketing, a sinister art of which she became a master. In her later years, Mary reflected on this decision to enter a career of crime as a "very fair expedient, whereby I might live, if not honestly yet safely; a mean betwixt the strokes of justice and the torments of poverty."

Mary Frith did not flirt with crime but plunged headlong into the trade of a pickpocket, being introduced to an actual criminal organization known as the Society of Divers (*diver* being criminal argot for "pickpocket"). She was carefully examined, her nefarious mentors scrutinizing her hands. It was noted that Mary had an exceptionally long middle finger, a sign of a born pickpocket in that this finger had to dig out the purse from the pocket of the unsuspecting victim.

After weeks of instruction, and still under the supervision of her teachers, Mary finally took to the streets. As a man of quality passed, a "bulk" would conveniently create a disturbance of some sort so that the man was distracted momentarily, and in that moment, Mary picked his pocket with swift precision. (Today the pickpocket's partner is called a "stall.") Such were Mary's high talents in picking pockets that she soon excelled her peers among the "cutpurses," then the common name for pickpockets in that purses carried in pockets too difficult to penetrate without detection required the pickpocket to simply cut away the entire pocket.

As Mary Frith's wealth from pickpocketing soared so did her reputation among the underworld, which, with dark pride, dubbed her "Moll Cutpurse," a name that would live in legend down through the eras of criminal history. And she was one with her fellow thieves, giving over her total respect for their felonious achievements. To Moll, they made up a "cunning nation of land pirates, trading altogether in other men's bottoms, for no other merchandise than bullion and ready coin."

Moll swaggered in her fame. She purchased with her stolen money the finest men's wardrobe the better shops could provide, and even took to smoking a pipe in the pubs she haunted, breaking, in her typical bawdy fashion, one more taboo for women. This minor vice Moll found most pleasurable, but, at least once, this habit of a lifetime backfired. Sitting in a grocer's shop, trading information with her fellow pickpockets, Moll asked the grocer's son to bring her a pipe to smoke. The youth obeyed with a mock bow, presenting her with a pipe filled with gunpowder, covered at the top with a layer of tobacco. Moll lit the pipe "and suddenly it fired in my mouth with such a blast and stench, belching and throwing out the ashes, that it was a little resemblance of Mount Aetna. I was all aghast but perceiving it was but a boy's roguery, I restrained my passion further than flinging the pipe at his head, but forsook the shop, resolving to blow up both master and man by engines and devices in convenient time." Moll stomped from the shop amid howls of laughter.

Whenever it tickled her fancy, the pipe-smoking, grandly swearing Moll provided voluntary entertainment for the public-at-large. Wearing her customary doublet and breeches, Moll easily qualified as a pioneer of female emancipation in manners and dress when, in 1605, she mounted the stage of London's Fortune Theatre, belting out bawdy songs while strumming a lute, and making lascivious speeches, an act that perhaps gives truth to the claim that she was the first professional actress in England. It was also an act that caused her arrest, according to the records of the *Consistory of London Correction Book*. Moll, also known as Frith, also known as Mary Markham, confessed to wearing men's attire, a minor offense that earned her a rebuke from authorities. (In Elizabethan stage practice the female roles were invariable played by male actors.)

Notoriety from this and other stage appearances, coupled with her underworld activities, brought Moll to the attention of Elizabethan playwrights Thomas Dekker and Thomas Middleton, who portrayed her in their 1607 drama, *The Roaring Girl*. Five years later another dramatist, Nathan Field, made her a despicable character in his *Amends for Ladies*, one whom the heroine, Grace Seldom, lambastes with the words—

Hence lewd impudent
I know not what to term thee, man or woman,
For nature shaming to acknowledge thee
For either, hath produced thee to the world
Without a sex; some say thou art a woman,
Others a man, and many thou art both
Woman and man, but I think rather neither
Of man and horse, as the old centaurs were
feigned.

Even vitriolic criticism, however, left Moll undaunted; she reveled in her career of crime, blithely continuing in its pursuit. Soon, though, she abandoned the risky role of pickpocket. At the time, she had been branded four times on the hands after being caught that number of times with her fingers in the pockets of rich men, a small enough retribution considering the thousands of purses Moll had filched.

Moll turned next to highway robbery, reasoning that the greater the hazards, the greater the spoils would be. For several years she joined one band of highwaymen after another, later forming her own gang. An excellent horse-woman, Moll fearlessly halted coaches after overtaking them, training a brace of pistols on the driver while her cohorts ordered the passengers outside where they were robbed of their purses and jewelry.

One of her victims, however, General Fairfax, proved truculent. When stopped near Hounslow Heath, he resisted handing over his purse and Moll shot him through the arm. Though wounded, Fairfax leaped upon the driver's seat of his coach and attempted to drive off. Moll shot two of his horses to death, then yanked the injured Fairfax from his perch and ripped away his purse, which contained two hundred and fifty jacobuses (a gold coin, struck in the time of James I, worth between ten and twenty-five shillings). Moll fled on horseback, the general and his servants hurling curses after her.

Fairfax walked to Hounslow, where he told his story to a squadron of king's guards who quickly set off in pursuit of Moll. They overtook the brigand near Turnham; Moll's horse had pulled up lame and she stood helpless in the road as the guardsmen surrounded her with drawn swords. She threw down her empty pistols in disgust and was taken to Newgate where she was condemned to death.

"A woman shot me?" the startled Fairfax replied when informed that the ugly highwayman attacking his coach had been none other than the notorious Moll Cutpurse. Though still recovering from his wound, the general broke into laughter, and, in his amused state, visited his assailant in Newgate where Moll awaited the hangman.

"I am informed that you are a person of means," Fairfax said to Moll as she sat in her cell.

"Yes," came her tart reply, "and you are aware of how it was obtained."

"Perhaps we can settle this affair," Fairfax proposed, ". . . for a considerable amount of money, that is."

Moll immediately arranged for a bribe of two thousand pounds to be delivered to Fairfax, whose need for money was political; he was backing Cromwell and his usurping roundheads in their war against King Charles I. Moll was released without comment by the authorities.

The experience frightened Moll badly. She had felt the breath of the hangman on her neck. Resolving never to get that close to the gallows again, she retired with her gold to a Fleet Street residence. There she established the Globe Tavern, which became the hub of criminals of all stripes—footpads, thieves, forgers, thugs, smugglers, highwaymen, pickpockets—who sat at Moll's tables guzzling ale and plotting capers.

These plans, of course, were revealed to Moll and her expert advice was asked. It was then that she thought of a safer way to glean dishonest gold. She hit upon the happy notion of becoming a fence, receiving and selling stolen goods. Her numerous associates responded by bringing her half the loot of London. For this she paid handsome prices but made double the amount she paid by selling the stolen heirlooms of the rich back to their owners, for, by then, she had become known to the authorities as London's master fence. (In the clubs and great halls of England, wealthy businessmen and nobles referred to her as "The Queen of Misrule.")

Not only did Moll encourage hundreds of thieves to make her their exclusive fence, convincing them that her contacts were of the high-

est stratum and her prices the best to be had, but she began to plan dozens of robberies as inventive as any ever conceived by a Dick Turpin or a John Dillinger. Moll provided her thieving partners with lists of the great merchants and tradesmen in England—obtained for a price from high-placed government contacts—and instructed her burglars to steal not goods but the business books of these men. "They are worth far more than a tapestry or gold watch," she cooed, knowing the merchants would pay fortunes to have the records of their transactions returned to them. They did.

Moll's own records were invaluable to her operations. She maintained a constantly updated list of the most popular courtesans in England and the wealthy gentlemen these ladies serviced. In secret rendezvous, the hideous-faced Moll would confront a beautiful harlot of high society, instructing her to carry on compromising correspondence with the married noblemen she visited. Moll would then instruct her house-thieves to steal these letters from the gentlemen's homes. She would next blackmail the men for great amounts of money before returning the letters. Or, often as not, she would keep the letters, especially the ones written by those who could cause her arrest, as insurance for her continued freedom of operations.

Fabulous wealth came to Moll Cutpurse, yet, other than buying more expensive male garments, she spent little on herself. She had long resigned herself to never having a husband. Even the lowest form of male criminal she approached sexually would shrink from her repulsive face and form. Her hatred for her own sexuality deepened and with it a hatred for all females.

Moll's contempt for the fairer sex she displayed in one of her more abhorrent sidelines, that of procuress. Men of great riches visited the Globe Tavern, asking Moll to provide them with young virgins. She took their orders as would a barmaid.

Alone, the powerful Moll would venture into the dark streets of London, find young girls, preferably those who had run away from rural homes and were seeking work in the great city, and try to cajole them into returning with her to her Fleet Street residence. Those who resisted

Another print of Moll Cutpurse, smoking her pipe.

she took by force, gagging and binding them, carrying them on her massive shoulders like so many sacks of potatoes. Once imprisoned in the rooms above the tavern, Moll had the girls service the gentlemen who visited her second-floor whorehouse. Any girl who resisted Moll personally flogged into unconsciousness.

Never having enjoyed the pleasures of sex, this perverted celibate would watch through peepholes in the walls of her many bedrooms while her white slaves were ravished by her brutal customers, gloating over the insufferable debasement of these girls. Such cruelty undoubtedly stemmed from Moll's resentment of her repulsive features and how they denied her the love of men.

Moll's great success convinced her that she was immune to the law. She walked through the better quarters of London in broad daylight, boasting of her criminal authority (though she never informed upon a single one of the innumerable criminals she helped support, which earned her a great trust among her underworld subjects). Swaggering into Drury Lane or St. Giles, Moll, bedecked in the finest breeches and doublet, puffed upon her pipe and bellowed ribald stories to uncomfortable gentlemen. Her presence became intolerable; the authorities finally arrested her, not for her many known offenses of robbery, white slavery, fencing, and blackmail, but, once again, because she had been "indecently and publicly wearing male attire."

Tried and convicted at the Court of the Arches in early February 1612, Moll was sentenced to do public penance. Dressed only in a white sheet, she was to stand in the square before St. Paul's Cathedral during the morning sermon on a Sunday and proclaim her remorse. Moll later remarked: "They might as soon have shamed a black dog as me with any kind of such punishment."

On the morning of her scheduled appearance in the square, Elizabethan historian John Chamberlain was present to record the scene, written in a letter to his patron, Dudley Carleton: "The last Sunday, Moll Cutpurse, a notorious baggage that used to go in man's apparel, and challenged the field of diverse gallants, was brought to [St. Paul's] where she wept bitterly, and seemed very penitent." It was, of course, all an act, for Moll had drunk three sacks before leaving her Fleet Street abode and was maudlin when she appeared before a great throng. Not only was her penance a travesty, she actually benefited monetarily from the affair; she had arranged to have scores of her best pickpockets in the square, and, while she sobbed and carried on, they looted the pockets of those who had come to deride her.

For the next two decades, Moll's supremacy among London criminals went unchallenged. She amassed one of the great fortunes of the epoch and no child in England was unfamiliar with her unsavory history. She became so rich that she did not feel required to sell much of the stolen loot brought to her door, paying for those items she liked and keeping them until, like some latter-day antique-collecting William Randolph Hearst, she had filled several buildings with paintings, statuary, furniture, jewelry, and, especially and ironically, scores of gilt-edged mirrors, items one would think she would avoid. But one mirror after another she hung in her residence until there was no room she could enter without seeing the image of her own misshapen body, her own ugly countenance, which she had somehow grown to admire.

Moreover, the wealthy Moll thought of herself in heroic terms, as a staunch supporter of the king, a brave loyalist to the marrow. In 1638, King Charles, after having put down a rebellion in Scotland, returned in triumph to London. On the day of his return, Moll supplied free wine to all on Fleet Street as a way of honoring her sovereign and displaying her sympathies. Then, half drunk, she stood waiting to greet the king as he marched with his retinue down Fleet Street. "And as the King passed by me," she later wrote with glee, in *The Life and Death of Mary Frith*, "I put out my hand and caught Him by His, and grasped it very hard, saying 'Welcome home, Charles!' His Majesty smiled, and I believe took me for some mad bold Beatrice or other, while the people shouted and made a noise, in part at my confidence and presumption and in part for joy of the king's return. The rest of that day I spent in jollity and carousing, and concluded the night with fireworks and drink."

In the following decades, Moll's purses grew even fatter and so did she, until her body was bloated with easy living. When she walked the streets, her ugly, evil-smelling person repelled one and all, so that passersby crossed the road rather than come near her.

At age seventy-three, Moll, afflicted with dropsy, knew the end was near. She made out her will, though by then there was little to leave. Of the thousands of pounds she had accrued through her sinister practices, only a few hundred pounds remained. Some of this Moll gave to the three maids still in her employ, telling them to use the money to enter honest work as weavers. The rest went to a distant kinsman, a Captain Frith, who commanded a merchant vessel. Along with the money, Moll sent a note to the captain, telling him to take to the sea no more, but to stay home and use the money in getting drunk—that way he would not drown at sea.

The last request of this first of the self-liberated females was as unusual as her entire life had been. For her burial she gave the following instructions: "Let me be lay'n in my grave on my belly, with my breech upwards, as well for a lucky Resurrection at Doomsday as because I am unworthy to look upwards, and that as I have in my life been preposterous, so I may be in my death. I expect not, nor will I purchase, a funeral commendation [a glowing eulogy], but if Mr. H——be squeamish and will not preach, let the sexton mumble two or three dusty clay words and put me in, and there's an end."

When the end came, in 1662, Moll Cutpurse, her diseased body too horrible to look upon, was buried in St. Bride's churchyard, close to the place of her birth. Her request was granted; she was placed in her coffin face downward, as if to hide her ugliness from God on Judgment Day, an ugliness for which she had taken an awful revenge upon society and established herself as a grotesque hallmark in the annals of crime.

An expensive white marble tombstone was placed over the grave of Moll Cutpurse, and on it an epitaph, reportedly written by none other than John Milton, though the stone was destroyed in the Great London Fire of 1666. The epitaph read—

> Here lies under this same marble,
> Dust, for Time's last sieve to garble;
> Dust, to perplex a Sadducee,
> Whether it rise a he or she,
> Or two in one, a single pair,
> Nature's sport and now her care;
> For how she'll clothe it as Last Day
> Unless she sighs it all away;
> Or where she'll place it, none can tell,
> Some middle place 'twixt Heaven and Hell;
> And well 'tis Purgatories found
> Else she must hide her underground.
> These relics do deserve the doom
> That cheat of Mahomet's fine tomb;
> For no communion she had
> Nor sorted with the good or bad;
> That when the world shall be calcined
> And the mixed mass of human kind,
> Shall separate by that melting fire,
> She'll stand alone and none come nigh her.
> Reader, here she lies till then,
> When truly you'll see her again.

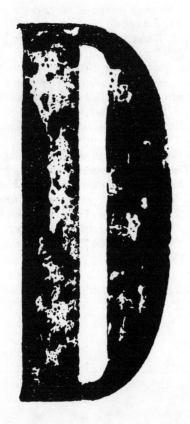

DAGOE, HANNAH

Thief ■ (? –1763)

Born in Ireland, Hannah Dagoe was a hardened petty criminal by the time she had emigrated to London at an early age. Preying upon the poor in Covent Garden, Hannah met an impoverished widow, Eleanor Hussey, and while Mrs. Hussey was absent from her home, the thief broke into the Hussey home and looted it, selling off every piece of furniture and crockery.

Hannah was caught some days later and tried for the theft at the Old Bailey. She was condemned to death, such being the harsh penalties for theft in Old England. Taken to Tyburn on May 4, 1673, to be hanged, Hannah cursed the crowds along the way and spat out oaths against the executioner who was traveling in the same cart.

When arriving at Tyburn and being placed beneath the gallows, Hannah, a powerfully built woman in her mid-thirties, broke free of the ropes binding her and punched the executioner, knocking him down. She then tore off her clothes and threw the garments to the cheering crowds; these would normally have been the executioner's payment, and the woman thus robbed the hangman in the last moments of her life.

"I dare you to hang me!" Hannah screamed as she struggled with the executioner in the cart. She drew up a handkerchief from her neck so that it covered her face just as the hangman got the rope around her. The frenzied woman then shouted that she would not wait for the signal for the cart to be drawn away but voluntarily jumped from the cart, intending to hang herself. Instead she broke her neck in an instant.

Thief Hannah Dagoe battling the executioner at her own hanging near Tyburn, England, in 1673.

DEAN, MARGIE

Bandit ■ (1896–1918)

Short and slight, olive-skined, with dark eyes and jet black hair, Margie Dean was one of the most notorious female American bandits of the days when the auto had just become the new tool of the bank robber. Born Margie Celano in the slums of Paris, she emigrated to New York while still a girl and soon became a shoplifter. She then moved on to Chicago, where she was caught stealing diamonds from a jewelry store and sent to Joliet Prison. Through another inmate, Eva Lewis, Margie was later introduced to the outlaw gang headed by Frank "Jumbo" Lewis.

Members of the Lewis gang included Roy Sherrill, ex-convict and sometime master of ceremonies in nightclubs; Roscoe Lancaster; and a tough named Dale Jones. When freed, Margie and Eva joined up with the bank robbers, striking at scores of banks in the Midwest, then ranging into Colorado. By this time Margie had married Jones and was usually serving as the getaway driver on bank holdups, waiting outside a bank in an idling car and speeding off when gang members ran from the bank and jumped into the car. It was the Lewis-Jones gang that first perfected this technique of bank robbery. The year was 1918.

On September 24, 1918, Jones, Margie, and Lancaster were trapped by Kansas City police in a house at 1904 Mont Gall Avenue. Margie and Jones escaped as police burst through the front door, but Lancaster put up a fierce gun battle, wounding two officers before being gunned down in an upstairs bedroom. As the dying Lancaster sank bullet-ridden to the floor, he croaked out to amazed officers, "Jones is nuts! He wants to get in the movies. I'm going now, but be sure to tell young fellows not to go this way because they all wind up like this!"

The comment regarding the movies led the Pinkertons and police to canvass Los Angeles. The Pinkertons had painstakingly learned that Margie wore only one particular perfume. From the owner of a fashionable perfume shop in Los Angeles, agents were able to locate a "Mrs. Forbes" who lived in a bungalow on Sierra Madre Avenue.

On November 24, 1918, police and agents staked out the address and soon saw Margie Dean and Jones emerge; the couple got into a Marmon touring car and drove off, two police cars loaded with officers following. When the Marmon pulled into a gas station in Arcadia, a suburb of Los Angeles, the police cars streamed in behind.

Spotting the police first, Margie Dean gave out a yell, then reached for a repeating shotgun that worked on a swivel. Jones drew an automatic. They opened up on the police who fired back. Deputy Sheriff George Van Vliet was struck in the face by one of Margie's shotgun blasts and blown out of his car. A dozen officers then riddled the Marmon, killing Jones and Margie Dean with gunfire far more withering than that which was to claim the lives of the outlaw lovers Bonnie Parker and Clyde Barrow more than a decade later.

DE MELKER, DAISY LOUISA

Murderer ■ (? –1932)

A trained nurse in South Africa, Mrs. de Melker poisoned her first husband, William Cowle, in 1923, after fourteen years of marriage, having decided to enhance her life with her husband's insurance money, 1,700 pounds. Four years later Daisy poisoned her second husband, Robert Sproat, but only after she convinced him to change his will, leaving his savings of 4,000 pounds to her instead of his mother.

Marrying for the third time to rugby player Clarence de Melker in January 1931, Daisy moved with her husband to Johannesburg with Rhodes Cowle, Daisy's twenty-year-old son from her first marriage. When Rhodes became obstreperous, demanding his inheritance, Daisy poisoned him with arsenic purchased, ostensibly to kill rats, from a local pharmacy.

When the druggist heard of Rhodes's agonizing death, he went to the police. The youth's body was exhumed and the poison found. The bodies of Cowle and Sproat were also dug up and signs of strychnine poisoning discovered. Mrs. de Melker was tried for the three murders and found guilty. She was hanged in Johannesburg on December 30, 1932.

DESHAYES, CATHERINE ("LA VOISIN")

Murderer ■ (? –1680)

The darkest side imaginable of any female criminal on record was personified and brought into hideous reality by a true-life monster named Catherine Deshayes, a self-styled French witch known as La Voisin. Her exploits in Paris in one decade, the 1670s, caused her to be labeled by her biographer, Frantz Funck-Brentano, a "strange and horrible creature—the last of the great sorceresses."

A murderer of thousands, La Voisin's power was immense, thorough, and almost unassailable, for she literally held the sway of government in her hands, a demoniac person who would not hesitate to arrange for the killing of any human being, no matter how highly placed, including the great "Sun King" of France, Louis XIV.

Little is known of La Voisin's early years. The first record of her existence reports her marriage to one Antoine Monvoisin, who hawked cheap jewelry in the squares of Paris. La Voisin encouraged her husband to open a shop on the Pont-Marie. The enterprise failed, and, to stave off abject poverty, La Voisin, as she later confessed to police lieutenant Nicolas de la Reynie, resorted to the occult. "It was chiromancy and face-reading that I learned at the age of nine."

At first, in the late 1660s, La Voisin's role of seeress proved innocuous, though she was an expert of physiognomy and a remarkable psychologist. Her reports on a person's past and her prophecies, especially in matters of love and sex, soon brought the middle-aged fortune-teller more and more paying customers, until she was able to purchase a handsome cottage at Villeneuve-sur-Gravois, a sparsely inhabited district between the ramparts and the St. Denis quarter of Paris.

As her popularity spread, La Voisin's cottage became the hub of the city's occult festivities. Well-to-do men and women, mostly married people with their lovers, flocked to the cottage, picnicking on La Voisin's garden lawns, then slipping into the house to have their love fortunes told. At first, the crafty fortune-teller divined fate through cards and a crystal ball. She would also consult the coffee grounds of her customer's cup. Most of her patrons felt pleased by her flattering remarks, and thought them no more than amusing fancies. But a few were persistent, demanding specific information, and La Voisin, for the price of her wisdom, presented more and more elaborate ceremonies, such as slaughtering small animals and reading their entrails for signs of the future.

Certain customers demanded results, im-

The only known likeness of France's arch-poisoner, La Voisin (portrait by Antoine Coypel).

mediate and direct. La Voisin was to be quoted in François Ravaisson's *Archives de la Bastille:* "Some women asked if they would not soon become widows, because they wished to marry someone else; almost all asked this and came for no other reason. When those who come to have their hands read ask for anything else, they nevertheless always come to the point in time, and ask to be ridded of someone, and when I gave those who came to me for that purpose my usual answer, that those they wished to be rid of would die when it pleased God, they told me that I was not very clever."

In addition to the useless love-philters La Voisin gave to patrons, she began to prepare certain poisons which would be administered to unwanted husbands and wives. By that time, the entire city of Paris was overrun with palmists, sorceresses, witches of all kinds. "Poison became a fashion," reported *Blackwoods* magazine three centuries later. "A certain elegance was observed in the sudden removal of an impediment to love or wealth, and neither beautiful women nor valiant men disdained so simple an aid to their schemes." Of the fortune-telling witches dispensing poisons to their customers, none approached La Voisin in popularity or success.

The wealthiest and most powerful people in France flocked to her door, and she, for exorbitant prices, handed out potent poisons to one and all. The first person of rank to visit the greedy witch was the Countess de Beaufort de Canillac, wearing a mask so as not to be identified. La Voisin told the countess that she could not tell her fortune from her hands; she was a face-reader. When the countess removed her mask, the fortune-teller thus identified her patron, and if she chose to blackmail the countess following her purchase of poison, she, like legions of others, became her victim. La Voisin, however, seldom resorted to blackmail since she would have to directly implicate herself. Her earnings were staggering for a person of her class, anyway, totaling more than 400,000 francs a year throughout the 1670s, about $50,000 in today's American money.

When friends, early in her career as a witch, reproached La Voisin, telling her that she should not commit poison by proxy, the woman would scream, "You are mad! The times are too bad. How am I to feed my family? I have six persons on my hands!"

The first known murder by poison of La Voisin was that of Judge Leféron. His wife, Madame Marguerite Galart Leféron, a woman of fifty, came to La Voisin, complaining that her husband not only bored her but was "insufficient" in bed, adding that she had a lover in his twenties, a Monsieur de Prade. (The lover saw La Voisin later and told the witch that he needed love potions to appease the ravenous sexual appetite of Madame Leféron, whose only interest for him was her money.) La Voisin provided a phial of strong poison and Judge Leféron died in agony on September 8, 1669. The alchemist, as La Voisin had taken to labeling herself, later told shocked police investigating her past, "It is quite true that Madame Leféron came to see me, most joyous at being a widow, and when I asked her if

The Marquise de Montespan, royal courtesan who sponsored much of La Voisin's murderous witchcraft.

the phial of liquid had taken effect, she said, 'Effect or not, he is done for!'"

The word went out. La Voisin's poisons worked, and fast. Scores of noblemen and royal-blooded women visited the alchemist, usually under the cover of darkness, slinking into the witch's new and sprawling residence on the rue Beauregard. The Duchesse de Bouillon visited her, as did the Duchesse de Lusignan. By that time La Voisin had plunged into every conceivable activity associated with witchcraft, performing for her occult-obsessed clients abortions and murders through poisons. Assisted by the infamous Abbé Guibourg, a sixty-year-old hunchbacked priest who had been defrocked, she performed hideous Black Masses for the likes of the Duchesse de Vivonne who wanted to devote herself and the unborn child in her womb to the devil; the Comtesse de Soissons (Olympe Mancini); the Duchesse de Vitry; women who asked Satan to work dark magic that would make them mistresses of the king, such as Madame de Polignac and the Comtesse de Rouse, both of whom were seeking the death of the current royal favorite, Louise de la Vallière.

The Princesse de Tingry came to La Voisin begging for love philters and charms that would make her more erotic to her many lovers. Madame Baron asked for evil charms that would make impotent a defrocked priest who had shunned her love for others'; Madame de Dreux required an abortion. Also to the witch's door came the Comtesse de Montmorency-Bouteville, Madame de Baucé (to whom La Voisin gave a severed human hand and a toad as charms), Madame de Gand, Madame d'Argenton, Madame de Chapelain.

The men of this corrupt aristocracy were also not lacking in La Voisin's ever-widening circle—the Comte de Longueval, the Marquis de Feuquière, the Chevalier de Varnens, the Duke of Buckingham in disguise, it was reported, and the Duc de Luxembourg, who insisted that La Voisin produce the devil so that he could have an extended conversation with him.

Of all the high and mighty personages La Voisin served, none approached the power and grandeur of her chief client, Françoise-Athénais de Rochechouart de Mortemart, the Marquise de Montespan, the new, ravishingly beautiful and devastatingly paranoid mistress of King Louis XIV. Louis' court was the most sumptuous in all the world, a monument to the splendor and absolute power on earth of kings, and at the heart of the court was the dazzling De Montespan, who, in the words of court biographer Madame de Sévigné, "holds all the cards." The de facto queen, Marie-Thérèse, and La Vallière, the preceding mistress, quietly deferred to De Montespan's love authority; they were then known as "the three queens." According to John B. Wolf,

Mademoiselle de la Vallière, Montespan's court rival and object of La Voisin's black magic.

one of Louis' many biographers, "They rode together in the same carriage; they lived together in the court."

But it was De Montespan who ruled the heart of Louis XIV, France's greatest king, and therefore the court and, in many respects, France itself. And, as we are to see, in her shadow stood La Voisin.

The king, who was to have seven children by De Montespan, openly escorted her everywhere. At thirty, she stunned all who entered her presence; she was "as beautiful as the day," and "a surprising beauty." She was "even more blonde than La Vallière, she had a beautiful mouth, beautiful teeth . . . and a brazen air." De Montespan surrounded herself with the great artists and writers of the day. She was the subject of dozens of famous portraits.

Yet there was an ugly side to this fabulous woman. Whenever that side was showing, she would set off in tirades of invective, directed toward those she thought were seeking her downfall. Even the king, whom she could charm in a second, was a fearful victim to her insane outbursts. That other, younger women at court were scheming to replace her became a raging fixation with the king's mistress. At first, to subdue her anxieties, De Montespan gambled away fortunes at the gaming tables of Paris. Then she began to eat excessively, gaining weight that was deadly to her sexual liaison with Louis. Her maid, Mademoisille Desoeillets, who had heard of the powerful magic wielded by an old crone named La Voisin, was dispatched to obtain some love philters to assure the royal mistress of continued kingly favor.

Apparently, De Montespan believed in these rather vile-tasting potions, for she soon visited La Voisin secretly, telling the alchemist her fears, particularly her apprehension that La Vallière might regain favor with Louis. She was given a deadly poison to settle the problem, and this, many historians insist, De Montespan used to murder La Vallière.

The royal mistress became a devoted follower of La Voisin, paying her enormous sums for her incantations, black-magic rites, and charms. According to many reliable accounts, including that of Paris Police Lieutenant De la Reynie, this untitled queen went so far as to actually participate in Black Masses herself, lending her naked body to the most disgusting rituals, even the ones that included the unconscionable murder of infants.

The defrocked priest, the Abbé Guibourg, assisted by La Voisin, conducted these abominable ceremonies in the witch's sprawling home. Guibourg was the illegitimate son of Henri de Montmorency, a large, big-boned man whose face reflected a sensual, malignant life-style. Writing in *The Geography of Witchcraft*, Montague Summers stated: "It was he who celebrated innu-

merable Satanic masses at the insistence of Madame de Montespan in order to secure her supreme power and eternal fidelity on the part of the King. A long black velvet pall was spread over the altar, and upon this the royal mistress laid herself in a state of perfect nudity. Six black candles were lit, the celebrant robed himself in a chasuble embroidered with esoteric characters wrought in silver, the gold paten and chalice were placed upon the naked belly of the living altar to whose warm flesh the priest pressed his lips each time the missal directed him to kiss the place of sacrifice (De Montespan's privates). All was silent save for the low, monotonous murmur of the blasphemous liturgy. The Host was consecrated, and then the Precious Blood. An assistant crept forward bearing an infant in her arms. The child was held over the altar, a sharp gash across the neck, a stifled cry, and warm drops fell into the chalice and streamed upon the white figure beneath. The corpse was handed to La Voisin, who flung it callously into an oven fashioned for that purpose which glowed white-hot in its fierceness."

Such was La Voisin's warped piety that, on these slaughterous occasions, she would insist that the infant to be sacrificed be baptized first. At her trial, La Voisin admitted that she had murdered more than two thousand five hundred children in Black Mass ceremonies, almost all of whom were purchased from the thousands of starving beggars and prostitutes of Paris eager to sell their children in order to purchase bread.

De Montespan's own regal robes were no more magnificent than the ones La Voisin wore for these chilling ceremonies. The witch's specially woven robe and cloak cost 15,000 livres (about $30,000 in today's American currency) and were "the talk of Paris." According to one chronicler, the "cloak was of crimson velvet studded with 205 two-headed eagles of fine gold, lined with costly fur; the skirt was of bottle-green velvet, edged with French point. Even her shoes were embroidered with golden two-headed eagles."

With the influenial De Montespan behind her, La Voisin flaunted her own power, ignoring all manner of propriety and law. She was constantly drunk and took dozens of lovers, one of whom was André Guillaume, the executioner of

Paris, who would later behead the mass poisoner Marie de Brinvilliers, and just barely escaped having to execute La Voisin. Guillaume, along with many costly gifts, supplied his witch-lover with the severed arms and legs of murderers he executed. From these grisly remains, La Voisin made long black candles which she burned at Black Masses.

A strapping Norman youth named Lesage became one of La Voisin's paramours; it was his duty to punish her in the streets of Paris, striking her abruptly without warning, knocking her to the street, kicking her, all of which were masochistic scenarios written by the witch herself. Another lover, Latour, was instructed to "brutalize" La Voisin's hapless dolt of a husband, who was beaten senseless every morning to edify the super-witch. Monvoisin was repeatedly poisoned by his wife, but La Voisin would suddenly stop the dosages when the man was on the verge of death, and seem to repent, running to church to confess her persecutions of the unsuccessful shopkeeper.

A veritable bevy of human monsters moved into La Voisin's residence—an Italian youth named Romani, one of La Voisin's lovers who specialized in torture; an incredibly ugly alchemist named La Trianon, reportedly a hermaphrodite whose black-magic practices were even more revolting than those of La Voisin, her mentor; scores of old crones assisting the super-witch in her dark chores—the place was a veritable witch's haven, all supported by the leading aristocrats of France.

Such blatant atrocities, however, could not long go undetected. Rumors of the Black Masses and mass murders and poisonings reached the ears of priests in the order of St. Vincent de Paul, a popular religious order actively working against heresy and witchcraft, and devoted to "converting sinners and removing scandals of all kinds." Members of the order began to investigate, interviewing nervous aristocrats who had supported La Voisin. On one occasion a group of priests burst suddenly into La Voisin's residence, finding the large hall used for the Black Masses and the charred bones of countless infants in a huge stove. Of these investigating priests, the fortune-teller later carped to authorities: "I have been persecuted for fourteen years; that is the work of the missionaries."

At first, no case could be established against La Voisin, who never once mentioned any of her elite sponsors, especially De Montespan. The religious authorities stepped back, preferring to observe La Voisin's actions. But their initial probe into her activities set off a hysterical reaction among the occultists and their patrons, particularly the anxious De Montespan, who somehow came to believe that the investigating priests had been urged on by her sovereign, Louis XIV, who was about to discard her for a new lover, Madame de Fontanges.

Summoning La Voisin to her, De Montespan raged for an hour against King Louis before giving the witch a sack full of gold to poison her sovereign. She pressed the witch for details on how she planned to murder the king. La Voisin had a clever plan. It was the ancient custom of the kings of France, the sorceress explained as she counted out her pay—100,000 gold crowns —to receive petitions from the lowliest of his subjects on certain days during the year. One of those occasions was fast approaching. She, La Voisin herself, would approach the king with a petition, the scroll of paper specially treated with poison. Once Louis handled the document, the poison would enter his system, the witch explained, and he would die within hours.

Bribing officials, La Voisin was promised an audience with Louis. On March 5, 1679, she traveled with Romani and another lover, Bertrand, to the king's palace at Saint-Germain. Her accomplice, La Trianon, had attempted to dissuade La Voisin from murdering the king, pointing out the terrible tortures reserved for those who committed regicide. La Trianon had cast her horoscope (a document later uncovered by De la Reynie's police) and foretold how the sorceress would be tried for crimes against the state. "Bah!" scoffed La Voisin. "There's one hundred thousand crowns to be gained!"

The attempt to murder Louis XIV failed. La Voisin was motioned to step forward and place the petition on a table near the king's throne. She refused, later telling associates that "the paper was useless unless it were placed in the king's own hands." She returned to her home on March 9, resolved to go again to the king on March 13, the following Monday, telling her un-

The resplendent King Louis XIV of France, whose magnificent reign was almost destroyed by La Voisin's mass murders and who himself almost perished at the poisoner's hands.

witting husband, "I must accomplish my design or perish in the attempt!"

"What?" replied Monvoisin, ignorant of the plot. "That's a good deal for a piece of paper!"

The day before La Voisin's second attempt on Louis' life, priests of the St. Vincent de Paul order, accompanied by De la Reynie and his police, burst into the sorceress's home, the murder plot having been told to them by an anonymous member of La Voisin's unsavory group. The witch was arrested, her documents seized. All the members of her household were also arrested. Hearing of the arrest, Madame de Montespan fled Paris.

La Voisin was tight-lipped and arrogant with the police, telling De la Reynie of her mass poisonings, murder, and black rites but refusing to implicate any of her aristocratic patrons. This was not the case with La Voisin's terrified daughter, Marguerite Monvoisin, who blurted out a nonstop list of France's mightiest personages as having been involved for more than a decade with her mother's sinister doings. Her statements were supported by Romani, Bertrand, La Trianon, and many others.

Presented with these horrendous statements, the king was stunned. When it was proved that his own mistress had attempted to murder him and Madame de Fontanges, he went into a stupor. Later Louis convened the Chambre Ardente to carefully investigate all charges.

Four hundred and forty-two persons, mostly aristocrats, appeared before the commission. Of those, two hundred and eighteen were imprisoned. Thirty-six persons were condemned to death by fire, beheading, or hanging—none of them from the aristocratic class, though twenty-six persons, some of noble birth, were banished.

Among those banished was the callous Madame Leféron, who was sent to a remote castle. Another was Madame de Dreux, who had poisoned her husband with La Voisin's preparations. This woman had two cousins sitting on the commission and was let off with a reprimand. The haughty killer was released from prison amid hurrahs from her peers. Wrote Madame de Sévigné, "It was a joy and a triumph and she was embraced by all her family and friends."

De Montespan's position was less definite. Her name came up repeatedly in interviews with the commission; Louis ordered the evidence against her suppressed, but reserved the decision of her fate for himself. In a brief interview, De Montespan met with Louis—the king was careful to have guards present—at which time the lovely courtesan gave the performance of her life, and her life, as she knew, depended upon it. She wept, cried, tore at her hair and gown, throwing herself at Louis' feet, begging for mercy, understanding, forgiveness; she had been driven mad, she choked, at the thought of being abandoned by him. Then, peering upward at the benevolent monarch through tear-swollen eyes,

De Montespan ruefully reminded Louis that the seven children she had borne him had been officially recognized by him as children of France, his children, and she, their mother, could not, for the sake of the throne, be humiliated by public accusations and trial, all of which would reflect terribly upon the crown and pose a threat to the monarchy.

Louis let off the shrewd De Montespan, banishing her to a distant château, warning her never to interfere with him again. The royal mistress departed with her life but continued her intrigues until her death.

No such royal clemency awaited the awful sorceress, La Voisin. She was tortured for three days—placed upon the rack, screws driven into her flesh in the torture chair, the Spanish boots applied to her. But throughout this excruciating pain, the superstar of black magic only laughed tauntingly at her keepers. (She did claim that the great poet Racine had poisoned his lover with concoctions he had obtained from her, but Racine, put through some nervous interviews, was never charged, La Voisin's statement thought by authorities to be a churlish smear at a writer whose work she disliked.)

De la Reynie advised the commission that nothing more could be learned from this vilest of women and the Chambre Ardente ordered her tongue cut out and that she be burned alive at the stake. La Voisin, wearing the simple linen shift of condemned prisoners, was taken to a public square in Paris on February 22, 1680, and tied to a stake, all the while spitting oaths at her executioners, the huge crowd assembled before her, and the absent King Louis. Madame de Sévigné was on hand to witness the gruesome spectacle, reporting in a letter to her daughter, the Comtesse de Grignan, that the witch "was bound with iron. All the while cursing, she was covered with straw, which she threw off five or six times, until at last the flames grew fiercer and she disappeared from sight. . . . She surrendered her soul to the devil very prettily."

The priest who had accompanied La Voisin to her death, later reported her last words to be, "I am loaded with so many crimes that I could not wish God to work a miracle to snatch me from the flames, because I cannot suffer too much for the sins I have committed."

Thus ended the life and crimes of the most evil of women of the most brilliant age of France.

DICK, EVELYN

Murderer ■ (1922–   )

Widowed at age twenty-four, Mrs. Evelyn MacLean married John Dick, a bus driver from Hamilton, Canada, but refused to live with him, insisting on staying with her mother. Mrs. Dick also continued to see her lover, Bill Bohozuk. On March 16, 1946, the body of the thirty-nine-year-old Dick was found, head and limbs missing.

The MacLean family, especially Evelyn, came under police investigation. A basket of ashes in the MacLean home yielded human bone fragments; the body of an infant was also found in a trunk in the basement. Evelyn, her mother and father, and Bohozuk were placed on trial for murdering Dick. Evelyn was convicted and condemned to death but won a new trial in which she was acquitted of her husband's murder. She was placed on trial again for the murder of her child, Peter. Evelyn insisted that Bohozuk had strangled the small boy. She was convicted of manslaughter and sent to prison for life.

DIVER, JENNY

Pickpocket ■ (1700–1740)

"What! and my pretty Jenny Diver too! As prim and demure as ever! There is not any Prude, though ever so high bred, hath a more sanctified look with a more mischievous heart. Ah! thou art a dear artful hypocrite." With these words, Macheath in

An artist's rendition of Jenny Diver as she stooped to lift the wallet from a drugged victim some time toward the end of her fabulous pickpocketing career.

The Beggar's Opera immortalized perhaps the greatest pickpocket in criminal history, the Irish-born Jenny Diver, whose dexterous fingers produced her fortune, and, in an uncontrolled state, brought about her grim fate as well.

Before taking the alias of Jenny Diver, this much celebrated criminal was known simply as Mary Jones. Her mother, Harriot Jones, was an attractive lady's maid who foolishly succumbed to a seducing aristocrat. Abandoned by relatives when pregnant, Harriot found refuge with Mother Wisebourne, a notorious madam, and gave birth to a daughter, Mary, in the bordello in about the year 1700. At five, Mary was deserted by her errant mother and stayed in several foster homes. Eventually, she was taken to Northern Ireland, where an elderly woman took the child under her wing.

Mary was sent to school at age ten, receiving what was reported to have been a good education, "instructed in the principles of religion and the knowledge of other things which was required in order to fit her for doing business."

By her early teens, Mary Jones's quick fingers began to earn her praise and money as she proved herself an extraordinary seamstress. There was nothing Mary could not do with a needle, and, as her guardian began to prosper through her efforts, the girl believed she could amass a fortune for her work in London. The passage to England, however, was expensive. Mary went to a young servant of a nobleman who had long been in love with her, telling him that she would marry him if he fled to London with her, paying their boat fare, of course. The youth promptly stole a gold watch and eighty guineas from his employer, and, meeting Mary at dockside, sailed with her for England.

Mary and her bridegroom-to-be arrived in Liverpool, where, under assumed names, they took a small room at an inn. A few days later, just as the two were about to leave for London in a rented cart, a messenger arrived from Ireland, alerting authorities to the theft committed by Mary's escort. The boy was found and arrested. Mary told the officers flatly that she was ignorant of the youth's theft and was released. She sent her duped friend his clothes while he was in jail awaiting return to Ireland, along with some of the money he had given her. Mary then left for London. The youth was taken back to Ireland, convicted and condemned, his sentence later reduced to banishment to America. None of this interested Mary Jones—she was on her way to London to make her fortune.

The notion of making it by means of her needlework, however, was quickly abandoned by the girl when she met Anne Murphy while taking a room in Long Acre. Anne had emigrated from Ireland some years before to establish herself as sort of a den mother to a pack of street thieves. She saw in the pretty young girl a natural actress, and, having heard the tale of Mary's woeful young companion, she also saw a larcenous heart with little or no feeling for her fellow human beings. After also observing Mary's incredible dexterity at needlework, Anne Murphy realized the girl's true criminal calling. She took her to the back room of a pub and introduced her to the most nimble-fingered group of pickpockets in London. Mary happily joined the group as an apprentice pickpocket and was given ten guineas on which to live until she began to pay her own way.

The girl was taken to several public squares in the better districts and there, for two hours a day, practiced filching purses and jewelry from her teachers, who pretended to be innocent passersby. So adept was the girl at taking purses that her criminal mentors were dumbfounded.

They never felt the slightest nudge, let alone saw the girl approach them in the crowds, as she picked their pockets, made especially deep to make her chore all the more difficult, and as they lost not only their purses but their jewelry. Mary was so masterful with her fingers, so quick and efficient, that the group named her the most amazing pickpocket alive. At the time, pickpockets were known in underworld parlance as "divers," and, as a way of showing their appreciation for her dark talents, they dubbed her "Jenny Diver," queen of pickpockets.

As her star rose, Jenny became rich. Her fellow gang members became her servants; her mentor, Anne Murphy, her general housekeeper. Biographer Arthur Vincent was to write of her in 1897 that, because of her ever increasing wealth, Jenny "was enabled to indulge to her heart's content the passion for handsome clothing which distinguished her down to the day of her death. Her education and natural advantages stood her in good stead in playing the *role* of a fine lady, and no feelings of jealousy prevented her companions from supporting her in the guise of servants in any enterprise that promised to result to the common advantage."

Hearing that wealthy Jews would be attending a special meeting in one of London's largest synagogues, Jenny, dressed in her finest gown, appeared in the throng, seeming to struggle toward the building's entrance. Her real objective, selected earlier by Jenny's cohorts as the target, was a wealthy young man who stood in the doorway of the synagogue.

Seeing Jenny as a handsome, fashionably dressed woman abused by the shoving, pushing crowd, the young man graciously reached for her hand with his own, as if to guide her through the entranceway. Jenny withdrew her hand from his gentle grasp almost instantly but in that split second she had, without his slightest knowledge, removed a huge diamond ring from his finger, in one movement passing the ring on to an accomplice while thanking the young victim for his courtesy.

"It is vain to get in," Jenny told the gentleman. "I will come again when there is less crowd." And with that she slipped back into the throng, disappearing. This singular theft became legendary among the criminal society of

London and earned for Jenny Diver an unchallengeable reputation as England's greatest pickpocket.

Jenny's acting ability matched that of her skillful fingers. But her performances were given only after many rehearsals and at a site that had been chosen with great care. Her favorite outings coincided with national holidays, especially royal celebrations. At such times—one being the day the king visited the House of Lords in a grand street celebration—Jenny would stuff two pillows beneath her large hooped gown and travel to a place along the procession route reserved for persons of quality. Alighting from her handsome carriage as a pregnant woman of means, her so-called servants going before her, she was always shown a prominent place from which to observe the festivities. At the height of the procession or the speeches, Jenny would suddenly collapse, writhing in agony, convincing all about her that she was in the throes of advanced labor.

The lords and ladies gathered around Jenny on these occasions invariably knelt to her aid, reaching out their hands. The apparently stricken Jenny would plead to remain still until the pain subsided. While sympathetic nobles clustered about her, making her comfortable, beautiful Jenny adroitly snatched up their jewels and purses, slipping them into special pockets sewn into her gown. At the same time, Jenny's confederates worked the outskirts of the crowd, merrily plucking away.

At one such outrageous performance, Jenny and her accomplices gleaned two diamond girdle-buckles, a gold watch, a gold snuff box studded with jewels, and scores of purses, all of it amounting to a great fortune with most of the loot going to Jenny, the star performer.

Jenny's stolen wealth enabled her to purchase a grand house, a fabulous wardrobe, and one of the finest carriages in London. Her fellow thieves were regularly employed as servants doubling as assistants in her imaginative schemes to rob the rich.

One of Jenny's more inspired ideas was the making of two false arms which were affixed to her elaborate gown. Wearing these artificial limbs, Jenny would be carried on a sedan chair by her servants into a meeting house or church,

being placed inside the circle of the rich. With her real arms and hands free to do her criminal work, Jenny would steal watches and purses, often jewelry, slipping her arms through slits in her gown while her false arms and hands lay clasped in her lap. She would then quickly pass the stolen goods to a confederate in the pew. On the few occasions when those who had been robbed cast suspicion upon her, the artful Jenny politely retorted that her hands had never left their position, and she was invariably excused with apologies.

No place, church or home, was above Jenny's invasion. The mansions of the rich were her favorite targets. Accompanied by only one servant—usually the man with whom she was having her current affair—Jenny would travel to the best districts, selecting a home she knew in advance housed great wealth. She would collapse in front of the building, feigning illness, as her footman raced to the door, banging loudly, and telling the mistress of the house that his lovely, well-to-do employer desperately needed help.

Jenny would be assisted inside, taken to the study at her request, the room where the greatest treasures of the house were most often kept, and then left alone, as her footman accompanied the household servants and mistress to fetch appropriate medicines that would revive the distressed woman. During their absence, Jenny would scoop up all things of value, from silver candlesticks to the cash box in the master's desk, hiding this booty in large sack-like pockets inside her gown. While Jenny was busy scampering about the study, her footman, excusing himself to get a drink of water or milk in the kitchen, pocketed the household silverware.

By the time the mistress of the house and her servants rushed back to the stricken Jenny, she would effect a miraculous recovery, regaining enough strength to stagger on the arm of her footman to the door. The footman would then call a carriage and shout loudly to the driver a fashionable address as their destination, further convincing the duped and kindly woman of the house that her brief guest was a lady of high status. Often, Jenny, to show her gratitude for the woman's kindness to her, would invite the woman and her family to dinner, giving the mulcted benefactress the phony adress. The carriage would rumble no more than a few blocks with Jenny and her footman before the driver was ordered to stop, his passengers hurriedly paying the fare and vanishing into a side street.

Never tiring of her role of elegant lady of fashion, Jenny attended all manner of high public functions but found the theater the most rewarding, both intellectually and financially. One night when leaving the theater, Jenny, about to enter her gleaming carriage, was stopped by a young gentleman whose fine clothes and ostentatious jewelry bragged his wealth.

"Might I be allowed the honor of attending you home?" he begged.

Beautiful Jenny gave him a polite no.

"But I must see you home."

"Please, sir, I am but recently married," Jenny told the gentleman, "and my husband is a suspicious person."

The rich first-nighter persisted, stating that his motives were purely chivalrous, that there were thieves and robbers about on the dark streets and she would need protection. Jenny, acting out her role to perfection, slowly yielded. The carriage took her and her admirer to a great house in Covent Garden, where the gentleman left her, but only after she promised to see him when her husband departed on a business trip scheduled for a few days later. During the carriage ride, Jenny had taken the young man's gold snuffbox, an item he later missed but never once suspected his beautiful companion as having taken.

Three days later the young gentleman, his pulse hammering, his mind racing with lusty images, was shown into the grand house in Covent Garden. Two members of Jenny's gang acted as servants. The role of Jenny's personal maid was played out by her mentor, the motherly Anne Murphy.

Following a sumptuous meal, Jenny and her gentleman retired to her bedroom. By then the young man was so delirious with the prospect of possessing this ravishing woman that he had not noticed how smoothly she had removed the diamond ring from his finger when she had greeted him at the door.

Inside the love chamber, the young man hurriedly divested himself of his expensive clothes, jewelry, and heavy purse, almost hurling himself into bed where Jenny awaited him. Minutes later, while the couple groaned out their carnal pleasures, loud knocking was heard at the bedroom door.

"Please, ma'am," cried out Anne Murphy in a plaintive voice. "It's your husband's carriage! He has returned unexpectedly!"

"My God, we must hurry!" shrieked Jenny. She leaped from the bed, snatching up not only her own clothes but those of her gentleman caller, including his diamond-studded sword, a gold-headed cane, his purse, and his other jewels. "Hide beneath the bed! I shall endeavor to persuade my husband to sleep apart from me this night. I will tell him I am ill. When he is asleep, I will return, my lover."

Dumbfounded and in shock, the gentleman slipped naked from the bed and crawled beneath it. Jenny raced from the room. Hours passed, and, when Jenny did not return, the duped lover tried the bedroom door to discover it locked. By noon the man was frantic and began to ring for the servants. The real servants and owners of the house did respond; they had to break down the door. In one terrible moment as the door was smashed open, the deserted lover, standing aghast and stark naked, was informed that the family and servants who lived in the house had been away for the day. Jenny and her cohorts had known of this family holiday, and used the mansion as a front. They had not only stolen everything of value from the suckered swain, but thoroughly looted the mansion.

For his pains the gentleman was compelled to pay the family for every item taken by the plundering Jenny and her gang. He did so willingly, begging the family never to reveal his stupidity in being swindled in a classic example of the old badger game.

All Jenny's thieving schemes, however, were not as easily expedited. In early 1733 she was caught lifting a gentleman's pocketbook near London Bridge and, giving her name as Mary Young, was throw into jail pending trial. In those ancient days, the techniques of criminal identification were primitive at best; it was next to impossible to pinpoint the thousands of thieves in London. Jenny had been arrested before, but, using many aliases—Jones, Murphy, Wills—she had always managed to escape conviction. This time a bevy of witnesses testifying against her sealed her fate. She was convicted and sentenced to transportation to America. Her confederates, however, using money she had supplied, bribed several officials so that instead of departing England by boat, Jenny simply went to the country for a rest.

No such chicanery worked for Jenny five years later, when, on April 4, 1738, she was caught red-handed attempting to steal a woman's purse in Canon Alley near Paternoster Row during the Festival of the Sons of the Clergy. She gave the name of Jane Webb and was quickly convicted. Authorities, thinking this her first conviction, sentenced her once again to banishment.

Jenny's downfall had been her age; her hands and fingers no longer worked with spritely action. And she had neglected her usual elaborate preparations. Jenny had not arranged for an accomplice to be nearby so that she could pass the stolen purse on. She was caught with the goods.

Also, by that date, Jenny's reputation was her enemy. She could no longer slip comfortably into the shroud of obscurity that up to then had cloaked her criminal activities. Said the London *Evening Post* of April 11, 1738, "She is one of the expertest hands in town at picking pockets; she used to attend well-dressed at the Opera House, play houses, etc., and it's reckoned made as much annually by her practice as if she had the finger of the Publick Money." The following week, the same newspaper reported that "among those that received sentences of transportation was the famous Jane Webb, *alias* Jenny Diver, reckoned the best hand in town; she belonged to a very great gang of pickpockets and formerly went by the name of Murphy."

Great activity on the part of Jenny's gang was noticed by the press, her accomplices frantically attempting to bribe officials high and low, perhaps even manage a spectacular escape, in order to prevent her from being sent out of the country. Stated the *Weekly Miscellany* on April 21, 1738, "She belongs to a large gang of pickpockets . . . who declare if it cost two

hundred pounds she shant go abroad." Said the *Post* in the same week: "Great interest is making to get the famous Jenny Diver off. . . . The gang spare no pains or cost, well knowing that in six months' time she'll pick pockets enough to pay all charges." The paper hinted that even "persons of figure" were attempting to have the charges dropped.

Nothing availed Jenny or her gang members. She was put aboard the galley *Forward* on June 7, 1738, and sailed for America. But she did not go penniless and without hope as was the case with most of her fellow thieves being transported. A great wagonload of trunks and boxes containing a fortune in jewels, money, and expensive goods, including "a fine sidesaddle trimmed with silver," accompanied her to Virginia.

No sooner had Jenny landed than she began to make plans for her return to England. Using her considerable wealth, she bribed a ship's captain to secrete her on board his ship, which sailed for Liverpool a year later. It never occurred to the street-hardened Jenny, her looks gone, her nimble fingers stiffening with arthritis, to retire in leisure with her ill-gotten gains. She had thrived upon her notoriety. Now she was frantic at the idea of losing the power she had exercised over her London gang members. She returned to recapture that power and to reestablish her position as the greatest thief of her day.

But when Jenny returned to London, her gang members had scattered, and she was reduced to stealing half-empty purses from middle-class passersby. The inevitable happened. On Sherbourne Lane, London, January 17, 1740, she was caught attempting to take the purse of a feisty young woman who struggled with her, knocking Jenny into the mud.

There would be no rescue attempts for Jenny Diver now. She was identified and convicted not only of stealing but of returning from transportation, an offense punishable by death. She was tried at the Old Bailey and sentenced to hang. Before her death, Jenny became penitent, and hortative, making religious declarations and advising her fellow pickpockets still at large to give up their evil pursuits. She had done evil all her adult life, she admitted freely, but now she was at peace, embracing the principles of the Protestant religion.

On the morning of Wednesday, March 18, 1740, Jenny Diver was placed in a mourning coach and, with a company of mounted troops leading the coach and a company of infantry following, taken to Tyburn. A great throng of spectators had gathered there to see the most spectacular pickpocket in British history mount the scaffold.

Strangely, the normally raucous, hooting crowd was silent during the woman's ordeal, with only a heavy murmuring running through the ranks, the sound of prayers being offered up for Jenny's soul. Jenny herself made no emotional display. She mounted the scaffold well dressed, wearing a veil. As the rope was placed around her neck, the forty-year-old woman whispered a few words to her religious adviser, the Reverend Broughton, words that went unrecorded.

It was over in seconds. No one cheered. Jenny's body was taken down and buried in St. Pancras' churchyard, a spot she had personally picked as her final resting place. Among those attending the last services at her grave was a man of apparent wealth. He wept openly. He was thought to be the young gentleman who had loved Jenny many years before, loved her still, even though she had shamelessly robbed him and left him standing naked to face her victims inside a great white London house.

DIXON, MARGARET

Murderer ■ (1670–1753)

Convicted of murdering her child, Margaret Dixon was hanged in Edinburgh. Her body was taken down, put in a wooden box, and taken away by friends for burial. The burial party stopped at an inn a few miles from Edinburgh for refreshments, taking the crude coffin into the inn with them. While drinking, members of the party were startled to see the lid of the coffin open and Margaret Dixon sit up. They ran wildly in all directions.

Margaret Dixon was bled (then a traditional doctoring technique) and put to bed. Within a day she was up and around and able to walk to her own home in Musselburgh. No one could explain her miraculous survival, and under existing laws the authorities were powerless to execute the woman again. The sheriff who had carried out the execution, however, was jailed for not performing his duties.

Dixon was thereafter a local celebrity, known until her death as "Half-hanged Maggie Dixon."

DONALD, JEANNIE

Murderer ■ (1896– ?)

Eight-year-old Helen Pristly was found dead, stuffed in a sack beneath the stairs of a rooming house in Aberdeen, Scotland, on April 21, 1934. Immediately suspected of murdering the girl was Mrs. Jeannie Donald, a thirty-eight-year-old housewife who had shown her dislike of the child, who lived next door. Only days earlier Mrs. Donald had struck the girl for annoying her.

Mrs. Donald was convicted of murder and sentenced to death, but her sentence was commuted to life imprisonment, and she was released in 1944. It was speculated that Mrs. Donald had literally frightened the child to death, leaping out at her when the girl was playing a prank by ringing Mrs. Donald's doorbell, that in her fright the child choked to death on her own vomit. To cover her act, Mrs. Donald molested the child to make it appear a rape killing, then threw the body into the sack and down the stairs. Mrs. Donald's own hairs were found in the sack.

DOSS, NANNIE

Murderer ■ (1905–1965)

A resident of Tulsa, Oklahoma, Mrs. Nannie Doss was one of the most peculiar mass murderers on record. She poisoned four husbands over several decades, and also murdered her mother, two sisters, two children, and several others for a total of eleven, killings to which she confessed when she was sentenced to a life term in 1964. She died in her cell the following year of leukemia.

Nannie proudly boasted at her trial that she did not, as the prosecution contended, murder for the small amounts of insurance she had collected on her victims. She had killed for true love, she insisted. "I was searching for the perfect mate, the real romance of life."

Nannie Doss of Oklahoma poisoned eleven persons, most of them for "romance."

DRUSE, ROXANA

Murderer ■ (1846–1889)

Mrs. Druse and her half-witted daughter, Mary, beat to death John Druse, a man in his seventies, chopping up the body and boiling down the remains in their frontier cabin outside Little Falls, New York, in 1889. Mrs. Druse's son, twelve-year-old John, Jr., later informed authorities. Mary was sent to prison for life. Mrs. Druse was promptly hanged after a speedy trial in which she put up no defense. She had remarked earlier that she felt she could successfully rid herself of her husband's body by boiling it into lard. "I didn't burn it," Mrs. Druse told officers, referring to the head of John Druse, which was never found, "for fear that the burning hair would bring the authorities." Her motive for the slaying was that her taskmaster husband worked her too hard on their hardscrabble farm.

DUBUISSON, PAULINE

Murderer ■ (1926–   )

After shooting her love Felix Bailly to death in his Paris flat on March 17, 1951, twenty-six-year-old Pauline Dubuisson tried to commit suicide by taking gas. She failed. The one-time medical student had murdered Bailly after learning that he intended to marry another.

Pauline Dubuisson smilingly accepting a life term from a French court in 1953 for killing her faithless lover.

The French jury, despite Pauline's proven promiscuity, judged the murder a *crime passionel*, and, upon her conviction, Pauline was sent to prison for life instead of being executed.

DUMOLARD, MARIE

Murder Accomplice ■ (1816– ?)

For more than a decade, Martin Dumolard, a farmer living outside the French village of Montluel, attacked and murdered several young women, ravaging the bodies and taking what belongings these poor peasant girls carried. Madame Dumolard encouraged her husband's murderous perversions and was given some of the victims' clothes to wear as payment for her complicity.

In 1861 Dumolard attacked a young woman named Marie Pichon, after promising to get her a job at a remote château where he said he worked. Marie was too fast for the man and escaped the lasso he tried to toss over her head on a lonely road, outrunning the man down a dark lane and gaining the safety of a nearby village where she told her story.

Dumolard was apprehended but refused to admit any crime. His wife broke down under interrogation and told the gruesome tale of her husband's murders. Both were placed on trial at Bourg in January 1862, howling mobs outside the courtroom demanding the Dumolards be killed at once.

The man was described as being "a strong and brutal peasant, with a large nose, thick lips,

Marie Dumolard who dressed in the clothes of her husband's victims. (Courtesy Tussaud's)

hollow eyes, and bushy eyebrows. A beard fringed his hard features. His wife, thin and slight, with shifty eyes and a cunning face, was placed at his side."

Clothes from at least ten victims were put on display in court—their victims may have numbered as many as twenty-five. Both were quickly convicted. Dumolard was executed, beheaded on March 8, 1862. The cold-hearted Marie Dumolard was sent to prison for twenty years.

DURGAN, BRIDGET

Murderer ■ (1844–1867)

An Irish immigrant, Bridget Durgan thought to replace her mistress, Mrs. Mary Ellen Coriell, in the affections of forty-four-year-old Dr. William Coriell, for whom she

England's awful Amelia Dyer, the "baby farmer." (Courtesy Tussaud's)

worked as a maid in New Market, New Jersey. Bridget attacked Mrs. Coriell with a knife while the woman was in bed, stabbing her forty or fifty times; the victim put up a terrific battle before dying of her wounds.

Quickly apprehended, Bridget claimed to have had an uncontrollable fit and to have murdered the woman in a semi-conscious state. A jury disagreed with this claim and convicted the maid, sentencing her to death. Bridget was hanged on August 30, 1867, before a crowd of more than two thousand. The local sheriff got Bridget drunk before dawn so that she would not become hysterical before spectators, who had paid handsomely to witness her death.

DYER, AMELIA ELIZABETH

Murderer ■ (1839–1896)

Advertising herself as a kindly woman who would board young children—she outlined her one-time career in the Salvation Army as a reference—Mrs. Dyer moved to Reading, England, in 1895. A number of infant bodies began to be discovered shortly after Mrs. Dyer's arrival, seven in all. These children had been placed in Mrs. Dyer's care. After collecting boarding fees, the woman later admitted, she simply strangled the children and threw the bodies into a nearby canal.

She was tried in May 1896, her lawyer unsuccessfully attempting to prove her insane. Mrs. Dyer was hanged on June 10, 1896, at Newgate Prison. Her victims may have numbered as many as fifteen; this monster had been a "baby farmer" for more than a decade. Before her execution Mrs. Dyer instructed the authorities, who were looking for corpses of other babies she might have killed, that there was one sure way to identify her victims. "You'll know all mine by the tape around their necks."

EASTERN JEWEL

Spy ■ (1906–1948)

Only during the bizarre, chaotic times of the Chinese warlords of the early 1930s could a calculating creature such as Eastern Jewel have lived and worked. A spine-chilling dragon lady by any standards, Eastern Jewel, perhaps more than any single person in the Orient, helped to set off the Second World War in the Far East, operating as a spy, a rabble-rouser, and a super-agent provocateur for the militaristic Japanese government, or, more specifically, for her Japanese lover. She would do anything for her lovers, intrigue against her own people, scheme toward the murder of high-ranking persons, or commit treason as easily as donning her top boots. It had been that way with her almost from birth.

Born a Tartar princess in 1906, Eastern Jewel was destined for a Japanese upbringing; her father, Prince Su, who controlled Inner Mongolia and was a descendant of Nurhachi, founder of the Manchu dynasty in 1616 (the year of Shakespeare's death), promised the girl to Naniwa Kawashima, his Japanese military adviser, to be raised as his own daughter. At age eight, Eastern Jewel, renamed Yoshiko Kawashima by her adoptive father, was sent to a primary school in Tokyo where she was given a Japanese education, one that included the learning of judo and fencing.

Prince Su died in Port Arthur in 1921; his wife, a concubine with no official identity, committed traditional suicide and followed the Manchu nobleman to the grave. The deaths of her mother and father seemed not to stir Eastern Jewel. By then she had become indifferent to her Chinese heritage and worshiped all things Japanese. Sex was also something the girl worshiped, and that at an early age.

At fifteen, she later bragged, Kawashima's seventy-five-year-old father raped her. She not only had an affair with her foster father but also seduced several young Japanese officers, including a Lieutenant Yamaga whom she genuinely

Eastern Jewel, then known as Yoshiko Kawashima, with her short-term husband Kanjurjab, on her wedding day in 1927.

loved. When Yamaga rejected her, Eastern Jewel, with considerable wealth at her disposal, took on many lovers. Oddly enough, Eastern Jewel agreed to marry the son of a Mongol prince, one Kanjurjab, in 1927; the wedding had been arranged years earlier by her father. Kanjurjab was an ineffectual youth, and, after being wedded in Port Arthur, Eastern Jewel stayed with the Mongol for only four months. According to Henry McAleavy, one of Eastern Jewel's biog-

raphers, the marriage was merely the acting out of ancient protocol: "She used to boast later that she had never allowed him to touch her during the few months they spent together."

Deserting her Chinese husband, Eastern Jewel departed Mongolia in 1928, first going to the cities of South China, then returning to Tokyo where in rapid succession she picked up and discarded several lovers. A member of the Japanese Diet took her to Shanghai where she quickly depleted his funds. The high-living Eastern Jewel had little fear of not finding someone to pay her way. She was extremely pretty, petite, and affected men's clothing, particularly uniforms, taking a delight in wearing riding breeches and shiny black boots. Dressed this way, Eastern Jewel attended a party in Shanghai where she was introduced to a huge, barrel-chested Japanese officer with a thick flowing mustache, Major Ryukichi Tanaka, head of the Japanese Intelligence Service in Shanghai.

Eastern Jewel was immediately attracted to

In the dress of a Japanese officer, Eastern Jewel poses with her lover Ryukichi Tanaka.

Eastern Jewel about to take off in a Japanese warplane to inspect the damage done to Shanghai in 1932, much of it through her spying efforts.

the man, although Tanaka politely rebuffed her initial advances, thinking that a Manchu princess was far beyond the social reaches of a Japanese line officer. Actually, the aggressive Eastern Jewel finally seduced Tanaka after telling him that she had discovered the boot fetish they both had in common. Tanaka, wrote David Bergamini in *Japan's Imperial Conspiracy:* ". . . loved to wear high black boots and she insisted that he wear them always. The boots scuffed the polish on the brightest dance floors of Shanghai, and ended each evening dangling over the end of a bed."

Tanaka, other chroniclers contend, desired

to denigrate all Chinese womanhood, for he had an abiding hatred for the Chinese people as a whole and, in seducing this Chinese princess, he took revenge upon a race he despised as weak and compromising. Biographer Umemoto insists that Tanaka, before consummating his first assignation with Eastern Jewel, donned Chinese garments and ordered his lover to wear the split skirt of the singsong girls of Shanghai. Eastern Jewel, after agreeing to dress in such fashion, demanded that Tanaka pretend to rape her, which he did, at the point of a gun, and in an open field outside the city. These were only minor perversions the couple practiced at the eve of their tempestuous love affair. Eastern Jewel, wrote McAleavy, "found in Tanaka a man who would drag her down by force into the slime where she longed to be."

In order to keep his lover in high style, Tanaka put Eastern Jewel on the Japanese intelligence spy payroll, sending her to a special school to learn English, which he thought would be an asset in her later espionage work. That work began in the fall of 1931 when Colonel Itagaki ordered Tanaka to create disturbances in Shanghai to screen the Japanese takeover of Manchuria. An incident in Shanghai would provoke the Chinese to act against Japanese businesses and thus provide the necessary counterattack of Japanese troops.

Using about $10,000 provided by Tanaka, Eastern Jewel hired dozens of Chinese thugs to break into Japanese homes and businesses in Shanghai, beat up inhabitants, and in general create mayhem. When the local police seemed either unwilling or unable to control the hoodlums, warships of the Japanese navy sailed into the harbor, and, using the perfect excuse of protecting their national interests, landed strong marine detachments which occupied sections of the city.

Short weeks later the Japanese employed Eastern Jewel to "persuade" the deposed boy emperor Henry Pu-Yi, last of the Manchu sovereigns and to whom she was related, to move from Tientsin to Mukden where he would rule as a puppet of the Japanese militarists who were about to take over Manchuria. Eastern Jewel flew from Shanghai to Tientsin and immediately went to Pu-Yi and his opium-addicted wife, Elizabeth. Under direct orders of Colonel Doihara, the local Japanese commander, the girl spy took it upon herself to frighten Pu-Yi half to death. She had confederates, posing as assassins, phone Pu-Yi and send him letters in which his life was threatened. When Pu-Yi called in Doihara to explain these threats, the Japanese colonel carried on a phony investigation in which he traced the would-be assassins to the camp of Chang Hsueh-liang, one-time warlord of Manchuria, Pu-Yi's arch-foe.

Eastern Jewel went further in her attempt to frighten Pu-Yi into accepting the puppet throne, putting snakes in the emperor's bed and then "discovering" a basket of fruit containing two bombs sent to Pu-Yi from a friend. Finally convinced that he was marked for assassination, Pu-Yi gratefully accepted Japanese protection and was smuggled, or kidnapped, into Mukden, assuming the titular throne in March 1932. Eastern Jewel had performed well, and the Japanese were so grateful they allowed her to wear the uniform of a Japanese officer and gave her the title of commander.

In early 1932 when Japan's fake war was at its height and Shanghai was being bombed incessantly by the Japanese air force, Eastern Jewel rejoiced at the deaths of thousands of her own countrymen. After the Chapai district had been destroyed, she flew over the bombed area in a Japanese fighter applauding and reveling. She later walked through the devastated area, laughing with Japanese officers, stepping over the bodies of women and children who had been slaughtered; no Chinese who witnessed the gloating of Eastern Jewel would ever forget the sight of her.

Years later, Eastern Jewel moved to occupied Peking where she dispensed favors to local Chinese who fell under suspicion of sabotage and espionage. The favors consisted of interceding with the Japanese on the part of those who stood accused of collaboration with the enemy, chiefly Chiang Kai-shek. For these favors Eastern Jewel demanded fortunes. The traitor grew rich. One rich Chinese merchant was brought before Eastern Jewel who accused him of receiving letters from Chungking, of itself sufficient to mark the man a collaborator with Chiang Kai-shek, whose armies occupied Chungking. She would forget the letters, Eastern Jewel told the merchant, and not report such devastating correspondence to the Japanese, for a payment of $60,000. The merchant could raise only $36,000. After paying this to Eastern Jewel, the man committed suicide.

In such activities, Eastern Jewel invariably gave a percentage of her extortion money to the local Japanese commander, Colonel Yamaga. In early 1943 Yamaga began to demand the lion's share of Eastern Jewel's spoils from her blackmailed countrymen. The traitor knew how to handle such impudence. She flew to Tokyo and told authorities that Yamaga had voiced

Henry P'u-Yi in Tsientsin before being terrorized by Eastern Jewel into cooperating with the Japanese.

tion in the world would induce me to lay a hand on her diseased carcass," he was quoted as saying. When Eastern Jewel heard this remark, retaliation was swift. Japanese troopers stormed onto the stage where Li was performing and dragged him by the heels through the streets before throwing him in prison on the trumped-up charge that he had stolen money from Eastern Jewel's handbag.

By war's end, Eastern Jewel was no longer the petite, pretty Manchu princess turned girl spy but a bloated syphilitic monster who preyed sexually upon children. When Chiang Kai-shek came back into complete control of China, Eastern Jewel went into hiding but was betrayed by a one-time lover she had forsaken. In 1948 she was hauled before a tribunal and in short order condemned to death.

"This woman deserves death as a traitor," intoned her chief prosecutor, "but most of all

P'u-Yi as the Japanese puppet emperor of Manchuria.

opposition to General Tojo's war schemes. Yamaga was ordered to stand court martial in Tokyo; Eastern Jewel testified against him and her word was enough to have him cashiered.

At this time and to the rest of her days, the traitor indulged in repugnant sex practices, taking on dozens of lovers, including members of her own Japanese bodyguard. She exercised a fierce lesbianism with dozens of singsong girls. Her favorites were young, heterosexual, virile actors, and these she would have brought to her mansion where she would beat them with whips, then compel them to make ardent love to her. One actor, a man named Li, refused to accept Eastern Jewel's invitation. "No considera-

because she rode in Japanese airplanes over bombed-out villages and laughed." Eastern Jewel was not given the military honor of a firing squad, but was sent to the block and beheaded.

EDMUNDS, CHRISTIANA

Murderer ■ (1829– ?)

A forty-two-year-old spinster living in Brighton, England, Christiana Edmunds had fallen in love with her family physician, a Dr. Beard. The physician had rebuffed the spinster, telling her to stay away from him. On August 10, 1871, Christiana sent a box of cakes to Dr. Beard's wife, but the servants ate the cakes, and they became ill. It was obvious to Beard that Christiana had tried to poison his wife. He went to the police who picked up the woman for questioning.

She was subsequently linked to the poison death of a young boy she had used to purchase chocolate for her—this to be mixed with the cakes she made for Dr. Beard's wife, along with strychnine she inserted into the cakes. To eliminate witnesses against her, Christiana had poisoned some chocolate and given it to her errand boys, making several seriously ill and killing a five-year-old.

Despite the fact that she came from a family of mental defectives—her father and brother had died in insane asylums, and there was a marked family history of hysteria and epilepsy—Miss Edmunds was placed on trial on January 15, 1872. She had stated, "I would rather be convicted than brought in insane." Christiana was convicted and sent to prison for life.

ELLIS, RUTH

Murderer ■ (1927–1955)

The murder tragedy of Ruth Ellis was a hallmark in British homicide, its aftereffects creating such a national storm of protest that the House of Commons was forced to a nervous decision as a direct result of this woman's senseless crime. The case centered about the debate of *crime passionel*, a crime the French understood well, the British not at all.

Born in the Welsh town of Rhyl in 1927 and raised in Manchester, England, Ruth Ellis was typical of many young women in England during World War II. She worked for a while in a munitions factory, held a job as a waitress, and, having a good voice, entertained troops as a dance-band singer. At seventeen she fell in love with an American flyer who was killed in 1944. Ruth delivered his child, a boy. Another child, a little girl, was the result of Ruth's 1950 marriage to a dentist. A short time later Ruth was divorced on the grounds of mental cruelty.

Having to support her two children, the uneducated Ruth took on modeling jobs, dyeing her auburn hair to peroxide blonde. She was more successful as a shill in nightclubs, earning about $22 a week by encouraging men to drink with her. Working in London's Carrolls Club in mid-1953, Ruth met the darkly handsome David Blakely, a racetrack driver who hoped someday to win at Le Mans. Their liaison was a loose affair. Ruth later insisted that Blakely pursued her and that she found it impossible to get rid of him. When she became manager of the Little Club, a plush and gold nightery in Knightsbridge, Blakely followed her there, cadging drinks from her. Ruth loaned him money, bought him clothes, and made a home for him in her small apartment.

In December 1953 Ruth had an abortion but Blakely proved sympathetic. "He was very concerned," Ruth later remembered, "and although he was engaged to another girl, he offered to marry me. I was really not in love with him at the time. I decided I could get out of the trouble I was in without him marrying me."

The couple stayed together, Blakely breaking off his engagement with the other girl and begging Ruth to marry him, but in 1954 she met a friend of Blakely's, Desmond Edward Cussen, and a love affair developed between the two. It was a strange arrangement. For almost a year, Ruth shuttled between Cussen and Blakely, each man aware of the other's involvement.

But in the end Blakely's temper got the best of him. The twenty-five-year-old driver—he was three years younger than Ruth—took to beating Ruth. On various occasions, he knocked her down, blackened her eye, broke her ankle. And yet they stayed together. Then Blakely began seeing other women, girls much younger than Ruth. Still they stayed together.

Some time later Ruth threw a surprise birthday party for Blakely. That night, as the couple undressed, she noticed "he had love bites on his back."

"What happened to your back?" Ruth asked her lover.

Blakely, ever the suave operator, retorted, "Oh, those—a sore loser bit me when I was playing darts."

"Get out of my flat!" ordered Ruth.

The next night Blakely was back, running into the Little Club and falling on his knees before Ruth Ellis. "Please marry me," he begged.

"No, your family wouldn't approve."

She took him back, but continued to see her other lover, Cussen. Blakely found Cussen and Ruth together on Christmas Eve 1954, in Cussen's apartment, and, as a result of the fight that night, Ruth vowed never to see Blakely again. But she did, as Ruth's trial later confirmed, going to hotels with the driver.

"Why did you do that when you had made up your mind to end the association?" asked a prosecutor at Ruth's 1955 trial.

Her answer was the classic line, "Because I was in love with him."

Blakely's ardor apparently cooled, and he again began seeing other women. On April 6, 1955, the racetrack driver went to Hampstead, telling Ruth that he had to see a mechanic who was building his racing car. Ruth became sus-

British bar girl Ruth Ellis, a $22-a-week shill with no illusions.

picious and followed Blakely, going to the mechanic's apartment. There was no answer to her knocking, but from behind the door she heard a woman's laughter.

Ruth returned to the Hampstead flat the next day and saw Blakely emerge with an attractive young girl, his arm affectionately around her. He drove off with the girl without seeing Ruth, who returned home with a strange feeling, a tightening of the stomach muscles. "I had a peculiar idea that I wanted to kill him," she later admitted.

On the evening of April 10, 1955, Ruth again went to Hampstead in a taxi, arriving about 9:30 P.M. near the Magdala public house. Just at that moment David Blakely, accompanied by a friend, car salesman Bertram Clive Gunnell, emerged from the pub. They had gone there for liquor to take back to a party that was in progress.

Blakely walked to the driver's side of the car just as Ruth approached him. He turned and gave her a nervous look, then began to run in front of the car. Ruth pulled a gun from her handbag and fired. Blakely by then was crouching in front of the car, attempting to hide, but Ruth ran up to him and emptied the gun into his bent-over body. He fell onto the road, dead.

Gunnell stood petrified, staring at the woman. Ruth turned to him, saying calmly, "Now call the police."

Constables took Ruth to a nearby station where without hesitation she blurted out her confession: "I am guilty. I am rather confused. It all started about two years ago when I met David Blakely at the Little Club in Knightsbridge."

A sergeant told her she would be charged with murder.

"Thanks," came her reply.

Ruth Ellis was examined and found to be sane. She stood trial at the Old Bailey on June 20 and 21, 1955. During her testimony, the prosecutor asked her the reasons for shooting her faithless lover.

"I did not know why I shot him," Ruth said. "I was very upset."

"Did you mean to kill David Blakely?"

"It is obvious. When I fired the revolver at close range, I intended to kill him." One bullet was fired only three inches from the victim.

Justice Havers, the presiding judge, concluded his summing-up to the jury with the statement, "The jealous fury of a woman scorned is no excuse for murder. That is the law of England." In record time, twenty-three minutes to be exact, the jury convicted Ruth Ellis of murder. She was sentenced to death by hanging, her execution to take place inside North London's Holloway Women's Prison, on July 13, 1955.

The death sentence caused a massive storm of protest. More than two thousand signatures were fixed to one petition for clemency and sent to the Home Office. All appeals on Ruth's behalf were turned down. Only a day before her scheduled execution, authorities heard a story that a man had driven Ruth to Hampstead on the night of the killing, given her the gun she used to shoot Blakely, and instructed her to murder her one-time lover. This story could not be confirmed and the execution took place as planned.

At dawn on July 13, a great crowd of more

Ruth Ellis with unidentified man shortly before she shot David Blakely to death.

than a thousand people clamored outside Holloway Prison. Many waved French newspapers which condemned the British authorities for taking the life of a woman who had been helplessly bound up in a *crime passionel*, papers that branded British justice "barbaric." In the jeering crowd was elderly Mrs. Violet Van Der Elst, dressed all in black and violently shoving aside the horses of the mounted police who sought to maintain order. Mrs. Van Der Elst had been protesting capital punishment since 1935. An aged violinist played Bach's "Be Thou with Me." He wore a sign about his neck which read, "No Alms Please." The crowd had begged prison officials to allow Ruth Ellis to be brought to one of the prison's great stone towers and, in sight of the crowd, to get on her knees and pray with the multitude. In answer to this, a guard announced, "She wants to pray alone."

At a little after 9 A.M., Ruth was brought into a large room where the scaffold waited. Her executioner was Albert Pierrepont, a Lancashire pub owner who made money on the side as England's last hangman. Ruth was given a glass of brandy, which she drank down rapidly. She was led to the rope and a white hood was put about her head. Minutes later she was dead, the last woman hanged in England. Ruth Ellis had gone to her death stoically, without a word.

The uproar over this execution did not subside, but mounted to the point where the House of Commons, in 1956, voted to abolish hanging in England, a move rejected by the House of Lords. One upper-crust member of Parliament reacted to the Ellis affair with typical aristocratic cynicism, shouting, "After the rigors of a public school education, hanging doesn't seem so bad."

EVERLEIGH SISTERS

Madams ■ (Ada, 1876–1960; Minna, 1878–1948)

Minna and Ada Everleigh were the darlings of the press during their thirteen-year heyday as the most stunning, class-conscious brothel madams of all America's whoredom. "The Scarlet Sisters," as the press affectionately labeled them, were also the most successful madams in American history, retiring with millions, and retaining a regal aura about themselves that lent color and fame to their stigmatized profession. And they were wonderful copy.

Kentucky-born, the sisters (Ada born in 1876, Minna in 1878) received good educations at the insistence of their widowed father, a successful lawyer. Also in the southern tradition, he arranged marriages for them, unions with two brothers, but the chosen husbands proved callous and, as Ada later put it, "brutes with unbearable characters." With their divorces tucked in their trunks, the girls joined an acting troupe in the mid-1890s, but were stranded in Omaha, Nebraska, when the show disbanded in 1898.

Omaha, however, was playing host to the Trans-Mississippi Exposition at the time and the boom was on. Both girls, then in their early twenties and extremely attractive, were not destitute; they had between them about $35,000, a sum received from their father after they agreed to his marriage plans for them. "We were looking for a nice town in which to invest our money," Minna Everleigh later said, and Omaha appeared to be just the city, with cowboys and tourists spending money at a furious pace. According to crime chronicler Herbert Asbury, "Everywhere they had gone the two girls had heard of the enormous fortunes which were being made by well-conducted brothels, and they decided that prostitution offered maximum returns with minimum risks."

As clear as the way seemed to the sisters, however, their transition from actresses to whorehouse proprietors was not all that abrupt. First they opened a stylish boardinghouse in Omaha. When they learned that the other so-called boardinghouses in the district were actually bordellos, they made the decision to convert their establishment as well. "We had already made our investment in the boardinghouse," Ada later admitted, "and it was simply a matter of doing the right thing with it."

That no thought of morality entered the minds of Minna and Ada Everleigh seems remarkable to us today. After all, this was the very age of morality, the prim and proper 1890s. Perhaps the fact that their father by this time had gone to Mexico City and died there, his paternal eye shut forever, allowed the girls to operate as madams without feeling they were embarrassing the family. (The name Everleigh, in fact, was a concoction of the sisters, taken from the way their grandmother had signed her letters to them when they were little girls: "Everly yours." From then on the Everleigh name was used exclusively in connection with their brothel operations; in all business and banking transactions, they used the name of Lester, and retired with this name, but, most probably, that

Minna Everleigh, all charm and wit. (UPI)

name, too, was an invention, and their real family name is lost forever to history.)

The Everleigh resort in Omaha flourished through the good taste of the sisters. The hardy denizens of this burgeoning cow town had never seen anything like it: the Tiffany stained-glass ceiling in the foyer, exquisite carpets in the girls' rooms, and a magnificently appointed bar with gilt-edged mirrors where customers were encouraged to drink only expensive wine or champagne. The real talk of the bordello was the $15,000 gold-plated piano which was played in the main salon by a professor of music attired in impeccable evening dress.

Even at this early stage in their career, the sisters were open and candid with newsmen, a cynical, tough breed with whom they identified

and whom they admired. When an Omaha reporter interviewed the alluring Minna as she sat on her ornate brass bed (this was the period in which the sisters worked the brothel before becoming exclusively madams), the Everleigh sister spread out her milky arms to take in the lavishly appointed room and exclaimed, "A girl has to start somewhere."

Minna was always the more loquacious of the two, the more outgoing and extravagant, who could be counted on for a stinging quote or a wry quip (although their Chicago banker, Oscar Swan, later told a reporter that he thought Minna was a little crazy; the sisters kept an account at the Central Republic Bank in Chicago decades after leaving the city, for they continued to hold considerable real estate and stock investments in the area). Ada was the brains behind the Everleigh sisters, a business genius who would manipulate their comfortable legacy into a great fortune. And it was Ada who would set the tone and standards of their bagnios, especially the palace they established later in Chicago, the world-renowned Everleigh Club.

With the exposition over, the sisters' clientele diminished, and they quickly decided to move elsewhere. They had doubled their nest egg in the space of one year and fielded about for a brothel in any major American city that would support the kind of super-class prostitution they envisioned. Throughout 1899 they traveled to New York, Washington, D.C., New Orleans, and San Francisco but found nothing that suited their tastes. Late that same year, the Everleighs arrived in Chicago and were informed that the luxurious bordello once operated by Lizzie Allen, Chicago's most famous madam up to that time, was available. Lizzie had spent $125,000 redecorating her Dearborn Street brothel in the Levee, the notorious red-light district of the First Ward. But Lizzie hadn't lived to enjoy her pleasure palace, having died in 1896. For a while Effie Hankins had run Lizzie's place but had proved inept, too cheap and gaudy for such a richly appointed sex spa. Lizzie's "man," a colorful rooster named Christopher Columbus Crabb and owner of the property, was fielding about for a new tenant just at the time the Everleighs appeared. He gave them a lifetime lease when they plunked down $70,000.

Chicago was about to experience the most amazing era of high-class prostitution in its low-life history. The sisters had a plan when they moved into their new bordello, which was two adjoining three-story buildings with a total of fifty rooms at 2131-33 South Dearborn Street (telephone CAlumet 412, a number that would be called from all points of the globe, even by Crown Prince Henry of Prussia, who came to visit the spectacular brothel in 1902). First, the Everleighs fired all the girls still working there. "They are unschooled strumpets, no class at all," reported Ada, exercising a snobbery that would soon alienate all her fellow tradesmen. The Everleighs discreetly let it be known that they were in the market for the most beautiful girls in the profession, flatly stating that any prospective boarder would soon, if she chose, retire rich. Ada made no bones about her high expectations, telling a reporter, "I talk to each applicant myself. She must have worked somewhere else before coming here. We don't like amateurs. Inexperienced girls and young widows are too prone to accept offers of marriage and leave.

"To get in, a girl must have a good face and figure, must be in perfect health, and must understand what it is to act like a lady. If she is addicted to drugs or drink, we don't want her. There will be no difficulty in keeping the Club filled."

In fact, the Everleighs, throughout their decade-long stay in Chicago, turned away hundreds of girls and had hundreds more on their waiting list. Thirty was the magic number of girls they settled on, and these young women, from all reports of the press and the keepers and players of the sprawling red-light district in the Levee, were the most stunning, graceful, intelligent females ever assembled under one bordello's roof; they were the superstars of American prostitution, and many of the more than four hundred girls who worked for the Everleigh sisters over the years did, indeed, retire with fortunes, or marry millionaires, titled gentlemen and statesmen, some of their offspring achieving the roster of Chicago's so-called blue bloods to this day.

The girls, their wardrobes carefully chosen by the sisters, were never dressed in a gaudy,

Ada Everleigh, the brains of the bordello business. (UPI)

garish fashion. Their expensive gowns might reveal a trim ankle or a bit of bosom, but they were bathed three times a day by black maids, their hair styled each morning, their fingernails manicured and toenails pedicured each day. At no time were these lofty sirens anything other than the most stylish and charming of ladies of the evening. The girls were also arrayed in glittering gems, necklaces, rings, bracelets, brooches studded with enormous diamonds, rubies, emeralds, all of which were "house jewels," owned by the Everleighs themselves and returned to the attic safe following each night's business. By the time the sisters retired, this collection of jewels, obtained from admirers over the years, was estimated to be worth more than a million dollars.

The girls themselves were allowed to keep

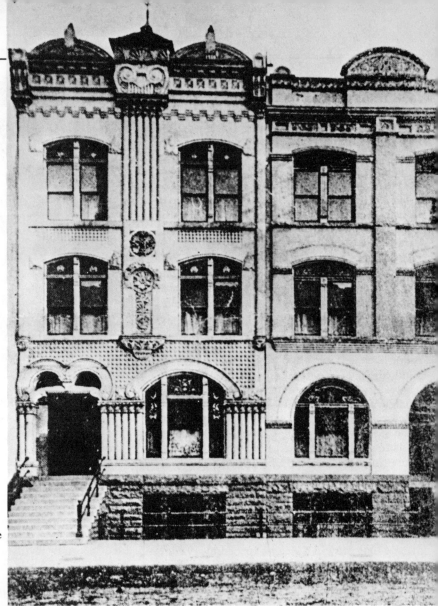

The Everleigh Club, a double three-story structure on Chicago's Dearborn Street that became the most famous whorehouse in the world—and the most expensive. (UPI)

any gifts of jewelry or other expensive bonuses their distinguished guests bestowed upon them. They split their weekly take with the sisters, and this ranged from $500 to $1,500 a week. These enormous sums were provided by the biggest spenders in America, from John "Bet-a-Million" Gates to the captains of industry and finance. A clerk might save up for a year to treat himself to one night of the glories the Everleigh Club provided.

And the club itself was a wonder to behold. The Everleighs spared no expense in the gilding of their mansion. When it officially opened on February 1, 1900, the sisters boldly led a bevy of newsmen through their new emporium, much the way a society hostess would guide guests through her home before a benefit or a tea. A fortune had been spent to rebuild the rooms, with special care taken with the reception areas, dining rooms, and large salons. These included the Persian Room, the Turkish Room, the Japanese Room, all festooned with priceless tapestries, carpets, hand-made furniture, gilt-edged mirrors, imported statuary and paintings, and a riot of velvet and plush that made any guest believe that he was anywhere but in a whorehouse. There was the Hall of a Thousand Mirrors and, especially popular, the Pullman Buffet, a great room constructed to resemble the interior of an exquisitely appointed Pullman car where guests ate from silver platters, dining on the finest cuisine available in Chicago (the Everleighs employed three master chefs) and were waited upon by black butlers in stunning livery. Three fully tuxedoed orchestras entertained guests in the main salons, playing such popular ballads as "Harem Life," "Love's Old Sweet Song," and an inane ditty called "Dear Midnight of Love." The composer of this last song was none other than Bathhouse John Coughlin, alderman of the notorious Levee district, who worked in tandem with his mentor and junior alderman, Michael "Hinky Dink" Kenna.

Alderman Coughlin's contribution to the world of music was nothing less (or more) than first-class kitsch, but it originated with one of Chicago's greatest bumbling boondogglers, and therefore the Levee, and the Everleighs with sarcastic grins, played it until guests begged the bands to stop. The prosaic refrain ran—

> Dear Midnight of Love,
>   Why did we meet?
> Dear Midnight of Love,
>   Your face is so sweet.
> Pure as the angels above,
>   Surely again we shall speak,
> Loving only as doves,
>   Dear Midnight of Love.

Bathhouse John and Hinky Dink were the epitome of corruption in Chicago. Totally unscrupulous ward bosses that they were, they raised graft, kickbacks, and payoffs to a high art under the equally corrupt mayoral regimes of Fred Busse and Carter Harrison. From the moment they decided to root themselves in the Levee, the Everleigh sisters knew full well the cost and the contacts. They would pay an average of $10,000 a year in protection, plus offering their spa free to any city or state legislator Bathhouse or Hinky Dink wanted wined, dined, and sexually edified. Between 1900 and 1911, these payoffs, calculated the ever-business Ada, would

The lavishly appointed music room inside the Everleigh Club.

cost the sisters an overall total of a quarter of a million dollars.

The go-between from the sisters to the alderman was Big Jim Colosimo, a 230-pound giant who began as a streetsweeper and, by virtue of his marriage to whorehouse madam Victoria Moresco, rose to the position of overall crime lord of the Levee and finally Chicago. (It was Colosimo who brought Johnny Torrio and Al Capone to Chicago, two men who would begin the bloodiest gang wars in American history and would be the original organizers of the present-day crime syndicate.)

Colosimo was on hand if any problem arose that the sisters could not handle—a rogue detective from another district demanding a payoff, a legislator insisting he receive a stipend of each week's take rather than waiting to be bribed through the official Bathhouse and Hinky Dink channels. "You sit tight," Big Jim would always assure the sisters on the phone. "I'll be right over." Minutes later Colosimo would appear winded on the front steps of the Everleigh Club, juggling jars of spaghetti, his own home-made tomato sauce, and Parmesan cheese. He would huff his way to the club's kitchen, and, while

Chicago's underworld boss, Big Jim Colosimo, who provided the strong-arm protection for the Everleigh sisters. Shown here with his showgirl-wife Dale Winter. (UPI)

Minna and Ada poured out their problems to him, he would prepare, in exactly nine minutes, his special spaghetti. The Everleighs hated spaghetti, particularly in the afternoon because it would spoil their dinner, but they sat at the kitchen table with Colosimo and "swallowed the clothesline," as Minna put it.

Colosimo would then tell the sisters that they had nothing to worry about, he would take care of the extorting cops and politicians, and, still gulping his spaghetti—he could eat spaghetti any time, all the time, even for breakfast—Big Jim would grab the phone and

set things right, roaring his authority into the mouthpiece. That authority had plenty of bite; Colosimo's army of hoodlums would break legs or arms, put a bullet into a man if necessary, on a moment's notice from their chieftain.

Through the years, the Everleigh Club was not free from bloodshed, despite all the precautionary efforts of the sisters, the powerful influence of Coughlin and Kenna, and Big Jim's strong arm. An enraged wife shot her husband to death after she found him aboard a New York-bound train with an Everleigh courtesan; they had just left the club. A butler shot and killed his employer on the club's steps one night, calmly telling his fatally wounded master, "You can afford the Everleighs but can't pay me my salary, sir?" The son of a railroad magnate got drunk in the club one night and staggered over to a cheap seraglio run by the notorious Vic (for Victoria) Shaw. The wealthy youth died at Shaw's, some said of morphine poisoning so that he could be rolled without trouble, and his body was smuggled back into the Everleigh Club, planted there so that the sisters and their girls would be labeled killers, especially to the coveted carriage trade. Ada and Minna were too fast for their ruthless competitors, however, and had the body taken back to Shaw's, then called the police, who found the corpse under Victoria Shaw's bed!

The average customer, however, had little doubt that he was as safe in the Everleigh Club as in his own mansion, with more inventive luxuries to please the senses than even home could offer. In every room a fountain would go on periodically, spraying perfume into the already incense-laden air. Gold spittoons, cleaned hourly by the army of Everleigh servants, gleamed next to every enormous bed.

Plays, musicals, and reviews would be performed by the talented and beautiful Everleigh maidens in the many parlors—the Gold, Copper, Red, Rose, Green, and Blue rooms. Customers would sit in chairs and on grand divans upholstered in silk damask and be surrounded by curtains of golden silk. Scores of canaries chirped in gold cages as the sisters greeted each guest, taking him into a private parlor alone, asking him what his pleasure might be. If the customer sought good food and superb wine, a dining area with a lovely dinner companion would be arranged. If female companionship of a different sort was required, Ada or Minna, not the guest, would select the girl for the hour or evening. Of course, the prices for that era of nickel beer and ten-cent-a-shot whiskey were staggering. The cheapest bottle of wine was $12, that of champagne, $20. No customer could go up the grand staircase to bedroom pleasures for less than $50 an hour. And those spending only $50 were not really welcomed into the club again. The cost of an overnight stay was $500 and up, depending upon the services sought.

One department store owner entertained a group of friends, dinner and spirits only, at a cost of $1,750 with every dish an out-of-season delicacy. His check (made out to "Cash") had been discreetly endorsed by the Utopia Novelty Company, when clearing the bank a few days later. Discretion was the hallmark of the Everleigh policy. The son of the mayor visited the club one night, got tight, and left an IOU for several hundred dollars. When he awoke at home the next day, he was too embarrassed to retrieve the IOU, sending an employee to redeem the note with cash. The sisters told the messenger that they did not know the son of the mayor, and had never received an IOU from him. Not until the mayor's son called personally for the note with cash in hand, did the Everleighs turn over the IOU to him.

In each courtesan's room, mirrors formed a canopy over the huge bed. There was always a convenient bowl of firecrackers at bedside which the guests and residents could set off to heighten the ecstasy of their lovemaking. (Use of mirrors was Ada's idea, the firecrackers were dreamed up by Minna.) Since it was an age of hairy faces, the girls held contests as to which one entertained the guest with the longest beard. Rulers were kept on hand in all the rooms for this purpose. As writer Alson J. Smith crudely put it, ". . . stories that the rulers were for other measurements are without foundation."

When the girls were idle, the sisters, especially Ada, encouraged her charges to read extensively from the library, which offered several thousand volumes on the most learned of subjects. "Maintain and improve your minds, girls," Ada would counsel.

An old but apt canard about Minna's sense of humor was the story she delighted in telling that involved a housepainter, a nervous type who had been called to the bordello to touch up some spots in the Red Room, where Minna had found several unsightly handprints on the wall above a bed. The painter shuffled into the kitchen, head down, not wishing to focus upon any of the delights the club had to offer, telling the Everleigh sister that he was a God-fearing, married man, and had only shown up because the boss ordered him to do so at the risk of losing his job.

"All right, all right," Minna said abruptly. "Come upstairs and I'll show you where a man put his hand last night."

The painter looked up, blushing beet red. "If—if it's all the same to you, ma'am, I'd just as soon have a glass of beer."

Newsmen weren't so shy. Reporters from Chicago's then many daily papers flocked to the club and were warmly treated by the sisters, who would relate the anecdotes of the night before, without, of course, ever mentioning the names of participants. One reporter, Ben Atwill, showed up in the early afternoon, letting himself in the back way. Standing outside a reception area, he peeked around a heavy drape to see Ada marching up and down in front of her charges, giving forth with her daily instructions: "Remember, girls, be polite and forget what you are here for. Stay respectable by all means. I want you girls to be proud that you are in the Everleigh Club. And remember, we will not tolerate the rough element. If an imposter sneaks by us and you discover you've got a clerk on a holiday or a man without a checkbook, excuse yourself politely and tell us. We'll handle it."

The reporters never had a checkbook, but they were given the best wine and food the club had to offer, at no charge, by the charming sisters, who had learned early that good press kept them in business. To that end, Minna published an expensive brochure, complete with photos of the illustrious establishment, and these were discreetly distributed among the male population of the upper crust. Everywhere the sisters went in Chicago they traveled in style. Their carriage was the most luxuriously appointed in the city with drivers bedecked in green velvet livery.

Though they always dressed in fashionable but modest streetwear when going about town, the Everleighs always took care to have one of their most beautiful girls accompany them. In summer, the elegantly attired girl would sit in the open carriage waiting for her employers to finish their banking or shopping, and serving as an excellent advertisement for their club.

Sunday evenings were reserved for the girls and their steady male admirers; the Everleighs called it "Beau Night." On such occasions, the sweethearts of the girls dutifully lined up at the club entrance bearing flowers and gifts and were admitted to their lovers' rooms with only nominal charges for food and drink—the Everleigh sisters certainly had no equals in the field of soft-heartedness.

Though gambling was allowed at the club—there was a room for poker and roulette—the sisters frowned on such activities. "Admitting that women are a risk," Minna complained, "I still say that men prefer dice, cards, or a wheel of fortune to a frolic with a charmer. I have watched men, embraced in the arms of the most bewitching sirens in our club, dump their feminine flesh from their laps for a roll of the dice." Minna went on to stipulate that all customers, whatever their station, were limited to a half hour of gambling, and this was strictly enforced. "Besides," Minna quipped, "gambling is illegal."

The more analytical Ada specified the perfect customer as "a married man in his fifties, well-to-do, a social leader, educated, mannered, respected." When the club closed years later Ada still clung to this perception: "If it weren't for the married men we couldn't have carried on at all and if it weren't for the cheating married women we could have made another million."

Married men and women, however, did not contribute as mightily to the downfall of the Everleigh sisters, and the entire red-light district, for that matter, as did the rip-snorting evangelists of the years just after the turn of the century. Religious leaders had long plagued the politicians to pull down the sex resorts of the Levee. W.T. Stead, the English reformer, visited the area in 1893 and wrote a book exposing the riotous Levee and its hundreds of red-light houses, an area where anything and everything

Chicago alderman John J. "Bathhouse" Coughlin, who served forty-six years on the city council representing the sinful First Ward and wielded the political clout that kept the Everleigh Club open for more than a decade.

went on and without police interference. Stead's book *If Christ Came to Chicago* was a huge bestseller, but it changed little.

"Do you want these girls in the district moving into the residential areas, next door to your families, your kids?" asked Hinky Dink Kenna, as a way of threatening reformers with worse prospects. "I guess not," added Bathhouse John. "We might as well keep 'em all down on the Levee where we can keep an eye on 'em." What Kenna and Coughlin meant, of course, was that they had no intention of parting with the most lucrative racket in the city; vice paid big, in the millions, and they intended to have and keep their share.

Lucy Page Gaston, a tobacco reformer, was well known to the Everleighs. She visited the club regularly in 1907. Minna was interrupted while talking to her head chef one day in the kitchen by an upset Miss Gaston, who rushed in from a reception area shouting, "Minna! Your girls are going straight to hell! You must stop them!"

"What can I do?" Minna replied in a pleasant voice.

"Make them quit smoking cigarettes!"

Another reformer in the Elmer Gantry tradition stormed into the club one night, and, much to the dismay of the sisters, the girls, and their nervous guests, fell to his knees in the main reception hall, praying aloud in soulful cries for "these poor damned souls" to be saved.

Ada calmly approached the man. "Why have you come here, sir?"

"Because there is a doubt in my heart," the zealot said, tears streaming down his cheeks. "I will experience for the first and last time in my life the great sins that are committed here in order that I speak with authority to my followers."

Giving him a knowing nod, Ada helped the man to his feet and motioned to one of her most attractive girls. The girl agreed to allow the reformer a special low fee of $25, and the couple went upstairs. Entering the Green Room, the reformer handed the girl a fifty-dollar bill.

"I'll have to get change," the courtesan said and left the man alone. She returned a few minutes later to find the reformer anxiously pacing the floor, rubbing his chin in deep thought.

"What's the matter?" asked the girl.

"I've changed my mind. Can't we just sit and talk for an hour or two?"

"Certainly," answered the girl, sitting down in a plush love seat, "but in that case you don't get any change."

Still the reformers heightened their blustering barrage against the wide-open whorehouses of the Levee, ninety percent of their attacks made squarely against the Everleigh Club. The most spectacular of these was made by the firebrand orator and religious crusader Gipsey Smith, who gathered about him on the evening of October 18, 1909, an immense crowd of between three thousand and twelve thousand followers. Chanting prayers and lifting their heads heavenward, the great throng marched by torchlight from the Seventh Regiment Armory at Wentworth Avenue and Thirty-fourth Street to Twenty-second Street, Smith in the lead with a booming Salvation Army band of a hundred tooting, drumming souls. As the religious crowds rippled through the neighborhoods, thousands more swarmed into their ranks, swelling the number of marchers to more than twenty-five thousand people. They marched into a dead Levee. All the doors were closed, the windows shuttered, the red lights turned off. Not a whore or a pimp stirred, except a few cowering cribsters who hid in basement doorways.

Holding a torch on high, Gipsey Smith walked to the steps of the Everleigh Club, knelt, and led the throng in a mass recital of the Lord's Prayer. "It gave me the very creeps," said whoremaster Ike Bloom as he hid behind an upstairs window of Ed Weiss's bordello, which was next door to the Everleigh Club. Oddly enough, the Everleigh girls in the second- and third-floor rooms, the windows of their rooms covered by heavy drapes, knelt in those rooms and prayed with Gipsey Smith and his legions. The evangelist then leaped to his feet, raised his hands, and led the crowds in singing "Where Is My Wandering Boy Tonight?" and "Nearer My God to Thee." Then, with Smith still leading, the crowds marched from the Levee to the Alhambra Theatre for a revival meeting.

A half hour following the departure of the reformers, the Levee sprang again to life. Windows and doors flew open; red lights flashed on; trollops, hoodlums, pimps, and gamblers spilled into the streets. Instead of ruining business that night, Gipsey Smith had given the Levee the greatest single evening of trade it ever experienced; thousands of neighborhood youths had followed his marchers into the area, and when the evangelists quit the district they had lingered on to patronize the whorehouses and gambling dens.

Minna Everleigh stood in the reception hall of her club trying to handle the crush that night, smugly telling a reporter, "We were certainly glad to get all this business, but I'm sorry to see so many nice young men down here for the first time."

The pressure built up with the formation of dozens of civic groups, sparked by Smith's crusade, all of them badgering Mayor Carter Harrison to close down the Levee, and, in particular, run the Everleigh sisters out of Chicago. He quietly resisted. None of it was news to him. Then, in 1911, when a special commission on vice was convened, Harrison was moved to act.

The commission reported scandalous conditions. Hundreds of brothels operated in Chicago and with plenty of police protection. There were more than five thousand working prostitutes, and these, like the brothels, were mostly centered in the Levee. The crime emanating from this district, from jack rolling to murder, from gambling to robbery, was awesome, cited the commission's report. Then, on a walking tour one night while showing some visiting dignitaries his city, Harrison was grabbed by his long coattails on Clark Street by a fee-desperate whore who attempted to drag him inside a cheap brothel. A few nights later the mayor watched bug-eyed as Vic Shaw rode down Michigan Avenue in a car fitted out with garish electric red lights. The madam sat perched on the rolled top of the car in a gown that showed most of her breasts. In fact, as the car moved down the stately, sacrosanct boulevard, Victoria Shaw's breasts inconveniently popped from their skimpy halter whenever the car hit a raised cobblestone, the painted hussy stuffing her flesh back into her dress with a carefree laugh. The final straw came when the mayor found Minna Everleigh's handsome brochure advertising the Everleigh Club sitting on his desk. (It was later contended that one of the sisters' Levee enemies, and these were legion, had bribed a city hall clerk to smuggle the brochure into the mayor's office.) Harrison roared for his administrators. "They've got to go," he bellowed as he waved the Everleigh brochure on high.

Harrison gave his historic order on October 24, 1911. He later wrote in his autobiography, *Stormy Years:* "The Everleigh Club was to be closed and kept closed during my term of office! It was perhaps the most widely-advertised bawdy-house in the world, I have been told the

most perfectly appointed. In its exploitation the terrible pair of sisters had published a small brochure giving a full description of its attractive features with full page half-tone illustration. . . . These were distributed far and wide, wherever existed a potential clientage. [Actually there were only about five hundred copies of the brochure available at the time Harrison popped the covers of the publication.] The book carried a caption to the effect that for the visitor to Chicago there were two outstanding points of interest; the Union Stockyards with the packing houses and the Everleigh Club."

Police Chief McWeeny received the mayor's order, but he refused to act on it. He called Coughlin and Kenna, telling them the disastrous

Michael "Hinky Dink" Kenna, First Ward powerhouse and mentor to the bumbling Coughlin. He challenged Mayor Harrison on the order to close the Everleigh Club.

Al Capone, who had the last, gruesome laugh on the Everleigh sisters.

"I really mean it, McWeeny!" Harrison shouted over the phone, exasperated.

"Yes, sir." The chief hung up, and then began passing the order down through his command, but he made sure the process was slow-going. Captain Wheeler, head of the Levee District, delayed as long as possible before assigning the order to a lieutenant to carry out. When Harrison heard of Wheeler's refusal to personally carry out the order, he went into a desk-kicking rage. "From then on," Harrison vowed, "he [Wheeler] was on my black list."

While the death rattle for the district sounded, news of the Everleigh Club's condemnation was leaked to the press, and afternoon editions soon bannered the story. The thousands of denizens in the Levee waited in shock.

"It must be a joke," said Vic Shaw.

"The Everleigh Club?" asked an incredulous Ike Bloom. "That'll be the last joint to go, not the first."

news. To the boondoggling aldermen this meant the end of the Levee and the end of their fabulous riches. Kenna, the boldest of the bold, marched into Harrison's office some hours later. He held up a copy of the mayoral order.

"On the square, mayor," Kenna said, "does this go? For keeps?"

Harrison stared the feisty little man down. "As long as I am mayor."

"Okay!" roared Kenna, tossing the order with disdain onto Harrison's desk and stomping from the office.

Harrison knew where Kenna had gotten the order and called up Chief McWeeny, asking his top policeman why he hadn't moved on the order.

"I just couldn't believe it," mumbled the chief.

"You can believe it now."

"Do you really mean it, mayor, or are you just upset—"

A cameo of Ada Everleigh when she began her career as a madam in Omaha in 1898. (Terrance Dureen)

Newsmen flocked to the Everleighs. Minna greeted them at the door sipping a glass of champagne. "Yes, yes, boys," she said calmly, "the mayor's order is real. I called Captain Harding of the Twenty-second Street Station, and he told me so." The reporters hung their heads in silence as if their benefactress were a tragic queen abdicating a great throne. "It's all right, boys," Minna went on, still sipping the champagne. "I don't worry. . . . What the mayor says goes, and I'm not sore about it. I was never a knocker and the police can't change my disposition."

That night hundreds of the club's most loyal customers flocked in to bid the Everleighs a final good-bye. The wine cellar was thrown open and the wildest bash the club ever gave tooted and hollered its hubbub into the dawn. By then the Everleigh sisters had packed up their exquisite clothing and jewels, and their precious heirlooms. They gave their girls and servants six months' pay and wished them luck. Movers hired by the sisters would arrive later to begin carting away the furnishings to be stored, though the sisters took some of it away with them, such as the gold-leaf piano.

Early on October 25, 1911, a detective arrived, hat in hand. Ada and Minna met him in the grand reception hall. "If it was us," the cop said in an apologetic voice, "you know how it would be. But we got our orders."

The rest of the Levee began to close up shop, too, brothel owners and managers not waiting for a police order. In a few short months the Levee was completely closed down, the red lights all turned out. But Minna Everleigh (reportedly against her sister's wishes) had the last word—or attack. She wrote out a statement, later published by the Chicago *Examiner*, in which she soundly attacked Kenna and Coughlin, her crooked aldermanic protectors, saying that the Everleighs had paid out more than $100,000 to stay open during their palmy years, and this was paid to the aldermen through their messenger, Sol Friedman. The aldermen tried a further shakedown, Minna insisted, when they sent around another lackey, Ed Little, asking for $20,000 to fix the mayor so the club would reopen. Minna had refused. More than $15 million in graft had been paid by the

brothel owners of the Levee since its inception, the Everleigh sister concluded.

But the recriminations mattered little. The sisters were off on a six-month European vacation. When they returned to America they settled in New York, buying a mansion on West Seventieth Street in Manhattan under the name Lester. Here they settled down with their priceless furniture, statuary, and paintings. They had a million in cash, half again as much in jewels, and, in their wall safe, more than $500,000 in IOUs from the most prominent men in the country. Not one of these notes was ever redeemed. To their sedate but curious high-society neighbors, the Everleigh sisters gave out the lie that they had inherited everything from their grandfather who had struck it rich in the California Gold Rush of 1849, and it was he who had collected the exotic paintings and statuary, which they kept for sentimental reasons. But the lies were harmless.

The sisters were always a source of amusement and nostalgia whenever a Chicago newsman appeared at their New York City doorstep to relive old times. The Everleighs gave a party every July 5 for decades for that very purpose, inviting journalist friends and some of their one-time girls, then in high social positions. On these occasions, a bevy of servants would serve champagne and a sumptuous meal, while the sisters sat reveling like queens, each adorned with $100,000 worth of glittering jewels. To the outside world they remained two retired spinsters named Lester, who grew old inside a charming mansion. They even held regular poetry meetings. The Lester Poetry Circle became quite the literary event of the week along West Seventieth Street.

Ada and Minna Everleigh lived long lives. Minna died on September 16, 1948, at the age of seventy-one. On her deathbed she turned to an old newsman and whispered, "We never hurt anybody, did we? We never robbed widows and we made no false representations, did we? Any crimes they attributed to us were the outcries of jealousy. We tried to get along honestly. Our business was unholy but everybody accepted it. What of it?"

Minna body's was shipped to Roanoke, Virginia, by Ada, who took a little cottage nearby

Minna Everleigh in her Omaha whorehouse as a "working" madam. Her bedroom reflects the rich taste of the "Scarlet Sisters." (Terrance Dureen)

The gilded bar in the Omaha bordello operated by the Everleigh sisters. Ada (shown at center) pitches a drunken client. (Terrance Dureen)

Chicago crime czar Al Capone, who "scammed" the shrewd Ada Everleigh. (UPI)

and waited for her own end, which came at the age of ninety-four on January 3, 1960. She was buried next to her sister under a tombstone marked "Lester."

There had been another sister who had died years before Ada and Minna. The Everleighs ordered a great tomb built to house her body. There was also a brother, "a ne'er-do-well," as Ada once described him bitterly. The sisters had bought this brother a handsome farm in the Midwest where he lived with his eleven children. "He isn't good for anything but raising children," Ada had once complained, and then added sor-

rowfully, "but I can't talk because I'm not even fit for that."

The Everleigh Club went long before its proprietors, smashed beneath the wrecker's ball in 1933. The wonderful club furnishings were auctioned off at Minna's death in 1948; the gold-leaf $15,000 piano was sold for $90, its buyer later scrapping it because he thought it jinxed. The Everleigh fortune itself, however, remained intact throughout the lifetime of the sisters. Even during the stockmarket crash of 1929 and the Depression-ridden 1930s, Ada Everleigh managed not only to hold on to their fortune through her shrewd investments but to almost double their holdings. There was one investment, however, where the businesslike Ada Everleigh had been suckered as easily as the greenest rube who ever stumbled into her club.

On the afternoon of May 12, 1920, Ada Everleigh received a call in New York from a man she had never met, but a man whose name she had heard in conversations with her one-time enforcer, Big Jim Colosimo. The caller was Al Capone phoning from Chicago to tell Ada through great sobs that Big Jim was dead, that he had been killed the day before.

"I want you to know, Ada," said a weeping Capone, "that Johnny Torrio and me are gonna do everything to get the guy who shot down Big Jim."

"Such as?"

"Well, Ada," Capone went on, his voice still choking, "we're getting up a fund to pay a lot of guys to look for the killer. Will you contribute?"

"Yes," came Ada Everleigh's reply, "put us down for $10,000."

She sent the money that night to Al Capone, the man who had actually shot and killed Big Jim Colosimo.

FAZEKAS, MRS. JULIUS

Murderer ■ (? −1929)

Little is known of Mrs. Julius Fazekas, a widowed midwife, before she came to the small village of Nagyrev, Hungary, in about 1911, except that she manifested criminal tendencies at every turn. The village and its neighboring hamlet of Tiszakurt was a peasant community situated about sixty miles southeast of Budapest on the river Tisza, a tributary of the Danube, with about 1,400 inhabitants, most of whom lived in neat whitewashed cottages and tended small gardens. Oddly, there was not a single church anywhere near the twin villages, or a hospital. Trained nurses were unheard of, let alone a doctor. Midwives serviced the medical needs of the simpleminded, superstitious residents, and Frau Fazekas was the primary midwife of the community.

In the early years of her residence in Nagyrev, Frau Fazekas busied herself with abortions; she was charged with ten of these illegal operations from 1911 to 1921 but always managed to be acquitted. In the light of horrible revelations a decade later, it is a wonder that Mrs. Fazekas even bothered with such poor-paying activities; her most lucrative business was derived from the poisons she prepared and sold, for the midwife was in the murder business, a thriving concern subscribed to by almost all the villagers and brought about by the advent of World War I.

With the absence of husbands and the coming of prisoners of war to camps near the village, the women experienced a sexual revolution that rocked the five-hundred-year history of their district and harkened back to their primitive Magyar culture. The gradual deterioration of morals in the female community eventually led to wholesale promiscuity, with the wives, ages twenty-five to seventy-one, taking on two and three lovers. By the time their husbands returned from the war they were unwanted men, the wives by then loathing the concept of conjugal life. In their mindless reasoning—and the area was about thirty percent illiterate—the only solution was to get rid of the husbands. The women flocked to Mrs. Fazekas for a remedy, and she had one ready-made.

Fazekas supplied doses of arsenic to the women for the comparatively small amount of between one hundred and five hundred penges. (A penge at that time equaled about eight cents, so the going price for murder was from $8 to $40.) The poison was easily obtained by the midwife; she merely boiled off the arsenic from flypaper which she bought in wholesale lots. According to one report, "The grocer of a neighboring town was able to later testify that more flypapers were sold in the midwife's villages than in the rest of the country."

The first known poisoning was in 1914, that of Peter Hegedus, a farmer living near Nagyrev. Dozens, then hundreds more followed as the murder mania spread. Wives murdered their husbands not only for the sake of lovers, but to obtain land; poisoned fathers, mothers, children, and, if the murderesses, numbering more than fifty, took issue among themselves, they attempted to poison one another. The province came to be known as "the murder district" of Hungary, and its inhabitants were to be labeled the "Angel Makers of Nagyrev." Behind all of it was the evil Mrs. Fazekas.

The midwife seldom spoke in public. She was a tall, heavyset woman with black brows and large, dark staring eyes, and who dressed in heavy shawls and long skirts. The untimely deaths began to mount in the villages but police seemed oblivious, even when several anonymous letters notified authorities that widespread murder was being committed. When officials did look into these claims, they discovered a death certificate properly made out for each one of those suspected of being poisoned. The cause of death was listed as pneumonia, heart disease, or senile decay. Investigations were halted. (It was later learned that the minor official who automatically signed the death certificates at the instructions of Mrs. Fazekas was the midwife's cousin.)

But the anonymous letters to the authorities continued. Then, in July 1929, a choir director in Tiszakurt insisted that Mrs. Ladislaus Szabo had served him poisoned wine, that he would

have died had it not been for the efforts of a visiting doctor who pumped his stomach. Then another man, an invalid Mrs. Szabo was caring for, hobbled to the police station to claim his "nurse" was poisoning him. Mrs. Szabo was arrested, and she quickly implicated Mrs. Bukenoveski who was also arrested and promptly confessed that, yes, she had purchased arsenic from Mrs. Fazekas in 1924 and had used the poison to kill her seventy-year-old mother. The woman went on proudly to tell shocked police that she had carried the body of her murdered mother in a wheelbarrow to the river Tisza and dumped the body into the water at night. The corpse was later found and the death attributed to drowning. The corpse of Mrs. Bukenoveski's mother was exhumed and the arsenic found.

Police went to the cottage of Midwife Fazekas and took her in for questioning. She insisted that she was not only ignorant of such horrid goings-on but totally innocent. Officers shrewdly set the midwife free and assigned agents to follow her. The police watched as Fazekas returned to her village, scurrying frantically from house to house to warn the female inhabitants, her customers, of danger. The police arrested everyone the midwife visited.

Two days later officers burst into the cottage of Mrs. Fazekas, one of them later describing it as "an evil-smelling den," with huge stacks of flypaper in the corners of every room. They discovered the midwife waiting for them, sitting calmly before the crackling fireplace, a fat, smiling, Buddha-like woman who nodded in the direction of the officers, then put a large chalice to her lips and gulped down poison. She was dead within a few hours. Her disciples did not escape punishment with such ease.

Thirty-eight women were arrested as a result of Fazekas' contacts with the murder ring, twenty-six of these later tried in Szolnok and sentenced, eight given death, seven life in prison, and the rest long prison terms. The statements of these women on trial horrified the civilized world as they blatantly admitted mass killings. (Estimates of the number of victims ranged from fifty to the more realistic number of three hundred.)

The most evil of the lot was the chief accomplice and disciple of Mrs. Fazekas, Susanna Olah, called Susi, or Aunt Susi, by her clients. She operated in Nagyrev a sort of franchise of the Fazekas murder business, dispensing arsenic, which her patrons called "Aunt Susi's Inheritance Powders." The women purchasing arsenic from Aunt Susi expressed genuine fear at her presence in court, claiming that her eyes "glowed ruby red at night," and telling the jury that she kept scores of poisonous snakes and lizards in her hut and these she had trained to creep into the beds of those who might inform on her.

Susi's sister, Lydia Olah, a misshapen crone of seventy, defied the charges of the court. According to *Posslyednia Novosti*, a Russian daily published in Paris, Lydia cried out during her trial, "We are not assassins! We did not stab our husbands. We did not hang them or drown them either! They died from poison and this was a pleasant death for them!" She was later condemned to death.

Hostility was expressed by all the defendants, along with what appeared to be a complete lack of moral sense. Defendant Rose Glyba was asked by the presiding judge if she knew the Ten Commandments. "No!" shouted Rose.

"Do you know the commandment 'Thou Shalt Not Kill'?"

"I never heard of it!" Rose shouted back to the bench and sat down angrily.

Each poisoner gave different reasons for her killings. Rosalie Sebestyen and Rosa Holyba admitted putting arsenic bought from Midwife Fazekas into their husbands' meals because their men "bored" them. They both received life sentences. Mrs. Julius Csaba claimed that she poisoned her husband because he was "always drunk and brutal." Strangely, the court interpreted this feeble excuse for murder as "extenuating circumstances" and gave Mrs. Csaba only fifteen years.

Some, like Mrs. Maria Szendi, exhibited a kind of warped early-day women's liberation attitude, screaming that she had poisoned Mr. Szendi because "he always had his own way. It's terrible the way men have all the power."

Mrs. Marie Kardos displayed a cold-blooded temperament when recalling for the court how she poisoned not only her husband, but her lover, too, when she grew tired of him. Mrs. Kardos, a wealthy and sophisticated woman by the standards of the village, next found herself burdened with her sickly twenty-three-year-old son. The forty-five-year-old mother gave the equivalent of $500 to Mrs. Fazekas for her special triple-strength arsenic, and this, in the form of medicine, Mrs. Kardos fed to her son. The less-than-devoted mother moved her son's bed outside one warm fall day, then brought the dying youth some soup. "I gave him some more poison," said Mrs. Kardos in court. "Suddenly I remembered how splendidly my boy used to sing in church, so I said, 'Sing, my boy! Sing my favorite song!' He sang it with his lovely clear voice, then suddenly he cried out, gripped his stomach, gasped, and was dead." Mrs. Kardos, having finished stunning the court with the telling of this incredible scene, reached down in the witness chair, pulled up the hem of her black skirt slightly, and adjusted her black silk stockings at the ankles, then brushed her patent leather shoes, part of the new outfit she had purchased for her day in court. She just as unconcernedly primped her dress while listening to the court condemn her to death.

Lydia Csery was also convicted of murder, killing her parents with Mrs. Fazekas' "remedies." Her father was heard by neighbors to scream to his dying wife, "May the Devil take Lydia! She has brewed us tea which has killed us!"

Maria Varga was found guilty of poisoning her husband, Laszlo, the first Hungarian soldier blinded in World War I. Mrs. Varga, forty-one at the time of her trial, admitted that she had taken on a youthful lover, Michael Ambrus, and had had sex with him repeatedly in her house while her blind husband raged about helplessly, knowing the couple were present. Mrs. Varga decided to rid herself of her troublesome spouse by going to Mrs. Fazekas, the "widow-maker of Nagyrev," and obtaining arsenic which she added to the blind war hero's food. He died in agony within twenty-four hours.

Though Mrs. Varga denied her guilt to her dying day in prison, she did tell the court that she saw her husband's ghost for years after his death: "He stalked about in the courtyard, tapping his white stick against the windows while

Mrs. Lipka had murdered her entire family to obtain real estate, and, by the time she was brought to trial, she was one of the richest women in the district. All she thought of was her land, even after she was found guilty and sentenced to death. "When can I go home?" she absentmindedly asked her lawyer. "They will auction off all my property while I am here." In her elderly fancies, Juliane Lipka believed she would be set free to live out her life with a young lover. According to one report, "this harridan hopes of marrying a young fellow of twenty-four despite her age and the fact that she is black-browed, pock-marked, squat and shapeless, with a most evil expression."

Mrs. Lipka, along with the other seven killers who were condemned, was hanged, her body put on display. The presence of these decomposing corpses swaying in the wind did much to bankrupt the murder business in the troubled Hungarian province of Theisswinkel.

Juliane Lipka, one of the many mass-murderesses of Nagyrev, Hungary.

his sightless sockets stared at me." The prosecution proved that five years later, having tired of her lover, Mrs. Varga poisoned Michael Ambrus to death.

Next to the disastrous Mrs. Fazekas and Susanna Olah, the worst offender of those standing trial was Juliane Lipka, then age sixty-six. Mrs. Lipka confessed to poisoning seven persons from 1914 to well into the 1920s. Her victims included her stepmother, aunt, brother, sister-in-law, and husband, Paul, whom she poisoned on Christmas Eve, dosing his traditional holiday drink of rum and tea. Ever the thoughtful neighbor, Mrs Lipka also helped Maria Koteles, the woman next door, to rid herself of an obstreperous spouse. "I was sorry for the wretched woman," stated the simpleminded Lipka, "and so I gave her a bottle of the poison and told her that if nothing else helped her marriage to try that."

FENAYROU, GABRIELLE

Murderer ■ (1850– ?)

To save her father's pharmacy in Paris, Gabrielle Gibon married Marin Fenayrou, a druggist, though she found the man repulsive and considered the marriage one of convenience. The marriage proved a mistake. Although Fenayrou first built the business up, he tired of his responsibilities and took to excessive drinking and gambling. Another assistant was hired, twenty-one-year-old Louis Aubert, with whom Gabrielle fell in love. Their affair lasted for eight years before Fenayrou began to be suspicious; since the husband lived in an almost permanent alcoholic stupor he noticed little.

When Aubert decided to marry another young woman, Gabrielle, bitter at being abandoned to her drunken husband, went to Fenayrou, confessed her infidelity, and then encouraged the man to kill her estranged lover.

Aubert's body, stabbed twice and the skull crushed, was found in the Seine by fishermen on May 28, 1882. It was common knowledge that Madame Fenayrou and Aubert had been lovers, and when the police questioned Gabrielle she quickly admitted her part in the murder, saying, "I am, in fact, a criminal. . . . I have done nothing but lie. . . . I have had enough. . . . I have suffered too much."

Marin Fenayrou had suffered, too, he said at his trial. He recounted how he had killed his wife's lover, saying to Aubert before stabbing him in the chest, "It is by the heart that you made me suffer and it is by the heart that you will die!"

The husband was sentenced to death; Gabrielle was sent to Clermont Prison for life. She was pardoned in 1903, at the same time as Gabrielle Bompard, who had been her only friend in prison.

FISHER, MARGARET

Thief ■ (1689– ?)

In September, 1722, a low-life thief and prostitute, Margaret Fisher, enticed a visiting Scottish businessman, one Daniel M'Donald, into the back room of a London pub, where she got him drunk and then filched thirteen gold guineas from his pockets. When sober, M'Donald and some officers found Fisher and brought her to the Old Bailey for trial.

The woman was convicted of stealing and sentenced to be put to death. She claimed to be pregnant, and upon examination, was proved correct. Margaret Fisher was pardoned.

FORCE, JULIA

Murderer ■ (1860– ?)

Insanity was obviously in control of Julia Force's mind on February 25, 1893, when she retrieved her father's Civil War pistol from the attic and shot her sister Minnie because Minnie's loud humming annoyed her. This berserk southern belle then shot and killed another sister, Florence, because the woman was "a tiresome invalid."

A jury hearing the case in Atlanta, Georgia, considered Julia sane and convicted her. She was sent to prison for life.

FROMME, LYNETTE ALICE

Assassin ■ (1950–)

A fringe member of the Manson family, Lynette Fromme, called "Squeaky," shaved her head, carved a cross on her bald pate, and sank into the drug world when Manson and others were sent to jail in 1969. Apparently desiring the same kind of notoriety gleaned by her lunatic hero Manson, Squeaky Fromme wedged into a large crowd greeting President Gerald Ford in Sacramento, California, on September 5, 1975.

Wearing a long robe and thrusting forth a .45 automatic not more than two feet from the President, she aimed but the weapon did not go off. Larry Buendorf, a courageous Secret Service agent, jumped in front of the President and grabbed the automatic. As she was being escorted from the scene, Fromme yelled, "This country is a mess! That man is not your Pres-

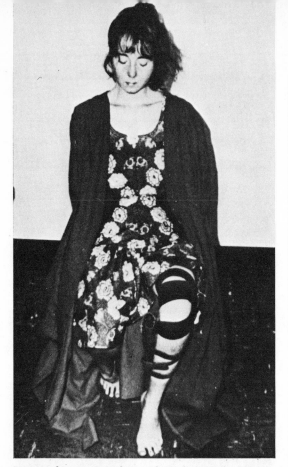

Manson hippie turned presidential assassin, Lynette "Squeaky" Fromme in custody.

ident! He's not a public servant. . . . It didn't go off. Can you believe it? It didn't go off."

She was sent to prison for life on December 17, 1975.

FULLAM, AUGUSTA FAIRFIELD

Murderer ■ (1876–1914)

Augusta Fullam, the thirty-five-year-old wife of Lieutenant Edward Fullam, a military accounts examiner in Agra, India, began an affair with Dr. Henry Lovell William Clark after meeting him at a military ball in 1911.

Clark, a forty-two-year-old physician in the Indian Subordinate Medical Service, told the marriage-weary Augusta that he found his wife repugnant and his four children nuisances. The Clarks were Eurasians. He loved only the beauteous Mrs. Fullam.

Not long after their love affair started, Augusta and Clark began a lengthy correspondence which would later clearly implicate them in murder. Clark himself wrote odd and contradictory notes to his wife when on assignment elsewhere in India, one of which read—

> I am fed up with your low disgusting ways, for I am quite sure you don't care a damn what becomes of me. With fond love and kisses to self, and the rest at home, I remain,
>
> Your affectionate husband,
> H. L. Clark

By early fall 1911 the situation had become impossible, and Mrs. Fullam had decided to kill her husband in order to live out her life in bliss with the attentive Clark. She wrote a reminder to herself on her memo pad (later found): "So the only thing is to poison the soup." Conferring with Dr. Clark, it was decided to select a poison that would simulate the effects of heatstroke. Clark provided large quantities of arsenic to Mrs. Fullam for this purpose. Though Augusta added generous amounts of the arsenic to her husband's soup, Fullam seemed to be made of iron. He got sick but survived. In desperation, Clark attended the stricken man and injected him with a dose of gelsemine (an alkaloid poison), which killed Fullam on October 19, 1911. The murderous physician then signed his victim's death certificate, giving the cause of death as "heatstroke."

There was one more person to be eliminated. The following year, the unsuspecting Mrs. Clark was attacked by four Indian natives, who broke into her bedroom on the night of November 17, 1912, and slashed her to death with swords. Clark had paid them a miserable 100 rupees for the killing (about $5 per assassin). Investigating police put Clark through a rigorous interrogation. He suddenly blurted out that he had a perfect alibi—he had been dining with

Mrs. Fullam on the night of his wife's murder.

Officers questioned Mrs. Fullam, who appeared extremely nervous. Her quarters were searched, and a large tin box was found beneath her bed. Augusta snatched the box from the hands of an officer. "That's Dr. Clark's dispatch box—you dare not touch it!" The box was opened by the officers, and inside they found more than four hundred letters Mrs. Fullam had written to Clark, all of them initialed by the co-murderer. The plot to kill their spouses was clearly spelled out in the letters; when read aloud in court, the letters served readily to condemn the pair. Also, arsenic was found in Fullam's body after it was exhumed.

Tried twice in Allahabad before a high court, both were found guilty of murdering Fullam and Mrs. Clark. After making a full confession, Clark was executed on March 26, 1913. Mrs. Augusta Fullam, who had turned "King's Evidence" in testifying against Clark, and who was pregnant with her lover's child, was sent to prison for life. She delivered the child and about a year later, on May 29, 1914, Augusta Fullam, soup poisoner, died in her cell. The cause of death, grim with irony, was heatstroke.

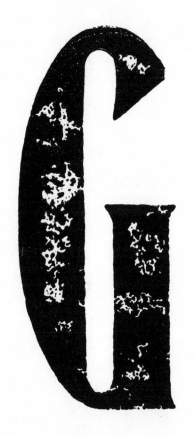

GEE, DOLLY

Embezzler ■ (1897–1978)

San Francisco never got over the shock. For five decades the city on the bay had boasted of having the first woman banker in America, one of the foremost businesswomen in the country who was honored and feted over the years as the pillar of the Chinese community in America's largest Chinatown. Chang Hor-gee, who Americanized her name to Dorothy "Dolly" Gee, was also one of the most spectacular embezzlers on record, taking more than $300,000 over a fifty-year period from San Francisco's Chinatown branch of the Bank of America. All of it, Dolly later sobbed, was done to preserve family honor.

It began in China where Dolly was born in 1897, the oldest of nine children. Her father, Charlie Gee, brought his family to San Francisco in 1901 where he opened a successful shoe store. Gee's hundreds of relatives and friends in China, knowing him to be a trustworthy sort, sent him money, quite a bit of money, to hold for them until they were able to immigrate to the United States. The banks in San Francisco at the time were not interested in deposits from Chinese. Charlie put the tens of thousands of dollars he received each year into shoe boxes.

The San Francisco earthquake and fire of 1906 forced Charlie Gee and his family to flee the city, embarking for Oakland on the ferry crammed with hysterical disaster victims. He and his family carried under their arms only shoe boxes. Once in Oakland, Gee went to the French-American bank. Since Chinese were not allowed inside, he begged a guard to have one of the bank's officers step into an alley.

When the puzzled executive appeared, Charlie Gee held out a stack of shoe boxes. "I have some money I must put into your bank. The San Francisco banks are finished."

"I dunno," mused the executive. "We don't encourage Chinese accounts."

"Please," Charlie begged. "I must put this money some place safe—in your bank."

San Francisco's banking queen, Dolly Gee of Chinatown, after her embezzlement conviction.

The executive peeked into one of the boxes and gasped. "How much money do you have here?"

"About one million dollars."

"Come with me, Mr. Gee."

With that the banking career of Charlie Gee commenced. The French-American bank not only accepted the money but made Charlie Gee an officer of the bank, in charge of all its Chinese accounts—on the provision that no Chinese ever enter its building; officials feared losing their Caucasian accounts should "streams of Chinese come through its doors." It was a simple ar-rangement. Chinese depositors gave Charlie Gee their money and he put it into his own account under his own name. He worked in a back room of the bank where he kept a set of books record-ing the proper ownership of the money. But only Charlie Gee could interpret these bank books since they were written in Chinese figures. Char-lie Gee, banker, prospered. Hundreds of Chinese people deposited their money with him in the alley next to the French-American bank each week. One night at home in 1914 the usually tire-less Charlie Gee complained about his ever in-creasing workload. His eldest daughter, Dolly, then in her third year at Oakland's Polytechnic High School, told her father that she would be more than willing to help him in the bank.

At first Charlie rebelled against the idea. That women should work outside the home was unthinkable for any traditional Chinese, but Charlie was a modern American, even though he had come from a family of bound feet. (The binding of feet in China, outlawed in 1911, was considered a mark of feminine beauty; fathers bound the feet of their little girls, crippling them, to show their status as good providers, that their women would never have to work in the fields and would remain docile and domestic. Dolly Gee's feet had been bound in China in 1900 when she was three.) A few days later Charlie agreed.

Dolly Gee went to work in the French-American Bank, or rather outside the bank, acting as a sort of door-to-door salesman in Chinatown, soliciting the accounts of merchants and businessmen. At first she met with stiff resistance; it was unheard of, keeping money in a bank run by Caucasians, let alone trusting it to a woman. But soon the tight-fisted residents of Chinatown began to have faith in Dolly, giving her their hard-earned dollars to put into "Charlie Gee's bank." The accounts controlled by Charlie Gee rose to more than $2 million, largely due to his daughter's street solicitations. The French-American Bank next opened a branch in Chinatown, placing Charlie and his energetic daughter in charge.

By 1919 successful Charlie Gee was known as the "boss of Chinatown." He traveled to China in that year, visiting Hong Kong and Canton, Dolly's birthplace. He opened the China Specie Bank in Hong Kong, and branches, especially those with importing/exporting departments, in Canton and Shanghai, before returning to San Francisco. Many Chinese who had dealt with Charlie Gee gave him money to deposit in his overseas banks. In 1929, the Bank of America took over the French-American Bank, and more and more Charlie Gee's daughter became the real genius of the Chinatown B of A bank.

The diminutive Dolly dedicated her entire life to her banking career. On a rare trip to New York in 1927, she met and married a Caucasian who remained in the shadows, his identity never disclosed. She divorced the man ten years later. "You know what broke up my marriage?" she later confided to a friend. "He wanted children and I didn't. I was selfish. The only thing I was interested in was my banking career."

And what a career it was. Over the years Dolly was repeatedly honored by the most distinguished organizations in the United States. At one fete she stated, "I find that the people put their money in the bank because of their confidence of those who work here, not because they know anything about the bank itself."

The Oriental branch of the Bank of America at 939 Grant Avenue boomed under Dolly Gee's direction, its assets jumping from $2 million to $20 million over three decades. Her father retired in 1929 and Dolly was left to run things, although Charlie Gee did show up regularly at the bank, spending a few hours each day in the accounting department where he continued to enter the day's business in his ancient Chinese figures. He died in 1956 and Dolly took over the books, also keeping the figures in Chinese.

Dolly was the empress of finance on the West Coast. Her clothes were always of the latest fashion. She drank scotch and smoked incessantly, a solid silver cigarette holder constantly clutched in her hand. At night the chic, gravel-voiced Dolly visited the posh P'ai Chiao clubs to play poker with dominoes, but her luck was always bad.

Ms. Gee's loan policy was probably the most liberal on the West Coast. According to one report, she "dished out hundreds of loans that put a financial base under half of Chinatown's enterprises during years when Chinese could not even get life insurance." Where she was liberal in loans, Dolly could also be notably effective in preventing withdrawals—the reasons for such toughness about the withdrawals were grimly evident in later years. In 1936, A. P. Giannini, head of the Bank of America, made some disparaging comments about the Chinese, which caused an immediate run on the Oriental branch of the B of A in Chinatown. Dolly confronted her irate depositors with a stoic face and a rough-and-ready speech which turned back the run.

A promoter, Dolly made sure the tellers in

her branch bank were all attractive young Chinese girls; males were used only for the counting of money. She further enhanced the bank in 1962 when she ordered the building completely remodeled, changing it into a pagoda-like structure with dragon-crested doors. She hired tiger dancers to set off firecrackers in the street and snake back and forth before the building to drive away evil spirits. As part of the celebration, Dolly finally became an American citizen.

All seemed well in Dolly's cozy world. Celebrations and luncheons in her honor were being prepared on the eve of her retirement in December 1963. But Dolly declined any kudos. Instead she went to R. A. Peterson, head of the bank. She sat nervously in front of the banker for several silent moments, then burst into tears. "President Rudy, you are going to hear something you won't like."

"Whatever it is, Dolly, go ahead."

She went ahead, telling Peterson a fantastic story of embezzlement, more than $300,000 worth since 1923, begun, she said by her father, whose banks in China had failed. Charlie Gee, not knowing the banks had gone under, continued to send these banks deposits of almost $100,000. To cover this loss, he began to juggle the books, paying necessary withdrawals from funds in dormant accounts. Dolly said her father told her of this ongoing embezzlement in 1929, and she attempted to help him make up the losses by gambling and funding highly speculative enterprises, but their investments all failed. They were compelled to keep up the fraud, conveniently hidden from bank examiners in the Chinese ledgers they kept. As interest accrued on the gutted dormant accounts, the amount embezzled snowballed to almost $400,000. Dolly had confessed to the startled Peterson, she said, because she could not bear being honored for a fraudulent career. Police authorities later sneered at this excuse, pointing out that upon Dolly's retirement she would have been compelled to reveal the true figures of her bank.

Following her confession, Dolly returned to her comfortable Stockton Street apartment. FBI agents arrived on Christmas Eve and placed her under arrest. She was taken to jail in her night-

gown. Some hours later, when the storm broke, Dolly inquired of a reporter, "Tell me, if I'm a criminal, do I still get social security? I haven't got a cent."

Dolly got five years at Terminal Island for embezzlement. Released in sixteen months, she returned to Chinatown and lived on a small pension, dying in obscurity in early 1978. The speculation for the embezzlement continues to this day. One law enforcement official guessed that the Gees were really sending money to China over the years in a scheme to finance immigrants to the United States. Another source pointed to the fact that Dolly was repeatedly taking short visits to Las Vegas in her last years with the bank, and the missing money really wound up on the green felt tables. Dolly insisted to her dying day that her motivation, as had been her father's, was strictly honorable. "We did it to save face in Chinatown. We had to save face."

An unnamed Chinese business leader smirked at Dolly's "saving face" remarks. "Who's going to believe something like that? Who did she think we were—a bunch of Charlie Chans?"

GIRIAT, MADAME

Thief, Murderer ■ (1866– ?)

A lady's companion, Madame Giriat was found gagged and bound by police investigating a break-in robbery at the home of wealthy Eugénie Fourgère at Aix-les-Bains on September 21, 1902. Her employer and the maid were found in another room strangled to death. All the jewelry belonging to Eugénie Fougère was gone.

Police followed Madame Giriat for days after the robbery-murders and finally brought her in for questioning before the Chief of Police in Paris. Within three hours she broke down and confessed that she had been part of a plot to steal her employer's gems, but she put the greater part of the blame on her lover, Henri Bassot, and a thug named César Ladermann, a resident of Lyons. Bassot, an ex-convict and part-time nightclub comedian, was arrested. Ladermann resisted police barging into his Lyons home and blew out his brains before officers could reach him.

Madame Giriat insisted that Ladermann was to enter the house through a kitchen window, which she had conveniently left open on the night of the killings. He was to merely tie up the women in the house and take the jewelry (which was in Giriat's possession when arrested). The unthinking brute, said the lady's companion, had strangled her poor employer and the maid for the thrill of it.

Taken to the scene of the crime to reconstruct events, as was then the French custom, Madame Giriat's actions were most suspicious. She entered the room in which Eugénie and the maid had been murdered, where, in the words of one reporter, "she indulged in the most disgusting levity." She leaped upon the bed, kicking the pillows and shouting hysterically, "Only to think that poor Eugénie was strangled on these pillows!" Madame Giriat described the murders in the room with such accurate detail that authorities could only conclude that she had been present when the women were killed and had undoubtedly assisted in those murders instead, as she had claimed, of being trussed up helpless in her own bedroom. Her lover, Bassot, confirmed police suspicions, saying that Giriat had planned the crime down to the last detail.

Both Giriat and Bassot were sent to prison for life.

GLABE, KAREN

Murderer ■ (1942–   )

A one-time airlines stewardess, Karen Glabe and her lover, Mitchell Link, of Arlington Heights, Illinois, decided to get rid of Karen's husband, Kenneth Glabe, a wealthy printing executive. Glabe had refused to give Karen a divorce so that she could marry Link, or, at least, that was the story the pair told Preston Haig, a former policeman hired for $5,000 to kill Glabe.

Haig stabbed Glabe to death on the night of June 21, 1971, but not until May 1979 did the police learn the true story of the unsolved murder. By then Haig was living in Roswell, New Mexico. Following an argument with her husband, Mrs. Haig informed Illinois police about Haig's role in the killing.

Turning state's evidence, Haig confessed the murder, saying that he had received only $700 instead of the $5,000 promised for the murder. Karen and Mitchell Link, then married and living in an upper-class section of Waukegan, Illinois, where Link practiced as a pharmacist, were arrested and placed on trial in July 1980. Both were convicted and sentenced to thirty-five to forty-five years in prison by Lake County Circuit Judge Robert K. McQueen, a sentence, angrily pointed out by prosecuting attorney Larry Helms, that would make the couple eligible for parole in eleven years and three months.

GOOLDE, MARIE VERE

Murderer ■ (1877–1908)

Two passengers alighting from the Monte Carlo Express in Marseilles on August 5, 1907, appeared nervous as they called a porter to remove a large trunk from their compartment. The stylishly dressed woman fidgeted with a heavy kit bag, seemingly reluctant to turn it over to the porter, who took the trunk from her husband. The trunk was taken to the baggage office in the depot and put in the care of a clerk named Pons. The couple left instructions that the trunk was to be sent on to Charing Cross, England. The man and woman took the kit bag with them, telling the clerk that he should send the bill for the shipping of the trunk to the Hôtel du Louvre de la Paix where they were staying.

An hour later Pons went into the storage area to make out the necessary papers for shipping the trunk when he smelled an overpowering odor. He ran his hand along the lip of the trunk where it was oozing a red liquid. The efficient clerk immediately went to the Hôtel du Louvre and confronted the couple, who had registered under the odd name of "Javasaah," saying that they were British.

The woman quickly told Pons that the trunk contained poultry and therefore the contents "might bleed a little." The clerk was still suspicious so he called the director of railway police from the hotel lobby. He was told to take the couple to the depot and open the trunk in front of them. Pons found the couple on the steps of the hotel, obviously preparing to flee. The man gripped the kit bag closely.

Pons persuaded the pair to accompany him back to the station. As they rode in a cab to the depot, the woman, who was dark featured and attractive, suddenly produced some money, offering it to both Pons and the cab driver if she and her husband were allowed to get away. Pons sneered at the awkward bribe.

Once in the station, the clerk summoned police, and the group went into the baggage room. The trunk was opened. Inside was found the torso and two severed arms of a woman. Gendarmes seized the man's kit bag. Its contents consisted of two legs and a head. Protesting loudly, the man and woman were arrested and taken to the police station.

The man huffily informed police that he was a British nobleman, "Sir" Vere Goolde, and that his wife was French, the former Marie Girodin, now Marie Vere Goolde. He would protest to the British consulate. The pretense lasted only a few hours. After contacting the authorities in Monte Carlo, police had most of the real story.

The couple had murdered a rich thirty-seven-year-old widow, one Emma Erika Levin from Sweden, who had loaned them money to gamble in the Monte Carlo casino. Knowing that she had valuable jewelry, the Gooldes had invited the widow to tea in the Villa Menesimy, where they had rented rooms with their twenty-seven-year-old niece, telling their victim that they intended to repay the 40 pounds they had borrowed. With the niece sent on an errand, the Gooldes had stabbed Mrs. Levin to death, then dissected her body in the bathroom, stuffing the remains in a trunk and kit bag. When the niece returned, she was told that her uncle had suddenly taken ill, Marie sobbing that he "has spit up quite a lot of blood," and that they must depart immediately to see a medical specialist in Marseilles. After the couple fled, the concierge entered the blood-splattered flat and found the dagger used to kill Mrs. Levin. Mrs. Levin's jewels were found in Marie's purse after her arrest.

Placed on trial in Monte Carlo, the real culprit soon proved to be Marie Vere Goolde. She had been an adventuress all her adult life. The thirty-year-old killer had been married three times. Her first two husbands had died mysteriously (there may have been more husbands who met the same fate). She had opened a dressmaking shop in London, where she had met the Irish-born Goolde. Seeking their fortune they went to Monte Carlo to win at the tables. Marie gambled away every cent they had while Goolde indulged in drugs, drink, and whoring. When broke they victimized the gullible Mrs. Levin. It had been Marie's idea to kill and dismember Mrs. Levin.

Both were found guilty. The niece was exonerated. The Gooldes were sent to the French penal colony at Cayenne, French Guiana, for life. Marie contracted typhoid fever in July 1908 and died. In September of the next year Goolde committed suicide.

GORDON-BAILLE, MRS. MARY ANN

Swindler ■ (1857– ?)

British swindler born Mary Ann Sutherland Bruce, Mrs. Gordon-Baille began her nefarious career in 1872 in Scotland, appearing in Dundee and leasing a mansion. Using this as a front, Mary Ann ordered all manner of expensive goods, from priceless paintings and tapestries to expensive silverware, always deferring payment. She promptly fenced these goods and left for Edinburgh where she repeated the same scam.

So successful was this confidence game that Mrs. Gordon-Baille played it for great riches throughout Europe, traveling to Vienna, Rome, Paris, Florence, and finally London. Here she met an elderly baronet in 1885, bilking him of more than 18,000 pounds. Next she returned to Scotland, where she presented herself as a philanthropist, telling the down-and-out Scottish farmers, known as "crofters," that she would buy up rich lands for them in Australia where they could relocate and enrich their miserable lives. In this way she raised enormous sums from wealthy residents as charitable donations. She did go to Australia but not to buy up lands; she and her newly acquired husband, Richard Percival Bodeley Frost, merely squandered the donations, then returned to England to implement check-cashing swindles.

She was eventually caught and tried for passing bad checks and given five years in prison; her husband was sentenced to eighteen months. Upon her release, Mrs. Gordon-Baille resorted to petty swindles to stay alive. After several arrests and prison terms, the once illustrious Mrs. Gordon-Baille disappeared.

GOTTFRIED, GESINA MARGARETHA

Murderer ■ (? –1828)

Always a headstrong child, Gesina Gottfried was used to getting her own way. Her upstanding parents had spoiled her; there was nothing Gesina could do that would make them think ill of her. During her youth in Bremen, Germany, Gesina had only to point, and the object of her desire was obtained for her by her parents.

As a young woman—she was extremely attractive, blonde, blue-eyed, and buxom—Gesina met a man named Miltenberg, a handsome young wastrel. Despite friends and relatives' warnings that the man was a notorious drunkard, she decided to marry him. Only her indulgent parents supported Gesina's ambitions to wed, and this she did in 1815.

From the beginning, the marriage was a disaster. Miltenberg drank himself into a stupor every day. Gesina's primary objection to her husband, however, was his inability to perform his marital duties. And Gesina was a woman who thrived on sex. At first, she merely took a lover, a man named Gottfried, but when her affair began to be noticed by neighbors, she resolved to eliminate her alcoholic husband.

Knowing that her mother used white arsenic to poison mice, she asked the trusting woman to purchase some of the poison for her from a druggist. (And if her plan went somehow awry, her mother would therefore be suspect.) Days later, when catching her husband already bleary-eyed and still guzzling his usual brew, Gesina dropped the arsenic into his beer.

Miltenberg's sudden death was no surprise to anyone. His alcoholic intake was enormous, and his painful demise was attributed simply to drink. Now Gesina was free to marry Gottfried. But the lover balked. She had had two children by Miltenberg and the lover refused to assume responsibility for them. Gesina powdered their milk with white arsenic and both died within a week, their deaths credited to a sudden illness.

When the tear-streaked Gesina, so tragically widowed in youth, announced her intention to marry Gottfried, her parents did the unthinkable. They objected, stating that it would be a public disgrace for a woman so recently widowed, as well as bereaved of her two small children, to rush into a new marriage. She invited her parents to lunch in her home to discuss the matter and promptly poisoned the elderly couple. As in the cases of her husband and her children, the authorities suspected nothing. Gesina's parents simply perished from old age, their deaths attributed to "inflammation of the bowels."

Now nothing stood in the way of Gesina's marriage to Gottfried—nothing, except Gottfried himself. The mass poisoner found out in shock that her lover still held back, offering one weak excuse after another to avoid taking the marriage vows. According to Lee Adam Hargrave, writing in *Woman and Crime*, Gottfried was not the oafish type, and perhaps suspected his sex partner's lethal nature; "he must have entertained some doubts about the deaths of Gesina's relations, which had followed so rapidly upon each other."

The calculating Gesina, however, was not one to take rejection in stride. Though she was a rare beauty who could attract a host of worthy suitors and was financially well off with the estates of her husband and parents in her grasp, Gesina resolved that Gottfried and only Gottfried would be her next husband. And to that fanatical end he became her next victim.

The poisoner had become so expert in administering white arsenic that she knew exactly how much poison would cause instant death and how much would provide only for a lingering illness. It was the latter course Gesina chose to compel Gottfried to marry her.

Day after day Gesina dosed Gottfried's food, until, bedridden and totally dependent upon her, the ailing man called his "beautiful nurse" to his bedside.

"I have done you great injustice," Gottfried told Gesina. "I should have taken you for my bride, and now I am dying."

"There is still time, my love," soothed Gesina. She sent for a priest and a lawyer. The priest performed a hasty deathbed wedding ceremony. The lawyer had Gottfried sign over all his wordly possessions to Gesina, his wife of a few minutes, using documents Gesina had ordered from the lawyer weeks earlier. Gottfried died in agony within the hour but with a smile on his face, thinking as he slipped into eternity that he had done "the right thing."

And Gesina Gottfried went on doing "the right thing" for her own ends, that is, poisoning her way through life. Having taken so many lives, no life was dear to her. Her brother, a dissipated soldier, came to stay with her briefly. Because his habits "disgusted her," Gesina poisoned him to death. A doctor termed his end the result of venereal disease. Before serving him her favorite white arsenic in a dish of stew, of course, Mrs. Gottfried had been careful enough to have her brother sign over all his savings to her.

A wealthy suitor then plied Gesina with presents and attention. Though she had a great dislike for the man, Gesina pretended affection, making the swain all sorts of tasty homemade dinners. He, too, died in poisonous pain, but not before arranging to leave his lovely Gesina his entire fortune.

An old friend of Gesina's had loaned her money, and when he politely asked for repayment, Mrs. Gottfried traveled to Hamburg to visit him, repaying the debt with arsenic. The creditor died before Gesina left town.

Such financial dealings were not always appropriate, and, by 1825, Gesina had been forced to operate on more legitimate levels in her business affairs. She had taken a large house in the Pelzerstrasse in Bremen in that year, having the house mortgaged. When she could no longer keep up the payments, the bankers foreclosed and Gesina's house was sold to a master wheelwright named Rumf.

The wheelwright was a kindly man, and, having sympathy for the handsome widow, allowed her to stay on in the house. His large family would need a housekeeper, Rumf stated. Gesina accepted the post with alacrity.

Neither the many children of the new owner nor his wife, who was expecting another child, offered any challenge to the happy Frau Gottfried. She worked hard to make the place comfortable for the Rumfs, paying particular attention to their meals.

Mrs. Rumf soon gave birth to a son, but only days later she mysteriously died, even though the doctors had stated she was in the best of health. Complications of childbirth, murmured the attending physician. Then the Rumf children began to die, one after another, of strange illnesses that baffled consulting doctors.

By early 1828 no one was left alive in the house except Rumf, Gesina Gottfried, and a few servants. And by then Rumf himself was constantly ill. One day the wheelwright ordered one of the many pigs he kept in the backyard killed and cooked for his dinner. He was amazed. It was the first meal in a long time that had not upset his stomach. He cut off a portion of sparerib and stored it in a cupboard. When retrieving the sparerib for a meal the next day, March 28, 1828, Rumf noticed that it was coated with a strange white powder. He then remembered seeing a similar white powder on a salad Gesina had prepared for him and, in the form of a sediment, in some homemade soup Mrs. Gottfried had made with her own delicate hands. Rumf hurriedly wrapped the meat in paper and took it to the police. Tests were made and the powder was quickly determined to be white arsenic.

A magistrate accompanied Rumf to his house and interviewed the servants, paying special attention to Frau Gottfried. For the first time in her murderous career she was confronted with direct suspicion. Her reaction was extreme nervousness. The magistrate arrested her and ordered her to jail pending a charge of murder.

When Gesina Gottfried stepped into the dock at her trial, there was a gasp from those in the court who had known her. Only days before her arrest she had appeared as an attractive, buxom middle-aged woman, youthful freshness still apparent in her face. The woman in the dock was a toothless old hag, "almost a skeleton," bearing sunken cheeks and hollow eyes. This frightening metamorphosis was later explained when it was learned that Frau Gottfried had disguised her withered body with thirteen corsets. She had made up her face with pearl powder

and rouge and had worn false teeth. Commented one reporter, "It was appropriate, though, that she should be physically as well as morally hideous."

Gesina offered no defense. In the course of the trial, she confessed not only to poisoning the Rumf family but to having murdered at least thirty other persons, and she boasted of each killing as if it were a badge of honor she had been compelled to wear secretly down through the years. Yes, the murders had given her gratification, she admitted, even a strange sort of ecstasy, one similar to a sexual climax. Only an exceptionally strong-willed person, she cried out to a bewildered court, could have performed as she did.

Found guilty and condemned, Gesina Margaretha Gottfried displayed the same iron will she had at her trial when she was led up the stairs to the scaffold and the executioner, who stood masked and leaning on a huge axe. She acted as if she were an equal to the nobles guillotined during the French Revolution, an aristocrat of murder full of invincible courage, when all the while her actions were undoubtedly that of a woman of monstrous vanity, a vanity that had motivated one of the most horrendous murder careers in German history. The arch-poisoner said not a word as she bent over, baring her neck on the block, and was beheaded in one swift stroke of the axe.

GRAHAM, BARBARA

Murderer ■ (1923–1955)

Four-time-married Barbara Graham habitually consorted with known criminals, a type which suited her best as drinking companions and as a source of thrills. On March 9, 1953, Barbara and four others attempted to rob an allegedly wealthy widow named Monohan in Burbank, California. Barbara pistol-whipped the woman, demanding to know where her jewels were hidden. Mrs. Monohan died from the vicious blows, and the gang went away without finding any gems.

When the thugs were finally rounded up, John L. True, a member of the gang, testified that Barbara was the killer of Mrs. Monohan. Barbara Graham, after much fanfare to save her life, was executed on June 3, 1955, in San Quentin's gas chamber.

GRESE, IRMA

Murderer ■ (1923–1945)

Working on a farm and later as a nurse, Irma Grese was to become the epitome of Adolf Hitler's vision for young German womanhood, resolute, unyielding, and devoid of compassion. She was also the epitome of inhuman sadism, torture beyond belief, and extravagant murder. Embodied in everything Irma Grese did were the words of Hitler, "We are a race of savages and have no pity."

Irma came from a good, hardworking family and, at an early age, was shocked by the licentiousness of the corrupt Weimar Republic, a directionless and doomed democratic government that had brought Germany to financial chaos following World War I. Like many well-intentioned but unthinking German youths, Irma joined Nazi youth groups in defiance of her father's wishes, believing Hitler would set a sound moral leadership for her country. She soon became immersed in her politics and the military superiority of Germany, obsessed with the half-baked theories of the Nazis, replacing a normal sex life with her fanatic activities in the party. It would be later pointed out with justifiable reason that Irma, when in absolute charge of more than thirty thousand helpless female prisoners at Auschwitz, manifested her sexual urges in the form of the most bestial sadism and killings committed by any woman in this century.

The terrible Irma Grese wearing her SS boots in the office compound of the Belsen concentration camp, 1945.

She was initiated as a concentration camp supervisor in Ravensbruck in 1942, then moved on to Auschwitz. (On the one occasion that she returned home during this period, her father beat her senseless after learning that she worked in these death camps.) The plain-looking, big-boned Irma arrived at Auschwitz at the height of the Nazi commitment to eradicate the Jews. She attacked this problem with unswerving fanaticism. Rising promptly at 7:00 A.M., seven days a week, Irma dressed in her man's SS uniform, slipping on heavy hobnailed boots. She strapped on a pistol and snatched up a whip. She was ready for work.

Even the mental torture Irma worked on prisoners was excruciating. She obtained lists of those scheduled to be sent to the gas chambers. Knowing full well when the prisoners would be sent to their death, Irma toyed with the inmates. She would say to one, "You're lucky—you have another two weeks." When the woman or child would appear relieved, Irma would smile and order the inmate killed at once. She dangled doom like a worm before a trout, telling another, "Your turn comes on Friday, so think about it."

She played barbarous games to amuse herself. At dawn Irma would place a shovel or pick outside the barbed wire enclosing a sand pit where hundreds of Jewish women labored each day. When the women were at work Irma would point to one and order her to retrieve the tool on the other side of the loosely stranded wire; she was always careful to select a woman who did not understand German. When the inmate would step through the wire to get the tool, the guard in the tower would shout a warning in a language the inmate did not understand. When the prisoner did not respond but went blindly to retrieve the tool, the guard shot her to death. On these frequent occasions, Irma's laughter rattled along with the deadly bursts of machine-gun fire.

Constant companions of this nightmare figure were two savage Alsatian hounds. Irma ordered these dogs, which were kept half starved, to attack and kill any prisoner who displeased her. As the dogs pinned the prisoner to the ground, Irma would jump on the inmate's stomach full force, then literally kick the woman or child to death. Often as not she whipped prisoners to near death in a wild frenzy which would burst from her without warning at any moment.

Though she later claimed that her pistol was never loaded, she was seen on numerous occasions to shoot prisoners to death at will. When spotting one woman staring at prisoners being unloaded from trucks, Irma took out her pistol, walked up to the woman, smiled, asked if she was enjoying the view, then blew away her face. Two young girls refused to leave their barracks while others were lining up in front of gas chambers. Irma dragged them screaming from

Wearing the number 9 about her neck, war criminal Irma Grese, along with other Nazi criminals, stoically listens to charges against her during her trial.

beneath their beds. The girls leaped from windows and began running wildly across the concentration camp compound. Irma shot both dead in their tracks.

When seeing a woman sobbingly talk to her little daughter through barbed wire, Irma rushed to the woman and beat her to death. Like the hellish Ilse Koch, Irma followed the perverse fad of having the skins of murdered prisoners made into lampshades. Reported Gerald Sparrow, "In her own house Irma had had the skins of three victims made into the most attractive lampshades, because she discovered that human skin, though it was tough and durable, also let the light through in a most pleasing way."

In 1945 Irma Grese was transferred briefly to another horror camp, Belsen, and was captured by Allied troops at the close of the war.

Condemned to death, the "Beast of Belsen" was hanged in the prison at Hameln, West Germany, in 1945.

Survivors of the death camps came forward in scores to testify against her at her war crimes trial. She faced her accusers stoically, calmly telling her judges, "Himmler is responsible for all that has happened, but I suppose I have as much guilt as the others above me." But she displayed no regret, no remorse. To her all the inmates of the satanic camps in which she ruthlessly murdered were nothing more than subhuman *"dreck."* Her philosophy was that of another war criminal, Hermann Göring, who proclaimed, "I have no conscience. My conscience is Adolf Hitler."

The reality of the woman's incredible sadism was clearly revealed as the damning testimony spilled forth. She listened but did not react as survivors of her brutality told how she delighted in selecting female prisoners with large breasts and how she would then cut their breasts open with her whip. She would next take these bleeding women, according to historian Raul Hilberg, writing in *The Destruction of the European Jews,* "to a woman inmate doctor who performed a painful operation on them while Irma Grese watched, cheeks flushed, swaying rhythmically and foaming at the mouth."

A British court, many of its members nauseated at the horrifying testimony, condemned the bestial Irma Grese to death. She was hanged on December 13, 1945, in Hamelin, Germany.

GRIEVE, ELIZABETH HARRIET

Swindler ■ (1735– ?)

A sharper all her life, London-born Elizabeth Grieve's most profitable confidence game was pretending to be well-connected at the British court. She let it be known that Lord

North was her cousin; the Duke of Grafton, a close relative. Lady Fitz-Roy was also a relative, she insisted, as was Lord Guildford. Through these bogus relatives, Elizabeth said she could grant any favor, for a price, of course.

Several tradesmen paid the woman hefty sums to obtain government positions for them. When Elizabeth did not deliver as promised, she was hauled before a court in 1774 and her scam exposed. She was transported to America for life and there disappeared during the American Revolution.

GRIFFIN, JANE

Murderer ■ (1680–1720)

A London housewife, Jane Griffin's uncontrollable temper guaranteed her doom. While slicing up a chicken for her children's supper, Jane suddenly remembered that she had lost the cellar key and, wanting to retrieve some potatoes, went upstairs to ask the maid if she had it. The maid, with whom Jane had been arguing, shouted at her. Jane, at a split-second's impulse, drove the butcher knife still in her hand directly into the maid's heart, killing her.

For this spur-of-the-moment madness, an act that would certainly be considered manslaughter today, Jane Griffin was hanged.

GRINDER, MARTHA

Murderer ■ (1815–1866)

O bviously mad, Mrs. Grinder poisoned her neighbor, Mrs. Carothers in Pittsburgh, Pennsylvania, feeding the woman food laced with arsenic when supposedly nursing her. She confessed to the crime,

saying she had enjoyed watching her victim die in agony and wished she could have "done more [murder]." She was hanged on January 19, 1866.

GROESBEEK, MARIA

Murderer ■ (1937–1970)

M arrying Christiaan Buys in 1953 in South Africa, Maria argued constantly with her husband in what became a seventeen-year battle that culminated in February 1969 when Marie fed Buys ant poison. He died in a hospital on March 28. Arsenic was found in his body, and Maria was arrested and tried. It was then learned that Maria had recently met twenty-year-old Gerhard Groesbeek, and, failing to get her husband's consent to divorce so that she could marry her young lover, she murdered Buys. Her only defense was that she "wanted to make him [Buys] thoroughly sick."

Maria was convicted, and hanged on November 13, 1970, a Friday.

GUNNESS, BELLE

Murderer ■ (1860–1908?)

A farming woman who lived outside La Porte, Indiana, Belle apparently murdered her husband, crushing Gunness's skull with a hatchet, when she felt he could not provide the things in life she desired. She told a coroner's jury that the hatchet "slipped from a shelf" and accidentally buried itself in the poor man's head. She was believed and acquitted, though one of her three children habitually

Mass killer Belle Gunness, shown with her three children, circa 1900.

skipped up and down the streets of La Porte chanting, "Momma killed Daddy with a hatchet!"

At the turn of the century, Mrs. Gunness began to advertise for a husband in the lovelorn columns of the Chicago newspapers, stating, "Rich, goodlooking widow, young, owner of a large farm, wishes to get in touch with a gentleman of wealth with cultured tastes. Object, matrimony. No triflers need apply."

Belle was neither rich nor good looking, and her farm was rather small, but that didn't stop dozens of men from applying for the marital position. Over the years, Belle selected more than a dozen such men, who journeyed to La Porte only to be drugged to a deep sleep, then strangled by the powerful Belle who took their money and

then chopped up their bodies, feeding the remains to the hogs and burying the bones in her pigsty.

Not until April 28, 1908 did Belle's murderous lovelorn scheme come to light. The bodies of her children were found, along with what most believed to be her corpse, after a fire devastated Belle's farm house. Searchers inadvertently discovered the remains of her thirteen victims. (The true toll might have been close to twenty.) It was later speculated that, tiring of her murder game, Belle burned down her own house, substituting the corpse of a female friend for her own, and departed with her loot (an estimated $30,000, equivalent to $200,000 today) to live out her life in comfort in San Francisco, though the woman was never identified as a resident of that city.

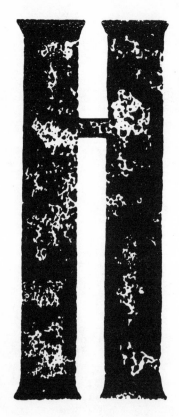

HAHN, ANNA MARIE

Murderer ■ (1906–1938)

Born in Germany, Anna met and married Phillip Hahn, a young telegraphist, in 1924. The couple moved to the United States with their young son in 1929, settling in the large German community of Cincinnati. It was in the many beer gardens frequented by German-Americans that the beautiful, blonde Anna lifted her pleasant contralto voice in song and met the rich, elderly gentlemen of her community.

Many of these men were ailing and Anna volunteered to look after them, assuming, without either formal education or practical experience, the role of nurse. One by one, under Anna's "loving care," the old men began to die. Relatives grateful to the attentive Anna left the self-made nurse thousands of dollars from the estates of the deceased. When elderly Ernest Kohler died in her care in 1933, Anna was left his large house, as the old man had specified in his will.

The first floor of this building was occupied by Dr. Arthur Vos, and, as the new owner of the builder, Anna had occasion to visit the physician's offices regularly. Vos discovered one day that many blank prescription forms were missing. When the doctor complained to Anna, she merely shrugged and said, "Maybe one of your patients took them."

Times were hard as the Depression deepened in the late 1930s. Anna Hahn felt the financial strain like everybody else but resolved to keep herself and her family in comfort. She took on the care of a half dozen old men, racing from one home to another to "nurse" them. They died like flies. On June 1, 1937, Anna began to care for sixty-eight-year-old Jacob Wagner. The old man died the next day. A few days later, another old man in her care, seventy-year-old George Opendorfer, passed away. Both men had died with similar symptoms, great stomach pain and vomiting. This was brought to the attention of Cincinnati Police Chief Patrick Hayes, who ordered an autopsy on Wagner's body. Poison was found. When the bodies of Anna's other patients were exhumed, four varieties of poison were found in the corpses. Anna was brought to Hayes for questioning.

She was indignant at the suggestion that she had anything to do with the deaths of the wonderful old men who had left her their fortunes for the attention she gave them in their final hours. "I love to make old people comfy," she said. It wasn't her fault that most of these elderly gentlemen died of dysentery, was it? "I know it's very peculiar, but why pick on me, chief?"

"We searched your place, Mrs. Hahn," Hayes told her. "We found enough poison to kill half of Cincinnati."

"I have been like an angel of mercy to them," Anna said through quivering lips before bursting into tears. "The last thing that would ever enter my head would be to harm those dear old men."

Anna's husband came forward to inform police that his wife had stolen the prescriptions from Dr. Vos, forged the physician's signature on them, and then ordered the poisons from local druggists, sending her twelve-year-old son to fetch the prescriptions. Phillip Hahn said that Anna had twice tried to insure his life for $25,000 but that he had refused. He himself had been taken ill after that, with the same symptoms as the old men Anna cared for; somehow he had survived.

Anna Hahn was tried for murder, the press making much of her good looks, calling her "the beautiful blonde killer." She was convicted and sentenced to death. She showed no emotion during the trial and only shrugged when learning that she was to be electrocuted in May 1938.

The mass poisoner—she may have murdered as many as fifteen elderly men—was oddly full of cheer as her date of execution approached. She refused to see her husband or child on the last night of her life, but asked if the newspapermen covering her trial could join her in a farewell party. This was granted, several sheepish reporters filing into Anna's cell to sip punch and munch unenthusiastically on little cakes.

"You gave me a 'good show' at my trial,

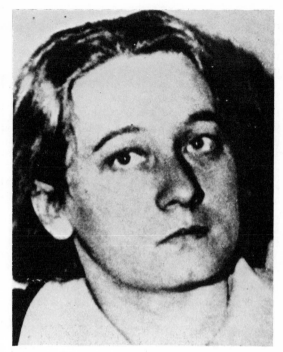

Cincinnati's mass poisoner Anna Marie Hahn.

boys," Anna told them. "The least I could do was to throw a bash for you. I guess I'm not much like a 'beautiful blonde' now, huh? Well, give me a good write-up when it's all over."

The same reporters were absent the next morning when Anna Hahn sat down in the electric chair. They had turned back their passes to the prison warden.

HAMILTON, MARY

Bigamist ■ (1705– ?)

Mary Hamilton is to this day, perhaps, the most peculiar female criminal in the record books. In 1746, Mary Hamilton was dragged before a court in Taunton, England, and accused by her spouse of being a bigamist. In fact, not only was she a bigamist, having married fourteen times in the past decade, but, to the baffling consternation of the judges, she had married fourteen persons of her own sex.

The Hamilton woman, dressed in men's clothing, including an expensive male wig, did not deny the charges brought against her by her wife, Mary Price, but defied the judges to pinpoint a law prohibiting her strange practice. Mary Price, the indignant wife, told the court that she had been married three months to Hamilton before learning that her husband was a female, that Hamilton had acted out the role of a man so well that the woman believed her spouse to be a male in every way, "a fellow creature of the right and proper sex."

Apparently Mary Price was of an extremely shy nature, for it was three months before she proposed coition with her modest "husband," and, during the night, the woman learned to her shock and dismay that another woman was in her marriage bed.

The court decided that Mary Hamilton was a bigamist, but the recorded verdict of its blustering members leaves no doubt as to their judicial quandary. The court decided "that the he, she, prisoner at the bar, is an uncommon notorious cheat; and we, the Court, do sentence her or him, whichever he or she may be, to be imprisoned six months, and during that time, to be whipped in the towns of Taunton, Glastonbury, Wells, and Shipton-Mallet." These were towns in which "Mary, the monopolizer of her own sex," had married other women. Authorities waited until the winter months before the woman was whipped through the towns, in order to make her punishment all the more uncomfortable.

HARRIS, CHARLOTTE

Murderer ■ (1819– ?)

Charlotte Harris's distinction in the annals of female criminals lies solely in her escape from capital punishment for the premeditated murder of her husband. She was tried and sentenced to death by hanging in 1848, but, because she was pregnant, the carrying out of her sentence was delayed until she gave birth to her child. During her waiting period the Society for the Abolition of Capital Punishment not only pressured the Home Secretary with delegations to plead Charlotte's case but bombarded Queen Victoria with petitions for a reprieve which more than forty thousand women signed. The Queen relented; Charlotte Harris's sentence was commuted to life imprisonment.

HARRIS, PHOEBE

Coiner ■ (1755–1788)

Phoebe Harris had been a coiner most of her life, a particularly repugnant crime to the British government, in that coins of the realm were defaced, which usually meant the cutting away or filing off of the raised features of the noble faces of royalty on coins. (These bits of gold or silver were then melted down and sold by the coiner.) Caught in the act of coining, Phoebe was condemned to death in 1788. The type of execution that was meted out to her was medieval and, even in the words of a chronicler of the day, "a barbarous event."

She was taken from her cell into a large open area next to the Old Bailey where twenty thousand persons waited to see the spectacle. A small, rather pretty woman, Phoebe trembled and her face turned ash-white as she was tied to a stake, her neck pinioned to an iron bolt fixed to the top of the stage. Great mounds of faggots were placed around the stake. After the frantic woman prayed for a few minutes, the steps upon which she stood were drawn away and she was left to strangle to death. A half hour later the kindling was lighted and a great fire consumed her body for four hours as the low-life crowd cheered. One report had it that "the flames presently burned the halter, the body fell a few inches, and hung then by the iron chain."

Phoebe Harris was the last person executed in this form of capital punishment in England, hanging and burning at the stake repealed in 1793.

HART, PEARL

Bandit ■ (? –1925)

Pearl Hart's solitary distinction as a bad woman was the fact that she was the last person to rob a stagecoach in America, holding one up outside of Globe, Arizona, with a local drunk named Joe Boot in 1897. She was quickly apprehended and spent five years in the Yuma Territorial Prison for her impetuous act, more of a prank than a serious crime.

HARVEY, MARGARET

Thief ■ (? –1750)

Dublin-born Margaret Harvey took employment as a maidservant in London. It was her misfortune to get drunk in St. James' Park during festivities celebrating the end of the war with France. She was persuaded to go to a pub, where she stayed the night. When she sobered, she was afraid to return to her employer. Margaret continued to drink and some days later stole a sailor's gold watch. An inept thief, Margaret Harvey was caught and promptly tried and sentenced to death.

The sentence was delayed until Margaret gave birth to a child, the bastard son of the very man she had robbed. Before her execution on July 6, 1750, Margaret Harvey was visited by relatives and friends from Dublin who gave her so much brandy that she was totally drunk when she stood on the scaffold. As the hangman placed the rope about her neck, Margaret Harvey shouted, "I wished to God I had never stepped on these evil shores!"

HAYES, CATHERINE

Murderer ■ (1690–1726)

Undoubtedly the most macabre murder on record in the early eighteenth century was committed by a shrewish housewife, Catherine Hayes, whose homicidal aim was solely that of money. Callous, greedy, incestuous, British-born Catherine Hayes stands out in the scrolls of murder as a peculiar killer whose singular crime was so heinous as to make her shudderingly memorable.

Born outside Birmingham in 1690 as Catherine Hall, the young girl ran away from home at age fifteen. Some army officers quartered at Great Ombersley in Worcestershire spotted the buxom girl as she walked the road, and, offering her gold pieces, enticed her to their camp where she willingly became their common whore, servicing the sexual needs of a score of the officers, sometimes in groups. Tiring of the girl, the officers drove her from the camp. For some years, according to one historian, "She ran about the country like a distracted creature."

Little is known of Catherine's activities as she grew into womanhood, but there are sketchy

The head of John Hayes on display in St. Margaret's Square, 1726; authorities hoped to identify the murder victim in this manner.

reports that she worked alternatively as a domestic servant and a prostitute, eventually finding her way to the door of a wealthy farmer named Hayes in Warwickshire where she applied for a job as a servant. Hayes hired the woman against the advice of his wife, who thought the new domestic too attractive and voluptuous. She would seduce their boys, she warned. Mrs. Hayes was correct. In a few months, Catherine had taken the eldest son, John Hayes, to her promising bed, happily introducing the youth to the pleasures of the flesh. The twenty-one-year-old John, a carpenter by

trade, and two years Catherine's junior, fell madly in love with the household servant. In 1713 he secretly married her. Catherine's reaction to the state of wedlock was typical of all her future marital obligations—dedicated infidelity. On the couple's wedding night, Catherine arranged for several of her former officer lovers to break into the bedroom of the inn where she and her new husband had retired. Under pretext of drafting the bewildered Hayes into the army, the officers dragged the young man off while several of their number lingered to once again enjoy Catherine's sexual acrobatics. Hours later Hayes was returned, with apologies from his military abductors, told that it had all been a mistake.

News of these scandalous events reached Hayes's father, who, after first berating his son, provided the couple with a cottage on his large farm, conferring upon them a handsome allowance. Catherine was warned by her father-in-law to conduct herelf as a decent wife or be turned over to authorities.

For six years the couple lived the country life. But Catherine was discontent, and made life as miserable for her husband as possible, taking traveling merchants and peddlers as hour-long lovers whenever the chance arose. She nagged Hayes day and night, demanding luxuries he could not afford. She carped about the dull country living, that life would be better, and she nicer to Hayes, if they could but move to London. The shrewish Catherine finally had her way. In 1719 her husband took her to London to begin a new life.

In London Hayes prospered, displaying a talent for commerce, becoming rich as a coal merchant and part-time money lender and pawnbroker. Catherine began to enjoy the luxuries she had always coveted. Her husband bought a modest building near his offices on Tyburn Road, and she was given an ever increasing allowance to purchase fine foodstuffs and custom-made clothes. Yet she still made no signs of being content, scolding Hayes for not making more money. She demanded servants, a carriage. Hayes found it all intolerable and finally lashed back at his wife by beating her, then witholding money from her. The more aggravating Catherine was to Hayes, the more niggardly her husband became with her allowance. By early 1725, the two thoroughly hated each other. Catherine made no pretense to friends about her animosity toward her husband, telling one that "it was no more sin to kill him than to kill a mad dog. Some time or other I will give him a jolt!"

Preparation for that jolt began some weeks later when Thomas Billings, a youthful tailor, appeared at Catherine's door looking for lodgings. She prevailed upon her husband to rent Billings a room. It was later reliably stated that Billings was Catherine's illegitimate son and had come to her at her bidding. No sooner was the youth settled in the Hayes house than Catherine began carrying on a torrid love affair with him, sneaking from her own bed to Billings's room after her husband fell asleep.

Once, when Hayes traveled from the city on business, Catherine and Billings ceased their lovemaking long enough to give several expensive parties, spending Hayes's hard-earned money with abandon. The coal merchant returned unexpectedly to view one of these drinking orgies. Hayes exploded, thrashing his wife so viciously that she was bedridden for days. Inexplicably, the husband never once asked Billings to leave his home.

The affairs of John Hayes became even more confusing with the arrival of Thomas Wood, a friend of the merchant's from Warwickshire, who asked for lodging. He was given a room and promptly became Catherine's second lover. The scheming Catherine had already decided to kill her husband. Wood, she concluded, would be the perfect instrument in that murder.

She began by poisoning Wood's mind against his friend, telling him that her husband had killed two of her newborn children in Warwickshire. Adding to this lie, Catherine whispered to her new lover, "And he has also murdered a man, a business rival." She proposed that Wood join her and her son in murdering Hayes, dangling before the penniless man the prospect of receiving almost the entire Hayes estate of 1,500 pounds after the killing.

On March 1, 1725, Billings and Wood, sitting with Catherine and John Hayes, suddenly made a strange wager. They had just come from a pub where they had each drunk six pints of wine and were, as Hayes could see, stone sober. Both men bet that Hayes could not drink an equal amount without becoming intoxicated. Foolish as the bet appeared, Hayes snatched it up, his merchant's mind already adding the guinea to his coffers.

Catherine, who had been encouraging her husband to take on the bet, departed with Billings and Wood, going to a local pub to buy the six pints of wine. As they were returning, she told her lovers that "this would be the best time to murder the man."

Hayes drank his six pints in record time and collapsed to the floor. The plotters jumped forward but stopped in their tracks when their victim sobered for some moments, stood shakily to his feet, and then wobbled into the bedroom, collapsing on the four-poster.

Stealthily, Catherine, Billings and Wood crept into the bedroom. They stood for some while in silence, watching Hayes snore himself into a deep sleep. At one point he rolled over onto his face and at that moment Billings stepped forward and brought down a coal hatchet on the back of the husband's head. The blow did not kill Hayes, but fractured his skull, producing such agony that the husband kicked his feet wildly and shrieked out his pain.

A Mrs. Springate, who rented rooms above, heard the noise and came down to the Hayes apartment to complain. A cool-headed Catherine met her at the door. "Pay no mind," Mrs. Hayes told Mrs. Springate. "Mr. Hayes has some noisy guests. They will be leaving soon."

As Catherine cooed her words to Mrs. Springate, Billings and Wood were busy sitting on the struggling John Hayes, repeatedly burying the hatchet in his head until he lay silent and quite dead. When Catherine reappeared in the bedroom she found both men quaking with terror. The bed upon which the dead man sprawled was sopped with blood and blood even blotched the ceiling, jets of it having shot upward with each blow from the hatchet.

Billings and Wood panicked even further when Catherine told them they must get rid of the body. The watch might see them carrying the body in the street, they said. They would have to drop the corpse and run for it then, and the watchman would certainly recognize Hayes's chopped-up cadaver and be at their doorstep within the hour. Catherine had a plan,

The execution of murderess Catherine Hayes. The executioner botched the job so that the woman burned alive.

a grisly one. No one could recognize a corpse without a head. They must decapitate Hayes and dispose of the head. Then they could take their time in disposing of the body wherever they chose.

The idea was so aversive to the two men they both threw up. The iron-nerved Catherine waited patiently for her accomplices to calm down, watching them in the dim light of a single candle, quietly explaining what they must do. She ordered Billings to bring a bucket and a large carving knife from the kitchen. Wood was told to move Hayes's body so that the head hung over the edge of the bed. When the bucket was brought, it was placed under the head to catch the great quantities of blood that spurted forth as the men, under Catherine's close instruction, cut it off with the knife. The headless corpse was then allowed to bleed into the bucket. Wood began to wrap the head in a pillowcase.

"There is still danger," warned Catherine. "The head might be recognized. I think it best I boil it, boil the flesh from the face."

"Disgusting!" grunted Wood.

"There's no time for that," urged Billings.

"All right," sighed the cautious Catherine. "Throw it in the river for the fish."

As Billings and Wood hurried from the bedroom with the head in the bloody bucket, rags covering it, Catherine Hayes began to scrub the bedroom floor stained with her husband's blood. She carried several buckets of water to the second-floor apartment from street level to wash down the sink where the blood had been poured from the bucket. All this she did in the manner of a housewife at daily chores, except that it was in the dead of night. When Mrs. Springate called down to ask what the noise was all about, the quick-witted Catherine shouted up the stairs to her, "My husband is going away on a trip and is preparing to leave." To reinforce this fabrication, Catherine kept up a line of chatter, as if saying good-bye to her dear spouse, telling him to "watch out for brigands, and dress warmly against these bitter March winds."

While Catherine carried water to her apartment and held loud conversations with an imaginary husband, Wood and Billings, their nerves jangled, walked briskly with their grisly bucket along the river bank. When they reached Horseferry Wharf, they spotted a watchman coming toward them. Without thinking, Wood hurled the bucket and head into the Thames, but the tide was out and the remains thudded into the mud. Both men fled. The watchman looked over the embankment and quickly spotted the head, which he retrieved, showing it to a gathering crowd and asking who its owner might be. Hours later authorities ordered the head washed and the hair combed. It was then impaled upon a pike and placed on exhibit in St. Margaret's Square in hopes that someone might identify it.

Returning to the Hayes house, Wood and Billings were so rattled that they threatened to bolt, but Catherine's iron nerve held sway. She ordered the men to cut off the limbs of the corpse and place the remains in a trunk. More hours of gruesome labor ensued until the body was hacked up according to Catherine's specifications. The two men next lugged the trunk to a pond in the Marylebone fields where they tossed it into the water.

Wood, his nerves shattered, immediately left for the country where he went into hiding. Billings returned to Catherine to take up his duties as lover, illegitimate son or not. Meanwhile, great crowds assembled each day to view the impaled head of John Hayes. A man named Robinson thought he recognized it and went to the Hayes home, informing Catherine of his discovery. The woman pooh-poohed his statements, telling him, "My husband is in good health—go look at a head on a pole, indeed! And I advise you to take care of your statements. They may make a great deal of trouble for you." Robinson shrugged as he was shown the door.

But he would not be the last visitor with such news to the Hayes home. A man named Longmore, who had viewed the head, came to the house, insisting that it was the head of Catherine's husband.

"Oh, such wicked times," moaned Mrs. Hayes. "Reports of murder everywhere. Why, a woman's body was just found this morning in the fields. But the head of my husband on a pole—oh, no. He's off in the country on business." Longmore, too, left, saying no more about the matter.

That was not the case with a man named Ashby, a close business friend of John Hayes. Ashby grilled Catherine as to the whereabouts of his friend, whom he hadn't seen in days and who had missed an important business appointment with him.

Catherine became confidential with Ashby, pretending to tell him, quite reluctantly, a great family secret. She whispered, "Some time ago my husband happened to have a dispute with a man, and from words they came to blows, so that Mr. Hayes killed him." Poor man, Catherine choked. He had to flee, traveling to Portugal where he was living incognito.

Ashby believed none of it, and went to the authorities. He was shown the head, which had now been removed from display because of putrefaction and placed in a jar of gin. After Ashby identified the head as that of John Hayes, he accompanied several officers to what had been the poor man's home.

The officers charged into Mrs. Hayes's

Catherine Hayes at about the time of her marriage.

apartment, finding her in bed with Billings. She hurriedly dressed. Billings sat on the bed wearing only his stockings.

"Have you been sleeping with this woman?" an officer asked the young man.

"No, I've been mending my stockings."

"What? Naked, and in the dark?"

Catherine, Billings and Mrs. Springate, who was thought to be an accomplice, were all arrested, charged with murder, and jailed. Mrs. Hayes screamed her innocence from her cell, telling a magistrate that she wanted to see the head that had been on display. She was taken to the offices of a barber-surgeon named Westbrook, who was keeping the head in the jar.

Looking at the head for a moment, Catherine suddenly lunged forward, caressing the jar, kissing it, and shouting, "Oh, it's my dear husband's head! It's my dear husband's head!"

Magistrate Lambert thought to frighten the woman into a confession, calmly telling

Catherine Hayes, Billings, and Hood decapitating the hapless John Hayes.

Westbrook to "take the head from the jar so that she might touch it." It was then a common belief that if a murderer touched his victim after death, guilt would somehow be revealed. Mrs. Hayes knew full well of this superstition and was not alarmed. When the head was taken from the jar she lovingly reached for the blackened face, kissing it passionately. "Please," she begged Westbrook, "may I have a lock of its hair?"

Westbrook, convinced of the woman's guilt, sardonically replied, "You've already had enough blood from this man."

Not knowing what histrionics to display, Catherine Hayes resorted to the only tactic left her—she fainted, or pretended to faint. She was returned to her cell. Days later the rest of the much dismembered John Hayes was discovered at Marylebone and the headless corpse shown to the weeping widow. Catherine went into a crying jag, still insisting upon her innocence.

About this time Wood returned to London and was quickly apprehended by officers. He, too, was charged with murder. Where Catherine and Billings held steadfast to their pleas of innocence, Wood quickly broke down, confessing the entire ghastly murder, detailing its steps for the authorities and attempting to place the complete blame on Catherine Hayes, stating that she had insisted on killing her husband because he was "an atheist and a free-thinker." All were speedily tried, convicted, and condemned to death, except for Mrs. Springate who, obviously innocent, was released.

The murderous trio were sentenced to die on May 9, 1726, but Wood died in prison of the fever before his execution, a fate more lenient that what the authorities would have meted out. Billings was taken before Catherine Hayes and hanged in irons, his body later removed to a gibbet to hang for days, still in its chains, as a warning to other would-be murderers.

The architect of the murder plot knew what was in store for her and sought to cheat the executioner. A friend, at her request, smuggled a small phial of poisonous acid to her. As she prepared to drink it while walking in an exercise cell, another inmate, thinking it smuggled wine, snatched the phial from Mrs. Hayes and placed it to her own lips. The acid burned the woman's lips, and, with a yell, she dashed the phial to the stone floor. The arch-murderess would die as the state had decreed after all.

Catherine Hayes met her own executioner, Richard Arnet, with cool demeanor, asking him of Billings in a low voice, "Have you killed my dear child yet?" Arnet did not answer, but merely lifted a huge arm in the direction of the open cell door. Catherine walked unsupported to the courtyard and to a cart which carried her to a square in Tyburn. There a huge throng had collected to watch her end, which was to be a particularly agonizing one.

She was to be strangled by hand and then burned. After tying her to the stake, Arnet lit the brushwood about her legs, then placed a rope around her neck and began to strangle her but the faggots blazed up and burned his hands. With a shriek, Arnet let go of the rope. The flames shot upward as Catherine kicked furiously at the brushwood, attempting to push the roaring kindling away from her, all the while crying out in such piercing, plaintive shrieks that the whole crowd was seen to wince as one body at the horror of it. The woman was literally burned alive, roasting for four hours until she disappeared into ashes inside the smoldering fire.

HEADY, BONNIE B.

Kidnapper ■ (1912–1953)

Enamored of criminals, Bonnie Heady had a long history of associating with gangsters in the Midwest; her husband, a one-time bank robber, had been killed while making a prison break. She saw in holdup man Carl Austin Hall, a way to bring more excitement into her dull life. Heady teamed up with the alcoholic Hall upon his release from the Missouri State Prison on April 24, 1953. He had gone through a $200,000 legacy and needed money, Hall explained to the overweight, pinch-faced woman. And he had a plan to make a quick fortune, something he had dreamed up in the long hours of his prison term. They would kidnap the six-year-old son of Robert Greenlease, a rich car dealer in Kansas City.

Pretending to be the aunt of Bobbie Greenlease, Jr., Bonnie Heady took the child from his private school on September 28, 1953. She and Hall then drove the boy to a lonely field where Hall strangled and shot Bobbie to death while Bonnie strolled through a meadow. They then drove to Bonnie's small home in St. Joseph, Missouri, where they buried the child in Bonnie's flower bed.

The Greenlease family received a ranson demand for $600,000 the next day, the largest such demand in American history. It was paid on October 4, 1953, after much confusion, created for the most part by the kidnappers who were rarely sober during this period. Hall then

Bonnie Heady in custody following the kidnapping of Bobbie Greenlease, Jr., in 1953.

Bonnie's kidnapping partner, Carl Austin Hall. The two died together in the gas chamber.

deserted Heady in a hotel room after an all-night drunk. He drove around aimlessly in cabs in St Louis, drinking heavily from a flask; he drunkenly bragged about the kidnapping to a cab driver and the cabbie turned him in to authorities.

Bonnie Heady was picked up just hours later and, after admitting they had killed the boy, both were placed on trial for murder and convicted. They were sent to the gas chamber at the same time in the Missouri Penitentiary on December 16, 1953. Bonnie Heady became the first woman ever executed for kidnapping in U.S. history. Less than half the enormous ranson the kidnappers had collected has been recovered to this date.

HEARST, PATRICIA CAMPBELL

Bank Robber ■ (1955–   )

The daughter of newspaper czar Randolph Hearst, Patricia was kidnapped on February 2, 1974, by members of the Symbionese Liberation Army, a fanatical left-wing terrorist group. In the following weeks the so-called victim released tape recordings in which she lambasted her parents, calling them "pigs" of wealth, and identifying herself with the SLA.

Bank robber Patricia Hearst in a pensive mood. (UPI)

The SLA, under the hazy threat of killing Patty Hearst, demanded a ransom of $2 million in foodstuffs, which were eventually distributed to minorities in California, albeit many who received these food packages were not among the needy. (At the time the then Governor of California, Ronald Reagan, stated, "I hope they get botulism.") Many later concluded that this ransom was a political device to embarrass capitalists such as Hearst, a sleazy scam to which Patty Hearst, by then involved with the SLA, gave wholehearted allegiance.

In April 1974 Patty Hearst and other SLA members robbed the Hibernia Bank in San Francisco, Ms. Hearst captured on the bank's videotape, menacing the employees with a carbine. After her capture by authorities in a San Francisco apartment on September 18, 1975, Patricia Hearst was charged with bank robbery. A long legal battle ensued, resulting in Patty's conviction for armed robbery; she was sentenced to serve in a California prison for seven years. Using every legal effort at their command, the powerful Hearst family failed to have Patty's conviction overturned.

Through lawyers and influential friends, the Hearst family pressured President Jimmy Carter to commute the bank robber's sentence. Carter, along with the Department of Justice, succumbed to the pressure, and a presidential commutation was granted, freeing Patty in February 1979. She had served only twenty-two months and seventeen days.

The sensational events surrounding Patty Hearst seemed to be taken rather cavalierly by Patty herself. When being interviewed following the presidential commutation, Patty wore a T-shirt emblazoned with large letters reading, "Pardon Me." At the time she said to newsmen, "I don't see anything wrong with being Patty Hearst." This, of course, was the whole point. Had she been the daughter of anyone less powerful than Randolph Hearst she would undoubtedly be in prison serving her sentence at this writing.

HICKS, MARY AND ELIZABETH

Witchcraft ■ (Mary, ? −1716; Elizabeth, 1705−1716)

In the dark, superstitious witchcraft era of England, many illiterate and gullible women practiced black magic to intimidate their equally unsophisticated neighbors into making small donations to "witches" in order to maintain their spiritual good health. One such practitioner was Mary Hicks, who admitted to authorities that she had sold her soul to the devil. Further, she insisted that her nine-year-old daughter, Elizabeth, had also made the same dark bargain. Incredibly, the raving woman was believed. Mother and daughter were hanged at Huntington on Saturday, July 28, 1716.

HILL, MILDRED

Swindler ■ (1881− ?)

A confirmed con artist, Mildred Hill operated a phony marriage scam from Washington, D.C., during the early 1940s. She selected the prettiest girl of her ten children to use as a come-on in a matrimonial scheme in which she sent out the girl's picture as her own, writing that she was looking for the perfect mate. She would then meet prospective husbands, introducing herself as her own mother. She would milk the sucker for as much money as he might have, saying that she must have an operation before her daughter's wedding plans could be completed.

Inevitably, Mrs. Hill would sadly report later that her daughter had eloped with a used-

A sad Mildred Hill in custody after her swindle was exposed.

HILL, VIRGINIA

Narcotics Peddler, Mob Associate ■ (1916–1966)

She was beautiful, ruthless, and a danger to every man who ever loved her, a "kiss of death," according to one law enforcement officer who documented her notorious career. She was the mob girl and the bag lady of the international crime syndicate, a lover of poetry and a worshiper of hard cash. To Virginia Hill, gambling, drugs, and murder were nothing more than the elements of dark commerce. It was only business.

The home in which Virginia Hill was born on August 26, 1916, was similar to almost every other house in Lipscomb, Alabama—run-down, small, and confining. Her father, Mack Hill, was an itinerant handyman whose love of the bottle ruled his life. At the urging of his wife, Margaret, the family moved to nearby Bessemer, but the Hill home in this struggling community was nothing more than a shanty. Mack and Margaret Hill continued to have and raise children, ten in all, Virginia being the oldest of the four girls. She was a tomboy and enjoyed going barefoot, a fact newsman Lee Mortimer would later point out and embellish, saying that Virginia arrived in Chicago *without shoes*, which, of course, was ridiculous, like most of Lee Mortimer's reporting. Virginia never forgave Mortimer for that gratuitous statement and hated all newsmen by virtue of it.

When Margaret Hill left her lush of a husband, she took the children with her, and Virginia wound up being mother to the brood while Margaret worked. Resenting her surrogate-mother role, Virginia rebelled, and using her meager savings, ran away to Chicago in 1933. The seventeen-year-old girl had blossomed into a beauty, with long, rich chestnut hair, a voluptuous figure, and a butter-melting southern drawl. She had hoped to find some sort of show-business work at Chicago's World Fair but settled for a waitress job in a restaurant along

car salesman, leaving the sucker high and dry. So successful was this hustle that Mrs. Hill began to use a mimeograph to copy the hundreds of letters she sent to potential marks. She was finally tripped up by postal authorities and received a five-year sentence in 1945 for using the mails to defraud.

the midway. (Oddly enough, she could have waited on the much wanted bankrobber, John Dillinger, who spent a great deal of time at the fair with his girl of the moment, Mary Longnaker.)

Virginia Hill might have remained a waitress for the rest of her life had it not been for a thirty-three-year-old, myopic little fellow named Joseph Epstein. When the fair closed down, Virginia took another waitress job in a Loop restaurant at Randolph and Clark streets. One evening the mild-mannered Epstein walked to the counter, ordered a cup of coffee from her, and immediately fell in love with Virginia Hill. Nothing in this man's makeup ever induced Virginia to reciprocate that love. He was scrawny, hawk-nosed, and balding, and he wore thick glasses without which he groped about like a blind man. But he had money, more money than Virginia Hill had ever seen in her life. And that was enough to convince her to live with him.

She moved into an apartment Epstein provided and was soon wearing expensive gowns, furs, and jewelry. Her handbag was always stuffed with rolls of bills provided by the ever generous Epstein. Though when testifying before the Kefauver hearings almost twenty years later, she denied knowing the source of Epstein's fabulous wealth, Virginia was well aware of the nature of the cornucopia controlled by her adoring Joe. It was mob money, Capone money.

Epstein was a bookie, in fact Chicago's most prominent and successful bookie. In 1930 he had been adopted by Jake "Greasy Thumb" Guzik, Capone's most trusted lieutenant, and had been put in charge of the Chicago mob's wire service. Epstein was a genius with figures; he had a computer for a brain. He was a sort of broker to every bookie in town. Through his operation, the wire service made untold millions, and Epstein's share was all he could carry home each night.

Through Epstein Virginia's backcountry manners were smoothed out. She became his hostess at the many parties the wire service king gave, and at these parties the girl from Alabama met and befriended the top mob figures in the country—Frank Nitti, Tony Accardo, and the Fischetti brothers in Chicago, Joe Adonis, Lucky Luciano, and Frank Costello in New York. All belonged to the newly established crime syndi-

Mob girl Virginia Hill in a publicity still when she was a starlet at Columbia Pictures.

cate, and all who met the attractive Virginia were impressed at her street savvy, her special physical presence, and her quick mind. To these calculating men she was something more than just another "dumb broad."

When Virginia began taking pleasure trips, Epstein was more than happy to provide expense money—thousands of dollars, and with no questions asked. He remained her private bank until the day she died, undoubtedly out of the strange love he had for her. Epstein was happy just to see the girl periodically. He took delight in knowing that she was his product, a criminal pygmalion, as it were. And that was enough for him.

Though Virginia became the mistress of the Mafia killer Joe Adonis, also known to intimates as "Joey A," her role changed by the late 1930s. At that time she was constantly on the move by plane and train, traversing the country a dozen times a month. Her new position was that of bag girl. It was Virginia's responsibility to deliver cash, tens of thousands of dollars, to various syndicate leaders around the United States. These amounts were loans to city chieftains for various legitimate enterprises in which the syndicate wished to invest. Or they were payoffs for gambling debts, or, most important, the amounts were used as huge banks to set up nationwide bookie operations.

Still in her early twenties, Virginia Hill grew rich. She sent money south to her impoverished family, and when she, and especially her lavish parties, began to attract too much attention from the press, she claimed that a mythical husband, George Rogers, had died and left his handsome estate to her, a lie which caused the press to refer to her as "the heiress, Virginia Hill." The parties that drew the hot-eyed attention of the press took place in New York, at various syndicate-owned nightclubs. Virginia would toss about hundred-dollar bills, tipping waiters with rolls of bills, leaving hundreds on the bar as a tip after taking but one drink. At such times the southern siren would kick off her heels and shake wildly about on the dance floor, always choosing a Mexican partner if she could. She later married two Mexican nationals and kept close ties with them, the reason being not affection but drugs—a Mexican connection established by Virginia Hill that would bring the syndicate millions each year.

By 1938 Virginia headed west, going into the lucrative fields of Los Angeles at the instructions of Adonis, Costello, and other New York syndicate heads. She took an apartment and promptly married a rhumba dancer, Carlos Gonzalez Valdez. This marriage lasted only a short while. Virginia stormed into Valdez' dressing room one night before he was to perform and had him sign an official-looking document—he did not read English—and departed. Valdez had signed an uncontested divorce agreement.

In Hollywood, to establish the right contacts, Virginia enrolled in an acting school run by Columbia Pictures. She also threw fabulous parties. One at Ciro's cost $4,800 for the night. She paid in cash. Her nightly tabs at the swanky Mocambo Club on Sunset Boulevard never dipped below $1,000. She was still playing the role of the heiress, spreading the mob's money about to enchance her status with Hollywood's elite. Later she would date such stellar personalities as Victor Mature, Gene Krupa, Bruce Cabot, John Carroll, many of these men earnestly asking her to marry them.

Just after the bombing of Pearl Harbor, the parties stopped. Virginia was summoned to Chicago by the mob. Her departure was explained in heroic terms—she was on her way to enlist in the services of the Red Cross in the windy city. Innocently, the *Los Angeles Times* reported, "Virginia Hill said adieu to her nightclub spending . . . her $7,500 parties that had all Hollywood gasping, in order to devote her time, energy and money to defense. Besides joining the Red Cross, she has devoted the greatest portion of her fortune to defense bonds. . . . According to her cancelled check stubs, Miss Hill has contributed more than $70,000 to the country's nightclubs in the last year. 'And that ain't bandages,' she said."

The real purpose of Virginia's return to Chicago was to confer with mob bosses as to how to set up narcotics smuggling from Mexico into the United States. She was given letters of introduction to certain Mexican politicians and militarists and then returned to the Coast, at which time, the stories go, she met the love of her life, the brainy, volatile, and flamboyant gangster, Benjamin "Bugsy" Siegel. Their meeting was never reliably recorded. Some say she first met Siegel in a New York bar while drinking with her then current lover, Joe Adonis. Siegel had criticized her for drinking in the afternoon and she had dismissed him as an oddball. Adonis had cautioned her at the time: "That is the most dangerous man in America."

According to Florabel Muir, California gossip columnist writing in *Headline Happy*, "Not long after Benny Siegel decided to make Hollywood his home, Virginia Hill showed up on the cinema horizon, although there is nothing in the record to indicate they had anything more than a speaking acquaintance."

Siegel had gone west in the mid-1930s to aid Jack Dragna, then mob chieftain for the Coast, in setting up modern wire services for California gambling. He had also been instructed by his mentor, Meyer Lansky, one of the syndicate's board members, to open up narcotics traffic via Mexico. This was the real way Siegel and Hill met. She was to travel extensively between Mexico and Los Angeles, setting up smuggling contacts and routes and reporting to him. That they fell in love was incidental to the wishes of their crime bosses in the East. Siegel was given the names of Virginia's Mexican contacts and supervised the smuggling of hard drugs from that point on, sometimes personally making actual delivery.

Of this period, Harry J. Anslinger, head of the Federal Bureau of Narcotics, wrote in *The Murderers*, ". . . On the West Coast he [Siegel] acted as a vice president and unofficial 'agent' of the mob. Owner of the multi-million dollar Flamingo Club in Las Vegas, Nevada, Bugsy was shot to death in the home of a woman named Virginia Hill, who achieved a measure of 'standing' when she appeared before Senator Kefauver's TV Committee. We had known for some time that Siegel was interested in narcotics and we had a conspiracy case against him that was about to be sprung when he was slain. One dealer, Francisco Orbe, told our agents after Bugsy's murder, 'He gave me $20,000 to buy a shipment of heroin for him in Mexico City. I made the delivery to Siegel himself. I was to get sixty thousand dollars as my cut of the profits. He's dead and I'm still waiting for my money.' "

Virginia Hill never had to wait for money. It was always there, plentiful, endless packages from Epstein containing no less than $10,000 per mailing in thousand-dollar bills, plus the thousands Ben Siegel lavished upon her. For the next six years, until Siegel's assassination in 1947, Virginia Hill lived a fairy-tale life, buying thousands of dollars' worth of jewels and furs. She never wore the same designer original twice, nor a pair of $300 shoes, nor a hat, nor

Virginia Hill arriving at the Los Angeles air terminal, circa 1945, on the move for the mob.

gloves, nor a purse. She maintained several luxury apartments and penthouses in Beverly Hills, along with a mansion, leased from one of her admirers, Juan Romero, at 810 Linden Drive. Romero also owned Rudolph Valentino's "Wolfe's Lair" where Virginia also sometimes stayed. As the forties flitted by, Virginia's lifestyle became even richer, thicker with luxury. She continued as the syndicate's chief link with

The national crime syndicate's first West Coast chieftain Benjamin "Bugsy" Siegel, who was to become the love of Virginia Hill's life.

cate. He called it The Flamingo, which was Virginia's nickname. Its grand opening was to be studded with hundreds of Hollywood stars and movie executives, social contacts Virginia and Ben had carefully cultivated over the years. But only a few dignitaries showed up, one being movie star George Raft—but Raft had been Siegel's boyhood chum and was obligated to attend. Then, when the hotel was open and running, the dealers and other casino personnel stole enormous amounts from Siegel's gaming tables, rigging games for their friends, or failing to report the proper take each night.

The syndicate hierarchy, especially the bosses in Chicago who had invested heavily in The Flamingo, felt the Las Vegas enterprise was a miserable failure; they demanded Siegel return their money. In a typical display of violence, Siegel threatened his superiors, including Charles "Lucky" Luciano. He ignored the many cautions of his childhood crime mentor, Meyer Lansky, the man with whom he had risen through the ranks of New York's mobdom.

Siegel blatantly told his syndicate investors to "go to hell," and that he would repay their investment in The Flamingo when he "was good and ready." He paused long enough to slip south of the border with Virginia to marry his torrid mistress, or so she later claimed. Siegel returned to Las Vegas and attempted to shore up his failing casino but nothing he did seemed to help. His gangster past followed him everywhere, a murderous past that became widely known, not only to Las Vegas residents but to potential customers who stayed away from The Flamingo by the score.

Virginia Hill also stayed away, shunning her lover and refusing to go near The Flamingo, living out of the Romero house at 810 Linden in Beverly Hills. She and Siegel argued incessantly these days, over women who paid too much attention to the pretty-boy gangster, such as actress Marie "The Body" MacDonald. But mostly they argued about the enormous upkeep of The Flamingo. Virginia advised Siegel to abandon the project, to sell out to the Eastern bosses and stay with the gambling and narcotics rackets they had built up, but he would not let go of his dream, for it had become a part of his very self-image. If The Flamingo failed, Ben

the Mexican narcotics smugglers and as the bag lady who transported enormous sums about the country. But, in 1945, she also became involved with Ben Siegel's grand dream of constructing and running the most lavish gambling casino and hotel in then dirtwater Las Vegas.

The casino was built at a cost of millions, money Siegel borrowed both from legitimate businessmen and from members of the syndi-

Siegel failed, and such a thought was intolerable to the vainglorious gangster.

Finally the mob girl flew to Las Vegas and confronted Siegel. She had had enough of his broken-down dream, she told him. She was leaving for Paris where the scion of a champagne-producing family would entertain her.

"You're not going," came Siegel's order.

"You don't own me, Ben Siegel," Virginia roared back, expressing the philosophy of her life in a single sentence. She left that day for Chicago to meet Epstein and then went on to Paris. It was June 10, 1947. Ten days later, as the handsome gangster sat brooding in Virginia's Beverly Hills home, wondering if his "wife" would return to him and reading the *Los Angeles Times*, someone sent bone-shattering carbine bullets into his body, blowing away an eye, killing him instantly.

Much has been said about this obvious syndicate "hit," and many sources later speculated that the plans for Siegel's assassination were known to Virginia Hill, that it was because of her knowledge that she forced the argument with him and went off to Paris in an apparent huff, all of it an act to save her own face and possible involvement in the murder, which remains unsolved to this day. She never said an unkind word about her one and only true love, however, falling into a dead faint at a party in

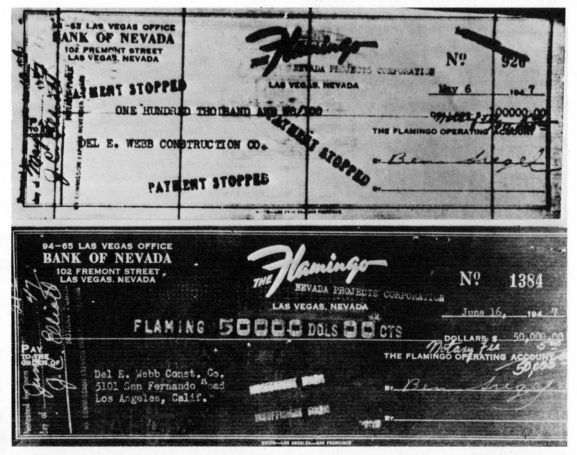

The hard reality of Bugsy Siegel's failure with his fabulous casino-hotel, the Flamingo, named after Virginia Hill: two checks, totaling $150,000, signed by Siegel and made out to the Del E. Webb Construction Co., which built the Flamingo, both of which bounced.

Bugsy Siegel's violent end inside Virginia's swanky Beverly Hills home, June 10, 1947.

Paris when informed of Siegel's death. Later, when returning to the States, Virginia shouted at badgering newsmen, "His name *wasn't* Bugsy Siegel, it was Ben, Ben Siegel! And he was no ganster—what do you know? Why, that man loved poetry! There was a poem both of us kept—" She fumbled inside her handbag, then gave up. "Aww, you jerks wouldn't understand anyway!"

More and more after that Virginia returned to Europe, meeting with Luciano in Italy in 1949, a meeting in which she practically ordered the all-powerful Mafia don to instruct his Sicilian lieutenants to treat her with more respect, according to one report. The mob girl visited all the European capitals, keeping up the appearance of a playgirl whose only desire was pleasure. Invariably, she ended most of her trips in Switzerland where, one reliable source had it, she made her regular deposits for the syndicate in unnumbered Swiss bank accounts.

The notoriety of the woman and her mob connections was so overpowering that by the time of the Kefauver hearings in 1951, watched by millions on television, she had become the star attraction of the senatorial probe into national crime activities. From her appearance and conduct she enjoyed every damning minute of her day before the cameras. On March 15, dressed in a wide-brim hat, fox fur, and a tailored suit, the mob girl walked into the hearing room in New York's Federal Court Building at Foley Square. Before the thirty-four-year-old Virginia were arranged her inquisitors, a bevy of senators making up the Kefauver Committee, officially known as the Special Committe to Investigate Organized Crime in Interstate Commerce.

She was late in arriving and was chastised by a member of the committee, but the chivalrous Senator Estes Kefauver, a wearer of coonskin caps from Tennessee, apologized for her, saying that Virginia "comes from Alabama and in the South it is an old-fashioned custom and an old southern custom for the ladies to keep the gentlemen waiting as long as they want to." She was then sworn in and the grilling began, questioning that seemed to exhilarate Virginia as she gave the committee wisecracks and wit.

She was asked how she made a living, how she could afford her expensive wardrobe, jewels, travel.

She replied, "Well, I worked for a while. Then the men I was around that gave me things were not gangsters or racketeers or whatever you call these other people. The only time I ever got anything from them was going and having fun and maybe a few presents. But I happened to go with other fellows. And for years I have been going to Mexico. I went with fellows down there. And like a lot of girls that they got. [Her reference here was undoubtedly to the expensive call girls.] Giving me things and bought me everything I want. And then when I was with Ben, he bought me everything."

"By *Ben* you mean Ben Siegel?"

"Yes, and he gave me some money, too, bought me a house in Florida. And then I used to bet horses. They asked me how much. I don't know. I figure whatever was close. [This was a reference to the IRS audits continually being made at this time of Virginia's bloated and

Virginia peering from her suite in the Westminster Hotel in Paris to see if the coast is clear of news photographers. This photo was snapped sixteen days after Siegel's assassination in California.

body in the narcotics traffic. But since I have been going to Mexico a lot of people have approached me and tried to give me those things. One fellow came one time and said he had a lot of H. and C.—which I don't know what H was, he told me it was heroin and cocaine. I told him to get out of the house [in Mexico]. He told me don't I know people. I said they'd break my neck if I mentioned such a thing. I had people who used to come in and say, 'Don't you want some?' I had an awful time getting rid of people down there that offered it to me."

The committee was especially eager to learn what Virginia knew of the business conducted by her gangster playmates.

"Just one thing," she was asked, "... you have testified now about a lot of details of your own finances and your own business. But are you really not in any position to give this committee any of the details you must have heard about the business of Siegel or Adonis?"

"But I never knew anything about their business," Virginia replied, her curving eyebrows arching. "They didn't tell me about their business. Why would they tell me? I don't care any-

seemingly unexplainable income.] I don't know if it is right or wrong. I paid income tax on that. That money I used to save it. When I am supposed to be out giving these parties, it was fellows that I was going with. They paid for things that I did. I didn't pay for it. If I was paying for it, I wouldn't have gone in the first place. After all, I didn't have to give my own parties, I don't think. But I have never had any businesses in my life. Whatever I have ever had was, outside of betting horses, was given to me."

Senatorial inquisitors then pushed Virginia hard on her relationships with known drug peddlers in Mexico. They wanted to know all about her trips to Mexico.

"Well," she answered matter-of-factly, "since it's been in the papers, I didn't know any-

A smartly tailored Virginia Hill smilingly testifying before the Kefauver Committee, March 15, 1951.

thing about business in the first place. I don't even understand it."

"The reason I ask you is that you seem to have a great deal of ability to handle financial affairs."

"Who, me?"

"You seem to have taken very good care of your own finances."

"I take care of myself."

"And, frankly, it is hard for me to believe, sitting here, watching you in the last half hour—"

"Whether you believe it or not, I don't know anything about their business. I wasn't interested. And, in the first place, if they ever started to talk about anything, I left, because I didn't want to know."

"It just seems impossible."

"Maybe it's impossible, but it's true."

In a separate closed session, members of the committee attempted to pin down Virginia's grand sources of income, or rather the reasons why such income was provided for her.

"Why should these men give you such large sums of money?" inquired Senator Charles Tobey of New Hampshire.

"I'd rather not say," Virginia said with a smile.

The elderly Tobey leaned forward, angry and frustrated with her evasions. "I insist you tell this committee."

Virginia Hill stared back at the entire committee, defiant and uttering one of the few truths of her entire testimony. "All right, then, it's because I'm the best goddamn lay in the country!"

The IRS had a hard time believing that Virginia Hill made all her money either with phenomenal luck at the race track or in bed and promptly began to investigate her financial background, learning that she had, within a decade, gone through more than $500,000 while paying hardly a penny in taxes. She countered by marrying a Sun Valley ski instructor, Hans Hauser, and moving to Europe. She had a child, Peter. While Virginia lived in Europe, refusing to return to the United States to face charges of fraudulent tax returns, an auction was held in which all her belongings, her furs, gowns, shoes, household furnishings, and the jewels she had neglected to pack in her haste to

"Get the hell away from me," Virginia Hill had shouted to news photographers a minute before this photo was taken and just after having been told that the IRS had auctioned off all her belongings to settle back taxes.

leave the country were sold off to the highest bidder to satisfy government claims against her.

Virginia spat out venomous remarks about the IRS and the United States, but remained in Europe, finally settling down in Salzburg, Austria. She also continued to receive her allowance from Joe Epstein in Chicago, a reported $3,000 a month.

Her fifteen-year exile in Europe ended on March 25, 1966, when she took an overdose of sleeping tablets. Virginia had tried to commit suicide many times in her stormy crime career, mostly by taking pills, but there was always someone around, as she knew there would be, to save her from herself. In 1966, she strolled to a snowbank and died; no one came to rescue her.

Exiled in Europe, Virginia Hill, older but no wiser, in a pensive mood.

While in Europe, Virginia had received more than $250,000 in cash from Epstein, according to newspaper reports. Yet her estate showed only a pittance. At the time of her death, the forty-nine-year-old Virginia Hill Hauser was separated from her fourth husband, and was living in a hotel room with fifteen-year-old Peter who was supporting the both of them with a waiter's wages.

It was suggested by *The New York Times* in one report that Virginia had died under mysterious circumstances. The *Spokane Daily Chronicle* went further, stating that the mob woman had intended to write her memoirs, "a project which might have aroused fears of exposure among some of the unsavory playmates of her salad days."

None of this was true. Virginia Hill didn't reveal anything to the Kefauver Committee and had never talked with anyone else. She kept her mouth shut, and that, coupled with Joe Epstein's weird undying love, was the reason why she was supported by the mob almost to the end. And there was a note that supported the suicide, saying that she was "fed up with life."

And Virginia Hill had lived her chosen life fully, breathing empty sighs for twenty years after the violent death of her one true love.

HINDLEY, MYRA

Murderer ■ (1943–   )

Myra Hindley was a healthy, seemingly normal girl when she went to work as a typist for a chemicals firm in Manchester, England, in 1961. She met and became infatuated with an oddball clerk in the firm, twenty-five-year-old Ian Brady. Though Myra made several advances to Brady, the dark-haired, thin-faced clerk shunned her. When he finally did agree to take Myra out, Brady, a raving sadist obsessed with pornography, Hitler, and murder, learned that the blonde typist had definite masochistic tendencies.

Within weeks Brady had persuaded Myra to pose before cameras with timing devices he had set up in his apartment, assuming pornographic positions with Brady. The couple kept a scrapbook of their pictures together which displayed their acrobatic sex.

In time, Myra and Bradley were wallowing in their sadism and masochism, consumed by the desire to commit any sensual act that would satisfy their perverted urges. Brady then insisted that they murder at random for the perverted thrill it would bring them. Children in the area began to disappear.

In November 1963, twelve-year-old John Kilbride was reported missing. Bradley and Myra had abducted the boy. They killed Kilbride and buried his body in a shallow grave on the moors. Next they abducted Lesley Ann Downey,

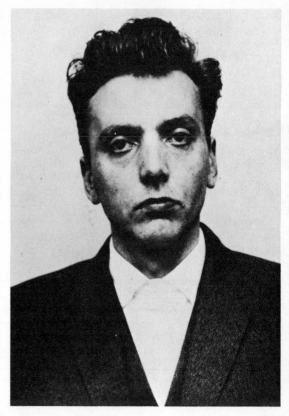

The "Moors Murderers" Myra Hindley and Ian Brady.

murdering her on December 26, 1964, burying her on the moors as well.

The couple waited until October 1965 to again express their maniacal streak. By then Myra had moved into her grandmother's house, which was closer to the moors where the sadistic couple had hidden their victims. Brady, on October 6, picked up seventeen-year-old Edward Evans, later described by Brady as a homosexual. Under some pretext he took the young man to the home of Myra's grandmother. Myra, at Brady's instructions, had also lured her seventeen-year-old brother-in-law, David Smith, to the scene. When Smith walked into the living room of the small house, he was paralyzed with shock at seeing Brady suddenly take an axe to Edwards, who was sitting on a sofa. The boy's screams as the axe was brought down on him again and again were so piercing that Smith

covered his ears. Brady struck Edwards fourteen vicious blows, smashing his head. Blood was everywhere.

With a sinister smile, Brady turned to Smith—he and Myra had undoubtedly wanted to make him an unwitting accomplice to the murder—and said, "It's done. It's the messiest yet. It normally only takes one blow!" A few weeks earlier, Smith had been introduced to the quirks of Myra and Brady, his head filled by the couple with the perverted philosophy of the Marquis de Sade. Brady had also told Smith that he had murdered "three or four persons," but Smith later said he had not then believed his statement. He did believe the awful carnage spread before him on the night of October 6.

Myra hurriedly got a blanket from upstairs. She calmed her ailing, almost deaf grandmother, who was in bed and inquiring about the noise, by telling the old woman that Brady had dropped a tape recorder on her foot. Going downstairs, Myra spread the blanket on the floor. Brady, who had tied chicken wire about the throat of his mangled victim, dragged the corpse by the neck to the blanket and wrapped it in the blanket. Smith stood by, pretending to enjoy the grisly scene, listening to Brady's disgusting quips, as he swaddled the corpse. "He's a bleeder, isn't he?" Brady laughed. He pointed to a place on the floor blotched with the insides of Evans's head. "Isn't he a brainy swine?" Myra laughed hysterically at that one.

Smith sat petrified on the edge of a chair, thinking he would be the berserk couple's next victim. After the body was dragged upstairs to an unused bedroom, Smith sat with Brady writing out an elaborate scheme to get rid of the corpse. (A police inspector later said of Brady that he "was the type who couldn't go on a picnic without putting it all down on paper.")

Finally Smith said matter-of-factly, "Well, I think I'd better be going home now." To his amazement Brady shrugged, wished him goodnight, and promised "more fun" the next day in secreting Evans's body. Smith rushed home, vomited, then blurted out the story to his wife, Maureen, Myra's sister. The couple called the police.

Officers rushed into the grandmother's house on Wardle Brook Avenue hours later, finding the body in the upstairs bedroom, exactly where Smith said it would be. Investigators then went to Manchester Central Station; Smith had told them that Brady kept two large suitcases in storage there. These were found and inside were pornographic books, photos, and two tape recordings.

One tape recorded the actual murder-in-progress of little Lesley Ann Downey. The hardened police officers listening to this gruesome tape gagged as they heard the voice of the little girl begging to be returned home, begging her kidnappers to stop hurting her. After killing the girl, the murderers had added a Christmas soundtrack to the tape as background music, the songs of "Jolly Old Saint Nicholas" and "Little Drummer Boy."

Photos found in one suitcase showed the ten-year-old girl standing naked, gagged, looking into the camera with terrified eyes. It was later determined that Brady and Myra had sexually abused the child before killing her, as was the case with the Kilbride boy. One photo showed Myra Hindley posing happily with her dog beside the grave of John Kilbride; the surrounding countryside in the photo enabled police to locate the site within hours. The bodies were shortly recovered and Brady and Myra taken into custody.

They appeared in a Chester court nattily dressed and staring blankly. When asked why Myra had blindly participated in Brady's horrendous crimes, the young woman, her large eyes ringed with dark circles, exclaimed, "I loved him. . . . I love him still. If he asked me to do something, I always went along with him eventually."

With Smith's testimony damning them, both were convicted—the all-male jury took only two hours and twenty-two minutes—and sentenced to life imprisonment on May 6, 1966; during the time the bestial killers awaited trial, the death penalty had been abolished in England. Though the murderous pair admitted the killings of Kilbride and Downey, they refused to admit having abducted two other children, never found, Pauline Reade and Keith Bennett, but everything pointed to these two children as being other victims of the "Moors Murderers." (The most thorough and chilling account of this monstrous case, albeit novelized, is Emlyn Williams's *Beyond Belief*.)

The killers are in prison at this writing and, fortunately, have no hope of parole.

HOUSDEN, JANE

Coiner ■ (? –1712)

A hardened criminal in her midthirties, Jane Housden was brought before the bar at the Old Bailey to be sentenced after her conviction for coining (see the Phoebe Harris entry explaining this offense). A sailor and adventurer named William Johnson, who had long been Jane's lover, appeared in court just as Jane was placed in the dock to hear her sentence.

Johnson swaggered to the dock, brushing aside guards, so that he could speak to Jane. A turnkey named Spurling grabbed Johnson's arm, telling him curtly, "You must wait until the hearing is finished before you can speak to the woman."

With a snarl, Johnson drew a pistol from his greatcoat and, in front of the entire court, shot the turnkey dead in his tracks, Jane Housden shouting encouragement to Johnson. Guards overwhelmed the killer, and, since the court was in session and scores of witnesses to the deed were present, both Housden and Johnson were instantly put on trial for murder, convicted, and condemned within minutes, the victim still lying in a pool of blood before the bench.

Housden and Johnson were taken to the scaffold on September 19, 1712. Even though there could be no doubt whatever as to their guilt in the Spurling murder, Housden and Johnson spat out curses at the crowd and shouted their innocence until they dangled dead. Johnson, as a traditional method of warning to other would-be flouters of the law, was hanged in chains near Holloway, between Islington and Highgate, his body left to rot in public view.

HOUSDEN, NINA

Murderer ■ (1916–   )

A rabidly jealous wife, Nina Housden hounded her bus-driver husband, Charles, at every turn, screaming curses at him if he so much as looked at another woman. The couple lived in a small apartment in Highland Park, Michigan, and, from all appearances, Housden was a dutiful husband, regularly turning over his $65-a-week paycheck to his wife. Yet the beautiful, dark-featured wife continued to plague Housden, phoning to check on his move-

Jane Housden encouraging William Johnson to shoot turnkey Spurling in court at the Old Bailey in 1712.

ments at work and at a bowling alley, where he indulged in his only pleasure.

Unable to stand these conditions, Housden filed for divorce and moved out. Just weeks later, a few days before the divorce was to be granted, Nina called Housden on December 18, 1947. She begged to see him "one last time." Housden relented and returned to the apartment where Nina pumped him full of so much liquor that he passed out. The woman then yanked a clothesline from beneath the couch where she had hidden it and knotted it about her husband's neck, strangling him to death in his stupor.

Rolling back the carpets, Nina put down a layer of newspapers, then piled Housden's corpse on these; she brought forth a cleaver and carving knife and spent the night hacking the corpse into pieces, which she then wrapped in gay Christmas paper. These bundles she piled into the back seat of her car and drove off, heading for her native state of Kentucky, thinking to dump the grisly "Christmas packages" in the wilds.

She had car trouble in Toledo, Ohio, and drove into a repair station. The mechanic informed Nina that it would take at least two days to make the repairs. "It's okay," she replied. "I'll live in the front seat until you're done. I'm low on cash and can't afford a motel."

The mechanic shrugged at this unorthodox arrangement but allowed the woman to stay in his garage while he worked on the car. Nina slept in the front seat, munching ham sandwiches and swilling cheap wine.

On the second day of the repairs, the mechanic slid from beneath the car and complained about the terrible odor coming from the back of the car.

"Well, it's your fault for taking so long," snapped Nina. "Those Christmas presents back there are for my folks. It's venison and the meat is spoiling. If you don't finish soon, you're gonna wind up paying for the spoilage!"

That night, with the protective Nina snoring in the front seat, the mechanic inspected one of the packages and found a human leg in the last stages of decomposition. He raced off to a police station. Nina was arrested, returned to Michigan where she was declared sane, and tried for the murder of her badly henpecked husband.

Upon her conviction and sentencing to life imprisonment, the jealous housewife turned to reporters and said, "Charlie wasn't a bad egg. He just made the mistake of running around with other women."

HOWARD, LADY FRANCES

Murderer ■ (1593–1632)

Lady Frances was a perfect player in the high court dramas of the Jacobean era, the time of James I of England, whose court was once described as "a royal cesspool of lust, intrigue and murder and James was a fit monarch for such evil days." James was as unsavory in appearance as he was in sexual appetite. Fat, unwashed, and odorous, he had an enormous tongue which lolled out of his flabby mouth and gave him the constant look of a wild beast crazed by thirst. He also had unbridled homo-

sexual tendencies, and practiced his various perversions with the handsomest male courtiers available. His favorite was one Robert Carr, a court page. James showered Carr with money and jewels, then, in return for Carr's favors, made him Viscount Rochester. Carr became the second most powerful man in England, aided by a penniless but intellectually gifted knight, Sir Thomas Overbury, his confidant.

Frances Howard, then only fifteen, appeared in James's court; the noble-born Frances—she was the daughter of the Countess of Suffolk—was a voluptuous siren who turned the head of every male, including Carr. She was described at the time as being an "oversexed young beauty who attracted the court gallants like flies round a honeypot." She became Carr's mistress, falling in love with James's favorite, mostly through the efforts of Overbury who, like Cyrano, wrote the love letters Carr sent to her. The fact that Frances was then married to the young Earl

Frances Howard at about the time she joined the royal court of James I.

of Essex did not interfere with her trysting with Carr.

To ensure her husband's continued indifference to her affair, Frances, who had an intense belief in witchcraft, sent for a notorious widow, Mrs. Anne Turner, a practitioner of occult rites. Frances implored the woman to supply her with some sort of magical potions to render her husband impotent. Mrs. Turner introduced Frances to Dr. Simon Forman, who, for exorbitant fees, supplied so-called "debilitation powders," which were used to dose her husband's food and which were spread throughout his bed linen over a period of two years. These powders appeared to work; the Earl of Essex made no advances upon his wife, and Frances promptly used his condition to petition the king for an annulment. James agreed, stating that Carr and Frances should afterwards be married. (That way James could keep Carr at court and continue to enjoy his homosexual relationship with him.)

Carr's consul and friend, Sir Thomas Overbury, openly criticized the annulment plan, further enraging his sponsor, Carr, by stating that Frances Howard would be his ruination. "She's nothing more than a common whore," Overbury stated bluntly. Such candor was Overbury's undoing. Under the pretext of saying that Overbury was plotting against the Crown, James ordered Overbury sent to the Tower of London. Of course, there would be no trial. Guarded day and night, the principled scholar was prey to anyone who wanted to end his life, and that person was Frances Howard.

She began to poison her nemesis slowly, sending Overbury tarts and pots of jelly, along with bottles of wine, all of it liberally laced with such exotic poisons as rose algar, lapis constitis, cantharides, and white arsenic. These were graciously given to the prisoner by Sir Gervase Helwys, commander of the Tower, and the head keeper, Richard Weston, both of whom were in league with Frances Howard. The poisoned tarts were so potently peppered with corrosive poisons that, on one occasion, the curious Weston lifted the crust on one of the tarts and his finger was almost burned away.

Overbury's constitution was sturdy, in fact, almost superhuman, for even though he ate the

food and drank the wine Frances sent to him, he survived for five months. The prisoner erupted with boils and festering sores and was in constant abdominal pain. He well knew he was being poisoned and, through a loyal servant, obtained antidotes, chiefly *aurum potabile*, from Dr. Francis Anthony, a close friend.

Frances increased the amounts of poison, sending Overbury roast partridges awash with sublimate of mercury. Still the man hung on. Mrs. Turner did what she could for the frustrated Frances, going to an apprentice apothecary, James Franklin. The young druggist guaranteed that his inventive poisons would do the trick; he sent along aquafortis, powder of diamonds, and poisons drawn from spiders. Still the stubborn Overbury lived.

"There must be an end to this man!" Frances screamed one day, and sent for a sympathetic physician, one Dr. Mayerne, who prepared a clyster, and the solution, sublimate of mercury, was administered by Paul de Lobel, an apothecary. Overbury's piteous suffering ended on September 15, 1613. Three days following the murder, Frances's marriage was annuled and a short time later she was married with great ceremony in Whitehall. James made Carr the Earl of Somerset, Frances becoming Lady Somerset.

Frances enjoyed as much power and deference at court as she would had she been a reigning queen; she and Carr literally ran the court. They became fabulously wealthy with James bestowing great lands on them. All would have gone as planned had not de Lobel, the apothecary who had injected the poison into Overbury's bowels, become sick and left for Holland. Knowing he was dying, the druggist wanted to clear his conscience; he made a deathbed confession that detailed the elaborate murder of Sir Thomas Overbury. He named all concerned with the murder plot.

Keeper Weston was arrested, tried, and hanged. Mrs. Turner was tried at Westminster Hall and also condemned. She went to the hangman in an expensive frilly gown with cuffs dyed with yellow starch, which she had made famous. The hangman, as a complement to Mrs. Turner's fashion setting, also wore cuffs dyed with yellow starch.

Frances after becoming Lady Somerset.

they would name him as a conspirator in Overbury's murder, which he was.

Still, the killers were made to do penance of sorts and were kept in the Tower, though comfortably, until 1622; they then retired to country life in Oxfordshire. Carr would live until 1645 and be honored at his burial in the Church of St. Paul's, Covent Garden. Frances Howard, Lady Somerset, had died thirteen years earlier. During their country life, Carr and Frances grew to hate the sight of one another. They did not speak for the last five years of Frances's life. Lady Somerset did not escape irony in her death. At thirty-nine Frances endured a uterine disorder that caused her flesh to rot, boils to cover her once beautiful body. The illness was lengthy and produced great pain, an agony that was likened to that of being poisoned.

HUTCHINSON, AMY

Murderer ■ (1733–1750)

Born into near poverty on the British Isle of Ely, Amy Hutchinson received a formal education until age twelve when she was sent to work as a servant. At sixteen she fell in love with a local youth, but he left to seek his fortune, and Amy married John Hutchinson, a sickly old man. When the youth returned from London on the day of her wedding, Amy resolved to murder her husband in order to be with the young man she loved. She dosed the old man's ale with arsenic and he died some days later, buried with little ceremony.

Amy immediately took up with her old lover, but gossip about the affair caused an investigation into Hutchinson's death. The body was exhumed and the poison found. Amy was tried and condemned, confessing to the murder shortly before she was strangled and burned on November 7, 1750.

Not until May 24, 1616, was Frances Howard tried for the murder of Overbury. James had done his best to stall the trial but gave in to pressure from powerful nobles. She was prosecuted by no less a light than the Attorney General, Sir Frances Bacon, who, mindful of the king's wishes, treated the beautiful woman with more kindness and gentleness than was ever shown to any other female felon in British history.

Wearing a dress of "black tammel, a cypress chaperon, a ruff and cuffs of cobweb lawn," Frances wept openly when the indictment against her was read. She trembled and quickly admitted her guilt. She was condemned. Carr's trial followed, and though he staunchly denied his guilt, he too, was convicted and ordered executed. King James pardoned them both, undoubtedly fearing that if he did not intervene,

ILY, NICOLE

Murderer ■ (1932–   )

Enacting childhood fantasies of spies, secreted fortunes, and shadowy underworld figures, Nicole Ily, a sixteen-year-old Parisian schoolgirl, encouraged two classmates, Claude Panconi and Bernard Petit, to shoot another classmate, Alain Guyader, son of a French author and civil servant, in December 1948. Guyader was mortally wounded with a shotgun Petit had taken from his home; his father was a police inspector in Paris.

It took more than twenty-eight months before the police unraveled the oddball killing. The students finally admitted their guilt. Panconi, who did the actual shooting, supposedly to save the "honor" of Nicole, received a ten-year sentence. Petit and Nicole Ily were sent to prison for three years.

IRWIN, ESTELLE MAE

Bankrobber ■ (1923–   )

Running away from her Topeka, Kansas, home in 1937 to join apprentice robber Bennie Dickson in Los Angeles, fifteen-year-old Stella Mae Irwin learned quickly the art of robbing banks. Dickson had already done seven years of a ten-year term for taking $1,147 from the State Bank of Stotesbury, Missouri. After marrying Dickson, Stella moved with her husband back to Dickson's home in Lake Benton, Minnesota, living in a cottage owned by Dickson's father. In the wilds, Dickson taught Stella how to become a crack shot and an expert getaway driver. When her "studies" were completed, Stella Mae, tucking her blonde locks under one of her husband's hats, jumped into a car with Dickson and roared off toward Elkton, South Dakota, only a few miles across the state line from Lake Benton, Minnesota; the pair entered the Corn Exchange Bank on August 25, 1938.

Finding that the vault was controlled by a time lock, the robbers sat on the floor, holding at bay employees and customers coming into the bank. The vault opened at exactly 3:00 P.M. Dickson and Stella Mae scooped up $2,174.64, every penny on hand, and locked the customers and employees in the vault; these people were fortuately rescued before suffocating.

Driving leisurely from town, the Dicksons went to Topeka, shed their overalls, and purchased snappy new clothes and a new car. They were at the height of fashion when they stepped into the Northwest Security National Bank of Brookings, South Dakota, on October 31, 1938. They followed the assistant cashier into the bank minutes after he unlocked the front doors. They lined up employees filing in to work and were then told that only about $2,000 was on hand, the rest being in the vault, which, with its automatic timing device, would only open two hours hence. The Dicksons said they would wait until then. They compelled the employees to get behind their cages and do business as usual with customers while the bandits stood nearby covering them with guns hidden from view.

Before the day's business began, Dickson cautioned, "Listen, you boys. You stay where you are until I tell you to move. I'm going to cut all the wires in this joint, so nobody can call for help. But my partner is Annie Oakley's little sister. She can hit the narrow end of a pin at a hundred yards and loves to do it. So keep your feet on the ground—the ground they're on now!"

For two hours the bandits loitered in the bank lobby as more than fifty customers came and went, conducting their banking business without the slightest notion that Dickson and Stella Mae were standing about with guns trained on the employees. When the vault did open, the bandits ordered two bank officials to pile all the cash and securities into a large sack and carry it to their car parked in front of the bank. The vice president and assistant manager of the bank did as they were told, going to the car with Dickson and throwing the sack into the rear of the car through an open window.

Through the bank window, Stella Mae, her automatic still trained on the other employees, saw Dickson slide behind the car's wheel and motion to her. She grabbed a sack of money—it contained less than $2,000—and said, waving the gun in her hand, "Say, you—we're taking those two guys with us, just in case. If one of you makes a move or lets out a squawk, I'll let 'em have a bullet from this."

With that Stella Mae sauntered to the street and got into the car beside Dickson, ordering the two bank officials to stand on the car's running boards. The car drove slowly out of town with the terrified officials holding on for dear life. They were freed without harm some miles outside Brookings. Dickson and Stella Mae drove off toward a deserted farm outside Tyler, Minnesota, only a few miles across the state line and not far from Lake Benton. With childish glee they counted the take from their second bank robbery—$17,529.99 in cash and $29,640.50 in securities.

The couple did not frighten at reading newspapers that announced that the FBI was looking for them. They drove to Detroit and went on a shopping spree. Then Stella drove to Topeka to see her parents. Bennie Dickson made the mistake of returning to a garage that he had rented to house the car he had used in the Brookings robbery. He was identified on this visit and, when he returned a few days later with Stella Mae, the couple were traced by police and FBI agents to a nearby tourist camp. Officers tried to arrest Dickson as he was backing his car out of a garage, but he evaded them in a barrage of gunfire. Stella Mae escaped on foot through the woods, working her way to a small town outside Topeka, where she and Dickson had agreed to rendezvous if such an emergency arose. Dickson appeared with a superficial head wound. He drove to Clinton, Iowa, and there forced a motorist to exchange cars with him, driving back to pick up Stella Mae. They then headed for Topeka where they abandoned the stolen car and drove off in a new car they had purchased earlier in Detroit.

The Dicksons felt they were safe and they still had most of the money from the Brookings robbery, yet they failed to realize that their description had been sent throughout the nation.

Two officers in a police car recognized the pair as they drove along a rural road in Michigan. The police pursued, Dickson gunning his car for all it was worth.

When the police began firing at Dickson's car in the high-speed pursuit, Stella Mae nervelessly grabbed one of the many rifles the couple always carried and jumped into the back seat, firing from the rear window. A bullet creased her head but she merely wiped away the blood and, taking careful aim, fired a bullet into the left front tire of the police car, sending the vehicle careening into a ditch.

By nightfall Dickson had commandeered a farmer's car, taking the farmer along as hostage. They drove into Indiana, and somewhere near South Bend exchanged cars with two more farmers, taking these bewildered men along too, as hostages. The car in which they were traveling was too crowded, so Dickson put one man into the trunk. When the car slowed at a railroad crossing, the farmer jumped from the unlocked trunk and ran off to give the alarm. At that point, the Dicksons released the other two farmers and headed for Hammond, Indiana.

In Hammond, Bennie Dickson rented a private garage, stored the stolen auto inside, and then purchased an old Ford for $40. Slowly the bandits drove south, going to New Orleans where they planned to settle down. Instead, they made the mistake of moving to St. Louis where Bennie Dickson was known to visit some of his underworld friends. On the evening of April 6, 1939, FBI agents cornered Dickson as he was walking away from a hamburger stand, carrying dinner to Stella who waited in a car a block away. Told to put up his hands, Dickson went for his two guns. He was shot to pieces by agents in a withering barrage of bullets.

Seeing the one-sided battle, Stella roared away. She escaped the St. Louis dragnet by driving to Kanas City with a travel-agent client who thought she was merely "hooking" a ride. Here Stella Mae was picked up by agents on April 7, 1939, as she walked the streets aimlessly, trying to figure out what to do, and only twenty-four hours after her husband had been shot down.

Oddly enough, the seventeen-year-old did not offer any resistance, but meekly surrendered to the FBI. "Sure-shot Stella" was tried and convicted in South Dakota for bank robbery and received a ten-year sentence.

JACKSON, MARY JANE ("BRICKTOP")

Prostitute, Murderer ■ (1836– ?)

Born in New Orleans, Mary Jane Jackson became a prostitute at fourteen. Her thick, flaming-red hair earned her the nickname of "Bricktop," but her ability to punish men physically made her the most feared trollop in the city, the toughest woman the French Quarter would ever know.

Having been the mistress of a bartender on Poydras Street, Bricktop was evicted one day by her lover. The tall, husky woman raced into the bar and beat up her lover so thoroughly that, at fight's end, the bartender was missing an ear and part of his nose. She then applied for a position in Archie Murphy's Dance-House on Gallatin Street, where her lethal ways frightened most potential customers. During this time, about 1856, Bricktop beat a man to death while wielding an enormous club. She next killed a seven-foot rail-thin New Orleans character named Long Charley with a knife she had had specially designed, one with two five-inch blades on either side of a center grip of German silver. According to one account, "with this fearsome weapon clutched in her fist, she could slash, cut, and stab in any direction without changing the position of her hand."

The woman was an unpredictable hellion and bad for business, Murphy finally concluded, driving her from his bordello. Bricktop opened a little brothel of her own in Dauphine Street, taking in three women almost as terrible as herself—Delia Swift, a murderous harlot popularly known as Bridget Fury; Ellen Collins, a scrappy little battler; and America Williams, a six-foot amazon of a whore who cracked heads for the sheer joy of it. No male customer welched on paying these awesome women their due. Next to Bricktop, Bridget Fury was the most feared woman in the Quarter at this time. She had entered whoredom in Cincinnati at age twelve, and there was no kind of depravity she did not practice. When a customer refused to pay her price in 1858, Bridget followed the man to the Poydras Street Market and buried an axe in his skull in full view of hundreds of shocked residents. She was sent to prison for life for this murder.

About a year later, on the afternoon of November 7, 1859, Bricktop, Ellen Collins, and America Williams were drinking in a beer garden at Rampart and St. Peter streets. Eating lunch at the next table was Laurent Fleury, who had the poor judgment to criticize the women's sloppy drinking habits.

Brandishing her knife, Bricktop swore at Fleury. Not knowing that this was the most dangerous strumpet in New Orleans, Fleury reached over and slapped Bricktop. In a flash all three women were on him, punching, kicking, clawing, screaming for his blood. The owner, Joe Seidensahl, ran to his customer's defense, but the women drove both men into a backyard and there slashed them to pieces, Bricktop doing most of the cutting with her famous knife. A man in an upstairs window tried to drive off the attacking women by firing a shot at them but they merely vented their fury on him by driving him from the window with a shower of bricks and rocks.

Police came streaming into the area as little Ellen Collins scrambled over a fence to make her escape. Bricktop and the behemoth America Williams were arrested, but only after two dozen officers managed to wrestle them to the ground. Both were dragged yelling oaths from the unconscious Seidensahl and Fleury. Seidensahl recovered in the hospital but Fleury died from the terrible wounds inflicted upon him by Bricktop. Both Bricktop and America Williams were held for trial but were released when the coroner could not determine the cause of Fleury's death, his ambiguous decision heavily influenced by money slipped to him from Bricktop's lawyer, who insisted Fleury had perished from heart trouble.

Bricktop's one great love flowered at this time when she met a prison turnkey, John Miller, while awaiting trial for the Fleury murder in the old Parish Prison. Miller, born in Gretna across the river from New Orleans, was a twenty-nine-year-old thug who had managed

boxers and had killed a man in a fight in Gallatin Street for which he was given a two-year prison term. He had bribed officials who made him a prison turnkey after he had served his time. Miller wanted this position so that he could collect bribes from inmates wanting favors.

When the Fleury murder charges were dropped, Bricktop left with Miller, who quit his prison job, retiring to his miserable hovel in Freetown where their love-hate relationship raged for more than two years. They fought constantly, knocking each other about, even knocking each other unconscious, and then, with equal fury, fornicated in front of the broken-down cabin to the chagrin of local inhabitants. Miller got the worst of it in a two-day battle in October 1861, when Bricktop slashed him with her infamous knife. She then left for New Orleans.

Recovering from his wounds, Miller implored the terrible trollop to return to Freetown which she did. He was obsessed with revenge, and, on the night of December 5, 1861, he attacked Bricktop with a cowhide whip, shouting, "You're getting too fresh, whore! You need a good thrashing to cure your evil ways!"

In seconds, the fearless Bricktop wrested the whip from her lover and began beating him with it. Miller had a ball and chain affixed to the stump of his left arm and he swung this deadly weapon at Bricktop's head. She ducked, grabbed the chain, and pulled Miller toward her. As he was yanked forward, Miller pulled a knife and tried to cut the woman's throat, but she chewed his hand and got hold of the knife. With a mighty shove, Bricktop slammed her lover into a wall and drove the knife into him five times. Miller slid to the floor, dead.

Bricktop was arrested and jailed. Commented the *Picayune* on December 8, 1861, "Both were degraded beings, regular penitentiary birds, habitual drunkards, and unworthy of any further notice from honest people." The *Daily Crescent* urged authorities to lock up Bricktop for life, adding, "This woman has been concerned in several murders, and is remarkable for bestial habits and ferocious manners. By the law making an example of her the community will be rid of two nuisances."

Though sent to prison for murdering Miller,

Bricktop again enjoyed astounding good fortune. She was released by Union General George F. Shepley, the military governor of the state, following the fall of New Orleans in 1862; Shepley, in an act of contempt for the South, freed all the felons. Bricktop, realizing she would again be jailed for life once the Union troops left the city, fled New Orleans and was never seen again.

JEANNERET, MARIE

Murderer ■ (? —1884)

A Swiss nurse, Marie Jeanneret was an attractive young woman when she poisoned her first victim in 1866, a friend named Berthet. A sadist, she killed for the perverse enjoyment it gave her, on one occasion using her favorite poison, belladonna (also called deadly nightshade), to murder an entire family named Juvet. Her sinister reputation was summed up by a Dr. Binet, who, unable to prove murder against the clever nurse, once advised a patient who was considering employing Marie, "Don't have anything to do with her. All her patients die."

Another physician, a Dr. Rapin, finally voiced his suspicions about Marie to authorities and the woman was arrested. Bodies of her deceased clients were examined and several types of poison were found. Marie had used atropine (a derivative of belladonna), morphine, and antimony, a mineral. Though convicted of murdering seven people, Marie Jeanneret swayed the jury in her favor and received only twenty years in prison. She died in 1884.

JEFFRIES, ELIZABETH

Murderer ■ (? —1752)

E lizabeth Jeffries was about eighteen when she went to work for her uncle, who had amassed a small fortune in London as a butcher and had retired to a comfortable estate in Walthamstow. It was Elizabeth's job to oversee the estate and manage the servants. Jeffries was harshly demanding of the young woman, but he promised to leave his entire estate to her in his will. Then whenever she displeased him, he threatened to eliminate her from his will. This seesaw situation finally prompted Elizabeth to arrange for her uncle's murder.

Having promised John Swan, a servant in the Jefferies house, 100 pounds for shooting the uncle, Elizabeth pretended to neighbors that highwaymen had forced their way into the Jeffries house on July 3, 1751, shot Jeffries, and looted the place of the family silverware. (Swan had shot Jeffries, Elizabeth had placed the silverware in a sack and secreted the loot.) The story was believed at first.

Swan later got drunk and drew suspicion from authorities. He was arrested and implicated Elizabeth. Both were tried at Chelmsford, on March 11, 1752. Elizabeth wrote out a lengthy confession and was condemned with Swan. Both were taken to Epping Forest and hanged on March 28, 1752. The gibbet upon which Swan was hanged was later moved next to a well-traveled road and the body was ordered to be allowed to rot in chains, so that all passersby would be warned.

JEFFS, DOREEN

Murderer ■ (? −1965)

Doreen Jeffs murdered her infant daughter Linda in November 1960 in Eastbourne, England, then faked the child's kidnapping. The body was quickly found and the mother confronted. She pleaded guilty to infanticide, but her defense attorney successfully argued that Mrs. Jeffs was "a woman who committed an offense while under the stress of childbirth." Linda Jeffs had been born prematurely a month before her murder.

Mrs. Jeffs was sent to a mental institution and was later put on probation. She tried to commit suicide by taking gas but was interrupted. In January 1965, Mrs. Jeffs, after folding her clothes neatly at the edge of a cliff overlooking the English Channel near Beachy Head, hurled herself into the ocean. Her body floated to shore some days later.

JEGADO, HELENE

Murderer ■ (? −1851)

A cook and housekeeper who murdered for the thrill of seeing her victims die in agony, Hélène Jegado began her career some time in her late thirties, working as a maid for clergymen in France. When displeased with the members of any household in which she was working, Hélène simply seasoned their food with arsenic. One family of seven was wiped out in this way, including Hélène's own sister.

In 1849, Hélène traveled to Rennes, France, and went to work as a cook in the home of university professor Théophile Bidard. When one of the servants died in agony, Hélène, for some odd reason, told Bidard that there was no need to hire another girl to replace the dead servant, that she, Hélène, would perform this girl's duties as well as her own.

Rosalie Sarrazin subsequently joined the Bidard household as housekeeper, nominally Jegado's superior. The illiterate Hélène watched in envy as Sarrazin did the family bookkeeping. In July 1851, Sarrazin became violently ill, vomiting and writhing in great pain, and then died. Bidard, suspicious of his cook, called the police. When they appeared, Hélène shouted, "I am innocent!"

"Of what?" replied an inspector. "Nobody has accused you."

The accusations came later when poison was found in the body of Rosalie Sarrazin and when arsenic was found in at least twenty-three other victims of the murderous cook. (She may have been responsible for more than sixty deaths by poison.)

Tried at Rennes in December 1851, Hélène was found guilty. She was beheaded by the guillotine.

JONES, ELIZABETH MARINA

Murderer ■ (1926–   )

The dull gray life of Neath in South Wales, a mining district, caused Elizabeth Marina Jones to run away to the lights of London in 1943. There she worked as a barmaid, movie usherette, waitress, and finally, under the nom de sex of Georgina Grayson, a stripteaser in sleazy clubs where within a year she had met an American GI, Karl Gustav Hulten. He had been AWOL for weeks, had stolen a truck and a gun, and was impersonating an American officer, calling himself "Lieutenant Ricky Allen."

The Swedish-born Hulten had been raised in Chicago before joining the paratroopers; his conduct in the U.S. Army was less than enviable. He had proved himself incorrigible and slovenly at every turn. When first meeting the bountiful

Miss Jones, he easily convinced her that he could provide the thrills in life she was seeking. As an example of what he intended, he hopped with Elizabeth into a car for hire driven by thirty-four-year-old George Edward Heath on October 7, 1944, and ordered the part-time cabbie to "drive around anywhere, maybe to the top of King Street."

Pretending to get out at their destination, Hulten pulled his automatic and shot the driver in the back. He then jumped behind the wheel, and, as Heath moaned his way to death, the excited Elizabeth Jones rummaged through the cabbie's pockets, taking his small earnings for the night. The couple dumped Heath's body near Staines and drove off.

The car was identified two days later with Hulten behind the wheel. He was arrested and taken to U.S. Army officials and interrogated by the Criminal Investigation Department. He staunchly denied killing Heath. Then Elizabeth Jones was picked up for questioning. She subsequently confessed but put the greater blame on her GI boyfriend, the ignorant stripteaser flatly telling London police, "Well, how was I to know—he told me he was a gangster from Chicago and that he was the head of his old mob which had moved to London . . . right here in London!" Hulten was turned over to British authorities and was tried and convicted for Heath's murder. He was hanged on March 8, 1945. The bosomy Elizabeth was reprieved from the hangman but sent to prison for life.

JONES, MRS. MARY

Kidnapper ■ (1884–1947)

Austrian-born Mary Jones was accused of kidnapping three-year-old Raimonde von Maluski from his home at 600 West 178th Street in New York City on March 29, 1925, as the boy watched a Salvation Army parade. She had been seen riding about the neighborhood in a taxi some days earlier, and was known to have a deep hatred for the Von Maluski family, the boy's father having previously charged her with stealing a diamond stickpin and $10 in cash from his home when she came to collect her husband's belongings.

Her husband, Harold Jones, assisted Von Maluski in maintaining the buiding where Von Maluski lived; Jones had been turned in to authorities for parole violation at the time by none other than Mary Jones. As irrational as the woman's actions seemed at times, she had been examined in Bellevue in 1920 and been judged sane.

Following Von Maluski's charges of theft against her, Mrs. Jones had attempted to hire three stew bums in the Bowery for $100. They would be paid after they had killed Maluski. When the bums refused—they later testified against her—it was concluded that Mary sought revenge by kidnapping little Raimonde, taking him to a secluded area where she killed the child and hid the body. She was charged with kidnapping. During her trial she confided to another inmate that the Von Maluski child "was dead and that's the end of it." She was found guilty.

When Mrs. Jones was sentenced to twenty-five to forty years in Auburn Prison, the woman put on a cynical smile but refused to make comment. "I believe you have killed that child," presiding Judge Collins told her. "You took that child in a taxicab away from the life of the city. . . . Since the child cannot be located, there is only one thing to believe—that you took him to a lonely place and killed him."

Mrs. Mary Jones made no comment. As she was being led to prison, she snapped to reporters, "The jury made a terrible mistake in finding me guilty of the boy's kidnapping."

The body of Raimonde von Maluski was never found.

JUDD, WINNIE RUTH

Murderer ■ (1909–   )

While working in a Phoenix clinic, Winnie Ruth Judd shot and killed her two best friends, Helwig "Sammy" Samuelson and Mrs. Agnes LeRoi, then dismembered the bodies of the two women and shipped the horrible freight to Los Angeles. When Winnie called for the trunk some days later in the baggage room of the Southern Pacific Railroad in Los Angeles, the clerk on duty grew suspicious; Winnie's manner was extremely nervous and the clerk also detected blood running from the trunk. When asked about the contents, the at-

Winnie Ruth Judd in 1971 after receiving her "out-of-state" parole. She had escaped seven times after becoming the notorious "trunk murderer."

Winnie Ruth Judd at the time of her sensational trial, October 23, 1931.

tractive Winnie shrugged and said she'd get the keys from her car so the trunk could be inspected.

She did not return to the baggage room but hurried to her car parked nearby and drove off. The alert clerk, however, managed to take down her license number and she was quickly apprehended. After the trunk was forced open and its grisly contents revealed, Winnie was charged with murder. Her trial took place in the winter of 1932. At first she insisted that the two women had unaccountably attacked her and she had killed them in self-defense, then panicked and shipped their remains out of Phoenix. When that story failed, Winnie's lawyer tried to plead her insane; her antics in court—she yelled and threatened to throw herself out of a window—convinced a jury and she was sent to a mental asylum for life. Winnie escaped several times and was finally released on December 22, 1971.

KELLY, KATHRYN THORNE

Kidnapper ■ (1904–)

Born Cleo Coleman in Saltillo, Mississippi, Kathryn wed while in her midteens but was divorced two years later. At seventeen she was running bootleg hooch for her mother, who at the time was operating out of Fort Worth, Texas. In 1924 Kathryn was married again, to Charlie Thorne, a local bootlegger. Their incessant fights ended in 1927 when Thorne committed suicide, though there was every reason to suspect Kathryn had more than inspired Thorne's self-destruction.

By the mid-1920s, Kathryn Shannon Thorne was a sophisticated, seemingly well-educated woman of gracious manners and bearing. Her native intelligence had always been superior to those around her. Most of it was gloss, however, a superficial style learned from the movies and popular magazines. The rest was cunning.

When Kathryn met the alcholic bootlegger George Kelly, there was nothing in their relationship that indicated much of a future for either of them, but Kathryn saw potential in the awkward, bumbling Kelly. For one thing he carried out her orders without a question asked. When Kathryn ordered George to get a reputation for himself as a bandit, Kelly promptly robbed several banks in Texas, Oklahoma, and the state of Washington, Kathryn acting as mentor to him and two others, she being the one who actually cased the banks and organized and detailed the plans for each robbery.

Beyond the easy money that flowed into Kathryn's hands as a result of these robberies, allowing her to indulge in extravagant purchases of cars, jewelry, and furs, her plan was to turn Kelly into a criminal superstar. To that end she bought him a machine gun from a Texas pawnbroker and compelled Kelly, by then her husband, to practice firing it each day. She would later hand out used cartridges from Kelly's weapon, impressing underworld figures with her husband's ferocity, telling them,

Kathryn Kelly on trial with her husband, George "Machine Gun" Kelly, in 1933.

"Here's a souvenir for you, a cartridge fired by Machine-Gun Kelly."

When Kathryn read about the increasing number of kidnappings throughout the United States, she resolved to move to "the big time." She badgered her husband into kidnapping a businessman from South Bend, Indiana. Kathryn had simply picked his name at random from a telephone directory. The Kellys held the man for a few days until discovering that his family had nowhere near the $50,000 ransom they were demanding for his release. Disgustedly, the Kellys freed the man and went to Kansas City to plan their next move.

Kathryn Kelly carefully researched the background of her next kidnapping victim and was soon convinced that millionaire oilman Charles F. Urschel did, indeed, have substantial money. Urschel was taken from the front porch of his Oklahoma City home on the night of July 22, 1933, by Kelly and Albert Bates. He was whisked to the remote Texas ranch owned by Kathryn's mother and stepfather, where he was held until a $200,000 ransom was paid to Kelly through a family intermediary in Kansas City. Urschel was released unharmed.

Urschel cooperated with FBI agents; the oilman's uncanny memory subsequently led to the apprehension of Kathryn's parents and brother at the Shannon ranch in Texas. Urschel though blindfolded, had remembered hearing a plane pass directly overhead each day during his captivity except Sunday, when a storm apparently sent the plane off course. Through meteorological reports and airline schedules, agents were able to pinpoint the Shannon ranch.

Urschel's survival had nothing to do with Kathryn Kelly. Within earshot of the blindfolded captive, she had argued with her gang members for the oilman's death, shouting, "What I think is that we're a bunch of saps if we turn this son-of-a-bitch loose! Kill the bastard! Then we won't have any more trouble with him!"

Kelly and Bates wanted no part of murder and finally talked the woman down. No doubt Kelly, who had served time for bootlegging, was thinking about the possibilities of being executed if Urschel were killed, now that kidnapping was a federal offense.

Following the kidnapping, Kathryn and Kelly drove north to St. Paul where they exchanged the ransom money for less than fifty cents on the dollar with "Boss" John J. McLaughlin and other criminal bigwigs in the area. (St. Paul, Minnesota, at the time, was the great haven for the 1930s outlaws, whose presence was tolerated for a price by a corrupt local government; hundreds of the most wanted felons in America, including the Barker and Dillinger gang members, used the city as a refuge.)

Kathryn used the kidnapping loot to buy a platinum watch with 234 diamonds, a $1,000 dinner ring, and an expensive designer-original wardrobe, complete with furs, and a new sixteen-cylinder touring car. She gave Kelly a new machine gun and a case of rye. The couple then moved aimlessly from Chicago to Texas and on to Kansas City and St. Louis. All the while Kathryn schemed to have her parents released from federal custody. She tried to exchange her husband for the Shannons with Kelly's slavish approval. The FBI would have none of it.

Hiding out in a cheap Memphis boardinghouse, the Kellys bickered constantly about their fate, Kathryn insisting that her husband, whom she had taken to calling "Pop-Gun" Kelly, turn himself in and save her parents. Perhaps there was still a way out of their predicament. Maybe they could escape to a foreign country.

For the first and only time ever, Kelly exploded, telling his calculating wife, "Now maybe you'll get it through your head what this heat is! I was the biggest damn fool in the world to ever let you suck me into this thing. Here I was, making grand a year knocking over those tin-can state banks. But that wasn't good enough for you. Now we've got heat smeared all over us. And you got me into this mess!"

Through a tip, police discovered the Kellys' hideout in Memphis and surrounded the boardinghouse on September 27, 1933. Memphis police sergeant W. J. Raney crept, gun in hand, into the rooms occupied by the Kellys. He was met by a smiling George Kelly, who rubbed sleep from his eyes and said, "I've been waiting for you." He was that relieved to be captured. The FBI had no hand in the capture. (The tale J. Edgar Hoover often told later of his agents bursting into the rooms to confront the snarling Kelly was the director's total fabrication and typical of his dogged search for the limelight; Kelly never said, "Don't shoot, G-Men!")

Kelly and Kathryn were tried and convicted, Kathryn posing happily for newsmen during her trial adorned in elegant black satin gowns which showed off her handsome figure. Both were sent to prison for life, Kelly dying in Leavenworth in 1954, full of regret for the kidnapping that made him famous.

No remorse was ever uttered by the cold-blooded Kathryn Kelly. She was finally released from the Cincinnati Workhouse in 1958 and returned to Texas to visit old haunts and former friends. She may be alive at this writing, address unknown, living in the Lone Star State, remembering the whirlwind crime wave she helped create in the Terrible Thirties.

KENT, CONSTANCE

Murderer ■ (1844– ?)

Of all the murderers of the Victorian era, none shocked the world more than the demure and proper schoolgirl, Constance Emilie Kent. Her act of homicide was so heinous and her plot to commit the act and cover it up so calculating that it branded her in the minds of law-abiding British citizens as a special kind of

Constance Kent, as a schoolgirl of sixteen.

That the Kents enjoyed the better things of life was due to the well-paid government position, that of deputy inspector of two cloth factories, of Samuel Savile Kent. Kent was the local Rich Man, a position he reinforced with a pompous and huffy bearing that endeared him to no one. His gruff manners made him disliked by the managers of the factories he inspected, and his truculent attitude incurred the wrath of his neighbors. Kent closed off any view of his mansion by having a large fence erected at the edge of his property, making the villagers living in humble cottages nearby all the more aware of their lesser social position, and branding them trespassers. Kent even took to patrolling the little stream bubbling through his property, gun in hand, and pot-shooting (though never successfully) at poachers after his fat trout.

Kent's authority at home was unquestioned, and, in the words of Douglas G. Browne, writing in *The Rise of Scotland Yard*, "He was what has come to be regarded as the typical Victorian father, very much the head of the family, and a selfish if on the whole well-meaning tyrant."

This stern patriarch married twice. His first wife gave birth to four children, two of whom died in infancy before 1836. In that year, the first Mrs. Kent suddenly went mildly insane, though her mental imbalance was not such to cause her to be confined. Her husband thought to cure her of her hallucinations by making her repeatedly pregnant. Four more children were born, all of them dying within a few months.

At this point, to bring some relief to his mentally plagued wife and the young surviving children, Kent at long last consented to hire a governess, a Miss Pratt, an attractive woman whose voluptuousness may actually have caused Mrs. Kent's mental condition to further deteriorate, especially when seeing the governess in close conversation with her employer. The dutiful Mrs. Kent nevertheless bore two more children, Constance in 1844, and William in 1845, both of whom survived. Then, in 1852, having lived most of her adult life with a thundering lord and master, and given birth to ten children, Mrs. Kent died.

Her husband was held blameless for the miserable mental state in which Mrs. Kent went to her grave, the local parson intoning at her

monster, one who could easily lurk in the shadows of their own sweet homes, murmuring plans of murder in dark hallways, beneath staircases, behind pantry doors. The sixteen-year-old Constance was no foreigner wheezing anarchy, but the epitome of British upper-class mores; she was attractive, intelligent, well mannered, and most of all, respectful. She was also, one might add, in light of her guileful deed, a malignant creature without compassion, without remorse.

Constance lived comfortably, with her parents, six brothers and sisters, and three maidservants, in a three-story mansion-like home called Road Hill House. The house was airy and bright, and was surrounded by quiet green acres of meadow and woodland through which ran a stream of pristine waters. Nearby was the peaceful village of Road (now called Rode), five miles from the town of Trowbridge in Somerset, England.

funeral that all of it was due to "the mysterious working of Providence." (This remark was later to evoke the wry comment of crime writer Edmund Pearson in *Murder at Smutty Nose* that "there seems to have been some grudge against women in the mind of Providence during the Eighteenth and early Nineteenth centuries, as will appear by the examination of dates on tombstones in any graveyard.")

Samuel Kent lost no time in marrying the beautiful and sympathetic Miss Pratt, his three daughters, two of whom were in their twenties, serving as bridesmaids. Constance was then nine. The prolific Mr. Kent then proceeded to produce with his second wife three more children by the year 1860, the favorite being Francis Savile Kent, who in that year was a precocious three-year-old. And the second Mrs. Kent was, at the time, about to deliver her fourth child. In fact, her incapacity had compelled Kent to hire a nurse, Elizabeth Gough, to look after the smaller children of the house.

The Kents slept in a second-floor room, a small daughter in a crib nearby. The nursery was across the hall. Here slept Miss Gough, a one-year-old girl, and Francis Savile Kent. The two grown daughters by Kent's earlier marriage roomed together on the third floor. Also on the same floor but in separate rooms were William, age fifteen, and Constance, sixteen. In smaller rooms on the third floor slept the cook and housemaid.

All was quiet in the house on the evening of June 29, 1860, an early-summer night full of warm breezes and the gentle sounds of tree limbs swaying. As was the custom, the twelve persons inside the mansion had said their prayers together in the drawing room after supper before retiring. Nurse Gough was the last to stir, arranging the bedclothes of the children in her care before slipping into bed. At about 5:00 A.M. Saturday morning, the nurse awoke as dawn crept across the lawns of Road Hill House. She checked the baby, then looked to the cot where Francis Kent slept. It was empty, the impression his small form had made upon the blankets still visible. Nurse Gough was not alarmed since she knew it was Mrs. Kent's habit to sometimes come to the nursery in the dead of night and carry her favorite child back to her own bed.

Elizabeth Gough rolled over in bed and went back to sleep. An hour later she was up and dressed, and had read from her Bible.

Softly, the nurse went to her mistress's bedroom door on the second floor, knocking quietly. Mrs. Kent came to the door and the nurse inquired, "Should I take Master Savile now?"

"But he's not here," Mrs. Kent replied, becoming alarmed.

Elizabeth Gough blinked puzzlement. "He's not in the nursery, ma'am."

With that Mrs. Kent raced downstairs in a frantic search for the child while the nurse hurriedly climbed the stairs to the third floor where she woke the other children. The grown daughters reported having seen nothing of the child. The same claim was made by William. "I have no suggestions to make," stated Constance when asked about the boy.

By this time the entire household was in a panic. The only thing amiss was a window found open in the drawing room, one that Samuel Kent had closed before going to bed. As he peered through the open window and across the lawn to a cluster of trees, it occurred to Kent that his son could well have been kidnapped by villagers enraged by his attacks on poachers. He told his family of this and the members nodded solemnly. Kent dressed hurriedly, then ran to his carriage, whipping his horses in a fast gallop toward the police station in Trowbridge.

In his absence, Mrs. Kent scolded Elizabeth Gough. "You should have told me at once when you discovered Savile missing."

Nurse Gough, a patient domestic, said nothing. When serveral hours later Mrs. Kent repeated the charge of neglect, the vexed nurse threw up her hands, and in a sorrowful voice cried out, "Oh, ma'am, it's revenge!" When asked by her mistress to explain her words, the nurse shook her head and remained silent, a silence that was to frustrate Scotland Yard in the weeks to come. Elizabeth's startling comment, although the nurse was never to make a direct accusation any time after the tragedy, did express her abiding suspicions of one member of the household.

While Kent raced for the police, the alarm spread among the villagers in Road. They flocked to the mansion, searching the grounds.

Two men, ironically two fishermen who had been scared away from the trout stream by Kent's wild shooting, parted some thick shrubbery and opened the door to a servant's outhouse no longer in use. On the floor was blood. Inside the vault was the body of Francis Savile Kent still wearing his nightgown. His killer had so severely slashed the boy's throat that he was almost beheaded. There was also a deep wound in the left side of the boy's chest.

By the time the boy's body had been returned to the mansion, Samuel Kent had arrived with police from Trowbridge, Inspector Foley in charge. After a mad hour of supposition, Foley concluded the murderer was a member of the household and told this to Samuel Kent.

"Sir, I want permission to search your house," asked Foley.

"Of course," replied Kent, "but I'm sure that some stranger has killed my child."

Foley's so-called search of the premises was to order the women disrobed by the wife of one of his policemen, their bodies closely scrutinized for the murder weapon. Of course, none was found. One of Foley's officers suddenly whispered to the inspector to follow him to the back kitchen. There the inspector was shown "a blood-stained woman's shift," which the policeman had found stuffed into a boiler hole. Foley, wholly inexperienced with detective work, stupidly ordered the shift to be put back into the boiler hole, chastising the officer with a wagging finger and some grunts about "personal property."

The inspector, only an hour later, blundered horrendously again when he found a bloody imprint from a hand on a windowpane, the very window that had been found open in the drawing room, and, to the everlasting mortification of Scotland Yard, hurriedly took out his own handkerchief and wiped the print away. He explained with a smile to some of his men that this was necessary "in order not to frighten the family."

An inquest was held a few days later with the villagers openly speculating as to the killer's identity. Many insisted that Samuel Kent had murdered his own son for inexplicable reasons, but such feelings stemmed from their dislike for his landed-gentry ways. Others, though not making any specific charges, voiced their dislike for William and Constance Kent, so much so that the coroner's jury called them to testify. Because of the hostility of the crowd, the coroner adjourned the hearing to the Kent mansion.

William Kent had nothing to contribute. He had heard nothing on the night of the murder, he had seen nothing. Constance sat calmly in a drawing room chair and gave much the same testimony. She was quite the young lady while testifying, registering shock and sorrow at the death of her half brother, dabbing her eyes with a lace handkerchief. "I learned he was missing from Elizabeth Gough," she said deliberately, looking with a steady gaze at the nurse, who was wringing her hands distractedly. "Everyone was kind to Francis," she said to the jury. "I never heard of anyone wishing him ill. I played with him often. I was very fond of him and I believe he was fond of me."

The jury then returned a verdict of murder against "some person or persons unknown." But in the mind of the considerate Inspector Foley, the identity of the inhuman child killer was not unknown. With his rural policeman's mentality, in absence of a butler, he fixed the guilt upon Nurse Gough. He arrested her for murder, but the woman's background and manner proved spotless coupled to the hard fact that she had no motive whatsoever for killing the child. She was released.

While the police, led by the blustering Inspector Foley, wallowed in wild speculation and got nowhere, the case became a *cause célèbre* in the press. Scotland Yard's failure to charge a likely suspect, let alone produce any kind of logical evidence, brought down upon the police agency a boiling storm of protest and criticism. On July 15, the Yard responded by sending one of their best men, Detective-Inspector Jonathan Whicher, to handle the case personally.

Whicher, though lacking a great deal of formal schooling, was a perceptive policeman, unusually gifted, in fact, with an incisive, deductive mind, a man who knew human nature well and whose suspicions had proved most often correct. His appearance in Trowbridge caused open resentment and antagonism from the hapless Inspector Foley, who said nothing to Whicher about the bloody shift or the handprint.

(Both men would later be profiled in Wilkie Collins's haunting novel, *The Moonstone*, the fumbling Foley as Superintendent Seegrave, and Whicher as Sergeant Cuff. Collins also used the idea of the bloody shift when a character in the novel, Franklin Blake, brushes against the door of Rachel Verinder's bedroom, staining his nightgown with paint.)

No help was offered to Whicher by Foley or the local police. The detective-inspector set off on his own investigation. For days, Whicher doggedly pursued evidence against only one person in the Kent household. After lengthy talks with Constance Kent, Whicher had been convinced of her guilt. But he had to prove it.

The available evidence, thanks to the stupidity of Foley, was less than meager, but Whicher did his best. He read with great interest in the *Somerset and Wilts Journal*, the local newspaper speculating on the case, that "a somewhat unusual number of servants have been discharged from this establishment [the Kent household], a fact which some have thought affords a probable clue to the murder." Whicher went in search of these ex-domestics in the nearby towns of Bristol and Frome. From them, along with the villagers in Road, he learned that the older Kent children were not favored by the parents, and there was much resentment on their part, especially on the part of Constance.

From Constance's classmates in a boarding school only two miles from her home, Whicher learned that Miss Kent was strong-willed, imperious, and delighted in the idea that some had compared her appearance to that of Queen Victoria as a young woman. Further, she nurtured the village rumor that her father, Samuel Kent, was the illegitimate son of the Duke of Kent, Queen Victoria's father, and that she was therefore of royal blood herself. (There is no foundation for this gossip; Samuel Kent's father was proved to be a carpet manufacturer in London.)

The classmates quoted Constance as saying to them, "It may be nice for you to go home on holiday but not for me. My home is . . . different." Added to this were Constance's critical remarks about the other children, the children of her stepmother.

Whicher's investigation turned up a curious tale about Constance and her younger brother William. When Constance was about thirteen, she had convinced her brother to run away with her. On that occasion she had gone to the very same outhouse where Francis's body would be found four years later, cut off her hair, and dressed in boy's clothes. She then led William on a ten-mile walk to Bath, intending to go to sea. Both were picked up and held by local police until retrieved by their father. Though William was in constant tears over the escapade, Constance's demeanor in the police station was cool, self-confident, even insolent in her attitude to the solicitous policemen. She refused to apologize to her father when he arrived to fetch her and William home and for weeks afterward expressed no regret for her escapade.

Though such children's mischief was not unheard of, Whicher coupled this running away with Constance's attitude toward her stepmother and the affections the second Mrs. Kent neglected to show her. One day while Constance was at school, Whicher made a thorough search of her room. Under her mattress he found some yellowing copies of the London *Times* of July 1857.

The three-year-old newspapers, when shown by Whicher to the Kents, produced some nervous remarks. The papers contained stories of the trial of Madeleine Smith of Glasgow, Scotland, a woman accused of murdering her lover, one Emile l'Angelier, and her acquittal, albeit most thought the woman guilty. At the time of Smith's trial, the Kents had hidden the copies of the *Times* in a writing bureau, they told Whicher, not wanting any of their children to read such sordid stories. The emergence of the long-forgotten newspapers in Constance's room was certain proof in Whicher's mind that the sixteen-year-old was keenly interested in the dark activities of Miss Smith, an interest Whicher felt was abnormal. And then there was her mother's insanity.

All this added up to little real evidence, Whicher knew. His most potent piece of evidence turned up some days later. When interviewing the Kent maid, Whicher learned that one of Constance's nightgowns was missing. On the Monday following the murder, the maid was preparing the usual basket of clothes to be taken to a washerwoman in the village. At that time Constance gave the maid the nightgown she had been wearing over the weekend, and, presumably, at the time of the murder. She casually asked the maid before she left the room to "look in her pocket [of the nightgown] to see if she had left her purse there." The maid shrugged, rummaged through the laundry basket, and checked the nightgown thoroughly, finding no purse. Then Constance had asked the maid to "go downstairs and fetch a glass of water" for her. The dutiful house servant went off on the errand. By the time the laundry reached the washerwoman in the village, Constance's nightgown was gone.

Whicher smiled at the subtle craft of Constance Kent. He deduced that the girl asked the maid to check the nightgown in search of the purse to make sure the maid examined the gown closely, knowing she would later report that it had no peculiar stains and that, indeed, the garment had gone to the washerwoman's. Her request for water was a ruse; during the maid's absence, Constance took back the nightgown from the laundry basket and returned it to her drawer, the loss of the nightgown then firmly becoming the responsibility of the maid and the washerwoman. More importantly, Whicher reasoned, this particular nightgown was not the one worn on the night of the murder; that gruesome-looking garment had been undoubtedly stained by the spurting blood of three-year-old Savile Kent and had been destroyed, leaving Constance with only two nightgowns. She had, through her clever laundry ruse, in effect created a third nightgown, having taken one of the two remaining fresh nightgowns from her drawer, worn it over the weekend, slipped it into the laundry as her third nightgown, removed it, and worn it over again as the second of her three nightgowns.

On July 20, 1860, and armed only with this evidence, Whicher arrested Constance for the murder of her half brother. The inspector knew

Crowds gathering to hear the news of the Kent arrest and impending trial outside Newgate Prison where Constance was detained in 1864.

his case was shaky, but he counted on Constance, in the shock of arrest, to break down and confess. She was, after all, an adolescent girl whose sophisticated pose and nervy manner would easily shatter under close interrogation. For the first time in his career, Whicher was wrong.

Constance Kent was calm at her hearing before the magistrates on July 27, insisting that she had been in her room the whole night of the murder, that she knew nothing of the pitiable death of Savile Kent. On the witness stand she looked anything but a murderer. Whicher grudgingly admired the iron in the girl, remembering the words of Dr. Stapleton, who had known Constance from early childhood and had seen her "strong, obstinate and determined will," her "irritable and impassioned nature," and her "powerful physique."

When Whicher's evidence was put before the court, those in attendance scoffed, many laughing loudly, some hooting criticism. Most of the villagers saw it all as the desperate ploy of a policeman without a case. Whicher, thundered Constance's defense counsel, a Mr. Edlin, was despicably "a man eager in pursuit of the murderer, and anxious for the reward which has been offered," a sum of a hundred pounds offered by local magistrates. He ridiculed Whicher's investigative abilities, and the fact that a respected detective would stoop to put up as evidence the gossip of Constance's classmates. Almost on cue, Constance then broke down, sobbing, "I am innocent! I am innocent!"

Constance's outburst produced revulsion against Whicher in the courtroom; many shouted that Scotland Yard was persecuting a defenseless, innocent, sweet-minded girl. A faint smile was seen to play about the small mouth of Constance Kent as she listened to Whicher being lambasted. She was released by the court, her father going the two-hundred-pound bail, and promising to produce her when called upon. Though not an acquittal, the decision of the magistrates clearly indicated that Constance was, in their minds, entirely blameless. The pretty girl walked from the courtroom in her best dress as spectators stood and applauded her.

Following this fiasco, abuse was heaped upon Inspector Whicher, press and public alike clamoring for his dismissal from Scotland Yard. Though pressure from his superiors was never made public, Whicher resigned from the Yard, going into early retirement for reason of "ill health," he said.

The miserable nurse, Elizabeth Gough, who had been under sort of open arrest from the beginning, was again brought before the magistrates and tried. By this time she had moved to a neighboring town and become a seamstress. Again, nothing could be proved against her and the poor woman was freed, though popular feeling was that she was the murderer.

To escape the notoriety of the unsolved murder, Samuel Kent moved his family to Wales. Constance was sent to a convent in France. It so happened that she returned to England in 1963 for a religious retreat, staying as a paying guest at St. Mary's Home in Brighton, which was under the direction of the Reverend A. D. Wagner. Something during the course of the next twelve months, a spiritual event never recorded for posterity, moved the heartless Constance Kent to confess the murder of her half brother. On April 25, 1864, accompanied by the Reverend Wagner, Constance, who by then was an attractive young woman, walked into the magistrate's office on Bow Street and, as calmly as she had denied the murder almost four years earlier, admitted her guilt to Chief Magistrate Sir Thomas Henry.

Her astounding confession was printed in the London *Times* two days later. It formed the better part of a letter to the newspapers from the doctor who examined her mental condition. The doctor's letter read—

Constance Kent says that the manner in which she committed her crime was as follows: A few days before the murder she obtained possession of a razor from a green case in her father's wardrobe, and secreted it. This was the sole instrument which she used. She also secreted a candle with matches, by placing them in the corner of the closet in the garden, where the murder was committed. On the night of the murder she undressed herself and went to bed, because she expected that her sisters would visit her room. She lay awake watching, until she thought that the

Constance Kent at the time of her confession.

household were all asleep, and soon after midnight she left her bedroom and went downstairs and opened the drawing-room door and window shutters. She then went up into the nursery, withdrew the blanket from between the sheet and the counterpane, and placed it on the side of the cot. She then took the child from his bed and carried him downstairs through the drawing room. She had on her nightdress, and in the drawing room she put on her galoshes.

Having the child in one arm, she raised the drawing-room window with the other hand, went around the house and into the closet, lighted the candle, and placed it on the seat of the closet, the child being wrapped in the blanket and still sleeping, and while the child was in this position she inflicted the wound in the throat. She says that she thought the blood would never come, and that the child was not killed, so she thrust ths razor into its left side, and put the body, with the blanket around it, into the vault. The light burnt out.

The piece of flannel which she had with her was torn from an old flannel garment placed in the waste bag, and which she had taken some time before and sewn it to use in washing herself. She went back to her bedroom, examined her dress, and found only two spots of blood on it. These she washed out in the basin, and threw the water, which was but little discoloured, into the footpan in which she had washed her feet overnight. She took another of her nightdresses and got into bed. In the morning, her nightdress had become dry where it had been washed. She folded it up and put it into the drawer.

Her three nightdresses were examined by Mr. Foley, and she believes also by Mr. Parsons, the medical attendant of the family. She thought the bloodstains had been effectually washed out, but on holding the dress up to the light a day or two afterward, she found the stains were still visible. She secreted the dress, moving it from place to place, and she eventually burnt it in her own bedroom, and put the ashes or tinder into the kitchen grate. It was about five or six days after the child's death that she burnt the nightdress.

On the Saturday morning, having cleaned the razor, she took an opportunity of replacing it unobserved in the case in the wardrobe. She abstracted her nightdress from the clothes basket when the housemaid went to fetch a glass of water. The stained garment found in the boiler hole had no connection whatever with the deed. As regards the motive of her crime, it seems that, although she entertained at one time a great regard for the present Mrs. Kent, yet if any remark was at any time made which in her opinion was disparaging to any member of the first family, she treasured it up, and determined to revenge it. She had no ill-will against the little boy, except as one of the children of her stepmother.

She declared that both her father and her stepmother had always been kind to her personally, and the following is a copy of a letter which she adressed to Mr. Rodway [Constance's lawyer] on this point while in prison before her trial:

Devizes, May 15th.

Sir:

It has been stated that my feelings of revenge were excited in consequence of cruel treatment. This is entirely false. I have received the greatest kindness from both the persons accused of subjecting me to it. I have never had any ill-will towards either of them on account of their behavior to me which has been very kind.

I shall feel obliged if you will make use of this statement in order that the public may be undeceived on this point. —I remain, Sir,

Yours truly,
Constance E. Kent

To Mr. R. Rodway.

She told me that when the nursemaid was accused she had fully made up her mind to confess if the nursemaid had been convicted; and that she had also made up her mind to commit suicide if she herself were convicted. She said that she had felt herself under the influence of the devil before she committed the murder, but that she did not believe, and had not believed, that the devil had more to do with her crime than he had with any other wicked action. She had not said her prayers for a year before the murder, and not afterwards until she came to reside at Brighton. She said that the circumstance which revived religious feelings in her mind was thinking about the sacrament when confirmed.

An opinion has been expressed that the peculiarities evinced by Constance Kent between the ages of twelve and seventeen may be attributed to the then transition period of her life. Moreover, the fact of her cutting off her hair, dressing herself in her brother's clothes, and then leaving her home with the intention of going abroad, which occurred when she was only thirteen years of age, indicated a peculiarity of disposition, and great determination of character, which foreboded that, for good or evil, her future life would be remarkable.

This peculiar disposition, which led her to such singular and violent resolves of action, seemed also to colour and intensify her thoughts and feelings, and magnify into wrongs that were to be revenged any little family incidents or occurrences which provoked her displeasure.

Although it became my duty to advise her counsel that she evinced no symptom of insanity at the time of my examination, and that, so far as it was possible to ascertain the state of her mind

The all-male jury deliberating in the Kent case.

Constance Kent's cell in Millbank Prison where she spent more than twenty years for her unspeakable crime.

at so remote a period, there was no evidence of it at the time of the murder, I am yet of opinion that, owing to the pecularities of her constitution, it is probable that under prolonged solitary confinement she would become insane....

John Charles Bucknill, M.D.

So the dogged Inspector Jonathan Whicher had been right all along, but his vindication was of little consolation to him. A sixteen-year-old killer with a Machiavellian mind had destroyed his career. Whicher was later offered the 100-pound reward, but he refused the money, proving, at least to himself, that he was first, last, and always an honest detective—and a great one.

Constance Kent, who had been judged sane, was put on trial, and was quickly convicted on her own confession. She was sentenced to death, but this sentence, given her age at the time of the crime, was immediately commuted to penal servitude for life. In 1885, after serving twenty years, she was released from Millbank Prison. Constance was then a graying woman of forty-one.

From that point on, the trial of Constance Kent vanishes forever. She is said to have gone to another convent, or traveled to another country, perhaps America. No one ever knew for certain, or by that time cared—no one except an enfeebled ex-detective-inspector of Scotland Yard, who stated that he would like to have looked upon the face of Constance Kent one more time to see if that demure smile of confidence and triumph still lingered.

KLIMEK, TILLIE

Murderer ■ (1865–1936)

A member of Chicago's Polish community, Tillie had worked in sweatshops since childhood. She obtained her first husband, John Mitkiewitz, through a marriage broker. After twenty-six years of wedded toil,

Tillie, a massive woman with the strength of three men, rebelled, quitting her job after knocking out the foreman of her plant. She forced Mitkiewitz to go to work.

In 1914 Tillie took out a $1,000 insurance policy on her husband. That summer Mitkiewitz died after eating Tillie's special stew. Neighbors were somewhat shocked in that Tillie had predicted his death, long claiming that she could read the future.

Railroad worker John Ruskowski married the suddenly rich Tillie, but, as Tillie told her friends, he too was "not long for this world." Ruskowski died within three months. Next came Joseph "Blunt Joe" Guszkowski who died in 1916 after gorging himself on Tillie's famous stew. Husband number four was Frank Kupczyk, who died in 1920.

A suspicious neighbor, Rose Chudzinski, thought Tillie's ability to predict the deaths of her husbands had nothing to do with being a clairvoyant and said so. Rose suddenly got ill a week later and died. In all these deaths, including that of Rose Chudzinski, Tillie managed to collect fat insurance payments.

In 1921 this female bluebeard married husband number five, Anton Klimek. Six years later Klimek fell ill, Tillie nursing him with her famous stew. The overweight seeress wasted no time in selecting a funeral dress. The clerk asked her who had died.

"My husband," replied Tillie.

"Oh, I'm so sorry," consoled the clerk. "When did he die?"

"Ten days from now," said Tillie.

Acting on these remarks repeated by the clerk to police, officers broke into Tillie's modest apartment to find Klimek near death, a bowl of Tillie's steaming stew at his bedside. His stomach was pumped and he survived. The stew was analyzed and found to be loaded with arsenic. The bodies of Tillie's other four husbands were exhumed, and arsenic was found in all.

Tillie's trial was a circus. The woman played to the press, posed for pictures in court, and generally ignored the charges against her. After she was convicted, Tillie worked her great weight onto a chair in court and bellowed, "I'll never stand on the gallows!" This prediction also came true; she was given a life sentence, dying at the Illinois Women's Prison in Dwight in 1936.

KNIGHT, MARY

Murderer ■ (1749–1788)

Mrs. Knight, a farm widow living in Warwick, England, was accused by her nine-year-old son of murdering her smaller child, Roger. The boy told authorities how his mother had beaten his younger brother when Roger failed to glean enough corn, Mary placing the boy in a pantry as further punishment. When the older son was told that he could play with Roger, he discovered that the young boy was cold.

Mary Knight, discovering the boy dead, wrapped the body in her apron, and took it to the well outside the house where she dumped the corpse. She ran inside her small cottage and threw into the fire the stick she had used to beat the boy. Neighbors saw the woman toss the small body into the well and immediately retrieved it. They entered the cottage and pulled the stick from the fire.

The stick was placed in evidence at Mary's trial which was swift. She was condemned, and on August 24, 1778, hanged at Warwick.

KOCH, ILSE

Murderer ■ (1917–1971)

Born and bred in Dresden, Germany, Ilse Koch began working in a cigarette factory at age fifteen, giving half her wages to her impoverished family. Two years later she went to work in a bookshop. A voluptuous blue-eyed

Ilse Koch, under arrest for atrocities, being taken from the Buchenwald concentration camp in 1945.

blonde, by then, she was enthralled by Hitler's storm troopers and had joined the Nazi Youth Party. The bookstore was an official branch of that party and the elderly owner pandered to the racist tastes of the Nazis. He told the naive Ilse that he would introduce her to classic literature but instead gave her obscene books to read to heighten her passions for the young storm troopers who visited the store to purchase Hitler's *Mein Kampf* and other party-approved dogma. (This tactic, of course, was in keeping with Hitler's program in the mid-1930s to promote youthful marriages, which in turn would produce more babies for the Third Reich.)

Ilse had many affairs with SS men but was singled out by Heinrich Himmler, the dreaded leader of the SS and Gestapo, for marriage to his then top aide, Karl Koch. Himmler entered the bookstore with Koch in 1937, spotted the oversexed Ilse, and ordered Koch to mate with her.

Himmler himself arranged for their marriage later that year.

A thick-set, bullet-headed man with the manners and morals of a pig, Koch assumed command of the new Buchenwald concentration camp outside Weimar. After his wedding, he took his youthful bride to a magnificent villa near the camp and promptly forgot about her—except to produce two children through their union in compliance with party dictates. Koch then began indulging in orgies with women at Weimar, staggering "sex feasts" costing fortunes. Ilse was left to her own diversions.

At first she spent her time riding to the hounds in Brandenburg. Then she flirted with Koch's junior officers, finally having affairs with a half dozen at a time, staging her own orgies where she would drink with several SS officers until taking them all into her bed. Her appetite for sex was insatiable, and her desire for perversion and sadistic acts obsessive. The prisoners at Buchenwald became her playthings.

Not until the war was in full progress did Ilse give vent to her incredible depravities. Ilse also took particular delight in sunbathing naked at her villa, where potential SS lovers would ogle her, and close to the camp, where she could tantalize the prisoners. She would greet all incoming trucks and trains standing semi-nude next to lines of male prisoners, mostly Jews by then, wiggling her hips, fondling her large breasts, and making lewd remarks. If one prisoner dared look up at her, he was beaten senseless. On one such occasion, guards noticed three prisoners glance up from the ground to stare at the "Bitch of Buchenwald." Two were beaten to death on the spot with clubs, the other was pushed face first to the ground, a guard standing on his neck grinding the man's face into the mud until he suffocated to death. Smirking, Ilse filled out a report that these men had been executed for giving her lascivious looks.

For sport, Ilse Koch encouraged the guards to participate in random mass slayings. One day, at her urging, guards opened up with pistols, shooting at prisoners as one would scurrying turkeys in a barnyard. Ilse was beside herself with ecstasy and grabbed a pistol, helping to murder many of the twenty-four prisoners killed that day.

Ilse brought a young female relative to live with her in her camp villa and ordered the girl to watch for attractive male guards newly arriving at Buchenwald and arrange orgies for her mistress. Ilse also forced the girl to participate in these acts.

One afternoon Ilse spied two male prisoners working without their shirts. Both had livid tattoos on their backs and chest. She ordered that the prisoners be killed immediately—they were taken to the camp hospital and murdered by injections that night—and their skins prepared and brought to her. Thus began one of the most heinous hobbies the world had ever known. Isle's fascination for human skin, particularly that bearing tattoos, never abated. She had lampshades made from the skin, with which she adorned her living room. Skin from other selected victims went to make up pairs of gloves which Ilse proudly wore on her delicate hands.

Ever inventive, Ilse ordered the heads of executed prisoners to be severed and, in an elaborate process, shriveled down to grapefruit size. Dozens of these grotesque human trophies decorated the sideboards of Ilse's dining room, where she dined each day with her children.

At the close of the war, Ilse Koch was arrested and tried as a war criminal, although she fared far better than her counterpart from Belsen, Irma Grese. She was placed on trial in 1947–48 in Nuremburg before an American military court and sentenced to life in prison, a judgment that prompted deep resentment the world over. A U.S. review board, headed by the military governor of the U.S. zone, General Clay, ordered her release two years later. The worldwide protest to *that* action was of hurricane proportions. President Truman ordered a special investigation, but authorities finally declared that offenses by one German against other Germans could not be considered a war crime.

It was left to the German people to judge the woman. She was placed on trial again in 1950–51 in Augsburg, Bavaria, charged with murdering 45 prisoners and being the willing accomplice in another 135 concentration camp homicides. The woman standing in the dock was anything but beautiful. Her Titian hair was now a straggly

Ilse Koch, the "Red Witch" of Buchenwald, at her 1950 trial.

dirty blonde, her features were bloated, her body a lumpy sack. She had no defense, really, and blamed her husband for everything, which was convenient in that Karl Koch had long ago been executed by the Nazis for embezzling party funds to pay for his orgies.

Ilse stood in the dock terrified, her eyes darting to the open windows. Outside, hundreds were screaming incessantly, "Kill her! Kill her!" She appealed for mercy from the court, stating the tired excuse that she had no knowledge of what went on at Buchenwald. "I was merely a housewife," she sobbed. "I was busy raising my children. I *never* saw anything which was against humanity!"

When confronted with photos showing mounds of corpses at Buchenwald, Ilse screamed, "Lies! All lies!" She had seen nothing, she had done nothing. The dozens of camp sur-

vivors who testified against her were impostors, actors, she said, playing out roles assigned to them by the Allies.

Halfway through the proceedings, Ilse Koch pretended to go into an epileptic state, forcing her body to twitch uncontrollably, responding to nothing, a blank stare masking her emotions. Doctors who examined her told the court that she was in perfect health. In her cell, Ilse laughed at one physician, telling him that he was enjoying her "First-class comedy act."

Yet Ilse persisted in the pretense, faking illness that prevented her from leaving her cell bed to hear the court declare her guilty of all the charges. She was to be imprisoned for life, and that decision too, caused this horrible woman to convulse with laughter; she had, unlike Irma Grese and others, escaped the headsman. Her eerie cackle was stilled by her death in 1971.

LABBE, DENISE

Murderer ■ (1926–   )

The home into which Denise Labbé was born was humble and poor but kept clean by her hardworking parents, and there was always enough food for the family. Her father, a postman in the quaint village of Melesse, near Rennes, France, had been shell-shocked in World War I. Following the news in 1940 that France had been invaded by Germany, the man became hysterical and drowned himself in a canal, fearing that he would again have to undergo the horrors of Verdun.

Denise went to work as a housekeeper for a local butcher but left to take a factory job in Rennes in 1942. She vowed that she would "rise out of the gutter," and to that end worked hard at her university studies in Rennes on her off hours. She vastly improved her lot in 1946 when she was given a secretarial post at the National Institute of Statistics in Rennes. She continued her studies at the university but began having numerous affairs. According to one of her biographers, Derick Goodman, "she was not faithful to any of her lovers and even seemed to take pleasure in deceiving them." Such infidelity frightened off any would-be husbands among the student population. A married doctor also had an affair with the promiscuous Denise, and a child, Catherine, was born out of wedlock.

Leaving her daughter in Rennes with her parents, Denise moved to Paris and continued work at the institute. She returned to Rennes for a May Day celebration in 1954, and there she met and became totally enamored of a strange twenty-four-year-old man named Jacques Algarron, who was an officer cadet at the Saint-Cyr School.

Algarron was the illegitimate son of a military man and had been ridiculed by his classmates for his lack of heritage. To ward off the jeers, the cadet had assumed an arrogant posture and adopted a weird philosophy that was a combination of Nietzsche and black magic. He thought of himself as an invincible

France's notorious Denise Labbé, who murdered her own child in a "love ritual," and her demented lover, Jacques Algarron, who demanded the killing.

superman and that women were nothing more than slaves to any man. After several months he had convinced Denise that she was his love pawn.

At Algarron's slightest suggestion, Denise performed every known deviation of the sex act, degrading herself on any level he desired. Further, the cadet ordered Denise to pick up strange men and bring them back to her apartment for impromptu fornication which Algarron watched from hiding. When the men departed, Algarron would sit imperiously in the room as Denise groveled at his feet, begging his forgiveness for her infidelity, an infidelity arranged and urged by the cadet-lover himself. All this gave Algarron a sense of absolute power over Denise, and yet he soon grew tired of her blind obedience.

To satiate his desire to control the young woman absolutely, Algarron next demanded that Denise murder her two-and-a-half-year-old daughter, Catherine. "It's the only way you can

prove your love to me," the young egotist told her.

At first Denise resisted the idea but finally gave in, and twice she began to drown her child but changed her mind at the last minute. Then on November 8, 1954, Denise took Catherine to a stone wash basin in the backyard of her mother's home in Rennes and held the child's head underwater until she was dead. Minutes later her mother and sister returned prematurely from a shopping trip. Denise sobbingly informed the horrified women that Cathy had drowned accidentally in the wash basin. Her body was still dangling over the edge of the basin when the women rushed into the yard. A doctor and a fireman, summoned at once, removed the child from the basin but failed to revive her with artificial respiration.

Police were suspicious of Denise from the beginning, especially after the woman told them she had seen her daughter fall into the water but was powerless to help the child because she had fainted. Officers nodded solemnly, then dismissed her. She raced to Paris to inform Algarron that his wishes had been obeyed.

The catalyst of the deed only shrugged, saying, "I find it all very disappointing. It means nothing at all to me now."

Police summoned Denise upon her return to Rennes and the woman broke down, confessing her crime. "Yes," she sighed, "I killed my daughter, but it was a ritual murder." With that she implicated the indifferent Algarron who was also arrested.

The couple met again while being arraigned for trial. Denise called her sinister lover a cultist devil, adding, "It is you who forced me to kill my daughter. You cast a spell over me from the moment we met. You told me there could be no great love without sacrifice and that the greatest sacrifice of all was death. You even added, 'The price of our love must be the death of your daughter. Kill for me. An innocent victim must be sacrificed.' You promised to marry me if I killed Cathy, but you threatened to abandon me if I did not kill her."

Jacques Algarron only stared coolly back at the woman as a magistrate and gendarmes gaped at the strange lovers.

"What have you to say?" the magistrate finally asked the would-be superman.

"The girl is completely out of her head," Algarron said calmly.

Algarron maintained the same cool attitude when he and Denise faced trial at Blois in May 1955. The esteemed but elderly Bâtonnier Simon defended the woman, ardently addressing the court with a plea that amounted to temporary insanity; his client had been totally under a spell cast by the evil-minded Algarron. He undoubtedly saved Denise's life. The jury took three hours before delivering a guilty verdict, but added that extenuating circumstances merited the court's mercy for Denise Labbé. She was sent to prison for life instead of going to the guillotine. The perverse Algarron drew a twenty-year sentence.

Marie Lafarge, playing the part of "the reviled one," as she called herself, at her murder trial in 1840.

LAFARGE, MARIE

Murderer ■ (1816–1852)

Rats scampered in packs across the floor of the great entrance hall. Overpowering odors of decay and animal excrement assailed the delicate woman in her Paris finery as she stood horrified in the doorway of the château Le Glandier, her new home. The burning insult to the twenty-four-year-old bride was complete. Not only had she been persuaded to marry almost *in absentia* a brutish, conniving man, but she had been tricked into believing she was to live in a grand estate. Instead she was greeted by a dilapidated mansion that resembled the ruins of a monastery. Marie's terrible vengeance for being so deceived would spawn the most sensational murder trial in France in

that courteous era, and split the nation almost in two as citizens everywhere argued her guilt or her innocence.

It was another cruel joke played upon Marie by heartless fate. As in the past, Marie Fortunée Capelle had reached out for grandeur only to uncover lies and find disillusionment. Like many an unfortunate child before and after her, from infancy on, Marie lived within France's high society but was never ever a real part of it.

Born in Picardy in 1816, Marie's background was distinguished, but not distinguished enough to be acceptable in the king's court. She was only an extension of France's royalty. Her mother, the Baroness Capelle, as she lay on her deathbed in 1835, reminded Marie, "You are not like other children. They are commoners and you are of royal blood." Marie, since childhood, had been told and retold countless times that her maternal grandmother was a natural daughter of the king's father, Philippe Egalité, and his mistress Madame de Genlis. Marie's father was Colonel Capelle, who had fought in the Old Guard and was one of Napoleon's favorite officers. One of her aunts was married to a high-ranking Prussian diplomat, another to Monsieur deGarat, Secretary-General of the Bank of France. As a child Marie was coddled by the cream of French society—the Duchess of Dalmatia (Madame Soult), the Princess of Echumhl (Madame Ney), Madame de Cambaceres, and others.

Great social cruelty was practiced against this sensitive child. One minute she was given the attention of those who peopled her mother's fanciful, carefree world, and the next she was shunted to the back room, snobbishly rejected by those at court not wishing to remember the sexual caprices of their kings.

By the time Marie was a teenager she was moving through French society completely unsure of her place, recognized but only with a nod or a nervous glance. To deal with her perplexing situation she retreated into a fairy-tale world, where princes and their ladies fair never spoke of position but only of love.

Marie's father died in 1828. Following the death of her mother, Marie was politely handed from one aristocratic relative to another, staying with each for only a short time. Her family reeked of wealth and status, yet she was treated as an unwanted orphan.

Marie attended one of the best schools in Paris where she learned the etiquette of the genteel tradition. Her classmates were the daughters of the powerful and wealthy, and the girl always felt a slight envy; their social places were fixed, their futures unblemished by doubt. Their worlds, unlike her own, were never threatened by imminent collapse.

One of these girls, Marie de Nicolai, became Marie's closest friend, even though her heritage placed her at the core of the great French nobility. According to historian Marie Belloc Lowndes, writing in *McClure's* magazine, "In those halcyon days of early girlhood the two Maries were inseparable and loved each other as sisters loved."

The two regularly went to church alone together, and, following one mass, they encountered a young poet, Félix Clavé, who was half Spanish. They flirted with the impoverished young man of letters, and he wrote to them, chiefly to Marie de Nicolai, of his love, intimating in some of his more torrid missives that he and Mademoiselle de Nicolai had shared moments together that no decent chaperone would have ever permitted. At times Marie Capelle acted as intermediary between Clavé and her bosom friend, Marie de Nicolai, carrying letters between them. For unexplained reasons, Marie kept three of the most compromising missives. These letters, contended those who came to hate the name of Marie Lafarge, would later be used as deadly blackmail weapons.

The letters might have served Marie Capelle as substitute suitors. For her there were no noble-blooded swains seeking her favors when she reached the age of the debutante, even though her kindly Aunt de Garat bought her costly gowns. Marie received no invitations; she had nowhere to go. At this time Marie had grown to become, if not pretty, quite distinguished looking. Major Arthur Griffiths, writing in *Mysteries of Police and Crime*, described her as "tall, slim, with dead-white complexion, jet-black hair worn in straight shining pleats, fine dark eyes, and a sweet but somewhat sad smile."

The only festive events attended by Marie were those held at the resplendent estate of her friend Marie de Nicolai, who, like the rest of her classmates, had married an aristocrat, the Vicomte de Léautaud, and moved into a fabulous château.

During one of Marie's visits some of her friend's jewelry disappeared, and the police were summoned. Sûreté Chief Allard personally conducted the many interviews with the household staff and the guests, including Marie Capelle, who told the suspicious detective that she knew nothing of the lost diamonds. Allard concluded his investigation by informing the Vicomte that, in his opinion, only one suspect could have taken the gems, and that was Marie Capelle. Ridiculous, roared the Vicomte. This sweet girl was his wife's dearest friend. They had known each other since childhood. He refused Allard's request to arrest the girl, insisting that Marie be allowed to finish her visit without another mention of the missing jewels.

When she returned home, Marie was informed by her aunt, who had become frantic to marry off the twenty-four-year-old woman, that she intended to place her name in the registry of the De Foy Matrimonial Agency in Paris, which regularly issued listings of eligible, well-educated females from upper-class families who sought responsible, well-to-do husbands. Marie wanted none of it, and told her aunt that such practices were for cattle, not human beings. She stormed into her room and, behind the closed door, opened her handbag where she found the De Léautaud diamonds. Marie was to say later that she had absentmindedly placed the diamond necklace in her handbag instead of returning it to the De Léautaud vault. When home she placed the diamonds inside her own jewelry box and forgot about them.

She did not forget about her aunt's threat to put her on the matrimonial block. She had had enough of affairs of the heart.

Only short months ago she had broken off with a lovesick chemist's son named Guyot. Their association, like so many of Marie's previous romantic flings, had been whimsical, Marie caring more for the high-minded letters she wrote to Guyot than for the time she actually spent with the youth. One of her more character-revealing missives to Guyot read—

If you know anything that wounds the heart more than being forgotten . . . if you know a way of being indifferent to such suffering, tell me. But no. One lives by illusions. This one was very sweet, and the awakening which always comes came for me also. A caprice of eight days, then nothing. And I had believed in you. Oh! The world must be very false.

Discovering the existence of Guyot, Marie's aunt became indignant, telling Marie, "You have disgraced the family." Marie responded by lapsing into a delicate swoon for days, a habitual ploy, critics later argued, whereby Marie evaded any criticism. When some weeks later Guyot pleaded to marry his dream woman, Marie turned him away, telling him, "It is impossible for me to marry a commoner."

Other suitors approached the idealistic Marie, most of them at the urging of her loyal friend, Marie de Léautaud. One was the handsome Georges Delvaux, a prosperous subprefect, but he too was rejected by Marie, who politely informed him that marrying a civil servant was quite beneath her station.

Meanwhile her Aunt de Garat worked to find Marie a suitable husband. Her industry was rewarded when Charles Joseph Pouch Lafarge answered the advertisement concerning Marie that had been offered by the De Foy agency. Lafarge represented himself as a man of extensive real estate holdings, an ironmaster, whose forges at La Glandier in the province of Corrèze in the south of France had brought him great wealth, and whose estate was shown to Marie through drawings provided by her suitor. The elaborate drawings depicted marvelous terraces, palazzos, and exquisite Gothic ruins. From a promontory, a rambling but charming château dominated the hundreds of acres in Lafarge's realm.

At last a marital spark ignited inside the reluctant heart of Marie Capelle. But it was Lafarge's promising estate, the wonderful drawings completed by Anna LeBrun, an artist who lived at Le Glandier, that intrigued the status-seeking woman. She imagined the place to be her private kingdom, one reserved for her since childhood. At long last, she would surpass her classmates. She would become the regal mistress of a great manor house, governing hundreds of peasants grateful for her benevolent guidance. Certainly the man Lafarge was as elegant as the lands he owned. Marie fell in love with this suitor before ever meeting him.

Some time earlier, Marie had written some truly brilliant essays for various newspaper columns. It so happened that the great writer Alexandre Dumas père had read them, and eagerly so, subsequently taking up a correspondence with the talented romantic. When Marie's long-awaited salvation arrived, she was ecstatic, and wanted to share her joy with the illustrious man of letters. She wrote—

M. Alexandre Dumas:

My thoughts, my friend, have voices. Some of them sing, some of them pray and others lament. My eyes seem to look within. I can hardly understand myself, and yet, in my exaltation, I understand everything, light, nature, God. . . .

If, instead of writing, I decide to sew, my needle trembles in my hand as if it were a pen in the hand of a great writer. It seems to me then, that I am an artist to the depths of my soul, and could show inspiration even in a hem. . . .

But upon meeting Charles Lafarge for the first time, Marie lost all interest in the man, if not her dreams of the Le Glandier fairyland. A large, oafish-looking man of twenty-eight, Lafarge had had a minimum of education. His manners were coarse and awkward. He knew nothing of literature, music or art.

Lafarge was also a fraud. Learning that Marie Capelle had a dowry of 100,000 francs (today's equivalent of $20,000), and desperately needing money to support his failing foundry as well as finance a new smelting process he had developed, Lafarge had determined to marry himself out of his financial difficulties. He had once before been motivated to marry for the same reasons, having wedded the daughter of a Monsieur de Beauford and used her considerable dowry to enlarge his plant, but these funds dwindled. When his wife died in 1839, the De Beauford funding ceased altogether.

After meeting Lafarge, Marie at first resisted

the marriage. But he pressed the matter without letup, as did Marie's aunt, who was almost hysterical with wanting to rid herself of her niece. In fact, only three days after the couple were introduced, Aunt de Garat forced the publication of the marriage banns. Marie consoled herself with thoughts of the glittering Le Glandier estate awaiting her. The following week she became Mrs. Marie Lafarge and left by carriage for Le Glandier with her husband and her maid, Clémentine Servat.

The trip presaged what was to come in her relationship with Charles Lafarge. Her new husband ordered food from a wayside inn, and when knives and forks were not readily available, he ate with his hands, ignoring the use of napkin or

Marie Lafarge hiding from her husband on their wedding night.

handkerchief and licking his fingers. He openly yawned in Marie's face when he grew tired, and, when she attempted to engage him in polite conversation, he curtly said, "For God's sake, stop talking!"

The bleak, run-down mansion and surrounding gray countryside of Le Glandier soon loomed into sight, and its dismal, almost hopeless appearance shattered forever Marie's bright hopes. Stunned, she stood in the doorway to the wretched manor house as her stern-face, distrusting mother-in-law walked toward her to greet her. Also on hand were Charles's hawk-nosed sister, Amena, and Anna LeBrun, the artist who had so cleverly drawn Le Glandier not as it truly was but as it had looked six hundred years earlier when monks chanted through its halls and tended its lost gardens.

When Anna LeBrun stepped forth to greet the new mistress, she took Marie's hand unsmilingly and without warmth, holding it only briefly. Of course, Anna had been in league with her employer to make the estate appear what it was not in order to trap another dowry. It was known to most in Le Glandier that the artist thought of Charles Lafarge as her own property. She also undoubtedly thought that after this upstart Parisian was no longer of financial service, Anna LeBrun would, somehow, become the third and final mistress of the Lafarge estate. The only female present who showed genuine kindness and affection for Marie was Emma Pontier, Charles's young cousin. Emma tried to make the thoroughly disgusted Marie at home, but the new bride retreated quickly to her room, slammed the door, and locked herself and the maid Clémentine inside.

When she refused to come out for dinner, Charles went to her door, begging her to come downstairs. He whispered angrily, "Marie! Do you realize how great a shame and affront you are putting on me? For heaven's sake, come out and behave like a reasonable woman!"

As Lafarge stood jiggling the door's handle, an envelope was shoved underneath it. He read Marie's letter with mounting, eye-popping fury:

August 25, 1839

Charles:

I do not blame you! I do not wish to say anything against you. All I beg you to do is to allow me to leave you. Our marriage has been a terrible mistake. I take all the blame of it on myself. Nay, more—I here and now make you a shameful confession.

Pity me, Charles. I love another man. And this man, my lover, has followed us during the whole of our wedding journey. Oh, Charles, forgive me, but I have seen him. I have had secret meetings with my love. I used to creep out when you were asleep. I am ashamed, deeply ashamed of my wickedness! But, Charles, you cannot wish me, knowing this, to stay with you. I do not ask to have back my fortune. I only ask you to let me go away. I will sign any documents you like, and I swear I will never trouble you again. Oh, Charles, on my knees, I implore you to be merciful and to grant my prayer! Forget the miserable Marie who has treated you so terribly.

Get two horses ready: I will ride to Bordeaux and then take a ship to Smyrna. I will leave you all my possessions. My God, turn them to your advantage—you deserve it. As for me, I will live by my own exertions. Let no one know that I ever existed. . . . If this does not satisfy you I will take arsenic—*I have some*. [This statement, when the letter was later offered up as evidence at her murder trial, weighed heavily against Marie Lafarge.] Spare me, be the guardian angel of a poor orphan girl, or, if you choose, slay me, and say I have killed myself.

—Marie

At first, Lafarge was incensed. He thought to batter down the door, but Madame Lafarge soothed her son's anger, sending him downstairs to dinner. She finally convinced Marie to open the bedroom door. Charles's mother then slowly drew out Marie's confession that there never had been a lover, that she had invented the wild tale to escape her marriage and the horrors of Le Glandier. Within the hour, the confrontation was over, "Marie having become transformed from a savagely determined, hysterical young woman into a kindly, well-conducted bride."

To placate Marie, Charles, on the advice of his lawyer, provided her with subscriptions to Paris newspapers, put the local lending library at her disposal, and ordered his servants to clean up Le Glandier as best they could. Further, the money-bent husband promised Marie that he would not claim his "marital privileges" until the estate was repaired to his wife's liking and he had arranged ample loans to put his forges back into full-time operation.

In return Marie took it on herself to do her share in improving conditions at the wretched estate. "She would refurnish, refurbish, replant, and restore," reported crime writer Francis Lipsig. "She would chase the poultry out of the kitchen and stop the six daily meals. Decent plumbing would be restored. She would discard the florid sailcloth drapes and send for cool, white curtains from Paris. . . . She would gather together the crazy-quilt social life of Le Glandier, make a patch here, a seam there, and redesign it as a miniature Paris in the wilderness."

But nothing of the kind happened; Marie's industrious plans were for the most part ignored by the Lafarge family. Workers on the estate, long resigned to poverty and a hopeless future, merely shrugged when she ordered them about, then laughed behind Marie's back.

Marie's piano was shipped from Paris at her request, but the Lafarges, except for Cousin Emma, proved a poor audience, leaving the mistress of the house to play late into the night, and without encouragement, in the dimly lit grand hall. Only Emma and the maid Clémentine sat in the shadows listening to the haunting waltzes of Chopin, Strauss, and Liszt, which trailed in echoes from the delicate fingers of Marie Lafarge.

Though in reality sad and embittered, Marie painted quite a different picture for her aunts in Paris. To Aunt de Garat she wrote—

I have accepted my position, although it is difficult. But with a little strength of mind, with patience, and my husband's love, I may grow contented. Charles adores me and I cannot but be touched by the caressess lavished on me.

To another aunt, her florid prose conveyed total bliss:

All my new family are delightful and kind to me. I am admired. I am adored . . . I am always in the right. . . . Charles . . . hides a noble heart beneath a wild and uncultivated exterior. I am still a spoilt and happy person. I am received with enthusiasm everywhere. Really, I thank God from the bottom of my soul both for Charles, whom he has given me, and for the life which is opening out before me. . . .

But what actually yawned before Marie Lafarge was a scheme to rid herself of the dreadful Le Glandier and an even more repugnant husband, her letters of love and happiness apparently written with the intention of veiling her dark plans.

When she learned that Charles would be leaving for Paris in December 1839, Marie abruptly drew up a will in which she bequeathed her entire fortune to him and asked her husband to do the same for her. He did, consigning all of Le Glandier to her upon his death. Giving Charles a part of her small dowry for expenses in Paris, Marie further aided her husband by also giving him letters to powerful friends of her family, missives in which she begged these landed gentlemen to assist her husband in raising funds to restore his iron works. This, too, was part of Marie's ruse to appear the loving and supportive wife. Before departing for Paris, Lafarge, a schemer almost of Marie's equal, secretly made out a second will which negated the first and in which he left Le Glandier to his mother, this move undoubtedly made at the urgings of the elderly Madame Lafarge.

Only a few days after Charles journeyed to Paris, on December 12, 1839, Marie posted a letter to druggist named Eyssartier in nearby Loubressac. It read:

Sir:
I am overrun with rats. I have tried nux vomica quite without effect. Will you, and can you, trust me with a little arsenic? You may count upon my being most careful, and I shall only use it in a linen closet.

The arsenic, four grams of full strength, was sent to Marie. A few days later Marie went to her mother-in-law and sweetly asked Madame Lafarge if she would bake some little cakes for Charles, the kind he liked, so that these could be sent to her darling husband in Paris. It would bring him some Christmas cheer to know that the family was thinking of him, a *"repas sym-*

Marie plying her husband with "medicine."

pathique" is how Marie phrased it. Madame Lafarge thought it was a good idea and set about baking the cakes.

Then Marie asked the truculent Anna LeBrun to paint a miniature portrait of her. The portrait was placed in a box along with the five cakes Madame Lafarge had baked and a letter from Marie. The box was sealed by Marie's mother-in-law in front of at least six witnesses, and sent along to Charles in Paris.

The package arrived at the Hôtel de l'Univers, where Charles was staying, on December 18, 1839. When he opened the box he found one large cake only, about six inches in diameter. He broke off a large chunk and ate it. Within hours he was seized with terrible cramps. Hotel servants found him writhing on the floor of his suite, and, no matter what they did, they could not stop his vomiting. Doctors were called, and for almost two weeks the young man "purged"

himself, unable to hold anything on his stomach. He complained of eating a spoiled cake which he had thrown out before becoming ill. Attending physicians diagnosed dysentery, which produced the "cholera-like vomiting."

By January 3, 1840, Lafarge had regained enough strength to make the journey back to Le Glandier. He had raised 28,000 francs for the restoration of his iron works, he informed his wife, but he did not mention to Marie that while in Paris he had forged her name on several letters of credit.

It didn't matter. Marie Lafarge needed no further injury to feed her seething wrath. On the day Charles arrived and went immediately to bed, Marie was all tenderness and concern over her poor sick husband. That same day Marie asked the druggist Eyssartier for more arsenic to deal with the armies of rats infesting Le Glandier; she was sent sixty-four grams. And when the family physician, Dr. Bardon, examined Lafarge, Marie asked the doctor for even more arsenic.

"Why do you need such poison, madam?" Dr. Bardon inquired.

"For the house, which is ridden with rats," Marie replied coolly.

She was given the arsenic. That night Charles Lafarge insisted that only his devoted Marie nurse him, prepare his meals, and see to his comforts. Marie cooked Charles a dish of venison and truffles. Hours later he was again attacked by the "Paris sickness," as Dr. Bardon called it.

Marie continued to nurse Charles and the patient continued to worsen. Though relatives and servants were constantly in the bedroom, Marie, it was later charged, managed to feed arsenic to Charles in all his food and drink. The poison in Marie's possession was never a secret. Denis Barbier, Charles's secretary, delivered a packet of arsenic to Charles himself, the poison ordered by Marie. Rats had been racing about above the bedroom, Charles had complained, disturbing his sleep. Charles handed the poison to Marie, and she placed the arsenic in her pocket.

With each swallow of wine or chicken broth, Lafarge grew more ill. By this time, almost everyone in the Lafarge household had begun to suspect Marie of foul play, these suspicions rein-forced by the acid comments of the artist Anna LeBrun who was enraged that Charles had selected Marie to nurse him, not his trusted Anna. She was also smarting over the fact that Marie had not paid her for the miniature por-trait she had completed in such haste for Charles's Christmas package.

On January 10, 1840, another physician, Dr. Massénat, gave the desperately weak Charles an examination, stating that Lafarge was in the throes of cholera. "Give him an eggnog to strengthen him."

Anna LeBrun entered the sickroom as Marie was preparing this drink and later testified that she saw Marie "mixing something whitish out of a tiny malachite box into a glass."

"What is that you are preparing?" asked Anna.

"Orange-blossom sugar. It will help settle Charles's stomach."

With that Marie slid the malachite pillbox into a dress pocket and handed the drink to Lafarge. He took only a few sips and set the glass down. When Marie left the room for a few min-utes, Anna inspected the glass to find strange white flakes floating on the surface of the drink. The artist took the glass to Dr. Bardon who was downstairs. The physician put a few flakes to the tip of his tongue. Even though he felt a burning sensation, Dr. Bardon casually explained away the flakes—"Some plaster probably fell from the ceiling into the drink."

Anna felt this explanation so preposterous that she became determined to watch Marie day and night. The next morning Anna found Marie stirring something into a glass of milk she was about to give Charles.

"What are you doing there?" challenged the artist.

Marie gave her a sideways glance and then drank the entire glass of milk. Wrote one jour-nalist later, "Who was to know better than Marie Lafarge that it would take a good deal more than a few drops of arsenic in that glass to finish off a human being?"

Days later Anna witnessed Marie putting a white powder into a large bowl of soup prepared by Lafarge's mother and then spoon-feeding this to Charles, who cried out, "Oh, Marie! What are you giving me? It burns like fire!"

The remainder of this soup Anna secreted away, showing it to Charles's mother, his sister Amena, and cousin Emma, loudly proclaiming that Marie was clearly poisoning Lafarge to death.

Madame Lafarge confronted Marie, who appeared unmoved at such a monstrous accusa-tion. She, in turn, called Alfred, the groom, who confirmed that all the arsenic Marie had ordered from the druggist and that provided by the doc-tor had been made into rat paste by himself and that he had personally placed this paste through-out the nooks and crannies of Le Glandier to kill rats. The family members dropped their charges. Emma, ever loyal to Marie, apologized for such evil thoughts.

An artist's conception of Lafarge's mother accusing Marie of poisoning her son.

Yet Charles Lafarge sank deeper into his strange illness, so weak by the night of January 13, 1840, that he could hardly speak. Another doctor was called. Dr. Lespinasse, who traveled to the gloomy country estate through a raging storm. Upon entering the sickroom, Lespinasse was informed by Amena Lafarge that Charles's wife had just left the room after having given Charles a glass of sugar water. Lafarge had drained the glass at his wife's insistence. At the bottom of the glass, Amena had found a white precipitate. The doctor examined Lafarge and then solemnly reported to family members that in his opinion Charles Lafarge "is indeed being poisoned to death—all the symptoms show it. But it is too late to save him. He is a dying man."

And die Charles Lafarge finally did, in the early morning hours of January 14, 1840. Dr. Bardon was in attendance. Marie left the room before her husband died, going to her own bedroom to retire. When Lafarge breathed no more, Madame Lafarge called her daughter-in-law to the side of the still-warm corpse. She railed and ranted against Marie, accusing her of killing her beloved son. Marie remained cool, only giving Madame Lafarge a silent stare. Her calm, reserved dignity only incited the family members to even more rash accusations.

Dr. Bardon thought the family had gone berserk with their shouts of arsenic poisoning. "Impossible!" he cried out to them. "You must all be wrong. It would be abominable to suspect a crime without more to go upon." More evidence, as the months rolled by, would be forthcoming, and out of it, the greatest controversy in a criminal trial that France had ever experienced.

Only hours after Lafarge's death, family members summoned Magistrate Moran from Brive. Meanwhile Marie adorned herself in mourning clothes and perfunctorily busied herself with her financial papers, sending her maid Clémentine to a notary with Charles's will, asking that it be processed. She did not know that it had been invalidated by Lafarge's second, secret will.

Emma was the only family member to visit Marie in her dark, dank room. She feared that her wonderful Marie might be implicated if found to possess any arsenic, and so, in an act of youthful protectiveness, she took the malachite pillbox without Marie's knowledge. Emma also instructed Alfred to hide the remainder of the arsenic in his possession. The groom buried this in a remote area of the estate.

Moran arrived at Le Glandier on January 15, accompanied by his clerk, Vicant, and three gendarmes. Anna LeBrun was ready for him. She gave him the eggnog, sugar water, soup, even some of Charles's vomit that she had managed to preserve for inspection.

When Moran questioned the groom, Alfred admitted that he had buried the arsenic given to him by Marie. He dug this up and turned it over to the magistrate, along with the rat paste he had placed about the estate. The three doctors, Bardon, Massénat, and Lespinasse, were requested to perform an autopsy.

The doctors kept Lafarge's stomach for examination. The rest of the body was buried in the Reynac cemetery. Using the apparatus newly invented by James Marsh which helped to evaluate the presence of poisons in various substances, the doctors determined that arsenic was present not only in the stomach of the deceased but in the soup, milk, eggnog, and vomit saved by Anna LeBrun. Surprisingly, when the physicians examined the rat paste and arsenic turned over to them by the groom Alfred, they found no traces of arsenic at all, not a gram.

By January 25, 1840, Moran felt he had enough evidence to charge Marie Lafarge with murder and he ordered her arrest. Accompanied by her faithful maid Clémentine, Marie was taken to the Brive jail.

Announcement in the press of the arrest for murder created a wave of shock that overwhelmed commoner and aristocrat alike. Aunt de Garat immediately hired the most celebrated lawyer in Paris at the time, Alphonse Paillet, and his brilliant associates, Charles Lachaud and Théodore Bac. In Lachaud's case, Marie approached the remarkable young advocate herself, pleading with him to take her case in the following letter:

Sir:
When I was still happy, careless, gay, I heard you defend a poor woman accused of theft, and your words brought tears to my eyes. Now that I

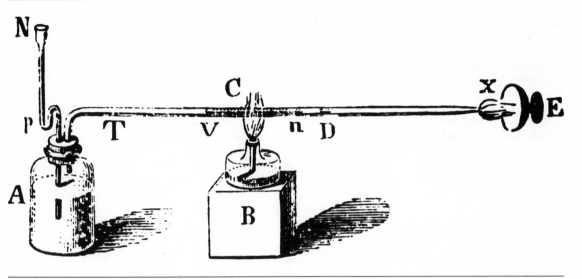

The Marsh apparatus, developed in 1836, used significantly for the first time in the Lafarge case to determine arsenic poisoning.

am wretched, careworn, and sad, I call on you to help me. I am suffering from the burden of an awful and a false accusation. Make me smile again, and fill with light the eyes that have wept so many bitter tears during the last few days.

Immediately upon receiving Marie's letter, this generous-hearted, ardently romantic lawyer packed his bags and left for Brive, in Corrèze, where the accused murderess was to be tried.

During her long detention in jail while the prosecution prepared its elaborate case (actually the first great criminal case in which the testimony of toxicologists would be the final determining factor in the jury's verdict), Marie Lafarge consistently maintained that she was being unjustly persecuted. She even let it be said that the charges had been brought against her to discredit her family's claim to the throne of France. Overnight, the woman became an *cause célèbre*, and French citizens everywhere became emotionally and intellectually involved in her case. "Until the *affaire Dreyfus*," Colin Wilson wrote more than a century later, "few cases in France were to cause such popular controversy; France split into those who were pro-Marie and

those who were anti-. . . . Many people declared Marie Lafarge a saint, and there were many who vouched for her charm and fascination. Others saw her as a spoiled and pampered liar who may have killed her husband to avoid having sexual intercourse with him."

Then, at the height of the controversy, the De Léautauds officially charged Marie with the theft of the long-missing diamond necklace. The jewels were found in Marie's bedroom at Le Glandier and her guilt appeared obvious. Marie's lawyers refused to handle the jewelry-theft case, insisting that the murder charge be dealt with first. The authorities, however, proceeded to try Marie *in absentia* on July 9, 1840.

From her cell Marie gave all manner of reasons why the De Léautaud jewels were in her possession. First, she stated that her good friend Marie de Léautaud had given them to her to pawn for money, these funds to be used to buy off the poet Félix Clavé, who was blackmailing Madame de Léautaud, using compromising letters she had sent him that later threatened to ruin her marriage. Then why were the jewels still in her possession? Marie was asked. Well, the much harassed woman countered, after learning that Clavé had gone to the Levant and would no more trouble her friend, Madame de Léautaud informed Marie that she should keep the diamonds as a token of her gratitude in helping to keep her name honorable.

Nonsense, retorted the De Léautauds; the jewels had been stolen from them by Marie Capelle Lafarge, plain and simple. They refused to drop their charges, and Marie was convicted of theft and sentenced to two years in prison. Clémentine, the frantically devoted maid, insisted that she accompany her mistress and lived with her in a small suite of rooms at Montpellier Prison, an act that made her a legend in France. (It was later claimed that Clémentine was Marie's murder accomplice, but there was little or no evidence to support such a theory.)

To half of France Marie was being railroaded, pilloried, and inhumanly persecuted; she was a political martyr of royal blood whom revolutionaries wished to eradicate for their own ends. Even Marie subscribed in her wild dreamings to this thinking, calling herself in her prison memoirs (*Heures de Prison*) *"la pauvre calomnyée"*—"the poor reviled one."

More than six thousand letters were sent to Marie at Montpellier as she awaited the opening of her sensational murder trial. Most of the letters expressed unswerving support of her. Many of them, many scented with cologne, came from high-born, wealthy gentlemen offering marriage, or, if that was not acceptable, at least she was welcome to the fortunes at their command to carry on the legal fight for her freedom. Marie was deluged with lingerie, perfumes, delicate foodstuffs and wines, and a great deal of money, perhaps as much as 200,000 francs (about $40,000 today). The woman had achieved the recognition of her dreams and she reveled in it, playing the part of the grande dame, bearing up under her terrible burden with the dignity of a regal Marie Antoinette going fearlessly to the guillotine.

As her lawyers feverishly prepared her defense, Marie took up an intense correspondence with her lawyer Charles Lachaud, then only twenty-two years old, but a legal genius who would one day become the greatest lawyer in all France.

At the eve of her trial, Marie wrote to him from prison:

> Now, praise God, the end is nigh and I can count the hours until the moment when I will be either restored in innocence to my noble friends or else transformed into a radiant martyr, worthy of heaven.

Such confident self-esteem, along with Marie's apparent sharing of her most intimate thoughts with Lachaud, caused the impressionable young lawyer to take on her defense with a vengeance. Then his natural empathy soon sidestepped into a personal passion for the delicate, cultured woman, one that would eventually blossom into undying love.

Lachaud's love and the grueling work he and Bac (also rumored to be in love with Marie) and Paillet performed on their client's behalf seemed at first to turn the tide in Marie's tedious seventeen-day trial.

Decous, the public prosecutor, opened the trial with a devastating account of Marie's background, especially the ruinous marriage with Lafarge. He then presented her wild letter, written that first night in Le Glandier, in which she spoke of her fabricated lover, her plans to leave the hapless groom, her intent to commit suicide, and how she possessed arsenic with which to accomplish her ends. This letter, when introduced as evidence, caused a roaring commotion in court.

From that night on, Decous continued, Marie had played with death, actively making plans to murder her husband to escape the marriage, all the while pretending to have had a change of heart and acting the role of the perfect wife to Charles Lafarge. She had begun her slow murder, Decous outlined, by substituting the one large cake that had been laced with arsenic for the small ones in the Christmas package sent to Lafarge in Paris, and had dosed him to death with poison after he returned home. Decous also produced Marie's malachite pillbox in which arsenic was found. This had been reluctantly turned over to him by Emma Pontier, Charles's cousin, after family members discovered that it was in her possession. Shown the pillbox and the arsenic therein, Marie waved it away as she

Marie's lawyer Charles Lachaud was so much in love with his client that he was willing to abandon his spectacular career.

stood heroically in the dock, stubbornly and illogically insisting that the contents of the pillbox were nothing more than gum arabic.

The next damning piece of evidence was offered up by the Lafarge groom, Alfred. In court he presented the "arsenic" left over from the rat pastes he had prepared from the poison Marie had given him. But, after examination, the substance proved to be bicarbonate of soda, harmless, and, like the samples of rat paste tested and exhibited in court, containing no arsenic at all.

Marie appeared to be innocently puzzled: "Why in the world is the court so concerned about bicarbonate of soda? Surely it is not dangerous. I've taken it myself many times."

"Well," said Decous in a patient voice, "explain its presence, then, where rat paste was needed."

"If I could, couldn't I establish my innocence here and now?" replied Marie sweetly, unruffled. "I am here precisely because I can't explain it, you see?"

"A charming response, but that is not the answer, Madame Lafarge."

Marie turned to the courtroom at large and rendered one of the many nonsensical comments during her trial that further confused all issues, speaking as if to herself a revelation of great magnitude: "Now I understand why the rats continued coming. Bicarbonate would never stop them."

It was all very simple, thundered Decous. Marie had obtained the arsenic and substituted soda in its place to be mixed as rat paste by the unwitting Alfred. She had kept the real arsenic in her pillbox and other places and used it to systematically poison Charles Lafarge.

Marie's defense attorneys roared back that the defense had not really proved that Charles Lafarge's body contained arsenic, that the rural doctors who examined the stomach of the deceased were wholly inept in carrying out such refined experiments.

That point was well taken, nodded the clever Decous. He had anticipated just such a move on the part of Marie's lawyers and was prepared. "Fortunately," cooed the prosecutor, "the investigation of poison murders has recently been revolutionized by advances in the science of chemistry. Probably the defendant would not stand before this court at this moment had not science given us the means to prove the presence of poison where hitherto it could not be detected in the very bodies of the victims."

And with that the science of toxicology made its first important bow in the courts of the world, setting an earthshaking precedent in proving the guilt or innocence of those accused of murdering by poison. Two noted chemists, Dubois and Dupuytren, at the behest of the prosecution, had inspected Lafarge's stomach, testing it with the apparatus invented by Englishman James Marsh, which had been only four years in existence. This device converted arsenic drawn from body fluids and tissues into arsinc, and, if used properly, the delicate apparatus could reveal the approximate amount of

Dr. Mathieu Orfila, the great forensic doctor whose word settled the sensational Lafarge murder case.

arsenic contained in the examined portions of human body.

Decous' use of the famous chemists, however, backfired. The two chemists entered the courtroom wearing solemn black robes. After a detailed and, to the public at hand, perplexing explanation of their science of toxicology, Dubois turned to the anxious jury and stated, "We have applied a number of different procedures, chiefly those recommended in the works of Monsieur Orfila." (At the time, Dr. Mathieu Joseph Bonaventure Orfila was the dean of French chemistry and the world's leading toxicologist). Dubois then described how he and

Dupuytren, following Orfila's instructions to the letter, had charred the remains of the deceased and removed those tissues to be examined minutely.

"But careful though we were and punctilious in every detail of the tests," droned Dubois, "we achieved no result whatsoever. . . . The conclusion was that in the materials presented to us no trace of arsenic is contained."

The courtroom erupted in total pandemonium. The Lafargists were jubilant. Marie clasped her hands together and raised her eyes to heaven as if her hour of deliverance had come. Paillet, Lachaud, and Bac "wept tears of triumph." According to criminologist Jürgen Thorwald, "Mounted couriers bearing the news of the testimony sped to the nearest telegraph office in Bordeaux."

Decous, however, was not finished. Renowned though Dubois and Dupuytren might be, they were human, the public prosecutor pointed out, and they could commit human error. In the whole of France, he insisted, there was only one man who could settle this matter, the master scientist himself, the great Orfila, whose word in the world of toxicology was final and absolute. Defense attorney Paillet could not protest; Orfila was his personal friend.

Orfila agreed to travel from Paris to Brive, where he conducted experiments on new tissues taken from Lafarge's exhumed body. The original organs had been so mistreated by the previous experts, Orfila complained, as to make them useless. Following the experiments of Dubois and Dupuytren, Lafarge's stomach had been cavalierly kept not in a jar but in a drawer of a court clerk where it decayed, its paper-shuffling guardian unconcerned even with the organ's overpowering odor.

With doors guarded and the original experts on hand at his request to watch his precise experiment, Orfila worked through the night of September 13. He appeared in court the following afternoon. "We have come to give our accounting to the court," the great Orfila intoned before the awed spectators. "I shall prove first that there is arsenic in the body of Lafarge; second, that this arsenic comes neither from the reagents with which we worked nor from the earth surrounding the coffin; also that the arsenic we found is not the arsenic component which is naturally found in every human body."

Orfila's comments registered a wave of shock throughout the court, and the once confident Lafargists were paralyzed. The great scientist went on to explain that only the bones of every human contain a minute amount of arsenic and Lafarge's bones were not examined. So careful were Orfila's experiments that he had even tested the soil surrounding Lafarge's interred coffin, knowing that arsenic can be found in some soil and that it sometimes works its way into a buried casket. There was no evidence of arsenic in the soil surrounding Lafarge's coffin, Orfila reported, nor in the coffin itself, the casket being an expensive air-tight model.

In the silent courtroom, Orfila went on to illustrate how the earlier chemists had erred, and how his own experiments had produced such drastically different results. "It is not impossible to explain the diversity," Orfila said. Dubois and Dupuytren had used the delicate Marsh apparatus for only an hour, and this extremely delicate apparatus was subject to all manner of disturbances—a mere draft of wind could alter the results. At the risk of alienating two famous scientist, Orfila pointed out that Dubois and Dupuytren had failed to use potassium nitrate in which to incinerate the residue of the solid matter, and most of the arsenic he, Orfila, had discovered, was lodged in this residue.

Presiding Judge de Barny interupted impatiently, asking, "Do you consider the amount of arsenic obtained by you to be sufficient to indicate murder by poisoning?"

Orfila's response was elaborate. He stated that, in conjunction with other facts—the symptoms of Lafarge's illness, the manner in which Marie obtained the poison, and the existence of the samples of Lafarge's food and drink which were heavily laced with arsenic—his experiments proved, yes, that Lafarge had been murdered with arsenic poison.

It was over. Alphonse Paillet shrieked

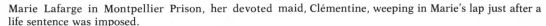

Marie Lafarge in Montpellier Prison, her devoted maid, Clémentine, weeping in Marie's lap just after a life sentence was imposed.

Marie Lafarge upon her release and shortly before her death.

uselessly, "There is more than a half milligram of arsenic in the chair the judge is sitting on right now!" But the attorney was utterly defeated and knew it. So did Marie Lafarge, whose normally staunch composure went to pieces. She collapsed in bitter tears and was taken away to her cell where she lay prostrate, wracked with sobs for two days.

A few days later Marie Capelle Lafarge faced Judge de Barny and received her sentence: hard labor for life and exposure in the dreaded pillory at Tulle. Marie rose in the dock and said only, "Gentlemen, I am innocent." Her appeal was rejected, but King Louis Philippe reduced her sentence to life imprisonment, no hard labor, no public exposure. Marie's connection with the blood royal served her after all.

Marie went back to Montpellier Prison in October 1841. Clémentine stayed with her for a year until ordered to leave. Marie's cousin, Adèle, joined her for long periods of time in her suite of cells. The prisoner busied herself with her memoirs and the writing of a tragedy, *The Lost Woman.* She continued her correspondence with Alexandre Dumas and other leading literary lights, but her mail from admirers dwindled. After ten long years, the raging battle between Lafargists and anti-Lafargists became nothing but distant echoes; Marie was a forgotten woman.

Only her devoted, lovesick lawyer Charles Lachaud remained faithful. One of her last letters to him cautioned him to "guard my heart, for the past has not touched it. It belongs to the future." The lawyer offered to quit his promising legal practice and move near to Montpellier Prison to see her when he could, even if she would not marry him. In one of her more unselfish acts, Marie wrote a note to her lover-from-afar, telling Lachaud to forget her, and "I cannot spoil your career."

In 1852, ill with tuberculosis, Marie appealed to Napoleon III and the emperor released her. She traveled alone to a small spa at Ussat in the Pyrenees, where within six months she died, without confessing and still wholly inside her own ancient fantasies, never having uttered a single word about the deliberate murder that had brought her the wrong kind of fame.

Though he had married and settled down, lawyer Charles Lachaud ordered that flowers be placed upon Marie's grave every day as long as he lived. His fellow advocate, Théodore Bac, who had also fought to save Marie a decade earlier and who may also have been in love with her, gave an unexpected response when news of Marie's death was brought to him. Said Bac, "You may think as ill of her as you can, but even then you are probably not thinking ill enough."

LALAURIE, MADAME DELPHINE

Murderer ■ (1790–1836)

She was one of the cruelest women on record in the antebellum South; that no one would dispute when discussing the ravishingly beautiful and sadistic Madame Delphine Lalaurie of New Orleans. A member of Louisiana's powerful McCarty family, Madame Lalaurie married three times, her last husband, Dr. Louis Lalaurie, a mousy little man who cowered at her every word.

Madame lived in a resplendent mansion on Royal Street where she kept a dozen slaves hopping at her slightest command. Her slaves feared her so much that they would not look Madame in the eye. To do so was to risk horrible punishment. All her slaves, residents noticed, appeared emaciated, starved, scarred as if from severe whippings. Only her mulatto butler appeared healthy and sound.

None, however, dared criticize Madame for the poor appearance of her slaves. She was Southern nobility, the very cornerstone of New Orleans society. When the great Lafayette visited the city in 1825, he dined in Madame Lalaurie's mansion.

Beyond her wit and charm, her great style and hospitality toward visiting dignitaries, the people of New Orleans began to hear rumors of demonic sadism, of unbridled madness. In 1833 one of Madame's neighbors watched in horror one night as Delphine, whip in hand, chased a small Negro child into her courtyard, beating the girl mercilessly. She chased the terrified slave child throughout the courtyard, her whip cutting the girl's flesh at every crack. Then back into the house as the woman pursued the child up three flights of stairs, the sound of her terrible whip marking the floors ascended. The bleeding child was next seen on the roof of the Lalaurie mansion scrambling madly over the eaves, Madame close at hand, laughing hysterically and whipping the girl until the slave, to escape her tormentor, hurled herself into space and downward to death on the courtyard flagstones.

Police were summoned by the horrified neighbor and found the girl's crushed body at the bottom of the Lalaurie well. Delphine was taken into custody. As punishment, typical of those slave-holding days, Madame Lalaurie was merely fined, but to uphold Southern tradition and honor, her slaves were taken away from her and resold to, it was thought, more considerate masters.

Delphine got around this quaint custom by having her relatives buy back her own slaves, returning these hapless creatures to her premises. Residents living near the Lalaurie mansion kept a watchful eye but saw only the mulatto butler moving about; the other slaves were nowhere to be seen. Then a fire broke out in the mansion on the morning of April 10, 1834. Answering the alarm, firemen with crude engines rushed to the scene, along with many of Delphine's distinguished neighbors, including Judge J. F. Canonge and Felix Lefebvre. These two men led a group of neighbors into the smoke-filled mansion, where Madame Lalaurie greeted them, telling them precisely which valuable pieces of furniture to remove.

In the kitchen, Judge Canonge found Madame's seventy-year-old cook unconscious and manacled to a twenty-foot chain. He and others broke the chain and carried the slave to the courtyard. Reviving, she told them she had started the fire, thinking it better to die in flames than live another day with Madame's cruelty.

"Are there any more slaves inside?" asked the Judge.

"In the attic."

The men ran inside the house and started up the stairs. Madame Lalaurie shouted to them to "mind your own business!" They ignored her. Several locked doors leading to the attic had to be broken down. Inside the garret, Canonge and Lefebvre found seven slaves, four men and three women, chained and crippled with awful wounds. They wore spiked collars that had torn their flesh and they were in an exhausted and starved state. The neighbors looked about in horror, examining the many tools of torture littering the floor. As they broke the chains of the slaves and carried them out, they learned exactly how Madame Lalaurie had turned her home into a torture chamber, how she had whipped her blacks, beaten them with iron bars, torn and gouged their flesh with hideous instruments. When she had tired she had ordered her mulatto butler to continue the torture and he had done so with relish as Madame stood by in an ecstatic swoon, her eyes glazed, spittle dripping from her gaping mouth.

The fire was extinguished and the furniture replaced. Madame was seen through the windows of the great house by an angry crowd of more than two thousand assembled outside watching her move nonchalantly about, replacing furniture, chatting with sympathetic relatives. When police failed to appear to arrest this ogre, the crowd began to shout curses and oaths. The mulatto butler closed the heavy shutters of the house, then locked the steel gates to the courtyard. Someone in the torch-bearing crowd shouted that the woman should be lynched.

Some minutes later, the courtyard gates flew open and out rushed Madame's sleek black carriage, the butler whipping the two horses in a frenzy. Delphine sat inside the closed carriage, her face hidden by a veil. Hundreds of men from the predominantly white throng ran after the carriage, but failed to catch up with it. The mob then broke into the Lalaurie mansion and smashed the furniture, tore the priceless paintings and tapestries. By the time the sheriff and deputies arrived, accompanied by troops, the mansion was a wreck.

By this time Delphine had reached St. John Bayou. There her slavish husband waited for her with a schooner and the couple sailed for their estate at Mandeville on Lake Pontchartrain. The mulatto butler, returning to the mansion, was met by a mob. The butler was dragged from the carriage, which tore him to pieces; his carcass was then hanged from a willow tree. Such was the anger of the mob that members tore even the elegant carriage to pieces.

Madame never returned to New Orleans. With her husband's great wealth she and Lalaurie moved to New York, but her reputation followed her and she went on to Paris where she thought her past was not known. The foreign press, however, along with American newspapers, had revealed her maniacal history, and, when the Lalauries entered their private box at the Paris opera, they were booed and hissed with such anger that the couple fled in fear.

Delphine Lalaurie did face retribution of sorts; she fell from her horse while hunting wild boar at Pau in 1836 and broke her neck.

LEBRON, LOLITA

Terrorist ■ (1920–   )

A rabid Puero Rican nationalist, Lolita Lebron led three men to the gallery of the House of Representatives on March 1, 1954. Lebron, a thirty-four-year-old mother of two children and a sewing machine operator by trade, suddenly produced a Puerto Rican flag and waved it frantically. Many of the 143 members of the House then on the main floor looked up curiously.

Lebron dropped the flag and whipped out a Luger, firing rapidly at the congressmen, as did her companions, Irving Flores Rodriguez, Rafael Mirando, and Andres Figueroa Cordero. The representatives scrambled for cover, hiding beneath desks, racing for the exits. Five congressmen were wounded, the most serious being Representative Alvin M. Bentley of Michigan. A bullet passed through his entire upper torso, puncturing a lung and the diaphragm.

Bystanders leaped upon the terrorists and held them down until officers put them under arrest. Lebron and the others were given seventy-five-year prison terms. All the congressmen who were injured recovered from their wounds.

Reacting to clamoring pressure from Puerto Rican minority groups, President Jimmy Carter commuted the sentences of Lebron and the others on September 6, 1979. They were released the next day, Lebron telling newsmen that she had no remorse over her senseless shooting.

Terrorist Lolita Lebron under guard only minutes after shooting up the House of Representatives chamber in Washington, D.C., on March 1, 1954.

LEE, JEAN

Murderer ■ (1917–1951)

An Australian call girl who had become famous with GIs during World War II, Jean Lee went into the badger game in the late 1940s, aided by her pimp and lover, Robert David Clayton. Joining the voluptuous redhead and her protector was a thug named Norman Andrews.

On the night of November 7, 1949, this scheming trio encountered William George Kent, a seventy-three-year-old bookmaker, in a Carlton Hotel lounge. Jean Lee flaunted her ample charms and soon convinced the old man to take her to his room. There she got him drunk and tried to rifle his pockets, but Kent, even in his stupor, doggedly held on to his money.

Jean let her two friends into the room. The men tore the money from Kent's grasp then savagely tortured him, tying his thumbs together, kicking him, and slashing him with a broken bottle. They left him dead and went off to a Sydney bar to celebrate. After Kent's mangled body was found, hotel employees described the trio, and the three killers were soon under arrest. After two trials in which all turned on one another, the trio drew death sentences. All three were hanged at Pentridge Jail on February 19, 1951.

LEHMANN, CHRISTA

Murderer ■ (1922–   )

Insanity was manifest throughout Christa Lehmann's heritage; her mother had been locked up in an asylum by the time Christa had reached her teens. Her father, Karl Ambros, a taciturn cabinetmaker, wholly neglected his child. Christa's stormy youth was pockmarked with petty thefts, which culminated in a prison term, which the girl was allowed to serve on probation.

In 1944, Christa met and married a dissolute tile setter, one Karl Franz Lehmann, who, only weeks after the honeymoon, proved to be a confirmed drunkard. Christa had several affairs in her hometown of Worms, Germany, but they led only to depression and seething anger over her seemingly hopeless situation.

On February 15, 1954, Christa purchased five chocolate truffles filled with cream and handed these out to neighbors. One she gave to Eva Ruh, a seventy-five-year-old widow who lived with her daughter Annie Hamann, also a widow, and Uschi Hamann, Annie's nineteen-year-old daughter. Eva Ruh put the truffle on a

This unusual photo shows poisoner Christa Lehmann (arrow) at the funeral of one of her victims. The man at left in the gray jacket, studying her reactions, is a German detective.

plate in the refrigerator. When Annie came home from work, she found the delicacy and took a bite, spitting most of it out and saying, "It's bitter!" An hour later Annie Hamann clutched her stomach and groped toward her bed, screaming, "Mother—I can't see anymore!" She writhed with cramped for terrible minutes, then died.

When authorities arrived they also found the family dog dead in the kitchen. The dog had eaten the truffle dropped by Annie Hamann. Police were called but inspectors were baffled, particularly when forensic scientists examined the body and found no known poison. Kurt Wagner, a university scientist, eliminated strychnine and other alkaloids. Wagner then recalled reading about a new organic phosphorus

compound known as E-605 which was used as a chemical insecticide. This agent, Wagner concluded, could have caused the convulsions experienced by Annie Hamann. When testing for this poison, Wagner did, indeed, discover E-605 in the victim's body.

Detectives, of course, suspected Christa Lehmann but were prevented from arresting the woman in that there seemed to be no motive for her poisoning the victim, who was Christa's close friend. Further, the other four truffles Christa had handed out to other neighbors had produced no ill effects.

In checking into Christa's background, it was soon learned that her husband, Karl, had died in convulsive agony on September 17, 1952. At the time a Dr. Wattrin had determined the cause of death to be the rupture of a stomach ulcer, an affliction Lehmann was known to have. More curious was the fact that Christa's father-in-law, Valentin Lehmann, had also died in convulsions, on October 14, 1953, falling to the street in intense pain from his bicycle only twenty minutes after leaving the house where he lived with Christa.

A careful watch was kept on Mrs. Lehmann, inspectors following the woman everywhere. They watched as Christa stood in the crowd around Annie Hamann's grave during burial services, great tears coursing down Mrs. Lehmann's lean face. Then, having no other suspect, police took the woman in for questioning.

Christa denied having had anything to do with the death of her friend, Annie. She was jailed pending a trial at which police had little hope for a conviction. Their prospects did an abrupt turnaround on February 23, 1954, when Christa called her father and a priest to her cell. She confessed that she had delivered *one* truffle poisoned with E-605 to the Hamann house. She had meant to kill the elderly Eva Ruh, who had criticized Annie Hamann for associating with Christa. Her friend, however, had accidentally eaten the truffle instead. Later, Mrs. Lehmann casually told police, "By the way, I also poisoned my father-in-law, and I killed my husband, too."

She had purchased the new insecticide, several boxes of it, from Meyer's the Chemist in Worms. "The boxes were marked 'poison.' That was all I needed to know."

Her trial was quick. Christa refused to repudiate her confession, leaving her defense attorney helpless. She was convicted on September 20, 1954, and sent to prison for life.

When the sensational Lehmann story broke, scores of people in Germany, which was then undergoing a terrible depression, purchased the poison E-605 and committed suicide.

Alternating between defiance and sorrow in court, Christa Lehmann admits murdering three persons in 1954. (Wide World)

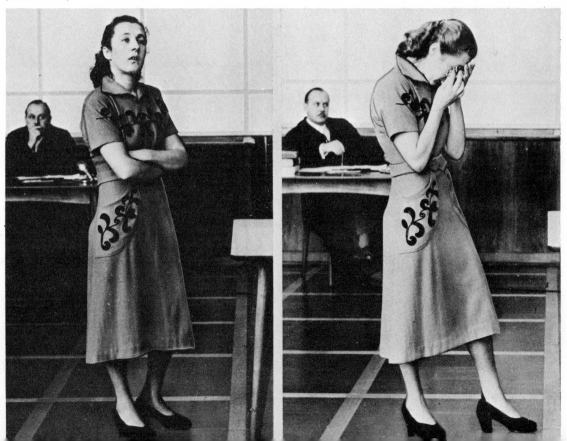

LEHNBERG, MARLENE

Murderer ■ (1955–   )

A secretary living in Capetown, South Africa, nineteen-year-old Marlene Lehnberg had two driving ambitions—she wanted to become a successful model, and she wanted to marry a man named Christopher van der Linde. The fact that Van der Linde was already married and, though flattered by Marlene's attentions, had no intention of seeking a divorce did not deter the beautiful Miss Lehnberg.

Marlene attempted the old dodge of calling Van der Linde's wife, Susanna, and telling her she was having an affair with her husband, a statement easily determined by the wife to be a lie. Next Marlene insisted that she was pregnant, but this fabrication also failed to produce the divorce the pretty secretary so longed for.

Murder seemed the only answer to this befuddled girl. She sought out an impoverished black, Marthinus Choegoe, promising him her car, some cash, and her own body if he would kill Mrs. van der Linde. The thirty-three-year-old Choegoe broke into the Van der Linde home on the night of November 4, 1974, and stabbed the victim to death in her sleep with a pair of scissors.

Police had little difficulty in tracking down Choegoe. He had a noticeable limp and had been seen hobbling from the scene of the murder. Choegoe confessed and named his employer. Marlene insisted she had nothing to do with the death, but Choegoe had had the foresight to keep a note she had sent him which read, "If you think it will be better or quicker, then use a knife but the job must be done."

Choegoe and Marlene Lehnberg were found guilty and given life terms.

LINE, ANNE

Heretic ■ (? –1601)

A middle-aged woman, Anne Line was loyal to the Catholic Church, which at the time was undergoing a great persecution in England. She not only harbored much hunted Catholic priests but allowed these priests to conduct masses in her home. She was caught by authorities as she was helping a priest to escape and was thrown into Newgate Prison, then quickly condemned as a heretic under the law that forbade the harboring of priests.

Anne was taken to Tyburn in 1601 and hanged. Before her execution she kissed the gallows, prayed aloud, which angered the assembled crowd, then stated, "Where I received one [priest], I would to God I had been able to receive a thousand."

LUSK, GRACE

Murderer ■ (1878– ?)

A spinster schoolteacher, Grace Lusk of Waukesha, Wisconsin, fell in love with a local horse doctor, David Roberts, exchanging affectionate letters with the married man throughout the spring of 1917. Mrs. Roberts, a tough-minded woman, caught on to Grace's love for her husband and confronted the thirty-nine-year-old teacher.

"I suppose you know about that girl who died in an attic room after an operation, after she had been too interested in my husband?" snapped Mrs. Roberts.

"And you lived with him after that?"

"Why, certainly," Mrs. Roberts told the shocked Grace. "I am a respectable woman! You, on the other hand, happen to be a bitch, a slut whom the dogs follow down the street!"

Grace Lusk calmly pulled forth a .25-caliber automatic and fired two shots into Mrs. Roberts's angry heart. She then tried to shoot herself but only blew off a fingertip and suffered a superficial chest wound. She was arrested.

While Grace awaited trial, Roberts told newsmen, "I did not deceive her or lead her on. We were not children. But I did some poor calculation. Other women have thought they cared for me, but I was married and they knew their liking for me would come to nothing permanent. So the affairs usually faded away. I thought it would be the same with Miss Lusk, but it wasn't. I loved my wife. She was the only woman I ever loved. We all make mistakes."

The everloving Grace responded with, "I care not what I have suffered or what my future will be—I love him and I will never cause him any trouble."

A jury found Grace guilty of second degree murder on May 29, 1918. The defense had tried to show that a streak of insanity coursed through the Lusk family, Grace's great-grandmother, Louisa Bond, having been confined in the Wisconsin State Insane Hospital in 1864. Their argument failed.

Upon hearing the verdict that brought her a life sentence, Grace glared into the face of the elderly prosecutor, D. S. Tullar, as she was being led from the court. She halted before the seated man, peering with hate down upon him. Then she lurched forward, nails clawing, tearing the prosecutor's face open so that blood ran down his face, screaming, "You lied! You lied my life and my love away!" Officers finally managed to pull Grace off the screaming Tullar.

She began serving her term in Waupun Penitentiary on June 19, 1918. Each night she was heard by guards to pray loudly in her cell. It was always the same incantation: "Oh God, send Dr. Roberts to me! Make him know that I love him still. I love him, I love him, I love him! I want him in spite of everything!"

Grace Lusk was pardoned by the Governor of Wisconsin in 1923.

LYLES, ANJETTE

Murderer ■ (1917–)

Authorities in Macon, Georgia, investigated a rash of sudden deaths in the small town of Cochran in the spring of 1958, their investigation centering about a forty-one-year-old restaurant owner, Mrs. Anjette Donovan Lyles. They had begun the investigation after receiving an anonymous letter stating that Mrs. Lyles's daughter Marcia was being poisoned. (The letter writer was later identified as Mrs. Lyles's cook, Carrie Jackson.)

Sheriff's deputies were too late to save Marcia, but the little girl's body was examined and

Mrs. Anjette Donovan Lyles, shown with daughters Marcia Elaine (left) and Carla. Mrs. Lyles poisoned Marcia and three others to death.

arsenic was found. Mrs. Lyles's two husbands and a mother-in-law had also died under mysterious circumstances and after these bodies were exhumed, arsenic was also found.

Mrs. Lyles, a buxom, outgoing woman who practiced black magic and voodoo as hobbies, had collected insurance money on all her deceased relatives. When confronted with the discovery of arsenic in the bodies, Mrs. Lyles said she knew nothing about it, that perhaps in the case of the little girl, Marcia had been playing "doctor and nurse" and swallowed arsenic by accident.

Mrs. Lyles was placed on trial. The prosecution convincingly argued that she had murdered for financial gain. The woman was found guilty and sentenced to death, but state psychiatrists later determined her to be insane. She was sent to the State Hospital at Milledgeville, Georgia, for life.

LYONS, SOPHIE

Swindler ■ (1848–1924)

America's first great lady of con, one of the most audacious swindlers of the nineteenth century, distinguished herself not only as a feminine hallmark of crime but the epitome of the reformed crook, one who died having made great fortunes on both sides of the law. Such was the spectacular life of Sophie Levy Lyons.

Born in New York City on December 24, 1848, the child Sophie, from the moment she could walk, was taught the subtle art of shoplifting by her mother, a dedicated crook, who went under the aliases of Sophie Elkins and Julia Keller. Her father, Sam Levy, was a housebreaker and spent more time in prison than out. Sophie took a warped pride in the criminal background of her family. One grandfather, named Elkins, was a second-story man in England. Sophie later boasted in her book, *Why Crime Does Not Pay,*

that Elkins was "a cracksman to whom Scotland Yard took off its cap."

A pretty child who was to grow into a beautiful woman, Sophie proved adept at shoplifting and pickpocketing at an early age. "All during my childhood," she once told a newsman, "I did little but steal and was never sent to school. I did not learn to read or write until I was twenty-five years old." At one time, after talking to some girls in a park, Sophie got the notion that stealing was immoral and refused to shoplift. At that her father grabbed a poker and seared her arm. Sophie obediently returned to thieving.

Surrounded on all sides by crooks, Sophie knew no other society than the criminal. When Maury Harris proposed to Sophie, he proudly informed her that he was an accomplished pickpocket. The sixteen-year-old girl was impressed; pickpockets were considered artists of

Sophie Lyons in her early twenties, after graduating from shoplifter to con artist.

the underworld at the time. Sophie quickly married what she thought to be a star in the criminal profession. But Harris was less proficient at his trade than his boasts would have it. He was caught red-handed trying to filch a wallet and imprisoned for two years. Sophie promptly forgot him. A short time later she met the love of her life, Edward "Ned" Lyons, an English-born burglar eleven years older than Sophie. Ned himself was enchanted by the apprentice thief. Sophie, at the time, was described as "an exceedingly beautiful girl with brilliant dark eyes, and auburn hair that flowed to her feet when shaken from its coils."

As for Lyons, he was a superstar in the underworlds of two continents. He had pulled some big jobs both in England and in America. He had been one of the gang that had burglarized the Ocean Bank in New York on June 27, 1869, netting the gang $786,879, a job masterminded by George Leonidas Leslie. Lyons had been taught his trade by Johnny Hope, an elderly mentor to the boldest of bank burglars. Lyons also worked with New York's cream among criminals—Johnny Hope's son Jimmy, Banjo Pete Emerson, Harry Raymond, Worcester Sam Perris, and Abe Coakley. This group, Lyons leading the way, robbed the Philadelphia Navy Yard in 1870, taking from the vaults more than $150,000. Ned Lyons was as idolized by the underworld of that era as rock stars are by teenagers today. In 1924, *The New York Times*, when offering Sophie's obituary, summed up this peculiar attitude: "There is nothing like that world today, but at the time there was a conscious pride about the big crooks, and they married as in a caste and often passed their craft from father to son or from mother to daughter. Sophie, then, was something of a catch. So was Ned Lyons."

Big, strong, sporting a thick red mustache, Ned Lyons was a walking anachronism. Here was a man who had fought in the worst hellholes in England and America as a brawler, having had one ear bitten off in a drunken donnybrook, an unscrupulous, desperate thief who never hesitated to rob any institution no matter the risks. Yet he insisted, after marrying Sophie, that his wife never again steal a penny. He would provide everything. She would live in

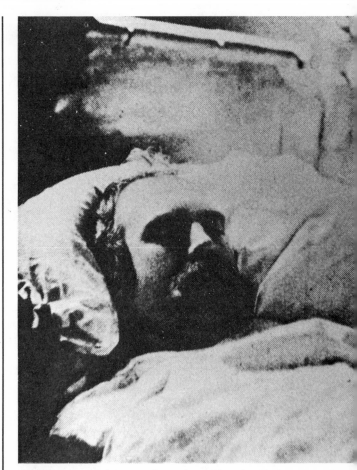

Bank burglar Ned Lyons, shown in a prison-hospital bed recovering from wounds, the only photo ever taken of this master criminal.

style. He bought her a fashionable home on Long Island and surrounded her with all a woman of that day might want. There were servants, expensive china, imported rugs and furniture.

Sophie, however, proved incurable. When Ned left the house to case a job, Sophie would slip out and travel to Manhattan for the day, hunting for wallets, jewelry, expensive lace, anything her nimble fingers could snatch and hide. She would then fence the items of each day's work with Fredricka "Marm" Mandelbaum, the millionaire fence and mentor to thousands of professional crooks, before returning home to take up the pose of wife-in-residence, calmly awaiting the arrival of her burglar husband. When Lyons began to find Sophie's loot, he reasoned that motherhood would motivate his wayward spouse to stay at home. Sophie gave birth to a son, George, late in 1870, but six months later she went back to her old ways, taking a train to see some friends in Portsmouth, New Hampshire. She did not tell Ned that her real aim was to work the sprawling fair in that town as a pickpocket. The youthful beauty was caught in the act by an alert fair detective.

Taken to the Portsmouth jail to be booked, Sophie put on an act that overwhelmed a roomful of detectives. The record of that arrest was kept and cherished by the arresting detective who witnessed Sophie's spectacular act:

> She was then only nineteen years old, but her phenomenal talent as an actress was already developed. She could mold her face to every shade of emotion. She could make her eyes at will a fountain of tears. She treated us to a moving display of her art. She was by turns horror-stricken, proudly indignant, heartbroken, and convulsed with hysterics. Who could press a charge against such a blushing, trembling, sobbing young beauty piteously claiming that it was a dreadful mistake, painting the agony of her dear husband and parents at the bare suspicion of her spotless innocence, and subtly hinting at the grave censure that would surely fall on her maligners? It was her shrewd calculation that the authorities in charge of her case would prefer to let it drop quietly, and so they did. Either conclusive evidence was lacking, or it was judged to be an unusually clear case of kleptomania, for the artful Sophie was suffered to disappear.

Released, Sophie returned to the fair, disguising herself as an old crone. She left Portsmouth with a bagful of wallets and watches.

Sophie's obsession with stealing, even when she didn't need the money, earned her a six-month jail term in early 1871 after she was caught scooping up diamond rings in a New York jewelry store. She was sent to Blackwell's Island. Little George was put in the care of Sophie's mother, who later turned him into a sneak thief. (George Lyons was to remain a crim-

inal all his days, sent to prison twice for long terms, and eventually dying in a cell. "Cut off in his prime, he was," Sophie would later lament.)

Luck had held for Ned Lyons for more than two decades, but shortly after Sophie's imprisonment, the master bank burglar looted a safe of $150,000 and was arrested, informed upon by a fellow gang member. He was given seven years in Sing Sing. Only weeks after her release from Blackwell's Island, Sophie was again under arrest, this time for grand larcency. She was convicted on October 9, 1871, and sent to Sing Sing for five years. Some of her friends properly speculated that Sophie had designed it all the way, that she purposely allowed herself to be caught so that she could be near Ned Lyons in prison.

It was later apparent that Sophie had gone to prison not just to be near her husband but to effect his escape. Within weeks, Sophie had ingratiated herself to the head matron of Sing Sing's female division, becoming the matron's personal servant. Prison regulations were lax in that era, and warders were allowed to do whatever they wished with their prisoners. Instead of wearing the required prison uniform, Sophie dressed in the costume of a maid and spent most of her time walking the head matron's children, even strolling outside the prison walls at will.

During one stroll, Sophie made contact with John "Red" Leary, a member of Ned Lyons' gang. She quickly explained her plan for Ned's escape. Some days later Leary arrived at Sing Sing, pretending to be Lyons' lawyer. He was given an official pass and interviewed his "client" for only a few minutes before leaving. When asked to return the pass, "lawyer" Leary mumbled an apology about having lost the document. Leary walked out of Sing Sing with the pass stuffed behind his upper teeth. Within days, a clever forger had manufactured a fresh pass with another name and a future date on it. This, along with a suit of clothes and a wig, was smuggled into Sing Sing by a trusty. A day later, Ned Lyons, bank burglar, simply walked out of prison.

Somewhat artless, prison authorities failed to connect Lyons' escape with Sophie, and she continued her duties as maid uninterrupted. While walking the matron's children outside the prison walls some days later, Sophie was met by an old Indian peddler, who crushed a piece of paper into her hands and winked. The peddler, of course, was Ned Lyons, and he, too, had a plan. Sophie was to take the wax Ned had passed to her inside the paper and make an impression of the key of the main prison door in the female division. This she did, passing the wax impression to Lyons a week later. Lyons soon returned a key to her, and, on the snow-swirling night of December 19, 1872, Sophie unlocked the prison door and ran to the nearby roadway where a sleigh was waiting. The jubilant Lyons took Sophie into his arms and wrapped a fur coat about her, one stolen just the day before. Man and wife then skidded away in the sleigh, sipping on brandy, laughing and kissing, as Ned Lyons lashed a team of horses into a fierce gallop, their trail obliterated by a driving snowstorm.

The lovers fled to Canada where they took up permanent residence, and for some years foraged only among safes and vaults to pay their living expenses. Ned then met a wealthy pawnbroker, in whose safe, he learned, rested a fortune. Sophie uncharacteristically argued with her husband at this time, telling him she was weary of the criminal life. She begged him to make the pawnbroker job his last. Ned agreed. Dressed as a man, Sophie went along on the job with Ned, dropping through a skylight with him, breaking into the safe with him, and then fleeing with more than $40,000, most of which was in gold.

But it was not Ned Lyons' last job. Sophie failed as miserably to reform her husband as Ned had failed years earlier to convince Sophie to go straight. The two stayed together for several more years, but they argued incessantly, and, when they finally returned to the United States, Ned and Sophie separated.

Then Ned returned, full of reconciliation and ideas. The Long Island fair of 1876 was in full swing, "thousands of suckers waiting to be plucked," according to Ned. Sophie, down at the heels, agreed to work the fair with her estranged husband. The reunion proved disastrous. On October 26, 1876, both were caught picking pockets and were returned to Sing Sing where they finished out their sentences.

During this long prison term, Sophie saw little of Ned Lyons and resolved to end her marriage. Once released, she decided, she would work as an independent operative and on a higher level than Ned Lyons had ever achieved. She would concentrate on being a blackmailer, a confidence artist, a bank thief, and in these unsavory realms Sophie was indeed to become supreme, becoming known as the Queen of Crime. She embarked on her new career immediately upon her release from prison.

Sophie admitted later that she had prepared well for her salad days of the 1880s. "My early training, under such expert bank robbers as Ned Lyons, Max Shinborn, and Harry Raymond made me extraordinarily successful in this variety of crime. The cleverest men in the business began to have respect for my judgement, and were continually inviting me to take an important part in their risky but very profitable ventures."

Sophie abhorred violence and told her new confederate, Billy Burke, that he was never to use force in any situation. "I can't stand the sight of blood," she reminded him. Sophie next outlined her method of looting banks. Holding up cashiers with guns, blasting safes open, all of that was out. Guile and cunning could achieve the same effect.

Sophie obtained lists of all the circus parades scheduled for several months, especially in small towns. She and Burke would then case a small local bank that had only a few employees. When the parade began, Sophie would position herself across the street in an advantageous position. She would note when all the bank employees came to the windows to watch the parade, then signal Burke, already at the rear of the bank and possessing a key to the back door. He would quickly enter the bank, rifle the cash drawers, and, if there was enough time, the vault, then slip out the back while the bank employees still had their faces glued to the windows to see the marvels of the circus dance by. Sophie's take was usually between $10,000 and $25,000 on such occasions, and there were many of these. (Burke, whom Sophie later married, worked as an underling, receiving a meager amount for carrying out Sophie's dictates.)

Sophie Lyons during her heyday as a supreme swindler.

Another inventive trick originated by Sophie Lyons was the carriage ruse. Dressed as a grand dame, she would arrive in a small town in a resplendent carriage, stopping in front of a county bank at noontime when only one clerk was on duty. Burke, acting out the part of a servant to this regal woman, would go into the bank and tell the clerk that his millionaire employer desired to open an account in the bank, that she had just bought half the county. She also required information on valuable stocks the bank was handling. Unfortunately, explained Burke, his mistress could not leave her carriage because she was lame. Would the clerk be kind enough to step into the street? The clerk invariably did go to the carriage where Sophie enmeshed him in a drawn-out conversation while Burke leisurely plucked every dollar

from the cashier cages.

As her success broadened, Sophie's fame soared. She went to Europe, pulling off fabulous capers in all the major capitals, everything from bank burglary in Paris to running stolen gems in Amsterdam, the jewels hidden in the false bottoms of trunks Sophie herself designed. Her reputation during the 1880s became such that William S. Devery, Chief of the New York Police Department, held a special press conference to label Sophie as the "Queen of Crime." Blustered Devery to newsmen, "Sophie Lyons is one of the cleverest criminals that the country has ever produced. She has carried her operations into nearly every quarter of the civilized globe and is known to the police of every European capital. She has been arrested hundreds of times since she was first picked up by the police in 1859 at age twelve. And don't you believe that nonsense about her reforming. For her that's impossible."

While enjoying the luxuries her enormous thefts had brought her—a villa on the Riviera, a townhouse in Manhattan, a ranch in the West—Sophie took the time to educate herself, hiring professors by the score to tutor her. She learned to speak four languages fluently and became an avid reader, schooling herself in art, literature, and music. Her manners and speech polished, Sophie moved among the upper-crust American society in Europe, accepted unwittingly by the Vanderbilts, the Ryersons, and the Whitneys as the daughter of a gold prospector who had struck it rich in the West.

When Sophie, who at the time was using the alias of Mary Wilson (she also used the aliases of Kate Wilson and Fannie Owens when pulling off jobs in Europe), was caught by a Parisian gendarme with her hand in a man's pocket near the Arc de Triomphe, and taken to the police station to be booked, the social lions of the American colony in Paris recoiled in shock and indignation. It was a terrible mistake, Sophie and her super-rich friends insisted. The American ambassador was called; he quickly took up Sophie's defense. This was a cultured woman of means. How dare the French authorities think such a person guilty of a low crime? Sophie played the injured innocent to the hilt and, when the American ambassador demanded her unconditional release, the Prefect of Police apologized, kissing Sophie's hand and begging forgiveness as he led her to a carriage. She was given a police escort back to her hotel, the gendarmes bowing and scraping all the way.

That day in her hotel, Sophie busied herself with another scheme, to steal some priceless diamonds from Mrs. Herbert Lorillard, a society matron of enormous wealth. Sophie later related the theft of the Lorillard jewels, valued at nearly $500,000 in her memoirs: "Mrs. Lorillard was occupying rooms adjoining mine, and I was trying to get her jewelry. She had two maids with her, one of whom had to keep watch over two satchels containing the jewels.

"The maids were honest girls, and we could not do any business through them, but we followed the party from place to place, expecting some time that the girl would forget to take proper care of the satchels, and then our opportunity to steal them would arrive. A few days after Mrs. Lorillard had settled in this hotel she attended some reception in Paris, and, of course, her jewelry bags had to be taken from the hotel safe, where they had been placed for safety.

"Mrs. Lorillard picked out the particular pieces of jewelry she wanted to wear at the reception and closed up the bags, turning them over to the maid to place in the safe. The maid came out of the apartment with the two bags, and I met her in the hall and began to ask her some trivial questions. She stopped to talk with me and laid down the bags. While I kept her engaged in conversation a comrade of mine crept up, substituted another bag for one of the jewelry receptacles and slipped off. I continued to talk a little longer, and then the girl and I parted.

"My associate went to another hotel and concealed the jewelry, while I stayed there in my room, not wishing to attract attention by leaving at such a critical time, for, after the robbery was discovered, if it had been found that I had left at the same time it would have been natural for suspicion to be directed to me."

The next day, when Mrs. Lorillard discovered the jewels missing, the hotel was in an uproar, detectives swarming through every room, searching. Not a trace of the missing jewels was found. At this time, the French police were par-

ticularly careful not to offend the sacrosanct Sophie, though they did search her room at her happy invitation. After fencing the Lorillard jewels, Sophie's cut came to well over $250,000, enough money to keep her in style and operation for years.

But Sophie's high living soon wiped out her handsome fortune, and she was compelled to return to America where she took up the trade of the blackmailer, which made her several fortunes. She also found enough time to reunite with Ned Lyons, producing three more children, two girls and a boy, before finally ending her marriage.

Some very inventive methods were used by Sophie as a blackmailer. When a wealthy Boston merchant fell in love with her, she lured him to her hotel room where she locked him in a closet and demanded that he write out a check to her for several thousand dollars.

"Well, you can keep me inside this closet then," shouted the merchant from behind the door. "The police will come looking for me eventually."

"Yes, and find you in my closet," replied Sophie. "And how will that look to your wife?"

In moments a check made out to Sophie for $5,000 was slipped beneath the door. Sophie, however, refused to let her sucker out of the closet until her associate, Kate Leary, the wife of Red Leary, ran to the bank, cashed the check, and returned with the money.

Even inventive methods, though, do not always bring success. In Detroit, a rich public official lusted after Sophie, but when she attempted to blackmail him, the official raced home and shut himself up. Sophie followed the man, sitting for hours outside his house on a horseblock, humming and softly calling the man's name. A theatrical agent passed by and became curious. Sophie handed him the lie that the man inside the house was the father of her child and refused to support the little one. The theatrical agent grew livid with anger, shook his fist in the direction of the official's house, and shouted, "You come out here right now, you cad, and help the woman you've wronged!"

The official came out on the front stairs. He held a hose in his hand and this he turned on Sophie, the blast of water knocking her off her perch. For good measure, the official next raced down the stairs and thrashed the interfering theatrical agent.

Arrested many times and having served several prison terms, some time during the early 1890s Sophie Lyons witnessed the onset of her career's decline. Officially she retired and re-formed, but police believed that her retirement was involuntary, that she had been forced into it by her own fame. Said one police official at the time, "With advancing years her remarkable beauty faded away. She became addicted to the opium habit, and dissipation marked her face indelibly. Of late years, she has had little oppor-tunity for plundering, for her face is so well known in all the large cities of America and Europe that she is constantly watched for, if she is not arrested on sight."

One of Sophie's last great attacks upon the American financial system was to establish her own bank, along with a female associate of the unlikely name of Carrie Mouse. Carrie fronted the operation, opening a large, well-furnished bank in mid-town Manhattan, The New York Women's Investment and Banking Company. Sophie financially backed the operation and ad-vertised in the daily press. These ads offered "widows and other women of means" invest-ments guaranteed to return from fifteen to twenty percent. A swarm of gulled women applied. Interested investors were referred to Sophie, who lived in a palatial mansion (rented for the occasion), and was waited on hand and foot by servants. Yes, of course, Sophie told the suckers, the investments made on her behalf by the bank had brought on these riches. And with a sweeping gesture of an arm that glittered with diamond rings and bracelets, she indicated the entirety of her lavish living quarters.

Before this bubble burst, the phony bank took in more than $200,000, but much to Sophie's chagrin, her partner, Carrie Mouse, absconded with the profits, badly shortchanging the Queen of Crime. It was the last straw. "If you can't trust your fellow crooks," sighed Sophie, "it's time to get out of the profession."

Sophie got out and stayed out, moving to Detroit where she made uncannily successful in-vestments in real estate which made her more than a million dollars. She did not hoard this money, but provided good educations for her two daughters, Florence and Esther, whom she had sent to Canada during her thieving years to be raised in a convent, spending $20,000 on their education. Esther repaid Sophie's love and sup-port by writing to her one day and telling her that she hoped her mother would never visit her at school or the other girls might find out just who Sophie Lyons was. Sophie continued to support Esther but never spoke to her again as long as she lived. A story exists that Esther later married, then came to poverty and was reduced to pushing a hand organ through the streets of Detroit. Sophie passed her on one of those streets years later "with her eye in the air."

By that time, 1897, Sophie had turned liter-ary lioness, becoming a society columnist, America's first, for the *New York World*. Sophie was a regular transatlantic passenger on the finest liners sailing to and from Europe. She had maintained the social contacts established dur-ing her years as an intercontinental thief and swindler, and these contacts held her in good stead as a columnist, providing a constant flow of society information. She maintained her villa on the Riviera and was always accompanied by two maids. She hobnobbed with royalty, in-cluding the Prince of Wales, and was an integral part of Europe's social elite, attending the most important parties and functions, all of which she wrote about in her popular syndicated column.

Sophie also turned to another type of writ-ing, publishing small booklets in which she urged her fellow crooks to reform, begging pro-fessional criminals to "tread on the past as you would on a doormat." She also tried to better the lot of the criminal by establishing a home in Detroit for children whose parents were in prison, funding this home year after year. She sent a grand piano to the Detroit House of Cor-rections. She spent thousands of dollars in estab-lishing and stocking prison libraries throughout the country.

Billy Burke, Sophie's one-time confederate, married her and Sophie reformed him, too. They stayed together in Detroit until Burke's death in 1919. Many stories were presented by Sophie and her police friends that attempted to explain the reason for Sophie's own reform. Explained Sophie in 1910, "Twenty years ago I heard the

Portrait of a reformed Sophie Lyons who became America's first society columnist.

voice calling. I now own forty houses, but I want something more than property. I want the respect of good people."

A retired New York police captain at that time gave another story, telling *The Success Magazine* that, as a young patrolman, he found Sophie Lyons inside a fashionable church.

"And what are the likes of you doing in here?" the cop had asked the con woman.

Sophie looked up from her kneeling position, her hands clasped in prayer. "As you can see, I'm here to worship."

"Well, Sophie. If you want to get religion you'll have to go to the Salvation Army. We can't let you stay here with all the swells."

"If I have to get it at the Salvation Army," thundered Sophie, "I'll do without."

It was this rejection, in a house of worship, the police stubbornly claimed, that caused Sophie Lyons Burke to reform.

On the night of May 8, 1924, Sophie, then seventy-six, received three men alone in her Detroit home, all of them thieves she had been attempting to reform. They had no thought of anything other than the rumors that hinted Sophie's fortune was hidden in her home. When she refused to turn over her valuables and money, they attacked the woman, crushing her head with pistol butts. Neighbors heard Sophie shout, "Quit! Don't do it!" When the neighbors rushed into the house, the thieves escaping out the back door, they found Sophie on the floor in a coma. That same night in Detroit's Grace Hospital, Sophie died of a massive brain hemorrhage.

A few days later court officials opened Sophie's huge safe deposit box. In it they found her will, huge amounts of cash, and scores of gem-encrusted rings, bracelets, brooches, pins, along with stocks and bonds wrapped inside the American flag; a note pinned to it read, "God bless this flag." The estate was estimated to be worth between $750,000 and well over a million dollars. Sophie's will provided generously for all her children except her daughter Esther, the daughter who had expressed shame for her mother. To this daughter Sophie left "$100, and a silver purse to keep it in. That is all."

MACLEOD, MRS. A

Forger ■ (? −1726)

A mysterious woman of apparently considerable means, attractive, in her midthirties, and always dressed fashionably, Mrs. Macleod came to the attention of Scottish authorities in early 1726 when she presented a check for 58 pounds, then a considerable amount, to a landowner named Petrie in Leith. Since the check was made out to George Henderson, a respectable Edinburgh merchant, and signed by the Duchess of Gordon, then endorsed over to Mrs. Macleod, Petrie, without question, made payment to Mrs. Macleod, who was a tenant in one of his buildings.

The check sooned proved a forgery, but when faced with this charge, Mrs. Macleod insisted that the merchant Henderson was the culprit. They were both brought to trial with Mrs. Macleod's attorney providing witnesses who testified that the merchant had had several meetings with the female prisoner and that they had seen Henderson give her the check and endorse it in her name.

During the trial a carpenter, David Household, was found hiding on a ship for London. Upon questioning, he confessed that he had been Mrs. Macleod's accomplice in forgery and fraud, but that she had thought up the clever swindle on her own. She had studied Henderson's attire and makeup and given Household a coat and wig identical to that which the merchant habitually wore, then had the carpenter impersonate Henderson in front of witnesses as he endorsed the check which Mrs. Macleod had earlier forged.

Henderson was released, Household was sent to prison, Mrs. Macleod was sent to the gallows. Forgery in Scotland was then considered an "artful and horrid contrivance" and therefore a capital crime.

The beautiful Mrs. Macleod went unruffled to the hangman; she wore a large black robe with a large hoop and carried a large white fan.

With great composure, the woman stood on the gallows and put the rope around her own neck. "I'm innocent," she murmured at the end.

MAJOR, ETHEL LILLIE

Murderer ■ (1890–1934)

In the spring of 1934, Arthur Major, a truck driver who lived in the Lincolnshire village of Kirkby-on-Bain, England, sat down at the edge of a gravel pit to have his lunch. Another worker sat down next to him and watched Major bite into a sandwich, then spit out the mouthful and comment ruefully, "I'm damned sure that woman is trying to poison me." He threw the sandwich away.

Moments later some birds lighted on the sandwich and Major's co-worker was astonished to see the birds drop dead after pecking away at the discarded food. It was no surprise to Arthur Major; oddly, even though he knew his wife, Ethel, was trying to kill him, he had continued to live with the woman.

Ethel Major, however, only stayed with her husband during the evening hours. Then when it was time to go to bed, she and her fourteen-year-old son journeyed to the home of Ethel's father to spend the night. The ritual had been going on for months, ever since the couple had begun arguing about Ethel's long-ago indiscretion.

Mrs. Major was not a born killer by any means. Her father, Tom Brown, was a Lincolnshire gamekeeper, and he provided a good home for his wife, three sons, and only daughter, living on the estate of Sir Henry Hawley. Ethel received a solid education and, upon leaving school, worked as a dressmaker. In 1914 Ethel became pregnant but never revealed the identity of the father. To prevent local scandal, the Brown family announced that little Auriel was Mrs. Brown's baby, not Ethel's, and the child was raised as Ethel's sister.

Ethel Lillie Major in 1914.

Four years later, a badly wounded hero, Arthur Major, whom Ethel had known briefly as a child, returned from France. Ethel happened to meet him again and fell in love with him. The couple wed when Major was on leave, June 1, 1918. The following year a son, Lawrence, was born to them. Mrs. Major never mentioned the fact that her "sister" Auriel was really her own child, a fact that did not surface until 1934 when local gossip reached Major's ears.

Major confronted his wife with the story, and she admitted her maternity. Who was the father? Major demanded to know. Ethel refused to divulge the name. After that the marriage became a nightmare of constant argument and ac-

Mrs. Major at the time she murdered her husband in 1934.

cusation. Ethel told neighbors that her husband had turned into a drunk and a bully, and she was sure that he was seeing another woman. (Later, at her trial, Mrs. Major produced letters purportedly written to her husband by a neighbor, Rose Kettleborough, the supposed mistress; Rose denied ever writing such letters and there was every indication that Ethel had written them herself.)

On several occasions Major claimed that his wife was trying to kill him. On May 23–24, 1934, according to later evidence, Mrs. Ethel Major succeeded. Her husband came home from work

ill. He lay in bed twitching, foaming at the mouth, his back bending into a bow of intense pain. A physician was called. Dr. Smith found Major sweating in bed, convulsive, unable to speak coherently.

When Dr. Smith asked Ethel what her husband had eaten, Mrs. Major replied, "I gave him corned beef, his favorite." Then she added, "My husband has been having fits at intervals for a year or two." Smith concluded that Major was suffering from a form of epilepsy and gave him a sedative. He seemed to improve.

The next day Ethel informed Dr. Smith that her husband had died. The physician wrote out a death certificate, stating that Arthur Major had died of "status epilepticus." Plans for Major's burial were made hurriedly by Ethel. All would have gone according to plan had not a busybody neighbor interfered.

This person wrote a quick note to local police which read—

Have you ever heard of a wife poisoning her husband? Look further into the death of Mr. Major of Kirkby-on-Bain. Why did he complain of his food tasting nasty and throw it to a neighbor's dog, which has since died? Ask the undertaker if he looked natural after death.

Fairplay

The note spurred police to have the dog examined and the burial of Arthur Major postponed. Another neighbor, Mrs. Elsie Roberts, confirmed the fact that a dog owned by a Mr. Maltby, who lived next door to the Majors, had been fed by Mrs. Major on the day of her husband's death. Ethel, she said, had come to her back door with scraps of food, throwing the remains to the dog. "Mrs. Major watched the animal eat the food," said Mrs. Roberts, "then she tossed her head up, laughed loudly, and went in."

The dog and parts of Arthur Major's body were sent to Dr. Roche Lynch, a London pathologist, who quickly determined that there were .12 grains of strychnine in the dog and 1.27 grains of the poison in the dead man. Scotland Yard's Chief Inspector Hugh Young had Mrs. Major brought in for questioning. He asked her what she thought had killed her husband.

Ethel shrugged, then said, "It must have been that corned beef he insisted on eating. I hate corned beef and think it is a waste of money to buy such rubbish. I prefer a piece of fat bacon."

"Do you think he might have been poisoned?" inquired Young.

Ethel arched her eyebrows at that one and blurted out, "I didn't know that my husband died of strychnine poisoning."

"What did you say?"

"I have never had any strychnine poison."

Young took some time before saying, "I have never mentioned *strychnine*. How did you know that?" (Up to that moment only Roche, Young, and a few other officials were aware of the strychnine found in Major's body.)

Mrs. Ethel Major realized her fatal *faux pas*, quickly stating, "Oh, I am sorry. I must have made a mistake. I did not understand what you said. I am still of the opinion that he died of poison in the corned beef."

Young immediately began a search for strychnine among Mrs. Major's belongings but came up with nothing. Then, on a hunch, he contacted Mrs. Major's father, gamekeeper Tom Brown. Yes, Brown admitted, he kept some strychnine. He used it to kill vermin, but it was always kept in a locked box and he had the only key. Then Brown remembered that there had been another key, but he had lost that more than ten years earlier.

Inspector Young returned to the Major home and conducted a thorough search. After several hours he unearthed an old purse in which was nestled a key that did not fit any of the doors in Ethel Major's house. He took the key back to gamekeeper Brown, who immediately recognized it as the one he had lost long ago. When trying it on his poison box, it opened the lock easily. Inspector Young had sealed his case against Ethel Lillie Major.

Norman Birkett defended Mrs. Major; he had never lost a murder case in his life. The Major case was his first defeat. Birkett could mount no defense for the woman after the evidence was heard. Mrs. Major was convicted, the jury recommending mercy, though there were never any obvious extenuating circumstances to warrant such a request. The poisoner was condemned, nevertheless, and hanged at Hull Jail on December 19, 1934.

MALCOLM, SARAH

Murderer ■ (1711–1733)

A London laundress, Irish-born Sarah Malcolm suddenly went berserk in the home of Mrs. Lydia Dunscomb, her eighty-year-old employer. On the night of February 5, 1733, Sarah, a powerfully built woman, crept into her mistress's bedchamber and strangled Mrs. Dunscomb while she slept. To eliminate any witnesses, she next strangled Elizabeth Harrison, age sixty, and cut the throat of another servant, seventeen-year-old Ann Price.

After ransacking the Dunscomb home, she fled, only to be caught carrying the stolen items. Throughout her trial, for what came to be famous as the "Temple Murder"—Mrs. Dunscomb's house situated as it was in Tanfield Court in the Inner Temple of London—Sarah denied her guilt. The evidence against her, however, was overwhelming, and she was sentenced to death.

On the day of her execution, March 7, 1733, Sarah, as stoic as she had been throughout her ordeal, rode in an open cart down Fleet Street. There, between Fetter Lane and Mitre Court, a gallows had been erected in the middle of the street in order that she be hanged as close as possible to the scene of her murders, as was then the custom. A great crowd stared in awe at Sarah, who refused to respond to their cries. She had, however, painted her cheeks thickly with rouge for the occasion.

Among the dignitaries on hand was the painter Hogarth, who had visited the killer in her cell and had drawn her portrait. After Sarah's execution, he commented that he thought her "capable of any wickedness."

MANNING, MARIA

Murderer ■ (1825–1849)

Two men had offered themselves for marriage to the twenty-four-year-old beauty. Because the young woman's only aim in matrimony was to make herself rich, she was forced to resolve only one issue: Which man had the most money? The choice she eventually made led the Swiss-born Maria into disaster, and, in a wild attempt to reverse her fortunes, into one of the most calculating murders in the annals of Scotland Yard.

Born Maria de Roux of Swiss-French parentage, Maria was accustomed to a life of luxury. She was the personal maid of Lady Blantyre who was the daughter of the Duchess of Sutherland; all about her were the trappings of wealth and security—so much so that she developed a deep dread of poverty and financial struggle.

Once in 1846 when Maria was on the channel boat going to Boulogne to join Lady Blantyre, she attracted the attention of another passenger, Patrick O'Connor, from Tipperary, Ireland, who spotted her trim figure and made advances. Obviously in his cups, O'Connor boldly told Maria that he had glimpsed her trim ankles when a sea breeze blew up her long dress and he liked what he had seen. Instead of being insulted, Maria was charmed by the man and suggested that he get in touch with her when she and her mistress returned to London.

O'Connor called for Maria at Stafford House some months later, taking her to dinner and giving her inexpensive gifts. He informed the maid that he was a customhouse officer, but he did not mention that he had obtained his position through bribery. Maria informed the love-hungry O'Connor that there was another man in her life; she had recently met one Frederick George Manning, a guard on the Great Western Railway.

Maria continued to see both men, and in the following weeks each begged her to marry him. Maria loved neither man, but she had a strong

Maria Manning, a maid to British aristocracy who turned to murder.

desire to wed, having tired of serving her wealthy employer. The only question in her mind was which one had more money. At first, Maria thought O'Connor to be the likelier prospect. He spent his money freely and spoke of large savings. On the other hand, O'Connor drank a great deal, and Maria finally concluded that no such apprentice alcoholic could hold on to his funds for long. She opted for Manning, the railway guard.

Frederick Manning had actually persuaded the woman that he would soon be a wealthy man. Though his guard's salary was but a pittance, he had ways of making extra money (all of them illegal). Further, Manning whispered that when his beloved mother died she would leave a great fortune to him, and this, in turn, would go to Maria upon his death. The maid was convinced, and promptly agreed to wed Manning. The ceremonies were held in St. James' Church in Piccadilly. Immediately after the ceremonies, Manning presented his wife with his most valuable wedding gift—his will, in which he left everything to his "very dear and beloved wife."

The weak-willed Frederick Manning, Maria's cowardly murder accomplice.

Content that her future was secure, Maria tucked the will into her purse and went off with Manning to Taunton to run the White Hart Inn. Manning proved an inept landlord, and the couple soon had to sell the property. They then returned to London, moving into a two-story house in Minever Place, Bermondsey. By then Maria had discovered that Manning had lied—there was no rich mother or any great fortune to inherit. She had made a terrible mistake and married the wrong man. Yet there was still time, she thought, to right the situation. She sent a letter to her former love, O'Connor. He, indeed, did have a great deal of money, she had discovered, especially in foreign railway stocks.

O'Connor, regretting that he had not been more insistent on marrying Maria, jumped at the opportunity to see her again. In fact, he was overjoyed in being able to partake of her sexual favors without having to take on the responsibilities of an official wife. O'Connor went often to the Manning house where both Maria and Frederick fully accepted him, telling neighbors and their one boarder, a medical student named

Massey, that O'Connor was "a dear friend of the family."

Frederick Manning's behavior as the cuckcolded husband was not as perplexing as it appeared. On the verge of bankruptcy, he had readily agreed with Maria that the rich O'Connor could serve them well in one capacity or another, Maria would determine which.

To the medical student Massey, Manning confided over drinks that O'Connor was "a wealthy man, worth probably twenty thousand pounds. He's made a will in favor of my wife, you know. They're old, dear friends." On another pub-lounging occasion, Manning slapped the student on the back drunkenly and cryptically advised the youth: "For God's sake, never marry a foreigner, for if you do she will be the ruin of you!"

Arcane, too, were the questions Manning put to Massey. He asked the medical student what effects chloroform and laudanum would produce in a person. "Could a person under the influence of these drugs properly sign a check, say for five hundred pounds?" "What is the most vital part of the human body? I mean, what part is the most vulnerable to attack?" "Have you ever witnessed an air-gun being fired, Massey, and, if so, can such a weapon kill a man?" All these wild queries Massey attributed to too much brandy, a drink favored by Manning and one that made him a bit foolish and garrulous at times. The young man thought the husband a harmless, lonely soul, who forced ridiculous conversation for the sake of companionship.

On July 28, 1849, Manning came to Massey's room and sheepishly told him that he would have to give up his lodging that day. Mrs. Manning's elderly mother was coming to stay with them. The student packed his bags and left without complaint.

No relative of Mrs. Manning visited the house on Minever Place that day or any other, but there did arrive a deliveryman who brought a crowbar to Maria Manning and was paid for it in cash. The delivery was witnessed by the departing Massey, who also heard Manning say to his wife at the time, "Get O'Connor to come here and get him to drink large quantities of brandy when he comes."

Interviewed months later, Massey remem-

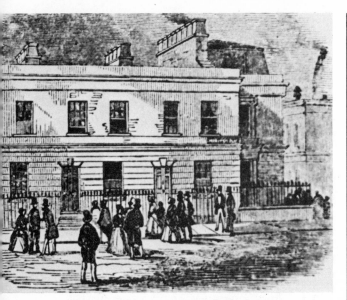

The stylish Manning house at Miniver Place which became a notorious London murder site.

bered another strange delivery five days before he was asked to leave the Manning house. A bushel of lime was delivered to the house, and Mrs. Manning promptly paid for this, too. And another tradesman later told Scotland Yard that he had made a delivery of a large shovel to Mrs. Manning on August 8, 1849.

On that day Maria Manning sent a note to O'Connor, which was delivered to his rooms in Greenwood Street, Mile End. It read—

Dear O'Connor,
    We shall be happy to see you to dine with us today at 5 o'clock.

Yours affectionately,

Maria Manning.

Greater London Dock,
Wednesday morning

O'Connor did go to see the Mannings that night, but he unexpectedly brought a friend named Walshe, who stayed for dinner and then cigars and brandy until midnight when he left with the honored guest. The Mannings behaved nervously throughout the evening. Remarked George Dilnot in *Celebrated Crimes:* "The presence of Walshe must have interfered with the arrangements of this estimable couple." Undaunted, the Mannings insisted that O'Connor dine with them again, the following night, Thursday, August 9, 1849. Maria intimated that she would prefer he come alone.

The customhouse officer knew what that meant; he and *Maria* would dine alone, another charming prelude to Maria's extramarital sex. On Thursday night O'Connor was seen by friends crossing London Bridge en route to Miniver Place. Neighbors of the Mannings saw him go to the back door of Maria's house, where he smoked a cigar while talking to Mrs. Manning before entering the house. It was the last time Patrick O'Connor was seen alive.

Inside the Manning House that night, Maria told O'Connor that dinner would be ready soon. "I want you to wash your hands," Mrs. Manning told O'Connor, and led him down into the kitchen, a lower-level room. As O'Connor turned toward the wash basin Maria affectionately put one hand on his shoulder. She lifted the other hand, which held a pistol, placed the weapon behind O'Connor's ear, and fired. He crumpled to the flagstone floor, as Maria, smiling broadly, raced upstairs.

Manning greeted her in the upper level of the house. Still smiling, Maria told her husband, "Thank God, I've made him all right at last! It'll never be found out, as he and I were on such good terms. No one will have the least suspicion of my murdering him."

From that instant, the couple began a falling out. Manning studied the woman who was his wife and then said, "It doesn't convince me—I'm quite sure you'll be hanged for it."

Maria snorted: "I think no more of what I've done than if I'd shot a cat on the wall. Anyway, it won't be you that will have to suffer."

When Manning went into the kitchen he suddenly drew back in horror. Though O'Connor had a bullet in his head, he was still alive, struggling to speak. In the next minute, Manning coupled his fate to Maria's by finishing O'Connor off. (He later laconically told inspectors from Scotland Yard, "I never liked him, so I battered his head with a ripping chisel.")

O'Connor's body was covered with lime,

then buried in the kitchen beneath two flagstones. The cold-bloodedness of the Mannings was then to be demonstrated sharply; only minutes after burying O'Connor, the couple sat down to a goose dinner, feasting in the very room where they had murdered and buried their dinner guest, a man who would never taste the flesh of goose again.

Maria lost no time in going after O'Connor's wealth. The following morning she appeared at O'Connor's Greenwood Street address. Miss Armes, the landlady, met her at the door.

"Is Mr. O'Connor in?" Marie asked sweetly.

"He's not returned from the docks yet," replied Miss Armes.

"I must go upstairs to his room. I've come to see him on urgent business. I will wait for his return."

Miss Armes reluctantly unlocked O'Connor's room for Maria, who closed the door in the landlady's face, locking it from the inside. Then, with the keys she had taken from O'Connor's body, she unlocked her victim's trunk and cash box. She took several hundred pounds in currency, two gold watches, and two gold chains. Maria found a bankbook which showed that O'Connor had three thousand pounds saved but realized this was useless and tossed it back into the cash box. Her frantic search of the trunk was rewarded with the discovery of many foreign railway certificates and bonds. These, too, she pocketed before returning home. She had spent no more than fifteen minutes inside O'Connor's room.

Once home, Maria angrily told her husband that she was sure that O'Conner had other foreign bonds that amounted to more than five thousand pounds. The next day, Saturday, she again returned to O'Connor's room, and, using another pretext, once again gained entry, but her search unearthed no new bonds. When she returned home that day she ordered her husband to impersonate O'Connor and sell off the railway shares.

"But I don't even look like O'Connor," protested Manning.

Maria waved away his objections: "The man is dead, so there can be no witness against you."

Manning, after bolstering his courage with several bottles of brandy, managed to sell off some of the railway shares, obtaining about a hundred and ten pounds. The experience so unnerved him that he refused to attempt to sell more. Maria brandished a butcher knife in front of his nose and shouted that he had better sell the shares within a week or face her wrath. He would try, Manning promised her halfheartedly.

On Sunday, August 12, two men came to the door of the Manning house. They introduced themselves as customhouse officers, friends and co-workers of the missing O'Connor. They asked if the murderers had seen O'Connor. Maria feigned surprise. Why no, they had had dinner with the charming man on Wednesday night last and had not seen O'Connor since. The Mannings were then informed that their memories must be failing. Some of O'Connor's friends had seen him cross London Bridge on *Thursday* night, and he had told them that he was "dining with Maria." The friends must be mistaken, replied Maria politely. Before the men left, Maria expressed deep concern over their friend O'Connor, begging the men to tell them any news of the dear man as soon as they learned of his whereabouts.

Seconds after the men departed, Manning turned to his wife and said, "Those men aren't from the customhouse—they're detectives from Scotland Yard!"

"How do you know such a thing?" asked Maria, wide-eyed.

"They exerted too much authority in the manner of their questions. Sure as you are a woman we shall be arrested."

Maria's face went white. "Don't tell me that or I shall faint!" With that, Maria realized that they must flee and fast. She instructed her husband to go to a man named Bainbridge, a family friend, and sell the household furniture to him for whatever price he would pay; they would need all the cash they could lay their hands on to escape to New York in America. Manning dutifully set off to see Bainbridge. When he returned he found his house a mess. Neighbors informed him that his wife had, only an hour before, raced from the house, her arms loaded with boxes and bags. She was last seen departing in a cab with three or four trunks on its roof. Maria had deserted her partner in crime, a move totally in keeping with her character.

Manning also decided to flee, and, grabbing

only a few items, left for Waterloo, where he caught the boat train for Jersey. The only money in his pocket was the thirteen pounds he had gotten for his furniture from Bainbridge. Maria had taken everything else.

Within days the police were investigating O'Connor's disappearance with the kind of doggedness that had made Scotland Yard famous. Visiting his rooming house, detectives had learned that a woman answering Maria Manning's description had ransacked the victim's room. Next they entered the Manning house, and one alert sleuth, Inspector Barnes, quickly spotted something suspicious. "We went into the back kitchen," Barnes' report later stated, "which was flagged all over with large flagstones. I observed a damp mark along the edges of two of the stones, which induced us to take out our knives and try the mortar. I found it was wet. Burton [another detective] did the same. I then told Burton I should not be satisfied until those two stones were taken up; and Burton went out and borrowed a shovel and a crowbar, and a boathook without a handle." Beneath

the stones, of course, the police found the body of Patrick O'Connor, buried in lime, a bullet through his head and other wounds inflicted on his head by another weapon. The mad search for the Mannings commenced.

Scotland Yard got its first real clue to Mrs. Manning's whereabouts on August 20 when a cabman, answering the Yard's appeal for information, came forward, telling inspectors that he had taken Maria to the South-Eastern Railway. In the depot, Mrs. Manning had checked two trunks, with instructions that read, "Mrs. Smith, passenger to Paris. Hold till called for." She had then driven on to the Great Northern.

Superintendent Haynes personally inspected the trunks Mrs. Manning had left behind and found dresses and linen marked "Maria de Roux," along with letters from O'Connor to her. More luck blessed Haynes when he interviewed personnel of the Great Northern Railway at King's Cross. Two train officials distinctly recalled seeing a woman answering Maria's description, a woman in a highly agitated state who nervously spoke English and French. She

Scotland Yard detectives discovering O'Connor's remains in the Manning kitchen.

had taken the 6:15 A.M. train to Edinburgh on August 14. Haynes telegraphed police in Edinburgh. The superintendent was amazed at the response; within hours he received a wire from Edinburgh's Superintendent Moxhay. The woman known as Maria Manning was in custody and was being returned to London.

Upon her arrival in Edinburgh, Mrs. Manning had attempted to sell O'Connor's stolen railway certificates, having gone to the brokerage firm of Hughson and Dobson. She had called herself Mrs. Smith, and, to make herself more credible to the distrusting Scottish businessmen, informed the brokers that a Mr. Robertson, a native of Scotland, was her father. Her thick French accent did not support this claim, the brokers thought, and they became suspicious. Moreover, the firm had received a letter from London warning them that certain French railway stock had been stolen and to be wary of anyone trying to sell the certificates. The brokers called Superintendent Moxhay and this led to Maria's quick arrest. In her possession were O'Connor's stolen railway certificates.

Upon her arrival in London, a white-faced Mrs. Manning was met by Superintendent Haynes who asked her about her husband. Maria glared at him with her eyes burning and blurted out, "I have nothing to say!" She was charged with murdering O'Connor and taken to the Horsemonger Lane Jail.

Frederick Manning remained at large for another week. He had gone to the Channel Island of Jersey, assuming the name of Jennings. He first took rooms in St. Helier, but when he met a man who had known him in London, he fled to the tiny town of St. Laurence, overlooking St. Aubin's Bay, and rented a room from an elderly couple. Drinking heavily, two or three bottles of brandy a day, he drew suspicion to himself everywhere he went.

The acquaintance who had met Manning in St. Helier notified police after reading the London papers announcing the O'Connor murder and the search for Manning. Detective-sergeant Langley was sent by Scotland Yard to Jersey. He had been selected for this job since he knew Manning personally.

The culprit was finally traced to the St. Laurence rooming house. On the night of August 21, 1849, Langley, accompanied by Centenier Chevalier, the high constable of Jersey, and some other local officers, crept up the stairs of Prospect Cottage to Manning's room. The door was ajar. The men entered quietly to see Manning asleep in bed. Chevalier put the candle he was carrying on the table.

"That's the man!" cried Langley. "Seize him!"

Chevalier threw himself across Manning's prone body. With a start, Manning half sat up in the bed, his eyes wide in shock. "What are you about?" he shouted. "Do you mean to murder me?"

As Chevalier and other officers pinned Manning to the bed, Langley came forward into the dim light of the candle. Manning recognized him immediately. "Ah, sergeant, is that you? I am glad you have come. I was going to London to explain it all."

"That's good of you."

"Is the wretch taken?" (Manning meant his wife.)

"I do not know," replied Langley.

"I suppose they will find a great deal of money on her—thirteen or fourteen hundred pounds at least."

"I do not know, but you must consider yourself under arrest."

"What for?"

"For the shocking affair that has taken place in your house, Manning."

"Very well, but I can explain it all, but surely you will not put the handcuffs on me."

As he was being taken downstairs, Manning turned to Langley and yelled: "*She* shot him!"

"What became of the body?" inquired Chevalier.

"She had a grave dug for him," answered the terrified Manning.

Langley accompanied Manning to Southampton by boat where Superintendent Haynes met them. They then took the train to London. On the journey, Manning said to Haynes, "If my wife confesses will I be set free?"

Replied Haynes, "You must excuse me from answering such a question."

"I'm sure she will confess when she sees me," sighed Manning to no one in particular, "especially if a clergyman is present."

Haynes finally cautioned Manning: "This is a very serious affair. You are not required to say anything to incriminate yourself."

"I am aware of that. I was very foolish to go away, for I ought to have stayed and explained it all. . . . She is a very violent woman. . . . I've been afraid for my own life. . . . Maria would follow me around at night in the dark of the house with a drawn knife in her hand. She vowed revenge on O'Connor. He persuaded us to take the house in Minever Place. He had told her that he would take a room to offset the expense. He only slept there one night and then refused to remain longer. She vowed revenge, you see?"

"I can say nothing about it," Haynes replied sleepily. Before nodding off in the rattling train car, the superintendent made sure that Manning was securely handcuffed to both Langley and himself.

When Manning finally arrived in London, he was taken to a police court where Maria had been brought to face him. The husband gave his murderous wife a theatrical wave.

"Have you anything to say to your husband?" asked an officer.

Maria gave Manning a short look of contempt and answered "No!" Both prisoners were then taken to jail. From that moment on the two expressed hatred for each other, each blaming the other entirely for the O'Connor murder. Stated Leonard Gribble in *Famous Judges and Their Trials*, "Maria swore that her husband alone was responsible, but no one believed that this obviously strong-minded woman had been influenced for a moment by the crawling, nervous wreck who stood in the dock. He made a miserable show, whining for mercy and feebly protesting his innocence until the whole court was sick of him."

The Manning trial opened at the Old Bailey on October 25. The question was not a matter of guilt or innocence for the pair, but who had been more responsible for the murder. Their separate lawyers continually shifted and sidestepped, each attempting to fix the blame on the other's client.

Said advocate Wilkins, who represented Manning, "Mrs. Manning had from the beginning to end taken as much pains to improve upon and cheat her husband as to cheat everyone else."

Mr. Ballantine, Mrs. Manning's counsel, retorted, "As to the efforts made to throw the whole blame on the woman . . . it originated in the attempt made by the male prisoner to shift the crime from his own shoulders—if there it rested—to those of the woman he was bound to protect."

Manning clearly showed that he expected Maria to assume the complete blame for the killing, casting pleading glances at her from the separate, distant dock in which he stood, or rather, where he pathetically sagged against a railing. Maria ignored his presence, standing stiffly, sneering contemptuously at Chief Justice Cresswell.

Following a two-day trial, the jury took no more than three-quarters of an hour to bring in a verdict of guilty for both defendants. Maria Manning, dressed all in black, lost her stoic composure. She shrieked at the jury, "You have treated me like a wild beast of the forest!"

Chief Justice Cresswell began to say, "You have been convicted of the crime of—"

Maria interrupted him, shouting, "No! No! I can't stand to hear that said! There is no law or justice here! You ought to be ashamed of yourselves! There is no justice and no right for a foreign subject in this country. There is no law for me! When I consider that Mr. O'Connor was more to me than my own husband, that I have known him . . . and that he has always felt the greatest respect for me, I call upon you to think and consider whether it is likely that I should have murdered him."

"You have been convicted of the crime of murder," finished Justice Cresswell.

"I tell you, my Lord," Maria rushed on, gasping for air, throwing her voice in a scream to the four corners of the courtroom, "this verdict the jury has returned will rest on their conscience hereafter. I am not treated like a Christian! If I had wished to commit murder, how much more likely it is that I should have murdered that man," and Marie pointed her finger like a dagger toward Manning in the dock opposite her," that man who made my life a hell upon earth ever since I have known him, than

A wax reproduction of Maria Manning at the time of her trial. (Courtesy Tussaud's)

ston in *The Bench and Dock* reported that "it is a fact that Maria Manning was often in the same room as Queen Victoria, for the young monarch and Lady Blantyre, Maria's mistress, were very intimate, and whenever her ladyship was on a visit to her Majesty they were constantly in and out of each other's rooms."

Victoria did study Maria's appeals, along with the trial records of her case. (This was the only trial, during her long reign, other than that of François Courvoisier, a Swiss butler who had murdered his master, Lord William Russell, who had been her friend, in which the queen took a special interest.) In the end Victoria concluded that Maria had certainly killed O'Connor. She refused to grant Mrs. Manning a reprieve.

When news of Victoria's decision was brought to the anxious Maria, the prisoner spat and gritted her teeth. "The Queen is no lady. I am surprised at her," she said.

Manning tried many times to establish some contact with his wife as they waited for the hangman, but she refused his letters. Finally, only days before the scheduled execution, Maria made one more desperate attempt to escape execution, imploring the weak-willed Manning to clear her of any responsibility for O'Connor's murder. She wrote to him, "All I have to beg of you is to state facts, as you know that I was not in the house when O'Connor met with his death, but I was gone out to see for him, and during that time he called in my absence and was shot by that young man from Guernsey [a fictitious scapegoat], who was with you in the back parlour smoking, but that I did not know anything about it until the Saturday." Her ploy failed. Manning refused to support such nonsense. If he was going to die, so was Maria.

On execution day, Manning and Maria mounted the scaffold together. The husband begged Maria to forgive him for not taking all the blame. As a sign that she did, Mrs. Manning kissed him. Then she turned haughtily to face the immense throng that had come to see her hang. It was the largest crowd ever assembled to witness a public hanging in England, estimated to be between thirty thousand and fifty thousand people.

This execution was the most agonizingly

that I should have murdered Mr. O'Connor, who would have married me the next month—yes, the next week—after I became a widow!"

Maria turned as if to leave the dock, but the attending officers prevented her, turning her back to face the court to hear her sentence of death, which was to take place at Horsemonger Lane Jail on Tuesday, November 13, 1849, a public hanging. Through her sobbing, Maria once more shouted, "Oh, base and shameful England!" With that she took up a handful of rue which had been sprinkled on the dock railing and threw it at the court. She was quickly taken from the dock. Manning's response was tame; he merely bowed to the judge and left meekly with his wardens.

From her prison cell, Maria fought against the execution, furiously writing appeals to Lady Blantyre and to the Duchess of Sutherland. When she received no response, Marie sent an appeal to Queen Victoria herself. Charles King-

memorable on record. Crowds had begun to gather for the spectacle two days before the scheduled execution. Entrepreneurs had erected spectator platforms for those willing to pay exorbitant prices, and there thousands who were. Barriers were thrown up, but five hundred constables found it next to impossible to control the crowds once the condemned couple appeared. The crush of bodies was unbearable; among the spectators who were trampled, hundreds required hospitalization. A thirty-year-old woman, Catherine Read, was smashed against a barrier and crushed to death, suffering a ruptured blood vessel near the spleen.

Thousands of respectable people attended the double hanging as if it were a festive outing. They included the entire memberships of the most fashionable clubs in London, gentlemen and ladies using binoculars to get a better view of the dangling, twisting bodies of the Mannings. When this gentry stood accused of being insensitive, *The Daily News* defended the upper-crust Victorians the following day: "As regards the matter of opera glasses, unless the art of witnessing an execution is proved to be discreditable and bad in itself, it is mere trifling to condemn people for employing the best means they can to enable them to see plainly what they have come to see."

Through their binoculars, high-born women of fashion focused upon Maria Manning. She stood on the scaffold next to her husband with great dignity, saying nothing as the rope was placed about her neck. What intrigued the ladies of fashion and occupied their chatter was what Maria was *wearing* to her own execution, which was a black satin dress trimmed with black lace and a black veil. Disgraceful, muttered the women of fashion; satin was then the most popular fabric in women's styles. And satin went completely out of fashion the second Maria dropped through the trap.

The event was long discussed as an extraordinary happening. Everyone had a tale to tell about his own experiences in the crowd. A Dr. Manning, who was later to become a cardinal, was watching the execution from a platform when he was recognized by a wealthy merchant. Though the physician was in no way related to the condemned, the merchant turned to him and exclaimed loudly, "What a dreadful thing it must be, doctor, to have a criminal in the family!" This comment evoked gales of laughter in the throng.

There was one man present, however, who found the gruesome spectacle anything but humorous. For author Charles Dickens, the scene was repugnant, unbearable. For weeks Dickens had been urged by friends to witness the execution but had begged off attending. He was finally persuaded to appear and found the experience traumatic. (Dickens was later to profile Maria as the murderous Frenchwoman, Hortense, in *Bleak House.*)

The great novelist vividly re-created the scene in a letter published later in *The Times*, one in which he exercised his enormous prestige in calling for an end to public executions for all time. Dickens wrote—

I believe that a sight so inconceivably awful as the wickedness and levity of the immense crowd collected at the execution this morning could be imagined by no man, and could be presented in no heathen land under the sun. The horrors of the gibbet, and of the crime which brought the wretched murderers to it, faded in my mind before the atrocious bearing, looks, and language of the assembled spectators. When I came upon the scene at midnight the shrillness of the cries and howls that were raised from time to time, denoting that they came from a concourse of boys and girls already assembled in the best places, made my blood run cold. As the night went on screeching and laughing, and the yelling in strong chorus of parodies of Negro melodies with substitution of "Mrs. Manning" for "Susannah" and the like, were added to these. When the day dawned, thieves, low prostitutes, ruffians, and vagabonds of every kind flocked on the ground with every variety of offensive and foul behavior. Fightings, faintings, whistlings, imitations of Punch, brutal jokes, tumultuous demonstrations of indecent delight when swooning women were dragged out of the crowd by the police with their dresses disordered, gave a new zest to the general entertainment. When the sun rose brightly—as it did—it gilded thousands upon thousands of upturned faces so inexpressibly odious in their brutal mirth or callousness that a man had cause to feel ashamed of the shape he wore, and to shrink from himself as fashioned in the image of the devil. When the two miserable creatures who attracted all this ghastly sight about them were turned quivering into the air, there was no more emotion, no more pity, no more thought that two immortal souls had gone to judgment, no more restraint in any of the previous obscenities, than if the name of Christ had never been heard in the world and there were no belief among men but that they perished like the beasts.

I have seen habitually, some of the worst sources of general contamination and corruption in this country, and I think there are not many phases of London life that could surprise me. I am solemnly convinced that nothing that ingenuity could devise to be done in this city, in the same compass of time, could work such ruin as one public execution, and I stand astounded and appalled by the wickedness it exhibits. I do not believe that any community can prosper where such a scene of horror and demoralization as was enacted this morning outside Horsemonger Lane Gaol [jail] is presented at the very doors of good citizens, and is passed by unknown or forgotten.

Though it would be more than ten years before Parliament abolished public executions, the outrage expressed by Charles Dickens of the Manning spectacle did more to effect the cancellation of public hangings in England than any other influence.

But during that long-ago day of death, there were many who thought the event extremely worthwhile and who made a great deal of money from the death of Maria and Frederick Manning, and not just the relatively small sums earned by the food vendors and toy mongers. The publishers of the Catnach Press, devoted to sensational murders and scandals, sold more than two and a half million broadsides detailing the Manning execution.

In the end, the attitude of the British public at large toward Maria Manning was summed up by a subscriber to *The Times* who wrote, "Thank God she wasn't an Englishwoman!"

MAREK, MARTHA LOWENSTEIN

Swindler, Murderer ■ (1904–1938)

The motive for Martha Marek's bizarre slayings was a pathological greed of astounding proportions. She intended to live well no matter the cost, even if the cost included human lives. No doubt, Martha's beginnings were the roots of her own evil, having been a foundling and then taken in at an early age by an impoverished Viennese couple. She went to work in a dress shop in Vienna in 1919 where, a few years later, a kindly old man, Moritz Fritsch, took pity on the beautiful girl and made her his ward.

Fritsch was wealthy, the owner of a large department store, and even though he was seventy-four, he had little qualms in taking his lovely Martha to bed. In return for her favors, Fritsch sent Martha to expensive finishing schools in France and England, where being surrounded by upper-crust society girls served to whet her appetite for the finer things in life.

Upon her return to Vienna, Martha again went to live with Fritsch but shortly met a handsome young engineer, Emil Marek, with whom she carried on a secret affair. When Fritsch died he left his stately mansion at Mödling, along with all his money, to Martha, as he had promised.

Martha reveled in her new riches, but she and Marek, who married her in 1924, went through everything in short order; their extravagant living soon compelled then to sell the Fritsch house. Out of funds, they devised a weird insurance fraud. Martha insured her husband against accidents, obtaining a 10,000-pound policy on Marek. The "accident" arranged by the Mareks was a bloody one, calling for Marek to actually chop off his own leg with an axe while splitting wood. Apparently he had difficulty in

Mass killer Martha Marek of Austria pleading for her life in a Vienna courtroom in 1938. She insisted she was lame and going blind, demanding pillows, blanket, and footrest. Note the swastika armband on courtroom guard, a sign that the Nazi regime was in power.

finishing the job, pleading with Martha in his semi-conscious state to take off the rest of his leg. Finally, Marek's leg was amputated below the knee. The insurance investigators were suspicious from the beginning, when docter stated that Marek's leg showed three separate cuts and that the accident clearly had been staged. Then the couple were charged by police with attempted fraud. Martha, to cover her bungling, tried to bribe a male nurse to say that the insurance company had bribed the doctor treating her husband to make the many wounds on her husband's leg. She then called a press conference and announced her "findings."

The charges of fraud were dropped against the Mareks, but they were convicted of bribing the nurse and served four months in prison. The insurance company finally settled, paying only 3,000 pounds, which was just enough to cover the extensive court costs in the mismanaged scheme.

Moving to Algiers, the Mareks tried to run several businesses, but all failed. By the time they returned to Vienna, they had two children. So poor were they by this time that Martha was reduced to selling vegetables in the street. Desperate, she looked about for financial salvation. This came momentarily in July 1932 when Emil died, supposedly of tuberculosis. Martha collected a small amount of money on his life. A few weeks later her seven-year-old daughter Ingeborg died, and her death, too, provided insurance money.

An aging aunt, Susanne Lowenstein, then asked Martha to look after her. She was dead within months with symptoms similar to that of

Emil Marek in that the old woman could hardly swallow and her limbs were numb. Again Martha was enriched; the old woman had left her house and modest fortune to her. The money evaporated in one spending spree, and Martha was soon forced to open the Lowenstein house to boarders, taking in a man named Neumann and a dowager named Kittenberger. The elderly woman died a short while later, her insurance money, amounting to no more than $300, left, of course, to Martha. This paltry sum was certainly inadequate for the high-living Mrs. Marek. In 1937, she entered into another swindle. She had the expensive paintings in the Lowenstein house removed to a warehouse, a secret operation taking place in the middle of the night. The next morning Martha called police, stating that the paintings had been stolen. She then put in a claim for the artwork.

Assigned to investigate was Viennese detective Ignatz Peters, who, ironically enough, had worked on the amputated-leg claim years earlier. Knowing Martha's fraudulent ways, Peters canvassed the city warehouses and soon uncovered the paintings. Martha was thrown into jail. After reading of Martha's arrest, Mrs. Kittenberger's son approached police, telling them he thought Martha Marek had poisoned his mother for her insurance.

In response, Peters not only ordered Mrs. Kittenberger's body exhumed but had the bodies of Susanne Lowenstein and Emil and Ingeborg Marek dug up as well. All were riddled with thallium, a rare poisonous chemical compound first discovered in 1861. Peters then remembered that Martha had another child, a son, and he soon found the boy boarded out in a poor district of Vienna. The detective was just in time; the boy, who had recently been insured by his mother, was dying of thallium poisoning. He was rushed to a hospital and saved.

Martha was brought to trial in 1938, charged with mass murder. It was quickly proved that she had been buying the poison regularly from a Viennese chemist. Mrs. Marek, pleading innocence to the last, was condemned. Capital punishment had been restored in Austria when Hitler had taken over the government. Martha was sent to the block on December 6, 1938, where she was beheaded by an executioner

wielding an axe far more accurately than she had on her late husband. It took only a single stroke.

MASON, ELIZABETH

Murderer ■ (? –1712)

A servant girl who thought to inherit her godmother's estate by murdering her, Elizabeth Mason mixed yellow arsenic into the coffee she served Mrs. Jane Scoles on Easter 1712. The woman, who had never shown anything but kindness to her goddaughter, died in agony a few hours later. Elizabeth then tried to poison a Mrs. Cholwell, her godmother's closest friend, believing this woman might inherit Mrs. Scoles's property. Mrs. Cholwell grew ill but called a druggist who forced her to drink great quantities of oil which expelled the little arsenic she had swallowed.

Elizabeth was arrested a short time later, named by the druggist who had sold her the poison, ostensibly to rid the Scoles household of rats. She was tried on June 6, 1712, after having confessed and was hanged at Tyburn twelve days later.

MATA HARI

Spy ■ (1876–1917)

No other spy, particularly no other female spy, ever aroused as much public interest, demanded as much press, and earned, deservedly or not, as many glamorous legends as Margaret Gertrude Zelle MacLeod, better known as Mata Hari. Her reputation was

A publicity shot of the ill-starred spy Mata Hari.

After having completed her formal education at eighteen, Margaret left the convent, and within a few weeks, met and was "swept off her feet" by a dashing Dutch officer, Captain Rudolf MacLeod, a man over forty whose uncle was an admiral; MacLeod, as he liked to boast, had often been presented at the court of The Hague, and had chatted with Queen Wilhelmina.

Margaret and her handsome officer were married in 1895 and immediately departed for Java where MacLeod was stationed as a colonial officer. Life proved difficult in the Dutch East Indies settlement of Banjoe-Biroe, a hot, rainy, uncomfortable place. MacLeod's charm faded fast as his young wife, pregnant with his child before their marriage, endured the captain's round-the-clock drinking; he consumed more than a quart of gin a day. Further, MacLeod cultivated many mistresses, native girls, bringing these women into his home at all hours. When Margaret gave birth to her son, Norman, on January 30, 1896, her husband was merrymaking in the next room with a native girl. At least this was to be Margaret's angry claim in a divorce court years later.

Following the birth of the child, MacLeod's conduct worsened. He attacked his wife, beating her with fists, kicking her at the slightest remark. (MacLeod had been in the habit of beating his native office workers for years, and his attitude was no different toward Margaret, whom he came to regard as his sexual servant.) On many occasions, boozy with gin, MacLeod would suddenly grab Margaret by her long hair and drag her around on the floor as a form of amusement.

With boredom closing in one day, MacLeod suggested that he and Margaret make money by playing the badger game with the rich plantation owners in Java and Sumatra. He would arrange for these men to visit Margaret, she would provide the sex, then they would both blackmail the victim. "Man is an animal," Margaret later quoted her husband as saying. "Let's make the most of it."

Margaret would later state in her divorce petition that she had been nothing more than a confused, naive girl when agreeing to prostitute herself for MacLeod. "My husband picked wealthy men as suitable objects for black-

certainly self-conceived and self-executed, for this little Dutch girl gone wrong aimed for immortality no matter the cost, and she bravely paid the price for her fanciful exploits before a French firing squad on October 15, 1917. From that moment to this the enigma of Mata Hari, so-called seductive super-spy, persists, although the true facts surrounding her espionage career are less than remarkable.

Born in Leeuwarden, Holland, on August 7, 1876, Margaret's parents, Adam Zelle and Antje van der Meulen, were rich Netherlanders who lavished attention and gifts upon their only daughter. At fourteen, Margaret's mother died and her father sent her off to a convent school.

mail. . . . One gentleman was a great admirer of my eyes and I led him on as I was told. . . . I was able to collect several thousand guilders."

Despite Margaret's whoring and her husband's pimping, the couple found time to produce another child, a girl, Juana-Luisa, in May 1898. A few years later, tragedy struck. A treacherous native housekeeper named Parama poisoned young Norman in retaliation for Captain MacLeod's public whipping of the housekeeper's brother before a regiment of troops.

By 1902, the couple, their marriage a disaster, had returned to Holland, where they immediately brought divorce proceedings against each other. MacLeod was willing to grant the divorce but attempted to maintain custody of the daughter. In court Margaret called her husband a drunk, a mental and physical bully, and a debauchee. MacLeod's response to these charges was a counterattack. He shouted to the bench, "But your honor, how was I to know that I was marrying a goddamned whore?" This was considered by some an odd stance in that the captain had arranged for Margaret's assignations, even with Hamid, the Sultan of Java, in order to collect blackmail.

"My wife brought shame on me," MacLeod moaned to the judge. "She spent night after night in a sultan's palace. Our son was killed during her absence from our home. I hold her entirely responsible. By her negligence, I consider her guilty of murder. She has never been a fit mother!"

To this Margaret pleaded, "I had nothing but suffering from this man. My body is covered with the scars of his beatings. On my breast I carry a horrible scar from a dagger wound inflicted upon me by this wretch during one of his insane outbursts. Though he pretends kindness now, he never gave a thought to the children, only for his many mistresses."

Margaret was awarded custody of her daughter but little else. The court ordered MacLeod to give her a small financial settlement, which he did after much grumbling. Margaret placed the daughter with an aunt in Holland and spent her last florins on dancing lessons. She had decided that she would support herself as an exotic dancer, an Oriental dancer. She remembered well the dancing she had seen performed in Java and Sumatra, which placed special emphasis on the use of the legs, arms, and eyes, her best physical assets.

With her father's help, Margaret worked for months performing acrobatic exercises until her body was supple and lithe. She would work at ballet with a private tutor until she collapsed from the strain. By October 1903, Margaret felt ready to perform the mystical dances of Shiva (or Siva), and left to seek employment in Paris. She met with utter failure and, for a while, supported herself as a stripper in low-class nightclubs. During most of 1904, she became a common streetwalker. On rare occasions, she earned a few francs by posing as an artist's model. Octave Guillonet interviewed her for a modeling job and was amused at Margaret's airs. She introduced herself to him as "Lady Gresha MacLeod." Guillonet had her disrobe and pose for some minutes, then dismissed her, advising her to take up any kind of job that would not expose her breasts. "They are hopelessly underdeveloped," remarked the painter. Margaret spat out a curse and left the studio.

After that she fell even lower, working in a cheap brothel, where, in late 1904, she was examined by a Dr. Bizard, who, ironically, was to become her mentor in her death cell at Saint-Lazare in 1917. He treated her for gonorrhea and was, at the time, impressed by her intelligence. After listening to her tales of the sad past, Dr. Bizard suggested she return to Java and find herself a reputable man to marry.

Instead, Margaret returned to Holland, pressing family friends and an ex-lover, Karl Breitenstein, for funds; she had known Breitenstein briefly after her divorce. Flush with money and a new wardrobe, she again went back to Paris, installing herself in the fashionable Hotel Crillon, in a suite of rooms that would soon deplete her funds, but Margaret was gambling on a great bluff and a stunning new identity; she was no longer Margaret Gertrude Zelle. She was now Mata Hari, her stage name meaning either "eye of the morning," or "child of the dawn," whichever version Margaret cared to tell.

To her swanky abode, Mata Hari summoned Emile Guimet, owner and operator of the popular nightclub, Musée Guimet. When the entrepreneur met her he became instantly enthralled by her charms. She was by then a worldly, sophisticated woman who knew exactly how to titillate a man's desires, having learned well her trade in sex along Paris boulevards. It must have amused the siren to know that Guimet had failed completely to recognize her from a previous meeting. Years earlier he had barely looked at her when she auditioned for him as Margaret Zelle and was summarily dismissed as untalented.

Not only did Guimet adopt Mata Hari as his protégée, he made her his mistress as well, sponsoring her debut in his club in 1905, a debut that sent Parisian reviewers and critics into swooning ecstasies of praise for her interpretive dancing, a shuddering shedding of veils with agonizing precision down to Mata Hari's quivering naked flesh.

The dancer's whole presentation scheme lay in the ignorance both critic and average viewer displayed toward East Indies dancing. Though she had studied the movements of Sumatran dancers and researched some of the religious rites practiced in the East Indies, Mata Hari, for the most part, made up fantastic gobbledygook to explain her background and her act. Mata Hari's dark, coarse features, instead of repulsing the aesthetic sense of Parisians, all the more convinced most who saw her perform that she was the genuine article.

Her actual dance was spectacular enough to captivate her audiences. She would appear in the dim light, swaddled in many red veils, before a small altar upon which squatted a statue of the Indian love god Shiva, and then begin to snake and slither her legs and hips and arms in an increasingly rapid undulating motion as she stripped one veil after another from her tall form, the throbbing dissonant music in the background accompanying her sensual movements.

Mata Hari, as the lights grew dimmer, would eventually twist free of all her silken veils, appearing naked except for golden bracelets and breastplates—to hide her flat chest—and anklets which were studded with pearls. She wore long, dangling pearl-encrusted earrings and pearl-encrusted headgear. As the beat of the music increased, Mata Hari would then move wildly to the center of the stage, the audience gasping as she fiercely contorted her pelvis and hips, the snake music growing louder and louder, her sinuous arms seeming to float in the air, her legs and hips pulsating with a pace so furious that her knotted leg muscles appeared to almost break the skin. Finally, as the music reached an ear-popping crescendo, Mata Hari collapsed before the altar of Shiva, exhausted, as was her audience, which was then in complete darkness.

Journalist H. Aston-Wolfe, writing in *L'Echo de Paris*, told readers the following day of the amazing performance: "To my astonishment I saw the form of a beautiful woman materialize behind shimmering gauze of gold and silver. Softly, almost imperceptibly, with infinite grace, she began to dance. One by one the enveloping veils were torn away, rising like birds of fluttering reluctance to the ground, until the dancer stood before us, covered only with heavy glittering chains and necklets of gleaming stones."

Said another reviewer, "There is something eerie about her. Nude dancing is, of course, designed to arouse passion and desire—usually in the man for the dancer. But Mata Hari made you think that you were actually satisfying your desires with her."

And still another critic gushed, "Mata Hari glided over the oval stage until, in a quivering frenzy, she dropped in a heap before the gilded image of her immobile lover [the statue of Shiva]. Crimson draperies licked her writhing body like flames . . . a priestess of love . . . a high priestess of sin."

Mata Hari's erotic charms were summed up by a sixty-year-old journalist who almost suffered a stroke witnessing her debut: "On a stage, covered with flowers, carefully lighted, five Hindu musicians played on strange instruments, a music that was enervating and spasmodic; and the invited guests, ravished, in ecstasy, could not stop their applause at the voluptuous attitudes and lascivious gestures, the feverish quiverings, the almost epileptic contortions of the dancer, whose suppleness was such that at first she seemed like a serpent, until she leapt up from the ground, full of life, and changed into an exquisite woman."

The one-time streetwalker was suddenly the

rage of Paris. Magazine and newspaper interviewers flocked to her side, jamming into her Hotel Crillon suite, which now boasted a rich Oriental decor. To these reporters, Mata Hari gave her well-rehearsed lies: "I was born in the south of India near Jaffnapatam on the Malabar coast, of a Brahmin family. My mother was a dancer in the Temple of Kandaswamy . . . she died in giving me birth. The priests who adopted me gave me the name of Mata Hari, which means 'child of the dawn.' From my earliest days I was shut up in the great underground world of the god Shiva. Here I was trained to follow in my mother's role as the chief dancer to perform the holy rites. The high priestess, my stepmother, who regarded me as one predestined for eternal glory, dedicated me to the god Shiva, the love god, and taught me the great eastern mysteries of love and faith, one spring night in the time of Sakty-Pudja."

All of it was nonsense, of course, but everyone loved this sensuous sex goddess and printed her every word. Not one editor bothered to check the fact that the god Shiva (or Siva) and its temples originated and was worshiped in Ceylon, not India. Nothing mattered except that Mata Hari had become the image of wonderful sin to a society bored with Victorian morality. Not only did Mata Hari become the idol of Paris, enjoying enormous salaries for her dances in clubs and theaters and in the mansions and palaces of the rich, but she became a figure much sought after to complement the ranks of the nobility. She snaked through her improvisational dances in the aristocratic drawing rooms of Prince Murat, Prince del Drago, Count Barraccini, the Duchess of Eckmuhl, the Chilean Embassy, being paid fortunes for her performances. Most of the aristocrats who invited her into their resplendent homes became her lovers, lavishing upon her priceless jewels, gold, furs. She was gossiped about and envied by every female in Paris; she was the object of exhilarating lust from men of all ages. And Mata Hari lived up to her reputation as a nymphomaniac, receiving two to three lovers a day.

Louis Damur painted her twice, once clothed and then in the nude. (The nobleman who had commissioned the nude painting paid Damur $1,000 for the portrait; this same painting was sold at auction three decades later for $40,000.) Damur wrote excitedly to a friend after first seeing Mata Hari dance, "The little breasts only were covered with chiseled brass cupolas, held in place by thin chains. Glittering bracelets encrusted with precious stones were on her wrists, arms and ankles. The rest of her was bare, fastidiously bare, from the nails of her fingers to her toes.

"Dominated by the ornamented bust, the plastic and firm stomach showed a sexless suppleness in symmetric curves which from the armpits under the raised arms traced themselves to the haunches. The raised legs were ideal, like two fine columns of a pagoda. The kneecaps, amber-colored, seemed plated with gold-leaf that had rosy reflections. . . . I can never forget her dancing."

She was mobbed everywhere she danced, at the Olympia, the Casino de Paris, the Folies-Bergere. Thousands of males begged her to accept their riches; for they would give anything for the favors of the "Red Dancer" (her silk veils were red). She danced the Dance of Love, the Dance of Sin, the Dance of Death. With her newfound riches, Mata purchased a villa at Neuilly, and took luxurious apartments in Montmartre. She was attended day and night by a bevy of groveling servants, all in Hindu livery, and her carriage was one of the most ornate in Paris, decorated in Oriental fashion.

She had her critics but they withheld comment about her until long after she was in disgrace; she was much too popular to castigate during her heyday. One of her astute critics was the French writer Colette who often saw her perform before aristocratic audiences. Said Colette many years later, "I have watched her from her first appearance in Paris, when she danced . . . between the columns of a temple, slender and bare as herself. She scarcely seemed to dance, but disrobed herself progressively, twirling a tall and dusky body, slim and proud.

"A little later she appeared at a Hindu fete in a garden, bare under a great June sun, riding a big white horse, richly caparisoned with saddlery encrusted with real turquoises. Her skin, amber by night, seemed mauve by daylight, but patchy—from artificial dyeing. Paris swallowed her, and raved about her chaste nudity, retelling anecdotes that Mata Hari had uttered about her hot Asiatic past. She was invited everywhere, men fought to pay her way. She would arrive almost naked, dance vaguely with eyes cast down, and then disappear wrapped in somber draperies."

Mata Hari left Paris to perform in other cities—Vienna, Rome, London, and Berlin. For two years this self-taught dancer swept fame and fortune into her purse. She became for men everywhere the living, pulsating symbol of sex. And she reveled in her success. In Berlin, Crown Prince Wilhelm had her brought to him so that she could perform privately. So taken with Mata Hari was the prince that during their brief but tempestuous affair, Wilhelm gave her diamonds and emeralds worth $100,000. He flaunted her against his father's wishes, once keeping her at his side when reviewing military maneuvers. In 1907 he brought Mata Hari to his officer's mess and had his mistress perform naked on the tables for his private guardsmen.

When Wilhelm tired of the dancer, he handed her down to the Duke of Brunswick, a future brother-in-law. Months later the once-loyal mistress was entertaining on a lower level still, appeasing the appetite of Berlin Police Chief von Jagow. The bald and beefy Von Jagow, who was to later become an adjutant to Colonel Walter Nicolai, head of German intelligence (*Nachrichtendienst*) during World War I, actually fell in love with Mata Hari, although he could not really afford her extravagant tastes. Their liaison would last until the end of Mata's life, an end that very liaison brought about.

During Mata Hari's heyday as a dancer she became the most famous and best-paid courtesan in Europe, with statesmen and aristocrats vying for her favors. One of France's great lawyers became her pawn. A French cabinet minister dallied with the dusky harlot. A Russian Grand Duke kept her in a palace. According to Alfred Morain, Police Chief of Paris, "At one time during her career, letters sent by her from Paris to her friends in Madrid and Amsterdam were written on paper bearing the address of the Minister for Foreign Affairs!"

Mata Hari's success as a dancer brought about a rash of Oriental and East Indies performers, all attempting to imitate her Asiatic gyra-

tions. Though the years 1905 to 1912 belonged to the Red Dancer in the realm of interpretive Eastern dancing, her imitators soon crowded her off the stages of music halls and nightclubs, causing her to rage against "these imposters! How dare they soil the image of Shiva with their fake ceremonial dances! Sacrilege, sacrilege!"

But there were still triumphs to be enjoyed. Mata Hari, after all, was an excellent dancer, even though her style was decidedly unorthodox. She practiced constantly, especially ballet, demanding of her body incredible feats as she used the exacting techniques of the Russian ballet. True, the Russian prima ballarina Pavlova towered above all, and interpretive dancers Isadora Duncan and Ruth St. Denis had mighty followings, but Mata Hari held a separate arena of attention all to herself. Her success at the Paris Opera Ballet and in Madrid, Vienna, and Berlin proved that. After her magnificent performance of the classic ballet *Bacchus and Gambrini* at La Scala in Milan in 1912, there were no doubts left among the critics that she was a one-of-a-kind dancer. Critics witnessing this performance responded with such praise as, "Mata Hari interested the audience greatly. She exuded an exotic elegance and noble gestures . . . slow harmonies which evoked profound admiration by the serious nature and purity of her art."

Not unlike any other performer the world over, Mata kept a scrapbook containing the notices of all her appearances, which she was able to fill rapidly. (This scrapbook, auctioned in 1955, was purchased by a Hollywood producer for several thousand dollars.) Mata also kept another file which contained hundreds of letters from the most powerful men in Europe, all compromising, of course, as well as copies of her own obscene and profane letters to these men. One could easily speculate that she intended to use this correspondence for future blackmail, although there is no evidence that she ever did. Perhaps she simply did not have time for such felonious pursuits. By the end of 1912, reliable records indicate, Mata Hari was involved in more important matters. She had gone into the spy business.

The manner in which the famous dancer and illustrious courtesan entered the dark circles of espionage is in debate to this day. After

The naked, except for breastplates, Mata Hari, as she performed in her heyday.

World War I, the German Intelligence Service minimized her efforts on their behalf, and Scotland Yard laughed at the thought of her spying abilities, but the French Deuxième Bureau insisted she not only was a super-spy but had caused the death of more than 200,000 French soldiers at the Battle of the Somme, turned over to the Germans the plans of the British tank, and caused the sinking of dozens of Allied ships through her crafty efforts. But, of course, the French shot her and had to have a good reason for executing the first woman spy of modern times.

Berlin's Police Chief von Jagow was the link to Mata Hari's involvement in espionage. Her own sense of adventure and love of risk, perhaps an innocent and romantic attitude before the opening of the "war to end all wars," was her motivation. It is understandable, given the fantastic career she had built on sham, that Mata Hari considered espionage nothing more than another melodrama, another piece of acting to be enjoyed, and, of course, an avenue in which she could earn fabulous sums, for money, not Shiva, was her true god.

During 1912 and 1913, Mata Hari's career as a dancer was all but over and she undoubtedly knew it. Yet in Germany her name was still magic, and it was here that she scored such stunning sexual triumphs with Crown Prince Wilhelm, who thought so much of her that he insisted photographers take pictures of them together in Silesia, and at the Cologne opera. She was also photographed with another paramour, the Duke of Brunswick, a handsome young Prussian nobleman. She was, during this period, referring to herself as the Duchess von Zelle, and waited on with great pomp at her elegant apartment in the swanky Adlon Hotel in Berlin.

Mata extended the lies about herself by hiring a genealogist of dubious reputation to prove that the Zelle family had branches reaching into English and German royalty, that she was related to William IV, the Prince of Wales, and even Queen Victoria. Claims to such grand ancestry mattered little to German intelligence officers, particularly Von Jagow, who loved her and kept her as his mistress months before the beginning of the war. In fact, she was seen driving with him amidst the cheering throngs of Berlin on the day war was declared.

Later, when being cross-examined by a French military tribunal, Mata Hari insisted that her first meeting with Von Jagow was a trivial matter that had to do with her naked performances. "I met him at the music hall where I was playing," she said. "In Germany the police censored costumes worn by artists. Someone complained that I was insufficiently attired. Herr Von Jagow arrived to inspect my costume."

Of course, the idea that Berlin's Chief of Police would busy himself with such perfunctory matters as costumes worn by exotic dancers is absolute nonsense. Von Jagow, despite his protests following World War I, had visited Mata Hari to recruit her services as an espionage agent. She had been "scouted" by Walter Canaris, a young, aggressive military attaché who would later head the Abwehr, the naval intelligence agency in Hitler's Third Reich. Canaris realized that the Dutch-born Mata Hari had complete mobility throughout Europe and that she had many lovers who held lofty positions in the military and diplomatic services of the Allies, men from whom she could easily obtain important information. Further, Canaris learned of Mata's real background and knew her to be partial to Germany and Germans in general, the people who had most sustained her success. It was Canaris who began the dossier on Mata Hari and urged Von Jagow to enlist her on Germany's side.

Von Jagow not only recruited the Red Dancer as an agent of the German Intelligence Service led by Walter Nicolai but assigned her the code number of H.21. The prefix *H*, Allied intelligence later learned, applied only to those agents recruited by Germany *before* August 1914 and the opening of hostilities.

A conspicuously unexplained gap of time in the life of Mata Hari occurred between late 1912 and the spring of 1913. She appeared in no musicals or reviews; her movements during this period are to this day shrouded. One report has it that she voluntarily enrolled in the German spy school outside Lörrach, near Munich in Bavaria. Here she was allegedly taught the art of espionage, from the making of tiny bombs inside cigars to the coding and decoding of top secret messages. By spring, the dancer was once again in Berlin, becoming the center of that capital's social events. The following year Mata Hari was still in Berlin, living yet in luxury at the exclusive Hotel Metropole. At the outbreak of the war, Von Jagow gave her her first assignment, ordering her to return to her native Holland and instructing her to re-enter France. She would receive further instructions at her villa in Neuilly.

Once in Amsterdam, Mata found it all but impossible to cross the French border; only those with approved military passes could enter the country. She decided that the best way to convince authorities to allow her into France was to plead non-belligerency. Going to the French consulate in Amsterdam, the dancer insisted that her home was in Neuilly, her friends were there, her career was in France. She showed letters to herself from high-ranking French politicians and military men. The French consul agreed to ready her papers, but it would take some time. During her wait, at Von Jagow's instructions, Mata Hari seduced one of the most important trade merchants in Amsterdam, learning from the duped lover the number of food shipments sailing from Holland to England, along with a complete list of merchant ships designated as supply vessels for France and England, sending this information to Berlin through her contact, Major Specht, a German intelligence officer.

Not until July 1915 did French officials approve of the dancer's re-entry into France. Mata Hari, for arcane reasons, did not simply cross the border but embarked on a Japanese ship in Amsterdam and sailed down the European coast, rounding Spain and then Italy. From Italy, she entered France, only a few days after a wire was sent to the Deuxième Bureau from the Italian Secret Service. The wire read:

> While examining the passenger list of a Japanese vessel at Naples we have recognized the name of a theatrical celebrity from Marseilles named Mata Hari, the famous Hindu dancer, who purports to reveal secret Hindu dances which demand nudity. She has, it seems, renounced her claim to Indian birth and become Berlinoise. She speaks German with a slight Eastern accent.

The moment Mata Hari appeared in Paris, agents were assigned to follow her everywhere; the telegram from the Italian authorities had branded her a suspicious foreigner, and it was quickly concluded that she was a spy for Germany. Her new papers listed her birthplace as Belgium, a criminally false statement that prompted the Sûreté-Générale in Paris to stamp her papers, "To be watched."

Agents tailing the woman discovered nothing, except that she lived lavishly and spent most of her nights with important members of the foreign office and other ministries, persons too important to be questioned by police. None of her actions suggested espionage. What the French did not realize was that Mata Hari obtained from these high-placed individuals vital information on supplies, troop dispositions, and even recruits being trained as reinforcements and that this information was sent along to Von Jagow in Berlin in the diplomatic pouches of certain so-called "neutral" countries.

Just when agents tailing Mata Hari were about to give up, they learned that, in late 1916, the woman had, through her friend, Jules Cambon, department chief of the French Foreign Office, obtained permission to travel to Vittel, near the front, close to important airfields. She traveled as a member of the Red Cross and nursed several wounded flyers hospitalized in Vittel, paying particular attention to a Russian aviator, Captain Marov, who had been blinded. When agents protested the pass given to

Mata Hari, Minister Malvy pooh-poohed their apprehension, writing, "Mrs. MacLeod, a prominent Dutch *artiste*, has the right to undertake this highly meritorious mission to perform for the benefit of our wounded Allied heroes."

The French agents nevertheless doubled their efforts to trap Mata Hari but again came up empty-handed. After seven months she returned to Paris without incident, but it was later determined that Mata Hari, after interviewing dozens of officers in Vittel, had learned of the great French offensive to be mounted in that sector, had warned the Germans, and had thus caused the deaths of as many as 200,000 French soldiers when their Somme offensive was crushed by a forewarned Geman army that had lain in wait for the attack.

Although nothing concrete could be proved against the woman, Captain Georges Ladoux of the French counterespionage service called her into his offices for a showdown. "Madam," the French officer said with utmost courtesy, "you are under suspicion by all the Allied Powers. You are to be deported, returned to your native Holland."

It was at this juncture that Mata Hari made her fatal mistake. She dropped the mask of innocence and begged Ladoux to allow her to spy for France. She could be extremely useful, she insisted, and, as a way of proving that she had special access to German military matters, she begged Ladoux to send her to the German general headquarters. "I will obtain any secret intelligence the French General Staff might require. I know Governor General von Bissing very well."

"How well do you know Von Bissing?"

"At one glance," smiled the dancer, "and he will be my victim."

Inside Mata Hari's reaction to the threat of deportation then was the tacit admission that she knew well the art of spying. In the words of Richard Wilmer Rowan, writing in *Secret Service*, it was "the one emphatic clue she was to give of having practiced in the field of international espionage; for she behaved like a professional spy, like the meanest hireling trapped during the war, vowing she had never worked for the Germans but gladly would enlist with the secret services of France."

Ladoux pretended to believe Mata Hari, that she would do anything for her "beloved France." The captain of the Deuxième Bureau agreed that she should spy against the Germans, but not at Stenay. She should travel to occupied Belgium, obtaining what information she could in Brussels. Mata Hari accepted this assignment and was given the names of six agents ostensibly working for France. Of course, all these agents, the French knew, were double agents, taking pay from the French and supplying useless information to Paris under the direction of the Germans, their real masters. Mata Hari was to take letters to all six agents, but it was learned that she got in touch with only one of these agents and this man was shortly arrested by the Germans and shot.

The French were baffled. The agent in Belgium was certainly not a true French spy; his reports had obviously been dictated by German intelligence. Then why had the Germans shot him? The answer came some weeks later when British intelligence informed the French that a resident spy of *theirs* had been arrested in Brussels and executed, that he had been betrayed by a woman answering the description of Mata Hari. So the man in Belgium was a legitimate Allied agent, after all, but had been working for the British, not the French. Ladoux concluded that Mata Hari was certainly a German spy, and a shrewd one. He gave orders for her arrest the minute she set foot on French soil.

But Mata Hari was by then headed in a different direction. With incredible bravado, she sailed for England, and was taken at her insistence to Scotland Yard, demanding an interview with Sir Basil Thomson, head of intelligence and the Criminal Investigation Department. To this most reserved of men, the alluring forty-year-old dancer confided that she was an espionage agent but not for the Germans.

"If not for Germany, madam, then for whom do you work?"

"I have been sent to England by the Deuxième Bureau," Mata Hari calmly told Thomson. "The Germans did not send me to spy in England—I have been sent by the French!"

Thomson did not register the shock he felt at the moment. Slowly, he realized that the woman either was insane or was part of some sort of spectacular espionage gambit contrived by German intelligence. He was having none of it. "France is our ally," Thomson told her in a grave parental voice. Years later, while writing *My Experiences in Scotland Yard*, he would remember escorting the doe-eyed dancer to his office door, reproaching her with the words of a father to a delinquent child: "Madam, if you will take the word of one nearly twice your age, give up what you have been doing." With that Mata Hari's mission to England, whatever it might have been, came to an abrupt end. She left for Spain via Holland.

In his meticulous fashion, Thomson wrote a detailed account of his amazing encounter with Mata Hari and sent this off to the Deuxième Bureau. French intelligence agents soon reported that the dancer had fully ignored Sir Basil's advice and, almost immediately after registering at the posh Palace Hotel in Madrid, begun consorting with German agents, becoming intimate with Captain von Kalle, the German naval attaché stationed in Spain, and the military attaché, Von Kron. She was, from all reports, busy earning her living as a courtesan and looking for new espionage assignments. She failed in both respects.

Her beauty gone, the Germans in Madrid amused themselves with the dancer, but to them she was no longer the beau ideal of sexual adventure. She was now a hard-looking woman, almost gaunt, her features severe, her attitude shrewish and demanding. She was also far too notorious at that time to ever again be used effectively as a German spy. Mata Hari lobbied the other countries having spies in Spain—Madrid was a hotbed of espionage activity—but was rebuffed. She went back to the Germans, demanding they pay her for her services and assign her to another field of operation. Von Kalle asked for instructions from Berlin.

The war in early 1917 had begun to take its financial toll on German intelligence and funds were running low. Mata Hari had been paid over the years an enormous amount of money, perhaps as much as 400,000 marks. Her demand for more funds from her luxury suite in Madrid irked Von Jagow but he did wire the German embassy in Madrid that H.21 was to proceed to France where, through a friend in a neutral legation, she would be paid 15,000 pesetas for her work in Spain. (That work was never specified, unless it had been the dancer's job to check on the efficiency of German spies in Madrid, an unlikely assignment.)

It was this wire from Von Jagow that spelled doom for Mata Hari. The French intercepted the message, and, knowing the German diplomatic code by then, determined that H.21 was, indeed, Mata Hari. They followed the dancer upon her return from Spain, tailed her to the neutral legation, and stayed with her as she returned to the Hotel Plaza Athénée on the avenue Montaigne. On the morning of February 13, 1917, Commissioner Priolet, accompanied by his secretary and two policemen, called on the dancer in her hotel room, bursting through the door to find Mata Hari sitting in bed, eating her breakfast. She was ordered to dress while her suite was searched. The check for 15,000 pesetas was found—she hadn't had time to cash it—and it was this check that proved the grim fact that she was agent H.21.

Mata Hari appeared unruffled by her arrest, giving Priolet two bunches of wild violets as the group left her rooms. She chatted with the commissioner in the car about her new apartment in the avenue Henri Martin as they sped toward the Palais de Justice. Her demeanor did not change an hour later when she underwent her first cross-examination.

Mata Hari only registered astonishment, falling back on her old story of being an innocent *artiste* who knew nothing of international espionage. The charge was ridiculous, absurd. She was still protesting when she was locked in a padded cell in the ancient prison at Faubourg Saint-Denis. The padded cell, of course, was a precaution against suicide; the French hoped to obtain vital information from Mata Hari before disposing of her.

Not until July 24–25, 1917, was Mata Hari brought before a closed-door quasi-military hearing. Sentries had been placed at the entrances to the hearing room with instructions to shoot anyone who came closer to the doors than ten paces. President of the Court was Colonel Semprou who commanded the Garde Républicaine. Also in attendance was Lieutenant Mornet in the role of Commissioner for the Govern-

ment (Judge-Advocate-General), and Major Massard, of the Deuxième Bureau. Edward Clunet was appointed by the court to serve as Mata Hari's lawyer, and he undertook his job with enthusiasm; in fact, Clunet became the dancer's impassioned champion and did everything in his power to save her.

Semprou opened the hearing with the charge: "On the day that war was declared, you had breakfast with the Prefect of Police [Von Jagow] at Berlin, and then drove with him through a shouting crowd."

Mata Hari, dressed all in black, sat confidently facing the court. "It is true," came her calm reply, "I had met the Prefect in a music

Mata Hari in the altogether after one of her erotic dances.

hall where I danced. That is how we got to know each other."

"A little later the Prefect charged you with a confidential mission and gave you thirty thousand marks."

"That is true. He was the man and gave me thirty thousand marks. But not for the reason you impute. He was my lover."

"We know that. But this amount seems rather large for a simple gift."

"Not to me."

"From Berlin you came to Paris, passing through Holland, Belgium, and England. What were you going to do in Paris?"

"My reason was to keep a watch over the removal of my goods from my villa at Neuilly."

"Immediately after that you spent seven months close to the front."

"At Vittel, where I was a nurse. I devoted myself to looking after a Russian officer, Captain Marov, who was blinded. My wish was to rebuild my life by the bedside of the unhappy man I loved."

"You were in the company of many officers. We have found many letters in your lodgings, from well-known Parisians, but mostly from aviators. Why were you so interested in the company of officers, madam?"

"Men who were not in the army did not interest me at all. My husband was a captain. An officer in my eyes is a superior being, a man who is always ready for any adventure, for any danger. When I loved, it was always soldiers, and it did not matter what country they came from, because to me a fighter belongs to a special race above civilians."

Semprou thought for a moment that this remark was addressed to him, a solicitation, then dismissed the idea. "The flying officers also came after you. They flattered you and courted you. How did you manage to get from them for nothing the secrets they had? It is certain that you told the enemy the places where our airplanes would put down our secret agents. Through this you have killed many men."

"I don't deny that I continued, while I was in the Red Cross, writing to the head of the German Secret Service, who was in Holland. It is not my fault that he had that appointment. But I wrote nothing about the war. He got no informa-tion from me. My relationships with the soldiers was out of sympathy for their plight. Others—well, I did it for money."

"Hundreds of thousands of marks were paid to you—"

"As a courtesan, yes! I confess it, but never a spy!" For a moment Mata Hari lost her composure, leaning forward as if to plead with the officers who sat stiffly in front of her. "Harlot, yes, I am that! But traitoress—never!"

"An innocent person does not so readily offer to spy, unless that person knows well the art of spying." Semprou gave her a decisive point of the finger. "And you offered to counterspy for France!"

Mata Hari's head whipped backward slightly, as if she were stunned. "Yes," she finally managed.

"And how would you have been useful to France?"

"By using my connections for her! I have already explained to the chief of the Second Bureau [Ladoux] the exact points in Morocco where the German submarines have landed arms. It was interesting."

"Very interesting, in fact," intoned Mornet, "but all these matters you have referred to could not have been known to you without your being in connection with Germany."

The dancer stuttered out a reply, something about learning top secrets of a German diplomatic dinner, overhearing important details. Then she dropped her head for a moment, then lifted it and shouted to the court, "After all, I am not French! I have no duty towards this people. My services were useful. That is all I have to say. I am only a poor woman whom you are trying to entrap into confessing faults she has not committed." Suddenly she twisted her head in Mornet's direction, a snarl on her lips as she raised her arms in his direction and shouted, "That man is bad!"

Semprou ignored the outburst and went on to relate how Mata Hari had been instructed to contact the six Belgian agents and how one of them—the only true Allied agent—had been shot by the Germans after she had visited with him.

"I recall nothing of such a man," Mata Hari said in a dull voice.

Semprou had saved the real evidence for

last. "At the order of German Headquarters you were notified in Madrid that you were to be paid 15,000 pesetas, money waiting for you here in France, and you came to France and collected those funds."

Shaking her head, Mata Hari gave the court a frantic look, then blurted out, "I was the mistress of Von Kalle, head of German intelligence in Madrid. That payment was a love debt, that's all."

"But the remittance was sent to the order of H.21. That is a number on the list of German spies. That was your number. That is what you were known as."

Now the dancer's composure was shattered. Her trim body quaked in the chair, her large doe-eyes blinked uncontrollably and her mouth quivered as she finally answered, "That—that is not true! I—I am telling you that—it was—it was to pay—to pay for my nights of love. It—it is my price. Please, believe me, gentlemen."

Witnesses were then called, all of them providing the court with damning testimony. Edward Clunet, the defense attorney, gave an impassioned speech on Mata Hari's behalf but the lawyer conceded her guilt, although he did attempt to portray her as a naive pawn in the hands of the clever, insidious German spymasters. Before he could further implicate her, Mata Hari stopped Clunet, and asked to make a final statement.

In a clear voice, the dancer said, "Please note that I am not French, and that I reserve the right to cultivate any relations that may please me. The war is not a sufficient reason to stop me from being a cosmopolitan. I am a neutral, but my sympathies are for France. If that does not satisfy you, do as you will."

A half hour later Mata Hari stood before the court. Semprou, without the slightest trace of emotion, told the dancer she had been found guilty of espionage. "Margaret Gertrude Zelle —you are condemned to death."

"It is not possible," Mata Hari muttered. "It is not possible!" The dancer then asked if she could made her appeal against the judgment of the court. Semprou nodded and Mata Hari confidently walked to the clerk of the court and signed her petition for appeal. She was smiling when she left the court.

Clunet worked energetically to get the decision reversed. Scores of powerful men in government and the military petitioned the court for leniency. These, of course, were Mata Hari's ex-lovers; they may have been concerned that the dancer would use against them letters she had kept if they did not go to her aid. Even in Holland, a prime minister attempted to get Queen Wilhelmina to intercede on the part of the Dutch-born Mata Hari, but the queen, like the French courts, had nothing more to do with the convicted spy.

In her prison cell at Saint-Lazare where she had been removed after her trial, the dancer remained in excellent spirits, thinking that she would somehow be saved, that the men she had so sexually edified would do the gallant thing and rescue her. Even when Edward Clunet tearfully informed her that she was to be shot as a spy on Monday, October 15, 1917, the woman displayed little concern.

Her attitude continued to be one of little or no apprehension. The day before her execution, Dr. Bizard, who had treated her for venereal disease almost fifteen years earlier, visited the spy in her cell and discussed dancing with her. Sister Léonide, who had been assigned to be the woman's cellmate to make sure Mata did not harm herself, turned toward the prisoner at this moment and said, "Show us how you dance." Mata Hari rose, a great smile on her face, and loosened her dress. She then began to dance about the cell before Bizard and Sister Léonide.

At 4:00 A.M. the following morning, Commandant Julien entered Mata Hari's cell and asked Sister Léonide to wake the dancer. The nun began to weep and Julien himself went to Mata Hari's cot and shook the prisoner awake. She stared up at him, crouching on the cot, her fists clenched.

"Zelle—be brave," Julien told her. "The President of the Republic has rejected your appeal. The moment has come for carrying out the sentence."

Mata Hari's voice began in a whisper, then rose in volume as she repeated over and over the same remark she had made following her trial: "It is not possible! It is not possible!" She then looked at Sister Léonide who was sobbing. "Don't cry, sister. I shall know how to die without weakness. You shall see a good end!" Looking at Julien and the guards, she then stated with some haughtiness, "Gentlemen—allow me to dress."

Mata Hari put on her warmest gown, complaining, "It is cold. I slept so well. Another day I would not have forgiven them for waking me so early. Why do you have this custom of executing people at dawn? In India it is otherwise. It takes place at noon. I would much sooner go to Vincennes [the place of execution] about three o'clock after a good lunch. Give me my nice little slippers, too. I always like to be well shod."

She powdered her face, then asked for a priest and spoke to him for some moments. Turning, she ordered Sister Léonide to bring in the guards. One report typified her as arrogant to the end: "One might have said she was holding a reception. Clad in a tailor-made costume, she held herself proudly erect, and drew on her gloves calmly."

Cocking her head toward Julien she announced, "Gentlemen, I am ready."

She was told by an officer that Article 27 of the French Penal Code demanded she declare herself pregnant, if that were the case. (In that event, she would have been spared until delivering the child.) The prisoner muttered something about having had nine abortions, then laughed and, pointing to the cots where Sister Léonide and another nun had constantly slept on either side of her, said, "Assuredly, no. How could that happen?"

"Do you have any statement to make?" Julien inquired.

"None. And if I had, don't you think I would keep it to myself?" She did hand Julien several sealed envelopes, farewell letters to her closest friends, all males, including a missive to her beloved Captain Marov, the blind Russian aviator.

She was taken down the passageway by Penaud, the chief warden, but broke loose from his grip, pulling his hand from her arm, shouting, "Let me be! Don't touch me! I don't wish it! I am not a thief. What manners are these?" She was allowed to walk free. She then whispered to Sister Léonide, "Little mother, don't leave me."

Suddenly Mata Hari spied a gas jet on the ceiling, seven feet from the floor. Capriciously she leaped upward and touched the gas jet. Then she said with a smile to Sister Léonide, "I'll bet you couldn't do that, little mother. You aren't big enough."

As she emerged, Mata Hari saw more than one hundred persons at the exit waiting to see her. She gave the crowd a big smile and gushed, as if she were attending one of her own premieres, "All these people! What a success!"

Her attitude did not alter when she arrived at the execution spot in Vincennes. Dr. Bizard managed to give the woman a glass of brandy to drink and this Mata Hari gratefully took. Next she calmly raised her skirts a bit and sidestepped pools of water as she made her way to a post and turned, erect, proud, seemingly fearless, to face a firing squad of twelve men. Sister Léonide was still at her side.

"Embrace me quickly and let me be," Mata Hari told the petite nun. "Stand to the right of me. I shall be looking at you. Adieu!"

She refused a blindfold and waved away the officer who attempted to tie the post cord about her waist. She was still smiling when the firing squad, standing twelve paces away, sent their bullets into her. As Mata Hari slumped to the ground, an officer walked to her crumpled form, placed a pistol behind her ear, and fired a round into her head, the traditional coup de grace.

Lawyer Clunet, weeping great tears, ran to the body, and lifted the dancer's limp hand, kissing it. "It's terrible," he moaned. "She did not deserve death."

No one claimed the body and the corpse was dragged through the mud to a cheap wooden coffin. The remains of the illustrious Mata Hari were removed to a medical center, and there a student performed his first appendectomy on the corpse, noticing that she had been struck by only four bullets. Apparently the members of her firing squad, even though it was purposely made up of seasoned veterans—four sergeants and four corporals, the rest privates—had been loath to kill this famous courtesan-spy. This was borne out in 1925 when one of the privates, no more than an eighteen-year-old *poilu* at the time of the execution, admitted that he could not bring himself to shoot "so brave a woman," and had purposely aimed high over her head. Others in that death squad had undoubtedly duplicated his act.

Glamorous stories persisted for years about the dancer's end. One had it that a man named Pierre de Morrisac had arranged for Mata Hari to meet a soldier's end, that of being shot instead of guillotined, so that she could easily survive the execution, that De Morrisac convinced the dancer that he would have blank cartridges inserted in the rifles of the execution squad and she was to pretend to die; he would afterward claim her body and spirit her out of the country. This then was the reason many gave for Mata Hari's incredible display of courage at the end; she was certain that she would not be killed.

Like so many others, the De Morrisac story was apocryphal, designed to further enhance the enigma of the immortal Mata Hari. There was never any real doubt that she was certain of her own death. This was verified by the French journalist, Georges de Parcq, who had known the dancer for years and had covered many of her spectacular performances, and who visited the prisoner the day before her execution. At that time, Mata Hari begged him for a favor.

"You have been a good friend to me," she told De Parcq. "I have a child, a girl. She is in a convent in Holland, and, of course, I shall never see her again, Georges, and I wonder, when the war is over—would you go and see her and be her friend?"

"Willingly. You have my word of honor," promised the writer. "I will do everything I can."

Mata Hari then gave the journalist a miniature of herself in a frame of tiny pearls, a locket which had been made by Fossard, the renowned Swiss miniaturist. "Will you give this to my little girl?"

One month after the war ended, De Parcq delivered the locket to a girl in Holland whose only image of Mata Hari was that of a glamorous and exotic dancer, a creature of love, who had spied for the losing side.

Ruby McCollum walking from the courtroom where she was tried for murdering her white paramour, Dr. LeRoy C. Adams, in 1952. (Wide World)

McCOLLUM, RUBY

Murderer ■ (1915–   )

A black resident of Live Oak, Florida, Ruby McCollum killed Dr. C. LeRoy Adams, a white local political bigwig, in 1952. Mrs. McCollum, alleged to have had a child by Dr. Adams, was imprisoned for two years, then removed to a mental asylum after being adjudged insane. Credited with saving Mrs. McCollum from the electric chair was Frank Cannon, a white country lawyer, who worked without pay. The controversial killing was the subject of a book by William Bradford Huie, *Ruby McCollum: Woman in the Suwannee Jail.*

Mrs. McCollum was subsequently released to the custody of her daughter.

MEINHOF, ULRIKE

Terrorist ■ (1934–1976)

A founder of the Red Army Faction, a radical left-wing group of political fanatics in Germany, Ulrike Meinhof came to prominence in 1970 when she and others, in a daring strike against German police, freed terrorist-arsonist Andreas Baader. (The group was forever after known as the Baader-Meinhof Gang.)

Ulrike was the daughter of a museum director and had become a well-known left-wing journalist at the time she embarked on her terrorist crusade, a paramilitary spree that involved bloody bank robberies which gleaned for the gang more than $250,000 which was used to finance its senseless operations.

German police and troops finally tracked down the gang. Meinhof was taken alive on July 15, 1972, and in the possession of several pistols, a submachine gun, two live grenades, and a bomb. Despairing while being held at Stammheim Prison in May 1976, Ulrike tore some towels in her cell, joined the ends into a makeshift rope, and hanged herself.

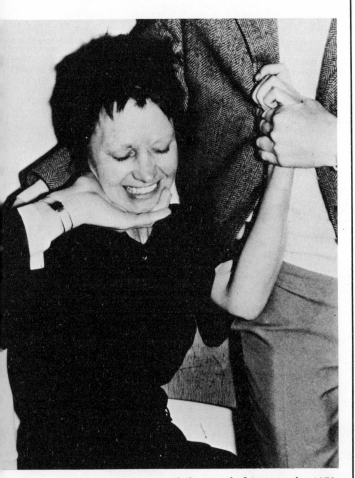

German terrorist Ulrike Meinhof in custody, 1972. (Wide World)

MERCIER, EUPHRASIE

Murderer ■ (1823– ?)

Among the quaint habits of rich single women of the nineteenth century was the practice of hiring lady companions to help them while away their uneventful days. One such companion was Euphrasie Mercier who proved one of France's most eccentric murderers, since childhood a woman whose extreme cunning had bordered on insanity.

Euphrasie had been raised by a religious zealot in the province of Nord, along the Belgian frontier. Her father gave his children extravagantly religious names—Euphrasie, Zacharie, Camille, Honorine, and Sidonie. The last three of these children, through their fire-eating father, became possessed of religious mania and were later determined to be insane. The children wrote the pope constantly, stating that they had committed the most horrendous of sins, offenses they wholly imagined. They also insisted that they were in direct communication with God. Camille, one of the Mercier sons, tried to convince everyone that his brain had been absorbed by a steam engine. Only Euphrasie and her brother Zacharie seemed to have escaped the family mania.

When Euphrasie's father died she was left an inheritance of 16,000 pounds, but she mismanaged this hefty sum in the upkeep of her lunatic family and the Merciers were soon destitute, wandering for decades throughout Europe with Euphrasie supporting them by means of the most menial of jobs, and always living on the brink of disaster. The situation was little improved in 1882 when Euphrasie opened a boot shop in Paris. That enterprise, too, was about to fail, when Euphrasie, then sixty years old, made the acquaintance of Elodie Ménétret, a forty-two-year-old woman who had had many lovers and had profited through their generosity.

Elodie visited Euphrasie's shop on the boulevard Haussmann to have some boots repaired when she saw a woman pass by the shop leading a dog. She had just recently lost her dog, Rigolo, and thought the dog passing by was hers. She ran to the street but the woman and dog had disappeared. Elodie concluded that the woman might return along the boulevard Haussmann and asked Euphrasie if she might stay in her small shop a few hours each day in hopes of seeing her lost dog again. Euphrasie agreed and the women became friends in the next week, with Euphrasie pouring out the woeful tale of her zany family, while Elodie kept her vigil by the shop window. To the trusting Elodie the elderly woman appeared kind, religious, and terribly at odds with fate. She confided that she had just purchased a home in Villemomble, a fashionable suburb of Paris, and, being lonely, invited Euphrasie to move there with her as her lady's companion. The shopworn Euphrasie accepted with alacrity, and the women moved into the house in March 1883.

Within a month, Elodie Ménétret had cause to regret her invitation. Her companion, instead of bringing comfort and a feeling of security to the association, frightened Elodie half out of her wits. "I feel ghosts present in this house," Euphrasie would murmur every so often. "They have no mercy on fallen women." This remark was an obvious reference to Elodie's tainted past. At other times Euphrasie would graphically describe gruesome murders: "Solitary women such as yourself, madame, have been strangled to death in their beds by killers looking for gold and jewels." Euphrasie knew full well that Elodie possessed some extremely valuable jewels given to her by past admirers, along with about 3,500 in pounds, her on-hand nest egg.

Alarmed by such talk, Elodie, on April 18, 1883, went to a neighbor, Mademoiselle Grière, and together the two women made an itemized list of Elodie's jewels, along with her other valuables. Each kept a copy of this list. At the time, Elodie told her friend, "The bootmaker frightens me. I have dismissed her, but she obstinately refuses to go, saying she only wants food and lodging."

But, of course, Euphrasie Mercier wanted much more. On April 25, a friend called at the Ménétret house and was met by the lady's companion. "She is dead to the world," Euphrasie informed the friend. "She has entered a convent, and I have sworn not to divulge the place of her retreat." It was the same story to all subsequent visitors. Euphrasie closed the door in their faces and kept the house shuttered, closed off from the world. Finally, Elodie's sister complained to the police and the commissary at Montreuil summoned the lady's companion to his office for questioning.

Euphrasie appeared before the police officer without the slightest trace of nervousness. She showed him a note she claimed Elodie had written. It had no date and read, "I quit France—I leave all to Mlle. Mercier—let her transact my affairs." The handwriting was examined and considered to be that of Elodie Ménétret, although it appeared scratchy, as if written nervously. The police, however, were satisfied that nothing was amiss and sent Euphrasie back to her comfortable quarters. Within a week, the mad Mercier brother and sisters were ensconced in the Ménétret house and were seen wandering about in Elodie's clothing. Elodie's possessions, including her jewelry, were pawned by Euphrasie who even represented herself in some of these transactions as Elodie Ménétret. She obtained Elodie's power of attorney by visiting a notary in Luxembourg, pretending to be Elodie and insisting that her good friend Euphrasie Mercier have her power of attorney. When the notary seemed suspicious, Euphrasie stepped into the street for a moment and bribed two strangers, a hairdresser and a musician, to swear she was, indeed, Elodie Ménétret. With this power of attorney Euphrasie demanded monthly payments from Elodie's former lovers, which they duly paid.

No one interfered with Euphrasie until 1885 when she introduced two more members of her family to the Ménétret house; she would later discover this to be an act of self-destruction. The two new members were Adèle Mercier, daughter of Euphrasie's brother Zacharie, and a young nephew, Alphonse Chateauneuf, the illegitimate son of the insane Honorine and the Comte de Chateauneuf. Euphrasie was particularly fond of the nephew, who was a deserter from the French army; he had been smuggled out of a Brussels garrison by Euphrasie herself, disguising the nephew in women's clothing.

From the first, the nephew noticed something sinister afoot in the Mercier household. His oddball aunts babbled about "the dead coming to life," and "misfortune will someday come out of the garden." The nephew too began to focus on the garden, especially a bed of dahlias, which Euphrasie would let no one tend but herself. She also made sure no dog coming with visitors even got near the dahlia bed. At dinner, the nephew would watch his aunt's eyes traverse the table, then always stray to the window which gave her a full view of the dahlia bed.

Even more disturbing were his aunt's weird religious rites practiced during the evening. A banner embroidered years earlier by Honorine in honor of the Virgin Mary hung in the living room. On several occasions Chateauneuf witnessed his Aunt Euphrasie prostrate herself before this banner and kiss the floor sixteen times while crawling backward on hands and knees. She would then rise and run to a window, throw it open, and shout into the garden, "In the name of God, get hence, Beelzebub, Lucifer, and thou, Satan! Hence with your legions of devils! Back, judges, commissaries, Assize Court! Back, ye terrors that beset me! Back, phantoms of my garden! Family of Ménétret, rest in peace, in the peace of God, and the glory of the elect! Amen!"

After such emotional ceremonies, the nephew would plague his aunt as to the whereabouts of Elodie Ménétret. Her only answer was, "Gone away somewhere—I don't know." Chateauneuf's darkest suspicions were reinforced when a stray dog got into the garden and began digging furiously at the bed of dahlias. Euphrasie went wild with rage when she spotted the animal and almost killed the dog as she drove it off with a hoe.

A few days later the nephew asked his aunt for a considerable loan. When she refused, Chateauneuf threatened to reveal a disastrous family secret. Still Euphrasie refused. The nephew went to Brussels and, piecing his theories together, wrote to magistrates in Paris through an uncle of Elodie Ménétret that the good lady had been murdered by his aunt, he was sure. He deduced that his Aunt Euphrasie had poisoned Elodie with match ends, burned her body, and buried the remains in the garden beneath the dahlia bed. He went further, telling the uncle that he was even sure of the room in the Villemomble home where the killing had taken place and had inscribed on the wall, "Mademoiselle Ménétret killed here!"

In short order Euphrasie was arrested. Investigators stalked through the villa and began digging up the garden. Charred bones were found beneath the dahlias, along with some teeth, one of which had been gold-filled. The teeth were taken to Elodie's Parisian dentist, who identified them as belonging to his patient. A greasy substance found in front of the fireplace proved to be similar to that in restaurant chimneys where meat was cooked. An expert examined the bulbs of the dahlias in the garden and reported that the flowers had been disturbed in the spring of 1883, almost to the week of Elodie's disappearance. Investigators also found wedged behind a mirror a newspaper clipping, Le Figaro of October 18, 1881, which told the story of how the body of a murdered priest in Imola, Italy, had been found buried in the garden of the murderer, a man named Faella. This article, police concluded, had been saved by Euphrasie and had suggested the method of disposal for Elodie Ménétret's remains.

More damning statements were provided by the gibbering sisters. An architect came forward to state that he had inspected the Ménétret house recently at Euphrasie's request, with some thoughts to improving the place. At the time, the mad Mercier sisters walked after him chanting and shouting strange invocations.

"Why don't you call the commissary of police," the architect remembered telling Euphrasie at the time, "and have these mad women taken away."

"The commissary, indeed!" Honorine had shouted, and with a mad laugh, she had added, "If once he came here, Euphrasie would never see the light of heaven again!"

Euphrasie Mercier's trial began on April 6, 1886. Her traitorous, blackmailing nephew faced her in court, accusing her of the murder of Elodie Ménétret. Adèle Mercier seconded Chateauneuf's accusations. The charred bones police claimed to be the remains of Elodie Ménétret were on exhibit in the courtroom in a large jar.

Insisting upon her innocence, Euphrasie repeated the lie that her friend Elodie had entered a convent. When informed by the court that the police had scoured every convent in France without finding her, the accused only shrugged.

The evidence against the woman was overwhelming. After an hour and a half of deliberation on April 10, 1886, the jury found Euphrasie Mercier guilty of murder, robbery, and forgery, but with extenuating circumstances. She was given the maximum sentence for a prisoner of her age, twenty years in prison; she would perish in her cell.

Euphrasie died cursing the name of Alphonse Chateauneuf, her disloyal nephew. The nephew had undoubtedly sent his aunt to justice out of revenge at not being given the loan he had requested. Being an enterprising scoundrel, the nephew still found a way to make money from the heinous act of his murderous aunt. During Euphrasie's sensational trial, Alphonse Chateauneuf enriched himself by slipping out of the courtroom at every recess and peddling a pamphlet he had quickly published, one entitled "The Mystery of Villemomble."

MERRIFIELD, MRS. LOUISA

Murderer ■ (1907–1953)

Just after their marriage in the spring of 1953, Louisa (born Louisa Highway) and seventy-four-year-old Alfred E. Merrifield, Louisa's third husband, went to work as servants for a Mrs. Ricketts in Blackpool, England. Their employer was a grouchy, ailing woman nearing eighty, who told deliverymen that the Merrifields were squandering her money on rum and unnecessary food. On April 14, Mrs. Ricketts died, a not unexpected event. What was strange was the fact that Mrs. Merrifield had not called the doctor until the next morning, though it was well known that the woman was desperately ill.

"I didn't want to go out into the night, not at that time of night," Mrs. Merrifield later testified. "Not to be looking for doctors. I was up and down with her five or six times that night. . . . Next thing I heard her up again, and she was in the hall, on the floor. I picked her up. I got her into bed. She said she thanked both my husband and me for what we had done for her. Those were her last words."

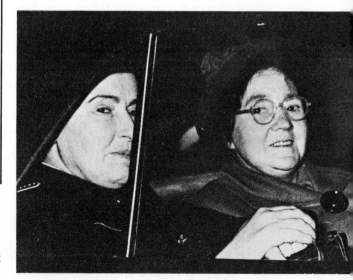

The happy, gossipy Mrs. Louisa Merrifield, being taken to prison to await her murder trial in 1953.

Mrs. Merrifield, no longer jolly, hears her death sentence.

Suspicious authorities investigated, especially when they heard that Mrs. Merrifield was arranging for her deceased employer to be cremated in a hurry. Examining the body pathologists found traces of phosphorous poison, normally used to kill vermin. A spoon found in Mrs. Merrifield's purse had on it a residue that could have been produced with a mixture of phosphorous poison and rum. Mrs. Merrifield had previously stated that she had given the old woman rum on the night of her death.

The smiling Mrs. Merrifield was put on trial in Manchester on July 20, 1953. She had long before convicted herself out of her own mouth.

Neighbors came forward to testify to Mrs. Merrifield's remarks. One stated that the housekeeper, meeting him on the street, had bubbled, "Oh, David! I've had a slice of real luck. Where I'm living the old lady has died and left me her bungalow, worth 3,000 pounds." She also stated that she would get a mortgage on the place and open up a swanky nursing home on the Blackpool promenade.

"We're landed!" she had exclaimed to a Mrs. Brewer when meeting her on the street. "I went to live with an old lady and she died and left me a bungalow worth 4,000 pounds."

Louisa's varied estimates on the worth of the Ricketts property aside, these remarks would not have been out of the ordinary—Mrs. Ricketts had, it appeared from her will, left everything to the Merrifields—except that Louisa had made her announcement a month *before* Mrs. Ricketts died.

Louisa's nonstop gossiping tongue had blared her plans to total strangers. To a person she had never met before in her life, Mrs. Merrifield told the story of going to work for Mrs. Ricketts with her husband, telling this dumbfounded person who was waiting for a bus that her doddering spouse was having an affair with her employer. Gritting her teeth, Mrs. Merrifield had said at the time, "If it goes on again, I'll poison the old bitch and my husband as well. She was leaving the bungalow between me and my husband, but he's so greedy he wants it all on his own."

The truth of the matter was that Mrs. Ricketts was about to fire the Merrifields but Louisa beat her to the punch by poisoning the old lady. Mr. Merrifield, it was later determined, had nothing to do with Louisa's scheme. He was released. His wife of only seven months was hanged on September 18, 1953.

METYARD, SARAH

Murderer ■ (? –1768)

A London milliner, Sarah Metyard, and her daughter, also named Sarah, were found guilty of murdering several young female apprentices sent to them from workhouses, chiefly one Anne Naylor who was beaten to death by the sadistic women, then stuffed into a box. The corpse decomposed and the stench caused the women to burn the body. The younger Metyard finally informed on her mother. Both women hanged at Tyburn on July 19, 1768.

MILLER, LUCILLE

Murderer ■ (1930–   )

San Bernardino housewife Lucille Miller staggered to a lonely house on the night of October 8, 1964, to inform the resident and subsequently police that her husband, Dr. Gordon E. "Cork" Miller, had burned to death inside the family Volkswagen parked off a nearby road. The husband, a thirty-nine-year-old successful dentist, was found a charred cinder by police. Mrs. Miller stated that the car suddenly erupted in flames and she had barely escaped; her husband, who had been taking sedatives, was unable to save himself.

When investigators found an empty gasoline container in the back seat of the wreck, and a charred four-foot weed stalk nearby, Mrs. Miller was arrested and charged with her husband's murder. His death, it was shortly concluded, was coupled to the death of Mrs. Elaine Hayton, wife of well-to-do lawyer Arthwell C. Hayton, with whom Mrs. Miller had been having an affair.

Mrs. Hayton had been found dead in her bed after Mrs. Miller had "nursed" her during an illness. Seconal was found in Mrs. Hayton's body. She had been drugged and then asphyxiated by Lucille, who wanted her out of the way, along with her husband, so that she could marry Hayton.

Miller's fate was similar. After his wife drugged him, she splashed gasoline throughout the inside of the family car, then, using the weed stalk as a long taper, ignited the vehicle while her husband sat unconscious inside. Attorney

California housewife Lucille Miller, convicted of murdering her husband, is all smiles upon being paroled in 1972.

Hayton, who testified at Mrs. Miller's trial, insisted that after a brief tryst with the woman he had wanted nothing to do with her; he had been on Catalina Island at the time of his wife's death.

Lucille Miller was sentenced to life imprisonment at the California Institute for Women at Fontana. She was paroled, May 10, 1972.

MILOSAVLJERIC, LJUBINKA

Murderer ■ (1917–   )

A railroad switchman's daughter living in Badrdan, Yugoslavia, Ljubinka Milosavljeric organized a band of Communist partisan fighters during World War II, and, following the war, rose to lofty positions in the Communist hierarchy, becoming minister of education in the Serbian government, chief censor of the country's press, and head of the Control Commission which kept party members in tow.

Ljubinka's one true love was Momcilo Cupic, who had joined her underground group in 1941. Years later Cupic became a diplomat under Tito, married, and raised a family. In early April 1955, the two met again at a party reunion; they had not seen each other in four years. Cupic walked Ljubinka home. While he was saying good night, his former lover pulled out a pistol and emptied it into the surprised man. The jilted Ljubinka was put into an asylum for the murder.

MODERS, MARY ("THE GERMAN PRINCESS")

Swindler ■ (1643–1673)

T he word *adventuress* may not have been coined in honor of Mary Moders, but she more than exemplified its meaning: an intelligent, beautiful, audacious woman. As a dedicated criminal, Mary also proved herself one of the greatest actresses of her era. Born on January 11, 1643, to one Moders (or Meders), a chorister of the cathedral at Canterbury, she lived in obscurity with her humble parents until early womanhood.

Little is known of Mary's youth, except that her father taught her to read, a then uncommon practice among the lowly born. Young Mary then proceeded, methodically and avariciously, to read her way through hundreds of books available in the church library. Particularly charmed by the romances of daring knights and their ladies fair, she favored such gothic stories as *Parismus and Parismenus, Don Belianis of Greece*, and especially *Amadis de Gaul*, a book portraying the character Oriana with whom Mary became obsessed. As a teenager she began thinking of herself as a princess or a highborn lady of quality, a fancy that became so entrenched within her mind that she later convinced herself she was indeed a princess. The legends *Cassandra* and *Cleopatra* were also among Mary's favorite stories, and she took on the cunning and guile of these characters, too. The girl's memory was phenomenal; she could recite whole books without error.

As a displaced intellectual, Mary felt that her marriage at an early age to an apprentice shoemaker named Stedman was leagues beneath her. She bore the young man two children but both were sickly and died in infancy. Stedman's troubles increased as Mary demanded finery and gifts he could not afford. She carried herself as a person born of the blood royal, insisting upon splendors and extravagances she felt were her birthright.

One day Mary suddenly abandoned the hapless groom and fled to Dover. There she encountered a surgeon named Day whose coffers were full. She married this man, too, and, after bleeding him of his life's savings, she prepared to leave, but was apprehended and a charge of bigamy lodged against her.

Tried at Maidstone, Mary Stedman Day, nee Moders, worked her wiles in court, presenting an eloquent defense. Since Stedman could not afford to travel to the trial—Mary was quick to point out his absence—the case was dismissed for lack of evidence. The beautiful Mary immediately departed for Europe, going first to Holland, then to the free-wheeling city of Cologne, Germany. There Mary entered a brothel, then politely called a "house of entertainment." Her exquisite beauty and haughty airs soon earned her her own suite of rooms in the bordello, in which she reigned not as a princess but as a queen. She discriminated among the many gentlemen seeking her sexual favors, selecting only those she knew to possess great wealth. One of those was an elderly lecher who had a large and wealthy estate near Liège; he showered presents upon the conniving Mary, money, jewels, even his most prized possession, a gold chain with a priceless medal given to him for exceptional services to Gustavus Adolphus, the King of Sweden, by Count Tilly.

The old man lost all reason, his passion for Mary controlling his every move. In the words of the *Newgate Calendar*, "The foolish old dotard urged his passion with all the vehemence of a young vigorous lover, pressing her to matrimony, and making her very large promises." Mary pretended disinterest. Then, putting to use her consummate skills as an actress, appeared to relent slowly under his demands that she marry him, giving the old man a lusty sense of triumph with sigh-filled phrases such as, "You are shattering my will, sir." Knowing incisively when to present the "convincer" in her sexual con game—and Mary was to prove one of the first great confidence tricksters in history—the adventuress surrendered to the old man's pleas in bed, blurting at his enfeebled climax, that "I am yours!" Her submission, the doddering suitor believed, was brought about by his sexual prowess; thus Mary had worked the old man's vanity to blend with his lust for her, convincing him that he had won her through a mythical virility.

They would be married within three days, she promised, but she would need money for the preparations, a great deal of money. The old man withdrew most of his savings and gave the gold to Mary. Hours after he left her side, she packed the money and jewelry the old man had witlessly given her and departed for Utrecht, then to Amsterdam, where she sold the old man's gold chain and medal and some of the jewelry, then to Rotterdam where she sailed for England.

Upon her arrival at Billingsgate, in March 1663, Mary inquired where she might find a res-

Mary Moders, known as "the German Princess," the first great female confidence trickster, shown here acting upon the British stage in 1663.

taurant suitable for a "lady," and was directed to the fashionable Exchange Tavern, a gathering place for rich young men of high society. Unaccompanied, Mary's shapely person immediately caught the attentions of the young swains, who made suggestive remarks about the questionable virtue of a well-dressed lady breakfasting in such a place.

It was at this moment that Mary Moders proved herself a supreme actress. Her eyes welled with great tears as her voice quivered: "Think of your sisters, gentlemen, being in a similar position. . . . You would not treat me so if you knew my story. . . . I am not a wanton and would not be here but for my father's cruelty."

Touched and ashamed, the young gentlemen apologized and, showing the politeness of their class, begged Mary to tell them the details of her plight; perhaps they could help. With the aplomb of the born confidence queen that she was, Mary haltingly wove a fantastic tale for the attentive young men, telling them she was a highborn lady of quality, a role she had rehearsed since childhood. The specifics of her tale, that she was the daughter of one Lord Henry von Holway, a prince of the German Empire, were invented on the spot by Mary's fertile imagination, aided by all the romantic novels she had put to memory long years past, the words from those books rushing back to flood her scenario with an excruciating confession. Her tyrant of a father hated the nobleman with whom she had fallen in love, and had banished her. (This part was to prove prophetic of her actual fate.)

"Certainly, any gentleman may suppose what a mortification it must be," wept Mary in her magnificent role, "to a woman born of such noble parents, and bred up in all the pomp of a court, under the care of an indulgent father, to suffer as I now do. Yet why did I say indulgent father? Alas! Was it not his cruelty that banished me, his only daughter, from his dominions, only for the desire of marrying a nobleman of the court, whom I loved to excess, without his knowledge?"

She appeared as if her sorrow were too much to bear, let alone talk about, that she was on the verge of collapse. The gentlemen, so moved by Mary's story, emptied their purses onto the table before her, and, despite her feigned efforts to refuse the gold, insisted that she, the "German princess," accept their aid. With that the myth of the abandoned German princess was firmly planted. Reluctantly, Mary accepted the generosity, and was soon residing in the best suite of rooms the inn had to offer, her expenses absorbed by the much impressed owner, Mr. Ling, whose wealthy brother-in-law, John Carleton, a man of immense wealth, was soon introduced to the German princess. Carleton was smitten at first sight and proposed marriage. Mary resisted momentarily, telling Carleton that marriages between princesses and commoners were unheard of, but she slowly succumbed to his on-the-hour arguments to be wed.

Following their marriage by only a few days was a letter anonymously sent to Carleton's father. It read—

Sir,
    I am unknown to you, but hearing that your son, Mr. John Carleton, hath married a woman of pretended fortune and high birth, I thought fit to give you a timely notice of what I know, and have heard concerning her, that she is an absolute cheat, hath married several men in our county of Kent, and then run away from them, with what they had. If it be the same woman I mean, she speaks several languages fluently, and hath high breasts, which is all from your humble servant unknown.

Once again, Mary was arrested and charged with bigamy. Her trial at the Old Bailey, like the previous one in Maidstone, was brief. She was again released for lack of evidence since neither Stedman nor Day, her other husbands, appeared to testify against her. Upon her release from Newgate, her notoriety already having swept England, Mary was offered the position of actress if she would enact upon the stage the role she made famous. (Three hundred years later, the offer would have certainly been a motion picture contract.) The playwright Holden had hurriedly written a drama based upon Mary's life.

Mary Moders became the theatrical rage, appearing in *The German Princess* to enormous crowds (and also at private performances), audaciously summing up her character and life perspective in the play's epilogue:

I've past one trial, but it is my fear
I shall receive a rigid sentence here;
You think me a bold cheat, put case 'twere so,
Which of you are not? Now you'd swear I know.
But do not lest that you deserve to be
Censured worse than you can censure me.
The world's a cheat, and we that move in it,
In our degrees, do exercise our wit;
And better 'tis to get a glorious name,
However got, than live by common fame.

The old Marshalsea Prison where the German Princess was held captive.

Her appeal in this drama reached businessman and intellectual, commoner and nobleman. Samuel Pepys, the great British diarist, became one of Mary's most devoted fans, amused and somewhat fascinated as he was by this bold creature cavorting upon the stage. In his entry of April 15, 1663, he wrote, "To the Duke's house and there saw *The German Princess* acted by the woman herself; but never was anything so well done in earnest, worse performed in jest upon the stage." Pepys saw the play again on May 29, traveling to Creed to see Mary perform at the Gate House, Westminster. On June 7, he wrote, "My Lady Batten inveighed mightily against the German Princess, and I as high in defence of her wit and spirit; and glad that she is cleared at the Sessions [court]."

Though she earned a good deal of money as an actress, Mary's ambitions were too twisted to permit her an honest career. Of the many admirers who came to her backstage after performances, Mary selected only the wealthiest beaux. These men Mary bilked of hundreds of pounds, threatening to expose their cyclone affairs with her to their wives. One elderly admirer was gutted of his entire fortune by the crafty Mary, who, after telling him he was not fit company for a princess, rifled the man's safe and trunks, stealing his savings, silver plate, gold seals, and watches. The old man at the time was so overcome with emotional distress that he drank himself into a stupor while Mary looted his mansion.

Leaving the stage, Mary cheated one man after another, sometimes employing what would later be termed "the badger game." She would entice a wealthy man to her apartment, then have an accomplice pretending to be her husband barge into the room, raging that he would kill them both. Invariably, the compromised male paid handsomely to be spared his life and raced off.

When this practice became too dangerous, Mary spent years bilking merchants of expensive goods, ordering priceless lace, silverware, and jewelry under various disguises, all being that of a lady of wealth, having these goods sent to false addresses where she would receive the goods,

St. Sepulchre's Church, close to where Mary Moders was executed.

give the delivery man a fake check, then depart, leaving the real occupants of the house, who were on vacation at the time of her scam, to face the wrath of the mulcted merchant.

As the years passed, Mary's once stunning beauty withered, and along with it the money-making ability it had brought her. To make ends meet, she was reduced to stealing silver tankards from the better inns and reselling them. Once she was caught taking a tankard from Covent Garden, and thrown, as a pretty thief would be, into a dungeon of a cell at Newgate. Mary was no longer a *cause célèbre* among the socially prominent. She had proved herself nothing more than a woman of crime, and, as such, was shunned by her former admirers. Convicted of robbery, Mary Moders was condemned to death,

but, through the intercession of an anonymous person of considerable influence, the sentence was commuted to banishment from England, then called "transportation."

Mary was put aboard a ship with common criminals, the dregs of the British jails, and sent to Jamaica. Smuggled to her, however, was a sack of gold from another old-time admirer, and, after about two years, Mary used this money to secrete herself aboard a British merchant ship, and returned to England, where once again she took up her old criminal practices.

Accidents and irony were her undoing. A man named Lancaster, who had been a jailer at the Marshalsea Prison, was asked to inspect several London boarding houses in the hopes of discovering some stolen goods. Though these goods had nothing to do with Mary Moders, Lancaster spotted the woman walking up some stairs in an expensive nightgown and, by the light of the flickering candle she held in her hand, recognized her as one of his former prisoners. "Why, you're the German Princess," he exclaimed in wonder. Knowing Mary had violated her transportation, the jailer placed her under arrest and took her to prison.

Unable at her trial to give any vindicating excuses for returning from transportation, Mary was sentenced to be executed, her violation then a hanging offense (among dozens of what we would today consider lesser offenses wholly undeserving of capital punishment). In desperation, Mary "pleaded her belly," as one historian put it, saying she was pregnant and that her unborn child could not be executed, which she knew full well to be the law. The courts appointed several midwives to inspect her and they quickly found her to be lying.

On January 2, 1673, the once bright star of the British stage, adroit confidence trickster, and highly paid harlot was driven to Tyburn in an open cart along with the hangman. It was her final performance and the thirty-year-old woman played it to the hilt. She drank a glass of gin before mounting the scaffold, turning briefly to a group of women spectators standing nearby, and saying in a clear, calm voice, "Ladies, your failings consist of falling, and mine in filching, yet if you will be so charitable as to forgive me, I will freely forgive you." Haughty to the last second, Mary Moders died with the unperturbed grace of the princess she thought herself to be, uttering no cry of remorse as the rope was placed about her neck.

She dangled for an hour, was then cut down and placed in a cheap coffin, which was buried in nearby St. Martin's Churchyard. None of the mighty men she had known in her short and spectacular lifetime attended her execution or burial. Her epitaph was chiseled onto an inexpensive stone above her grave, written by a wag whose offbeat wit would haunt her grave for eternity with the words:

The German Princess, here against her will,
Lies underneath, and yet, oh strange, lies still.

MOORE, SARA JANE

Assassin ■ (1930–)

On September 22, 1975, a forty-five-year-old divorcée, Sara Jane Moore, who was standing outside a San Francisco hotel, pulled a .38 revolver from her purse and began shooting at President Gerald Ford, her aim spoiled by a marine in the crowd of onlookers. At her trial, Mrs. Moore's oddball background came to light.

The woman had held a job as a bookkeeper a year before the attempted assassination, supporting her nine-year-old son. She suddenly left this job to work for the food-giveaway program forced by the SLA's alleged kidnapping of Patty Hearst, telling one and all that God had spoken

Would-be assassin Sara Jane Moore in prison for life. (Wide World)

directly to her, telling her to feed the needy with Hearst's goods.

Fired from this work, Mrs. Moore next went to the FBI; she informed agents that her contacts with underground radicals would make her an ideal undercover agent and informant. Strangely enough, the bureau believed her and she was put on the FBI's list of informers. Instead of informing on the terrorists, however, Mrs. Moore bought a gun and joined them, her erratic efforts culminating in her abortive attack on President Ford.

She was sent to the Federal Correctional Institution at Alderson, West Virginia, for life. In 1980, Sara Jane Moore told reporters that her assassination attempt was a "valid political tool." She went on to state that her current ambition was to devote herself to writing and speaking.

MYRTEL, HERA

Murderer ■ (1868– ?)

Everything in the life of Paul Jacques was orderly and filled with comfort. He was one of the most successful silk merchants of his day, and the fruits of his middle-aged labors had brought him a thriving business in Mexico and Europe, servants, and money in the bank. Jacques was in good health and was plagued by only a single fear, more an apprehension, really—he did not trust his wife, and had not trusted her for some time.

One evening in January 1914, Héra Myrtel Jacques had summoned the family maid, Georgette Picourla, ordering the girl to take a tureen of soup to her husband who was working in his study. Héra quickly dropped some white powder into the soup, standing between the table with the tureen of soup and the maid. Georgette, however, managed to see that extra ingredient shaken into the soup and asked what Madame Jacques was doing.

"Oh, it's just some special flavoring I know he likes, Georgette," Héra said casually.

The maid delivered the soup to Jacques, telling her employer with a cheery voice, "I hope you like the flavoring Madame put in your soup." Georgette remained a few moments in the study to see Jacques take only a taste of the soup. When the maid was gone, Jacques sat staring at the soup his wife had prepared for him. After the brew had cooled, he poured some of the soup into a glass bottle, slipped the bottle into a handbag, and left his spacious apartment at 107 rue de Sèvres, going immediately to a Paris chemist he knew well.

The chemist analyzed the contents in the glass bottle within an hour, reporting to Jacques, "This substance contains a corrosive sublimate of some kind—a lethal poison. Where did you get it, Paul?"

"It was served to me at dinner," Jacques said wryly.

"My God, you ought to sue the restaurant!"

Most any man, upon learning that his wife had attempted to poison him, would have taken some decisive action, but Paul Jacques thought of his life and his family as the essence of propriety and would endure anything this side of the grave to prevent scandal from tainting that family image. He was also a meek, retiring person, who had succumbed to his wife's total domination since the first moment he fell to her charms. Though he had been married to Héra for more than twenty years, he had often admitted to close friends that he "did not know the woman, never would understand the dark corners of her mind."

The corners of Héra Myrtel's mind, in fact, had been darkening progressively ever since her youth, and hidden in the murk was a past littered with dead men. Born on October 25, 1868, in Lyons, France, and christened Marie-Louise Victorine Grônes, the girl was sent at an early age to be educated by nuns in a nearby convent. Completing her education in her early twenties, Marie-Louise returned home to find her father's silk business floundering. She went to work for the failing firm, traveling to Mexico in 1892 at age twenty-four in an attempt to secure contracts.

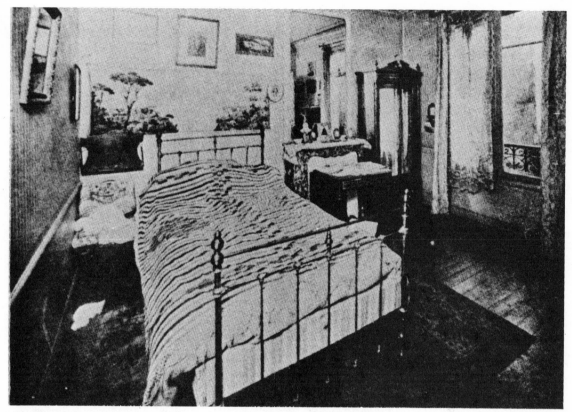

The bedroom in which popular novelist Héra Myrtel murdered her husband.

Notoriety, not business, attended Marie-Louise's life in Mexico. The dark-complected woman attracted several wealthy young Mexican businessmen. One, it was reported, killed himself over her rejection of his affections. On another occasion, the woman was found by federales in a remote hacienda with a dead man at her feet, a rich merchant with a bullet through his heart. Bandits, the woman claimed through hysterical sobbing, had arrived and killed her lover. The investigating officers were most sympathetic and admitted that, yes, bandits had been causing a lot of trouble in their country for decades; she received an apology and was escorted home.

In Mexico City, Marie-Louise met the silk merchant Paul Jacques, a man almost twice her age. Jacques instantly fell in love with her, and asked that she marry him. This suited Marie-Louise's plans, especially since Jacques was planning to return to France to settle down. The couple moved to Paris where, in 1904, a daughter, Paule, was born.

Paris at the time was overrun with foreign artists and writers. Literary and art salons blossomed on every corner. Bored with motherhood, Marie-Louise became preoccupied with the artistic community and spent most of her energy writing romantic stories and poetry. She penned a romantic novel under the nom de plume of Héra Myrtel, and, when this book met with some success, she was commissioned to write several more. With her popularity, Héra became the center of a small literary circle chiefly made up of failed writers and painters supported by rich dilettantes; she had little or no time for her husband and child, but that suited Paul Jacques who hired a nurse for his daughter and retreated into his study to conduct his business at leisure. He realized that his wife was taking on lovers to feed her bloated vanity but it mattered little to him, as long as he was left in peace. He realized she had married him for convenience and security.

Héra's many love affairs were short-lived and without any deep emotional bonds. She was not a person who could sustain affection for anyone. Soon she was longing to return to Mexico, knowing that she would be received there not as the daughter of an almost bankrupt French businessman, but as a successful novelist. When she put her desire before her milksop of a husband, Héra was startled to hear him refuse. He was quite content to stay in Paris, and that is where he meant to stay. "As my wife," he reminded her dryly, "you will stay here also with our child." Such a dictate was not only unacceptable to Héra but unthinkable. She had made up her mind to return to Mexico, and if Jacques attempted to block her ambition, well, there was only one alternative.

On the evening of March 5, 1914, the maid Georgette was summoned to the Jacques' master bedroom by Héra, who was standing over her husband's body. A bullet had been sent through his right temple. He was quite dead. "Jacques has committed suicide, poor man," Héra announced to the queasy maid. "Fetch the concierge." Georgette stumbled downstairs to get the landlady, a Madame Chambre. When the concierge arrived, Georgette next to her, the maid was surprised to see the body of her employer propped up in a chair, a pistol on the floor next to him. Blood drenched Jacques' face and clothes. "Madame Chambre," announced Héra, "my husband is dead, and he was quite alone. Georgette found him dead when she took him his chocolate." At this the maid almost swooned but kept silent.

When the concierge raced for the gendarmes, Héra put her arm around the stunned maid and said in a soothing voice, "When the police come tell them you found him lying shot in the chair when you brought his chocolate. I don't think I could stand being questioned."

Georgette did as she was asked, thinking Héra the victim of a great tragedy. The maid's vague statements to the arriving police cast no suspicion on Madame Jacques. Jacques' death was ruled a suicide. (Years later Georgette's testimony regarding the doctored soup and Héra's odd requests about the body's discovery would point to a more sinister motive for Jacques' end.)

Billing herself a "mystical novelist," Héra embarked for Mexico with her daughter, Paule, whom she introduced to literary types in Mexico City as Paulette. Madame Jacques soon liquidated her husband's considerable estate in Mexico and with these funds set up a salon peopled only by those who showered flattery upon Héra Myrtel. Through a rich dilettante, a Madame Laforce, Héra met a mysterious handsome man named Charles Bessarabo (a Rumanian of dubious interests, probably criminal, who had changed his name from Weissmann). In no time, Bessarabo proposed marriage to the aging Héra. She promptly accepted, and the couple made plans to return to Paris in 1916.

Bessarabo, a ne'er-do-well and opportunist, confided to a friend before his marriage to Héra, "Money, fame, and beauty—I shall have them all at the same time."

Replied the friend, "You couldn't give me enough money to make me marry that woman. I shiver at the thought of it. I've read about what happened to her husband. I'm sure that what happened to him will befall any other man she weds."

"Suicide?" Bessarabo laughed. "I know myself too well to do that."

The couple sailed for France, arriving in Paris and moving into luxurious quarters at 3 place La Bruyère, where Héra set up a new literary salon, inviting any males into private conference who pretended to be serious writers but who were, for the most part, lounge lizards and draft dodgers attempting to escape service on the Western Front, for, by then, France and the rest of the world was at war with the Axis Powers. As she had with Jacques, Héra cuckolded Bessarabo with increasing regularity, expressing "the single desire of satisfying her taste for luxury and pleasure," according to Alfred Morain, head of the Paris police. "Her husband

Police photos of Héra Myrtel.

became to her merely a source of money, and she made him aware of this fact.... Probably he shunned the company of his wife, who only came to him with demands for money, created violent scenes, and threatened to kill him."

Héra's nymphomania astounded Bessarabo, who complained to a friend, "I don't understand her vitality and I don't know how she can keep going on the way she does. She never tires." The husband never seemed to tire of being humiliated. When Héra's so-called literary guests, all males, arrived to dine with the "high priestess of a feminist cult," as one admirer called her, Bessarabo was ordered to eat his supper alone in his room which he dutifully did. If Bessarabo dared to challenge her actions, Héra would scream, "I'll have your skin!"

One night in 1918 Bessarabo awoke to feel hands about his neck, cutting off his wind and choking him to death. He stared up to see his wife kneeling on his chest, her face contorted, wild-eyed, frothing at twisted lips as she leaned down to strangle him. With a superhuman effort, Bessarabo threw the woman to the floor. She lay motionless in a heap, weeping and saying, "I don't know what came over me."

Inexplicably, and like Jacques before him, Bessarabo continued to live with this hellion, even though her outbursts became increasingly threatening. On July 8, 1920, when Bessarabo arrived home for dinner, he inadvertently walked into his wife's salon to find her scantily clad, applying perfume to her sagging body, undoubtedly preparing herself for another lover, he assumed.

Héra grabbed an automatic pistol from a nearby table and pointed it at her husband, yelling, "Get out—or I'll lay you out!" Bessarabo dove for the floor just as a bullet whistled over his head. Héra then threw down the pistol, and, without looking at her trembling spouse, went to a table set for dinner and began to eat, unperturbed and obviously very hungry.

Bessarabo's nerves were beginning to show strain. To his friend, a man named Berlioz, he remarked, "I can only survive provided she does not deal with me as she has the other [meaning Jacques]."

The much harassed husband finally told Héra he could no longer tolerate the threats against his life and that he intended to leave her.

"You walk out on me and I'll expose you," Héra replied, undoubtedly referring to Bessarabo's shady business dealings. The cuckolded husband became so fearful that he locked himself in his room for three days, having his meals catered. Next, Bessarabo hired a chauffeur, a man named Croix, to drive him everywhere. But despite all his precautions Bessarabo could not escape the inevitable.

Croix called for his employer on the morning of July 31 but found him gone. Héra and her daughter arrived at their home at 3 place La Bruyère at 11:00 A.M. that day. (The chauffeur later stated that Madame Bessarabo appeared as if she were in a daze; for years Héra had indulged in drugs, becoming particularly fond of hashish, which may have explained her euphoric state that morning.)

"Bessarabo had to go away on business," Héra told Croix.

"But he specifically asked that I pick him up at nine this morning."

Héra gave the chauffeur her icy stare. "I told you—he's off on a business trip. He'll return on August 2. You're dismissed."

Croix brooded over these strange happenings until August 2, 1920, and, when Bessarabo failed to get in touch with him, the chauffeur went to the police, relating the curious disappearance of his client. Knowing some of Bessarabo's marital problems, Croix detailed his employer's apprehensions to the inspectors. Héra Myrtel Bessarabo was brought in for questioning.

The story the inventive Héra gave out left the officers astonished. Bessarabo, Héra insisted, had returned home on Friday, July 30, at midnight, and got up at seven the next morning, telling her that he was going away on business and that she was to pack several trunks for him and deliver these to the Gare du Nord for train shipment. Bessarabo failed to show up at the train station, Héra said, so she went off with a female friend for lunch, then returned to the Gare du Nord where Bessarabo met her.

"He took the large trunk, then disappeared into the train terminal. I returned home. An hour later a cabman arrived with this trunk with instructions from my husband that it should be sent to Nancy." Obedient in a way she had never been to her husband's wishes, Héra declared that she immediately took the trunk to the Gare de l'Est and shipped it off to the city of Nancy. "I have not seen Bessarabo since," Héra shrugged. "He must have gone off to Switzerland with his mistress." Héra could not name the mistress but was sure her husband had one. "Every successful businessman in Paris has a mistress," she added, "is that not true?"

Inspectors went to Nancy, and quickly located the trunk. The contents made the hard-boiled cops nauseated. From their official report: "The trunk was opened and found to contain the body of a man, bound with a yellow strap and naked save for a red flannel waistcoat. The face was bleeding and swollen, it seemed to have been hammered, and there was a wound behind the head from which the brains were escaping."

Confronted with this evidence, Héra promptly confessed to shooting Bessarabo, then trussing up his body and shipping it off in the trunk. She stated that her gruesome deed was a *crime passionel*, that her husband had accidentally dropped a letter from his mistress, his typist, Mlle. Nollet, which she read and became so infuriated that, blind to reason, she picked up a revolver and shot him to death. The daughter, Paule, had been awakened by the shot, Madame Bessarabo said, and rushed into the bedroom, crying, "Mother—what have you done?" Héra had triumphantly answered, "It's only justice!"

Both Héra and Paule were placed on trial for murder on February 15, 1921. The trial was almost as sensational as that of Landru, the notorious Bluebeard. In fact, Landru's attorney, Moro-Giafferi, also argued Héra Myrtel's doubtful case, while Paule was represented by Raymond Hubert, another famous criminal lawyer.

During the proceedings, Paule shocked the court by leaping to her feet and screaming, "I must and will tell the truth." She then placed the slaying at her mother's feet. Héra Myrtel continually interrupted her daughter's gushing words by shouting, "Shut up! Shut up!" But Paule would not be stopped. Her mother's motivation, the daughter insisted, had nothing to do with any mythical mistress. When she had rushed into the murder room at 8:00 A.M., she had found Héra, revolver in hand, calmly stating, "What could I do, my child—it was either he or I." Moreover, Héra had ordered her daughter to drag a trunk from the attic and place the body of her stepfather into it. Héra had then bound up the trunk and taken it to the train station where she had ordered Paule to "ship it anywhere so that it won't be found for a long time."

Following Paule's indicting testimony, Héra changed her story, giving several versions, hinting that the unrecognizable body in the trunk was not that of Bessarabo. The jury believed none of Héra's forced fancies and found her guilty of murder but with "mitigating circumstances," the jury members leaning toward Héra's crime-of-passion claim. Madame Bessarabo was sentenced to twenty years in prison; Paule, who was later universally scorned for "shopping" her mother, was ordered set free.

Héra rose in court to solemnly state, "I wish to thank the jury for acquitting Paule. But I swear to you that I also am not guilty. Bessarabo is alive and in America. The man in the trunk was his enemy."

Bessarabo was indeed the man in the trunk, according to the Paris police and the jury that tried the novelist-turned-murderess. Héra Myrtel gave more mysterious stories about that body, all different, for years, until she died in prison, taking her self-concocted murder enigma with her to the grave. Paule became a tragic street waif in Paris, then disappeared.

NATHANIEL, CATHY

Murderer ■ (1946–   )

A thirty-year-old prostitute, Cathy Nathaniel, along with her co-worker, Bernice Albright, picked up Chicago lawyer Steven Ticho in a bar on May 3, 1979, returning with Ticho to his apartment on the sixty-fifth floor of the John Hancock Building. Midway during the assignation, Albright left Ticho's apartment and returned to her own place at 929 N. Hudson, an apartment she shared with Nathaniel.

Cathy left later, but only after shooting her client in the back of the head. She returned home, retrieved Albright, and went back to the Ticho apartment. Both women looted the place while Ticho's body lay sprawled in blood before them. Cathy went on a shopping spree with Ticho's credit cards the following day and was arrested.

Convicted of murder on October 25, 1979, Cathy Nathaniel was sentenced to thirty-five years in prison by Criminal Court Judge James M. Bailey, a term considered by many to be flagrantly lenient. Judge Bailey's final remarks to the stoic Cathy following the sentence consisted of a barrage of personal indictment, concluding with, "I think you have no remorse. I question whether you have any morals at all."

NEEDHAM, MOTHER

Procuress ■ (? –1731)

A toothless, horrible harridan who provided young girls for London's lowest whorehouses, Mother Needham preyed upon farm girls coming to the city seeking employment, drugging the girls and hauling them to bordellos. This early-day white slaver, who had been watched for more than ten years by the police, was finally caught in the act of smuggling a girl into a whorehouse in April 1731.

Mother Needham was quickly convicted and placed in a pillory at the corner of St. James Street and Park Place near the West End. Constables tried to ward off oath-shouting mobs, but for two days the old woman was constantly pelted with rocks and stones, finally dying of her injuries.

NEWELL, MRS. SUSAN

Murderer ■ (1893–1923)

The Newells argued and battled constantly in their one-room Glasgow apartment. In June 1923, John Newell complained to police that his thirty-year-old wife had attacked him. The following day, Mrs. Newell was seen pushing a handcart down the streets of Coatbridge, a Glasgow suburb. Piled on the cart was a bundle, and sitting on top of the bundle was Mrs. Newell's eight-year-old daughter, Janet.

A kindly truck driver, seeing the woman struggling with the cart, offered Mrs. Newell a lift. She accepted with a smile and she, her daughter, the bundle, and cart were put aboard the truck. The driver let his passengers off at the corner of Duke Street in Glasgow. As they were removing the bundle, a woman leaning out of a nearby window saw a human foot protruding from the end of the bundle, a human head from the other.

A policeman was called. The constable followed, seeing Mrs. Newell dump the bundle at the head of a boardinghouse stairwell. She then went to a six-foot wall, climbed it and let herself down, right into the arms of the waiting constable.

Police took the woman, her child, and the bundle to the police station. Inside the bundle, trussed like a chicken, was the body of newsboy John Johnstone, thirteen. The boy had last been seen alive when entering Susan Newell's apartment to collect for his papers that morning.

Janet Newell innocently told the court at Mrs. Newell's trial that her mother had strangled the boy in a fit of rage—apparently she did not want to pay the few pennies he asked for his newspapers. The little girl, at her mother's direction, had helped Mrs. Newell stuff the body into the sack. Defense attorneys tried to prove their client insane but failed. She was convicted and sentenced to death.

Angry and defiant to the last, Susan Newell was hanged at Duke Street Prison in Glasgow on October 10, 1923. She was the first woman to be hanged in Scotland in fifty years. Upon the scaffold Mrs. Newell proved truculent, telling the mild-mannered executioner, John Ellis, that she absolutely refused to wear the traditional white cap over her head. She went through the trap glaring, her face turning purple, her tongue protruding as she dangled.

Judiciary Building in Glasgow where the brutal child killer, Susan Newell, heard her death sentence.

NEWMAN, JULIA ST. CLAIR

Swindler ■ (1818– ?)

After spending her childhood in the West Indies, Julia Newman, who was of Creole ancestry, was sent to France where she was educated. She then moved to London and made her living chiefly by fraud and theft. Julia was repeatedly charged with renting rooms then selling off her landlady's household goods. On March 11, 1837, she was sent to Millbank Prison for swindling. She was nineteen.

Julia Newman, though an accomplished singer and musician, and a young woman of impeccable manners when in a peaceful mood, proved herself to be one of the most incorrigible inmates in the annals of British penology. She tore apart the books she was given to read, attacked her keepers, incited other prisoners to rebel, hurled her food at warders. She attempted suicide several times. Then she began to starve herself to death and had to be force-fed.

She was considered insane, put into a straitjacket, and kept in solitary confinement. Julia chewed herself out of the jacket. In despair, British authorities finally released the woman, banishing her from England. Julia was put aboard the convict ship *Nautilus*, and sent to Australia where she disappeared.

NICHOLSON, MARGARET

Assassin ■ (1727–1826)

On August 2, 1786, King George III of England alighted from his coach at the gates of St. James' Palace. Fifty-nine-year-old Margaret Nicholson came forward asking if she could present a petition. The king paused a moment to listen to the unkempt wom-an. Margaret quickly produced a knife and plunged it downward at the king but her aim was faulty and she merely tore the sleeve of his coat. She tried to strike again but guards pinioned her arms.

Wild and incoherent, Margaret was dragged screaming before a court where she stated that the Crown was rightfully hers and she had merely been reclaiming her proper title. "If my legal rights are not granted," she threatened the court with a wagging finger, "England will be bathed in blood for a thousand generations!"

"What exactly are your rights?" asked one of the judges.

"That is a mystery," Margaret hissed with a smile. She then nodded to the two judges, Lord Mansfield and Lord Loughborough, and scolded: "You boys should not treat your mother this way."

"What?" exclaimed Mansfield.

"You're both my sons, you know that?"

Margaret was ordered from the court. She was taken to Bethlehem Hospital, where she was judged hopelessly insane. Margaret Nicholson was kept behind bars for forty-two years, dying just short of her hundredth birthday on May 28, 1826, pathetically begging attendants to recognize her queenly station in life: "Won't someone bring my crown to me now?"

NOZIERE, VIOLETTE

Murderer ■ (1915– ?)

A spoiled and only child, Violette Nozière received the best of educations her railway engineer father could provide. Nozière and his wife would tolerate the most abominable behavior in their daughter. If she chose to hang about Parisian cafes and nightclubs instead of applying herself to her studies, such conduct was condoned. If she chose to squander her allowance on frivolities, that, too, was permitted.

The nineteen-year-old also liked to spend money on men, impressing them with the false claims that her father was a director of a railroad, her grandmother owned a château, and that she was an heiress. Not having enough money to convincingly enact such a preposterous role, Violette became a prostitute, spending her nocturnal earnings the next day on gullible male students hanging about the seedier cafes of the Latin Quarter. It was here, on the boulevard Saint-Michel that Violette met eighteen-year-old Jean Dabin, a fellow student. She fell in love with him, promising him an expensive sportscar and a lavish holiday abroad. More than 180,000 francs would soon be hers, Violette informed Dabin. What she neglected to say was that the amount was her father's entire savings and she would have to murder the old man to get it.

The prospect of parricide had not bothered Violette. In the spring of 1934 she had actually practiced poisoning both her parents, giving her father six ground-up tablets of Veronal, and three to her mother in their morning coffee. She had told them she was giving them a "nice, new tonic." As they were pill addicts, they delighted in Violette's new "patent medicine." The drugged coffee had only made the Nozières drowsy, but in this coma-like state they were unaware that their much loved daughter had set fire to the living room drapes and then raced into the hallway to scream for help to the other tenants, crying, "Fire!" When a neighbor responded, Violette hurriedly told him, "I think the electricity must have been short-circuited."

The fire was put out and the Nozières were revived. Violette's father was not to survive his daughter's next "experiment." On August 23, 1934, the girl dosed Nozière's coffee with twenty Veronal tablets; she gave her mother six. Then she went to sleep in the chair next to the couch upon which her parents slumbered toward death. Checking the pulses of her parents about 2:00 A.M., and finding no hint of life, Violette again went racing into the hallway, shouting, "Gas! I think the pipe has burst." (She had been careful to turn on the gas in the stove.) Before neighbors responded, Violette secreted the 1,000 francs she had taken from the corset of her unconscious mother.

The plan was not a complete success. Madame Nozière survived, but her husband, the trusting train engineer, was dead by the time a physician arrived. The two "accidents" had caused suspicion on the part of police, but Violette, sensing her own danger, fled to spend a week making the rounds of her favorite cafes and, in particular, waltzing at the Bal Tabarin.

Her face, by then, adorned the front pages of every newspaper in Paris. One of the men Violette picked up recognized her and turned her over to gendarmes. When she was charged with murdering her father, Violette sneered and said, "I'm glad I killed him—he was a satyr!"

Her trial was brief. She was quickly convicted and, upon hearing the jury's verdict, Violette pounded her fists in the dock and yelled, "Curse my father! Curse my mother!"

She was sentenced with great pomp, her end decreed to be a ceremonious return to France's medieval type of execution. Said the judge in grave tones, "She is to have her head cut off in death upon a public place in Paris. She shall be taken there barefooted, clad only in her chemise and with her head covered by a black veil. Before the execution shall be done, let the clerk in a clear voice read aloud this Judgment."

Guards began to lead Violette to prison. Suddenly, she whirled about and shouted to a gendarme, "Fetch my handbag with my powder, rouge, money! I must have dropped it in the prisoner's box!"

Violette's nonchalance reflected the attitude of a higher court which commuted her sentence to life imprisonment.

OGILVIE, CATHERINE

Murderer ■ (1746–　?　)

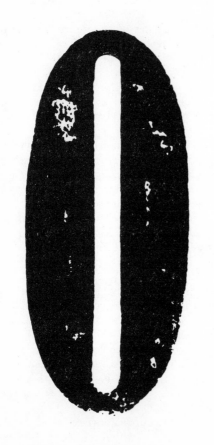

The daughter of Sir Thomas Nairn of Dusinan, Scotland, Catherine was considered a prize matrimonial catch. She was a beautiful and radiant young woman of great charm and intellect. She also proved, only three weeks after her marriage to wealthy Thomas Ogilvie on January 31, 1765, to be deceitful, faithless, and lethal.

Soon after the Ogilvie nuptials, Thomas's younger brother, Patrick, an army lieutenant, returned from the East Indies. The handsome young man was soon seen by servants and friends to be at Catherine's side most hours of the day. They kissed and petted in public as they strolled the vast Ogilvie estate at East Miln. The couple even openly slept together, not even bothering to close Catherine's bedchamber door.

Thomas Ogilvie was an amazingly cooperative cuckold. He was totally aware of the affair raging between Catherine and his brother under his own roof but did nothing. When his brother departed, Ogilvie made arrangements for Patrick to take over the greater part of his estates, *plus* his wife, Catherine, writing to his brother, "My wife cannot be happy without you."

It was all the more incredible that Ogilvie's understanding and generosity was repaid by murder. (Apparently Patrick was not satisfied with most of the estates but intended to have all the Ogilvie property, which would only come to him when his older brother died.)

Catherine wrote Patrick, asking him to send her some white arsenic. The brother sent the poison in a package marked "salt." The arrival of this package alerted one Anne Clarke, a relative staying with Ogilvie, who suspected that her kinsman was marked for death. She warned Ogilvie not to take any food or drink offered by his pretty wife. The trusting Thomas, however, accepted a pot of tea his wife served him and promptly died, writhing in agony.

Anne Clarke called authorities and arsenic

was found in Catherine's rooms, along with passionate letters between her and Patrick Ogilvie. The brother was arrested and tried for murder with his lover. Both were found guilty, Ogilvie hanged at Grass Market in Edinburgh on November 13, 1768. Catherine, also condemned, cheated the hangman for some months until she delivered Patrick's child. Her execution was then to take place, but a servant of the Nairn family, an ancient butler who had always been close to the woman, smuggled an officer's uniform to his mistress, along with keys to her cell, and she escaped to London.

With her faithful servant, Catherine Nairn Ogilvie managed to board a packet boat bound for Calais. She was never seen again.

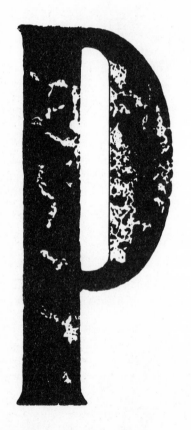

PARKER, BONNIE

Bandit ■ (1911–1934)

Much has been written and even sung about this ninety-pound, yellow-haired Texas vixen, most of it sentimental slop that lionizes one of the most psychopathic bandits to terrorize the American Southwest. Born in Rowena, Texas, Bonnie Parker lived a dirt-poor existence until meeting Clyde Barrow in a Dallas cafe where she was working as a waitress in January 1930. At the time she was still married to an outlaw named Ray Thornton, who was serving a ninety-nine-year term for murder.

Marriage had never hindered Bonnie in the past; long before Thornton was imprisoned she had carried on several affairs at once, and for money. Barrow, whose background and upbringing were as deficient as her own, offered Bonnie excitement. They immediately embarked upon a series of petty holdups, robbing grocery stores and tin-can banks. In March 1930 police captured Barrow and sent him to Eastham Prison from which he was paroled on February 2, 1932.

Bonnie had waited for him, but not patiently; she had had many lovers during her hiatus as an armed robber. Joining Bonnie and Clyde at this time were Buck Barrow and his wife, Blanche. These country bumpkins then unleashed a crime wave through the Midwest and Southwest, their largest bank robbery netting them $1,500. Buck Barrow was killed in an ambush by a large posse at Dexter, Iowa, on July 24, 1933, and Blanche Barrow was captured. From that moment Bonnie and Clyde had less than a year to live.

The couple went on robbing and killing (credited with no fewer than fifteen deaths,

Bandit Bonnie Parker "getting the drop" on her murderous boyfriend, Clyde Barrow, while the two were being hunted in five states. The photo was taken by Buck Barrow, Clyde's brother; the entire Barrow gang was Kodak crazy.

mostly police officers). They lived for the sheer joy of taunting the law, both resigned to the fact that they would, in turn, be shot to death by officers. To that end, Bonnie wrote long-winded, maudlin verse. One bit of doggerel called "Suicide Sal," found after the gang escaped a Joplin, Missouri, hideout under a hail of bullets, was widely published by newspapers and gave the murderous pair an unjustified image of persecuted down-and-out farm folks striking back at a cruel society.

Nothing could be further from the truth. They loved killing and robbing and had no scruples whatsoever. This was reflected in their personal life. Though together, they shared partners, mostly male, who worked with them on and off. They indulged in a mania to take snapshots, posing menacingly while loaded down with guns. Both were neurotic about weapons and thrilled to possess and fire them. To obtain any high-powered automatic weapons meant ecstasy for the couple.

"Blackie" Audett, Kansas City gangster, told the author of meeting Bonnie and Clyde in the home of Herb Farmer, who supplied many of the outlaw gangs of the early 1930s with rapid-fire weapons. He had just sold Clyde Barrow two submachine guns and a Browning automatic rifle, perhaps the most deadly weapon ever used in that gangster-ridden era.

"They sat in Herb's living room," said Blackie, "like a couple of kids playing with those guns, running their hands over them, inserting clips and laughing. I thought they were crazy. Bonnie held the Browning and rubbed her legs against it like she was having sex. Maybe they were on the dope, I think. I didn't want to say too much to them. They killed a lot of people."

The killing stopped at Gibsland, Louisiana, on May 23, 1934, when an enormous posse, hidden in trees and shrubbery alongside the road ambushed the car in which Bonnie and Clyde were riding. Texas Ranger Frank Hamer and two dozen others opened up on the Ford V-8, pumping almost two hundred bullets into it. When the smoke cleared, they found the pair shot to pieces. Clyde was shoeless; he had been driving in his socks. There was a piece of sandwich in Bonnie's gaping mouth.

The back seat and trunk was an arsenal containing a shotgun, a revolver, eleven pistols, three Browning automatic rifles, and two thousand rounds of ammunition. On the stock of Clyde's shotgun were eleven notches. There was a pistol in Bonnie's hand, her favorite, and there were notches, too, on the grip, three of them.

PARKER, PAULINE YVONNE

Murderer ■ (1938–   )

A resident of Canterbury, New Zealand, Pauline Parker's best friend was Juliet Hulme. So close were these two teenage girls that their relationship became noticeably lesbian, a liaison their parents desperately sought to prevent. When the Hulmes decided to move to South Africa, Pauline announced her intentions to go with the family. Mrs. Honora Mary Parker refused to give her permission.

Wrote Pauline in her diary, "Why could not mother die? Dozens of people, thousands of people, are dying every day. So why not mother, and father too?" A later entry said, "We discussed our plans for murdering mother and made them a little clearer. I want it to appear either a natural or an accidental death."

The death of Mrs. Parker was anything but natural or accidental, police easily determined on June 22, 1954, after the girls raced into a tea shop to shout hysterically that Mrs. Parker had died after accidentally striking her head on pavement in a nearby park.

Police found the woman dead along a path, forty-five separate wounds on her head. In attempting to explain the dozens of lacerations, Pauline insisted that the additional wounds were made when the girls tried to drag her mother by the legs, ostensibly taking her for help, and how her head "kept bumping and banging."

Investigators would not buy the story. Detectives grilled Pauline for hours, one finally asking, "Who assaulted your mother?"

Teenage killers Pauline Parker (right) and Juliet Hulme of New Zealand.

"I did."

"Why?"

"I won't answer that question."

Juliet also confessed to the murder, telling police that "after the first blow was struck I knew it would be necessary to kill her." The weapon, a stocking with a brick inside, was found next to the corpse. Pauline's diary was found and further damned the murderous pair. Besides the entries discussing her earlier thoughts of murder, the sixteen-year-old had written, "We decided to use a brick in a stocking rather than a handbag."

Both girls at their trial in Christchurch appeared defiant and displayed no remorse. Because of their age, they were given indefinite sentences. Both were released in 1958.

PEARCEY, MARY ELEANOR

Murderer ■ (1866–1890)

The twenty-four-year-old Mrs. Mary Pearcey was a much kept woman. A resident of Kentish Town in North London, she was supported by Charles Creighton, but her one true love was a furniture mover, Frank Hogg, who had aspired to a better station in life. (Hogg was proudest of the fact that he was able to hand out printed business cards.) Hogg was unhappy with his wife, Phoebe, having married her only when she had accidentally become pregnant. Phoebe, on the other hand, felt jeopardized by Mrs. Pearcey, a regular visitor to her home.

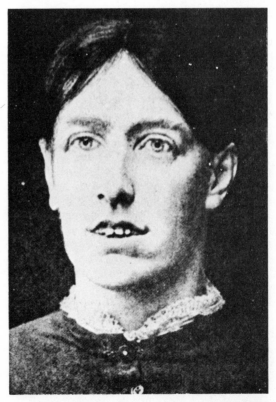

Mrs. Mary Pearcey, who used a baby carriage to dispose of her victims.

Neighbors saw Mrs. Hogg leave her home on October 24, 1890, pushing a perambulator which carried her eighteen-month-old daughter; it was the last anyone ever saw of Mrs. Phoebe Hogg. In the evening of that day Mrs. Pearcey was seen pushing the same baby carriage, but its burden was much heavier; not discernible in the dusk were the bodies of both Mrs. Hogg and her child.

Clara Hogg, sister to Mrs. Pearcey's lover, called on Mary late that night. Her sister-in-law had been found, her throat slit from ear to ear, on Crossfield Road, Hampstead. Would she accompany Clara to the mortuary to identify the body? Mrs. Pearcey nodded agreement. At the mortuary, Mary Pearcey became hysterical when looking down at her victim. She departed with a shriek. In the shadows stood a detective from Scotland Yard who took more than curious note of Mrs. Pearcey's strange conduct.

In the morning Phoebe's child was found dead, suffocated, a mile from where her mother was found, lying near Finchley Road in a garbage dump. The perambulator with bloodstained cushions was found a mile away from the body of the child.

Police went directly to Mrs. Pearcey's home to interview her. As one detective tried to question the woman, other officers searched the premises. Mary Pearcey did not object, but casually sat down at a piano and began to play furiously, singing loudly enough for half the neighborhood to hear. Officers found broken glass and furniture and bloodstains everywhere, particularly in the kitchen, where they also found two bloody knives and a chopper.

"How do you explain all the bloodstains, madam?" a detective asked Mary Pearcey. "What have you been doing?"

Mrs. Pearcey blithely looked up but did not cease to bang away at the piano, singing back her answer: "Killing mice, killing mice, killing mice!" (This conduct, prosecutors later claimed, was planned by the killer to establish her claim to insanity should such a defense be necessary.)

A police matron was brought in, and Mrs. Pearcey was searched; all her undergarments were soaked with blood. She was arrested and jailed.

The pieces of the crime came together quickly. Mrs. Pearcey had lured Mrs. Hogg and her child to her home and, in a jealous rage, had hacked the mother to death. (Neighbors later testified that they had heard screams coming from Mrs. Pearcey's home on the night of the murder. When they investigated, they found the curtains drawn over the windows. Mrs. Pearcey told the neighbors that the wailing had been her own. She was deep in grief over the death of her brother. This lie was accepted.) She next put the child in the perambulator and dumped the mother's body on top. The child apparently had received only superficial wounds and had actually been suffocated by the weight of her own mother's corpse. Mrs. Pearcey had then gone for a stroll, dumping the mother, child, and perambulator at one-mile intervals.

There had been no struggle during the murder, police determined. Mrs. Hogg had been knocked unconscious with three powerful blows to her skull; her throat had been cut later. Confronted with the charges, Mrs. Pearcey denied any guilt. She clung to her stand of innocence all the way to the scaffold. At her brief trial, Mrs. Pearcey's lawyers attempted to prove her insane, but the M'Naghten rules did not apply in that Mrs. Pearcey had no delusions, according to experts examining her.

In prison, awaiting her execution, the woman pined for Frank Hogg who had conspicuously kept silent during her trial. The discarded mistress begged Hogg to visit her but he refused. Mrs. Pearcey even arranged to have a visitor's pass sent to him but still he declined to see her. Mrs. Pearcey, during her last day on earth, wrote to her solicitor, stating that she still loved the man but added bitterly, "He might have made death easier for me!"

Standing with a rope around her neck on the morning of December 23, 1890, Mrs. Mary Pearcey's last words were cold and deliberate. She turned to the hangman and said in a calm clear voice, "The sentence is just, but the evidence was false."

PECK, ELLEN

Swindler ■ (1829–1915)

Known as the "Queen of Confidence Women," Ellen Peck, born Nellie Crosby in Woodville, New Hampshire, began her criminal career at age fifty-one, leaving her family and moving to New York City, where she lured into her clutches B. T. Babbit, an ancient soap millionaire. Ellen became the gullible man's mistress and soon absconded with $10,000 in negotiable bonds, which she sold, banking the proceeds. Further, when Babbit complained of misplacing the bonds, Ellen hired herself out to her victim as a detective. She would uncover the bonds, she vowed. Such an investigation, however, would be costly. Babbit gave Ellen $5,000 to cover her expenditures in tracking down the culprit. Mrs. Peck then vanished.

Babbit, incensed, put real detectives on her trail, and she was finally tracked down four years later. She was given a four-year sentence in 1884 for fraud. She resumed her swindling career immediately upon her release, conning a Dr. Jason Marks out of $20,000 in a matrimonial scheme. The bride departed before the nuptials. She went on to swindle a large but undisclosed sum from robber-baron Jay Gould. Police caught up with Ellen, and she was jailed for the Dr. Marks swindle.

In 1894, once more at large, Ellen impersonated the wife of Admiral Johann Carll Hansen of the Danish Navy and, as such, took out loans from banks of more than $50,000. This

America's most durable con woman, Ellen Peck, who was "compromising" gentlemen when in her eighties; her career spanned forty years.

scam was quickly followed by another caper when Ellen went to work for a Brooklyn physician, Dr. Christopher Lott, a man in his eighties, who had apparently not lost any of his sex drive. Ellen milked him of $10,000, but in the process provided the doctor with so much sexual entertainment that he was a physical wreck when she finally left him. (Dr. Lott became so debilitated that he had to hire a nurse to look after him; Ellen, before departing, learned that the nurse had $4,000 and, "forming an unnatural liaison with the nurse," managed to bilk the woman out of her savings.)

This amazing woman continued the practice of con until 1913, when she was arrested after bilking a Latin-American businessman. She had inveigled the man into her cabin while bound for Vera Cruz on a luxury liner, and for her promise not to inform the man's wife of their sexual encounter, was given the title to several coffee plantations. At the time, Ellen Peck was eighty-four years old, probably the most well-preserved lady confidence artist in history. She died two years later with more than a million dollars secreted away in bank accounts across America.

Mrs. Louise Peete, whose compulsion was to bury bodies.

PEETE, LOUISE

Murderer ■ (1883–1947)

Born Lofie Louise Preslar in Louisiana, Louise married several times before 1910, deserting each of her husbands (a few of whom committed suicide) and finally drifting into prostitution, specializing in blackmail from Texas to Boston. She then married Richard C. Peete, a Denver salesman, in 1915, and had a child the following year.

In 1920 Louise, abandoning Peete, took the position of housekeeper-lover to Los Angeles millionaire Jacob Charles Denton. When Denton refused to marry her, Louise promptly arranged for his death. On May 30, 1920, Denton was de-

clared missing; Louise, who went on living in Denton's twenty-room mansion, giving expensive parties, later put through claims for the missing man's millions. Suspicious police found Denton's body buried in the basement of his mansion. By then Louise had rented his house and returned to Denver.

Extradited from Colorado, Louise was tried and convicted of murdering the millionaire and was sent to prison for life, serving eighteen years, during which time her husband, Peete, killed himself. Upon her release, Louise was paroled to Mrs. Margaret Logan and her husband, Arthur, and went to live with them. In 1944 Mrs. Logan disappeared and elderly Arthur Logan was placed in an asylum by Mrs. Peete, who took over the Logan home in Pacific Palisades, California.

Parole officers noted something strange in the reports they received from Mrs. Logan; her signature, they quickly determined, was a forgery, in fact it was that of Louise Peete. Police came to the Logan home a few days before Christmas 1944 and dug up Mrs. Logan's body, which was buried in the garden. Louise said she was innocent, that Arthur Logan had "gone nuts one day and beat his wife to death." Humanely, she had buried the body and committed the old man. When a bullet wound was found in the skull of Mrs. Logan's corpse, Louise was charged with murder.

She was again convicted and sent to Tehachapi, then, in 1947, to San Quentin to be executed on April 11, the second woman in California history to go to the gas chamber. She insisted upon her innocence to the end.

PEROVSKAYA, SOFYA

Assassin ■ (1855–1881)

Blonde, slim Sofya Perovskaya, a leader of Russia's revolutionary sect called "The People's Will," masterminded the bombing attack on Czar Alexander II, which took place in St. Petersburg on Sunday, March 1, 1881.

Several men were directed by Perovskaya to stand along the route the czar's sleigh-carriage took on the Nevsky Prospect. Two bombs were thrown, the first missing Alexander and killing a newsboy and a Cossack guard. When Alexander began to change carriages, he paused to examine the slain, and another bomb was thrown directly at his feet, going off and mortally wounding him. He was taken to the Winter Palace where he died within hours.

Nikolai Rysakov, a member of the revolutionary group, informed on other members and six conspirators, headed by Sofya Perovskaya, who were quickly placed on trial and convicted. All were condemned, but one; Gesya Helfman was given life imprisment because she was pregnant.

Perovskaya and the others, including the informer Rysakov, were taken to Semenovsky Square on April 3, 1881. All were compelled to wear signs reading "Regicide." They were hanged before a silent throng of more than a hundred thousand people.

PFEIFFER, ANNA URSULA

Thief ■ (1813–1863)

One of the most jailed thieves in nineteenth century Germany, Anna Pfeiffer was a resident of Nuremberg. From an early age, she supported herself solely through theft, from pickpocketing to house burglary, earning for herself the dubious distinction of being imprisoned forty-one times from 1838 until her death in 1863.

PHILLIPS, CLARA

Murderer ■ (1899– ?)

Discovering that her husband, Armour Phillips, a wealthy Los Angeles oil-stock salesman, was having an affair with Mrs. Alberta Meadows, a beautiful twenty-two-year-old widow, Mrs. Phillips opted for murder on July 6, 1922. She and a friend, Peggy Caffee, got drunk that afternoon, then intercepted Mrs. Meadows as she was coming out of a department store. Clara offered her rival a lift, which was accepted.

The women drove along a lonely road, Clara finally confronting Mrs. Meadows. A fight ensued. Mrs. Meadows, after having been knocked from the car by Clara, ran down the road, Mrs.

Clara Phillips, California's "Tiger Woman," shown at the time of her release from Tehachapi in 1935.

Phillips after her, taking a hammer from her purse. Mrs. Meadows fell to the ground when her high heel broke. Clara was on her, striking her repeatedly with the hammer until she was dead.

That evening Mrs. Phillips confessed the murder to her husband. Phillips, fearing for his own safety, pretended to help his wife by persuading her to flee town. He then called police, telling authorities that they could pick up Clara on the next train arriving in Tuscon, Arizona.

Mrs. Phillips was convicted in a sensational trial where she was dubbed the "Tiger Woman" by the press, after reporters heard how she had stalked her victim for days as would a tiger. Peggy Caffee testified against Clara, assuring the vengeance-seeking woman her sentence of ten years to life on November 16, 1922.

Clara Phillips was released from Tehachapi on June 21, 1935. A bevy of newsmen greeted her, photographers shouting, "Hey, tiger woman! Look this way for the cameras, tiger woman!"

PLACE, MARTHA

Murderer ■ (1848–1899)

The first woman ever to be executed in the electric chair (at Auburn Prison, New York), Martha Place had taken an axe to her seventeen-year-old stepdaughter, Ida, on February 7, 1898, killing her. She waited until her husband, William, came home, preparing dinner for him as usual. When William Place arrived that night, Martha attacked him with the same bloody axe and wounded him, but he managed to escape to the street.

She was sentenced to die in the electric chair on March 20, 1899. Mrs. Place petitioned the then governor of New York, Theodore Roosevelt, for a commutation but Roosevelt declined. Mrs. Place was electrocuted on schedule.

PLEDGE, SARAH

Murderer ■ (? –1752)

Upon their marriage, James and Anne Whale moved to Horsham, England, taking rooms in a house owned by Mrs. Sarah Pledge, a voluptuous widow. Sarah made advances to Whale, who ordered her never

Mrs. Martha Place (third from left) entering the death chamber in Auburn Prison, New York. She was the first woman to be executed in the electric chair.

again to enter his apartment. Mrs. Pledge next approached Anne Whale, and the two soon formed a lesbian relationship. It was afterwards suggested that Mrs. Pledge's sole purpose in establishing this liaison was to engineer the death of James Whale.

One day in the summer of 1752, Mrs. Pledge came to Mrs. Whale and said, "Nan, let us get rid of this devil!"

"How can we do it?" replied Mrs. Whale.

"Let us give him a dose of poison."

At first the women caught and roasted spiders, mixing this vile preparation with Whale's beer, but the man only grew a bit queasy. Arse-nic was next mixed into Whale's pudding and he died within hours. A physician examined the man and determined that he had been poisoned. Taken into custody, Mrs. Whale promptly confessed the murder. Both she and Mrs. Pledge were condemned. Sarah vowed that she would fight the hangman and was dragged shouting oaths from the court.

The double execution, however, on August 14, 1752, in Horsham went as authorities planned. Mrs. Pledge was properly repentant before being hanged. Mrs. Whale was then strangled at the stake and burned to ashes. She was twenty-one years old.

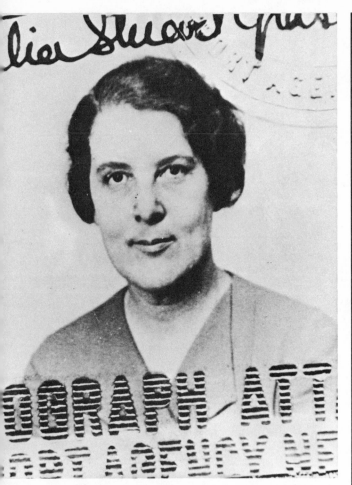

Missing-person photo of Soviet spy Juliet Poyntz.

POYNTZ, JULIET STUART

Spy ■ (1896– ?)

A fanatical member of the American Communist Party, Juliet Poyntz, born and bred in Omaha, Nebraska, maintained her quarters in New York. From there she traveled several times to Moscow where she was taught the art of spying. Returning to New York, she had the task of recruiting other Americans who would be willing to obtain secret government and military information.

With the advent of Stalin's repressive measures and witch hunts in Russia during the mid-1930s, Juliet Poyntz reportedly quit the Communist Party, declaring herself an avowed enemy of Stalinism. Some time in early June 1937, Juliet left her New York City apartment in the American Women's Association clubhouse and was never seen again. Her disappearance was not reported until her lawyer, Elias Lieberman, declared her missing six months later.

Carlo Tresca, editor of *Il Martello* (*"The Hammer"*), who had known Miss Poyntz well, stated that she had been "lured or kidnapped" aboard a Soviet freighter bound for Russia and had been liquidated. Tresca's claim was never substantiated; the editor himself was assassinated a few years later.

RABLEN, EVA

Murderer ■ (1905– ?)

A gin-guzzling flapper, Eva Rablen tired of her husband, Carroll, early in her marriage. The man, deaf from wounds suffered during World War I, was in the habit of accompanying his wife during her nocturnal prowling about Tuttleton in Tuolumne County, California. Carroll Rablen would dutifully sit in the car while his wife frequented speakeasies and dancehalls.

The husband was sitting in the car on the night of April 26, 1929, while Eva danced the Charleston at a local gathering. She walked from the hall at midnight and handed her husband a cup of coffee. He died in screaming agony a half hour later. A police search of the hall uncovered a bottle of strychnine which was later traced to a Tuttleton druggist. The poison had been sold to Eva Rablen only days earlier. The residue in the coffee cup and the dead man's stomach were examined and the poison found.

Eva's trial was in keeping with the hectic Jazz Age, held in an outdoor dancing area and attended by thousands of sensation-seeking spectators. She admitted her guilt and was sent to prison for life.

RANSOM, MRS. FLORENCE

Murderer ■ (? – ?)

A ttractive, middle-aged Florence Ransom had been having an affair with Lawrence Fisher, of Piddington, England, for some time before moving in with her lover in early 1940. Fisher's wife, Dorothy, and nineteen-year-old daughter, Freda, lived in nearby Matfield. For some inexplicable reason, Mrs.

Ransom, carrying a concealed shotgun, went to the Fisher cottage on the night of July 9, inveigled Mrs. Fisher and her daughter into the garden and shot them both. As she reloaded and fired more bullets into the dying women, the Fisher maid, Charlotte Saunders, ran outside to investigate. Mrs. Ransom then shot and killed the maid.

While fleeing, Mrs. Ransom dropped one of her white leather gloves, which was later found and traced to her. Witnesses later stated that she had been near the Fisher cottage on the night of the murder. Mrs. Ransom was sentenced to death and later removed to Broadmoor, a prison for the criminally insane.

RAPHAEL, SYLVIA

Spy ■ (1938–   )

A beautiful Israeli intelligence agent, Sylvia Raphel and five others flew to Norway in 1973 with the purpose of assassinating Ali Hassan Salemeh, thought to be responsible for the slaughtering of Israeli Olympic athletes in Munich during the 1972 games. Through a case of mistaken identity, a blameless Moroccan was killed instead of the intended victim. Sylvia, arrested while using her cover name of Patricia Roxbourgh, was sentenced to five and a half years in prison, having been expertly defended by Anneaus Schjodt, one of Norway's stellar lawyers.

Schjodt, who had fallen in love with his sultry client, managed to have Sylvia's sentence reduced to twenty-two months. They were married upon her release.

RENDALL, MARTHA

Murderer ■ (? –1909)

In 1906 a railway worker in western Australia, Thomas Morris, angered over his wife's slovenly habits, drove Mrs. Morris from his home, substituting her with a housekeeper, Martha Rendall. He married Martha some months later and soon the Morris children began to die.

Three of the children, Anne, Olive, and Arthur, all under age thirteen, developed sore throats. Martha made it her job to constantly swab their throats. The children shrieked in agony before their deaths. When Arthur died, an attending physician insisted upon an autopsy; Martha insisted she be present when the dissection was performed. Nothing was found.

In April 1909 young George Morris was given a cup of tea by Martha. The brew was so hot that it scalded his throat, which Martha insisted be swabbed immediately. Fearing the fate of his sisters and brothers, George fled the home, running to authorities and telling them that Martha was going to murder him, too.

Police investigated and discovered that Martha had purchased, between 1906 and 1909, huge amounts of hydrochloric acid from druggists; she had used this to swab the throats of the Morris children, thus killing them. Never having had children, the woman, jealous over the attentions Morris gave his own, had sadistically murdered what she had construed to be rivals for her husband's affections.

Martha Randall was executed in Fremantle Jail, the only woman ever hanged in western Australia.

ROBINSON, HENRIETTA

Murderer ■ (1816–1905)

The lack of background in the story of Henrietta Robinson, America's most mysterious murderess of the nineteenth century, was the precise reason why the public was so intrigued with it. The woman was the great enigma in the annals of homicide in the United States, and the possibility that Henrietta was insane, or cleverly pretended to be, served all the more to further darken the riddle of her life.

Henrietta had been living in Troy, New York, for more than a year, in a small cottage across from Lanagan's grocery store at River and Rensselaer streets. Few people in Troy knew the woman and no one knew her well. She was rumored to be the mistress of a powerful New York State official. An expensive, privately owned carriage with its shades drawn was sometimes seen parked late in the evening outside Henrietta's home; small-town gossips had it that her sponsor was paying her one of his infrequent nocturnal visits.

In March 1853, a social was held in Troy, and, to the surprise of all, particularly the women who had organized the dance, Henrietta appeared, entering the dance hall alone and sitting in a corner, studying the dancers with her dark, flashing eyes. The local lotharios were agog at Henrietta's beauty, and they argued among themselves as to who would be the first to dance with her. A young fellow named Smith then approached the woman, bowed, and asked her to dance. Henrietta shook her head but Smith persisted, leaning low and whispering something to the woman. She turned scarlet, stood up, and brushed past the youth, leaving the hall.

It was common knowledge that Mrs. Robinson was a kept woman, and the nature of Smith's remark may have reflected upon her dubious social status. Worse, gossiped the neighbors, the impetuous youth had probably suggested an assignation, and, being treated as a common whore, Henrietta left the dance in a rage. Her appearance at the dance, it was noted, was only nights after Henrietta's mysterious sponsor visited her for the last time, a tall, distinguished-looking gentleman, wearing a cloak and top hat. There had been an argument, loud shouting heard by neighbors, something about the gentleman's wife and children, something about Henrietta's being abandoned.

Some days following the dance, Henrietta Robinson entered Lanagan's grocery store, after seeing Smith go inside. Smith was standing at the counter ordering some foodstuffs when Henrietta marched into the store, going up to him and pulling a pistol from her handbag. She placed the barrel against the startled youth's temple.

An artist's sketch of Henrietta Robinson, known as the "Veiled Murderess," drawn a year after she inexplicably dosed her neighbors' beer with arsenic. (Courtesy Troy, New York, Public Library)

"You insulted me some nights ago," Henrietta said in a monotone. "Admit it."

Smith kept his terror-filled eyes glued to a shelf of canned goods in front of him. "I admit it, I admit it," he replied in a quavering voice.

"If you ever insult me again," Henrietta told him slowly, "I will pull this trigger."

"I believe you," Smith said.

With that Henrietta put away the pistol, but stood staring at the Lanagans who had been momentarily petrified by her actions. Timothy Lanagan then dashed from behind the counter, upbraiding Henrietta, telling her that Smith was his good friend and that if she ever again threatened anybody in his store he would have her arrested. Lanagan and his wife took hold of Henrietta's arms and led her to the door, shoving her rudely outside.

During the next few weeks Henrietta rarely appeared in public, except to order her food supplies from the Lanagans. It was apparent from her behavior that she seethed with hatred for them. She also began to drink heavily and late at night. Her cottage ablaze with light, neighbors heard her loudly singing songs in a foreign tongue.

In early May, Henrietta Robinson's attitude toward the Lanagans changed abruptly. She attempted to talk with Mrs. Lanagan in a friendly manner whenever she entered the store, but Mrs. Lanagan distrusted her and filled her orders swiftly, ushering the woman from the premises as soon as possible.

On May 15, 1853, Mrs. Robinson went to the local druggist, William M. Ostrom, asking to purchase poison. She told Ostrom that she wanted to get rid of rodents in her house. He sold her two ounces of arsenic.

Ten days later, Henrietta entered the Lanagan grocery. She appeared happy and insisted that the Lanagans become her friends, that they forget her impulsive outburst against Smith. She proposed buying them a beer. The Lanagans eyed each other nervously then agreed it would be a good idea to patch up their differences. After all, Henrietta was really one of their best customers. She always paid her bills. She had money, a lot of money, thousands in a local bank, they had heard. Yes, they would have a beer.

Henrietta and the Lanagans retired to the kitchen in the back of the store where Catherine Lubee, whose sister was married to Mrs. Lanagan's brother, was making dinner. Mrs. Lanagan fetched the beer, a large pitcher, and some glasses.

"Do you have some sugar?" Henrietta asked Mrs. Lanagan as she brought the beer to the kitchen table. "I'd like to sweeten my beer with it." Mrs. Lanagan nodded and went into the store to get the sugar. During her absence, Henrietta told Timothy Lanagan that she was hungry. Did he have a hard boiled egg handy? Lanagan went to fetch an egg. Catherine Lubee left the kitchen too, to get some potatoes for dinner.

Mrs. Lanagan returned with a saucer filled with powdered sugar but left the kitchen in a hurry when a customer came into her store. Henrietta was then alone at the kitchen table. By the time the Lanagans and Catherine Lubee returned, they found that Henrietta had mixed the sugar with the beer and had poured them each a glass of the inviting brew.

"To your good health," Henrietta toasted. Lanagan and Miss Lubee lifted their glasses, draining them. Mrs. Lanagan was about to drink but was again interrupted by the arrival of another customer and went back into the grocery store. A minute later Henrietta was walking past Mrs. Lanagan, on her way out of the store. "I have some errands. Sorry I can't stay. Don't forget to drink your beer."

When she returned to her kitchen, Mrs. Lanagan looked at her glass of beer and noted the white flakes floating on the surface of the drink. "I don't like sugar in my beer," she told her husband and threw it out.

"It tasted kind of funny," Timothy Lanagan complained before returning to work.

"Yes," added Catherine Lubee. "You'd think it would taste sweet, not bitter. It was so bitter."

Soon Timothy Lanagan began vomiting. At 5:00 P.M. he begged his wife to send for a doctor. When Dr. Adams arrived, Lanagan complained of stomach cramps and intense pain, and that his mouth was burning. Mrs. Lanagan then saw Henrietta Robinson standing at the counter of her store. She rushed up to her, saying, "What have you done to my husband? You put something in that beer, didn't you?"

"Don't be absurd, Mrs. Lanagan. It must be the weather. Hot."

"You put poison in that beer! What have you done? You have killed the father of my children!"

"Oh, no, I wouldn't do any such thing!"

Mrs. Lanagan pushed Henrietta out the front door of her store, shouting that the police would soon arrest her. Two hours later Timothy Lanagan died in writhing agony. By then Henrietta was in Ostrom's drugstore.

"I'm in trouble," Henrietta told the druggist. Her hands shook and her lower lip quivered as she spoke. "Remember, I bought that arsenic from you to kill rodents, to kill rodents."

"What kind of trouble are you in, Mrs. Robinson?"

"They're accusing me of poisoning some people—the Lanagans."

"Why would you be suspected of doing such a horrible thing?"

"Revenge, that's it. Because I wouldn't loan the Lanagans a hundred dollars, so now they accuse me of murder. Can you imagine that, Mr. Ostrom?"

Ostrom only blinked at her from behind thick glasses.

"The entire neighborhood is against me, and I think they mean to do me harm. Who should I go to for protection?"

"Amasa J. Copp," Ostrom told her. "He's the chief of police."

"Good. I'll see him at once."

Henrietta did not have to seek out Police Chief Copp. He and several officers who had been called by the Lanagans, stopped Henrietta as she was walking home, and, in the middle of the street, arrested her for murder. She was charged with poisoning Timothy Lanagan to death. When Catherine Lubee also died the following morning, her death was also charged to Henrietta.

An autopsy by several doctors revealed arsenic in the bodies of Lanagan and Miss Lubee. A quantity of arsenic was then found hidden beneath a rug in Henrietta's cottage. One of the physicians, Dr. Reed B. Bontecou, went to the Troy jail and confronted Henrietta. "You know you have poisoned these people," he informed her. "I want you to tell me about it."

Henrietta ignored his remarks and began to chatter about the spring fashions in dresses. As the weeks went by, the prosecution prepared their case against the murderess. Dr. Bontecou interviewed Henrietta several times but got nothing out of her except incoherent sentences. "As far as I could judge, I could not see that she comprehended what I meant," the doctor later reported in court. "From the beginning to the end of my visits, on all occasions, I was satisfied that she was not a rational woman."

Once in court, spectators and officials alike were amazed to see Henrietta enter the dock dressed all in black. Even more amazing were the five heavy blue lace veils she wore, so that no one could see her pretty face. From the beginning of her trial to the end of her life, Mrs. Robinson would be known as "the Veiled Murderess," for she refused, except for a few seconds at a time, to remove the veils from her face, a practice that mystified the many journalists flocking into court to report on the sensational case.

Wrote one New York newsman, "Mrs. Robinson attracted all eyes. She was richly and fashionably apparelled, wearing an elegant black silk dress, white hat trimmed with artificial flowers, and spotless white kid gloves. Her face was shrouded with blue veils from the time she entered the courtroom until she left it."

One person who had seen Henrietta's face just before the trial began was Mrs. Oakes Smith, a phrenologist who had visited Mrs. Robinson in her cell. At the time phrenology was a much respected criminal science, which claimed to be able to determine the criminality of a person from mere physical makeup, a science thankfully forgotten today. Mrs. Smith's report to the court ran like this: "Phrenologically, her brain is low above the ears, and her coarse, black hair grows down upon the forehead even lower than that upon the bust of the celebrated antique of Clite. She has two projections in the region of what is called Constructiveness, extending backward which of themselves would be sufficient to throw a whole character out of balance. When you add to this brain a refined ladylike form, round and compact, with a temperament of the highest and most excitable kind, it will be easily seen that education might retard and modify her destiny, but would hardly serve to re-create her into a reliable or very safe character."

Judge Harris insisted that Henrietta remove her veils. She refused. The judge became angry, shouting for her to take away the veils. From beneath the veils came Henrietta Robinson's calm voice: "I am here to undergo a most painful and important trial. I do not wish to be gazed at."

The judge then implored H. Beach, Henrietta's lawyer, to persuade his client to remove the veils, but Beach shrugged, telling the court that Mrs. Robinson had been advised to cooperate but adamantly refused. Reported Beach, "Her reply to us is that, rather than sit here unveiled, she had rather incur any hazard, however great, and endure all possible consequences. The court will perceive that we are powerless in the matter."

Judge Harris then threatened the accused that officers would physically remove the veils if she did not do so voluntarily. A sound came from beneath the veils that was thought to be low laughter. Henrietta threw back the veils in such a way that part of her lovely face was exposed, but she quickly put a handkerchief to that part of her face and thus managed to conceal herself.

It went that way throughout the trial, Mrs. Robinson lifting her veil only for seconds so that witnesses could identify her. On one occasion, the druggist who had sold her the arsenic approached the woman to a position within a few inches of her, and Mrs. Robinson lifted her veils briefly. Druggist Ostrom fell back in horror. Henrietta had been smiling at him, a hideous, maniacal smile full of gleaming teeth.

When it came to establishing Henrietta's background, the court was at a total loss. Though many witnesses came forward and related conversations they had had with Mrs. Robinson in the past, every witness had a different, strange story to tell.

An Irish laborer named Riley stated that Mrs. Robinson had hired him to put up a fence in her yard and during their conversations she had told him that, like himself, she was a native of Longford, Ireland; that she was the daughter of Admiral Pagnum and had lived in Pagnum Cas-

tle before being made pregnant by a man named Robinson, the son of her father's steward. After that, she told him, she had departed in shame for America, being abandoned in New York City where she had become the mistress of a great politician, the mysterious man who provided her with money and the cottage in Troy. He had, in turn, also abandoned her. (Many later said that this last desertion caused Henrietta's mind to snap, compelling her to take vengeance on the nearest male, meaning Timothy Lanagan.)

Mary Jane Dillon, a dressmaker who provided Mrs. Robinson with gowns, swore before the court that Henrietta had given her several life histories, all different. "She told me she was a lord's daughter in Ireland," testified Miss Dillon. "She told me that she had been turned away from her father's castle for marrying a poor man. She then cried. Soon afterwards, something seemed to pass her mind, and she laughed, and danced about the floor. . . . She showed me a daguerreotype [an early form of photography] of her mother, a lady with a bundle of flowers. She said the flowers were gathered from the garden of the king of France. She said her mother gave her this likeness when her father turned her away. She told me another time that her mother died when she was a small child. . . . It was another time when she told me that her husband was a great lord in Ireland. . . . She said she could jump into the river and swim until she got tired, and then she had a cork which she could put between her teeth and rest in the water and not sink."

To others Henrietta had confided that she had been raised in a nunnery in England. To still others, it had been in a château in France, and that, in one way or other, she was related to great princes of Europe. Her raging paranoia was illustrated in her comments to many a Troy citizen about how doctors treating her for minor illnesses had given her medicine that was really poison—she had given some of this medicine to a dog once, she said, and the dog died immediately.

"How that woman laughed," said one female witness, a neighbor, "almost at anything, even a thought, and the laughing would begin. While laughing she would commence to dance. Her dancing was not regular; she kind of jumped around. I could not exactly call it dancing—'twas a figure I never saw danced before."

All of it added up to insanity in the eyes of Henrietta's lawyer, but his attempts to have Mrs. Robinson declared insane proved futile. She was convicted of the murder of Timothy Lanagan. Before Judge Harris pronounced sentence on her, Henrietta Robinson said from beneath her veil, "The Judge of judges will judge you!"

"Have you anything more to say?" Judge Harris asked.

"Yes, I have a great deal to say. . . . I have been persecuted. Shame!"

Judge Harris grew angry, blurting out, "Life is worth but little to you, Mrs. Robinson."

"Don't trouble yourself about that."

Judge Harris then sentenced Henrietta to die on the gallows on August 3, 1853. He added, "And may God have mercy on your soul."

"You had better pray for your own soul," Henrietta told the judge. She was led away laughing.

The governor of New York reviewed Mrs. Robinson's case and on the very day of her execution commuted her death sentence to life imprisonment. She was taken to Sing Sing and became a model prisoner. Two years later a newsman interviewed her, reporting that "she has dropped many eccentricities she portrayed before her sentence was changed to life imprisonment with one exception. We refer to the singular practice of concealing her face from visitors. In that respect she seems to be incurable. Whenever a visitor approaches her, she hastens to hide her countenance with whatever may be within her reach—sometimes a fan, and sometimes a piece of pasteboard, or whatever else is handiest."

Henrietta continued to be a nagging mystery. In the following decades newsmen probed her past only to come up with conflicting stories. She hid her face, said one, because she feared being recognized as a direct descendant of a European monarch. Another claimed she did not wish to be identified because her millionaire husband was still searching for her.

Wrote the editor of the Albany *Knickerbocker*, "The history of this woman has so much

mystery hanging about it that any little circumstance which helps to clear up the matter is not to be looked upon as otherwise than interesting."

She was moved from Sing Sing to Auburn Prison in 1873. In 1890, Henrietta gathered all her belongings and the wooden furniture in her cell and set it all on fire. Wardens rushed to her cell to put out the fire and prevented her from throwing herself on the blaze. For this attempted suicide, Henrietta Robinson was sent to the Matteawan State Hospital for the Criminally Insane.

Henrietta received no visitors during the last fifteen years of her imprisonment. Her lawyer, who had come to see her once a year, had died. She did receive a large box at Christmas each and every year during her fifty-two years in prison (a record for any female in U.S. prison history). The box contained foodstuffs and clothing, and, without fail, several blue veils. The sender remained unknown.

On May 14, 1905, Henrietta Robinson died quietly of old age in her cell. Records showed her to be eighty-nine years old, but there was precious little else about her the file yielded. She remained "the Veiled Murderess" to the very end, having drawn over her real identity and life a veil as inscrutable as the mysteries of the pyramids.

ROBINSON, SARAH JANE

Murderer ■ (? –1905)

Irish-born Sarah Jane Tennent used poison to settle differences and gain insurance money. After marrying a man named Robinson, Sarah poisoned her Boston landlord, and, in 1882, her husband. The widow next poisoned her sister Annie so that she could wed Annie's husband, Prince Arthur Freeman. When Freeman declined her marriage proposal, he, too, was poisoned.

Sarah also poisoned her own children, William and Lizzie, and seven-year-old Thomas Freeman, her sister's son, collecting insurance money on all her victims. A suspicious insurance investigator had the bodies exhumed, and arsenic was found in all the corpses. Sarah Robinson was tried and convicted for the murder of her brother-in-law. She died in prison in 1905.

RUMBOLD, FREDA

Murderer ■ (1913–)

The marriage between Albert and Freda Rumbold, of Bristol, England, was a strange one. The husband, his mother was later to testify in court, "was a very odd person, particularly at the time of the full moon." At her trial for murder, Freda told how she spent many a night in her daughter's bed or on the staircase landing, rather than sleep with her eccentric spouse. The lumber contractor apparently had strange sexual habits.

For her part, Freda spent a good deal of time forging her husband's signature to worthless checks and taking out loans in his name, building up a nest egg, the prosecution was to claim, to enable her to flee her family. The prosecution also insisted that Freda, thinking her felonies about to be discovered by her husband, decided to murder Albert Rumbold. She had asked friends who were about to go hunting to provide her with cartridges for a 12-gauge shotgun. Rumbold kept just such a weapon in his house.

On the night of August 25, 1956, Freda entered her husband's bedroom while he was asleep and blew away his head. She then locked the bedroom door, stuffed a towel sopped with cologne under the door, and put up a sign reading, "Please do not enter." What she hoped to conceal through these awkward measures is still in doubt (the cologne-soaked towel, perhaps, was to offset the strong odor of a fast decomposing body).

When relatives asked about Rumbold's whereabouts and got vague answers from Freda, the police were called in and promptly discovered the body. Mrs. Rumbold insisted that her husband had died in a domestic argument as they both struggled for the shotgun, but the manner of entry of the bullets into the deceased disproved her claim. She was sent to prison for life.

SACH, AMELIA

Murderer ■ (1873–1902)

Like the notorious "baby farmer," Amelia Dyer, Mrs. Sach was also in the murder business. Unlike Madame Dyer, Amelia Sach presented the appearance of a youthful and kindly person who doted on her own children. Then again, she only arranged for mass murder; the gruesome chore was carried out by her cohort, squat, ugly Annie Walters whose incredible stupidity brought both women to the gallows.

Amelia ran a "nursing home" in East Finchley, London, Her services consisted in providing a haven for unwed mothers to deliver their babies. She lured her helpless, frightened clients with the following advertisement:

> ACCOUCHEMENT: Before and during, skilled nursing. Home comforts.
> Baby can remain.

The last line, of course, was the real sales tool. Amelia told prospective clients that she could arrange for wonderful foster parents to take the children. There were additional fees, of course, from between 25 and 50 pounds. The desperate mothers were only too ready to scrape up and borrow the needed money.

After a child was born in Amelia's home, Mrs. Sach would tenderly bundle the baby in new blankets and turn the child over to Annie Walters, who, for a third of all fees, promptly killed the child, usually by giving the infant chlorodyne, then dumped the body into the Thames or buried the little corpse in a convenient garbage dump.

In 1902, Mrs. Sach turned over a baby born of an unmarried girl named Galley, telling Mrs. Walters to dispose of the child. The dim-witted Annie Walters, however, took the child home with her "for company." Mrs. Walters' landlord was a policeman, and when the constable inquired about the child, Annie told him that she was keeping the baby for a few days as a favor to a sailor and his wife who lived in Kensington.

"Isn't she a dear little girl," Annie said, showing the baby to the constable's wife. The wife found this statement peculiar, as, in changing the child's diapers, she had discovered the infant to be a boy.

Mrs. Walters came downstairs weeping a few days later to announce that the child had died at her side in bed. Her grief was so genuine that no questions were asked, the constable and his wife assuming that the child had been returned to its parents for burial. Not more than two months later Mrs. Walters came home with another baby. When this child also "accidentally" died in its sleep, the policeman grew suspicious and questioned Mrs. Walters. Frightened, Mrs. Walters excused herself and ran from the boardinghouse. She was quickly apprehended and taken to a police station. Investigators demanded she explain where the babies came from; illiterate Annie Walters claimed that a third child she was known to have had was given to a wealthy woman who met her in an elegant coach in the heart of Piccadilly. Mrs. Walters' statement read—

> I met the lady who was in a brougham. She said you have come. I said, yes, and she said get in and give her the baby. I gave her the baby and she drest it in fine lase robes and a boutful cloak, she said it will be a lovely baby. . . . She said to me I have a bottle of Shampain in my bag pour me out a glass and she drank that and gave me one. I said only a little I am not youse to that . . . then I got out she gave me ten shillings. I said let me know how you get home . . . good night.

The claim, police knew, was utterly preposterous. When several corpses of babies were found, coupled to the statements of Mrs. Sach's clients, both women were tried and condemned to death. They were hanged together in 1903 in Holloway Prison, the first women to be executed in that institution.

One of their hangmen, H. A. Pierrepoint, kept a diary of all his executions. His entry for Mrs. Sach and Mrs. Walters was as follows:

> These two women were baby farmers of the worst kind and they were both repulsive in type. One was two pounds less than the other, and there was

a difference of two inches in the drop which I allowed. One had a long thick neck and the other a short neck, points which I was bound to observe in the arrangement of the rope. They had literally to be carried to the scaffold and protested to the end against their sentences.

SADLER, DORA

Murderer ■ (1886– ?)

A nannie obsessively devoted to two children in the London home of Benjamin Katzman, Dora Martha Spalding Sadler vied for the children's affections with their mother. The jealousy of the woman became so intense that Mrs. Katzman gave Dora notice. On the night of November 11, 1923, Dora went to sleep with the two small children, Jean and Sonia Katzman, in their nursery, turning on the gas. In the morning Sonia was found dead; the baby Jean died a short time later. A note written by Dora read, "I am taking them both. I could not leave my Sonia to the creature she calls mother." The nannie was revived and later stood trial for murder; she was convicted and condemned. Her sentence was later commuted to life imprisonment.

SALOMEN, EDITH ("THE SWAMI")

Swindler ■ (1849– ?)

B orn in Kentucky, Edith Salomen learned the art of confidence games early from her swindling father, who called himself a professor. At the age of twenty, she traveled to Baltimore, where she convinced the press that she was the illegitimate daughter of the notorious courtesan-dancer Lola Montez and her mad lover, Ludwig I of Bavaria. The fawning newspaper stories about her drew the wealthy young men of Baltimore to her side, and she soon wheedled more than $200,000 out of a young suitor whose family was a cornerstone in Maryland society.

When the father of this duped swain had investigators prove Edith a fraud, she took to smoking opium in such quantities that she had to be hospitalized. While in the hospital recuperating and waiting for authorities to bring charges against her for fraud, Edith, one fine morning, jumped from her bed, stabbed an orderly, and ran raving through the hospital corridors, an act that convinced doctors she was, indeed, insane, which was her plan. She was sent to an asylum for a year. There she married a doctor named Messant, and he promptly signed her release papers. Messant died the following year and Edith moved into another field of con, hypnotic mysticism, she called it.

Her first victim was a wealthy, weak-minded mark, General Diss Debar, whom she married, taking on an entirely new name at the wedding altar: Ann O'Delia Diss Debar. Using her husband's prestige, Edith drew the cream of New York society to her salon on Madison Avenue, where she humbugged the gullible with crude séances. She would go into hypnotic trances and conjure any available spirit a patron desired to see cross over from the world of the dead. Her most noteworthy victim in this period was a half-senile New York lawyer, seventy-year-old Luther R. Marsh. Marsh had always wanted to become a great painter but was devoid of any real talent. Edith easily convinced him, for a price, that she could put him in touch with the late great master painters. The visage of no less an artist than Raphael soon presented itself to Marsh at one of Edith's séances.

Raphael, it appeared, was a ruthless businessman. He demanded from the other side, where expenses were obviously heavy, that Marsh fork over an enormous amount of cash if he was to paint a picture to which Marsh would subsequently affix his signature. The money was placed in a locked cabinet, Edith having the only key. In ten days' time, the painting would be completed on a blank canvas, also locked in the cabinet. A painting, still dripping with wet paint, was present in the cabinet when unlocked ten days later. Marsh, who was certainly no judge of art, readily accepted the work as genuine Raphael.

The ever gullible Marsh next ordered ancient tapestries woven in the cabinet by long-dead spirits. In addition, Edith conjured the ghost of Shakespeare for him, for a great sum of money; Shakespeare was kind enough to create an original ode for the gulled lawyer.

The procession of famous spirits continued to appear at Edith's command, and, at the expense of Marsh's wallet. Charlemagne appeared, wearing his famous crown; Cicero and others

Swindler Edith Salomen, adorned in her "Swami" robes.

came forward. His money gone, Marsh was quickly convinced by Edith to sign over the deeds on his expensive Madison Avenue property if he wanted to go on conversing with the great dead. He did, an act that prompted his relatives to intervene. Edith and her cronies were arrested and her séances and "communications" with dead spirits exposed as frauds. Edith was sent to prison for six months. When released, she promptly divorced her husband, the general, and took up a new identity, calling herself Madame Vera P. Ava.

Under this new title, Edith gave lectures on sex, combining these performances with segments of musical comedy, which she proudly announced were her own creations. So offensive were these "lectures" that audiences rebelled.

In Chicago a crowd rioted at one of Edith's performances, and she was compelled to escape through a window.

Using different names, Edith next embarked on a series of bigamous marriages, wedding a man named Smith in Kansas City, then deserting him when his funds were drained, and moving to New Orleans where she married a man named Jackson. In New Orleans Edith called herself the Countess Landsfeldt, and Jackson served at her side in setting up "psychic lectures," in which she brought forth once again the spirits of the famous dead.

Wrote one journalist of the day, "The most popular ghost was that of Frederick the Great, and for an extra charge of two dollars per head he appeared wearing the Imperial Crown of Germany, oblivious to the fact that that particular crown was in the possession of the Austrians." When this scam, too, was exposed, Edith returned to Chicago, billing herself as "Sister Mary," an ascetic mystic raising money for a nonexistent orphanage. She was run out of town, going to Capetown, South Africa, with Jackson, where she quickly set up a phony Theosophical University which dispensed degrees in "higher mysticism" to any who had the price for the scroll. Authorities closed the so-called university, and Edith moved on to England, establishing herself as "Theo, the Swami," selling her bogus religion, which she called "theocratic unity." She and Jackson bilked hundreds of dupes before Chief Detective Inspector Kane of Scot-

land Yard exposed the racket. "The Swami" was tried in 1901 and given seven years' imprisonment for the swindle. Upon her release, the overweight confidence artist returned to America where she disappeared. Before sailing she told unimpressed reporters at the dock, "I represent a principle. I am a principle for the unecclesiastical Court. The foundation that that principle represents is the Lord."

SAXE, SUSAN

Terrorist ■ (1947–   )

A Brandis University honor student, Susan Saxe became one of the most rabid anti-war activists of the late 1960s. She and others were involved in a 1970 bank robbery in Boston in which a patrolman was slain. Saxe spent five years as an underground fugitive until

Terrorist Susan Saxe. (Wide World)

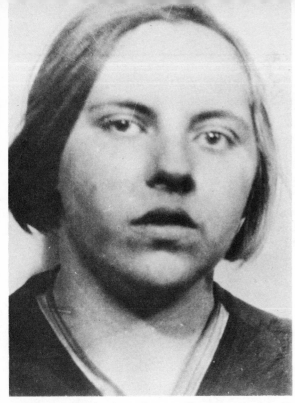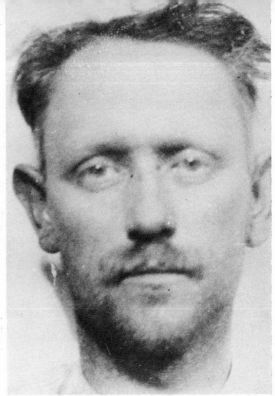

Bandit Irene Schroeder with her outlaw lover Walter Glenn Dague.

she was arrested in her Back Bay apartment in 1975. Police found a large supply of guns and ammunition on the premises.

Twenty-four witnesses for the prosecution testified at Saxe's trial. The defense was feeble. A deadlocked jury caused a mistrial. The terrorist finally pleaded guilty to robbery and manslaughter and was given a twelve-to-fourteen-year prison term.

SCHROEDER, IRENE

Bandit, Murderer ■ (1909–1931)

This plain-looking housewife met salesman and Sunday school teacher Walter Glenn Dague in late 1929. He was thirty-four, she twenty. Irene deserted her husband, taking her young son, Donnie, with her. Dague left his wife

and children in a small West Virginia town. The couple embarked upon a crime spree, robbing several stores and a few small banks, but taking in only enough money for gas and food. They lived out of a stolen car.

In Butler, Pennsylvania, the pair robbed a grocery store and fled. The grocer gave the alarm and two highway patrolmen, Corporal W. Brady Paul and Patrolman Ernest Moore, parked nearby, gave chase. When Irene spied the pursuing police car she calmly rolled down a car window, leaned out, and began firing. Dague fired back also, handling the wheel with one hand. Four-year-old Donnie Schroeder sat in the back seat thinking it all a game.

One of Irene's bullets struck Paul, killing him instantly. Dague managed to wound Moore. The police car careened into a ditch. Irene and Dague could only run after that, driving through roadblocks and ambushes all the way to Arizona, where a giant posse surrounded their car on a lonely road. They shot it out, surrendering only after they ran out of ammunition.

Donnie Schroeder became the state's chief witness, telling a policeman, "My mother killed

Irene Schroeder (center) on her way to Rockview Penitentiary in Pennsylvania to be executed in 1931.

a cop like you." Irene did not deny the murder. In fact, she attempted to assume complete blame for all the crimes she and her lover Dague had committed together. Both, however, were found guilty and sentenced to die. On their way to Rockview Penitentiary, Pennsylvania, by car, "the two constantly caressed each other," according to an accompanying newsman. As her date of execution—February 23, 1931—approached, Mrs. Schroeder displayed such reserve that journalists dubbed her "Iron Irene."

To the last she begged authorities in vain to spare her lover. When the prison chaplain arrived to walk the last mile with her, Irene smiled and said, "Don't worry about me. I'll be all right. You'd better go back to Glenn. I think he needs you more than I do." She preceded Dague by a few days.

When asked if there was anything that might be done for her, Irene, sitting down as easily in the electric chair as one would on a comfortable sofa, smiled and said, "Yes, there is something. Please tell them in the kitchen to fry Glenn's eggs on both sides. He likes them that way."

Within three minutes she was dead, the first woman electrocuted in Pennsylvania and the first female to be executed in that state since 1890.

SCIERI, ANTOINETTE

Murderer ■ (? – ?)

Other than the fact that she was born in Italy and came to France as a little girl, little is known about the early life of Antoinette Scieri, mass poisoner. Some time early in World War I, she learned the arts of nursing in a casualty clearing station at Doullens. It was here that she also began a life of crime, filching French and English money from wounded British officers under her care. Antoinette also took from the hands and fingers of her patients their watches and wedding rings. These she sold.

Antoinette's special fraud during these hectic times was to write letters home, pretending to be the wounded man and asking for money. The funds were invariably sent to the address the nurse provided. She went further, stealing an officer's paybook, writing army bankers for an advance of 5,000 francs, a scheme that ended in her arrest in 1915. She was sent to prison, then released some time in 1916.

Once she gained her freedom, Antoinette met and married an Italian soldier named Salmon. She bore him two children, but shortly after the war, Salmon left his wife after learning that she had been carrying on several affairs. Antoinette next took up with a brutish fellow named Joseph Rossignol who drank incessantly and beat her whenever urged by his devils. Though she had him arrested several times for assault, Antoinette always took Rossignol back. The couple produced one child and moved to the peaceful village of St. Gilles in southern France

in 1920. There Rossignol took a job as a laborer in the vineyards. Antoinette announced that "Nurse Scieri" was available to any and all who were ailing.

A portrait of her at the time was drawn by a contemporary scribe who declared that she "was no beauty. She looked a typical gypsy with her swarthy complexion and thick black hair which hung in ringlets around her face. Her face was heavy and pouched, and her eyes were almost mesmeric in the steadfastness of their gaze."

Within two years a number of strange deaths began to occur in St.-Gilles. On December 11, 1924, a fifty-eight-year-old spinster named Drouard died under Antoinette's care. A local doctor attributed her death to heart seizure. On Christmas Eve, a Madame Lachapelle died in great agony. Antoinette called in a doctor to sign the death certificate, saying, "She had a pork sandwich yesterday. She particularly asked for it, and, as she had been getting on well, I thought it would do no harm." The woman's death was listed as caused by ptomaine poisoning. Her husband died two days later of a heart attack, Antoinette insisted. The doctor dutifully agreed.

When Rossignol again beat Antoinette after a mean drunk, the nurse fed her husband a bowl of mussels. He was dead within hours. Nurse Scieri had little time to mourn; the sick needed her and she scurried off to comfort Marie Martin, a sixty-seven-year-old spinster, and her sister, Madame Doyer.

Said Antoinette to the sisters, "You must not worry about money. My mission is to heal and help the sick. Fees mean nothing to me." Oddly enough, this claim was true, for Antoinette had taken little or nothing in payment for her so-called nursing. Having given the two sisters cups of coffee, Antoinette watched as Marie Martin grew ill and died. Madame Doyer had poured the coffee into the sink when Antionette's back was turned. "It was bitter," she later said of the brew; her act undoubtedly saved her life.

Antoinette moved on to nurse the ailing wife of a man named Gouan-Criquet. When the seventy-five-year-old woman died, the husband called in a doctor named Clauzel, a physician unknown to Nurse Scieri. The husband told Dr. Clauzel that he had begun to grow ill from the time Antoinette came to care for his wife. Suspicious, the doctor called in police instead of perfunctorily signing the death certificate. Detectives found a bottle with green fluid beneath the bed of Madame Gouan-Criquet. It was analyzed as pyralion and ether, a mixture containing acetate of lead and used in killing weeds. More than three hundred people, chemists reported, could have been killed by this one bottle of deadly poison.

Police cautiously ordered the bodies of Antoinette's patients exhumed, including that of her common-law husband, Rossignol. All contained huge doses of pyralion. Antoinette Scieri was then arrested. She readily confessed but put most of the blame on her neighbor, Rosalie Gire. The neighbor was cleared, and, on April 27, 1926, Antoinette was condemned, the judge lambasting her: "You have been called a monster. But that expression is not strong enough. You are debauched, you are possessed of all the vices. You are also a drunkard, vicious, and a hypocrite and you have no shame. I do not believe judicial history contains the records of many criminals of your type."

Antoinette Scieri first screamed oaths at the judge, then shrugged and gave out a short laugh before being led back to her prison cell. Her death sentence was commuted to life imprisonment. The murdering nurse never explained her motives for killing six people.

SHERMAN, LYDIA

Murderer ■ (1830–1878)

Perhaps the most famous female poisoner in nineteenth century America, Lydia Sherman was an attractive housewife with a disarming manner. She killed every person around her and for the simple reason of greed. Lydia collected insurance monies on various families and lived in high style along New York's Tenderloin.

By the early 1860s Lydia was married to a policeman, Edward Struck, and had produced six children through the union. Tiring of her role of housewife, Lydia bought ten cents' worth of white arsenic from a druggist in the spring of 1864. When the pharmacist asked if she intended to kill rats, Lydia's response was, "Rats, my goodness, yes, we're alive with rats!" She then proceeded to poison Struck, and, following his agonizing death, her six children, collecting money on all.

The killing of seven people took time, of course. Lydia murdered her children, ranging in ages from nine months to fourteen years, over a two-year period, from 1864 to 1866. Doctors, convinced by Lydia's sorrowful demeanor, signed the death certificates matter-of-factly, listing the victims as dying from various epidemics, fevers, and bronchitis.

By 1868, Lydia had moved to New Haven, Connecticut, where she married a senile rich farmer, Dennis Hurlbut. She slowly poisoned the old man to death and inherited his small estate. By April 1870 Lydia was again low on funds and went to work as a housekeeper for well-fixed Nelson Sherman of Derby, Connecticut. Lydia soon had Sherman in her sway and convinced him to marry her. She tired of nursing the Sherman baby and put arsenic into the child's food. Little Frank Sherman died within hours. Next was Sherman's fourteen-year-old daughter, Addie; Lydia gave her two cups of "very strong tea," both laced with arsenic. The girl died in December 1870. Sherman himself, who had become a wasted alcoholic over the mysterious deaths of his beloved children, was given dozens of cups of chocolate before he, too, succumbed on May 12, 1871.

The local physician, Dr. Beardsley, unlike the apparently indifferent doctors in New York who had overlooked the real cause of death of Lydia's previous victims, became suspicious. He and two other doctors examined the bodies of the Sherman family and discovered them replete with poison. Believing her murders to be known, Lydia fled to New York, but detectives trailed her and returned her under arrest to Connecticut.

Lydia Sherman about to poison Dennis Hurlbut with her specially prepared wine.

"Queen Poisoner" Lydia Sherman in her prison cell, thinking back on her many murder victims.

"Queen Poisoner," as Lydia was dubbed by the press at her trial, was convicted of second-degree murder and sent to prison for life. In her cell she gave out a long and strange confession, admitting to eleven *known* murders, but she may have been responsible for the death of ten or fifteen more people. She died in Wethersfield Prison, May 16, 1878.

Typical of Queen Poisoner's lackadaisical confessions was her so-called reason for killing her husband Edward Struck. "I gave him the arsenic because I was discouraged. I know that that is not much of an excuse, but I felt so much trouble that I did not think about it."

SMITH, MRS. MARY ELEANOR

Swindler, Murderer ■ (1866– ?)

The earliest entry for a criminal offense in the case of Mary Smith was in 1910. This woman would later be known to police across the United States as "Old Shoebox Annie." She lived in San Francisco at the time and used her young son, Earl, to pass worthless checks. Earl would enter a store with a note from his mother to purchase certain items and leave a useless check as payment. The check was returned, of course, but Earl never came back.

Shoebox Annie had taken precautions in the event that Earl was caught. "People don't like to send a boy to prison," she instructed her son. Further he was to take all the blame for the passing of bad checks if cornered. When this happened, Earl skillfully played out the scenario written for him by his scheming mother, pleading and crying great tears as he sobbed, "Please don't have me arrested. I forged my mother's name to that check. If she finds out it will kill her." The ploy worked, again and again.

Earl's successful check passing put expensive clothes on Shoebox Annie's back. While in her late forties, she appeared more of a society matron with an ingratiating smile than the determined crook she was. She had been a thief for decades, earning her sobriquet through a device solely of her own invention.

Her unique method of shoplifting involved, naturally, a shoebox. She would tape some strong paper over a lidless box then wrap string around the sides of the box but not across the top. Then, having cut a slit in the paper, she could slip any item that caught her fancy into the box, which appeared to be a solidly wrapped purchase.

Earl, by 1914, had grown into a murderous thug, according to his mother's plan. A San Francisco cop interrupted the youth as he was about to beat a man to death for his wallet which contained four dollars. Earl was sent to a reformatory for three years. Not more than a week after he was released, Earl teamed up with his mother and they stole a car in Bozeman, Montana. Earl was caught and given a five-year term in the state prison; Shoebox Annie, as usual, went her merry way.

Paroled in 1920, Earl went back to his mother in Anaconda, Montana. The two of them had developed a murder-for-profit plan that, to their prosaic way of thinking, would prove impenetrable by police. As Mary Smith put it to Earl, "They can't prove murder unless they find the body!" With this thought in mind, the Smiths built a tank of sheet copper beneath their home and filled it with muriatic acid, a substance so corrosive that it was guaranteed to dissolve almost anything.

This task complete, Earl, who was then using the alias of Mayer, approached a wealthy oil-stock speculator, Ole Larson, telling him that he could sell him valuable stock. Larson took the bait and accepted a dinner invitation, arriving with a burgeoning wallet. He was delighted to sample some of Shoebox Annie's home cooking. Following dinner, Larson disappeared.

Police accused Earl Mayer of murdering Larson but the killer was prepared, snapping back, "You say I killed Ole Larson. If that's so, produce the body."

No corpse could be produced and Earl went free. His mother then told him that one of his old girl friends, a woman named LaCasse, had married into wealth and was living in Seattle. Earl traveled to Seattle. The LaCasse woman vanished. Police trailed Earl back to his mother's home in Anaconda and found the missing woman's jewels, furs, even her monogrammed underwear, but no trace of the woman.

Detectives confronted Mary Smith, all but stating that she and her son had murdered the LaCasse woman. Sneered Shoebox Annie, "All right. Prove we killed her. Find the body!"

The police, however, did not give up and followed the mother and son everywhere. Shoebox Annie and Earl moved to Seattle in disgust. For the next several years, Earl spent most of his time stealing cars and reselling them, turning over his profits, except for walk-about money, to his glinty-eyed mother.

One car in particular interested Earl in 1920, a bright blue roadster which had been advertised for sale. The seller was a young navy lieutenant, James Eugene Bassett, who disappeared while in Earl Mayer's company. The car had also disappeared, and an all-points bulletin went out, alerting police to look for the roadster. A week later an Oakland squad car pulled in front of a blue roadster, curbing the car. Inside sat a stern-faced old woman and a hollow-eyed cadaverous man with thinning hair.

A search of the car revealed Bassett's cuff links and watch. The victim's wallet was found empty, stuffed between seat cushions. Though police searched the Smith home on the outskirts of Seattle, they could find no body. Both Mrs. Smith and Earl were charged, however, with grand larceny. Earl's long prison record earned him a life term as a habitual criminal. Shoebox Annie, protesting her innocence to the end, drew an eight-year term.

In November 1938, when about to be paroled, Mary Smith was suddenly charged with the murder of Lieutenant Bassett. She faced another trial and a surprise witness, a cellmate to whom the garrulous old woman had confided the killing of Bassett. The witness had to shout in court above the screams and oaths of Shoebox Annie, but her story was heard and believed. She quoted Mary Smith as telling her the following tale: "Well, the truth is, we did kill Bassett. Earl brought him to the house. I already had water boiling in the kitchen in case I needed it to wash up any blood. Bassett had made out the bill of sale, and Earl had said he would give him a check when he came to the house. Instead, Earl hit him on the head with a hammer.

"Then we undressed him and dragged him into the bathroom. Earl had big tongs to do things like this, because he was afraid fingerprints might show on dead bodies. We drained the blood out of him and then Earl cut the body into pieces and we put them in a galvanized tub. We were careful not to get blood on anything. After a while we had dinner. Then we put the pieces of the body in gunny sacks and took them out into the country, and Earl buried them one at a time.

"But we were scared that night. The car ran into a ditch and some people came up and saw us. We thought sure we were discovered, but they went on, and we buried the body. We never heard anything from them. So everything was all right."

Other witnesses came forward to state that they had seen the mother and son burying sacks in an open field. Both Mary Smith and her dismembering son were convicted. A few days later Earl committed suicide in his cell, fearing that the state of Washington would demand his death.

The prosecution did insist on hanging Shoebox Annie. Ironically, this murderous harridan was saved by the very mother of her victim. Mrs. Bassett appeared at Mrs. Smith's trial and was asked by the prosecution, "Do you desire that the death penalty be inflicted?"

Mrs. Bassett replied, "No. I shall be content if she remains in prison."

Shoebox Annie went back to prison for the remainder of her life.

SNYDER, RUTH

Murderer ■ (1893–1928)

As murderers go, there was nothing at all spectacular about Ruth Snyder. She was a rather frumpy thirty-two-year-old housewife with dead eyes, a lantern jaw, and a head of peroxide blonde hair. Her lover and co-killer, Henry Judd Gray, was equally uninspiring, a little fellow addicted to dapper attire but generally frightened of his own shadow, an adult male who was in every sense a mama's boy with Ruth acting out the part of surrogate mother. (Gray's own mother staunchly defended him at his trial, even sitting on his lap for the sensation-seeking photographers of the Jazz Age.)

Snyder and Gray killed for sex, and that was the real reason their trial was so highly publicized. They had been carrying on a tawdry affair for two years. Both were married. Ruth decided that her unsuspecting husband, Albert, an art editor for *Motor Boating* magazine, must be killed. It was the only way she could be happy.

Gray had to get half drunk to sneak into the Snyder home in Queens, New York, on the night of March 19, 1927. He met Ruth in an upstairs closet to have a quick carnal bout before slipping into the bedroom where Albert Snyder slept. Gray smashed his victim on the head with a sash weight Ruth had given him, but Snyder awoke and put up a struggle. Screamed Gray, "Momsie, Momsie—for God's sake, help!" It was the cold-hearted Ruth Snyder who then rushed into the bedroom, grabbed the sash weight, and crushed her husband's skull.

Ruth's weak tale of intruders breaking into her house and killing her husband was suspected by police from the start to be a lie. She quickly broke down and confessed, but stated that it was all Gray's idea. Gray was arrested and confessed, blaming everything on Ruth.

The trial was a newspaperman's delight, and for days New York headlines screamed every tidbit of the sordid affair and inept murder. One wry journalist, Damon Runyon,

Granite-jawed Ruth Snyder, who committed the sensational murder of her husband in 1927.

dubbed the killing the "Dumb-bell Murder," because "it was so dumb."

Both defendants were found guilty and sentenced to die in the electric chair. While awaiting execution, Snyder and Gray told their rather tedious "autobiographies" to the newspapers. Ruth received 164 offers of marriage from men who begged to be dominated by her, provided she was reprieved. (Most of these oddball suitors undoubtedly remembered Judd Gray's courtroom statement: "She had this power over me.")

There was no reprieve. Both went to the electric chair on the night of January 12, 1928. Gray went first, terrified and trembling. Ruth Snyder followed, sitting down stonily into the chair. As the electrodes were fixed to her bare

Ruth Snyder's timorous lover and co-murderer Judd Gray, shown at his 1927 trial, being consoled by his mother.

legs and skull, she mumbled the words, "Father, forgive them for they don't know what they're doing." A mask was then placed over her face.

In the crowd of reporters on hand to witness the event was Basil Gray (no relation to Judd), a staffer for the *New York Daily News*. Defying prison regulations, Gray had strapped a small camera to his leg. A trip line ran up his leg to his wrist under his clothes. Just as the current was thrown into Snyder's body, Gray lifted his trouser leg, squeezed the plunger in his hand and snapped a photo of Ruth Snyder being thrown in a death shock against the restraining straps of the chair. This photo took up the entire front page of the *News* the next day with the headline, DEAD!—a hallmark in journalistic bad taste.

But even in worse taste was the bit of doggerel written by Ruth Snyder and published after her death, a bit of self-serving kitsch in which the killer attempted to whitewash herself **and** her crime while attacking the press:

You've blackened and besmeared a mother,
Once a man's plaything—A Toy—
What have you gained by all you've said,
And has it—brought you Joy?

SPARA, HIERONYMA ("LA SPARA")

Murderer ■ (? –1659)

I n 1659 members of the clergy in Rome went to Pope Alexander VII, having found it necessary to violate the rules of the confessional. Several women, the pope was informed, had confessed to poisoning their husbands, which explained the vastly increasing numbers of attractive widows in the city. There were also reports that unhappy marriages had abruptly ended of late with the husband dying in screaming agony.

Investigating officials soon uncovered an odd sect of women who met each night in the home of an ancient crone named Hieronyma Spara, a seller of perfumes and a self-proclaimed witch. After performing Dianic rituals, La Spara would provide powerful poisons to be administered to those husbands unwanted by members of her underground society.

A female papal spy entered the group, and was given poison with which to kill her husband after the woman complained about her spouse—La Spara charged the spy a great deal of money for the homemade deathbrew. Days later La Spara was arrested, and, under torture, outlined the work of her society. She, La Gratiosa, her chief accomplice, and three women who had poisoned their husbands were publicly humiliated, then hanged as witches and murderers. More than thirty other women belonging to the secret society were driven half naked through the streets of Rome, mercilessly whipped and beaten.

SPENCER, BARBARA

Counterfeiter ■ (? –1721)

A difficult child, born in St. Giles, England, Barbara was sent at an early age to apprentice with a weaver. Her violent temper soon caused her employer to return Barbara home. She quarreled constantly with her mother and then ran away to London where she became a counterfeiter. Having been apprehended and tried, she was amazed to hear herself condemned in court. (Counterfeiting, as well as coining, in that period was a crime of treason against the Crown in that the countenances of royalty were tampered with or defaced.)

Barbara was taken to Tyburn on July 5, 1721, where she angered the large throng by shouting curses back at spectators who threw stones and dirt at her. In the barbaric tradition of the day, Barbara Spencer was first strangled and then burned to ashes.

Following her burial, Barbara's mother announced that her daughter's very first offenses had involved running away to Tyburn to witness the executions of convicted criminals, the very spot where her horrible fate had been meted out to her.

SPINELLI, MRS. EVELITA JUANITA

Murderer ■ (1889–1941)

V icious, cold-blooded, and utterly ruthless, Evelita Spinelli, already a middle-aged woman, suddenly decided upon a career of crime and acted upon that decision with a vengeance. Called "the Duchess" by underworld characters in San Francisco, the widow Spinelli took up with Mike Simeone who became her common-law husband. At her direction Simeone recruited a gang of young thugs in the Bay area, all of them swearing allegiance to the Duchess as their iron-willed leader.

The Duchess proved her superiority over her minions from the start. She terrified them into obedience by putting on wrestling exhibitions in her home, tossing burly henchmen over her shoulder with ease. How Mrs. Spinelli developed such athletic prowess is unknown, and what was more puzzling was the source of her strength. She was scrawny and thin shouldered. The Duchess was also myopic and sported big ears and a long, pointed nose, which later prompted Warden Clinton T. Duffy of San Quentin—who was to order her execution—to describe her as "an enormous mouse wearing glasses."

Also among Mrs. Spinelli's hidden treasure trove of talent was an expert ability at knife throwing. She could whirl about and in the same movement hurl a knife with lightning speed, splitting a poker chip at thirty paces with unerring accuracy. The Duchess's word was law with her gang.

The Duchess pinpointed where the gang would commit their holdups, marking the spots on a San Francisco map, careful never to stage robberies in the same area twice. The gang also hijacked trucks with expensive goods and sold the goods through fences. When not working on what the Duchess thought to be an important job, gang members were instructed to roll at least five drunks a night and return the loot to Mrs. Spinelli. The Duchess herself picked up spare money by manufacturing blackjacks for other petty mobsters.

Things went along smoothly for the Duchess for some time, until the owner of a barbecue stand was murdered when her gang held up the place. The Duchess and her gang fled to Sacramento, taking rooms in the Arlton Hotel. With Mrs. Spinelli were her husband, Simeone, Gordon Hawkins, Albert Ives, and Robert Sherrard. The Duchess was nervous about the nineteen-year-old Sherrard. He gave every indication that he intended to give himself up to police and to tell all he knew about the murder.

The Duchess decided to take care of Sherrard herself and one evening slipped chloral

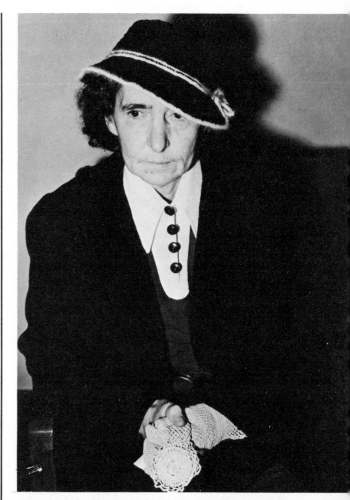

Mrs. Evelita Spinelli, San Francisco gang leader, under arrest.

hydrate into the youth's whiskey. When the "knock-out drops" took effect, the other three men, under Mrs. Spinelli's direction, carried the unconscious Sherrard to their car. The entire gang then drove to the Freeport-Clarksburg Bridge where Sherrard was thrown into the Sacramento River to meet a watery death.

All would have gone as planned had not Albert Ives broken down when arrested for a petty offense and informed on the Duchess, Simeone, and Hawkins. Though Ives himself was later judged insane and sent to the Mendocino State

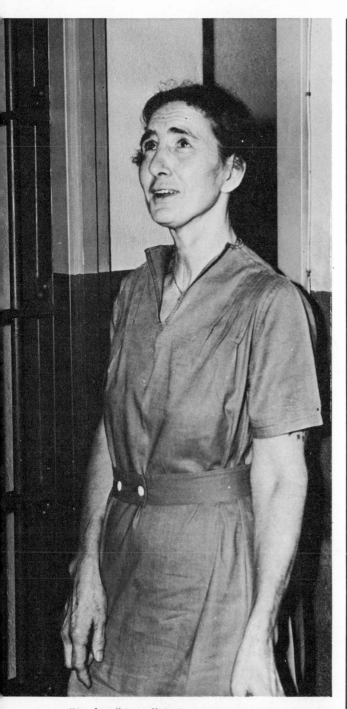

"Duchess" Spinelli in San Quentin awaiting execution in 1941.

Hospital for life, his testimony sent the other three to death row, the men to await execution at San Quentin, the Duchess at the women's prison at Tehachapi.

Mrs. Spinelli was reprieved from her death sentence several times but was finally scheduled to become the first woman to enter California's gas chamber at San Quentin on Novermber 21, 1941. (She was, in fact, the first woman ever to be officially executed in that state.) The Duchess was hard-bitten to the end. When asked if there was anything that could be done for her, she snapped, "Yeah—tell that son-of-a-bitch Simeone to tell the truth! He's the only one who can get me out of this!"

But no one could save the hard-hearted Duchess. She went to her execution almost on schedule. Actually she arrived prematurely at the gas chamber, before the necessary witnesses were in place. Warden Duffy asked Mrs. Spinelli if she wished to return to her cell while the sixty-six witnesses were brought into the death hall.

Without a flicker of emotion, the Duchess said, "No—we'll just stand here." In full sight were the two chairs inside the gas chamber, the chamber door open and waiting. Beneath the chairs the bags of cyanide suspended above the wells of sulphuric acid were plainly visible.

"Does this bother you?" she was asked.

"Oh, no," replied the stony-faced woman. She turned to Clinton Duffy. "The sun's out, isn't it, warden?"

"Yes."

"It's a beautiful day," she said flatly.

"Yes, bright and sunshiny."

"It sometimes gets so damp and foggy here." Incredibly, while the witnesses filed into the room, Mrs. Spinelli continued to chat about the weather while waiting for her own death.

When all sixty-six witnesses were present, Warden Duffy nodded to Mrs. Spinelli, saying, "It's time. . . . Keep your chin up."

The woman shrugged. "Okay." She walked calmly to one of the chairs in the gas chamber and sat down without a flicker of fright. She died a few minutes later with four photographs, showing her three children and that of a grandchild, strapped to her heart.

SPOONER, BATHSHEBA

Murderer ■ (1746–1778)

The daughter of General Timothy Ruggles and a devout Tory, Bathsheba hated her marriage to elderly Joshua Spooner from the start. It was a social marriage arranged between two prominent Massachusetts families. Bathsheba, an attractive woman, soon ignored her wedding vows and took up with a lover, one Ezra Ross, who regularly sneaked into the Spooner mansion near Worcester to meet his paramour.

During the Revolution, Bathsheba, continuing her affair with Ross, nurtured a special hatred for her husband. Spooner was a Revolutionary. She was loyal to the British king. She decided, for the sake of both her love life and her strong political beliefs, to murder her husband.

Two British soldiers, James Buchanan and Alexander Cummings, who had deserted, were taken in by Bathsheba on February 8, 1778. Promising them money, Bathsheba convinced the deserters to join in her murder plot, along with her lover Ross.

The murder was a clumsy affair. The three men simply beat old Joshua Spooner to death and threw his body down a well. The corpse was soon discovered and the British soldiers were found in a Worcester inn spending the money Bathsheba had given them. Spooner's watch was also found on Buchanan. Cummings was wearing the victim's hat.

Bathsheba and her cohorts were all tried on April 1, 1778, the first case of a capital offense under the new Constitution. All four defendants pleaded not guilty but were convicted and sentenced to be hanged on July 2, 1778. More than five thousand people thronged the streets of Worcester on the day of execution.

The beautiful Bathsheba went calmly to her death, though she protested the sentence, claiming that she was pregnant. As she had requested, an examination was conducted following her execution, and doctors discovered her claim to be true. A five-month fetus was found, the child of Ross or, perhaps, one of the British soldiers. No one ever knew which.

STARR, BELLE

Thief ■ (1848–1889)

Horse thief, fence, and mistress to many lesser-known outlaws of the Oklahoma Territory during the 1870s and 1880s, Belle Starr was the most overrated female bandit of her day. She reveled in a reputation she

Horse thief Belle Starr, dressed to kill.

never earned and had her photo taken wearing many guns. Except for whipping her prize horse **Venus**, whom she whipped mercilessly, Belle raised little terror in anyone.

Belle lived for a while with Cole Younger, of the Jesse James band, and reportedly had his child, Pearl. When Younger rode back to Missouri, Belle took up with outlaw Jim Reed. When Reed was shot down in 1874, she went to live with an Indian renegade named Blue Duck. Another Indian outlaw, Sam Starr, caught Belle's eye and they were married.

The Starrs concentrated on horse stealing and were tried several times for that offense, each receiving a six-month sentence in 1883. When Sam Starr was killed in a gun fight in 1886, Belle moved in with Jim July, another Indian on the wrong side of the law.

Belle, decked out in her velvet riding dress with guns strapped high on her hips, was shot from ambush and killed on February 3, 1889, while riding to her shack at Younger's Bend, an area in the Oklahoma wilds Belle had named after her one true love, Cole Younger. Her killer, probably a discarded lover, was never found. Few mourned her passing.

STEWART, MRS. FRANCIS

Murderer ■ (1831–1874)

Mrs. Stewart, for unexplained reasons, killed her infant grandchild in 1874. Hanged at Newgate, she became a first in Britain's history of capital punishment. She was the first grandmother executed for such a murder.

STOPA, WANDA

Murderer ■ (1899–1925)

Wanda killed for love, or the lack of it. In love with her artistic mentor, Y. K. Smith, a Chicago advertising executive who had rebuffed her, Wanda went to Smith's home in Palos Park on April 24, 1924, and rushed inside, where she fired several shots at Smith's wife, Vieva, the rival she sought to eliminate. Mrs. Smith ducked out of the way, but one of Wanda's bullets strayed into the garden and killed Henry Manning, the sixty-eight-year-old caretaker of the Smith estate.

The hysterical woman then raced to the

Flapper Wanda Stopa, who killed for love.

street and hopped into a taxi which she had waiting. Wanda Stopa was traced to Detroit and found in the Hotel Statler. While the detectives were breaking down her door, the beautiful Jazz Age flapper swallowed an entire bottle of poison. When they finally gained entry into her room, she was dead.

Wanda had been a brilliant attorney, having served as an assistant district attorney in Chicago; she was much respected in that she had struggled out of destitute conditions in Chicago's Little Poland. Wanda Stopa received a funeral nearly equal to that of a head of state, as all of Little Poland turned out to bid this tragic young woman farewell.

SWETT, JANE

Murderer ■ (1805– ?)

After a thirty-year marriage of constant battling with her alcoholic husband, Charles Swett, who had set himself up as an independent Baptist minister in Kennebunk, Maine, Jane Swett dosed her husband's whiskey with morphine, killing him on the night of September 23, 1866. She was sentenced to six years in prison.

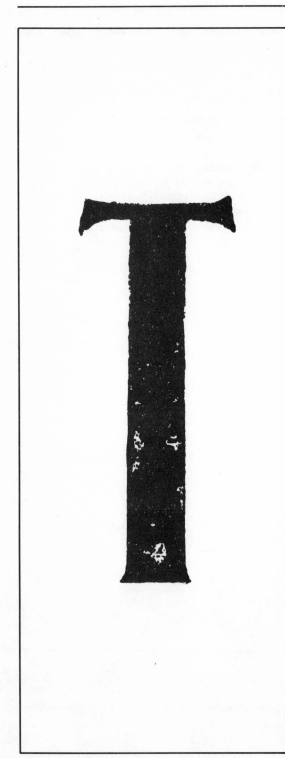

TARNOWSKA, COUNTESS MARIA

Murderer ■ (1878–1923)

From childhood, the Countess Tarnowska exhibited the kind of ruthless selfishness for which members of her noble class came to be loathed, a desperate greed that would bring about the death of numerous lovers who were overpowered by her lethal charms. Neither life nor death held any meaning for Maria. She used and discarded men like soiled lace handkerchiefs, and the more callous she became, the more her victims seemed to love her cold-blooded ways.

This vixen was born in St. Petersburg, Russia, in 1878, the daughter of a Russian noblewoman and Count O'Rourk, whose foreign ancestry in xenophobic Russia was explained by an early-day Irish adventurer, a soldier of fortune who had immigrated to Russia to become a military commander for Peter the Great. At the age of thirteen Maria Nicolaievna O'Rourk was sent to the School for Noblemen's Daughters, an elite institution in Kiev. Within two years, Maria had blossomed into a young woman who attracted the attentions of dozens of cavalry officers stationed nearby. Belying her years was a husky voice and the body of a mature woman. One of her many biographers described her at this time as being "physically a knockout. Her hair was auburn, her eyes deep blue, her features fine, and her complexion flawless. As for her body, a Parisian modiste, on an occasion when the countess was more or less on public display for an extended period, made the considered statement that she had the best figure of any woman in Europe."

Three suitors sought her hand, a prince and a baron, both of impoverished estates, and Count Vassili Tarnowska, a wild libertine with many mistresses and the well-deserved reputation of being a satyr. Count O'Rourk approved of either the prince or baron but warned his daughter against Tarnowska. Maria eloped with the count some days later, just after her sixteenth birthday. So madly in love with the girl was the count that he sacrificed his military career to run off with the alluring teenager.

When the couple returned to Kiev, they entered a gay court life of incessant parties and revels, but, as Maria's father had predicted, Tarnowska soon tired of his youthful bride and took a mistress. The count flaunted this woman in front of Maria. Her reaction was to take on several lovers, draining them of their funds with which the countess purchased jewels, the beginning of a gem collection that would later astound European royalty.

Although the Tarnowskas had two children born to them, the couple remained distant, pursuing their own love affairs. Maria feebly attempted a reconciliation with her roaming husband, but, when these efforts proved futile, she seduced the count's brother Peter, a naive youth who melted like butter under Maria's steaming advances. The countess carried on her torrid affair with Peter in her own home; Tarnowska was certainly aware of being cuckolded under his own roof but made no response.

Maria then sent Peter away, telling him, "Wait two months. If by that time you feel the same toward me, I will come to you." Within a few weeks the countess was involved with another man and wrote Peter that she was no longer interested in him. The day the lovesick Peter received this note he hanged himself.

Maria ignored the suicide, having by that time attracted the attentions of a wealthy financier who lavished jewels upon her, pleading with her to flee with him to the Urals. This man's gifts of priceless gems Maria hid away and then told him that, no, she must stay at her husband's side for the sake of her children—two youngsters the countess rarely saw. The financier blew his brains out. Receiving the news of the latest fatality of her affections, Maria merely shrugged and said, "He was a fool."

She next turned her attentions to a dashing member of the Imperial Guard, one Captain Alex Bozevsky, a satyr like her husband. So violent was Bozevsky's sex that even the countess, an agile acrobat in the bedroom, grew weary of her lover's tireless demands on her. In her peculiar logic, Maria decided that the only way to rid

herself of her overactive lover was to arrange for his death. Knowing that her husband would return shortly to the St. Petersburg mansion, she contrived to have Bozevsky visit her in her boudoir, and left instructions with a servant to have Tarnowska come there as soon as he returned home.

The duped Bozevsky rushed into Maria's bedroom to find her, arms open, wearing a diaphanous sapphire blue negligee. One impassioned scribe dwelt upon this spidery scene: "Revealed in all their seductive loveliness were the graceful lines of the body which had captivated the souls of so many men."

Running into the arms of her lover, Maria smothered him with fiery kisses, holding him even tighter when she heard her husband's footsteps outside her bedroom door. When Tarnowska threw open the door, Maria suddenly leaped back from Bozevsky, then playing the outraged wife, viciously hitting the startled captain of cavalry, screaming, "How dare you enter my bed chamber and assault me?"

Without a moment's hesitation Tarnowska, who always went armed, as Maria was aware, drew a pistol and shot Bozevsky, the wound in his chest causing blood to spurt onto the front of Maria's exquisite gown. As her lover collapsed into an unromantic heap on an expensive bearskin, Maria ran to the protective arms of her husband. When the couple discovered that Bozevsky was still alive, they called a wealthy physician friend, Dr. Dmitri Stahl, to attend to the captain. Stahl could do little; Bozevsky was dying. Maria, in the presence of Dr. Stahl, visited Bozevsky's deathbed, playing the part of the bereaved and star-crossed lover, sobbing, "What could I do, Alex? When my husband came in unexpectedly, I had to keep up appearances." Bozevsky died smiling and believing that his lovely Maria had been as much a victim of fate as had he.

Dr. Stahl at this moment leered at Maria and at once decided to have her no matter the cost. A drug addict himself, Stahl introduced the countess to cocaine, to which she would later become addicted. Tarnowska, through Maria's efforts, abetted by Stahl, was charged with murder and locked up. This was another plot by the scheming countess to rid herself of her unwanted husband and yet retain his estate and his fortune.

Stahl lent Maria a vast sum of money to arrange for her husband's exile to Siberia for murder and summoned a meek-mannered lawyer, Donat Prilukoff, to work with the countess in having Tarnowska's estate placed in her hands. To assure herself of unswerving loyalty from both men, Maria carried on simultaneous affairs with Stahl and the married Prilukoff.

The plot, however, failed miserably. Tarnowska was acquitted of the murder charge and promptly divorced Maria, giving her a small settlement and driving her from his mansion with a whip. She fled into the arms of Dr. Stahl who set her up in an apartment. Maria bled the doctor of his entire fortune within a few months, and when the impoverished physician begged her to marry him the countess reacted in her typical fashion: she spat in his face. Dr. Stahl, like others before him, borrowed a pistol and sent a bullet into his brain.

Now the lawyer Prilukoff came to the top of Maria's list of victims. Working her wiles on this reserved, unemotional man, the countess convinced Prilukoff to embezzle a huge amount of money from the coffers of a firm he represented and run away with her. He did her bidding, deserting his wife and three children, traveling with the dazzling countess to Vienna, Paris, Algeria, and then to Marseilles. The man found himself a slave to Maria, unable to leave her though he attempted several times to flee her conniving clutches.

In Marseilles, Prilukoff summoned his courage and momentarily escaped, boarding a train that would take him back to his family. His later statement to a startled courtroom in Venice gave some insight into how powerful was Maria's hold upon the man Maria contemptuously called "the Scorpion." Testified Prilukoff, "I had only gone a few stations when I heard a call of Maria. I tried to resist it, but it was too strong for me, and I got out of the train at the next station and returned to my beloved."

Though Prilukoff feared apprehension for his embezzlement, Maria easily convinced the weak-willed lawyer to return to Russia with her. Within weeks of their arrival, Maria snared another victim, Count Paul Kamarowsky, a rich and respected nobleman. Kamarowsky, a liberal-minded man, did not mind the ménage à trois and paid for the trio's luxury trip to Warsaw. Here Kamarowsky introduced Maria to his good friend, Dr. Nicholas Naumoff, whispering in the countess's ear, "Naumoff hates women—your wiles will not work on him."

The head-hunting Maria could not resist the challenge. She made Naumoff her prime love target. The doctor, a high-strung young man, was the son of the governor of Orel. Instead of rebuffing Maria's nymphomaniacal advances, Naumoff fell completely under her spell, so much so that he allowed full expression to Maria's sadistic urges.

Following one of their all-night orgies, Maria slid a pistol across the bed where her exhausted lover lay prostrate and panting. "If you love me," Maria told Naumoff, "you will shoot yourself."

Naumoff grabbed the gun. "Where?"

"Anywhere," Maria smiled, "just shoot yourself for me."

The sex-befuddled doctor then shot himself through the hand. Maria went wild at the sight of Naumoff's blood, becoming so sexually aroused that she hurled herself upon him before the lover could bandage his wound. On another occasion Naumoff sat dumbly on the edge of Maria's bed while she carved her initials in his arm with a razor, sterilizing the gashes with eau de cologne. "The sight of your blood," said the countess, "gives me immense pleasure—only when seeing your blood flow do I realize that you love me as much as I love you!" It is no wonder that the press and public alike reeled in shock when Naumoff later revealed these strange sex rites in court, practices that undoubtedly led to Maria's being labeled "the Russian Vampire," and "the Sphinx in Crepe."

Maria's excessive tastes and high living soon made it necessary for her to field about for substantial sums of money. Count Kamarowsky had given her a small allowance but when she had taken up with his friend Naumoff, the count had cut her off. Naumoff had already been bled white of his trust fund, so Maria returned to Kamarowsky, begging him to marry her. While the count considered, Maria convinced him to take out a life insurance policy of 20,000 pounds, equivalent at the time to about $100,000, naming her as the sole beneficiary. The countess then went separately to Naumoff and her old lackey, lawyer Prilukoff, telling each of them that she wanted Count Kamarowsky murdered.

To Naumoff, Maria presented the motive of avenging her honor, giving the young doctor the false tale that the count had ravished her repeatedly against her will, and stolen her jewels (she had already pawned most of her gems to pay for her exorbitant expenses). Naumoff vowed to kill his one-time friend.

"I will seek him out and challenge him to a duel!"

"No," cautioned Maria, "he must be murdered. In a duel anything might happen. You might be killed—then, my dearest, what would I do without you? No, you must shoot Kamarowsky. You must do it with a revolver, throw it away so it cannot be found when the deed is done, and then telegraph me in a false name."

Naumoff left immediately on his murder chore, going from Vienna to Venice, where Kamarowsky was vacationing. Maria then met with her stooge-like lover Prilukoff, telling him that the count must be murdered.

"Maybe I could get him to smoke a chloroformed cigarette," the lawyer mused.

"No," said Maria. "Use the dagger!" She went on to explain that Kamarowsky had taken out a life insurance policy in her favor and "when the count is out of the way we will spend the rest of our days together living on the money from his insurance."

Though slavish in his devotion to Maria, Prilukoff was not necessarily stupid. After some checking on his scheming lover's activities, he discovered that Maria had sent Naumoff to Venice to kill the count.

When confronted by the lawyer with her double-dealing, Maria simply explained that she had not really wanted Prilukoff—the man she really loved—to risk his life in killing the well-armed count and had sent Naumoff to perform the errand. "However," she added, her mind never at a loss for a new plot, "I want you, dear Donat, to go to Venice after all and arrange to have detectives at the scene of the shooting so they can arrest Naumoff. We will then be rid of both these pesky gentlemen."

Such an insidious plan appealed to the lawyer; he was on the next train for Venice, Maria accompanying him in case he were to lose heart. They arrived on September 1, 1907. Two days later Naumoff burst into the villa Kamarowsky had rented on the Campo Santa Maria del Giglio, brushing past the maid, Isabella Gregorio, and rushing upstairs to the count's room with a drawn revolver.

The maid heard Naumoff yell out, "Paul, you scum!" Then there were shots. Flattening herself against the wall of the staircase in fright, the maid watched bug-eyed as Naumoff raced down the stairs, his revolver smoking, and disappeared out the door.

The detectives Prilukoff had arranged to have at the villa—they had received an anonymous tip from the lawyer warning of an attack on Kamarowsky—were too late to prevent the murder, but they pieced the crime together in short order. The maid identified Naumoff, who was arrested at a train station as he prepared to flee Italy. Naumoff quickly confessed to the plot and, his will shattered, implicated the love of his life. Countess Tarnowska and Prilukoff were eventually located and extradited from Vienna to stand trial in Venice. Because of the effectiveness of lawyer Prilukoff's delaying tactics, the trial of the murderous threesome did not take place until March 1910. All three admitted their complicity, but each attempted to place the burden of the killing on one of the others.

The press had a field day with Countess Maria Tarnowska. Her every move in court was chronicled by scores of fascinated newsmen. The correspondent for the London *Mail* described Maria's physical appearance as "amazing. . . . Only Guy de Maupassant if he were alive, or Gabriele D'Annunzio, if he cared to, could describe the peculiar power of those weird black eyes. . . . I have observed her for thirty minutes while the clock of the court struck the hour and then the half hour, and I did not see those uncanny eyes blink a single time. And yet those inscrutable eyes appear to read one's very soul." The French reporters concentrated on the physi-

Under a murder charge, Countess Maria Tarnowska enters court under guard in March 1910.

cal litheness of the twenty-nine-year-old vampire. Said *Le Figaro* of Paris: "Her figure has the pure lines of a Greek amphora."

The trial itself was brief, with all three being found guilty and sentenced to prison terms: Prilukoff to ten years, Maria to eight years, and the much duped Naumoff, the actual killer, to only two years. The leniency of Naumoff's sentence was explained by the presiding judge who informed the press, "He was inhumanely coerced, tricked, and deluded into his foolish and vicious act."

Maria was sent to a rather comfortable cell in Trani Prison where she wrote verses about murder which were published in French magazines. She received more than fifty legitimate offers of marriage from wealthy men who begged to be her love slave; she answered none of these proposals.

Released in August 1912, her health shattered, Maria drifted from Vienna to Russia, then Paris, her cocaine habit dominating her life. The woman who had caused the death of at least a half dozen men died in obscurity in 1923. Maria's lovers and fellow murder conspirators, Prilukoff and Naumoff, faithful unto the grave, died only months after being informed of her death.

TAYLOR, LOUISA JANE

Murderer ■ (1846–1883)

The motive of Louisa Jane Taylor for poisoning an eighty-two-year-old woman to death has never been determined, but though her methods were awkward, her conduct stupid, the simple fact of her ponderous murder plan points to a dedicated slayer. The odd twist in the Taylor case involved the kind of poison the killer chose, one so obvious that its use was almost overlooked.

Mrs. Taylor's background remained sketchy despite the extensive probing of Scotland Yard and literary sleuths who looked into her life years later. At age thirty-six, Louisa Taylor, an attractive brunette, became a widow. Her husband, a retired dockworker twice her age, died in March 1882, leaving Mrs. Taylor with a small pension. In August of that year Louisa visited William Tregillis, a friend of her husband's, who lived at 3 Naylor's Cottages, Plumstead. Tregillis, an eighty-five-year-old naval worker, also retired and living on a pension, asked the kindly Louisa to stay with him and his wife, Mary Ann. It was understood that as a boarder Louisa would pay her rent by acting as a nurse to the ailing Mary Ann, a woman of eighty-two. Mrs. Taylor happily agreed. She slept with Mrs. Tregillis while William bedded down in the front room of the two-room apartment.

Within days, the old man began to notice small objects, bric-a-brac and pictures with expensive frames, disappear from the household. He thought he only imagined these items missing and chalked it up to senility. More annoying were the nocturnal visits paid to Mrs. Taylor by a young gentleman named Edward Martin, who told Tregillis that he was a watercress salesman. On such occasions Mrs. Taylor asked Tregillis to stay with his wife while she enjoyed her tryst; the old man grumpily complied.

Early in September, Tregillis told Mrs. Taylor, "I'm worried for my wife's health. If she should pass on, I'd be put in an institution."

Louisa's response was to rub the old man's shoulders soothingly and say, "We should leave her to fend for herself. She's an invalid. We can't do anything for her. Let us go away together."

"What? Are you suggesting—?"

"Yes, that we elope."

"I'm an old man," croaked Tregillis. "My wife is not dead. How could I expect to live with you? I would not come unless I married you."

Louisa politely dropped the subject and went back to nursing Mrs. Tregillis, though by September, her condition seemed to worsen, despite regular visits by a Dr. Smith. At each visit, Louisa asked the physician for large quantities of sugar of lead (lead acetate), explaining that she needed this for "injections" that would keep her complexion smooth. Dr. Smith gave Mrs. Taylor all the sugar of lead she wanted. The patient thereafter began to grow increasingly worse. Mrs. Tregillis would go into shivering fits, and she vomited almost all her meals, including the medicine fed to her by the dutiful Mrs. Taylor. Dr. Smith repeatedly asked Louisa to give him samples of the vomit, but the woman always found an excuse for not doing so, later stating that she found such a chore "nauseating and disgusting."

Louisa Taylor, notorious British poisoner.

When Tregillis mentioned to Mrs. Taylor that several keepsakes in the apartment appeared to be missing, Louisa Taylor ignored the comment and quickly confided that she had made out a will in which she was leaving 500 pounds to Tregillis. Though his faculties were dim, the old man was able to perceive this to be a ridiculous gesture.

"You're not half my age, so why leave anything to me? I'll die first, that's certain."

Louisa only smiled and showed the old man an official-looking document addressed to her, which stated, "Madam, you have had 500 pounds left you and can draw on it any day." The old man could only shake his head in wonder.

Meanwhile Mrs. Tregillis became so sick that she could hold nothing in her stomach, a symptom that completely baffled Dr. Smith. Never once, until it was too late, did the physician check to see if Mrs. Tregillis was being poisoned, even though all her symptoms indicated it. In the words of Jack Smith-Hughes, writing in *Eight Studies in Justice*, Dr. Smith "was destined for permanent fame as the doctor who supplied the poison and treated the victim without having his suspicions even momentarily aroused." Not until October 6, 1882, did Dr. Smith suspect poison. And even then his suspicions were aroused by other events, specifically when Tregillis called the police to his apartment to charge Louisa Taylor with stealing a pension payment of ten pounds.

He explained to constables that he had just received this payment, and, after cashing the check, was confronted by Louisa Taylor.

"Turn over the money to me, please," Louisa told him.

"Why should I do that?"

"Mrs. Tregillis wishes to see it and keep it under her pillow."

The old man respected his wife's wishes and turned over the money to Louisa. A few hours later the landlady downstairs reported to Tregillis that she had seen Mrs. Taylor leaving the building with the money in her hand. Tregillis sent the landlady for the police.

Dr. Smith arrived moments after constables appeared in the Tregillis apartment. Only then did he think something was terribly lacking in his treatment and call in a police doctor. Both doctors inspected the patient's gums, finding a dark blue line at the edge of the gums, the unmistakable sign of lead poisoning. At that moment Mrs. Taylor returned and was placed under arrest for theft, but she was not taken away until confronted by her patient.

Mrs. Tregillis pointed a wavering finger at the woman, saying that she had doctored her to death, that she had seen Mrs. Taylor put a powdery substance into her medicine and had given her two tablespoonfuls every four hours. "I told her it made me very nauseous, that it burned my throat and I wouldn't take any of it. She said, 'You must. What is the good of a doctor, if you do not take his medicine?'"

The old woman went on to tell the doctors and the police that she had continued to take the medicine, even though she vomited everything—"and it came up black and always burned my throat." Louisa Taylor stood like a trapped animal in a corner of the sickroom, shaking her head in denial.

On October 23, Mrs. Tregillis, as expected, died of lead poisoning.

After the body was shown to be full of lead acetate, Mrs. Taylor was charged with murder. She was quickly tried and condemned. Louisa Taylor never admitted her guilt and remained in a highly nervous state until she was led to the Maidstone Prison gallows on January 2, 1883.

For several reasons Louisa Taylor was a most unusual criminal. First, she made an odd choice of poison to kill her victim, for sugar of lead produces easily determined symptoms, and requires massive doses over a long period to take a life. Further distinguishing Louisa as an unorthodox poisoner was her apparent lack of a motive for the murder. Even if her guilt had gone undetected, Louisa stood to reap no more than Tregillis's small pension, one that the crafty old gent would not readily have turned over to her, anyway, and a pension that was half the amount of the one she was already receiving. The motive certainly was not to make herself rich.

Evidently, Louisa Taylor belonged to that group of the most sadistic of killers, a poisoner who enjoys watching the slow and agonizing death she administers to her own trusting victim. It undoubtedly gave Louisa a sense of great power to control the destiny of a fellow human being. But having this power also gave her a false sense of God-like authority and immunity from the law, a mistaken belief that finally placed the hangman's rope around her lovely neck.

TIERNEY, MRS. NORA PATRICIA

Murderer ■ (1920– ?)

Three-year-old Marion Ward was left to play with Stephanie Tierney, age six, along Elsworthy Road in St. John's Wood, London, on August 12, 1949. When the mother, Mrs. Basil Ward, returned from the bakery, the Tierney child was playing alone. She asked where Marion had gone.

"I don't know," came the reply. "She went off to play by herself."

The mother began a frantic search which broadened that night into a full-scale hunt by Scotland Yard. Three days passed before police found the child dead, her head crushed by what seemed to be a hammer. The body was discovered in a bombed-out house not far from the home of James and Nora Tierney. A clear print of a woman's shoe was found near the body and a cast was taken.

Mrs. Tierney, who lived next door to the Wards, was questioned by Chief Inspector James Jamieson of Scotland Yard. The woman was hostile from the first. At twenty-nine, Nora Tierney had a haggard look on her lean face; her red hair hung lankly down her cheeks, her eyes had a vacant look. "I can't help you," she told Jamieson. "I didn't see my neighbor's child on the day she disappeared."

After some parrying, Jamieson suddenly said, "I would like to see your shoes, madam."

Nora showed him to a closet and he selected a few pairs he thought would match the imprint of the woman's shoe found at the murder site.

Next Jamieson said, "If you don't mind, madam, we require parings from your fingernails."

"You require what?"

Jamieson explained and Mrs. Tierney nodded. She held out her hands, and tears began to run down her thin cheeks. Then she blurted out, "I-I-I will tell you the truth of what happened. I didn't do it. My husband did it. I saw him do it." She went on to explain that James Tierney had inexplicably hammered the Ward child to death in the bombed-out house while they were looking for light cords. She had tried to stop the man, Nora insisted, begging him and crying out, "What are you doing this for?" He had knocked her to her knees and she had fled, terrified. Later, Nora said, her husband came home, wiped his fingerprints from the hammer, and hung it up in the kitchen. She reported that they had had the following conversation:

"Will you say you done it?" he asked her.

"Why should I?" she replied.

"They hang men and they won't hang women. Besides, your fingerprints are on the hammer."

It took Scotland Yard little time to prove that James Tierney was nowhere near the scene of the murder and that his wife was lying. Mrs. Tierney was charged with the killing and went to trial at the Old Bailey (by then renamed the Central Criminal Court) in October 1949. Although she denied her guilt the prosecution proved that Nora's right shoe fit the print at the murder site. Further, fibers from a sweater worn by the child were found under Mrs. Tierney's fingernails.

The jury convicted the woman inside of ten minutes. She was condemned to death but later removed to Broadmoor Criminal Lunatic Asylum. The motive for the killing remains undetermined.

TOFFANIA, LA

Murderer ■ (1653–1723)

Like La Voisin, La Spara, and Mrs. Fazekas, La Toffania was a mass poisoner, an ancient woman when at the height of her murder trade, selling for high profit her specially prepared poisons designed to rid wives of unwanted husbands in Naples, Italy. The poison, known as "Aqua Toffania," was reported to be crystallized arsenic compounded with the harmless herb Cymbalaria, though victims given her poisons never exhibited the symtoms of arsenic poisoning.

La Toffania's activities did not come to the attention of authorities until 1719 when the Viceroy of Naples learned that scores of men were being poisoned by their wives and that La Toffiana was the supplier of the deadly drug. The old crone was ordered arrested, but as she had done in the past, she escaped to a nearby nunnery where she claimed sanctuary. (It was the peculiar belief of this woman that she could murder with impunity, then race to a church or nunnery and, once inside the holy building, be cleansed of any guilt.)

Demanding that she be surrendered to him, the Viceroy threatened the abbess of the convent where La Toffania was being sheltered. He was told that the woman would not be given up. The enraged Viceroy then sent a troop of soldiers into the convent to drag the mass killer out; she was then thrown into a dungeon to await trial.

The local archbishop became incensed that one of his convents had been violated and ordered La Toffania returned to the nunnery under pain of excommunication for the entire community, particularly the Viceroy. The Viceroy countered by surrounding the archbishop's palace with troops, informing the clergy inside that they would receive no food unless the threat of excommunication were repealed. The Papal Bull, a formal document of condemnation, was not forthcoming from the archbishop, and La Toffania was subsquently tortured into con-

fessing that she had poisoned or provided the poison that had killed more than six hundred people, almost all males. In her painful recital she mentioned dozens of high-born females who had been her clients. (None of these esteemed ladies was arrested.)

The Viceroy then acted upon his considerable anger toward La Toffiana for her heinous crimes by ordering her strangled to death and her corpse tossed over the wall of the convent where she had taken refuge. One of the world's greatest mass murderers, La Toffania was later used as the hideous protagonist in *Sidonia the Sorceress*.

TOPPAN, JANE

Murderer ■ (1854–1938)

No other class of killer is as treacherous as the medical murder. America's own Jane Toppan was one of this breed, an enigmatic killer whose victims were myriad and whose motives dwelled inside a dark madness.

Jane was born Nora Kelley in Boston in 1854. Her mother died when she was an infant and her father, Peter Kelley, a tailor, looked after Jane and her three sisters. Kelley was found one day in his small shop attempting to stitch his own eyelids, an act that earned him the unfortunate sobriquet of Kelley the Cracked. He was sent to an insane asylum and his daughters were taken in by their grandmother.

When the old woman found it impossible to care for the children, the four girls were taken to an orphanage. Mr. and Mrs. Abner Toppan visited the orphanage in 1859 and were immediately charmed by happy-faced Jane. They adopted the precocious five-year-old and cared for her as one of their own; the Toppans already had two grown daughters. (Little is known of the fate of Jane's sisters, except that one, Ellen, followed her father into an insane asylum in her twenties.)

The Toppans changed the girl's name to Jane and provided her with a fine home in Lowell, Massachusetts. Jane regularly attended the First Congregational Church with her parents. The Toppans were proud of their new daughter; she excelled in grade school and high school, and the folks in Lowell thought her to be one of the brightest young ladies in their quiet town. The inventive Jane provided the spark of life to skating parties in winter, and boating and picnic outings in summer. Young men sought her company, one of these swains capturing her heart.

The two became engaged, the youth giving Jane a ring with a bird engraved on it. Jane busied herself with wedding plans while her fiancé went off to seek an office job in Holyoke. Then disaster struck. Jane received a short note from the fiancé some weeks later in which he apologetically explained that he had, indeed found a job, but he had also married the daughter of his Holyoke landlady.

Taking the engagement ring from her finger, Jane hammered the symbol of her hopes to pieces. She could never talk about birds after that, or look at them. Once, when a relative showed her a picture of a bird, Jane shrieked, "Take it away! Take it away! I'm going to be sick!"

Despondent, Jane withdrew into herself, staying at home, refusing to see friends. She bought a book about dreams, and after reading it, made extensive notes and formulas wherein she convinced herself that she could foretell the future. These visions proved so disappointing that Jane tried twice to kill herself.

The Toppans showed her great understanding, allowing her to find her own way without prodding. At age twenty-six, Jane suddenly informed her foster parents that she was going to take up nursing. She immediately enrolled as a student nurse in a Cambridge, Massachusetts, hospital where she came to be regarded as an excellent trainee, eager to learn and devoted to her duty. She displayed a willingness to work long hours and to take on the most repugnant of chores without complaint. Jane soon became the most popular nurse at the hospital.

Some months later other nurses began to notice Jane's unnatural interest in autopsies performed at the hospital; her fascination with such anatomical experiments seemed to border on the ghoulish. Then a patient who was in Jane's care suddenly died, a man who had been recuperating rapidly. So did another patient Jane Toppan was looking after. Jane was called in to the chief surgeon's office for questioning. No official statement was ever made by the hospital but that very day Jane Toppan was discharged.

Nurse Toppan then applied for a job as a head nurse at another hospital in Cambridge, and was hired, but was quickly fired when it was learned that she was not a graduate nurse and had forged her certificate.

Even in disgrace, Jane received support and sympathy from the Toppans. But by then Jane Toppan had somehow developed an iron will. She needed no guidance in the pursuits she planned for herself. "I will go to the old and the sick," she told her parents, "to comfort them in their neediest hour."

From that day in 1880 to a much darker one in 1901, Jane Toppan served in the capacity of private nurse, working in scores of New England homes, gaining the confidence and love of her employers, at least those she left alive to give her that blind love.

On a sweltering July 7, 1901, Jane Toppan could be found among a group of mourners in a small cemetery in Cataumet, Massachusetts, watching a coffin being lowered into a grave. She was by then a middle-aged, rather plumpish woman with an expressionless face and a quiet manner. The services over, Jane joined with the other mourners in snatching up a handful of dirt and tossing it down upon the casket. Inside that casket was her patient, Mrs. Mattie Davis. Jane turned to view in silence from Cemetery Hill many sailboats skimming the blue waters of Buzzards Bay, and the little village of Cataumet, which was situated nine miles north of Falmouth.

Mattie Davis had been an old family friend and had visited Jane in Cambridge. She had suddenly grown ill and Jane had nursed her. The woman had died on July 4 and Jane had brought the body to the Davis home in Cataumet. Elderly Alden Davis, a retired sea captain, who had founded the town of Cataumet and ran the post office and general store, escorted the nurse from the cemetery, pleading with her to stay on at his home.

"I'd best be on my way," Jane told him.

"But the whole family is sick, we need you," Davis said, stating that his two married daughters, Mrs. Henry Gordon of Chicago, and Mrs. Irving Gibbs, whose husband was then at sea, had been stricken by a strange malady; he, too, had felt weak of late.

"Everywhere I go," Jane said slowly, "death seems to follow me. It would be best for all of you if I left."

"No," Captain David said in a commanding voice. "We need you."

Jane Toppan gave him a rare smile and agreed to stay on. What was in her strange mind at that moment was later recorded in a prison cell by Dr. Henry R. Stedman, an alienist; and they were spine-chilling words from Jane's own mouth. When she walked down that hill away from the cemetery on the arm of Captain Davis, she was thinking, "You had better wait a little while and I will have another funeral for you. If you wait it will save your going back and forth."

On July 29, 1901, Mrs. Annie Gordon was so sick, despite nurse Jane's constant care, that a Dr. Walters had to be called. While Captain Davis was at the telephone, Mrs. Gordon, her brow burning hot, her body writhing, came out of her coma for a moment to look into Jane's eyes, moaning, "I'm afraid, Nurse, I'm afraid."

"There, there," soothed Nurse Toppan as she inserted a hypodermic needle into Mrs. Gordon's arm.

A few hours later Dr. Walters came racing into the Davis home. Jane told him crisply, "I am afraid she is sinking."

Dr. Walters took the woman's pulse, then turned to Jane and Captain Davis with a puzzled look on his face: "This girl is dead."

Again there was a Davis burial on Cemetery Hill. Again Jane prepared to leave, but Captain Davis insisted she stay on.

"I feel I should have done something," Jane said. "Now I can't bear to look at those motherless tots," referring to Mrs. Gordon's two young children.

Captain Davis consoled her. "You mustn't blame yourself, Jane. You did everything that was humanly possible. You must stay with us."

The two deaths had drained Captain Davis's energy. For days, in searing August heat, the old man merely sprawled on a horsehair sofa in the living room of his large house. He could not eat, he could not sleep.

Then Jane came to him, saying, "You need some medicine." She held a glass containing a colorless, odorless fluid.

Davis waved her away.

"Now! Now!" Jane shoved the glass almost to his lips.

The old man drained the glass.

"You'll be fine in the morning," Jane told him.

The next morning Captain Alden Davis, head of Cataumet's first family, was found dead in his bedroom by his surviving daughter Mary Gibbs. His face was gray, utterly drained of blood it appeared, his mouth agape as if he had meant to call out in his final moment of life.

"It was a stroke," Jane informed Mary Gibbs matter-of-factly. "The grief did it."

Alone in the house with Jane, Mary Gibbs was seized by strange fears. Her husband, Captain Irving Gibbs, would not return from his sea voyage for weeks. The uneasy Mrs. Gibbs asked her cousin Beulah Jacobs to come down from Somerville to stay with her. Beulah arrived the next day but she could be of little comfort to her cousin. Mary Gibbs had been overwhelmed by the three recent tragic deaths in her family; for hours all the woman did was sit at a window and stare toward Cemetery Hill. Her cheeks were bloodless and there was fear in her eyes.

Nurse Toppan knew how to cure such depressions. She came to Mary in the sitting room, carrying a glass. "Dr. Walters prescribed this," she told Mrs. Gibbs. "It will do you good."

Mary drank the contents of the glass. Within the hour she called her cousin Beulah to her side, telling her, "I feel perfectly awful!" Beulah helped Mary to her room. In a short time Mrs. Gibbs lay tossing and moaning in bed. Her dilated eyes rolled in her head, unable to focus on Jane Toppan, who stood over her, nursing her.

By dawn, Mrs. Mary Gibbs was dead; the Davis family had been wiped out within the space of forty-five days by an unknown disease, according to a very confused Dr. Walters. Jane

Toppan shook her head, packed her bags, and went to Lowell, where a sick family urgently required her nursing skills.

When Captain Gibbs returned from his voyage to find his wife dead, cousin Beulah Jacobs drew him aside. "When your wife was dying," the cousin told Gibbs, "she tried to talk, but she couldn't—and she acted scared every time Nurse Toppan came near her." There was more, much more. Beulah related how she had sat sewing with Mary and Jane in the Davis house and how Jane had brought up a debt of $500 owed to the Davis estate. Now that the captain and his wife were dead, Jane had pointed out, it seemed only fair that Mrs. Gibbs should cancel her debt.

"I don't see why I should do that," Mrs. Gibbs had snapped.

"I do," Jane Toppan had said in a low voice before dropping the subject.

Then there was the matter of the autopsy, Beulah reported. Dr. Walters had thought to exhume Mrs. Gibbs's body to further examine it, but Jane had stopped him from doing so before she left Cataumet, telling the physician, "The poor child [Mrs. Gibbs] told me to look after her, and I'm going to do it, even now—there will be no autopsy, doctor. Such practices were against the religious beliefs of the Davis family."

Captain Gibbs wasted no time going to the police and pouring out his story to Detective J. H. Whitney. The detective had Mary Gibbs exhumed and then called in two physicians who performed an autopsy. E. S. Wood, a Harvard chemistry professor, examined tissues of the body and quickly determined that Mrs. Gibbs had been murdered, heavily dosed with morphine. When Dr. Walters was confronted with this discovery, the physician stated that, yes, all the Davis victims had showed the symptoms of morphine poisoning except one, the constriction of the pupils of the eyes, which was why he had been baffled by the deaths.

After receiving the report of the poisonings, Detective Whitney caught the next train for Lowell, Massachusetts, going to the home of O. M. Brigham, who had married Jane Toppan's late foster mother. Whitney was too late to save another life. By then Jane had "treated" her foster sister, Mrs. Edna Bannister of Tunbridge, Vermont. Mrs. Bannister, it was later learned, had stopped off to see Jane in Lowell en route to the exposition in Buffalo. "Why, Edna," Jane had told her when greeting her at the door, "you're looking terrible. Let me give you a tonic."

"Oh, I'm all right," Edna had said. "Don't bother."

Minutes later, Jane ordered Mrs. Bannister to drink something she had prepared, cooing with glass in hand, "Sister knows best." A few hours later, and only four days after the death of Mary Gibbs, Mrs. Bannister was also dead.

Whitney asked Brigham if he would call Jane downstairs, but the detective was told that Jane had left weeks earlier, called to the home of George Nichols in Amherst, New Hampshire, to look after Nichols' ailing sister. Whitney raced off to New Hampshire. He arrived at the Nichols home in Amherst on the stormy evening of October 29, 1901. Inside the Nichols home at that moment, according to one writer, Jane's "laughter rang through the trim New Hamphire sitting room . . . as she sat plumply before the fire, her glowing eyes traveling from sister to brother."

Jane answered the knock at the door. Detective Whitney stood in the rain looking at the nurse with a steady gaze. "Jane Toppan, the nurse?"

"Yes."

Whitney showed his badge. "You are wanted in Massachusetts for questioning in connection with the deaths of Mrs. Henry Gordon and Mrs. Irving Gibbs."

The nurse expressed shock, then added, "I am most eager to clear my name of any wrongdoing. Why, I've been a trained nurse for more than twenty years." She waived extradition and voluntarily went back to Massachusetts with Whitney, laughing off the ridiculous notion that she would ever hurt anyone, telling the detective on the train, "I have a clear conscience. I wouldn't kill a chicken, and if there is any justice in Massachusetts, they will let me go."

Jane was locked in the Barnstable County Jail after being charged with murder. While she awaited trial, proper families of wealth and prestige in Boston and Cambridge rallied to Jane's support, donating heavily to a defense fund established by Jane's Boston cousin, Mrs. J. E. Snow. All talked warmly about dear Nurse

Toppan, who had been recommended by scores of esteemed physicians.

Police throughout New England, at the request of Massachusetts authorities, began to exhume dozens of bodies, one-time patients of Nurse Toppan. Autopsies proved all had been poisoned with morphine and atropine. Scores of detectives visited pharmacies throughout Massachusetts and finally unearthed druggist Benjamin Waters in Wareham. The startled druggist checked his records and then admitted that he had indeed provided Nurse Toppan with morphine, a great quantity of the drug, 120 quarter grains over the years, to be specific. "But I'm sure everything is in order," Waters said. "I have doctors' signed prescriptions for every one of those morphine orders." The prescriptions were checked. Every one of them was a clever forgery written in Jane Toppan's own hand.

At this time, Dr. Stedman began dropping by to visit with Jane in her cell. The alienist, at the request of the Barnstable sheriff, was to probe her thoughts and report back to the authorities. Dr. Stedman at first chatted about trivial matters. Jane responded cheerily. The alienist felt that Jane's appetite for killing had increased at a terrible pace in the year 1901 and that, prevented by her confinement in jail from appeasing that appetite, she could be drawn into at least *talking* about murder, even if she was at the time prevented from killing.

In subsequent conversations, Stedman began to talk of sickness and death, asking the nurse how she felt when handling those problems in her profession. Jane delighted in discussing in detail the illnesses and agonizing deaths suffered by her patients. Seeing this spark of depraved enthusiasm, Stedman risked a single question, "Did you kill them, Jane?"

At first the stout, dark woman was silent, but then a horrible smile broadened her full cheeks. She fairly beamed and there was exultation in her words when she finally blurted out in a hiss, "Yes, I killed all of them! I might have killed George Nichols and his sister that night if the detective hadn't taken me away! [When Nichols heard this remark a few weeks later he collapsed on an Amherst street.] I fooled them all—I fooled the stupid doctors and the ignorant relatives. I've been fooling them for years and years."

Then she began a list of her victims, reciting their names with relish. Besides the Davis family and her foster sister, Mrs. Bannister, she had murdered the Brigham housekeeper, Florence Calkins, the Dunham family of Cambridge, Myra Connors of Woods Hole, Mrs. McNear of Watertown. The list, as far as Jane cared then to remember, went as high as thirty-one victims, but seventy was perhaps a more accurate number. Either way, Jane Toppan delightedly informed Stedman that she was the champion female poisoner in American history, an unsavory title she holds to this day. (Years later Nurse Toppan estimated more than a hundred people, saying that some of these killings, such as those of her early hospital days were only "practice murders.")

"Do you know what I want to be, doctor?"

"What might that be, Jane?"

"I want to go on and on and on." She fairly keened with the thought, rocking on a prison cot, possessed in ecstasy by her gruesome visions. "I want to be known as the greatest criminal that ever lived. That is my ambition!"

A prosecutor and a stenographer were called and Jane's every word was taken down.

"By the papers," sneered Jane to the prosecutor, "I read your statements about me poisoning people with arsenic. That's ridiculous! If I had used arsenic, my patients would have died hard deaths. I could not bear to see them suffer. When I kill anyone, they go to sleep and never wake up. I used morphia and atropia, the latter to hide the effects of the former." (Where morphine would cause the pupils of the eyes to constrict, atropine, or belladonna, would enlarge the pupils, making them appear normal and thus disguise the telltale sign of morphine poisoning, a sign never seen by the dozens of doctors who attended Jane's victims. This technique was first used by a Dr. Robert Buchanan of New York City who poisoned his wife for insurance money in 1892, a case widely publicized and one that certainly caught the eye of Nurse Jane Toppan who always kept up on the most useful medical news.)

Later Jane was as specific about her

techniques as any nurse might be in filling out a clinical report. She explained how she would first inject morphine into the arm of a victim. "Then came the wait. I would have to watch and watch and watch as the pupils contracted, and, at the right moment then inject the atropine and watch and watch until the puils were again wide and vacant. This was hard, precise work, all of it. I had to dose the patients slowly, a little at a time. It took days, sometimes weeks to kill them."

At the end of her devasting confession, and as an indication of her deep compassion for her patients, Jane Toppan added, "Most of the people I killed were old enough to die, anyway, or else had some disease that might cause death. I never killed children. I love them."

Her actual reasons for murdering these unsuspecting, trusting people were vaguely associated with euthanasia, said Jane. "They were sick and I eased their suffering." Once she shouted, "I had to do it. It relieved me."

Many reasons have since been given for the acts of this incredible mass murderess. A strong desire to be married might have prompted her. In the instances of her poisoning Mrs. Bannister, her foster sister, and Mrs. Davis and Mrs. Gordon, Jane had entertained the notion of marrying one of their husbands. Nurse Toppan's love of children prompted her to kill others, mothers of children she somehow thought she would adopt, much the way she had been adopted. And, of course, Jane must have had a dreadful sense of personal rejection, having been rebuffed by her own insane father, by a jilting Romeo, by hospital authorities, and this may have spurred her on to take revenge against an adult world that had mistreated her as a child and young woman. She admitted the joy of having the power of life and death. On many occasions she dosed her patients to the brink of death, then feverishly worked to bring them back to health, then slowly poisoned them to death, a ghastly teeter-totter game created in Nurse Toppan's tortured mind. There were other times, Jane lamented, when, after moderately dosing a patient with poison over several days, she was seized by regret, and, though the victim was hopeless, she exhausted herself in attempting to save that victim. Following these deaths, however, Jane felt no remorse. She would then go off to "save more people from life."

When Nurse Toppan's confession was published, the Back Bay families who had pressured authorities to release her suddenly had nothing more to say. The defense fund was dispersed back to contributors. Dozens of doctors who had been hoodwinked into signing death certificates for Jane over the years went into hiding from a howling army of reporters.

On June 25, 1902, Jane Toppan was put on trial. She clutched a hand rail for support. Dr. Stedman rose to testify that "Jane Toppan is suffering from a form of insanity that can never be cured."

With a furious shout, Jane raged against Stedman and the court: "The alienist lies! I am not crazy! And all of you know it! I know that I have done wrong! I understand right from wrong! That proves I am sane!"

The courtroom heard out her diatribe in silence. The following day Jane, according to the *New York Daily Tribune*, "was perfectly calm, and laughed and joked with her counsel."

Jane Toppan was sent to the Taunton State Asylum for the Criminally Insane. By 1905, Nurse Toppan was thought to be near death. Her behavior alternated between that of a simple, sweet child and that of a raving paranoiac, screaming that the nurses were trying to poison her. "It would be simple for them to poison me," Jane told a visiting reporter that year. "And *I* should know!" She worried herself into an emaciated state and became so frail that doctors gave her only a few weeks to live. Finally, one physician asked her why she was worrying. Jane replied, "Because I have no remorse for murdering all those people."

Like her patients before her, see-sawing between life and death, Jane suddenly recovered, but unlike her hapless victims, she continued to live out a long life, finally dying of old age at eighty-four on August 17, 1938.

"She never gave us any trouble," was the laconic reply of one of the asylum doctors to an inquiring newsman aasigned to write Jane's obituary. "She was just a quiet old lady."

Nurses who had retired from working at the

asylum, however, gave out a different story to reporters looking into the enigma of Nurse Jane Toppan. These elderly nurses all repeated the same story. Throughout the decades of Jane's confinement in the asylum, Nurse Toppan periodically would call one of the nurses to her cell-like room and whisper with a maniacal grin, "Get some morphine, dearie, and we'll go out in the ward. You and I will have a lot of fun seeing them die."

TRACY, ANN GIBSON

Murderer ■ (1935–   )

Cocktail waitress Ann Tracy fell in love with successful building contractor Amos Stricker in 1958. For two years the couple carried on a strange affair, Stricker sleeping with many women and later informing Ann of these other affairs in lurid detail. She begged him to stop, she later said at her trial, but Stricker exercised his sadism to the fullest when with her. Unable to bear the situation, Ann dined with Stricker on the night of November 13, 1960, at his surfside home in Laguna Beach, California. She then went to bed with him. As they were later sipping drinks, she shot him several times. She then propped her lover's corpse on a pillow and covered him with a blanket "as if he were sleeping."

Hours later Ann confessed the killing to a friend and was arrested. She was convicted of second degree murder and sent to the Corona Women's Prison for life.

TRIPP, GRACE

Murderer ■ (1691–1710)

After going to work as a maid in the London mansion of Lord Torrington, Grace Tripp met a sneak thief named Peters who persuaded her to open the kitchen door to the Torrington mansion one night while the family was away. The object was to steal the family silverware, but the housekeeper interrupted the pair and Peters slit the woman's throat while Grace held a candle aloft so that he could see to perform the murder.

They rifled the housekeeper's pockets and took about thirty guineas, then gathered up the silverware and fled, leaving the front door open. The crime was the sensation of London for days, undoubtedly because it had occurred under the roof of a respected lord. Police quickly tracked down Grace and Peters and both were tried and condemned.

Before she and Peters were executed at Tyburn, Grace Tripp told authorities that they were wrong to hang her; she had only held the candle. The housekeeper had not died directly by her hands. What was so wrong, after all? She only wanted the silverware to sell. With the proceeds from the sale of the silver, she intended to establish herself as a grand lady, one who would have servants of her own.

Grace Tripp went to the gallows on March 17, 1710, protesting to the end the severity of her punishment.

TURNER, JOYCE

Murderer ■ (1928–)

Mrs. Turner, a mother of six, operated the Hanover Kiddies' Nursery in Columbia, South Carolina, and generally supported her lazy husband, Alonzo. She complained long and bitterly to her neighbors Mrs. Audrey Noakes and Clestell Gay. Often she vowed in front of these women that she would kill Alonzo.

The three women sat drinking coffee in Mrs. Noakes's kitchen on a June night in 1956. The other women encouraged Joyce to kill her worthless husband, Clestell goading, "Well, are you going to do it, or not?"

With that, Mrs. Turner rushed to her own house nearby and shot her husband to death as he slept. She and her friends then told police that a "tall, white-skinned" intruder had killed Turner. Mrs. Turner remarked at her husband's funeral that he deserved to die since he ran around with other women.

Police investigated Turner's background and found no history of extramarital relationships. The murder weapon, a .22-caliber pistol, was next traced to Clestell Gay, the purchaser. All three women confessed and were sent to prison for life.

Mrs. Turner's hate for her sleep-loving mate had not abated at the end of her trial. She quipped to reporters, "Alonzo always told me that he wanted to die in bed. . . . I simply arranged for it."

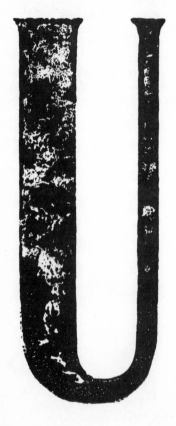

URSINUS, SOPHIE

Murderer ■ (1760–1836)

High-born Sophie Ursinus was a pillar of German society when she was arrested for murder. Police politely came to her villa outside Berlin and interrupted her game of whist; she dutifully went with arresting officers and calmly admitted that she had been feeding arsenic to one of her servants, Benjamin Klein.

The daughter of an Austrian diplomat, Sophie Charlotte Elizabeth Weingarten had married the elderly privy counsellor Ursinus of Berlin in 1779. The old politician politely looked the other way when his wife sought sex with a Dutch officer named Rogay. This affair ended when Rogay died at a young age, the cause being consumption, doctors stated. Sophie's husband died on September 11, 1800.

Deaths of an unusual nature surrounded the later life of Frau Ursinus. Her maiden aunt, Christina Regina Witte, perished under mysterious circumstances on January 23, 1801. All these deaths were subsequently laid at the door of Frau Ursinus. Her servant Klein, who had long been her confidant, told police that his mistress had fed arsenic to her husband to rid herself of a useless old man. She had poisoned her lover Rogay because he had intended to leave her. The aunt had been given arsenic so that Sophie could inherit her estate. When Frau Ursinus learned that Klein intended to leave her employ, she decided to murder him, too. He simply knew too much. (Klein recovered and was given a large pension by Sophie even after she was convicted of murder.)

Sent to prison for life for killing her aunt—the one case proved against her—Frau Ursinus lived out her life in the grand style she had always known. She was taken to the massive fortress at Glatz between the frontiers of Silesia and Bohemia and given the deluxe suite of rooms near the top battlements, an apartment usually reserved for the warden. Here she outfitted her rooms with comfortable furniture and was allowed servants. Oddly enough, she not only had great amounts of money from her husband's estate but was permitted, owing to her station in life, to keep the fortune inherited from Christina Witte, the very woman she had murdered.

Sophie was a bizarre sight as she moved across the open ramparts of the Glatz castle, adorned as she was in flowing silks and satins, peering contemptuously down on other prisoners, starving and chained, working below as ditchdiggers and gardeners. She continued for decades in her role of lady of quality, allowed to see important travelers fascinated with a mass poisoner of the upper classes. Sophie prattled on endlessly during these interviews, always maintaining her innocence.

While other criminal inmates suffered in the dungeons below, Frau Ursinus gave sumptuous parties in her suite, and these were attended religiously by aristocrats living on nearby estates.

During one of her lavish receptions, Sophie noticed a female guest peering suspiciously at her salad, seeing some grains of sugar sparkling on the lettuce. "Don't worry, my dear," Frau Ursinus cooed to her guest, "it's not arsenic."

Sophie died a natural death on April 4, 1836, and was buried with great pomp. The odor of sanctity was everywhere at her funeral, which was attended by hundreds of the high born. Sophie went to her grave in an expensive oak coffin she had purchased years earlier. She was clad in a white petticoat and a cap trimmed with blue ribbons. She wore her husband's wedding ring. Clergymen extolled her generosity to the poor of the district, omitting any mention of the murders that had brought her to the Glatz cemetery—dedicated by no less a personage than King Frederick William III. A large children's choir sang hymns in Sophie's praise as she was lowered into the earth.

VAN VALKENBURGH, ELIZABETH

Murderer ■ (1799–1846)

A resident of Fulton, New York, Elizabeth poisoned two husbands with arsenic, the second being John Van Valkenburgh. She laced Van Valkenburgh's tea with arsenic, the same method she had used when murdering her first husband. Van Valkenburgh died in March 1845. Confessing, Mrs. Van Valkenburgh stated that she had attempted to cure both husbands of their heavy drinking, adding, "I always had a very ungovernable temper." She was hanged on January 24, 1846.

VELGO, MARIE HAVLICK

Murderer ■ (1916– ?)

Marie Havlick was an uncommonly beautiful woman of twenty-one when she married Circuit Court Judge Jan Velgo and moved into his luxury apartment in Beno, Czechoslovakia. She had been swept off her feet by the judge, but she soon learned from a maid that Velgo had married her only as a matter of convenience, that there was a vacancy on the supreme court and, as a married man, his chances of getting the post were improved. He would quietly divorce Marie later. That way she would stand to inherit none of Velgo's substantial estate.

In desperation, Marie confided her fears to the family maid who put her in touch with a petty criminal, Wenzel Cerny. The pair met in a cafe and there Marie proposed that Cerny murder her husband. The crook demanded money and Mrs. Velgo promptly offered him the not-too-princely sum of 5,000 kronen (about $200). Down on his luck, Cerny accepted.

On the night of March 16, 1936, Judge Velgo returned to his apartment after a business dinner. As he entered, Cerny, who had been waiting for him, slugged Velgo, cutting open his head. He dragged the unconscious man to the bathroom where he dumped him into the tub. Cerny opened the tap and then held Velgo beneath the water, which turned crimson red from the head wound.

Cerny then prepared to leave the apartment but was suddenly shot by Marie, who had been hiding in a closet. (Their "deal" had called for her to be absent from the apartment at the time of the murder.) Marie then placed the gun in Cerny's hand as he lay in a pool of blood. She had attempted to make the whole affair look like a murder and subsequent suicide by the killer.

Just as she went toward the front door she heard the rush of feet. Marie ran to the bedroom and hid in a closet. Police, called by a downstairs neighbor who had heard loud noises, smashed down the door of the Velgo apartment and found the judge dead in the bathtub. Cerny, however, was still alive. Marie was found in the closet, pretending to have fainted after having been attacked by the intruder.

Though Marie attempted to pin the entire blame on her hired killer, Wenzel Cerny was not as doltish as he looked. "If you don't believe the girl put me up to it," he told arresting police, "you'll find her note to me sewn in the lining of my coat."

Detectives tore open the coat and found a note signed by Marie and addressed to Cerny; it detailed the financial arrangements the pair had made concerning the murder of Marie's husband. It read—

> I hereby agree to pay you 5,000 kronen for services, the nature of which is known to you and to me. In case of my death, this obligation will be covered by a provision in my will. You incur obligation to talk to nobody about this agreement, to show it to nobody, and not to state your claims to any third person. This debt may be collected neither in a legal way nor in a forceful way. In case of your death, your wife and son inherit all your claims. The above may be paid in monthly payments or in a lump sum. Upon full demand this note must be returned. In case of my divorce, this promissory note becomes null and void.
>
> Marie Havlick Velgo

The note was dated a month before the murder of Judge Velgo. Marie's handwriting was easily determined as that shown in the note to Cerny.

Cerny was convicted and sent to prison for life, but, amazingly, Marie, whose stunning beauty certainly influenced the all-male jury, was acquitted. She was tried a second time in October 1937, found guilty, and sentenced to twelve years in prison.

VIDAL, GINETTE

Murderer ■ (1931–   )

In early 1972 Gerard Osselin greeted the new tenants who moved into his apartment building in Montfermeil, a Parisian suburb. For some reason the twenty-nine-year-old factory technician was attracted to his new neighbor, Mrs. Ginette Vidal, then forty-one, dumpy, and sour-faced. Madame Vidal responded, and the couple soon left their families and moved into a townhouse in Clichy-sous-Bois.

There the possessive Ginette drew up one of the strangest love-murder contracts in recorded history. Under the terms of the pact Osselin and Ginette swore life-long fidelity to each other. Should either one of them break the pact by seeing another, the aggrieved party had the right to kill the other. In November 1972 Osselin began sneaking back to his wife, Mireille. Ginette suspected as much, and her suspicions were confirmed when she found a shopping list in Mireille's handwriting in her lover's pocket.

Calmly, the woman picked up a .22 rifle, went to the sleeping Osselin, and sent two bullets into his neck and head. For the next three days the woman pretended that her lover was still alive. She fondled the decomposing corpse and talked to it. She made dinner for two.

Alerted by Osselin's family, police eventually broke into the small house and arrested Ginette. Quickly, she produced the murder pact she and Osselin had signed. "This should be good in any court of law," she said smugly as she was led off to jail.

The contract, of course, had no legal standing in the French civil code in that it was "contrary to good morals," according to legal arbiters. Ginette was convicted and sent to prison for ten years. She was indignant to the end, stating, "I cannot understand that the court does not respect the last wishes of a dead man."

WADDINGHAM, DOROTHEA NANCY

Murderer ■ (1899–1936)

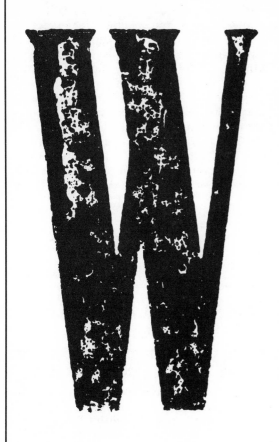

Using her maiden name of Waddingham, Dorothea opened a nursing home in 1935 on Devon Drive in Nottingham, England. She was a widow (once married to a Thomas Willoughby Leech), and her nursing skills were more imaginary than learned. Handling the heavy chores around the home was Dorothea's lover, Ronald Joseph Sullivan, a World War I hero whose servility to Nurse Waddingham was unaccountable; Dorothea had little to recommend her in the way of physical beauty, having pronounced buck teeth, a long and haggard face, and a stare that might remind one of a character out of a Bram Stoker novel.

The small home was accredited by the County Nursing Association, which also sent along to Nurse Waddingham her first two patients, Mrs. Baguley, age eighty-nine and suffering from senility, and her daughter Ada, age fifty and afflicted with creeping paralysis. A short time later Ada Baguley directed her solicitor to change her will, wherein she left her entire estate to Dorothea and Sullivan, about 2,000 pounds. Mrs. Baguley then died on May 12, 1935, cause of death listed as old age. On September 10, her daughter Ada followed the old woman to the grave. Her death was attributed to cerebral hemorrhage, brought on, Nurse Waddingham told the doctor, by gobbling down too many chocolates given to Ada by a friend, a Mrs. Briggs.

Nurse Waddingham alarmed authorities by her haste in having Ada Baguley's corpse cremated, producing a letter dated August 29, 1935, and purportedly written by Ada, in which she stated her desire to be cremated. The letter concluded, "And it is my wish to remain with Nurse and my last wish is my relatives shall not know of my death." This last remark was thought to be most suspicious by Dr. Cyril Banks, the medical health officer who had to approve of the crema-

amounts of morphine. Dorothea and Sullivan were arrested, the slavish lover freed later.

Dorothea Waddingham was tried at Nottingham on February 4, 1936. The calm nurse told the court that Dr. H. Manfield, who had signed the death certificates for both Baguley women, had directed her to give the patients morphine tablets. Manfield's testimony was brief and damning: "I never prescribed them. I never gave them."

Further pointing to Dorothea's guilt was her own admission that on the night before the younger woman's death she had fed Ada Baguley two heaping meals of pork, boiled potatoes, and fruit pie. If Ada had been suffering from the sharp abdominal pains that required doses of morphine that Dorothea claimed she was, the judge illustrated, no nurse with any common sense would have served such a dinner.

The jury voted for conviction but unaccountably recommended that mercy be shown the poisoning nurse. Dorothea Waddingham, nevertheless, was hanged on April 16, 1936.

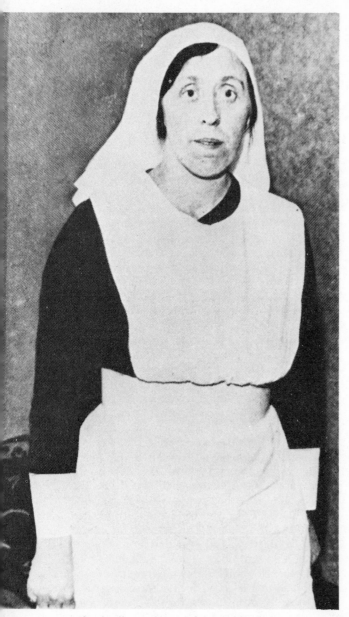

The deadly nurse, Dorothea Waddingham.

tion. (The letter was written by Dorothea, it was later proved.)

Dr. Banks ordered an autopsy on Ada Baguley's corpse, and subsequently on her mother's. Both bodies contained excessive

WATSON, ELLA ("CATTLE KATE")

Cattle Thief ■ (1866–1888)

Not too bright, Ella Watson had been a bar shill and prostitute until moving to Rawlins, Wyoming, where she met cattle rustler Jim Averill who set her up with her very own whorehouse. The bordello was really a front. Into the large pens behind the property, Averill and Ella herded hundreds of cows they had stolen from neighboring ranches, selling the beef for quick and heavy profits. Ella was soon known in the area as "Cattle Kate."

In July 1888 an angry group of vigilantes appeared at Cattle Kate's bordello. They threw

Cattle Kate Watson on horseback and posing in front of pens that contained the cattle she had rustled. (Wyoming State Archives)

the woman into a wagon, ignoring her curses, and drove to Averill's ranch nearby. Here Kate and Averill were made to stand on rocks, ropes around their necks, the ends of which were tied to a strong tree. "Jump!" ordered the leader of the posse.

Averill smiled. "Stop your fooling, fellows."

A humorless vigilante stepped up and pushed both Kate and Averill off the rocks. A newspaper later reported that "the kicking and writhing of those people was awful to witness." None of the vigilantes who hanged the hard-riding Kate and her lover were ever prosecuted, though every man was known to the good citizens of Rawlins.

WEBER, JEANNE

Murderer ■ (1875–1910)

The madness that possessed Jeanne Weber had many psychological names, from monomania to death wish, and her story is perhaps the darkest in twentieth century records dealing with female criminals, a murderous tale that for sheer horror went unequaled; she was a Hitchcockian nightmare.

In 1889 Jeanne Weber, then only fourteen, left the small fishing village in northern France where she was born and headed for Paris. She took odd jobs of a menial stripe until her marriage in 1893. Her husband, a borderline drunk, barely managed to keep his position as a timekeeper for a transport company.

Jeanne was a short, fat, lethargic housewife living in a rundown tenement district in Paris in 1905. She, her husband, and her seven-year-old son, Marcel, shared a small apartment in the Passage Goutte d'Or. Two of Jeanne's children had died, and this, sympathetic neighbors said, undoubtedly had led to her heavy drinking.

On March 2, 1905, Jeanne's sister-in-law, needing to go to the laundry, asked her to look after her two children, two-year-old Suzanne and eighteen-month-old Georgette. A neighbor came into the laundry some minutes later to inform the sister-in-law that Georgette had suddenly become ill.

The mother raced home and found the baby choking as Jeanne cradled the child in her lap, rubbing the girl's chest. The mother nursed the child for some time and, when she appeared to return to normal, again left for the laundry. Coming home three hours later, the mother found Georgette dead. A neighbor named Pouche directed the mother's attention to the black-and-blue marks on the child's neck but these were ignored.

Nine days later Jeanne was again asked to babysit for Suzanne. The gullible parents returned home to find the child dying, arms and legs contracted, teeth clenched. Suzanne died moments later. A doctor stated that the cause of death was convulsions.

On March 25, Jeanne burst in on her brother, Leon Weber, and, without being invited, sat down to breakfast. Mrs. Weber took advantage of Jeanne's presence by asking her to look after her daughter Germaine, age seven months. Jeanne smiled pleasantly and agreed.

A half hour later Germaine's grandmother, who lived downstairs, heard the child cry out. She went to the Weber apartment and found Germaine breathing hard, her face flushed. When the child calmed, the grandmother returned to her flat. Germaine cried out again and the grandmother again climbed the stairs to see her grandchild choking. When Jeanne departed, leaving the child with the grandmother, Germaine's condition improved. A neighbor, Madame Navet, came by and said to the grandmother, "What are those strange red marks on the baby's neck?" The elderly woman only shook her head in ignorance.

The following day, Jeanne returned, again offering to stay with Germaine. The Webers happily went shopping, leaving the sister-in-law holding the baby. Germaine was dead when they returned. A doctor said the cause of death was diphtheria.

Three days later, when Germaine was being lowered into her tiny grave, Jeanne's own son, Marcel, died in convulsions. Doctors said this, too, was the result of diphtheria, but they were at a loss to explain the red marks on the boy's throat.

Jeanne Weber had a large family. For years she had not bothered with her relatives, but on April 5, she invited two more sisters-in-law, the wives of Charles and Peter Weber, to have dinner with her. Mrs. Charles Weber brought along her son, ten-year-old Maurice. Following the meal, Jeanne asked the two women to run a few errands for her; Maurice should stay with her. His loving aunt would know how to take care of him. The sisters-in-law went on the errands, but Mrs. Charles Weber returned prematurely to find Maurice sprawled on a bed, his aunt standing over him and staring down coldly on the boy. The mother saw that her boy was unconscious and that black-and-blue marks encircled his neck. She turned to Jeanne, shouting, "You wretch! You have strangled my son!" She rushed Maurice to the hospital where doctors revived him. Mrs. Charles Weber then signed a complaint against the woman.

By the time Jeanne Weber went on trial the nation was in a frenzy at the horrid prospect of a child-killer being acquitted. Public opinion demanded she be condemned, which was probably why Henri Robert, who had been involved in the sensational Gabrielle Bompard case, leapt to Jeanne Weber's defense. The nine-day trial began January 29, 1906, while mobs of angry parents stood outside the courthouse calling Jeanne a satanic monster, giving her the sobriquet of *Ogre de la Goutte d'Or*. Jeanne sat in the dock with no expression on her heavy face.

The prosecution quickly mentioned other deaths that may have been caused by the Parisian housewife. Two other children, Lucie Aléandré and Marcel Poyatos, who had been left in Jeanne's care, had died. So had her own two little girls and son, Marcel. The woman was a weird maniac obsessed with killing children. In fact, the prosecution went on, she had murdered her own son, Marcel, after the deaths of the Weber children to dispel any suspicions of the neighbors and leave the door open for more child murders.

Defense counsel Robert scoffed at such ridiculous charges. Moreover, he left the defense solely in the hands of forensic scientists. To that end he solicited the opinion of Dr. Leon Henry Thoinot. The forty-seven-year-old Thoinot was considered the leading forensic scientist of the day. He performed an autopsy on Germaine Weber and quickly came to the conclusion that, though there were some abnormalities in the body, the baby had not been suffocated. Thoinot was aware of all the particulars involving Jeanne Weber, including the fact that she had been found holding her hands under the children's clothes and pressing against their chests. (A Dr. Tardieu had once published a paper in which he stated that it was possible to suffocate a person, particularly a child, by compression of the chest, but Thoinot ignored such a statement as wild theory.)

Thoinot appeared in court and, despite the overwhelming testimony against Jeanne Weber, swung the jury in her favor by stating, "Science cannot tell you how these children came to die, but everything points to a natural death and that the accused is innocent."

The jury deliberated briefly and then pronounced the woman not guilty. Madame Charles Weber screamed in court, "There is no justice!" That father of Lucie Aléandré stood on a pew and shouted, "She will begin again!"

Lawyer Robert shrugged off these cries of agony, gloating over his victory. Most in the courtroom were suddenly gripped by Robert's emotional oratory and began to clap, the applause rising to a thunderous ovation. Jeanne leaned from the dock, took her lawyer's hand, and kissed it. Her husband, who had been at the back of the court, suddenly erupted with drunken shrieks of joy, jumping over benches and running toward Jeanne, who was let loose from the dock.

"I didn't kill them!" the woman yelled as she ran into her husband's arms. "Say that you believe me now!"

Almost all believed Jeanne Weber at that moment, except for the parents of the dead children, who sank back in their seats in shock. The fickle mob tore up the courtroom in celebration, lifting Jeanne onto shoulders, attempting to carry her outside.

The noted French journalist Michel Darland wrote the following day, "In the future let no one forget that the fate of Jeanne Weber, the fate of an innocent woman, would have been sealed had she not lived in our age and in a Paris which is one of the greatest, if not the greatest, cradles of the exact science of forensic medicine. Science alone has won a victory for innocence and a triumph for itself; for the superiority of scientific knowledge over the testimony of witnesses and the detective work of the police has now been demonstrated."

Dr. Thoinot, along with his mentor, the esteemed Dr. Paul Camille Hippolyte Brouardel, published a long medical report entitled "The Jeanne Weber Affair" in the most respected French medical journals, a report that essentially awarded kudos to themselves for their infallible medical decision.

Despite his show of support in court, Jeanne's husband deserted her shortly after her acquittal. The woman was hounded by neighbors, who insisted on calling her the Ogre of the Goutte d'Or. She was shunned as if she were a leper. In February Jeanne threw herself into the Seine, claiming later that persons unknown had tossed her into the river, but one witness stated that she had only descended a few stairs to wet her dress. She then disappeared for fifteen months.

On April 17, 1907, a Dr. Papazoglou was called to the home of a poor peasant named Bavouzet near Villedieu in the province of Indre. Inside the small home, the doctor found nine-year-old Auguste Bavouzet stretched out on a bed. Sitting stone-faced and immobile next to the child was a heavy-set woman named

Moulinet who had become Bavouzet's housekeeper and mistress. Auguste was dead. He had been scrubbed and dressed in his best clothes by the housekeeper. The boy's collar was buttoned tightly to his neck.

Dr. Papazoglou pointed to the boy, asking the housekeeper, "Why did you do that?"

The round-faced woman stared back with black, expressionless eyes, then answered in a flat voice, "He vomited. He was dirty."

The physician noticed discoloration around the boy's neck. The red marks struck the doctor as so peculiar that he refused to sign a death certificate. Instead, he went to police, who assigned another doctor to inspect the corpse. Dr. Charles Audiat examined the body and then reported that Auguste Bavouzet had died of "convulsions." The matter was dropped.

Some days later Germaine, Auguste's older sister, who resented Madame Moulinet's sleeping in her dead mother's bed, rummaged through the housekeeper's bags and found newspaper clippings from the *Petit Parisien* with 1906 dates. All described the sensational trial of one Jeanne Weber who was accused of strangling three of her little nieces and almost suffocating her nephew. Some of the clippings showed photos of Jeanne Weber, who was none other than the housekeeper, Moulinet. Germaine ran to the police station in Villedieu, throwing the clippings on the desk of Inspector Auphand. "She did it!" Germaine shouted. "She strangled Auguste!"

Dr. Frederic Bruneau was asked to do a second autopsy on the Bavouzet boy. He concluded that the child had been strangled to death, that a handkerchief might have been placed around the boy's neck and twisted. Jeanne Weber, alias Madame Moulinet, was arrested on May 4, 1907, and taken to Bourges to await trial. When the Paris newspapers screamed headlines that Jeanne Weber had been arrested again for murder, Henri Robert quickly announced that he would again defend "this poor persecuted soul." The authorities in Indre were labeled country bumpkins and Dr. Bruneau was called an inept country doctor seeking the limelight. The wizard of forensic science, Dr. Thoinot, was again called into the case. He examined the Bavouzet child for a fourth time, even though the body was by

then in an extreme state of decomposition. Thoinot declared that the boy's death was due to typhoid fever.

Jeanne Weber was released in December 1907 and quickly vanished. Robert and Thoinot, grumbled authorities in Indre, had acted irresponsibly, attempting only to save their reputation. They were responsible for this monster being at large and only because they could not afford to have the woman they had championed and saved be convicted, said the provincial press. One editorialist stated sarcastically, "Jeanne Weber is free . . . and so are Thoinot and Robert."

On January 13, 1908, Henri Robert addressed the distinguished Paris Society of Forensic Medicine. He called Dr. Bruneau an ignorant and inept doctor and lauded Thoinot. "After eight months of pre-trial imprisonment," he intoned, "Jeanne Weber was released. You now know who bears the responsibility for that imprisonment."

Dr. Bruneau was ruined. Jeanne Weber went her mysterious way. She was seen working as an orderly in a children's hospital in Faucombault. Later, Georges Bonjean, President of the Society for the Protection of Children, gave Jeanne a job working in his Children's Home in Orgeville. Bonjeau, who had followed her case and was an admirer of Thoinot and Robert, believed the woman had been persecuted. The job he gave Madame Weber was a way of expressing his desire to "make up for the wrongs that justice has inflicted upon an innocent woman."

A few days after Jeanne went to work in the home under the name of Marie Lemoine, she was caught choking a sick child. Bonjeau fired her immediately, and fearing he would be made a laughingstock, said nothing of the event. Bonjeau's silence guaranteed the death of at least one more child.

Returning to Paris, Jeanne was arrested as a vagrant. She was taken before Chief Hamard, head of the Sûreté, to whom she blurted out, "I am the woman who killed the children in the Goutte d'Or!" Hamard ordered her brought before Prefect of Police Lépine, but, confronting Lépine, she denied ever having made such an admission. Lépine sent her to a mental asylum in Nanterre, where a Dr. Toulouse interviewed her and released her as sane.

There were still do-gooders offering the persecuted Jeanne Weber sanctuary against her oppressors. A man named Joly sent her a letter, offering her his lodgings, and Jeanne went to live with the man near Toul, becoming his mistress. Next she became an all-out whore, sleeping with scores of railway workers in Bar-le-Duc, finally going off with one, Emile Bouchery. They arrived as common-law man and wife in Commercy on the night of May 8, 1908, taking a room in an inn on the rue de la Paroisse. The inn was run by a friendly family named Poirot.

Jeanne helped Madame Poirot with the housekeeping while Bouchery took a job in the Euville quarries. One night Jeanne went to Madame Poirot, telling the woman that her husband was a drunken brute, that sometimes he beat her when he came home at night. Would Madame Poirot allow one of her children to sleep with her? That way Bouchery would not beat her. Kindly Madame Poirot agreed and sent her ten-year-old boy, Marcel, to stay with Jeanne. "I will see that he sleeps well," promised Jeanne.

At about ten o'clock that night Madame Curlet, one of the guests staying at the inn, was aroused from her sleep by loud noises coming from Jeanne's room. She went to the hallway, then threw open the door to Jeanne Weber's room. Before her was a sight that froze her flesh: Jeanne Weber was on the bed, straddling the boy Marcel, strangling him. The boy's face was almost black. Blood gushed from his mouth as death rattled in his throat. Jeanne Weber wore a maniacal smile coated with spittle which dripped from her heavy chin. She, the bed, and the boy were covered with gore. Three blood-stained handkerchiefs were hanging from the side of the bed. Though she wildly glanced in Madame Curlet's direction, the woman continued to twist tighter the blood-soaked handkerchief around the boy's neck.

Madame Curlet finally managed to let a piercing scream escape her lips. The Poirots came on the run; the innkeeper had to smash his fists several times into Jeanne Weber's face to force her to release her grip on the bloody handkerchief embedded in the flesh of his son's neck.

This time the esteemed Dr. Thoinot and the much vaunted lawyer Robert could not save Jeanne Weber. She was declared insane on October 25, 1908, and locked up in the mental hospital in Mareville while all France exploded in indignation over the grotesque fact that this monster had been allowed to roam free, seeking her helpless victims. Despite his gross errors, Dr. Thoinot never once admitted his responsibility for any of the deaths inflicted by this mass murderer.

Doctors studied Jeanne periodically, peeping through the bars of her cell, watching her go into fits during which she would claw at the air, froth at the mouth, place her long fingers around imaginary throats and squeeze, attempting to relive the sexual ecstasy of her murders, a perversion that had undoubtedly been the motive for her many slayings. (Jeanne Weber was credited with eight killings, but she may have murdered as many as twenty children or even more.)

One morning in 1910, asylum physicians came running to the sound of Jeanne's hideous wails of horror. They were too late. The woman was dead. Around her throat were her own fingers, her talon-like nails piercing the flesh, drawing her own blood in a gruesome deathgrip.

WEBSTER, KATE

Murderer ■ (1849–1879)

Nowhere in the dark history of Kate Webster can one find a soul who loved her. The universal dislike and disgust of this callous female is constant to this day; even Kate Webster's memory is despised. From her day to this, the chroniclers of crime have cast jaundiced eyes upon her image, invariably rendering her character as despicable. Some of the myriad comments about this incredibly cold-blooded killer include: "She had a peculiarly sinister face, with dark, gleaming and slightly oblique eyes." "She was dark, morose." "She was a

Kate Webster, the murderous maid. (Courtesy Tussaud's)

compound of primitiveness, sharpness, greed, mother love, histrionic genius, extravagance, economy, sexual love, love of finery, sullenness, revenge, mendacity, coolness, cunning, self-possession, ungovernable fury, demoniacal savageness, and over and above all, perhaps, superstition." All this for a woman who was convicted of murdering a solitary human being. The reaction to that single slaying, then, was undoubtedly connected to Kate Webster's method, a *modus operandi* more in keeping with a jungle beast than a human being of high civilization.

Born in Killane, County Wexford, Ireland, in 1849, Kate Webster's villainy surfaced in early childhood. Though raised by respectable, if poor, people, Kate was often caught in the act of stealing lace and cheap jewelry. When brought before her parents by constables, the child sobbed long and loudly, begging forgiveness from all injured parties and promising never to

filch again. This predictable scenario began to bore even the local priest, who was called many times to the Webster household to lecture the child.

When only a teenager, Kate sailed for Liverpool, using stolen money to pay for her passage. For several years she lived by stealing alone. But she was an awkward pickpocket, and at age eighteen was arrested and sent to prison for four years after a constable caught her with her hand inside a pedestrian's pocket. Upon her release, she looked for greener fields and traveled to London. A powerfully built woman by then, Kate appeared to have reformed, taking a job as a charwoman, though on and off she supplemented her small income through prostitution. While living in Kingston-on-Thames, she gave birth to a son whose father was never identified. Though Kate always appeared to genuinely love the boy, she never had the slightest intention of reforming for the child's sake. To pick up extra money she worked the trade of the lodging-house robber, taking a room in a lodging house for a few days, during which she would steal anything she could cart off to pawnbrokers, from furniture to lighting fixtures, before moving on to another rooming house. This career resulted in dozens of arrests and short prison terms. At the time of one arrest she was charged with thirty-six counts of larceny. In 1875 Kate was given an eighteen-month term in Wandsworth Prison. Free only a few months in 1877, Kate was again apprehended for theft and returned to prison for another short term.

By early January 1879, Kate had moved to Richmond, where she and her small son lived on the charity of a Mrs. Crease. Through her Kate obtained a job as a maid with the well-to-do Mrs. Julia Martha Thomas, who lived at No. 2 Vine Cottages, Park Road, Richmond. At first, the work went well. Kate performed her duties faithfully, her son continuing to stay with Mrs. Crease. Then Kate resorted to her old habits, neglecting her work and spending most of her time in nearby pubs, particularly one run by a Mrs. Hayhoe, the Hole-in-the-Wall Pub. (This habit of Kate's was especially irksome to Mrs. Thomas since she and Mrs. Hayhoe were not on speaking terms.) On Sunday, Mary 2, 1879, after only a month's service, Mrs. Thomas gave her imbibing maid notice and went off to afternoon church services with Kate hurling curses after her.

To all who saw Mrs. Thomas at church, it was clear that she was quite upset as she sat through services, her hands trembling, tears trickling down her cheeks. Mrs. Thomas returned home and went to her room. As she was removing her hat, the bedroom door burst open and Kate Webster, an axe in her hand, rushed forward.

Kate struck Mrs. Thomas in the head with the axe but only the side of the axe. Fighting for her life, Mrs. Thomas struggled with her murderous maid into the hallway and onto a staircase landing. There Mrs. Thomas lost her balance and fell, Kate pushing her, to the bottom of the stairs. Kate raced down the stairs wielding the axe, smashing in the head of Mrs. Thomas

before she could cry out for help. Leaving a trail of blood, Kate dragged the body into the kitchen. She had prepared well. A large copper pot was already boiling on the open fire. Stripping her victim, the maniacal maid went to work on the body with savage industry, cutting up Mrs. Thomas and boiling down her remains. While this awful brew was being prepared, the stench in the kitchen became unbearable. Kate stepped out for an hour or so, going to Hayhoe's Pub where she drank herself into wobbly-legged courage. (Said the reflective Mrs. Hayhoe weeks later when the crime was firmly affixed to her ghoulish customer, "I little thought when Kate came in and I chatted with her that she had left her mistress boiling in the copper." Kate then returned to the Thomas house, where she packaged the parboiled remains of her employer in a

Kate confronting her employer, Julia Thomas, axe in hand.

box and then inside cloth bags lined with thick brown paper.

Never before had Kate Webster worked so hard as a maid as that night when cleaning up after her own butchery of Mrs. Thomas, scrubbing the hallway and kitchen floors, scouring the copper pot in which she had boiled down Mrs. Thomas's body. The next day Kate made a roaring fire in the kitchen fireplace, feeding Mrs. Thomas's stubborn remains—mostly bones—into the blaze. Adorned in her mistress's clothes, Kate then scurried to a pawnbroker and sold Mrs. Thomas's gold bridgework with several false teeth attached for six shillings, which she promptly used to get drunk in Mrs. Hayhoe's Pub. At this time, according to Mrs. Hayhoe, Kate brought along two jars of a lard-like substance which she offered for sale to customers as "best drippings." There were no takers. (This special sale of ostensible animal fat—in reality the residue of the hapless Mrs. Thomas—was later to become a hallmark of horror in the murder annals of England.)

So brazen had Kate Webster become that she assumed the role of proprietor of Mrs. Thomas's house, telling a family named Porter in nearby Hammersmith that she had inherited "a small villa in Richmond from a dear aunt. Even though it's a cozy place, I'm eager to sell the furniture."

Henry Porter suggested John Church, a friend and used-furniture dealer, who would more than likely be interested in buying such goods. Kate agreed to see Church and left with Porter and his son Robert, who accompanied Kate to several pubs before her return home. En route, Kate excused herself momentarily from one pub and, lugging a large black bag, said she had to meet a friend for a short while, someone waiting for her on the other side of the Hammersmith Bridge. Twenty minutes later, she returned without the bag.

"Where's the bag?" asked Henry Porter.

"Oh, I left it with my friend," replied Kate.

The bag at that moment was at the bottom of the river, and inside that bag was the head of Mrs. Julia Thomas.

Robert Porter escorted Kate to the Richmond house to perform an errand for the kindly Irish maid. With her help, Robert carried a large wooden box from Mrs. Thomas's home to the Richmond Bridge. Kate explained that she was to deliver the box, as she had the black bag, to a friend. "Leave me with it in the middle of the bridge," Kate told the Porter youth. "You go back the way we came and I'll catch up after I've talked to my friend."

Robert Porter shrugged and began walking across the fog-shrouded bridge. He heard a dull splash, then the footsteps of Kate Webster hurrying after him. "Well, that's over," Kate said.

The next day the box, tied with heavy cord, surfaced along the riverbank. Curious fishermen pried the box open, then nearly collapsed as they beheld the cooked remains of a human being. Though the hue and cry of foul murder went up, no one suspected for a minute that the victim had been Mrs. Thomas, who was a recluse. Knowing this, Kate, during her nocturnal travels days after the murder, passed *herself* off as Mrs. Thomas.

John Church next arrived at the Thomas home and told Kate that he would be willing to pay her sixty-eight pounds for all the furniture therein. She agreed only if Church paid her eighteen pounds in advance, which he did. When Church arrived, on March 18, to take the furniture away, the next-door neighbor, a Miss Ives, grew suspicious and called police. Constables stopped Church from removing the goods and began a search for Kate Webster. But the maid was too quick for them, slipping out the back door and hurrying from town. She fled to her native village of Killane, Ireland, but by then her identity as the killer of Mrs. Thomas was certain and her destination easily guessed. Officers of the Royal Irish Constabulary arrested her in Killane on March 28, 1879; at the time the brazen slayer was still wearing Mrs. Thomas's clothes and rings. Equally audacious was Kate's staunch attitude of innocence. "Is anyone in custody for the murder?" she inquired of arresting officers. "If there isn't, there ought to be. It's very hard that the innocent should suffer for the guilty."

Kate Webster's gall was still in force when she was returned to England and entered the Richmond police station where she was brought face to face with the duped John Church, the would-be purchaser of Mrs. Thomas's furniture.

Before Church could utter a sound, Kate pointed an accusing finger at him and shouted to constables, "Here's your murderer!"

The dumbfounded Church, who had volunteered to identify the maid, was then placed under arrest, and, along with Kate, charged with the murder of Mrs. Thomas. He was released, a nervous wreck, a short time later after police learned that he was nowhere near the Thomas home on the day of the murder.

The trial of Kate Webster began on July 2, 1879, and lasted seven days. Throughout the ordeal Kate shouted her innocence, not only labeling Church the murderer of her mistress but trying to fix blame on her friend Henry Porter as well, insisting that he had been Church's willing accomplice. She alone was found guilty.

"I never done it!" shrieked Kate from the dock. Frantic, Kate then placed the guilt on an unnamed lover. When that failed and she was condemned, the maid insisted that she was pregnant and could therefore not be executed. A panel of matrons soon disproved this new lie.

Right up to the night before her execution, Kate continued her lies, wildly accusing anyone who came to her tormented mind of having committed the murder. Late that night, having exhausted all schemes to escape her punishment, Kate Webster admitted her guilt to the prison chaplain, Father McEnrey, and Captain Colville, governor of Wandsworth Prison. Mayor Arthur Griffiths later remarked that on the day of her execution, July 29, 1879, Kate Webster went sullenly to her death, "a defiant, brutal creature who showed no remorse and who broke out into the most appalling language" as she was led to the hangman.

WEISS, JEANNE DANILOFF

Murderer ■ (1868–1891)

Love, not avarice, was the root of the tragedy that befell Jeanne Weiss. Born out of wedlock, Jeanne was never acknowledged by her father as his own; her mother, an exile from Russia, died at age twenty-five. The little girl was raised by her grandmother in a small boarding house in Nice on the Riviera. At sixteen, in 1884, Jeanne met a handsome young French officer, Monsieur Weiss, at a ball in Nice. They were married two years later and Lieutenant Weiss was posted to the small dust-ridden town of Ain-Fezza, near Oran in Algeria.

As the tranquil years passed, Jeanne gave birth to a son in 1887 and a daughter in 1889. The Europeans in Ain-Fezza saw that Madame Weiss took her wifely duties seriously, and considered her a paragon of motherhood. Also, because she was never without her Bible, which she studied assiduously, to her neighbors Jeanne Weiss was the essence of piety.

In late 1889, a young engineer, Felix Roques, arrived in Ain-Fezza to work for the West Algerian railways. He made advances to Jeanne the first minute he met her at a social tea. Out of either whimsy or boredom, Madame Weiss responded, and began meeting Roques clandestinely. In a short time she was madly in love with her ardent paramour, abandoning everything, running to Roques at his command at any time of the day. She willingly became the engineer's sex pawn. Such conduct undoubtedly inflated Roques's self-image to kingly proportions. Jeanne Weiss was lost. According to H. B. Irving, writing in *Studies of French Criminals*, "She surrendered herself to him with an intensity of passion and a slavishness of devotion which are the abiding characteristics of certain ill-balanced, incomplete natures which are only themselves when they are acting under the impulse of one stronger than they are."

Jeanne became Roques's mistress on November 13, 1889, a date she had engraved on an inexpensive ring the engineer gave her. Lieutenant Weiss grew suspicious and tried to win back his wife's affections by arranging a trip to Nice for her and the children in March 1890. Jeanne went to live again with her grandmother. She was pregnant again, but with the child of Roques, not her husband. Roques himself returned to France and saw Jeanne often, taking a room near her in Nice.

Weiss joined his wife in August, when Jeanne gave birth to a little girl whom the lieutenant thought to be his child. The couple and the three children returned to Algeria the following month. By then the lover Roques had traveled to Madrid to set in motion a sinister plan he and Jeanne had conceived as early as May 1890—the elimination of Lieutenant Weiss. At first the lovers thought to drug Weiss with chloral, then shoot him in the mouth to make him appear a suicide, but Jeanne carefully pointed out that her husband's insurance policies were not payable should he take his own life.

"You have an alternative," Roques pointed out. "You can merely elope with me."

"No," Jeanne said. "I'm too good a mother to abandon my children. It is my husband who must be finished."

The conspirators resolved to poison Weiss, that is, that Jeanne would poison Weiss. On May 18, 1890, to be assured that Jeanne would live up to the bargain, Roques ordered her to write in a yellow morocco pocketbook the words, "I swear that I will murder my husband, that I may belong to you alone. [Signed] Jeanne."

When resettled with her husband in Algeria, Madame Weiss had second thoughts. She wrote her lover—

I am beset by sad and depressing thoughts. What I am about to do is very ugly; and yet, if one commits suicide, what is to become of the poor little ones? . . . Felix, I ask you, do you tell me whether it would not be better that we should relinquish our dreams of happiness?

Roques ignored this appeal and insisted in a return letter that Jeanne live up to her agreement. Weiss must be murdered. Ever the love slave, Jeanne agreed, writing back—

It is agreed, Felix, you shall be obeyed. Have I ever hesitated before anything except the desertion of my children? Crimes against the law don't trouble me at all. It is only crimes against Nature that revolt me. I am a worshipper of Nature.

Jeanne continued wavering through September 1890, unsure of her purpose in poisoning a husband who had been kind and generous to her, who had shown her love and respect. Roques sent a barrage of letters to Jeanne demanding she kill Weiss. On September 29 he wrote—

I can't believe that you are slackening. You promised to obey me. I implore you to obey me.

During the first week of October, Weiss began to grow ill as Jeanne, obedient to her lover's orders, systematically poisoned his food with arsenic. Weiss suffered from high fever, burning sensations in the head, convulsions, and excessive vomiting. Doctors prescribed Fowler's solution, and this was administered by Jeanne herself. She prepared all his food and drink and was careful to throw away what was not consumed. Meticulously she washed each bowl and glass from which her husband ate and drank. "Her tender solicitude was beautiful to see," one scribe later remarked sarcastically. "She nursed her husband morning, noon, and night, and let no one else come near him."

A close friend of Weiss's, Monsieur de Guerry, grew suspicious when he overheard the postmistress of Ain-Fezza discussing the "peculiar" letters exchanged between Madame Weiss and a man named Roques, letters which the post office employee had boldly read. De Guerry suspected that his friend Weiss was being poisoned and on October 9 summoned a doctor to investigate. Also on that day, Jeanne sent an important letter to Roques, and the postmistress, who had been alerted by De Guerry, turned it over to him. In shock De Guerry read Jeanne's words to her lover—

You may as well know what a fearful time I am going through at this moment, in what a nightmare I live. Monsieur has been in bed four days, and the best half of my stock is used up. He fights it, fights it by his sheer vitality and instinct of self-preservation, so that he seems to absorb emetics and never drains a cup or a glass to its dregs. The doctor, who came yesterday, could find no disease. "He's a madman, a hypochondriac," he said. "Since he seems to want to be sick, give him some ipecacuanha, and don't worry, there's nothing serious the matter with him."

The constant sickness obliges me to administer the remedy in very small doses. I can't go beyond 20 drops without bringing on vomiting. Yesterday, from five in the morning to four in the afternoon, I have done nothing but empty basins, clean sheets, wash his face, and hold him down in bed during his paroxysms of sickness. At night, I have got away for a moment . . . and sobbed like a child. And I am afraid, afraid that I haven't got enough of the remedy left and that I shan't be able to bring it off. Couldn't you send me some by parcel post to the railway station at Ain-Fezza? Can't you send four or five pairs of children's socks with the bill? I'll take care to get rid of the wrapper. Hide the bottle carefully.

I am getting thinner every day. I don't look well, and I am afraid that when I see you, I shan't please you. Did you get the photograph?

Forgive my handwriting, but I am horribly nervous. I adore you.

Du Guerry instantly went to the authorities with the letter. The Procureur de la République arrived at the home of Madame Weiss on October 10, and showed her the letter she had written to Roques. "Do you recognize that letter, Madame?"

Jeanne responded without a twitch. "Yes. Monsieur Roques has been my lover. He wanted to marry me or elope with me. I tried to pacify him by pretending that I was poisoning my husband."

A quick search of the premises revealed enough poison to kill several people. Realizing her lie was uncovered, Jeanne dashed to a closet, snatched up a bottle of corrosive sublimate, and took a large dose, but she was stopped by officials; this was enough, however, to make her ill for the next six months. Roques was arrested in Madrid some days later. He had made elaborate preparations to marry Jeanne once the murder was done. In his apartment police found her let-

ters supporting their murder plot, printed forms announcing their marriage, and all the legal documents required to make them man and wife. Roques quit the intrigue on October 20, 1890, when he seized a guard's weapon in a Madrid jail and blew out his brains.

Jeanne faced trial alone. Her letters and her own statements damned her but she clung to one defense—Roques had ruled her will and she had been nothing more than his helpless sex toy. It was a convenient ploy with Roques dead.

Weiss was portrayed by the defense as a sickly, ineffectual weakling who made life miserable for his wife, but the court and public alike scoffed at such defamations. The cuckolded and almost murdered husband took the stand briefly on May 29, 1891, to tell the court, "I desire, gentlemen, to make to you the following declaration. I speak that I may reply to certain calumnies that have appeared in the press [the newspapers had published stories to the effect that Weiss, ever the doltish weakling, was willing to drop all charges and take back his lethal wife]. I have never forgiven Jeanne Daniloff. I do not, and I never will forgive her. Henceforth she is nothing to me. Whatever her fate, I stay near my children. I only wish never to hear her name again."

Applause then shook the court, so thunderous that the president had to gavel down the noise, shouting, "No one is allowed to applaud here! Consider the accused!"

At the moment of her husband's condemnation, Jeanne was seen to chew on her handkerchief but was hampered by her gloves. The jury, following a short deliberation, found her guilty of attempted murder. She was sentenced to twenty years' penal servitude.

Early the following morning Jeanne managed to bite again into her handkerchief while in her cell; sewn into the hem of the handkerchief was a roll of cigarette paper containing strychnine. She had planned to poison herself if her husband would not forgive her, but had failed in her efforts in court. She had whispered to her lawyers following her sentence, "I shall kill myself, I must save my children. They must not have a mother alive who is in jail as a poisoner."

A female guard entered the cell to find Madame Weiss lying feebly on her cot. The prisoner asked for a drink of water and was given it.

Drinking quickly, Jeanne at first thought that somehow another drug had been substituted for the poison. "Oh!" she cried, "it's cruel! They have deceived me! They have given me quinine!" Her body then began to convulse wildly. Her back arched to a bow but the woman was joyful in her excruciating torment, exclaiming, "No, they have not deceived me. I am happy. Adieu!" She was dead at 4:00 A.M., May 30, 1891, a bizarre martyr to murderous love.

WHEELDON, ALICE

Assassin ■ (? – ?)

Along with fellow conscientious objectors Alfred and Winnie Mason, Alice Wheeldon decided, in 1917, to murder British Prime Minister David Lloyd George, who, they felt, was solely responsible for the excessive loss of life then being incurred during World War I. Alice planned to get close to the prime minister during a public rally and stab him with a needle dipped in curare, a deadly poison.

Winnie Mason, a gossipy type, mentioned the plot to a friend and all three assassins were arrested, convicted in the Central Criminal Court on March 10, 1917, and given prison terms.

WILLIAMS, ANN

Murderer ■ (? –1753)

A husband-killer, Ann Williams wanted her mate eliminated so that she could carry on an affair with her butler. She mixed white mercury into her husband's gruel and served it to the unsuspecting man. He was in

Husband-killer Ann Williams, burned at the stake for her crime in England, 1753.

such pain within hours that he ordered his servants to fetch a doctor. To this physician, Williams confided his suspicions that his wife had killed him. Upon Williams's agonizing death the following day, Ann was arrested.

Tried and found guilty, she was taken to Gloucester, England, and burned alive at the stake.

WILSON, CATHERINE

Murderer ■ (1842–1862)

A poisoning nurse, Catherine Wilson operated in and about London from 1853 to 1862. Ingratiating herself with ailing people of wealth, she would persuade them to make over their wills to her, then feed them various poisons. For a while Catherine lived with a man named Dixon. When Dixon began to drink and quarrel with her, Catherine poisoned him, too.

She aroused suspicion by begging tearfully that doctors refrain from performing an autopsy on her dead husband. "Don't cut my dear one up," she pleaded. "He was always horrified by the thought of his poor body being mutilated." Catherine had her way with the doctors as she had with the victims.

In early 1862 Catherine went to live with ailing Mrs. Sarah Carnell and her husband. She so tenderly nursed her patient that Mrs. Carnell made out a new will, leaving most of her property to Catherine. A short time later Catherine brought Mrs. Carnell a "soothing draught." The woman took one mouthful of the burning-hot brew, spat it out, and called her husband.

When Carnell rushed into the room, he and his wife gaped. The mouthful Mrs. Carnell had spat out had burned holes in the carpet. Carnell seized the glass as evidence as Catherine Wilson fled. Police arrested her some days later and

Housekeeper and poisoner Catherine Wilson.

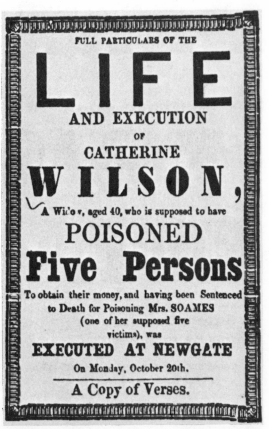

FULL PARTICULARS OF THE

LIFE

AND EXECUTION

OF

CATHERINE

WILSON,

A Widow, aged 40, who is supposed to have

POISONED

Five Persons

To obtain their money, and having been Sentenced to Death for Poisoning Mrs. SOAMES (one of her supposed five victims), was

EXECUTED AT NEWGATE

On Monday, October 20th.

A Copy of Verses.

Frontispiece of a pamphlet on Catherine Wilson.

charged her with attempted murder. The glass of fluid the nurse had given her patient contained enough sulphuric acid to kill fifty people.

Though Catherine was cleared of this charge—her defense attorney successfully argued that the druggist had given his client the wrong prescription—she was immediately re-arrested and tried for seven other murders. By then the bodies of her victims had been exhumed and examined, various poisons, from colchicum to arsenic, found in all.

Catherine Wilson was condemned and sent to the gallows outside the Old Bailey as on October 20, 1862, a crowd of twenty thousand waited to see her hang. She admitted not one murder nor shed a single tear.

WILSON, ELIZABETH

Murderer ■ (? –1786)

A resident of East Bradford, Pennsylvania, Elizabeth Wilson was so poor that she could not afford to feed her infant twins, only ten weeks old. She murdered the children, and her crime was quickly discovered.

Elizabeth's brother obtained a reprieve for his sister from the governor and rode wildly toward Chester, Pennsylvania, where the woman was scheduled to hang. The brother was slowed by muddy roads and arrived twenty-three minutes after Elizabeth had been hanged on January 3, 1786.

WISE, MARTHA HASEL

Murderer ■ (1885– ?)

M artha, a forty-year-old widow living on an impoverished farm in Medina, Ohio, fell in love with Walter Johns, a man much younger than herself. Martha's mother ridiculed her daughter for thinking of such "capricious romances" to the point where Martha poisoned the old lady on New Year's Day 1925.

When her aunt and uncle, Lily and Fred Geinke, also made fun of her affection for Johns, Martha spiked their coffee with arsenic in February 1925. In fact, Martha Wise was so incensed with the entire Geinke clan that she tried to poison the entire rest of the family, but the remaining Geinkes only grew ill.

Martha Wise, who insisted that the devil made her murder.

Authorities investigating the unusual deaths found the poison in the bodies of Martha's mother and the Geinkes. Joseph Seymour, the local prosecutor, confronted Martha, who was brought to his office. As the rain beat upon the office roof, Seymour repeatedly made the same charge: "You did, you did, you did, you did—"

"Yes, I did it!" Martha finally burst forth. "But it was the devil who told me to do it. He came to me while I was in the kitchen baking bread. He came to me while I was working in the fields. He followed me everywhere. It was the devil, I tell you! The devil!" She went on to admit not only to the murder of her mother and other relatives but to committing many burglaries in the area and also setting many fires. "I like fires. They were red and bright, and I loved to see the flames shooting up into the sky."

At her trial in 1925, Martha Hasel Wise was dubbed the "Borgia of America" while her defense attorneys fought boldly to prove her insane. To help the jury arrive at that verdict, Martha's lover, Walter Johns, willingly embarrassed himself by testifying that she was not of a balanced mind. Asking for an example, Johns told the court that during their lovemaking, Martha "barked like a dog!"

Martha was, however, convicted of first degree murder and sent to prison for life.

WORMS, PAMELA LEE

Murderer ■ (? —1852)

Mrs. Worms grew to hate her taskmaster husband Moses. In a fit of anger she poured arsenic into his food. At the moment, she was feeling angry toward her daughter, so she dosed the girl's meal, too. Pamela was arrested for the killings and condemned, hanged before a large crowd in Pittsburgh, Pennsylvania, on January 30, 1852.

WYNEKOOP, DR. ALICE

Murderer ■ (1870–1952)

One of the most sensational homicide cases of the Depression-torn 1930s involved an upstanding citizen of Chicago, Dr. Alice Wynekoop, who for years had been a respected physician and club woman, perhaps one of the most unlikely murder suspects on record and one who presented such a baffling, contradictory nature that to this day heads shake at the mention of her name. Dr. Wynekoop's murder saga began with a frantic phone call on the evening of November 21, 1933.

Called from her duties in the children's department of Cook County Hospital, Dr. Catherine Wynekoop answered an urgent phone call. Her sixty-three-year-old mother, Dr. Alice Wynekoop, was calling from home, her voice fluttering, unsure, as she told her daughter, "Something terrible has happened here. . . . It's Rheta. . . . She's dead. . . . She's been shot."

At about 10:00 P.M. that night, police officers, asked by Dr. Catherine Wynekoop to investigate, entered a gloomy mansion at 3406 W. Monroe Street. They were greeted by Dr. Alice Wynekoop and Miss Enid Hennessey, a schoolteacher who boarded with the Wynekoops.

"Something terrible has happened," Dr. Alice said to the officers. "Come on downstairs and I will show you." The police dutifully followed the woman downstairs and into an operating room where Dr. Alice practiced. The body of a beautiful young girl was lying on an operating table. The girl's clothing was piled in a heap on the floor next to the table. The body was wrapped in a thick blanket which one officer removed to see a bullet wound in the girl's breast. A .32-caliber Smith & Wesson was also on the table, under a cloth. There appeared to be burns on the girl's face, later claimed to be chloroform burns.

As the officers stood in the basement surgery, Dr. Alice could only mutter, "It must have been a burglar. . . . We've had robberies here be-

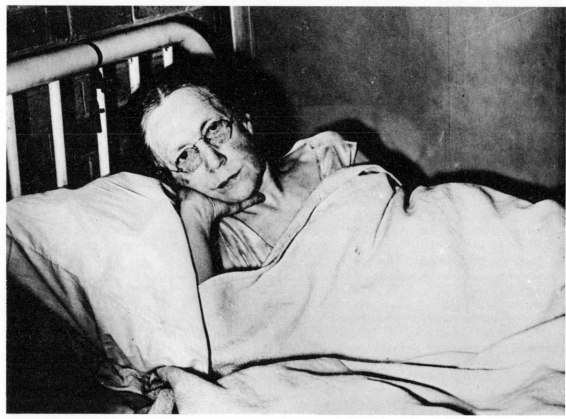
Dr. Alice Lindsay Wynekoop of Chicago in 1933, awaiting trial for murder in a jail hospital.

fore when burglars took some money and some drugs I keep in the glass case over there in the corner. . . . It must have been a burglar."

The red-haired girl on the table was Dr. Alice's daughter-in-law, Rheta Gardner Wynekoop, whose father, Burdine H. Gardner, was an important flour and salt merchant in Indianapolis. The girl's husband of only a few months, Earle Wynekoop, was a shiftless playboy and the darling of his hardworking mother, Dr. Alice. At the moment of the murder, it was later established, Earle Wynekoop was on a speeding train headed for the Grand Canyon, ostensibly to take scenic pictures for his budding career in photography. His companion was an attractive brunette.

The police arrested no one on the night of the murder, merely taking away the body.

Newsmen learned of the story within minutes of the corpse's arrival at the morgue. Captain John Stege, one of Chicago's finest homicide sleuths, began to sift through the evidence, and, having learned the Wynekoop family background, determined that Dr. Alice had murdered Rheta Wynekoop. He brought the elderly physician in for questioning.

Meanwhile, Earle Wynekoop, learning of his wife's death, returned to Chicago; he was met at the train station by a bevy of pencil-pushing reporters who badgered him for answers. The tall, darkly handsome Earle, enjoying the limelight, blustered brag and bravado, telling newsmen that "my wife was sickly, had tuberculosis and she was also mentally deranged. You know she once tried to poison my entire family by putting drugs and iron filings into our food?

The marriage, gentlemen, was an utter failure." When one of the reporters quizzed the lothario about his attractive companion, the girl accompanying Earle slipped away in the crowd. Wynekoop shrugged, waving a date book. "I've got fifty more like her listed here." Yes, he agreed with his mother's theory. His wife had probably been the victim of a burglar. "It's my opinion that she was murdered by a moron."

Questions of a different sort were at that moment being plied to the frail and nervous Dr. Alice Wynekoop as the police mercilessly grilled her hour after hour. At the same time, Captain Stege was putting together the history of the Wynekoop family.

He learned that Dr. Alice was one of the most respected physicians in Chicago. She had been a prominent social worker and club woman for twenty-five years, devoting much of her time to charity work. Dr. Alice had in all that time lived with her large family in the Monroe Street mansion, a towering three-story stone building which had been built in 1904 for her and her husband, Dr. Frank Wynekoop. When her husband died, Mrs. Wynekoop worked hard to support her own three children, Walker, Earle, and Catherine, as well as an adopted child, Mary Louise, who later died at an early age. Walker went on to become a successful businessman, and Catherine proved herself as skillful a physician as her mother and father had been, specializing in the care of children. Earle specialized in nothing but himself. He was, from early childhood, the favorite among Dr. Alice's brood. She spoiled him and indulged his every wish.

Earle Wynekoop never undertook a profession, but drifted about aimlessly, supported for the most part by his devoted mother. On a trip to Indianapolis, Earle attended a concert and spotted Rheta Gardner, a beautiful young violinist. He fell in love with her and married the eighteen-year-old girl a year later. Following a brief honeymoon, the couple moved into the Monroe Street mansion. Rheta was unhappy with the arrangement, especially when Earle began running around with other girls. The bride was confined to doing humdrum household chores, taking violin lessons, and treating herself to an occasional purchase of sheet music, her only joy.

She became a ward of Dr. Alice, who more and more resented the girl, coming to believe that her son had made a poor marriage.

Apparently, Earle felt the same, that the sickly, moody Rheta made him feel hemmed in and miserable. Prosecutors later stated that after talking with her son at great length about his unhappy marriage, Dr. Alice determined to murder Rheta so that Earle could find happiness elsewhere. Following this talk and only a few days before the murder, Dr. Alice wrote a note to Earle which indicated her traumatic state of mind—

Precious—
I'm *choked*—you are gone—you have called me up—and after 10 minutes or so, I called and called—no answer—maybe you are sleeping—you need to be—but I want to hear your voice again tonight—I would give anything I had—to spend an hour—in real *talk* with you—tonight—And I cannot—Goodnight.

This note, never delivered to her son, was placed in evidence against the mother. The state's attorney would later insist that the note indicated that Dr. Alice had come to a decision to murder her daughter-in-law.

Captain Stege produced more substantial evidence for the court following Dr. Alice's nonstop interrogation. On the morning of November 24, 1933, Stege entered the office of a Captain Duffy in the station where the woman was being held. Dr. Alice was stretched out on a couch, an overcoat covering her. She raised herself when Stege entered, blinking at him. Their dialogue began innocently enough.

"Good morning, doctor."

"Good morning, captain."

"Did you have any breakfast?"

"No, I don't want any, but I would like some coffee."

Stege turned to a policeman and told him to get Dr. Alice some coffee.

Then the elderly woman sat up and said to Stege, "Captain, what would happen if I told the story about killing Rheta?"

"Doctor, I don't want any story from you. All I want is the truth."

Dr. Wynekoop at age seventy-eight after having served fourteen years for the murder of her daughter-in-law.

Dr. Alice Wynekoop then confessed to killing Rheta Garner Wynekoop, but insisted that it was all an accident. Her statement was later introduced in court and branded a grand fabrication as a cover for the real murder. It read:

"Rheta was concerned about her health and frequently weighed herself, usually stripping for the purpose. On Tuesday, November 21, after luncheon at about one, she decided to go down to the Loop to purchase some sheet music that she had been wanting. She was given money for this purpose and laid it on the table, deciding to weigh herself before dressing to go downtown. I went to the office. She was sitting on the table practically undressed, and suggested that the pain in her side was troubling her more than usual. [This mysterious 'pain' was never explained before or after Dr. Alice's confession.] I remarked to her since it was a convenient interval . . . for an examination, we might just as well have it over. She complained of considerable soreness, severe pain and tenderness. She thought she would endure the examination better if she might have a little anesthetic. Chloroform was conveniently at hand, and a few drops were put on a sponge. She breathed it very deeply. She took several deep inhalations. I asked her if I was hurting her and she made no answer. Inspection revealed that respiration had stopped. Artificial respiration for about twenty minutes gave no response. Stethoscopic examination revealed no heartbeat. Turning the patient quickly on her side and examining posteriorly as well as anteriorly, there was no sign of life. Wondering what method would ease the situation best to all and with the suggestion offered by the presence of a loaded revolver, further injury being impossible, with great difficulty one cartridge was exploded at a distance of some half dozen inches from the patient. The scene was so overwhelming that no action was possible for a period of several hours."

Inside this reserved admission, Dr. Alice was claiming to have accidentally overdosed her patient with chloroform, and to cover her error, had shot the dead woman to make her death appear the murder of persons unknown, a fantastic statement on the face of it. The burns on the girl's face, originally thought to be from chloroform, were then determined to be powder burns from the revolver. Medical authorities later performed an autopsy on the body and found that it contained no chloroform whatever.

Earle Wynekoop visited his mother in jail before her confession. He was, at the time, placed in custody, but was allowed to see his mother. The following conversation was overheard by jailers.

"For God's sake, mother, if you did this on account of the bond of love between us, go ahead and confess."

"But, Earle—I did not kill Rheta."

"Mother—mother . . ."

Earle Wynekoop could not believe the confession, and he branded it false. He later made five separate confessions of his own, that he, not his mother, had murdered his wife. In one confession, Earle stated that he had only pretended to take the train to Arizona, but had doubled back to the Monroe Street mansion, slipped into the basement surgery, and waited for his wife to come into the room to weigh herself and then shot her dead. All these statements were proved false, and it was verified that Earle was, indeed, on that westbound train.

Further, Enid Hennessey, the teacher who boarded with the Wynekoops, appeared in court to state that she was in the house shortly after the time of the murder and that Dr. Alice had pretended that nothing was amiss. Miss Hennessey reported how the doctor had prepared a dinner of pork chops and mashed potatoes for herself and Miss Hennessey, and that after dinner the two women sat in the study calmly discussing some books Miss Hennessey intended to read, *The Forsyte Saga* and *Strange Interlude*, Rheta Gardner Wynekoop, all the while, lying dead in the downstairs surgery. The time of the murder had been fixed by Dr. Alice in her own confession as midafternoon. In her own words, Dr. Alice had stated that the "scene was so overwhelming that no action was possible for several hours." Yet she carefully prepared dinner and had a leisurely literary discussion while her daughter-in-law lay dead in the same house. Such conduct was paradoxical, and certainly perplexing to the jury that heard Dr. Alice's case.

Alice Wynekoop recanted her confession, insisting that she was only half conscious when making the statement after being grilled by police for more than sixty hours. The prosecution made telling points by illustrating how Dr. Wynekoop had been in desperate need of money and that upon her daughter-in-law's death she stood to benefit from Rheta's insurance policy. But Earle Wynekoop was the real reason why his mother killed Rheta, intoned the prosecutor—she would do anything to make her boy happy, and that included murder.

The jury spent only fourteen hours mulling over the case and concluded that Dr. Alice was guilty beyond a reasonable doubt. She was convicted of first degree murder and given a life sentence. She was paroled in 1949, and died two years later.

The object of her affections and motivation for murder, Earle Wynekoop, was set free. He took menial jobs to support himself and finally vanished.

ZILLMAN, BERTHA

Murderer ■ (? –1893)

Bertha's husband returned home one night and beat her and her children so severely that she poisoned him with arsenic the next morning at breakfast. She was quickly tried and sentenced to death, taken to Plötzensee, Germany, on October 21, 1893, to be beheaded.

One newspaper reported that "her dress was cut out at the neck down to the shoulders, and her hair fastened up in a knot, her shoulders then being covered with a shawl. At eight, the inspector entered Zillman's cell, and found her completely prostrate, incapable of putting one foot before the other. Two warders raised her up, and led her to the block."

BIBLIOGRAPHY

The exhaustive research for this book was not done only in libraries and archives throughout the United States, but culled and gleaned from the author's own files, exceeding more than a quarter of a million separate entries and a personal crime library of more than 25,000 volumes. Interviews and extensive correspondence with law enforcement personnel, convicted criminals, and experts in the various crime fields were also employed. Hundreds of different newspapers and periodicals throughout the world were consulted, specific dates too numerous to cite herein. Some of the most helpful published sources follow.

BOOKS

Abbott, Wilbur C. *New York in the Revolution*. New York: Charles Scribner's Sons, 1929.

Adam, Hargrave Lee. *Woman and Crime*. London: T. W. Laurie, 1912.

Adleman, Robert H. *The Bloody Benders*. New York: Stein and Day, 1970.

Adler, Freda. *Sisters in Crime: The Rise of the New Female Criminal*. New York: McGraw-Hill, 1975.

Adler, Polly. *A House is Not a Home*. New York: Rinehart, 1953.

Alix, Ernest Kahlar. *Ransom Kidnapping in America*. Carbondale, Ill.: Southern Illinois University Press, 1975.

Allen, L. B. *Brief Considerations on the Present State of the Police of the Metropolis*. New York: N.p., 1821.

Altick, Richard D. *Victorian Studies in Scarlet*. London: J. M. Dent & Sons, Ltd., 1956.

Amory, Cleveland. *The Last Resorts*. New York: Harper & Bros., 1948.

Angley, Edward. *Oh, Yeah?* New York: Viking Press, 1931.

Anslinger, Harry J., and Oursler, Will. *The Murderers*. New York: Farrar, Straus and Cudahy, 1961.

Asbury, Herbert. *The Gangs of New York*. New York: Alfred A. Knopf, Inc., 1927.

————. *The French Quarter*. New York: Alfred A. Knopf, Inc., 1936.

Asmodeus in New York. New York: N.p., 1868.

Aspinal, A. *Politics and the Press, 1780-1850*. London: Home and Van Thal, 1849.

Aydelotte, Frank. *Elizabethan Rogues and Vagabonds*. Oxford Historical and Literary Studies. Oxford: Clarendon Press, 1913.

Baker, General L. C. *History of the United States Secret Service*. Philadelphia: J. E. Potter & Co., 1889.

Baker, Pearl. *The Wild Bunch at Robbers Roost*. New York: Abelard-Schuman, 1965.

Baker, Peter. *Time Out of Life*. London: Heinemann, 1961.

Barnard, William F. *Forty Years at the Five Points*. New York: N.p., 1893.

Barnes, David. *The Metropolitan Police*. New York: Baker & Godwin, 1863.

Bateson, Charles. *The Convict Ships, 1787-1868*. Glasgow: Brown, Son & Ferguson, 1959.

Beccaria, Cesare Bonesana. *An Essay on Crime and Punishments*. Philadelphia: Philip H. Nicklin, 1819.

Becker, Jillian. *Hitler's Children*. New York: J. B. Lippincott, 1977.

Bedford, Sybille. *The Faces of Justice*. New York: Simon & Schuster, 1961.

Bell, J. Bowyer. *Assassin!* New York: St. Martin's Press, 1979.

Benson, Captain L. *The Book of Remarkable Trials*. London: Chatto and Windus, 1924.

Bergamini, David. *Japan's Imperial Conspiracy*. New York: William Morrow, 1971.

Berger, Meyer. *The Eighty Million*. New York: Simon & Schuster, 1942.

Berns, Walter. *For Capital Punishment*. New York: Basic Books, 1974.

Bierstadt, Edward Hale. *Curious Trials and Criminal Cases*. Garden City Publishing Co., 1928.

Bigelow, L. J. *Bench and Bar*. New York: Harper & Bros., 1871.

Birmingham, George A. *Murder Most Foul!* London: Chatto and Windus, 1929.

Bishop, George. *Executions*. Los Angeles: Sherbourne Press, Inc., 1965.

Blackstone, William. *Commentaries on the Laws of England*. 4 vols. London: A. Strahan, 1809.

Bleackley, Horace. *The Hangmen of England*. London: Chapman and Hall, Ltd., 1929.

Bloch, Herbert A., ed. *Crime in America*. New York: Philosophical Library, 1961.

Block, Eugene B. *Fifteen Clues*. Garden City, N.Y.: Doubleday & Co., 1965.

————. *The Fabric of Guilt*. Garden City, N.Y.: Doubleday & Co., 1968.

Blum, Richard H. *Deceivers and Deceived*. Springfield, Ill.: Charles C. Thomas, 1972.

Blumenthal, Walter Hart. *Brides from Bridewell: Female Felons Sent to Colonial America*. Westport, Conn.: Greenwood Press, 1962.

Bolitho, William. *Murder for Profit*. London: Jonathan Cape, 1926.

Bontham, Alan. *Sex Crimes and Sex Criminals*. New York: Wisdom House, 1961.

Bornstein, Joseph. *The Politics of Murder*. New York: William Sloan, 1950.

Boswell, Charles, and Thompson, Lewis. *Practitioners of Murder*. New York: Collier Books, 1962.

————. *Advocates of Murder*. New York: Collier Books, 1962.

Boucher, Anthony, ed. *The Quality of Murder*. New York: E. P. Dutton & Co., 1962.

Brace, Charles Loring. *The Dangerous Classes of New York*. New York: Wynekoop & Hallenbeck, 1880.

Bradley, John L., ed. *Rogues Progress*. Boston: Houghton-Mifflin Co., 1965.

Brearley, H.C. *Homicide in the United States*. Chapel Hill, N.C.: Univ. of North Carolina Press, 1932.

Brice, A. H. M. *Look Upon the Prisoner*. London: Hutchinson & Co, Ltd., 1930.

Brolaski, Harry. *Easy Money*. Cleveland: Searchlight Press, 1911.

Bromberg, W. *Crime and the Mind*. Philadelphia: J. B. Lippincott, 1948.

Brown, Ivor. *Dickens in His Time*. New York: Thomas Nelson, 1963.

Browne, Douglas, and Brock, Alan. *Fingerprints*. New York: E. P. Dutton & Co., 1952.

Brophy, John. *The Meaning of Murder*. London: Ronald Whiting & Wheaton, 1966.

Bullough, Vern L. *The History of Prostitution*. New Hyde Park, N.Y.: University Books, 1964.

Burton, Anthony M. *Urban Terrorism*. London: Leo Cooper, 1975.

Busch, Francis X. *Prisoners at the Bar*. Indianapolis: Bobbs-Merrill, 1952.

Byrnes, Thomas. *Professional Criminals In America*. New York: Cassell & Co., 1886.

Caminda, Jerome. *Twenty-Five Years of Detective Life*. London: John Heywood, 1895.

Campbell, Helen. *Darkness and Daylight*. Hartford, Conn.: A. D. Worthington & Co., 1892.

Camps, Professor Francis E. *The Investigation of Murder*. London: Michael Joseph, Ltd., 1966.

Canning, John. *50 True Tales of Terror*. New York: Bell Publishing Co., 1972.

Carpenter, Mary. *Our Convicts*. London: W. & F. G. Cash, 1864.

Carpozi, George, Jr. *Ordeal By Trial: The Alice Crimmins Case*. New York: Walker, 1972.

Cassity, J.H. *The Quality of Murder*. New York: The Julian Press, 1958.

Celebrated Murders. Chicago: Belford, Clarke & Co., 1879.

Celebrated Trials of All Countries. Philadelphia: E. L. Carey & A. Hart, 1843.

Chandler, Frank W. *The Literature of Roguery*. 2 vols. Boston: Houghton-Mifflin Co., 1907.

Chandler, Peleg W. *American Criminal Trials* Vol. II. Boston: Little, Brown & Co., 1841-44.

Christie, Trevor L. *Etched in Arsenic*. Philadelphia: J. B. Lippincott & Co., 1968.

Christoph, James B. *Capital Punishment and British Politics*. Chicago: Univ. of Chicago Press, 1962.

Churchill, Allen. *The Year the World Went Mad*. New York: Thomas Y. Crowell, 1960.

————. *A Pictorial History of American Crime*. New York: Holt, Rinehart & Winston, 1964.

Clarke, Charles. L., and Eubank, Earle E. *Lockstep and Corridor*. Cincinnati: Cincinnati Press, 1927.

Clayton, Gerold Francourt. *The Wall is Strong*. London: John Long, 1958.

Clinton, Henry Lauren. *Celebrated Trials*. New York: Harper & Bros., 1896.

Clutterbuck, Richard. *Kidnap & Ransom*. Boston: Faber & Faber, 1978.

Cockburn, J. S., ed. *Crime In England, 1550-1800*. London: Methuen, 1977.

Cohen, Louis H. *Murder, Madness and the Law*. New York: World, 1952.

Cohen, Sam D. *100 True Crime Stories*. Cleveland: World Publishing Co., 1946.

Colby, Robert. *The California Crime Book*. New York: Pyramid Books, 1971.

Collins, Frederick L. *The F.B.I. In Peace and War*. New York: G. P. Putnam's Sons, 1943.

Collins, Philip. *Dickens and Crime*. London: Macmillan, 1962.

Collins, Ted., ed. *New York Murders*. New York: Duell, Sloan & Pearce, 1944.

Cooper, Courtney Riley. *Ten Thousand Public Enemies*. Boston: Little, Brown & Co., 1935.

————. *Designs in Scarlet*. Boston: Little, Brown & Co., 1939.

Cooper, David D. *The Lesson of the Scaffold*. Athens, Ohio: Ohio University Press, 1974.

Corder, Eric., ed. *Murder My Love*. Chicago: Playboy Press, 1973.

Costello, A. E. *Our Police Protectors*. New York: C. F. Roper & Co., 1885.

Crane, Milton. *Sins of New York*. New York: Boni & Gaer, 1947.

Crapsey, Edward. *The Nether Side of New York*. New York: Sheldon, 1872.

Crook, G. T. *The Complete Newgate Calendar*. London: Privately printed for the Navarre Society, 1926.

Culpin, Howard. *The Newgate Noose*. London: Frederick Muller, Ltd., 1951.

Damore, Leo. *The Crime of Dorothy Sheridan*. New York: Arbor House, 1978.

Dean, John. *The Indiana Torture Slaying*. Chicago: Bee-Line Books, 1967.

de Ford, Miriam Allen. *Murderers Sane & Mad*.

New York: Abelard-Schuman, 1965.

Deindorfer, Robert G. *The Spies.* New York: Fawcett Publications, Inc., 1949.

de La Torre, Lillian. *Villainy Detected.* London: D. Appleton-Century Co., Inc., 1947.

—————. *Elizabeth Is Missing.* London: Michael Joseph, 1947.

Dellinger, Dave. *More Power Than We Know.* New York: Anchor Press/Doubleday, 1975.

Demaris, Ovid. *America the Violent.* New York: Cowles Book Co., Inc. 1970.

—————. *The Director.* New York: Harper's Magazine Press, 1976.

Deming, Richard. *Women: The New Criminals.* New York: Thomas Nelson, 1977.

Dempewolf, Richard. *Famous Old New England Murders.* Brattleboro, Vt.: Stephen Daye Press, 1942.

de Rham, Edith. *How Could She Do That?* New York: Clarkson N. Potter, 1969.

Derleth, August. *Wisconsin Murders.* Sauk City, Wis.: Mycroft and Moran, 1968.

de Toledano, Ralph. *J. Edgar Hoover.* New Rochelle, N.Y.: Arlington House, 1973.

Deutsch, Albert. *The Trouble With Cops.* New York: Crown Publishers, 1954.

Dexter, Walter., ed. *The Letters of Charles Dickens, 1845-1847.* 3 vols. London: Nonesuch Press, 1938.

Dickens, Charles. *Miscellaneous Papers.* 2 vols. London: Chapman and Hall, 1908.

Dickson, G. *Murder By Numbers.* London: Robert Hale, Ltd., 1958.

Dilnot, George. *Celebrated Crimes.* London: Stanley Paul & Co., Ltd., 1925.

Douthwaite, L. C. *Mass Murder.* New York: Holt, 1929.

Drummond, Isabel. *The Sex Paradox.* New York: Putnam's, 1953.

Duffy, Warden Clinton T. *The San Quentin Story, As told to Dean Jennings.* Garden City, N.Y.: Doubleday, 1950.

—————. with Hirschberg, Al. *88 Men and Two Women.* Garden City, N.Y.: Doubleday, 1962.

Duke, Thomas S. *Celebrated Cases of America.* San Francisco: James H. Barry Co., 1910.

Eldridge, Benjamin P., and Watts, William B. *Our Rival The Rascal.* Boston: Pemberton Publishing Co., 1897.

Elliot, Robert G., with Beatty, Albert R. *Agent of Death.* New York: E. P. Dutton, 1940.

Ellison, E. Jerome, and Brock, Frank W. *The Run for Your Money.* New York: Dodge Publishing Co., 1935.

Emery, J. Gladstone. *Court of the Damned.* New York: Comet Press, 1959.

Erickson, Gladys A. *Warden Ragen of Joliet.* New York: E. P. Dutton, 1957.

Erickson, Kai T. *Wayward Puritans.* New York: John Wiley, 1966.

Farley, Philip. *Criminals of America.* New York: Farley, 1876.

Felstead, Sidney Theodore. *Sir Richard Muir.* London: John Lane, Ltd., 1927.

Fink, Arthur E. *Causes of Crime.* Philadelphia: Univ. of Pennsylvania Press, 1938.

Fitzgerald, Maurice. *Criminal Investigations.* New York: Greenberg, 1953.

Flinn, John T. *History of the Chicago Police.* Chicago: Police Book Fund, 1887.

Fosdick, Raymond B. *American Police Systems.* New York: Century, 1920.

Foucault, Michel. *Discipline & Punishment: The Birth of the Prison.* New York: Vintage, 1979.

Fox, Lionel. *English Prison and Borstal Systems.* London: Routledge, 1952.

Franklin, Charles. *Woman in the Case.* New York:

Taplinger Publishing Co., Inc., 1968.

—————. *World Famous Acquittals.* London: Odhams Books, 1970.

French, Joseph Lewis. *The Book of the Rogue.* New York: Boni & Liveright, 1926.

Friedman, Michael, ed. *The New Left of the Sixties.* Berkeley, Calif.: Independent Socialist Press.

Fuller, Margaret. *Woman in the Nineteenth Century.* New York: W. W. Norton, 1971.

Funck-Brentano, Frantz. *Princes and Poisoners.* London: Duckworth and Co., 1901.

Furlong, Thomas. *Fifty Years A Detective.* St. Louis: C. E. Barnett, 1912.

Furneaux, Rupert. *The Medical Murderer.* London: Elek Books, 1957.

—————. *Famous Criminal Cases.* London: Roy Books, 1959.

—————. *They Died By A Gun.* London: Herbert Jenkins, 1962.

Gibney, Frank. *The Operators.* New York: Harper & Bros., 1960.

Gilliver, L. *Select Trials at the Sessions—House in the Old Bailey.* London: N.p., 1747.

Gish, Anthony. *American Bandits.* Girard, Kan.: Haldeman-Julius, 1938.

Glaister, John. *The Power of Poison.* New York: William Morrow & Co., 1954.

Glueck, Sheldon, and Glueck, Eleanor T. *500 Delinquent Women.* New York: Alfred A Knopf, 1934.

Goddard, Henry. *The Memoirs of a Bow Street Runner.* New York: William Morrow & Co., 1956.

Gollomb, Joseph. *Crimes of the Year.* New York: Liveright Publishing Corp., 1931.

Goode, Stephen. *Affluent Revolutionaries.* New York: Franklin Watts, Inc., 1974.

Goodman, Derick. *Crime of Passion.* New York: Greenberg Publishers, 1958.

Gowers, Sir Ernest. *A Life for a Life.* London: Chatto and Windus, 1956.

Graham, Stephen. *New York Nights.* New York: Doran, 1927.

Grathwohl, Larry. *Bringing Down America.* New Rochelle, N.Y.: Arlington House, 1976.

Gribble, Leonard. *Famous Judges and Their Trials.* London: John Long, 1957.

—————. *The Dead End Killers.* London: John Long, 1978.

—————. *Compelled to Kill.* London: John Long, 1977.

Griffiths, Major Arthur. *Mysteries of Police and Crime.* Vols. I, II, III. London: Cassell & Co., 1902.

Gross, Hans. *Criminology Psychology.* Boston: Little, Brown & Co., 1915.

Gross, Kenneth. *The Alice Crimmins Case.* New York: Alfred A. Knopf, 1975.

Guerin, Eddie. *I Was a Bandit.* Garden City, New York: Doubleday, Doran, 1929.

Guttmacher, Manfred S. *Sex Offenses.* New York: W. W. Norton, 1951.

—————, and Weihofen, Henry. *Psychiatry and the Law.* New York: W. W. Norton, 1952.

Hambly, Charles R. *Hold Your Money.* Los Angeles: Monitor Publishing Co., 1932.

Harding, Thomas Swann. *The Popular Practice of Fraud.* London: Longmans, Green, 1935.

Hardy, Allison. *Kate Bender, The Kansas Murderess.* Girard, Kan.: Haldeman-Julius, 1944.

Hart, Smith. *The New Yorkers.* New York: Sheridan House, 1938.

Hartman, Mary S. *Victorian Murderesses.* New York: Schocken Books, Inc., 1977.

Haskins, George Lee. *Law and Authority in Early Massachusetts.* New York: Macmillan, 1960.

Haswell, Jock. *Spies & Spymasters.* New York:

Thames and Hudson, 1977.

Hayward, Arthur L., ed. *A Complete History of the Lives and Robberies of the Most Notorious Highwaymen, Footpads, Shoplifts, and Cheats of Both Sexes.* London: Routledge & Sons, 1926.

Helpern, M.D., Milton, with Knight, M.D., Bernard. *Autopsy.* New York: St. Martin's Press, 1977.

Henriques, Fernando. *Prostitution in Europe and the Americas.* New York: The Citadel Press, 1965.

Hentig, Hans von. *The Criminal and His Victim.* New Haven, Conn.: Yale Univ. Press, 1948.

Hibbert, Christopher. *The Road to Tyburn.* London: Longmans, Green and Co., Ltd., 1957.

—————. *The Roots of Evil.* Boston: Little, Brown & Co., 1963.

Hilberg, Raul. *The Destruction of the European Jews.* Chicago: Quadrangle, 1967.

Hill, Elwin C. *The American Scene.* New York: M. Witmark & Sons, 1933.

Hinde, R. S. E. *The British Penal System, 1773-1950.* London: Duckworth, 1951.

Hirsch, Phil., ed. *The Killers.* New York: Pyramid, 1971.

Hist, David. *The Gun and the Olive Branch.* London: Faber & Faber, 1977.

Hogarth, Georgina, ed. *The Letters of Charles Dickens, 1833-1870.* 3 vols. London: Chapman and Hall, 1909.

Holbrook, Stewart. *Murder Out Yonder.* New York: Macmillan, 1941.

Holtzoff, H., ed. *Encyclopedia of Criminology.* New York: Philosophical Library, 1949.

Hooper, William Eden. *The History of Newgate and the Old Bailey.* London: Underwood Press, 1935.

Hooten, E. A. *The American Criminal.* Vol. I. Cambridge, Mass.: Harvard Univ. Press, 1939.

Hoover, J. Edgar. *Persons In Hiding.* Boston: Little, Brown & Co., 1938.

Horan, James D. *The Pinkerton Story.* New York: G. P. Putnam's Sons, 1951.

—————. *The Pinkertons.* New York: G. P. Putnam's Sons, 1967.

Horwitz, Irvin M. *Assassination.* New York: Harper & Row, 1972.

Hot Corn. New York: N.p., 1854.

House, Brant, ed. *Crimes That Shocked America.* New York: Ace Books, 1961.

Huggett, Renee, and Berry, Paul. *Daughters of Cain.* London: George Allen & Unwin, Ltd., 1956.

Hurwitz, Stephen. *Criminology.* London: George Allen and Unwin, Ltd., 1952.

Huson, Richard, ed. *Sixty Famous Trials.* London: A Daily Express Publication, 1967.

Irving, H. B. *Studies of French Criminals.* London: William Heinemann, 1901.

—————. *A Book of Remarkable Criminals.* London: Cassell & Co., Ltd., 1918.

Irwin, Inez Haynes. *Angels and Amazons, A Hundred Years of American Women.* Garden City, N.Y.: Doubleday, Doran, 1934.

Jackson, Joseph Henry. *The Portable Murder Book.* New York: The Viking Press, 1945.

Jackson, Robert. *The Crime Doctors.* London: Frederick Muller, Ltd., 1966.

Jacobs, Harold. *Weatherman.* New York: Ramparts Press, 1970.

James, H. K. *The Destruction of Mephisto's Greatest Web; or All Grafts Laid Bare.* Salt Lake City: Raleigh Publishing Co., 1914.

James, John T. *The Benders of Kansas.* Wichita, Kan.: Kan-Okla. Publishing Co., 1913.

Jenkins, Elizabeth. *Six Criminal Women.* London:

Pan Books, Ltd., 1949.

Jennings, Dean. *We Only Kill Each Other*. New York: Prentice-Hall, 1967.

Jesse, F. Tennyson. *Murder and Its Motives*. London: George G. Harrap & Co., 1924.

Johnson, Captain Charles. *Lives of the Most Noted Highwaymen*. Dublin: Tegg & Co., 1839.

Jones, Willoughby. *Weighed and Found Wanting*. Philadelphia: W. Flint, 1872.

Judges, A. V. *The Elizabethan Underworld*. London: G. Routledge & Sons, 1930.

Kahn, Samuel. *Sing Sing Criminals*. Philadelphia: Dorrance & Co., 1936.

Karpmen, Benjamin. *Case Studies in the Psychopathology of Crime*. Washington, D.C.: Mimeotorm Press, 1933.

—————. *The Sexual Offender and His Offenses*. London: Julian Press, 1934.

—————. *The Individual Criminal*. Washington, D.C.: Nervous and Mental Diseases Publishing Co., 1935.

Kavanagh, Marcus. *The Criminal and His Allies*. Indianapolis: Bobbs-Merrill, 1928.

Kershaw, Alister. *Murder In France*. London: Constable & Co., 1955.

Kilgallen, Dorothy. *Murder One*. New York: Random House, 1967.

Kingsmill, Joseph. *Chapters on Prisons and Prisoners and the Prevention of Crime*. London: Longman, Brown & Green, 1854.

—————. *A History of the Guillotine*. New York: Taplinger, 1959.

Kingston, Charles. *Remarkable Rogues; Some Notable Criminals of Europe and America*. London: Stanley Paul & Company, Ltd., 1921.

—————. *Famous Judges and Trials*. New York: Frederick A. Stokes Company, 1923.

—————. *The Bench & The Door*. London: Stanley Paul & Company, Ltd., 1925.

—————. *Dramatic Days At the Old Bailey*. New York: Frederick A. Stokes, 1927.

Kinsey, A. C.; Pomeroy, W. B.; Martin, C. E.; and Gebhard, Paul H. *Sexual Behavior in the Human Female*. London: Saunders, 1953.

Klein, Alexander, ed. *Grand Deception*. Philadelphia: J. B. Lippincott, 1955.

—————. *Double Dealers*. Philadelphia: J. B. Lippincott, 1958.

Knox, Thomas W. *Underground*. Hartford, Conn.: Burr, Hyde, 1873.

Kobler, John. *Some Like It Gory*. New York: Dodd, Mead, 1940.

Koestler, Arthur, and Rolph, C. H. *Hanged by the Neck*. New York: Penguin, 1961.

Laguer, Walter. *Terrorism*. Boston: Little, Brown & Co., 1977.

Laurence, John. *A History of Capital Punishment*. New York: Citadel Press, 1960.

Laurie, T. Werner. *The Newgate Calendar*. New York: G. P. Putnam's Sons, 1932.

Lavigne, Frank C. *Crimes, Criminals and Detectives*. Helena, Mont.: State Publishing Co., 1921.

Lavine, Sigmund. *Allan Pinkerton, America's First Private Eye*. New York: Dodd, Mead & Co., 1963.

Lawes, Warden Lewis Edward. *20,000 Years in Sing Sing*. New York: R. Long & R. R. Smith, Inc. 1932.

—————. *Meet the Murderer*. New York: Harper & Bros., 1940.

Lawson, John D., ed. *American State Trials*. 17 vols. St. Louis: Thomas, 1914-1937.

Le Brun, George P. *Call Me If It's Murder*. New York: William Morrow & Co., 1962.

Lening, Gustav. *The Dark Side of New York Life*. New York: F. Gerhard, 1873.

Lewinsohn, Richard. *A History of Sexual Customs*. New York: Harper & Bros., 1959.

Lewis, Alred Henry. *Nation-Famous New York Murders*. Chicago: M. A. Donahue, 1912.

Lindsay, Philip. *The Mainspring of Murder*. London: John Long, 1958.

Lipsig, Frances. *Murder—Family Style*. New York: Collier Books, 1962.

Logan, Guy B. H. *Rope, Knife and Chair*. London: Stanley Paul, 1930.

Lombroso, Caesar, and Ferrero, William. *The Female Offender*. New York: Appleton, 1897.

Loomis, Stanley. *Paris In The Terror*. New York: J. B. Lippincott Co., 1964.

Louderback, Lew. *The Bad Ones*. Greenwich, Conn.: Fawcett, 1968.

Lundberg, Ferdinand, and Farnham, Marynia F. *Modern Women, The Lost Sex*. New York: Harper & Bros., 1947.

Lunde, Donald T. *Murder and Madness*. New York: The Portable Standard, 1975.

Lustgarten, Edgar. *The Murder and the Trial*. New York: Charles Scribner's Sons, 1958.

Lynch, Dennis Tilden. *Criminals and Politicians*. New York: Macmillan, 1932.

MacDonald, Arthur. *Criminology*. New York: Funk & Wagnalls, 1893.

MacDonald, John M. *The Murderer and His Victim*. Springfield, Ill.: Charles C. Thomas, 1961.

Mackaye, Milton. *Dramatic Crimes of 1927*. Garden City, N.Y.: Doubleday, Doran, 1928.

Mackenzie, Frederic A. *Twentieth Century Crimes*. Boston: Little, Brown & Co., 1927.

Mariano, John Horace. *The Second Generation of Italians in New York*. Boston: Christopher Publishing House, 1921.

Marks, Harry, H. *Small Change*. New York: Standard Publishing Co., 1882.

Martin, John Bartlow. *Break Down the Walls*. New York: Ballantine, 1954.

Mayhew, Henry. *London's Underworld*. London: William Kimber, 1950.

Mayhew, Henry, and Binny, John. *The Criminal Prisons of London and Scenes of Prison Life*. London: Griffin, Bohn, 1862.

McAleavy, Henry. *A Dream of Tartary*. London: George Allen & Unwin, Ltd., 1963.

McClintock, F. H., and Gibson, Evelyn. *Robbery in London*. New York: St. Martin's Press, 1961.

McComas, Francis. *The Graveside Companion*. New York: Obelensky, 1962.

McCord, W., and McCord, J. *Origins of Crime*. New York: Columbia Univ. Press, 1959.

Meek, Victor. *Cops and Robbers*. London: Duckworth, 1962.

Mehnert, Klaus. *Twilight of the Young*. New York: Holt, Rinehart and Winston, 1976.

Merz, Charles. *The Dry Decade*. Garden City, N.Y.: Doubleday, Doran, 1931.

Minot, G. E. *Murder Will Out*. Boston: Marshall Jones, 1928.

Mitchell, David. *Pirates, An Illustrated History*. New York: The Dial Press, 1976.

Mitchell, Edwin Valentine, ed. *The Newgate Calendar*. Garden City, N.Y.: Garden City Publishing Co., 1926.

Monahan, Florence. *Women in Crime*. New York: Washburn, 1941.

Moore, Maurice, *Frauds and Swindles*. London: Gee & Co., 1933.

Morain, Alfred. *The Underground of Paris*. New York: Blue Ribbon Books, 1931.

Moreau, William B. *Swindling Exposed*. Syracuse, N.Y.: N.p., 1907.

Morland, Nigel. *This Friendless Lady*. London: Frederick Muller, Ltd., 1957.

Morris, Lloyd R. *Not So Long Ago*. New York: Random House, 1949.

Morris, Norval. *The Habitual Criminal*. Cambridge, Mass.: Harvard Univ. Press, 1951.

Morris, Terrence. *The Criminal Area*. New York: The Humanities Press, 1958.

Mueller, Gerhard O. W., ed. *Essays in Criminal Science*. New York: Rothman, 1961.

Murtagh, John M., and Harris, Sara. *Cast the First Stone*. New York: McGraw-Hill, 1957.

Nash, Jay Robert. *Bloodletters and Badmen, A Narrative Encyclopedia of American Criminals From the Pilgrims to the Present*. New York: M. Evans, 1973.

—————. *Hustlers and Con Men, An Anecdotal History Of the Confidence Man and His Games*. New York: M. Evans, 1976.

—————. *Among the Missing, An Anecdotal History of Missing Persons from the 1800s to the Present*. New York: Simon & Schuster, 1978.

—————. *Murder, America, Homicide in the United States from the Revolution to the Present*. New York: Simon & Schuster, 1980.

—————. *Almanac of World Crime*. New York: Doubleday, 1981.

Nelson, Victor. *Prison Days and Nights*. Boston: Little, Brown & Co., 1933.

Neustatter, W. L. *The Mind of the Murderer*. London: Johnson, 1957.

The Newgate Calendar. London: T. Werner Laurie, 1932.

Norman, Frank. *Bang to Rights*. London: Seeker & Warburg, 1958.

O'Ballance, Edgar. *Language of Violence*. San Rafael, Calif.: Presidio Press, 1979.

O'Brien, Frank M. *Murder Mysteries of New York*. New York: W. F. Payson, 1932.

O'Connor, John J. *Broadway Racketeers*. New York: Liveright, 1933.

O'Donnell, Bernard. *The Old Bailey and Its Trials*. London: Clerke & Cockeran, 1950.

—————. *The World's Worst Women*. London: W. H. Allen, 1953.

—————. *Should Women Hang?* London: W. H. Allen, 1956.

O'Donnell, Elliot. *Trial of Kate Webster*. London: William Hodge & Co., 1925.

O'Sullivan, F. Dalton. *Crime Detection*. Chicago: O'Sullivan Publishing, 1928.

Owen, Collinson. *King Crime*. New York: H. Holt, 1932.

Paine, Lauran. *The Assassin's World*. New York: Taplinger, 1975.

Pearson, Edmund. *Studies in Murder*. New York: Macmillan, 1924.

—————. *Murder at Smutty Nose*. Garden City, N.Y.: Doubleday, 1927.

—————. *Five Murders*. Garden City, N.Y.: Doubleday, 1928.

—————. *Instigation of the Devil*. New York: Charles Scribner's Sons, 1930.

—————. *More Studies in Murder*. New York: Smith and Haas, 1936.

Pelham, Camden. *The Chronicles of Crime*. London: Reeves and Turner, 1886.

Pinkerton, Allan. *Mississippi Outlaws and the Detectives*. New York: G. W. Carleton & Co., 1881.

Pinkerton, Matthew W. *Murder in All Ages*. Chicago: Pinkerton & Co., 1898.

Playfair, Giles, and Sington, Derrick. *The Offenders*. New York: Simon & Schuster, 1957.

Pollack, Otto. *The Criminality of Women*. Philadelphia: University of Pennsylvania Press, 1950.

Porges, Irwin. *The Violent Americans*. Derby, Conn.: Monarch Books, 1963.

Porter, Garnett Clay. *Strange and Mysterious*

Crimes. New York: McFadden, 1929.

Porterfield, Austin L. *Cultures of Violence.* Ft. Worth, Tex.: Manney, 1965.

Potter, John Deane. *The Fatal Gallows Tree.* London: Elek Books, 1965.

——————. *The Art of Hanging.* New York: A. S. Barnes & Company, 1969.

Powers, Edwin. *Crime and Punishment in Early Masschusetts.* Boston: Beacon Press, 1966.

Pringle, Patrick. *Hue & Cry, The Birth of the British Police.* London: Museum Press, Limited, 1955.

Quimby, Myron J. *The Devil's Emissaries.* New York: Modern Library, 1969.

Quinby, Ione. *Murder for Love.* New York: Covici-Friede, 1931.

Quinn, John Philip. *Fools of Fortune.* Chicago: W. B. Conkey, 1890.

Radin, Edward D. *12 Against Crime.* New York: G. P. Putnam's Sons, 1953.

Radzinowicz, Leon. *A History of English Criminal Law.* New York: Macmillan, 1956.

Rankin, Hugh F. *The Golden Age of Piracy.* New York: Holt, Rinehart and Winston, 1969.

Rapoport, David C. *Assassination and Terrorism.* Toronto, Can.: Canadian Broadcasting Co., 1971.

Rascoe, Burton. *Belle Starr.* New York: Random House, 1941.

Ravaisson, Francois. *Archives de La Bastille.* Paris: A Durant Et Pedone-Lauriel, Libraires, 1873.

Reckless, Walter. *The Crime Problem.* New York: Appleton-Century-Crofts, 1950.

Reid, Ed. *The Mistress and the Mafia.* New York: Bantam, 1972.

Reinhardt, James Melvin. *Sex Perversions and Sex Crimes.* Springfield, Ill.: Charles C. Thomas, 1957.

——————. *The Psychology of Strange Killers.* Springfield, Ill.: Charles C. Thomas, 1962.

Reith, Charles. *A New Study of Police History.* London: Oliver & Boyd, 1956.

Reiwald, P. *Society and Its Criminals.* New York: International Univ. Press, 1950.

Remarkable Trials of All Countries. New York: S. S. Peloubet & Co., 1882.

Reynolds, Ruth. *Murder 'Round the World.* New York: Justice Books, Inc., 1953.

Rhodes, Henry T. F. *Alphonse B. Bertillon.* New York: Abelard-Schuman, 1956.

Rice, Robert. *The Business of Crime.* New York: Farrar, Straus & Cudahy, 1956.

Roe, Clifford. *Panderers and Their White Slaves.* Chicago: Revell Pub. Co., 1910.

Rolph, C. H., ed. *Women of the Streets.* London: Secker and Warburg, 1955.

——————. *The Police and the Public.* London: Heinemann, 1962.

Rosefsky, Robert S. *Frauds, Swindles and Rackets.* Chicago: Follett Publishing Co., 1973.

Rosen, George. *Madness in Society.* New York: Harper & Row, 1968.

Roughhead, William. *Malice Domestic.* Garden City, N.Y.: Doubleday, Doran, 1929.

——————. *The Art of Murder.* New York: Sheridan House, 1943.

Rovere, Richard H. *Howe & Hummel.* New York: Farrar, Straus & Cudahy, 1947.

Rowan, David. *Famous American Crimes.* London: Frederick Muller, Ltd., 1957.

Rowan, Richard Wilmer. *The Pinkertons.* New York: Little, Brown & Co., 1931.

——————, with Deindorfer, Robert. *33 Centuries of Espionage.* New York: Hawthorn Books, 1967.

Rowland, John. *More Criminal Files.* London:

Arco Publications, 1958.

Royal, H. W. *Gambling and Confidence Games Exposed.* Chicago: Royal, 1896.

Runyan, Damon. *Trials and Other Tribulations.* Philadelphia: J. B. Lippincott, 1926.

Salgado, Gamini Norton. *The Elizabethan Underworld.* London: J. M. Dent & Sons, Ltd., 1977.

Sandoe, James, ed. *Murder, Plain and Fanciful.* New York: Sheridan, 1948.

Schmalhausen, Samuel D., and Calverton, V. F., eds. *Woman's Coming of Age: A Symposium.* New York: Horace Liveright, 1931.

Schultz, Donald O., and Scott, Stanley K. *The Subversive.* Springfield, Ill.: Charles C. Thomas, 1973.

Schultz, Gladys Denny. *How Many More Victims: Society and the Sex Criminal.* Philadelphia: J. B. Lippincott, 1966.

Schwarz, Dr. Fred. *The Three Faces of Revolution.* Washington, D.C.: The Capital Hill Press, 1972.

Scott, Sir Harold. *Scotland Yard.* New York: Random House, 1954.

Seagle, William. *Acquitted of Murder.* Chicago: Henry Regnery, 1958.

Seth, Ronald. *Witches and Their Craft.* New York: Taplinger, 1967.

Shackleford, William Yancey. *Belle Starr.* Girard, Kan.: Haldeman-Julius, 1943.

Sharpe, May Churchill. *Chicago May.* New York: The Macaulay Co., 1928.

Simpson, Keith. *Forty Years of Murder.* New York: Charles Scribner's Sons, 1979.

Sinclair, Andrew. *Prohibition.* Boston: Little, Brown & Co., 1962.

——————. *Era of Excess.* New York: Harper & Row, 1964.

Singer, Kurt. *Mata Hari.* New York: Universal Publishing Co., 1967.

Smith, Captain Alexander. *History of the Highwaymen.* London: George Routledge & Sons, Ltd., 1926.

Smith, Ann D. *Women in Prison.* Chicago: Quadrangle, 1962.

Smith, Edward Henry. *Famous American Poison Mysteries.* New York: Dial Press, 1927.

Smith, Matthew Hale. *Sunshine and Shadow in New York.* Hartford, Conn.: J. B. Burr & Co., 1868.

Smith, Sir Sydney. *Mostly Murder.* New York: David McKay, 1959.

Smith-Hughes, Jack. *Eight Studies in Justice.* London: Cassell & Co., 1953.

Soderman, Harry, and O'Connell, J. J. *Modern Criminal Investigation.* New York: Funk and Wagnalls, 1952.

——————. *Policeman's Lot.* New York: Funk and Wagnalls, 1956.

Sorenson, Alfred R. *Hands Up! or The History of Crime.* Omaha, Neb.: Barkalow Bros., 1877.

Sparrow, Gerald. *Women Who Murder.* London: Arthur Barker, Ltd., 1970.

Stern, Susan. *With The Weatherman.* New York: Doubleday & Co., 1975.

Streetwalker. London: The Bodley Head, 1959.

Stuart, William H. *The 20 Incredible Years.* New York: M. A. Donahue, 1935.

Summers, Anne. *Damned Whores and God's Police.* Ringwood, Victoria: Penguin, 1975.

Summers, Montague. *The Geography of Witchcraft.* London: Routledge & Kegan Paul, 1927.

Sutherland, E. H., with Cressey, Donald. *Principles of Criminology.* New York: Lippincott, 1954.

Taft, Donald R. *Criminology.* New York: Macmillan, 1956.

Tallant, Robert. *Voodoo in New Orleans.* New York: Macmillan, 1946.

——————. *Ready to Hang.* New York: Harper & Bros., 1967.

Tannenbaum, Frank. *Crime and the Community.* New York: Columbia University Press, 1951.

Teeters, Negley K., and Hedblom, Jack H. *". . . Hang By the Neck . . ."* Springfield, Ill.: Charles C. Thomas, 1967.

Terhune, Albert Payson. *Famous Hussies of History.* New York: World, 1943.

Thomas, William I. *Sex and Society.* Chicago: Univ. of Chicago Press, 1907.

Thompson, Basil. *The Criminal.* London: Hodder & Stoughton, 1925.

Thompson, C. J. S. *Poison Mysteries in History.* Philadelphia: J. B. Lippincott, 1932.

Thorwald, Jurgen. *Dead Men Tell Tales.* London: Thames and Hudson, 1965.

——————. *Proof of Poison.* London: Thames and Hudson, 1965.

Tozer, Basil. *Confidence Crooks and Blackmailers.* Boston: Stratford Co., 1930.

Train, Arthur. *True Stories of Crime from the District Attorney's Office.* New York: McKinley, Stone & MacKenzie, 1908.

Traini, Robert. *Murder for Sex.* London: William Kimber, 1960.

Trenery, Walter N. *Murder in Minnesota.* St. Paul: The Minnesota Historical Society, 1962.

Triplett, Col. Frank. *History, Romance and Philosophy of Great American Crimes and Criminals.* Hartford, Conn.: Park Publishing Co., 1885.

Trumble, Alfred. *The Female Sharpers of New York.* New York: R. K. Fox, 1882.

Turkis, Burton B., and Feder, Sid. *Murder, Inc.* New York: Farrar, Straus & Cudahy, 1951.

Tuttle, Elizabeth Orman. *The Crusade Against Capital Punishment in Great Britain.* Chicago: Quadrangle, 1961.

Tyler, Gus, ed. *Organized Crime in America.* Ann Arbor, Mich.: Univ. of Michigan Press, 1962.

Unger, Irwin. *The Movement.* New York: Dodd, Mead & Co., 1974.

Van Cise, Philip S. *Fighting the Underworld.* New York: Houghton-Mifflin Co., 1936.

Van Every, Edward. *Sins of New York.* New York: Frederick A. Stokes Co., 1930.

Vincent, Arthur, ed. *Lives of Twelve Bad Women.* Boston: L. C. Page and Company, 1897.

Wagner, Walter. *The Golden Fleecers.* Garden City, N.Y.: Doubleday & Co., 1966.

Waller, George. *Kidnap.* New York: Dial Press, 1961.

Walling, George. *Recollections of a New York Chief of Police.* New York: Caxton, 1887.

Washborn, Emory. *Sketches of the Judicial History of Massachusetts.* Boston: Little, Brown & Co., 1840.

Washburn, Charles. *Come Into My Parlor.* New York: National Library Press, 1936.

Weihofen, Henry. *The Urge to Punish.* New York: Farrar, Straus & Cudahy, 1956.

Wellman, Manly Wade. *Dead and Gone, Classic Crimes of North Carolina.* Chapel Hill: Univ. of North Carolina, 1954.

Wendt, Lloyd, and Kogan, Herman. *Lords of the Levee.* Indianapolis: Bobbs-Merrill Company, 1943.

West, Don. *Sacrifice Unto Me.* New York: Pyramid, 1974.

Whitehead, Don. *The F.B.I. Story.* New York: Random House, 1956.

——————. *Journey Into Crime.* New York: Random House, 1960.

Whitelaw, D. *Corpus Delicti.* London: Geoffrey Bles, 1936.

Wildeblood, Peter. *Against the Law*. London: Weidenfeld and Nicolson, 1955.

Wilkinson, George Theodore. *The Newgate Calendar*. London: Cornish and Co., 1814.

Wilkinson, Paul. *Terrorism and the Liberal State*. London: Macmillan, 1977.

Williams, Jack Kenny. *Vogues in Villainy*. Columbia, S.C.: Univ. of South Carolina Press, 1959.

Williams, Roger M. *The Super Crooks*. Chicago: Playboy Press, 1973.

Wilson, Colin. *A Casebook of Murder*. New York: Cowles Book Company, Inc., 1969.

Wilson, Rufus Rockwell. *New York: Old and New*. Philadelphia: J. B. Lippincott, 1902.

Wines, Frederick Howard. *Punishment and Reformation*. New York: Thomas Y. Crowell, 1919.

With the Pinkertons. New York: McFadden Publications, Inc., 1940.

Wolfe, John B. *Louis XIV*. New York: W. W. Norton, 1968.

Wolfgang, Martin E. *Patterns in Criminal Homicide*. Philadelphia: Univ. of Pennsylvania Press, 1958.

Woolcott, Alexander. *While Rome Burns*. New York: Viking Press, 1934.

Wright, Sewell P. *Chicago Murders*. New York: Duell, Sloan, & Pierce, 1947.

Wyles, Lilian. *A Woman At Scotland Yard*. London: Faber and Faber, Limited, 1952.

PERIODICALS

"Affluent, Educated and Deadly, Terrorist Shock Troops Are Laying Siege To West Germany." *People*, (November 7, 1977).

"America and the Sixth Commandment." *The Outlook*, (February 16, 1907).

"American Credulity." *The Outlook*, (December 3, 1910).

Anderson, Robert T. "From Mafia to Cosa Nostra." *American Journal of Sociology*, (November 1965).

Asbury, Herbert. "Days of Wickedness." *American Mercury*, (November 1927).

Banay, R. S. "Study in Murder." *Annals of the American Academy of Political Science*, 284 (1952).

Bell, Daniel. "Crime as an American Way of Life." *Antioch Review*, (June 1953).

"The Benders of Kansas." *Kansas Magazine*, (September 1886).

Berger, Meyer. "Lady in Crepe." *The New Yorker*, (October 5, 12, 1935).

"Beyond the Dream of Avarice." *Blackwood's Magazine*, (January 1908).

"Big Martha." *Time*, (March 14, 1949).

Bingham, T. A. "The Organized Criminals of New York." *McClure's Magazine*, (November 1909).

Blackman, N.; Weiss, J. M. A.; and Lambert, J. W. "The Sudden Murderer." *Archives of General Psychiatry*, 8 (1963).

Bourke, Charles Francis. "Pinkerton's National Detective Agency." *Strand Magazine*, (1905).

Brearley, H. C., and Seagle, W. "How Often We Murder and Why; Review of Homicide in the U.S." *The Nation*, (May 25, 1932).

Bullock, H. A. "Urban Homicide in Theory and Fact." *Journal of Criminal Law*, 45:565, (1955).

Burkholder, Edwin V. "Those Murdering Benders." *True Western Adventures*, (February 1960).

Burns, William J. "The Trail of the Bank Swindler." *Saturday Evening Post*, (January 13, 1925).

Butler, James Davie. "British Convicts Shipped to American Colonies." *American Historical Review*, (October 1896).

Carroll, Raymond, with Sullivan, Scott. "Femme Fatale." *Newsweek*, (May 19, 1975).

Carson, Charles. "One Underworld." *Author and Journalist*, (November 1945).

Cole, K. E.; Fisher, G.; and Cole, S. S. "Women Who Kill." *Archives of General Psychiatry*, 19 (1968).

"Comrades and Lovers." *Time*, (April 25, 1955).

Conrad, William, and Greenwood, Robert. "The Bender Legend." *Kansas Magazine*, (1950), pp. 27-32.

Cooper, Courtney Riley. "Mother of Crime." *American Magazine*, (December 1938).

————. "Shoe-box Annie." *American Magazine*, (July 1939).

Crapsey, Edward. "Our Criminal Population." *Galaxy*, 7 (1869).

Creel, George. "Unholy City." *Collier's*, (September 2, 1939).

Crosby, W. C., and Smith, Edward H. "Con." Series. *Saturday Evening Post*, (January 24, 31; February 7, 14; March 15, 1920).

Cruvant, B. A., and Waldrop, F. N. "The Murderer in the Mental Institution." *Annals of the American Academy of Political Science*, 284 (1952).

Dies, Jerome. "The Fine Art of Catching the 'Sucker.'" Series. *The Outlook*, (March 28, April 4, 11, 1923).

"Disciple of Despair." *Time*, (May 24, 1976).

Dougherty, George S. "The Public the Criminal's Partner." *The Outlook*, (August 23, 1913).

"Easier to Get Away with Murder?" *U.S. News and World Report*, (February 11, 1955).

"Electrodes for Two: Raymond Martin Fernandez and Mrs. Martha Beck." *Newsweek*, (August 29, 1949).

Ellison, E. Jerome, and Brock, Frank W. "Fabulous Frauds." *Reader's Digest*, (September 1936).

"Exit the Bobbed-Haired Bandit—Twenty Years." *The Literary Digest*, (May 24, 1924).

"Exposing the Frauds and Swindles." *The Literary Digest*, (January 9, 1937).

"Fleecing the Wise." *The Literary Digest*, (May 16, 1936).

"Fooling the People." *The Outlook*, (February 3, 1912).

"From a Family of Bound Feet." *Time*, (January 10, 1944).

Gibbons, T. C. N. "Sane and Insane Homicide." *Journal of Criminal Law*, 49 (1958).

Goldberg, H. "Crimes of Darkness." *Cosmopolitan*, (April 1959).

"Golden Age Fraud." *Time*, (January 1, 1973).

Gregg, Albert Stanley. "Pinkerton Tells How We Make It Easy For Swindlers." *American Magazine*, (September 1919).

Grinnell, C. E. "Modern Murder Trials and Newspapers." *Atlantic Monthly*, (November 1901).

"A Gun in Her Purse." *Newsweek*, (July 4, 1955).

"Hangman's Turn." *Newsweek*, (July 25, 1955).

Harris, John P. "Beautiful Katie." *Kansas Magazine*, (1936), pp. 43-49.

Henderson, Marie. "Murder Tavern." *The Great West*, (May 1968).

Hill, D., and Pond, D. A. "Reflections on 100 Capital Cases." *Journal of Mental Science*, 98:23, (1952).

Hoffman, F. L. "Murder and the Death Penalty." *Current History*, (June 1928).

Hopkins, Mary Alden. "Hungarian Borgias." *The Outlook*, (June 18, 1930).

Howe, William F. "Some Notable Murder Cases." *Cosmopolitan*, (August 1900).

"Hungary's 'Poison' Villages." *The Literary Digest*, (January 25, 1930).

"Imaginative Crooks." *Literary Digest*, (February 7, 1914).

James, M. "Annals of Crime." *New Yorker*, (December 6, 1941).

Jarman, Rufus. "The Pinkerton Story." Series. *Saturday Evening Post*, (May 15, 22, 29 and June 5, 1928).

Jeffery, Clarence Ray. "The Development of Crime in Early English Society." *Journal of Criminal Law, Criminology and Police Science*, 47:647-66 (March-April 1957).

Johnson, Pamela Hansford. "In Ghastly Transcripts, A Test of Our Times." *Life*, (August 12, 1966).

Landesco, John. "The Criminal Underworld of Chicago in the Eighties and Nineties." *Journal of Criminal Law and Criminology*, (September 1934, March 1935).

————. "The Woman and the Underworld." *Journal of Criminal Law and Criminology*, (March 1936).

Levy, Newman. "Easy Money." *Collier's*, (May 2, 1925).

Lindesmith, Alfred R. "Federal Law and Drug Addiction." *Social Problems* 7:48-57, (Summer 1959).

Lippman, Walter. "The Underworld: A Stultified Conscience." *Forum*, (February 1931).

Loth, David. "A Look at Famous Swindlers." *American Legion Magazine*, (August 1969).

Lowndes, Marie Belloc. "The Strange Case of Marie Lafarge." *McClure's Magazine*, (April 1912).

Lunde, D. T. "Our Murder Boom." *Psychology Today*, (November 1975).

Manchester, Harland. "Jane Toppan, Champion Poisoner." *American Mercury*, (March 1940).

Manchester, William. "Murder Tour of New England." *Holiday*, (May 1961).

"The Maximum Sentence." *Time*, (May 13, 1966).

Maynard, L. M. "Murder in the Making." *American Mercury*, (June 1929).

"Murders By Poison." *Harper's Weekly*, (November 8, 1902).

"Musings Without Method." *Blackwood's Edinburgh Magazine*, (May 1906).

Nobile, Philip. "The Case of the Murderous Mother-in-Law." *New York*, (August 7, 1978).

Northlander, J. Philip. "Ma Barker's Last Stand." *Midwest Magazine*, (June 21, 1970).

O'Connor, T. P. "Criminals I Have Known." *Harper's Weekly*, (January 10, 1914).

Palmer, John Williamson. "The Pinkertons." *Century Magazine*, (February 1892).

"Patty Is Free And Older." *Time*, (February 12, 1978).

Peters, W. "Why Did They Do It?" *Good Housekeeping*, (June 1962).

Peterson, West. "Sexpot On Trial." *Front Page Detective*, (September 1968).

"Poisoning In The Seventeenth Century." *The Nation*, (July 20, 1899).

Portley, Ed. "The Barrow Gang." *Master Detective*, (February 1945).

"A Rationale of the Law of Kidnapping." *Columbia Law Review*, 53:540, (1953).

"Red Roses from Roter Morgen." *Time*, (August 15, 1977).

"Robbery and Murder." *The Outlook*, (November 28, 1923).

Ross, Jack. "Everywhere I Go, Death." *Coronet*, (December 1954).

Rowe, Fayette. "Kate Bender's Fate Stil Mystery of Pioneer Kansas." *Wichita Eagle Magazine,* (September 26, 1954).

"The Russian Semiramis On Trial For Murder In Venice." *Current Literature,* (June 1910).

Saltus, E. "Champion Poisoners." *Cosmopolitan,* (February 1902).

Schur, Edwin M. "Drug Addiction in America and England." *Commentary,* 30:241-48, (September 1960).

Scoville, Samuel, Jr. "Trappers of Men." Series. *Lippincott's Magazine,* (December 1913; January, February, 1914).

"Sentimentality in Murder Trials." *Review of Reviews,* (November 1908).

Shipley, M. "Crimes of Violence in Chicago and in Greater New York." *Review of Reviews,* (September 1908).

"The Strange Story of Madame Lafarge." *Cornhill Magazine,* (January 1898).

Sutherland, Edwin H. "The Diffusion of Sexual Psychopath Laws." *American Journal of Sociology* 56:142-48, (September 1950).

Swallow, Richard. "Where Is the Infamous Katie Bender?" *Real Detectives,* (September 1932).

"The Tall, Cool Blonde." *Time,* (June 15, 1962).

"The Tenderloin." *American Notes and Quotes,* (August 1945).

Toland, John. "Sad Ballad of the Real Bonnie and Clyde." *The New York Times Magazine,* (February 18, 1968).

Tully, Jim. "Yeggs." *American Mercury,* (April 1933).

Turner, G. K. "The City of Chicago." *McClure's Magazine,* (April 1907).

"Vampire Of A Real Tank Drama." *The Literary Digest,* (October 13, 1917).

Waldron, E. "Murder Tour of the Midwest." *Holiday,* (August 1961).

Waldrop, F. C. "Murder as a Sex Practice." *American Mercury,* (February 1948).

White, Frank M. "New York's Ten Thousand Thieves." *Harper's Weekly,* (December 29, 1906).

White, Owen P. "Belle Starr, Bandit." *Collier's,* (February 2, 1932).

"A Woman Thief Who 'Came Back'." *The Literary Digest,* (June 7, 1924).

BROADSHEETS, BULLETINS, DOCUMENTS, PAMPHLETS, REPORTS

Beccaria, Cesare Bonesana. *An Essay on Crimes and Punishments.* Philadelphia: Philip H. Nicklin, 1819.

Brendan, Rev. *Life, Crimes, and Confessions of Bridget Durgan.* Philadelphia: C. W. Alexander, 1867.

British Museum. *Murders* (Collection of Broadsides Containing Accounts of Murders and Executions). London and Edinburgh: 1794-1860, 1830-55.

Butler, J. E. *The Trial of Jane M. Swett.* Biddeford, Me.: Union's Journal, 1867.

Chicago Police Problems. The Citizen's Police Committee, 1931.

Chicago Vice Commission Report, Chicago, 1912.

Citizen's Association of Chicago. *Annual Reports,* 1902-24.

Confession and Awful Disclosures of Elizabeth Van Valkenburgh. New York: N.p., N.d.

The Confession of Elizabeth Van Valkenburgh. Johnstown, N.Y.: G. Henry and W. H. Clark, N.d.

A Faithful Narrative of Elizabeth Wilson. Philadelphia: N.p., 1786.

The Grinder Poisoning Case. Pittsburgh: John P. Hunt, N.d.

Hearings Before the Permanent Subcommittee on Investigations: Organized Crime and Illicit Traffic in Narcotics. U.S. Senate, 1963.

Hearings Before the Special Committee to Investigate Organized Crime in Interstate Commerce. U.S. Senate, 1950.

Illinois Crime Survey, 1902, 1929.

The Life and Confession of Bridget Durgan. Philadelphia: Barclay & Co., 1867.

The Life and Confessions of Martha Grinder, the Poisoner. Pittsburgh: John P. Hunt, 1866.

The Life and Confessions of Mrs. Henrietta Robinson, the Veiled Murderess! Boston: Dr. H. B. Skinner, 1855.

Maccarty, Thaddeus. *The Guilt of Innocent Blood Put Away (Bathsheba Spooner).* Norwich: John Trumbull, 1778.

A Manual of Correctional Standards. American Prison Association, 1954.

The Poison Fiend! Life Crimes and Convictions of Lydia Sherman. Philadelphia: Barclay & Co., 1872.

The Record of Crimes in the U.S. Buffalo: Faxon & Co., 1834.

Report of the City Council Committee on Crime. Chicago: 1915.

Report of the Committee of 15 on Prostitution and Gambling in Chicago. Chicago: 1915.

Report of the Committee on Homosexual Offenses and Prostitution. H.M.S.O., 1957.

Reports of the Chicago Crime Commission. Chicago: 1919-1979.

Reports of the New York Crime Commission. New York: 1928-1979.

Reports of the Senate Select Committee on Improper Activities. U.S. Senate, 1958.

Seabury, Samuel. *Final Report in the Matter in the Investigation of the Magistrate's Court in the First Judicial Department.* New York: 1932.

Social Evils in Chicago, A Study of Existing Conditions with Recommendations by the Vice Commission of Chicago. Chicago: 1911.

Three Noted Women, Being Historical Sketches of the Lives of Lucrezia Borgia, and the Marchioness of Brinvilliers, Together with a Complete and Accurate Account of the Career and Confession of Lydia Sherman. New Haven, Conn.: Stafford Printing Office, 1873.

Truth Stranger than Fiction. Lydia Sherman. Confession of the Arch Murderess of Connecticut. Philadelphia: T. R. Callender & Co., 1873.

U.S. Senate Proceedings. *Terrorist Activity: Hostage Defense Measures.* Washington, D.C.: 1975.

Wilson, D. *Henrietta Robinson.* New York: Miller, Orton & Mulligan, 1855.

York, Mary. *The Bender Tragedy.* Mankato, Kan.: George W. Neff, 1875.

INDEX

Accardo, Tony, 191
Adams, Dr. C. LeRoy, 291
Adams, Mary, 2
Adams, Millicent, 3
Adler, John, 3
Adler, Lydia, 3
Adler, Polly, 4-5
Adonis, Joe, 191, 192
Aikney, Thomas, 59
Albright, Bernice, 310
Alexander II, Czar, 323
Alexander VII, Pope, 348
Algarron, Jacques, 230-232
Allard, Sureté Chief, 234
Allen, Lizzie, 144
Allen, Margaret, 5-8
Ambrus, Michael, 159-160
Anderson, Bella, 8
Ansell, Mary, 8-9
Anslinger, Harry J., 193
Antonini, Theresa, 9-10
Archer-Gilligan, "Sister" Amy, 10-11
Arden, Alice, 11-12
Arden, Thomas, 11-12
Arnet, Richard, 185-186
Asbury, Herbert, 143
Aston-Wolfe, H., 280
Aubert, Louis, 160-161
Audette, James Henry "Blackie," 15, 318
Auphand, Inspector, 380
Averill, Jim, 376-377

Babbit, B.T., 321
Bac, Theodore, 240, 242, 244, 246
Bacon, Sir Frances, 205
Baguley, Ada, 375-376
Baguley, Mrs., 375
Bailly, Felix, 132
Ballantine, (attorney), 272
Baniszewski, Gertrude Wright, 13
Banks, Dr. Cyril, 275, 376
Bannister, Edna, 365, 367
Barberi, Maria, 14
Bardon, Dr., 238, 239, 240
Barker, Dock, 15
Barker, Fred, 14, 15
Barker, Arizona Donnie Clark "Ma," 14-16
Barnes, Inspector, 270
Barrow, Addie, 8
Barrow, Blanche, 316
Barrow, Buck, 316

Barrow, Clyde, 316, 318
Barrow, George, 8
Barry, Mary Ann, 16
Barrymore, Lord, 89
Bassett, James Eugene, 345
Bassot, Henri, 168
Bateman, John, 16-17
Bateman, Mary, 16-20
Bates, Albert, 216, 217
Bathory, Elizabeth, 21
Beach, H., 332
Beaufort de Canillac, Countess de, 120
Beck, Martha, 21-22
Beck, Sophie, 22
Becker, Marie Alexander, 22-23
Beddingfield, Ann, 23-24
Beddingfield, John, 23-24
Beland, Charlie, 25
Beland, Lucy "Ma," 24-25
Beland, Willie, 25
Bender, Kate, 25-27
Bennett, Keith, 201
Bentley, Alvin M., 248
Bergamini, David, 137
Bessarabo, Charles, 306-308
Bevan, Catherine, 27
Bever, Lambert, 22-23
Bigley, Elizabeth. See Chadwick, Cassie L.
Bilansky, Ann, 27
Bilansky, Stanislaus, 27
Billings, Thomas, 182-184
Birch, A.O., 78
Birkett, Norman, 265
Bizard, Dr., 279, 289, 290
Bjorkland, Penny, 28
Black, Will, 11-12
"Blackie" Audette, 15, 318
Blakely, David, 140-142
Blandy, Francis, 28-29
Blandy, Mary, 28-29
Blankenfeld, Dorothea, 9-10
Blantyre, Lady, 266, 273
Bleicher, Hella, 78-79
Bluffstein, Sophie, 30
"Bobbed-Haired Bandit," 96-102
Bodeley, Richard Percival, 170
Bogle, Helen McDermott, 30-31
Bohozuk, Bill, 125
Bolton, Charles, 31-32
Bolton, Mildred Mary, 31-32
Bompard, Gabrielle, 32-33, 161, 378
Bonetti, Rosina, 33-34
Bonjean, Georges, 380
Bonmartini, Count, 33-34
Bonmartini, Countess Linda, 33-34
Bonner, Antoinette, 34
Bonny, Anne, 35-39
Bonny, James, 35-36
Boot, Joe. 186

Borelli, Gene, 39
Borelli, LaVerne, 39-40
Botkin, Cordelia, 40
Bouvier, Leone, 40-41
Bozevsky, Captain Alex, 355
Bradford, Eden, 44-46
Bradford, Priscilla, 41-47
Bradford, John Young, 41-44
Brady, Ian, 199-201
Branch, Elizabeth, 47-49
Branch, Mary, 47-49
Brécourt, Jeanne, 49-58
Brinvilliers, Marie de, 58-59
Broadingham, Elizabeth, 59
Broadingham, John, 59
Brouardel, Dr. Paul Camille Hippolyte, 379
Browne, Douglas G., 218
Brownrigg, Elizabeth, 59-64
Brownrigg, James, 60
Bruce, Mary Ann Sutherland. See Gordon-Baille, Mary Ann
Brudenell, Sir James, 89
Bruhne, Vera, 64-65
Bruneau, Dr. Frederic, 380
Brunswick, Duke of, 282, 284
Bryant, Charlotte, 65-67
Bryant, Frederick, 65-66
Buchanan, James, 351
Buchanan, Dr. Robert, 366
Bucknill, Dr. John Charles, 226
Bukenoveski, Mrs., 158
Burdock, Mary Ann, 67
Burke, Billy, 257-258, 260
Busse, Fred, 147
Butchill, Elizabeth, 67
Buttersworth, Jane, 47
Buys, Christiaan, 176

Caffee, Peggy, 323, 324
Caillaux, Henriette, 68-72
Caillaux, Joseph, 68
"Calico Jack," 36, 38, 39
Calmette, Gaston, 68-72
Calvert, Louie, 72-73
Cambon, Jules, 285
Cannon, Frank, 291
Canonge, J.F., 247
Capelle, Marie Fortunee, 233-234, 235, 236-237
Capone, Al, 147, 153, 156, 191
Carew, Edith Mary, 73-75
Carew, W. R. H., 74-75
Carey, Daniel, 98
Carleton, John, 299
Carnell, Sarah, 389
Carothers, Mrs., 176
Carr, Robert, 203-204, 205
Carson, Ann, 75-76
Carson, John, 75

Carter, President Jimmy, 189, 248
Casey, William, 99-100
Cataldo, Domenico, 14
"Cattle Kate," 376-377
Celano, Margie. *See* Dean, Margie
Cerny, Wenzel, 372-373
Chadwick, Cassie L., 76-77
Chadwick, Dr. Leroy, 76
Chadwick, Nancy Ellen, 6-7
Chamberlain, John, 114
Charles I, King, 112, 114
Chauveau-Lagarde, Claude-François, 105
Chesimard, Joanne, 77
Chiang Kai-shek, 138, 139
"Chicago May," 80-89
Childs, Clifford X., 94
Chivers, Elizabeth, 77-78
Coate, Pearl, 78
Choegoe, Marthinus, 252
Christofi, Mrs. Styllou, 78-79
Churchill, Deborah, 80
Churchill, May, "Chicago May," 80-89
Clark, Dr. Henry Lovell William, 162-163
Clark, Lorraine, 89
Clark, Melvin, 89
Clarke, Marion, 8
Clarke, Mary Anne, 89-90
Clavé, Félix, 233, 241-242
Clay, General Lucius, 228
Clayton, Robert David, 249
Clifford, Mary, 61-63
Clunet, Edward, 287, 289, 290
Coakley, Abe, 255
Coleman, Cleo. *See* Kelly, Kathryn Thorne
Colette, 281
Collins, Ellen, 209-210
Collins, Judge, 213
Collins, Wilkie, 221
Colosimo, "Big" Jim, 147-148, 156
Columbo, Frank, 90
Columbo, Patricia, 90-95
Coo, Eva, 95-96
Cooney, Cecelia, 96-102
Cooney, Edward, 97-101
Corday, Charlotte, 102-106
Cordero, Andres Figueroa, 248
Coriell, Mary Ellen, 134
Coriell, William, 134
Cormac, William, 35
Cornelys, Madame, 106
Costello, Frank, 191 192
Cotton, Charles Edward, 107
Cotton, Frederick, 107
Cotton, Mary Ann, 106-108
Coughlin, John "Bathhouse," 147, 148, 150, 152, 154
Courvoisier, François, 273

Cowle, Rhodes, 118
Cowle, William, 118
Cranston, William Henry, 28-29
Cresswell, Chief Justice, 272
Crimmins, Alice, 108-109
Csaba, Mrs. Julius, 159
Csery, Lydia, 159
Cummings, Alexander, 351
Cummings, Joyce Lisa, 42, 44-47
Cupic, Momcilo, 298
Cutpurse, Moll, 109-115

Dagoe, Hannah, 116-117
Dague, Walter Glenn, 339-340
Damur, Louis, 281
Danton, Georges Jacques, 102, 104, 105
Darland, Michel, 379
Davis, Alden, 363, 364
Davis, Mattie, 363, 367
Davis, Volney, 15-16
Day, Mary Stedman. *See* Moders, Mary
Dean, Margie, 117-118
Deane, Mrs. Joshua, 40
de Barny, Judge, 245, 246
Decous, public prosecutor, 242, 243, 244
Defoe, Daniel, 35
de Garat Madame, 233, 234, 235, 237, 240
Dekker, Thomas, 111
De Leautaud, Marie, 241-242
DeLuca, Frank, 92-95
de Melker, Clarence, 118
de Melker, Daisy Louisa, 118
de Nicolai, Marie, 233-234
Denton, Jacob Charles, 322
De Pareq, Georges, 291
Deshayes, Catherine "La Voisin," 118-125
Devery, William S., 258
Dick, Evelyn, 125
Dick, John, 125
Dickens, Charles, 274-275
Dickson, Bennie, 206-208
Dillinger, John, 191
Dilnot, George, 268
Diousidon, Judge, 41
Diver, Jenny, 125-131
Dixon, Margaret, 131
Donald, Jeannie, 131
Doss, Nannie, 132
Dowling, Delphine, 22
Downey, Lesley Ann, 201
Dragna, Jack, 193
Drouet, Jean-Baptiste, 104
Druse, John, 132
Druse, Roxana, 132
Dubuisson, Pauline, 132-133

Duffy, Clinton T., 349, 350
Dumas, Alexandre, 235, 246
Dumolard, Marie, 133-134
Dumolard, Martin, 133-134
Dunning, Elizabeth, 40
Dunning, John Presley, 40
Dunscomb, Lydia, 265
Durgan, Bridget, 134
"Dutch Gus," 83, 84-86
Dyer, Amelia Elizabeth, 134

Eastern Jewel, 135-140
Edmunds, Christiana, 140
Elkins, Sophie, 254
Ellis, Ruth, 140-143
Emerson, Banjo Pete, 255
Epstein, Joseph, 191, 195, 198, 199
Erlich, Jake, 39-40
Everleigh, Ada, 143-156
Everleigh, Minna, 143-156
Evrard, Simmone, 103, 104
Eyraud, Michel, 32-33

Fairfax, General, 111-112
Farmer, Herb, 318
Fay, Janet, 22
Fazekas, Mrs. Julius, 157-160
Fenayrou, Gabrielle, 160-161
Fenayrou, Marin, 160-161
Ferbach, Johann, 64-65
Fernandez, Raymond, 21
Field, Nathan, 111
Fielding, Sir John, 106
Fisher, Dorothy, 327
Fisher, Freda, 327
Fisher, Margaret, 161
Fleury, Laurent, 210
Foley, Inspector, 220, 221
Force, Florence, 161
Force, Julia, 161
Force, Minnie, 161
Ford, President Gerald, 161-162, 303-304
Forman, Dr. Simon, 204
Foster, Campbell, 107
Fourgère, Eugénie, 167-168
Fourquier-Tinville, Antoine-Quentin, 105
Freeman, Prince Arthur, 333-334
Frobisher, John, 72
Fromme, Lynette Alice, 161-162
Fullam, Augusta Fairfield, 162-163
Fullam, Edward, 162

Gargano, Gene, 93, 94
Gaston, Lucy Page, 151
Gates, John "Bet-a-Million," 146
Gaudry, Nathalis, 52-53, 56-58

Gay, Clestell, 369
Gee, Charlie, 164-167
Gee, Dolly, 164-167
Geinke, Fred, 390-391
Geinke, Lily, 390-391
George III, King, 312
George, David Lloyd, 388
Gibbs, Mrs. Irving, 364
Giriat, Madame, 167-168
Glabe, Karen, 168
Glabe, Kenneth, 168
"Golden Hand," 30
Goodman, Derick, 230
Goolde, Marie Vere, 168-169
Gordon, Mrs. Henry, 364, 367
Gordon-Baille, Mary Anne, 170
Göring, Hermann, 175
Gottfried, Gesina Margaretha, 170-172
Gouan-Criquet, Madame, 341-342
Gouffe, Toussaint-Augustin, 32, 33
Gough, Elizabeth, 219, 220, 223
Gould, Janice, 42, 44-47
Gould, Jay, 321
Graham, Barbara, 172-173
Gray, Basil, 347
Gray, Henry Judd, 346
"Greasy Thumb," 191
Greenlease, Bobbie, Jr., 187
Grese, Irma, 173-175
Grey, Frank, 99-100
Gribble, Leonard, 272
Grieve, Elizabeth Harriet, 175-176
Griffin, Jane, 176
Griffith, Arthur, 233, 385
Grinder, Martha, 176
Groesbeek, Maria, 176
Guerin, Eddie, 83-89
Guibourg, Abbé, 121, 122
Guillonet, Octave, 279
Guimet, Emile, 279-280
Gunness, Belle, 176-177
Gustavus Adolphus, King, 299
Guszkowski, Joseph, "Blunt Joe," 226
Guyader, Alain, 206
Guzik, Jake, "Greasy Thumb," 191

Hahn, Anna Marie, 178-179
Hahn, Phillip, 179
Haig, Preston, 168
Hall, Carl Austin, 187
Hall, Catherine. See Hayes, Catherine
Hamann, Annie, 250
Hamid, Sultan (of Java), 279
Hamilton, Mary, 179-180
Hamer, Frank, 318
Hargrave, Lee Adam, 171
Harris, Charlotte, 180

Harris, Judge, 332, 333
Harris, Maury, 254-255
Harris, Phoebe, 180-181
Harrison, Carter, 147, 152, 153
Harrison, Elizabeth, 265
Hart, Pearl, 181
Harvey, Margaret, 181
Hawkins, Gordon, 349
Hayes, Catherine, 181-186
Hayes, John, 181, 183, 184
Hayes, Patrick, 178-179
Haynes, Superintendent, 270-272
Hayton, Arthwell C., 297
Hayton, Elaine, 297
Heady, Bonnie B., 187-188
Hearst, Patricia Campbell, 188-189
Heath, George Edward, 213
Hegedus, Peter, 158
Helpern, Milton, 108-109
Henry, Crown Prince (of Prussia), 145
Henry, Sir Thomas, 223
Hicks, Elizabeth, 189
Hicks, Mary, 189
Hill, Mildred, 189-190
Hill, Virginia, 190-199
Himmler, Heinrich, 175, 227-228
Hindley, Myra, 199-201
Hitler, Adolf, 175
Hogarth, William, 265
Hogg, Phoebe, 320
Holden, (playwright), 299-300
Holyba, Rosa, 159
Hoover, J. Edgar, 217
Hope, Jimmy, 255
Hope, Johnny, 255
Horner, Governor Henry, 32
Housden, Charles, 202
Housden, Jane, 201-202
Housden, Nina, 202-203
Household, David, 262
Howard, Lady Frances, 203-205
Hubert, Raymond, 308
Hulme, Juliet, 318-319
Hulten, Karl Gustav, 212-213
Hunt, Richard, 80
Hurlbut, Dennis, 342-343
Hussey, Eleanor, 116
Hutchinson, Amy, 205
Hutchinson, John, 205

Ily, Nicole, 206
Irving, H. B., 385
Irwin, Estelle Mae, 206-208
Ives, Albert, 349

Jackson, Mary Jane, "Bricktop," 209-211
Jacques, Paul, 304, 305-306

Jacques, Paule, 305, 306, 308-309
James I, King, 203, 204, 205
James, Lester, 25
Jamieson, James, 361
Jeanneret, Marie, 211
Jeffries, Elizabeth, 211
Jeffs, Doreen, 212
Jegado, Hélène, 212
Johnstone, John, 311
Jones, Dale, 117-118
Jones, Elizabeth Marina, 212-213
Jones, Harold, 213
Jones, Mary, 61
Jones, Mrs. Mary, 213
Judd, Winnie Ruth, 214

Kamorowsky, Count Paul, 356-357
Kane, Chief Detective Inspector, 338
Kanjurjab, 136
Kardos, Marie, 159
Karpis, Alvin "Old Creepy," 14, 15, 16
Katzman, Jean, 336
Katzman, Sonia, 336
Kawashima, Naniwa, 135
Kawashima, Yoshiko. See Eastern Jewel
Kefauver, Senator Estes, 191, 193, 196, 197, 199
Keller, Julia, 254
Kelley, Nora. See Toppan, Jane
Kelly, George, 215, 217
Kelly, Kathryn Thorne, 215-217
Kenna, Michael "Hinky Dink," 147, 148, 150, 152-153, 154
Kent, Constance, 217-226
Kent, Francis Savile, 219-220, 223
Kent, Samuel Savile, 218-220, 223
Kent, William George, 249
"Kid John," 83, 84-86
Kilbride, John, 199, 201
Kingston, Charles, 273
Klein, Benjamin, 370
Klimek, Anton, 226
Klimek, Tillie, 226-227
Knight, Mary, 227
Koch, Ilse, 227-229
Koch, Karl, 227-228, 229
Kohler, Ernest, 178
Kunstler, William M., 77
Kupczyk, Frank, 226

Labbe, Catherine, 231
Labbe, Denise, 230-232
Lachapelle, Madame, 341
Lachaud, Charles, 57-58, 240, 242, 243, 244, 246
Ladermann, Cesar, 168

Ladoux, Captain Georges, 285-286, 288
Lafarge, Charles Joseph Pouch, 234-235, 238, 240
Lafarge, Marie, 232-246
La Gratiosa, 348
Lalaurie, Delphine, 247-248
Lalaurie, Dr. Louis, 247
Lambert, Magistrate, 185
Lanagan, Timothy, 330-331, 332-333
Lancaster, Roscoe, 117, 118
Langley, Detective-sergeant, 271
Lansky, Meyer, 193, 194
Larson, Ole, 344
la Vallière, Louise de, 121, 122
"La Voison," 118-125
Lawes, Lewis E., 96
Leary, John "Red," 256
Leary, Kate, 259
Lebron, Lolita, 248-249
LeBrun, Anna, 234, 236, 238, 239, 240
Lee, Jean, 249
Lefebvre, Felix, 247
Leféron, Judge, 120
Leféron, Marguerite G., 120, 124
Lehmann, Christa, 249-251
Lehmann, Karl Franz, 249, 250
Lehmann, Valentin, 251
Lehnberg, Marlene, 252
LeRoi, Agnes, 214
Leslie, George Leonidas, 255
Lespinasse, Dr., 240
Levin, Emma Erika, 169
Levy, Sam, 254
Lewis, Frank "Jumbo," 117
Lieberman, Elias, 326
Liebowitz, Samuel, 101
Line, Anne, 252
Link, Mitchell, 168
Lipka, Juliane, 160
Lippmann, Walter, 101
Lipsig, Francis, 237
Loeb, Richard, 7
Logan, Arthur, 322-323
Logan, Margaret, 322-323
Lonely Hearts Killers, 22
Long Charley, 209
Lorillard, Mrs. Herbert, 259
Lott, Dr. Chrisopher, 322
Loughborough, Lord, 312
Louis XIV, King, 121, 122, 123, 124
Louis XVI, King, 104
Louis Philippe, King, 246
Lowenstein, Susanne, 276-277
Lubee, Catherine, 330-331
Luciano, Charles "Lucky," 4, 5, 191, 194, 196
Lusk, Grace, 252-253
Lyles, Anjette, 253-254
Lyles, Marcia, 253-254

Lyons, Edward "Ned," 255-257, 259
Lyons, George, 256
Lyons, Sophie, 254-261

McAleavy, Henry, 136, 138
McCollum, Ruby, 291
McDonald, Mike, 83
Macé, Gustave, 54-57
McLaughlin, John J. "Boss," 217
Macleod, Mrs. A., 262-263
MacLeod, Captain Rudolf, 278, 279
McManus, "Kid John," 83, 84-86
McWeeny, Police Chief, 152, 153
Major, Arthur, 263-264
Major, Ethel Lillie, 263-265
Malcolm, Sarah, 265
Mandelbaum, Fredricka "Marm," 255
Manning, Frederick George, 266-269, 271-273
Manning, Henry, 352
Manning, Maria, 266-275
Mansfield, Lord, 312
Marat, Jean-Paul, 102-105
Marek, Emil, 275-277
Marek, Martha Lowenstein, 275-277
Marks, Dr. Jason, 321
Marov, Captain, 285, 288, 290
Marsh, James, 240, 241, 243, 245
Marsh, Luther R., 337-338
Marschall, Carl, 9-10
Martin, George, W., 101
Martin, Marie, 341
Mason, Elizabeth, 277
Massard, Major, 287
Massénat, Dr., 239, 240
Mata Hari, 277-291
Maybrick, Florence, 74
M'Donald, Daniel, 161
Meadows, Alberta, 323-324
Meinhof, Ulrike, 292
Ménétret, Elodie, 293-295
Mercier, Adèle, 295
Mercier, Euphrasie, 292-295
Merrifield, Louisa, 295-296
Metyard, Sarah, 296-297
Middleton, Thomas, 111
Miller, "Dutch Gus," 83, 84-86
Miller, Dr. Gordon E. "Cork," 297
Miller, John, 210
Miller, Lucille, 297
Milner, Sir Charles, 89
Milosavljeric, Ljubinka, 298
Milton, John, 115
Mirando, Rafael, 248
Mitchell, Lanyon, 92-94
Mitchell, Mary, 60, 62, 63
Mitkiewitz, John, 226
Moders, Mary "The German Princess," 298-303

Monier, Judge, 69, 70
Montane, Judge, 104-105
Montespan, Marquise de, 120, 121-122, 123, 124-125
Monvoisin, Antoine, 119, 123, 124
Moore, Reverend, 63-64
Moore, Sara Jane, 303-304
Morain, Alfred, 282, 307
Mornet, Lieutenant, 287
Moro-Giaffери, (attorney), 308
Morris, Thomas, 328
Mosby, Richard, 11-12
Mouse, Carrie, 260
Mowbray, William, 106-107
Murphy, Anne, 127, 129
Murphy, Peter, 27
Murri, Professor, 33-34
Murri, Tullio, 33-34
Myrtel, Héra, 304-309

Napoleon III, 246
Nathaniel, Cathy, 310
National Biscuit Company, 99
Nattrass, Joseph, 107
Naumoff, Dr. Nicholas, 356, 357, 358
Naylor, Anne, 296-297
Needham, Mother, 310-311
Newell, Susan, 311
Newman, Julia St. Clair, 312
Newton, Herbert, 76
Nicholson, Margaret, 312
Nicolai, Colonel Walter, 282, 284
Nitti, Frank, 191
Noakes, Audrey, 369
Norry, August, 28
Nozière, Madame, 313
Nozière, Monsieur, 313
Nozière, Violette, 312-313

O'Connor, Patrick, 266-269, 272
Ogilvie, Catherine, 314-315
Ogilvie, Patrick, 314-315
Ogilvie, Thomas, 314
Olah, Lydia, 159
Olah, Susanna, 159
"Old Creepy," 14, 15, 16
Opendorfer, George, 178
Orfila, Dr. Mathieu, 244, 245
O'Rourk, Count, 354
Osselin, Gerard, 373-374
Overbury, Sir Thomas, 203, 204, 205

Paillet, Alphonse, 240, 242, 244, 245-246
Panconi, Claude, 206
Parker, Bonnie, 316-318
Parker, Honora Mary, 318
Parker, Pauline Yvonne, 318-319
Parkhurst, Reverend, 82

Parsons, Leonard, 65, 67
Pearcey, Mary Eleanor, 319-320
Pearson, Edmund, 219
Peck, Ellen, 321-322
Peete, Louise, 322-323
Pepys, Samuel, 301
Perigo, Rebecca, 18, 20
Perigo, William, 18, 20
Perovskaya, Sofya, 323
Perris, Worcester Sam, 255
Peters, Ignatz, 277
Petit, Bernard, 206
Pfeiffer, Anna Ursula, 323
Phillips, Clara, 323-324
Pierrepoint, H. A., 336
Pierrepont, Albert, 143
Place, Ida, 324
Place, Martha, 324, 325
Pledge, Sarah, 324-326
Porch, Edith Mary. See Carew, Edith
    Mary
Poyntz, Juliet Stuart, 326
Praun, Dr. Otto, 64-65
Price, Ann, 265
Prilukoff, Donat, 356, 357, 358
Pristly, Helen, 131
Pu-Yi, Henry, 138, 139

Rablen, Carroll, 327
Rablen, Eva, 327
Rackham, John "Calico Jack," 36,
    38, 39
Raft, George, 194
Rankin, Hugh R., 36
Ransom, Florence, 327-328
Raphael, Sylvia, 328
Raymond, Harry, 255, 257
Read, Mary, 35, 36, 37-39
Reade, Pauline, 201
Reagan, Ronald, 189
Rendall, Martha, 328
Ricketts, Mrs., 295-296
Ringe, Richard, 24
Robert, Henri, 378, 379, 380, 381
Roberts, Mrs. David, 252-253
Robespierre, 102, 104, 115
Robinson, Henrietta, 329-333
Robinson, James, 107
Robinson, Sarah Jane, 333-334
Rodays, Fernand, 57
Rodriguez, Irving Flores, 248
Rodway, R., 224-225
Rogers, Governor Woodes, 36, 38
Roosevelt, Theodore, 324
Roques, Felix, 386, 387
Rosenthal, Herman, 82
Ross, Ezra, 351
Rossignol, Joseph, 341, 342
Roth, Celia. See Cooney, Cecelia
Rowan, Richard Wilmer, 285

Rumbold, Albert, 334
Rumbold, Freda, 334
Ruskowski, John, 226
Russell, Sir Charles, 107
Russell, Lord William, 273
Rysakov, Nikolai, 323

Sach, Amelia, 335-336
Sadler, Dora, 336
Saint-Croix, Gaudin de, 58-59
Saint Pierre, Georges de, 50-58
Salomen, Edith "The Swami," 336-
    338
Samuelson, Helwig "Sammy," 214
Sarrazin, Rosalie, 212
Saunders, Charlotte, 328
Saxe, Susan, 338-339
"Scarlet Sisters," 143-156
Schmidt, Axel, 3
Schroeder, Irene, 339-341
Scieri, Antoinette, 341-342
Scoles, Jane, 277
Seabury Investigations, 4-5
Sebestyen, Rosalie, 159
Secchi, Dr. Carlo, 33-34
Semprou, Colonel, 287, 288, 289
"Shakebag," 11-12
Shaw, Vic, 148, 153
Shepley, George F., 211
Sherman, Addie, 342
Sherman, Lydia, 342-344
Sherrard, Robert, 349
Sherrill, Roy, 117
Shinborn, Max, 81, 257
Siegel, Benjamin "Bugsy," 192-193,
    194-196
Simeone, Mike, 349
Simon, Batonnier, 232
"Sister" Amy, 10-11
Smith, Clara, 67
Smith, David, 200, 201
Smith, Earl, 344-345
Smith, Gipsey, 151
Smith, Mary Eleanor, 344-345
Smith, Oakes, 331
Smith, Richard, 75
Smith, Vieva, 352
Smith, Y. K., 352
Smith-Hughes, Jack, 360
Snyder, Albert, 346
Snyder, Ruth, 346-348
Snyder, Simon, 75
Sobcynski, Roman, 93, 94
Somers, Ann, 47-48
Spara, Hieronyma "La Spara," 348
Spencer, Barbara, 348
Spinelli, Evelita Juanita, 348-350
Spinelli, Simeone, 349
Spooner, Bathsheba, 351

Spooner, Joshua, 351
Sproat, Robert, 118
Stahl, Dr. Dmitri, 355, 356
Starr, Belle, 351-352
Starr, Sam, 352
Stead, W. T., 150
Stedman, Dr. Henry R., 364, 366,
    367
Stege, John, 392-393
Stewart, Francis, 352
Stopa, Wanda, 352-353
Stricker, Amos, 368
Struck, Edward, 342
Su, Prince, 135
Sullivan, Ronald Joseph, 375, 376
Summers, Montague, 122
Sutherland, Duchess of, 266, 273
Swan, John, 211
"Swami, The," 336-338
Swett, Charles, 353
Swett, Jane, 353
Swift, Delia, 209
Szendi, Maria, 159

Tanaka, Major Ryukichi, 136-138
Tardieu, Dr., 379
Tarnowska, Countess Maria, 354-358
Tarnowska, Count Vassili, 354-355
Taylor, Louisa Jane, 359-361
Tennent, Annie, 333
Thoinot, Dr. Leon Henry, 379, 380,
    381
Thomas, Dortohy, 38
Thomas, Julia Martha, 382-385
Thompson, Jane, 22
Thomson, Sir Basil, 286
Thorne, Charlie, 215
Thornton, Ray, 316
Ticho, Steven, 310
Tierney, Nora Patricia, 361
Tilly, Count, 299
Toffania, La, 362
Toppan, Jane, 362-368
Torrington, Lord, 368
Torrio, Johnny, 147
Tracy, Ann Gibson, 368
Tregillis, Mary Ann, 359-360
Tregillis, William, 359-360
Tresca, Carlo, 326
Tripp, Grace, 368
True, John L., 173
Truman, President Harry, 228
Tsamoutales, Nicholas, 43
Tullar, D. S., 253
Turner, Joyce, 369

Urschel, Charles F., 216-217
Ursinus, Sophie, 370-371

Van Der Elst, Violet, 142
Van der Linde, Susanna, 252
Vane, Charles, 36
Van Valkenburgh, Elizabeth, 372
Van Valkenburgh, John, 372
Varga, Maria, 159-160
Velgo, Jan, 372-273
Velgo, Marie Havlick, 372-373
Victoria, Queen, 180, 273
Vidal, Ginette, 373-374
Vincent, Arthur, 127
Von Jagow, Chief, 282, 283-284, 286-287
Von Kalle, Captain, 286, 289
Von Maluski, Raimonde, 213
Vos, Dr. Arthur, 178

Waddingham, Dorothea Nancy, 375-376
Wade, Charles, 67
Wade, George, 107
Wagner, A. D., 223
Wagner, Jacob, 178
Walker, Mayor James J., 4
Walker, John, 27
Walters, Annie, 335-336
Ward, Marion, 361

Wardle, Colonel Gwyllym Lloyd, 90
Waterhouse, Lily, 72-73
Watson, Ella "Cattle Kate," 376-377
Weber, Germaine, 378, 379
Weber, Jeanne, 377-381
Webster, Kate, 381-385
Weingarten, Sophie Charlotte Elizabeth. See Ursinus, Sophie
Weiss, Jeanne Daniloff, 385-388
Weiss, Monsieur, 385-386
Were, Martin, 80
Weston, Richard, 204
Whale, Anne, 324-325
Whale, James, 324-325
Wheeldon, Alice, 388
Whicher, Jonathan, 220-223, 226
Whitla, Willie, 30-31
Whitney, J. H., 365
Wilhelm, Crown Prince, 282, 283
Wilhelmina, Queen, 278, 289
Wilkins, (Attorney), 272
Williams, America, 209-210
Williams, Ann, 388-389
Williams, Emlyn, 201
Wilson, Catherine, 389-390
Wilson, Colin, 241
Wilson, Elizabeth, 390
Wise, Martha Hasel, 390-391

Wisebourne, Mother, 126
Witte, Christina Regina, 370-371
Wolf, John B., 121
Wood, E. S., 365
Wood, Thomas, 182-184, 185
Worcester, Sam Perris, 255
Worms, Moses, 391
Worms, Pamela Lee, 391
Wright, Harry, 95-96
Wynekoop, Dr. Alice, 391-395
Wynekoop, Dr. Catherine, 391
Wynekoop, Earle, 392-393, 395
Wynekoop, Rheta Gardner, 391, 392-395

Yamaga, Colonel, 138, 139
Yamaga, Lieutenant, 135-136
York, Dr. William, 25-26
York, Duke of, 89, 90
Young, Hugh, 264-265
Young, Myrtle, 22

Zelle, Margaret Gertrude. See Mata Hari
Zillman, Bertha, 396